D0848979

SHADOW WORLD

SHADOW WORLD

Resurgent Russia, the Global New Left, and Radical Islam

Robert Chandler

Cataloging-in-Publication data on file with the Library of Congress

ISBN 978-1-59698-561-2

Published in the United States by
Regnery Publishing, Inc.
One Massachusetts Avenue, NW
Washington, DC 20001
www.regnery.com

Manufactured in the United States of America

10 9 8 7 6 5 4 3 2 1

Books are available in quantity for promotional or premium use. Write
to Director of Special Sales, Regnery Publishing, Inc., One Massachusetts Avenue NW, Washington, DC 20001, for information on discounts
and terms or call (202) 216-0600.

In Memoriam

Esperanza Millas-Estany de Chandler

American patriot, Catalanist, anti-communist, best friend

CONTENTS

Books by Robert Chandler

The New Face of War: Weapons of Mass Destruction and the Revitalization of America's Transoceanic Strategy.

Counterforce: Locating and Destroying Weapons of Mass Destruction.

Tomorrow's War, Today's Decisions: Iraqi Weapons of Mass Destruction and the Implications of WMD-Armed Adversaries for Future U.S. Military Strategy.

War of Ideas: The U.S. Propaganda Campaign in Vietnam.

ACKNOWLEDGMENTS

THE STRATEGIC ANALYSIS presented in this book was drawn from more than four decades of reading, writing, and working to resolve a wide range of international security problems facing the United States. Over the years, I was blessed to work with many people who helped me improve my analytical skills and taught me to "see" beyond the apparent and behind the drawn curtain. To these colleagues and acquaintances who shaped my life's journey in several foreign lands and at home, I extend my deepest appreciation for their confidence and encouragement.

Among those who influenced me the most was Esperanza, my wife and life partner who passed away during the writing of this book. Raised in Fascist Spain, this Catalana had a life-long thirst for liberty and democracy. She left her mark on every page *Shadow World* through her admonition to me: "You must finish the book. The American people don't know what you know. You must explain to them how the 'cultural war' is undermining everything good about America." I have tried to satisfy her admonition by simply telling the story about what I see developing in the storm clouds looming before us at home and internationally. It is for the reader to judge whether I have done my job well.

Secondly, I am deeply grateful to Peter Siebelt of Loosdrecht, the Netherlands, for his never ending grace and confidence in sharing his thoughts, ideas, and documents that were essential in writing the chapters about the hate-America progressives, socialists, and Marxists in the United States and Europe. Peter is a good friend and colleague whose dedication to America is founded on his recognition of the deceit and deception by the hard Left in trying to tear down the United States. He was also the "best host in Europe" for this foreign visitor several times over the last two decades.

Thirdly, John Rees of the Maldon Institute was very helpful in sharing his years of experience in tracking, analyzing, and writing about America's socialists and Marxists. In addition, to sharing Maldon's first-rate analyses of threats and risks facing American companies and government, John also gave me a copy of his unfinished manuscript about the Institute for Policy Studies, also known as "the think tank on the Left." John's insights were extremely helpful to this writer in "breaking the code" underlying the Institute's strategy and goals. For all of his support and counsel, I am very grateful.

Fourthly, my thanks also go to "The Bear" for his counsel and friendship as well as assistance in locating difficult to find documentation that underwrite key arguments in this book. I benefitted greatly from his deep insight to the workings of the world behind the scenes and key aspects of important stories left untold.

Many others assisted my research in 1001 different ways, from forwarding articles, reports, and studies of important issues to me. Many have shared their experiences and observations about important aspects of our complex world. My appreciation is extended to them all.

Introduction

ONE-WORLD GOVERNMENT

AMERICANS IN THE EARLY twenty-first century find themselves locked inside a rapidly changing world of imminent dangers emanating from three main centers of activity: one is political, another is ideological, and a third is cultural (georeligious). Each hostile group uses propaganda and disinformation to present images in strategic deception plans designed to mask their actions to sap American geopolitical influence and reshape the realities of the world order. Americans face a circumstance similar that created by clumsy French bureaucrats, lazy journalists, and co-opted professors in the 1930s, when they all helped to lull France's people into believing that the Maginot Line provided them assured protection against German attack. Similarly, Americans are responding to the deceptive images spun by politicians, journalists, and intellectuals that all would be well in the world, if the United States would only stop doing things that make Americans unpopular. Meanwhile, Russians are offering a theatrical production of their friendship and cooperation with the capitalist West, progressives-socialists-marxists inside America are pursuing a slow-roll cultural revolution, and Saudi Arabia's Salafists (Wahhabi) are preparing America and Europe for their new status of "*dhimmitude*," or a gradual subservience to the "ideology of *Jihad* and the Islamic powers that propagate it."[1]

Shadow World is about the political forces hidden deeply in the shadows of international affairs. It examines a wide-range of America-haters, including those aging ones who survived the Cold War and others that have since been spawned by new transnational predators. America's unchallenged ascendance during the 1990s resulting from its position as the world's sole economic and military superpower triggered the development of a caldron of vicious political, economic, environmental, social, and cultural anti-American centers. This seething hatred for Americans coalesced into a loose network of mutual support through three main centers of anti-U.S. activity: (1) the Kremlin's hidden hand operating from the shadow world to create conditions favorable for Russia's long-term geopolitical objectives; (2) a radical progressive-socialist-marxist web of popular fronts, agents of influence, and covert operatives fostering an anti-capitalist cultural revolution in the United States and Europe; and (3) an Islamic Salafist multinational with interconnections between al-Qaeda and other terrorist groups dedicated to restoration of a world caliphate and Saudi Arabia's plans to place Europe, Russia, and the United States under Islamic suzerainty.

These three main activity hubs operate as independent centers of anti-Americanism, but there are many connections between them. Together they make up a "Faceless International" pursuing common goals of reducing U.S. power and influence in the world, while they compete for global geopolitical dominance. These shared strategic objectives offer opportunities for ad hoc support for one another, sometimes as the result of intermediaries coordinating activities and at other times simply parroting the policy line of the other. Russia, for instance, contributes to the radical Left's "peace movement" through its recycled Cold War ideological allies inside the United States. At the same time, anti-war protests against America's war on terrorism in Afghanistan and Iraq by the homegrown radical Left and abroad are supported by al-Qaeda and other terrorist groups. Russia, on the other hand, supports international terrorism in the form of arms transfers to enemy combatants through proxies and sub-proxies.

Against this backdrop, three major geopolitical contenders, each with sufficient resources to establish a new world order, are locked in a long-term, winner-take-all competition. Their weapons are words and culture, economic strengths and diplomatic skill, political action in the open and from the world's shadows, as well as guns and bombs. The ultimate victor will win the right to exercise its power and political authority over all of the Earth's six billion people.

Malachi Martin, an eminent Vatican theologian, was the first to describe the global competition that was underway to win control of all of the world's people. He declared in 1990 that "we are the stakes."[2] Since Martin alerted humanity to the globalist struggle for control of our lives nearly two decades ago, one georeligious competitor, the Vatican, melded with the capitalist West, while another, Islamic Salafism, emerged as a contender to establish global rule.

Much of Martin's narration about the early post-Cold War competition has spilled over into the contemporary chess match between the capitalist West, Russia and its strategic partners and Western agents of influence, and Islamic Salafism. For this we owe Martin a great debt of gratitude for giving us warning about the global geopolitical competition and urging us to take it seriously since it is our lives that hang in the balance.

Today's competitive triad holds all of us at risk, Martin said: our lives, our families, our jobs, our prosperity, our property, our schools, our communities, our religions, our cultures, our general well-being, and our national identities. Who we will be depends upon which contender eventually wins. Regardless of the victor, no aspect of our lives will be immune or left untouched. The contemporary three-way geopolitical competition, like the initial global chess match described by Malachi Martin in 1990, will result in ". . . the most profound and widespread modification of international, national, and local life that the world has seen in a thousand years."[3]

The first geopolitical competitor is the capitalist West led by the United States and Europe. Its geographic expanse stretches from the Pacific coast in North America, across the Atlantic, to the east European borders with Russia. This globalist competitor also includes the Vatican, Japan, and Oceana. The United States, emerging from the Cold War as the world's lone superpower, has served as a primary engine of economic globalization. Over the next fifty years or more, with appropriate adjustments by the industrial North to ensure the economic well-being of suppliers and workers in the Southern Hemisphere, as well as displaced U.S. workers, globalization could result in the elimination of sovereign borders in a single, world-embracing North-South global economy.

The second globalist competitor is led by Russia, which is still motivated, though secretly, by a Leninist, Party-State mentality. Moscow is joined by strategic partners that, together with Russia, make up a vast geostrategic quadrangle with China, Iran, and Cuba-Brazil-Venezuela.

The Kremlin's long-term strategic goals are enveloped in a hub of denial and deception. This major strategic deception involves a rather loose but strident quadrangle of friendship and cooperation between Russia-China-Iran-Cuba/Brazil (and Venezuela). These Russian proxies and sub-proxies have energy-hungry economies that portend robust future growth. Moscow's strategic partners are also dedicated to restructuring the world security order from its current unipolar structure to a multi-national system in which Russia will hold a chair of significant influence. The reach of this global competitor stretches from the Pacific coast of Eurasia to Russia's borders in eastern Europe and the Caucasus. It also stretches from the North Sea to Central Asia, which facilitates a predominant position over the energy-rich Caspian Sea.

Russia's strategic partners serve as activity centers or hubs for decentralized competitive actions in their respective regions of interest. Iran stands on the threshold of controlling a major Shiite nation consisting of the political states of Iran itself, most of Iraq, Syria, and Lebanon. This emerging Shiite nation will stand with Russia in the Kremlin's efforts to wrest control of the world's prices for oil and natural gas from OPEC. Russia is relying on the stealthy application of Antonio Gramsci's revisionist Marxist formula for transforming the cultures of target countries over time to create the conditions necessary for Moscow to assume global leadership.

Russia's goal is to create the conditions necessary for a peaceful convergence of Europe and Russia. The Kremlin's complex design for winning this strategic objective is based on engaging the Europeans in a broad series of complex commercial relationships. First among these European-Russian cooperative arrangements is Moscow's position as a principal supplier of natural gas and oil that drives the European economy. Moscow's strategy is supplemented by a vast array of progressive (socialist-marxist) agents of influence promoting the secularization of Europe and its cultural transformation to one more amenable to Antonio Gramsci's formula for acceding to power through the ballot box. The progressive-socialist-marxist agents of influence often use stealth and deceit to shape European ideas for accommodating the Kremlin's convergence goals.

The third global geopolitical competitor is Islam's Salafist (Wahhabi) fundamentalism centered in Saudi Arabia. The geographic expanse of Salafist influence stretches across the Maghreb and Middle East, through Pakistan, and into India to where the Muslim and Hindu worlds meet. The Salafists, through al-Qaeda, immigration, and religious missionaries reach into Europe, Bosnia, Macedonia, Albania, Kosovo, Chechnya, and other Muslim nations inside Russia, Central Asia, Africa, North and South America, and Southeast

Asia. The Salafist georeligious goal is to restore a global-girdling Islamic (Sunni) caliphate.

The georeligious objectives of the Salafists are focused on the creation of conditions necessary for the emergence of "Eurabia." Using the complementary tools of terrorism (al-Qaeda) and immigration, Salafist rulers look forward to the time when Europe will fall into their hands like a ripened plum. The conditions for winning Europe are expected to be created over time as the native European birth rate remains low and the immigrant birth rates are high. Over time, the Islamic immigrants will be able to accede to power through the ballot box and Europe will slide into a condition of neutralization or *dhimmitude*.

The loss of Europe to Russian or Salafist interests would be a crushing blow to the United States and gravely wound its ability to compete geopolitically. While Europe finds itself at the center of gravity in the struggle between the three globalist contenders, it remains a vital part of the capitalist West. Hence, Europe can anticipate that it will be protected by American power and influence, but only if it does not crumble from within. Both Russia and the Salafists have growing fifth columns inside Europe in readiness to rise up at the right time.

The Muslim Brotherhood of North America has successfully established a major presence in the United States and Canada. It operates behind an array of fronts that mask its anti-U.S. activities. A deep hatred for the United States and Americans is a strong motivating force. The Brotherhood's strategic goal is to destroy the United States "through long-term civilization-killing" that will eliminate all religions except Islam. The Brotherhood's self-described ". . . work in America is a kind of grand *Jihad* in eliminating and destroying the Western civilization from within. . . ." This civilizational jihad will be accompanied by terrorist attacks, quite possibly including a nuclear 9/11.

Shadow World illuminates (1) the details of the capitalist West led by the United States in pursuit of creating liberal democracies through political and economic globalization; (2) a Russian hidden hand that includes extraordinary disinformation and a vast left-wing conspiracy of denial and deceit; (3) and a radical Islamic Jihad in the name of Allah that extends its blood-sucking tentacles deeply into American society and across the globe. This geopolitical competition will determine which contender will win political authority over all the Earth's six billion people. The three-way globalist competition will likely run for fifty years or more in the twenty-first century. There will be many ups and downs in the long-term chess match, since each of the competitors hold strengths and exploitable vulnerabilities.

The capitalist West's response to the opening moves by Russia, the revolutionary Left within the United States, and violent militant Islamists already reflects the ongoing geopolitical chess match to determine which player will dominate the twenty-first century world order. The trends, policy shifts, covert actions, international terrorism, and anti-American coalitions add up to one certainty: A late twenty-first century borderless world under a single government is in the making. The open question is whether the new world order will be autocratic, democratic, or theocratic.

The ultimate winner of this global geopolitical competition is not yet apparent.

1

PLATO'S CAVE

PLATO EXPLAINED THE differences between images and reality in their simplest and perhaps purest form some 2,400 years ago. He selected the shadows made by a fire in a cave to explain the difference between what we see and the reality surrounding us in the sunlight outside the cave. Shadows are only imitations of really living things, the Greek philosopher observed. The shadows on the wall of the cave present the appearance of material things, not their true nature.

From this beginning premise, doubtlessly drawn from his own observations, Plato takes a second step, which helps us to understand deception in the modern world. If one held people as prisoners in a cave, Plato surmised, with chains preventing them from turning their bodies and heads, the fires behind and above them at some distance would cast shadows on the wall. Since restraints would hold the prisoners in place, the shadows could be used to manipulate and shape their perceptions, which would naturally lead to a phenomenon in which the images cast on the cave wall would become truth in the eye of the beholder. "To them," Plato concluded, "the truth would be literally nothing but the shadows of the images." As a result, the prisoners, once in the world of sunlight outside the cave, would find that they believe the "shadows of the images" more than the living creatures and actual things in the world around them.[1]

Plato's discussion in *The Republic* about the problems of distinguishing between image and reality provide a backdrop for the narrative in this analysis. For Plato, the puppets on the wall of a cave, shown as shadows from flickering fires behind the captive audience, served to mislead and manipulate the perceptions of objects and events. Today, we call such activities propaganda and disinformation, whose purpose is to deny and deceive.

Faceless International

The American people, held like the prisoners in Plato's cave, are being fed a constant psychological diet of images designed by Russia's clandestine specialists doing all they can do to constrain the growth of America's power and influence. At the same time, America's home-grown and international cultural Marxists or progressives-socialists-marxists—in ideological solidarity with Russia—are centered on tearing down what they call "corporate America," and Islamic militants are poised to crush what they see as the depravity of U.S. culture and enforce a status of *dhimmitude* before America's toxic perversion can infect Muslim societies. The arsenal of political weapons chosen in the assault on America by one or more of the three antagonists include subversion, propaganda (open and covert), disinformation, direct action (agitation) and active measures, terrorism, agents of influence, immigration, and a particular emphasis by all three groups on the life-blood of political warfare: denial and deception.

Since few in the United States are countering the images cast by these three hostile centers, Americans, when they are released from the dictatorship of the images cast inside Plato's modern cave and having reached the sunlight of reality, do not perceive the dangers swirling around them. Therefore, it will be difficult to correct the pictures that deceive Americans. These perceptions have been keenly shaped by the propaganda and disinformation spewed from the Russians, cultural Marxists, and Salafists. Americans can be expected to resort to the human psychological process of cognitive dissonance, which will screen-out factors in the real world that do not fit the images so carefully fed to them. The open question is whether these images are so strongly inculcated that they are resilient to correction that expose their baseline of denial and deceit. If the propaganda and disinformation programs against the United States by Russians, home-grown and international progressives-socialists-marxists, and radical Islamists are so strong that Americans will resist seeing the threatening realities operating deeply inside the world's shadows, their response options will be severely constrained.

Authoritarian Russia

Russian ruling elites and the people at-large have been rankled about the loss of Russian power and influence in the world after the December 31, 1991 disintegration of the U.S.S.R. Since the 1990s, the Kremlin foreign policies have been pursued on a dual track, one open rail and another underground. The Russian Federation's intelligence service remained extremely active inside the United States right from the beginning. Midway through its first decade, Russia's Federal Security Service (FSB), copycat successor to the KGB, had intensified its espionage activities in the United States. Russia maintained several of the Soviet Union's international fronts, such as the World Peace Council, World Federation of Trade Unions, and International Association of Democratic Lawyers to advance Russian national interests. Moreover, members of the American progressive-socialist-marxist movement have maintained their connections with the surviving Soviet-Russian fronts.

The FSB maintains a direct continuity with the KGB from the Cold War days when subversion, propaganda, forgeries, training terrorists directly and through third countries (e.g., East Germany), arms transfers to terrorist supporting regimes (e.g., Iran, Syria, Libya, Yemen, and others), and use of American radical Leftists as agents of influence were forged into sharp weapons of political warfare. During the Cold War, the Soviet Union funded the anti-capitalist, pro-Marxist movement through American agents of influence and popular fronts in the United States. This record leads one to question whether Russia has used this well-worn clandestine pathway to work with Western anti-globalization and anti-war groups in the early twenty-first century. Similarly, Soviet intelligence or their client states trained terrorists as far back as the 1970s, including those responsible for bombing the World Trade Center in 1993 and 2001.

The image presented to the West by the Kremlin's masters of deception shows a democratic, free-market, non-communist Russia that is safe for foreign investment of all types, from advanced technology to ordinary consumer goods. Russia also casts itself as a responsible member of international society that treasures close relations with the United States and Europe. This picture has been projected through the tumultuous days leading up to the December 1991 implosion of the Soviet Union, the wild days of Boris Yeltsin's years leading the country, and into the Vladimir Putin era of discipline and state control. When these two decades of post-Soviet Russia are viewed through a prism of historical analysis, some very interesting factors appear that contradict the Kremlin's well-spun image of Russia in the early twenty-first century.

Chapter 3, The Andropov Plan, tells the real story about the disintegration of the Soviet Union, which was more of a controlled implosion than a spontaneous reaction to a clash of major trends. The three main pillars of the Soviet system—the *nomenklatura* (the 1.5 million or so Soviet elites), the KGB (now with a happy-face as the FSB), and the Communist Party, a new version—all survived. The *nomenklatura* are now the new factory and industry owners and government officials; they are swimming in cash from the burgeoning Russian economy, especially since the increase in energy prices rescued Russia's resources-based society from the poor house. The state security organs, nearly a thousand former KGB officers, are running key departments of the Russian government. The new communist system—based on Antonio Gramsci's revisionist Marxism—is operating in stealth, deep inside the shadows of Russia's well-oiled clandestine world.

Russian officials never seem to tire from telling the West that "Communism died" with the Soviet Union. Marxism-Leninism did expire as a planned event of the restructuring or *perestroika*. But deep inside the warrens of the Gorbachev Foundation in Moscow in 2008 operated the cultural Marxism developed by Antonio Gramsci, the founder of the Italian Communist Party. Gramsci spent more than a decade scribbling his ideas about cultural Marxism in notebooks while an inmate in one of Benito Mussolini's prisons during the 1930s. The notebooks were picked up by his sister-in-law, a Russian, and turned over to the Soviet Embassy in Rome and then on to Moscow. From all accounts, the nine volumes of Gramsci's ideas collected dust somewhere deep in the libraries of the Soviet Communist Party, at least until Mikhail Gorbachev dusted them off and applied the new directions toward cultural revolution outlined by the Italian revisionist. The application of Gramsci's ideas was a key component of the "Andropov Plan," which underwrote Mikhail Gorbachev's *perestroika* or restructuring.

The Soviet-Russians were able to pull-off the gigantic ruse envisioned in the Andropov Plan through years of planning for the development of an unprecedented disinformation campaign that spun off the New Economic Policy of the 1920s and Lenin's reading of the gullibility of the capitalist West. The key was to conceal the coordination between the "new" Russia and Gramci's unique pragmatism in applying Marxist and Leninist ideas to engage Western governments through support of the Kremlin's disinformation strategy. Russia's ultimate goal of creating a socialist world order on terms acceptable to Moscow remains unchanged. Instead of Marxism-Leninism and violent revolutionary change, Russia flipped to the cultural Marxism aimed at the long-term transformation of Western values that would open the doors to socialist world governance. The Kremlin's ultimate goal is to emerge over the long-term as the world's dominant and controlling geopolitical power.

Progressives-Socialists-Marxists

The radical Left in the United States and abroad was thrust into ideological turmoil with the disintegration of the Soviet Union. The dictatorship of the proletariat and other power tools of Leninism were exposed as they existed—a means for the Soviet Communist Party's self-appointed ruling elite to exercise total control over the hapless populations of Russia, Ukraine, and other downtrodden peoples in areas ruled or controlled by the Kremlin. When the Soviet Union and its Communist Party died at the end of 1991, the peoples of Eastern Europe threw out their Kremlin-directed tormentors and the Berlin Wall came tumbling down. Russia seemed to be evolving toward democracy and the liberty that goes with free market economies. Cold warriors in the West were exhilarated. Champagne corks popped. The Cold War was over. Yet, the pieces of the new international jigsaw puzzle did not quite fit all that well. Right from the beginning, one could sense something was amiss but that "something" was well hidden.

In spite of the West's collective euphoria in the wake of the Soviet collapse, remnants of the communist regime were boiling in the shadows to reorganize, re-orient, and re-emerge onto the world scene. There was no reason to believe that all of the communists in the world would have dried up and been blown away by the wind with the demise of the Central Committee of the Soviet Communist Party. Yet, revolutionary socialists all over the globe began dropping "Leninism" and the hyphen linking it with Marxism, while they sought to create a "Marxist renewal and re-emergence." Antonio Gramsci's recipe of the stealthy pragmatism of moving quietly to "passive revolution" stood Marx on his head and called for a silent cultural revolution. "This involves," U.S. diplomat and educator Alberto M. Piedra explains, "dismantling or destroying the values of the past by slowly infiltrating the 'old' institutions and changing the mentality of the masses."[2]

In the United States, Marxists adopted the term "progressive" to mask their activities, an old popular front word that had been used by communists on and off since the 1930s. No one is really sure what is and is not a progressive, but it is clear that the word is used to sow confusion and provide political cover for those who may be socialists or Marxists. Many American journalists and other mindless peddlers of political correctness cannot bring themselves to say "progressive." They muddy the waters even further by wrongfully calling radical Leftists "liberals," which is an insult to both members of the ultra-Left and legitimate liberals. Since progressives use popular fronts to co-opt liberals to join their ideological crusade, they are in no hurry to correct the record when mistakenly or purposively called "liberals." When Tom Hayden, one of the raging radicals from the 1960s was introduced as a "liberal" on a television talk show in the late 1990s, he initially flinched at the innocent insult and then broke into a knowing smile without explaining that he patently was not a member of the liberal camp but a Marxist revolutionary.

When the Soviet Union passed from the world scene, Antonio Gramsci's political philosophy of penetrating existing cultures to transform society and its institutions through direct action and propaganda began underwriting a "renewed" Marxist doctrine. Gramsci's ideas had become so popular in Left-wing circles that the International Gramsci Society was established in 1997 to further the spread of his action program against free enterprise and democratic governments. This new brand of Marxism that began to evolve in earnest during the 1990s gradually matured into a cautious process of what the radical Left dubbed "Marxist renewal and re-emergence." One European analyst told me that he disliked attending the radical Left's open meetings in the mid-1990s. "They argued that Gramsci said this, Gramsci said that, Gramsci meant . . . Gramsci, Gramsci, Gramsci. They drove me crazy. Gramsci was all they talked about." Similar discussions took place in the United States behind closed doors in accordance with the prescriptions of Gramsci's stealthy, cultural Marxist doctrine.

Part Three of this book examines the conduct of the silent socialist revolution underway in the United States, Europe and Australia, and inside the United Nations. These six chapters do not stand alone, for each is an essential layer in Gramsci's "genius of Marxist pragmatism" against the West. For the ultra-Left, the United States is the main prize. Much of their pounding at the gates of America is directed toward undermining the country's values and traditional institutions in a widespread culture assault against the nation's political strengths that are drawn from its free economic engine. Since each layer represents the vital linkages among the radical Left members, one must consider the four-tiered layer cake as a subversive network of networks.

The upper-most tier of this political-ideological pastry blends the doctrinal tenets, underlying assumptions, goals, and policies that guide a unified effort by the successive levels. The driving forces in this top network are the "thought leaders" and other individuals in non-governmental organizations (NGOs), including anarcho-communists and anarcho-syndicalists. These are the strategists guiding the operational commanders who direct the Gramsci-embracing street fighters. By and large, one can expect to find these enablers in the darkest shadows of the world. Examples of leading members are the Washington, D.C.-based the revolutionary centers—the Institute for Policy Studies, the so-called "think tank of the Left," as well as the coopted mainstream media and politicians making up the Congressional Progressive Caucus and the "Shadow Party" hiding inside the Democratic Party that has been seized by George Soros and the sixties radicals.[3]

The radical Left selected appropriate political warfare tools to penetrate U.S. culture—"open spaces" in the social structure, public schools and universities, government, and a host of community organizations—in order to transform society and replace traditional American values and institutions with neo-Marxist values. Arnaud de Borchgrave, editor at large at United Press International and *The Washington Times*, explained the ultra-Left's renewal and re-emergence in 2001 by focusing on one of its most powerful driving forces.

The Washington left-wing think tank Institute for Policy Studies

(IPS) is . . . back in action. IPS was a major conduit for major Soviet disinformation themes throughout the Cold War and spent most of the past decade [1992–2001] licking its wounds and biding its time pending the next global anti-capitalist opportunity. It is now at hand.[4]

The second tier of the progressive-socialist-marxist cake consists of the key strategic partners of the upper-most level. Individuals and NGOs at this level operate more openly than at the first tier. These Leftists are the key operational planners who may be best seen as enablers of the guidance offered from the top. These second layer actors draw upon their own funding sources as well as those made available by the upper level. Although many may hug the shadows, they operate mostly in the open. Examples of the strategic partners of the upper level are the American Civil Liberties Union (ACLU), National Lawyers Guild, deep cover Leftists in the news media, and several thousand Marxist professors at American universities.

Both anti-globalization and anti-war activists are key drivers in the third tier of the radical layer cake. Most are members of NGO's protesting U.S. economic and political actions. Among the major topical areas is the environment, gender issues, race, immigration, animal rights, and a multitude of other groups. Examples include such NGOs as Moveon.org, Rainforest Action Network, National Organization for Women, La Raza, and Code Pink. These organizations often draw members focused on their single issue orientation, only to be co-opted by the progressive-socialist-marxist propaganda and disinformation.

The fourth tier in the so-called "progressive movement" is made up of street workers who are the radical Left's cannon fodder at direct action (agitation) and propaganda protests in the cities of North America, Europe, Oceana, and the developing world. Each of these activist areas are opposed to neoliberalism, globalization in the South, and conflicts in Afghanistan and Iraq. Among the large numbers of college student activists are many who are not motivated by ideology. Protesting is fun. As one student anti-Vietnam protester told me in 1969, marching in the streets of Washington, D.C., was all about "smoking a little grass and getting a little ass." This writer's many interviews of student and hard Left protesters since the December 1999 Battle for Seattle revealed that a large contingent simply ignored the communist credentials of the protest organizers. "We're not political," one coed cooed, "we are for peace."

Islamic Salafists

For nearly 1,000 years, from the seventh and eighth centuries to the seventeenth, Islamic warriors swept across the map from Portugal to northern India, North Africa, Spain and southern France, the Balkans, Turkey, and parts of Hungary and Poland. After the Ottoman Turks appeared on the scene, they kept the pressure on the West until they suffered a resounding defeat in a 1683 during a siege against Vienna. The Christian West's victory began a long retreat for the Islamic civilization, which reached its lowest point in the 1920s, following the end of World War One, when only four Islamic countries—Turkey, Saudi Arabia, Iran, and Afghanistan— were not reduced to some form of rule by non-Muslims.

Western retreat from colonialism, especially following World War Two, resulted in the independence of forty-five independent countries with sizable majorities of Muslim people. Hence, the contemporary "Islamic Resurgence," Samuel Huntington explained, is at its base a historical return to the violent clashes between Islam and Christianity, the same violence marking radical Islam and the West nearly 1,400 years ago. Huntington cited several factors as contributors to the contemporary Islam-West conflict: (1) rapid Muslim population growth resulting in a spike of unemployed and disaffected people, (2) greater confidence among Muslim peoples of the intrinsic worth of their civilization and values, (3) Muslim fear of the predominantly Christian West's efforts to universalize its values and institutions through economic and political globalization, (4) collapse of the Soviet Union as a common Western-Islamic threat, and (5) the contact and intermingling of Westerners and Muslims in today's world gave the latter a restored sense of identity and an appreciation of how their values differ from and were superior to those in the West.[5]

By the twenty-first century, Muslim disapproval and fear of being infected by what they considered a Western disease resulting from a gross depravity and decadence added a sixth element to Huntington's formula. Or, as Dinesh D'Souza properly described the Islamic hatred for the secular West in 2007, "the radical Muslims are convinced that America and Europe have become sick, demented societies that destroy religious belief, undermine traditional morality, dissolve the patriarchal family, and corrupt the innocence of children."[6] The multi-cultural pot between the Judeo-Christian West and the Muslim East began to boil over. "In Muslim eyes," Professor Huntington explained, "Western secularism, irreligiosity, and hence immorality are worse evils than the Western Christianity that produced them."[7]

Accommodating the United States and Europe into a restored world caliphate, or perhaps a network of cooperative caliphates, could result from two different actions by the Western countries. The first is preferable to Islam, since it entails surrender without resistance. The population, after their values and societal structures have been wholly undermined by the forward march of Islam, could simply roll over like whipped dogs and surrender to Islamic domination and convert to Islam. In this case, they would be accepted and ostensibly treated fairly.

A second alternative for the West would be invoked if the "infidel" population was defeated as a result of Islamic military action. The carrots would be sparser and sticks harsher in this eventuality. The defeated infidels could (1) convert to Islam and be "promoted" to first-level citizenship in Islamic society; (2) not convert and maintain their own religions, only Jews and Christians are eligible, in which case they would demoted to second-class citizenship and under varying circumstances that could be very harsh and with constricted freedom; and (3) those that neither convert nor maintain their own religion could be eliminated or subject to ethnic cleansing.[8] In Europe, as documented in persuasive detail by Bat Y'or, Europeans have already been conditioned to *dhimmitude*, and they are being neutralized from within by "passive submission to intellectual censorship, insecurity, internal violence, and even terrorism."[9] Europe is dying.

The assault against the West is drawn from the radical Islamic vision of a world caliphate in which the Koran serves the source of law for all peoples. This fantasy world is hardly new—it has been a part of Islamic doctrine from the beginning. Meanwhile, the Salafists in Saudi Arabia are using immigration as a weapon to colonize the United States through an array of covert measures. Underwritten by Saudi funds, immigrants to North America are assisted in the building of mosques, creating pockets of Muslim-dominated areas of the country, and slowly undermining American values in order to open greater societal space for Muslims. Terrorism and immigration are the double-edged sword in the Salafist/Wahhabi quasi-war against Judeo-Christian America, which in the long run will be unable to resist the imposition of Islamic universalism and living under the conditions of a world caliphate. Many members of the Saudi royal family, Arnaud de Borchgrave reminds Americans, consider Osama bin Laden a larger-than-life hero or "some sort of miracle man."[10] "Sleeper cells" of clandestine operatives connected to Wahhabi Islam and Saudi Arabia infiltrated the United States mostly since the mid-1980s. By 2008, the Saudi-Wahhabi presence within America was extensive.

Inside the United States, an overseas-funded terrorist support network of foreign image-makers "are creating a virtual army of supporters within our borders through aggressive recruitment of disaffected Americans, including minorities in the prison population."[11] Meanwhile, marching under the Left-wing banner of "political correctness" and wielding a curved sword to destroy America's civilization, the Saudi-Salafist lobby had already positioned itself politically within the United States by the time of the September 11, 2001 terrorist attacks. In the years following September 11, the Saudi-Salafist network disguised its presence and scored victory after victory through its clandestine spokesmen and lobbyists as it moved along a magical yellow brick road toward establishing a politically dominant Islamic community inside America.

Several high-ranking royal members of the House of Saud have funded Osama bin Laden through charities set up to launder such donations. Rand analyst Laurent Murawiec had rocked the Pentagon and many American Arabists in July 2002 when he indicted Saudi Arabia's crass duplicity:

> The Saudis are active at every level of the terror chain, from planners to financiers, from cadre to foot-soldier, from ideologist to cheerleader. Saudi Arabia supports our enemies and attacks our allies [and is responsible for a daily] outpouring of virulent hatred against the US from Saudi media, 'educational' institutions, clerics, officials—*Saudis tell us one thing in private, do the contrary in reality.*[12]

The Saudi-Salafist movement intensified its efforts to establish a workable fifth column inside America that would include a Wahhabi presence sufficient for recruitment of converts, exercise of political muscle through the democratic system, support al-Qaeda terrorists, and, over time, create the conditions needed for an Islamization of the United States.[13] "The Wahhabi presence in the United States," Senator Charles E. Schumer rightly concluded, "is a foreboding one that has potentially harmful consequences for our nation's mosques, schools, prisons, and even our military."[14]

Behind the golden hasps and locks on the Salafist doors in Medina and Mecca, is the toxic wellspring of anti-Western, anti-American hatred. Salafist clerics and some members of the Saudi royal family have been obsessed for years about neutralizing what they see as a corrupting influence of Western culture. Together, Wahhabis and members of other Islamist groups consider Islam as much a political ideology as a religion. This perspective offers Saudi Arabia a rationale for its global outreach through the creation and use of religious fifth columns around the world. Using the Saudi-Salafist/Wahhabi symbiosis as a political tool provides a super highway for funding Islamist schools, building mosques, recruiting new members, supporting terrorism, and creating charities to serve as fronts for nefarious purposes. Saudis, including members of the royal family, have aided and abetted Osama bin Laden's campaign against America through money transfers laundered through charitable organizations. "There was clearly Saudi money supporting Osama bin Laden and the terrorist group that he led," said Senator Carl Levin in July 2003. "And I think we've got to face up to that fact, the Saudis should face up to that fact and end it."[15]

Dore Gold's remarkable book, *Hatred's Kingdom,* provides the essential key to opening the secret door to the Saudi government's relationship with Salafist Islam and their off-the-books support for global terrorism, including al-Qaeda. "To put an end to the sorts of horrors that have been perpetrated by Osama bin Laden," Israel's former ambassador to the UN observed, "it is absolutely necessary to understand the unique environment whence the hatred sprang. A cold eye must be cast, therefore, on the internal dynamics of America's purported ally Saudi Arabia."[16]

It certainly is time for Americans to turn a "cold eye" toward those who profess to be friends and allies, while they build a hate-filled, clandestine fifth column inside American society. The political warfare waged by the Saudi-Salafist/Wahhabi symbiosis emphasizes disinformation and propaganda to keep American authorities guessing about Riyadh's loyalties, intimidation and money to silence moderate Muslims, and fronts and agents of influence to expand the political space for Islam's growth inside America. Meanwhile, Saudi officials, Salafist clerics, and Wahhabi fighters have been waging a "Reverse Crusade" against the United States since at least the 1980s.[17] Such Soviet-style disinformation and covert operations were never more sinister than the game being played by the Saudi-Salafist unholy trinity in which the third element, al-Qaeda, remains hidden in a shadow world of denial and deception. "We are in the midst of a jihadist offensive," William Kristol observed in 2006. "And the West is on its heels."[18]

Shadows on the Wall of Plato's Cave

The American people are being inundated with images designed by Russian propaganda and disinformation specialists, American progressives-socialists-marxists, and Saudi-Salafist/Wahhabi militants. The global geopolitical competition between the capitalist West, Russia and its supporting progressives-socialists-marxists in the West, and militant Salafism remains unseen. The image-makers in Plato's cave cast entirely different pictures than the realities in the world of sunlight. Americans so far have been blinded by the propaganda and disinformation, especially from Russia and its far Left agents of influence in the United States.

For Gramsci, victory would come after the Western "inner man" has become Marxized, the Christian superstructure destroyed, and traditional Western values replaced with the utopian goals of Karl Marx. "At the geopolitical level, the Gorbachevist design for a new world order envisages a condition in which all national governments as we now [1990] know them will cease to exist," Malachi Martin explained. "There is to be one central governing hub located in Moscow and dominated by the Communist Party of the World (CPW)."[19]

Tony Blankley, offering a clear-eyed perspective of the Islamist threat, writes in his 2005 book, *The West's Last Chance*, that "in much of the West . . . there is a blind denial that radical Islam is transforming the world." More ominously, he adds, "most European elites and far too many American politicians and journalists . . . are sheep who cannot sense the wolf pack in the woods; they see the odd wolf tail, but can't imagine wolves' teeth in their throats."[20]

$\boxed{2}$

CULTURAL REVOLUTION

"THE PARTY'S NOT OVER" proclaimed a tongue-in-cheek unifying theme of "Marxism 2000," an international conference of progressives-socialists-marxists held at the University of Massachusetts at Amherst.[1] Sponsored by the Association for Economic and Social Analysis that operated out of the Department of Economics, the September 2000 forum promoted

> . . . Marxian approaches to social theory and radical social change. We especially seek to stimulate and facilitate open discussions, rethinkings, and extensions of Marxism. In our view, they can and should form an important part of developing effective movements in the twenty-first century for an end to class exploitation and the current forms of political, cultural, and psychological oppressions (including those based on race, gender, and sexual orientation).[2]

Hundreds of participants sampled the radical agenda, which was rich in a range of topics suitable for America's social and cultural transformation to "move Marxism's future forward."

TABLE 2.1

MARXISM 2000—AGENDA (SELECTED)

- The Strange Pleasures of Destruction in Capitalist America
- "Class," "Race," "Gender" and Modernity
- The People: Multiculturalism and Renewal of the Left
- Welfare Capitalism and the American Family
- Cultural Policy, Economic Redevelopment, and the De-Sexualization of Public Space
- Gramsci on State, Civil Society, and Subaltern Struggle
- Marxism and Civil Society

- A Marxist View of the U.S. Constitution
- A Marxist Approach to the U.S. Congress
- State Terror, Prison Intellectuals, and Imprisoned Dissent
- Rethinking Labor: Towards a Labor Theory of Culture?
- Black American Cultural Revolution

- Democratic Coordination Structures, Incentives and Controls in the New Socialism
- Marx's Concept of Value: After the Cultural Turn

Most of the conference participants were university professors, including both presenters and attendees. They were an affable crowd and spoke big words about serious matters. Among them were several hard-nosed radicals, some could be heard arranging private evening discussions about revolutionary agendas. This writer inadvertently crossed-paths in the university parking garage with Zapatista Subcomandante Marcos, leader of the indigenous revolt in Chiapas, Mexico (At the time, I had not seen "Marcos" unmasked; a photograph of Professor Rafael Sebastian Guillen Vicente, the Mexican Marxist behind the balaclava, was later released by the Mexican government.).

It seemed almost everyone at the radical Left conclave was advocating some variety of socialism, Marxism, Maoism, anarcho-communism, and even Marxism-Leninism, although disagreement persisted over important differences between their respective doctrinal prescriptions. Orthodox communists warned conference participants about the dangers of wandering away from the basics of Marx and Lenin and others cackled endlessly about the ideas of Italian revisionist Antonio Gramsci. But most agreed that it was imperative to get a new left-wing movement underway as quickly as possible.[3]

The progressives-socialists-marxists and other latter-day radical Leftists agreed on the need to destroy the state as a part of the coming socialist revolution. There simply was no other way to achieve socialist governance in the United States than to crush the existing capitalist system. It was the prospect of this very same tearing down of the U.S. government that led journalist Alice Widener four decades ago to label all communists and Marxists "teachers of destruction." As in my experience at the Marxism 2000 conclave, Alice Widener found as early as 1965 that the radical Leftists attending the Socialists Scholars Conference were not peaceful reformers: "They instruct their pupils to be against the entire past and existing traditional social and political order of things."

The Socialists' first strategic aim was to launch the social and cultural revolution on all fronts, then accede to political power, and finally dismantle the bourgeois structure and replace it with political forms that would be representative of the working class. "The Marxist teachers of destruction seek to destroy our union as a people through fomenting every kind of discussion by means of 'class struggle,'" Widener observed. "They seek to destroy our domestic tranquility by aggravating discontent, envy, and all natural, genuine or fancied ills in our fallible human society, and by instigating riots and demonstrations certain to lead to violence."[4]

The political, economic, social, and cultural realities in the early twenty-first century, as compared to the late 1960s may differ in detail, but the over-all progressive-socialist-marxist goal of transforming American culture and destroying the existing form of constitutional democratic government from within remains unchanged.

More than four decades have passed since Ms. Widener offered her trenchant observations about the "teachers of destruction." During all of those years, nothing has been revised on the radical agenda, except the intensity level of the Left-wing pressures on traditional American values and the institutions of freedom that protect them. Although Widener did not use the contemporary catch-phrase "Culture War," she stood on the threshold of its birth and the subsequent Left-wing bludgeoning of American society and culture since the mid-1960s and 1970s. Quoting a position prepared for the Socialist Scholars Conference entitled "Towards a Socialist Strategy for the United States," Widener laid bare the structure and purpose of the effort to transform American society: "it is clear that the primary strategic perspective of American socialism should be to launch the social and cultural revolution on all fronts. This means desanctifying and putting into crisis all capitalist institutions and social relationships."[5]

The Marxist notion of violent upheaval and seizure of power in the United States was put aside as being a task too great.[6] Rather, the Socialist Scholars' goal was to prepare for that "glorious day" by fomenting a cultural transformation through the direct and indirect activities of a new revolutionary vanguard steeped in the revisionist Marxism of Antonio Gramsci. If the progressives-socialists-marxists transformed American culture, they would be in a position to achieve power with minimal violence through transformation *before* the ascension of the working class to political power.

"American Communists sought nothing less than the revolutionary transformation of society into a perfect egalitarian socialism that delivered material and cultural abundance without oppression of any sort," John Earl Haynes and Harvey Klehr—the deans of research and analysis of American Communism—concluded. "This was no gentle utopianism, however, but a messianic romanticism that hated the existing world with its myriad imperfections and looked forward to apocalyptic change."[7] A massive social transformation in the United States, what is popularly called the "Culture War," would prepare American society for this momentous event, while tearing down the federal government and shredding the Constitution through a "passive revolution" to make way for socialist governance.

The radical Left prosecutes two agendas at the same time. One is in the open world behind agents of influence masquerading as non-governmental organizations of ostensibly well-meaning social activists, whereas the other agenda goals are pursued from the darkness of the shadow world to transform cultures and ruling political systems. The open and covert activities designed to advance the Left-wing goal of creating a stateless world order reveal the basic socialist principles that are being honed to become predominant influences in the American people's lives. Within the Left-wing are elements with different degrees of radicalism. Some operate clandestinely from the shadow of popular front groups. For others, extreme actions must be taken to advance the cause of "social justice" in the face of well-entrenched political power in the industrialized countries. Most of these "teachers of destruction" are aligned with Moscow as a global geopolitical competitor, some knowingly in solidarity with Russia's goals and others conveniently unaware of their support for the Kremlin's drive for one-world, Party-State socialist governance.

Roots of the Contemporary Culture War

Today's culture war is designed by the revolutionary Left, the new "teachers of destruction," to enable them to accede to political power through stealth. Once they occupy key positions in America's liberal democratic government, they plan to crush the liberties provided for by the U.S. Constitution and Bill of Rights in order to destroy corporate capitalism in the name of the public good.

Three sketches of the Marxist roots influencing today's culture war expose the realities behind the Left-wing images presented to Americans. The first is "Critical Theory." It was developed by Marxist scholars at the Frankfurt School that reached back to its 1923 origin in Germany. Critical Theory provided the European intellectual driving force that underwrote many of the counter-culture events in the United States during the 1960s and 1970s. The second Marxist root to the contemporary culture war in American draws strength and guidance from the strategy and tactics for achieving power developed by Antonio Gramsci, an Italian communist. And the third Marxist root is made up by 25,000 to 30,000 radical professors ensconced on American campuses across the country who have turned their classrooms into political re-education camps. These radical professors, wrapped in the pseudo-intellectual robes of Critical Theory and Antonio Gramsci, make up America's contemporary "teachers of destruction." The revolutionary agenda of the Marxist professors in 2008 is the same as it was in the mid-1960s when Alice Widener warned that "the Marxist teachers of destruction seek to destroy our union as a people through fomenting every kind of dissension by means of 'class struggle' . . . They seek to destroy our justice. . . . They seek to destroy our common defense."[8] The difference today is that the "teachers of destruction" are several steps closer to undermining the cultural pillars of American society, setting the stage for their accession to power.

Critical Theory

Critical Theory helped to radicalize today's neo-Marxist culture war. Rooted in the Marxist-oriented ideas and activities of a German intellectual brain trust assembled in the 1920s, the New

Left radicals drew upon these early musings to sustain their assault on America. During the 1960s, Critical Theory rationalized the New Left's anti-capitalist and social change agendas. It accommodated multidisciplinary research in an effort to develop a social theory that would be sufficiently systematic and comprehensive to serve as a change agent for principal social and political problems of the present-day.[9]

The Institute of Social Research began as a part of the University of Frankfurt in Germany. Created to emulate the Marx-Lenin Institute in Moscow, European Marxism served as the theoretical basis of the Institute's program of study. Over the years, the Institute's variety of Marxist intellectuals conducted inquiries into empirical-historical open questions, a materialist supra-disciplinary social theory, and a critical theory of society.

The term Critical Theory was adopted by the Institute during its World War II exile at Colombia University in New York. Critical Theory was an attempt to synthesize specific elements of political economy and socialist politics. Since Americans were quite hostile toward any theory of socialist revolution and closeness to the Soviet Union, Critical Theory was chosen as a cover word for the Institute's commitment to the study of Marxism.[10] Hence, right from the beginning Marxist images cast on the wall of Plato's cave were aimed at manipulating American perceptions and hiding the reality that Critical Theory served as an intellectual dagger aimed at American hearts and minds.

Critical Theory begins with a premise that all inquiry, thought, political action, and "informed" political behavior must occur within a framework of reference that accounts for history, society, and a synthesis of philosophy, the sciences, and politics. By showing the relationship between ideas and theoretical positions in their social environment, critical theorists claim that they expose the roots of social processes. "Social theories, for Critical Theory," Douglas Kellner explains, "are thus forms of social practice which reproduce dominant forms of capitalist activity."[11] To take the summary view of Critical Theory one step further: "While traditional theory uncritically reproduces the existing society, 'Critical Theory,' by contrast, is an expression of activity which strives to transform it."[12] "It," in this case, being American society.

The Nazi seizure of power compelled members of the Institute of Social Research to flee Germany in 1933. After two years in Geneva, the Institute moved to New York (1935–41) and later California (1941–53). These intellectual Marxists established their presence at American universities, including Columbia, Princeton, Brandeis, and the University of California at Berkeley and San Diego. In 1953, the Institute of Social Research returned to the University of Frankfurt in Germany, although some of its scholars, most notably Herbert Marcuse, remained in the United States. During its years of exile, the Frankfurt School had become well-known for its theory of capitalism's growing strength over all aspects of social life and its development of new forms of social control.

German intellectuals at the Institute developed a "Critical Theory," which rejected Western civilization and tilted heavily to an imaginative, utopian, Marxist vision, which was totally disconnected from everyday American experience. The critical theorists insisted that the logic of their thinking was sufficient to "transcend" reality—the superior minds of the Institute's intellectuals, they argued, would fashion "truths" without the need for verification of theory by experimental evidence.

Critical Theory's influence on the New Left in the late 1960s and 1970s ensured that American society would be infected by this Marxist malignancy. While it addressed many aspects of social structure, Critical Theory, in the final analysis, proposed activities that would transform society into one far more amenable to Marxism. Critical Theory's "struggle for social change" was an important step in undermining the values, structures, and practices of America's free market and democratic principles.

Special attention was given to the "culture industries" of U.S. capitalism. To the Frankfurt Institute's Marxist thinkers, the culture industries used communication to manage the people's consciousness and mask social conflict behind the scenes. According to the Institute's scholars, the mass deception conducted by the culture industries manipulated popular acceptance of current society and served as an ideological indoctrination to reinforce existing cultural standards.

By identifying contradictions in society's belief in the existing system, these revolutionaries entertained a dream world where their rules based on Marxism would prevail. The cultural Marxists at the Frankfurt School set into motion—and then guided—the counter-culture revolution of the 1960s. Herbert Marcuse was among the most active in promotion of Critical Theory's social revolution among university students. The new strategy of revolution was focused on a unique dispersed disintegration of the capitalist governing system and the establishment of a classless world.[13] Marcuse's young disciples of the 1960s are now the tenured university "teachers of destruction," and their ruinous actions are aimed directly at American culture.

Herbert Marcuse offered opportunities to further develop and teach a radical Marxist brand of sociology centered on culture and consciousness as vital elements of revolution. By the 1960s, the University of California at San Diego-based Marcuse was known internationally as the "Guru of the New Left."[14] Within this radical Left context, Marcuse developed a comprehensive statement of the theory of a totally administered or one-dimensional society. He published *One-Dimensional Man* in 1964.[15]

Marcuse argued that mass media, culture, advertising, industrial organization and management, and modes of thought had a synergistic impact on the existing governing systems. These conditions resulted in an erosion of the ability for cultural thinking and creation of opposition to the capitalist-controlled system.

Marcuse questioned the very existence of a revolutionary proletariat in America and the predicted inevitable crisis of capitalism. This questioning of Marxism placed Marcuse at odds with the Old Left but in a loving embrace with the New Left. While advanced industrial society was deemed to possess the capacity for qualitative change, Marcuse posed the hypothesis "that forces and tendencies exist which may break this containment and explode on society."[16]

During the 1960s, Herbert Marcuse was celebrated worldwide as the "father of the New Left." Brandeis University refused to renew his tenured position, prompting him to take a position at the University of California at San Diego. He enjoyed great influence and popularity in the 1960s and early 1970s. His lectures, articles, and counsel to student radicals continued to call for revolutionary change and radical opposition to bourgeois society. According to David Horowitz, Marcuse's most famous essay, written in 1965, was about "Repressive Tolerance." Marcuse argued with regard to those possessing conservative views [of liberal government and individual liberty], that since they already reflected "an oppressive and already dominant social class," their speech and access to cultural platforms could be legitimately suppressed.[17]

The modern-day ultra-Left ideology of "Cultural Marxism" takes yesterday's Soviet Marxist-Leninist model and stands it on its head. Revolution on this alternative path no longer envisions a cataclysmic clash between workers and capitalists as the final act. Rather, contemporary revolutionary doctrine is far more dangerous: it is based on a nonviolent, persistent, and "quiet" transformation of American traditions, families, education, media, and support institutions day-by-day. The seizure of political and economic power remains a key objective, but this "final act" is really a first step in transforming the existing cultural order.

The Left's "rage against the system" is still dominated by "teachers of destruction" who counsel the disintegration of American culture. Herbert Marcuse was adamant that Marx's and

Lenin's traditional ideas were old fashioned and that "what we must undertake is a type of diffuse and dispersed disintegration of the system."[18] Antonio Gramsci's formula offered Professor Marcuse a practical application of "Critical Theory."

Antonio Gramsci

The strategy for Marxist revolution devised by Antonio Gramsci in the 1930s is quite evident in the contemporary struggle between the guardians of American values and traditions and the propaganda and disinformation spun by the ultra-Left. Gramsci's influence can also be found in the positions taken by the New Left in the 1960s and the 1970s. Likewise, followers of Gramsci are clearly present among today's puppeteers in Plato's cave, busying themselves with casting shadows of "political correctness" on the wall. Even though these deceptive images would never hold up in the glaring sunlight of reality, many Americans have been manipulated and find these deceptive shadows to be true depictions of life on earth. At its base, the "culture war" in America is a war of deception waged by the contemporary followers of Antonio Gramsci.

Born on January 22, 1891 in Ales, a town located in the Sardinian province of Cagliari, Antonio Gramsci suffered from ill health throughout his life and experienced deep financial insecurity during his youth. Nonetheless, he was judged to be of such superior intelligence that he won a scholarship in 1911 to study at Turin University. It was at the University that Gramsci had his first contact with and actively supported the Italian Socialist Party. After the Party split a decade later, Gramsci became an intellectual leader on the central committee of the Italian Communist Party. From May 1922 until November 1923, he was an Italian delegate to the Communist International in Moscow. When he returned home, Gramsci became a prominent leader of the Communist Party in Italy's parliament.

Because of his opposition to Italy's Fascist leader Benito Mussolini, Gramsci was arrested on November 8, 1926 and a year later was sent to prison for political dissidence. Following nearly a decade of illnesses that were never treated properly in prison, Gramsci died from a cerebral hemorrhage on April 27, 1937 at age forty-six. During his years in prison, Gramsci was able to smuggle thirty-three notebooks, more than 3,000 pages, of his thoughts about working class revolution. He explained in the notebooks why Fascism triumphed in Italy and why the Italian working class did not rise up against the capitalist superstructure and seize power during a political vacuum in 1921–22. These political writings, about nine volumes of notes, were supplemented by nearly 500 letters that he wrote from prison to his sister-in-law Tatania Schucht and a few friends.

Tatania resided in Rome and was the person most intimately associated with Gramsci's prison life, bringing him the clothing, food, and medicine he needed to survive. She exchanged thoughts and feelings with him in letter form and sent his notebooks via diplomatic pouch to Moscow. Gramsci's intellectual work did not emerge until after World War II, but by the 1950s his writings began attracting increasing attention and critical commentary, especially by Left-wing intellectuals.[19]

Pondering the events that brought Benito Mussolini to power and the meek acceptance by ordinary Italians, Gramsci concluded that they had been motivated to a quiet acceptance by the teachings of the Roman Catholic Church, which in Italy stood above all other societal influences in shaping the values shared by both workers (assumed to be oppressed) and the bourgeoisie. It was from this analysis and conclusion that Gramsci postulated a new pathway into the future for the proletariat, an ideology that some today call "Cultural Marxism."

Gramsci's years in prison gave him a chance to devise a new and more deceptive pathway to winning power over the ruling capitalists. Although he was a deeply committed Marxist in ideology, Gramsci believed that Marx and Lenin overlooked the importance of a key reality that bound the workers and bourgeoisie together: Christian culture. As John Vennari observed, Gramsci knew that "unlike the non-existent proletarian revolution, which existed only as a mirage of the future, Christian culture was a hard-rock reality that the people ate, drank, and breathed."[20]

Gramsci set out to provide a revolutionary blueprint that would pervert the Roman Catholic Church's values of goodness and forgiveness into a mind control tool in the hands of the new Marxists. He knew that the working classes were defined by their Christian faith and their Christian culture. Christianity, Gramsci recognized, blocked the way toward uprisings by the workers against the ruling class. No matter how strong might be their oppression, the working classes defined themselves in terms of their Christian faith. Christian culture liberated the working classes against even the most repressive secular abuses. While Gramsci shared the world views of Marx and Lenin concerning a future "workers paradise," he knew that it had to come about in a wholly different way than through violent revolution.[21] A high priority item for contemporary radical Leftists, therefore, is to destroy religion, a competitor for winning the "hearts and minds" necessary for Marxist revolution. For the Left, worship of God must be replaced by a worship of man, or "secular humanism."

Focusing on the fact that cultural values in the West are tied to Christianity, Gramsci's strategy centered on destroying the influence religious values have over people. This "hegemony" of Christianity, Gramsci argued, is manifested by civil society institutions that influence government and the will to openly resist recognized Marxist initiatives. These institutions include the churches of all denominations; education from grade school to university; the mass media—electronic, print, and Internet-based; the family; key nodes of popular culture; and others. The pathway to eliminating the hegemony of Judeo-Christian values, therefore, is through the activities of civil society institutions and the quiet destruction of the nuclear family. To establish a new hegemony based on Marxist utopian ideals, one must infiltrate these institutions, show people how Marxism touches their lives and then turns them away from Judeo-Christian values to an accommodation with secularization, which will ostensibly meet their spiritual or transcendent needs when their inner selves are Marxized. This approach has already proven enormously effective in Europe and has achieved significant gains in the United States.

Political warfare—not violence—is needed to challenge the dominant hegemony of the bourgeoisie. Capitulation will come after a long war of position fought across the associations and institutions of the capitalist civil society. It is important to recognize that "political warfare," in this context, means societal coalitions striking to gain control through a cultural and ideological struggle, as well as bouts in the political and economic arenas. When the working class and its coalition partners gain control, the character of hegemonic leadership changes to nurture the new moral and intellectual order based on Marxism.[22]

Lynne Lawner explains that Gramsci was well aware that his was a political strategy, one that would take a long time for consensus, or a new hegemony, to prevail over coercion. But Gramsci also was convinced that the strategy, strengthened by Marxism, would produce an enduring revolution once victory had been achieved: "Only a Marxist party, Gramsci maintained, could become that new organism of civil society—the party that is a *part* of society, operating dialectically in relation to other parts and capable of founding a State for all members of society precisely because of its daily dependence on the active, conscious consensus of the great laboring masses."[23]

Gramsci's blueprint for action serves as the driving force behind the contemporary culture war in the United States. Gramsci's overarching concept, John Vennari explains, is aimed at a complete secularization of American society to make way for Marxist hegemony controlling the minds of the population:

What was essential, insisted Gramsci, was to Marxize the INNER man. *To secularize him to the point of godlessness.* Only when that was done could you successfully dangle the utopia of the 'Workers' Paradise' before his eyes, to be accepted in a peaceful and humanly agreeable manner, without revolution, violence or bloodshed.[24]

Vennari's analysis and description cuts into the very heart of Gramsci's strategy and how it is being applied today in the United States with great success. This is an attack on the "Christian mind and Christian culture" in America, a stealthy assault that systematically touches "what is . . . [*inner*] and *immediate* to individuals and groups . . . in their daily lives." The modern-day Gramscists are orchestrating America's secularization from deep inside the world's shadows and seek to clean out the Judeo-Christian values held by most Americans. Only then will Americans be ready to Marxize their inner selves.

American and international progressives-socialists-marxists from the Soviet era tuned to Gramsci's ideas in the 1990s in order to shore-up their Marxist ideology, though Gramsci also drew on Leninism in developing his slow-roll strategy for communist revolution. The driving force behind the adoption of Gramsci's model, laced with dollops of Marxist dogma, though with a few practical amendments, has been based on two mutually reinforcing goals. The first objective is an on-going domestic campaign by American progressives-socialists-marxists to tear down what they consider the "corporate-controlled" U.S. government and replace it with a governance by the working class. This campaign is not new. Rather, it is an intensification of a long-term propaganda and agitation program that has been designed to undermine American values and foment a massive cultural transformation, with special emphasis on secularizing the minds of Americans as a way of neutralizing the strength of Christianity. This is an important function on the radical Left's agenda, for it dovetails with secularization efforts in Europe and elsewhere that drives humanity toward a Russian type of Party-State, which is directed toward eventual socialist world governance dominated by the Kremlin.

The second mutually reinforcing goal has a long pro-Soviet ancestry, especially among the ultra-Left in Europe. The idea behind the European Union has been to create a stateless civil society over time, one with greatly weakened national sovereignty and a concomitant strengthening of the central European authority. In the 1990s, Gramsci's revolutionary strategy, drawing heavily on key aspects of Marxism, became the European radical Left's model to replace Soviet Marxism-Leninism. Moreover, its doctrine was expanded from a Eurocentric model to a "Global Village," to a socialist vision that would provide global social justice, and finally to a stateless and secularized civil society exercising a bottom-up people's democracy. In plain words, in Europe, Gramsci's formula is the radical Left's scheme for world governance in a convergence with Russia and under a confederation of the United Nations, the European Union, and supporting institutions, such as the International Criminal Court, which was put into effect in 2002.

The United States is expected to join this new world order once the country's culture is sufficiently de-Christianized and Marxized. This is the case since Gramsci's strategy also absorbs Lenin's geopolitical vision of a world Marxist revolution falling under the control of a Party-State operational center. The culture war in America is but a single theater of operations, though perhaps the most important.

New Left

Members of the New Left in the early 1960s, said to be "shocked" by revelations of Stalin's murderous ways, romanticized Cuba's Fidel Castro. Over the years Castro slaughtered *only* about 16,000 "like noxious insects," as Lenin described his killings, for their political beliefs—a piker compared with Lenin's and Stalin's genocidal statistics.[25] By its own rationalization, the New Left captured the moral high ground of the communist movement by invoking "Marx as a political weapon" and challenging the Old Left.[26] But make no mistake. "From the beginning, the New Left was not an innocent experiment in American utopianism," David Horowitz cautions, "but a self-conscious effort to rescue the Communist project from its Soviet fate."[27] In spite of its differences with members of the Old Left and their totalitarian enthusiasm, the New Left refused to break ranks and remained loyal to "the revolt against bourgeois society."[28] Above all, the New Left "refused to concede that Marxism or socialism, both integral to the Communist idea, were themselves condemned by the Stalinist nightmare." Horowitz explains that among New Leftists "who were impatient to 'bring the System down,' it was Marxism that provided the convenient ax."[29]

The 1960s and early 1970s were tumultuous years for American communism. The Red offspring from the 1930s had come of age. This was a pampered generation—"Red Diaper" babies—that grew up in communist households where they had become brainwashed by Marxist-Leninist values. By breaking from the pro-Soviet Old Left making up the core of the American fifth column, the New Left dedicated itself to designing a distinct future for America.

American communists, responding to orders from the Soviet Comintern in 1935, adopted the popular tactic of camouflaging their activities and real intentions. Often referring to themselves as "progressives," communists were able to hide their true affiliation. Sometimes they wore the mask of benign liberals or reformists.[30] David Horowitz explained yesteryear's false presentation of the communists' political beliefs:

My parents and their comrades were indeed conspirators. . . . Their secret names and secret organizations, the elaborate network of front organizations they created to camouflage their agendas, their practice of infiltrating and subverting liberal organizations, and the disingenuousness with which they presented themselves as 'progressive' all added up to a suspicious case. And their hearts were loyal to the Soviet state. . . . For them, Russia was the incarnation of the socialist idea.[31]

Many New Leftists collaborated with America's enemies in the 1960s and 1970s. Thousands of the New Left worked with communist regimes and their intelligence bureaus. Cuban intelligence (the DGI), for instance, operated the Venceremos Brigades in which foreigners were brought to Cuba to help harvest sugar cane (The foreign volunteers also offered Cuba's intelligence service a large recruiting pool.). Other New Leftists had direct contacts with communist guerrillas in El Salvador, Eastern Europe, and Vietnam. Since they considered the U.S. to be the evil empire, cooperation with America's socialist enemies was a natural outgrowth of their loyalty to the revolution.[32]

"For us," Horowitz says, "the Cuban Revolution embodied first of all the hope of breaking with the tinted Stalinist past. We thought of Fidel as one of us."[33] Yet, 50,000 of the educated middle class left the country, including doctors, teachers, and lawyers. Subsequent repression in the 1960s resulted in political killings and some 30,000 Cubans who were deemed to be of questionable loyalty were thrown into rat-infested, filthy prisons. These measures led to a mass exodus aboard makeshift rafts to escape Cuba.[34] The New Left's hero Fidel Castro looked more like a cheap imitation of Stalin that the mythical revolutionary he had been made out to be.

Rejecting the Old Left's loyalty to the brutish Communist Party of the Soviet Union, the New Left embraced the Cuban Revolution, Black radicalism, "alienation," and the Third World. The American Communist Party kept the New Left at a distance in order to remain "a faithful handmaiden of Soviet policies."[35] The New Left "scorned the Old Left's dishonesty in hiding its agenda behind liberal and progressive masks," Horowitz lamented. "Liberals were the real enemy; progressive was a mealy-mouthed camouflage for a revolutionary agenda."[36]

Focusing on their own particular pathway to America's socialist future, radical Leftists in the 1970s and 1980s shared a world view of the ostensible inequities inherent in American capitalism that resulted in a society of grievous social contradictions and a self-perpetuating elite power structure. Lifting a chapter from Antonio Gramsci, the radicals strived to achieve a majority perspective or "ideological hegemony."[37] Martin Carnoy and Derek Shearer, for instance, argued for "Economic Democracy" that would shift control of investments from corporations to the public sector and then reconstruct economic decision-making to emphasize control by workers and consumers.[38] Yet another line of radical thought pressed closer to Gramsci's blueprint by advocating a "citizen movement" based on "organic intellectuals," or those drawn from the working class that would "lead to a self-consciousness about its 'historic role.'"[39]

Other Leftists, agreeing that American society held many flaws and that capitalism was "wasteful" and "repugnant," grasped Gramsci's formula in building a new "collective consciousness." These radicals or "coercive utopians," according to Rael Jean and Erich Isaac, would begin a new "cultural revolution" through ideological-cultural struggle.[40]

G. William Domhoff, a professor of psychology and sociology at the University of California at Santa Cruz, is particularly notable for filling his classroom for four decades with anti-capitalist, hate America's governing system invective. Domhoff's central thesis, borrowing more than a little from C. Wright Mills' *The Power Elite* (1956), is that the United States is ruled by a carefully interwoven governing class. The "power elite." Domhoff argues, are benefactors of corporate capitalism that has emerged to dominate the American economy. This "corporate feudalism," he says, led to a privileged few who attend private schools, maintain exclusive clubs, and "ride the hounds on their vast farmlands." For Domhoff, simply "turning the spotlight on the power elite is a revolutionary act."[41]

Nearly forty years after his writings in the late 1960s and 1970s Domhoff was still peddling his argument for creating blueprints to foster the post-industrial America. In April 2005, he was still pounding his well-worn drum: "those who have the money have the power," "money rules in America," the "upper class" dominates the federal government, and "working people have less power than in many other democratic countries." Defining the "power elite as leadership groups of the upper class," Domhoff arguably shows how these privileged persons dominate the federal government to serve their interests through use of corporate lobbyists, backroom super-lawyers, and industry-wide trade associations as the agents of power.[42]

The open question is how much academic pollution has Domhoff been responsible for over the years. Not only did his Marxist propaganda poison the minds of his students directly but thousands of others indirectly as well through the use of his writings by other Marxists in their classrooms across the country. Somehow Domhoff escaped being tagged by David Horowitz as one of "the 101 most dangerous academics in America" in his book *The Professors*. Professor G. William Domhoff is nominated here for consideration as the 102nd most dangerous. His past and present Marxism advocating of cultural revolution deserves no lesser sentence.

Peter Collier and David Horowitz placed their finger on the pulse of the New Left's unfulfilled expectations, when they noted that the 1960s have become the "decade that would not die." The New Left's tumultuous actions made it the "Destructive Generation," which contaminated American society that persists even today. Some accomplishments by the New Left were positive, but, Collier and Horowitz, agree that "there was a dark side too. . . . We had weakened our culture's immune system. Making it vulnerable to opportunistic diseases."[43]

One of those "opportunistic diseases" was the radical Left's contemporary subversion of America's societal strengths to motivate a massive cultural revolution. The doyens of Critical Theory and New Leftism opened wounds in American society that became infected with the Marxist strain of Antonio Gramsci. By sweeping away traditional American values, institutions, and the Constitution and Bill of Rights, the Gramsci Left remains poised in the shadows to accede to power via the electoral process. Once in power all things will become possible. Gramsci's formula for "passive revolution" makes it within reason to deliver America's head on a silver platter.[44]

Culture War

By the 1980s, the ever dangerous true believers in radical marxism, the "teachers of destruction," turned to transforming American universities into instruments for revolutionizing American culture. These messianic Gramscists formed an "academic cult" based on Antonio Gramsci's blueprint to obtain the levers of power necessary to follow a passive revolutionary pathway that would undermine America's Judeo-Christian values and traditional institutions.[45]

Burrowing into universities at a time when the radical professors were nearing tenure status, the new "teachers of destruction," served as Gramsci's "Marxist intellectuals." In this way, the excess baggage of Critical Theory, Antonio Gramsci, and the New Left found its way into academia where Marxist professors trained the next generation to carry on the stealthy campaign of transforming American culture over the long term. Their goals, following Gramsci's formula of operating quietly and out of sight, is to destroy the Judeo-Christian values and the nuclear family that stand in the way of their Marxist fantasy world. These contemporary "teachers of destruction" have not abandoned their pursuit of destroying the

American political system—they simply went underground and into civil society positions in academia, the media, politics, unions, business, and non-profit organizations; others entered government.

Three major categories underwrite the ultra-Left's Gramsci formula for the cultural transformation of America: anti-Christianity, the family (feminism, abortion, homosexuality, and sexualization of children), and re-education (pre-school through university).

Anti-Christianity

Christianity is the most important superstructure in the United States that must be eliminated for Gramsci's blueprint to be successful. Gramsci prescribed a unitary Marxist attack against Christianity," Malachi Martin explained, "for Gramsci meant that Marxists must change the residually Christian mind. He needed to alter that mind—to turn it into its opposite in all its details—so that it would become not merely a non-Christian mind but an anti-Christian mind."[46] This meant to erase any individual or group thought about God or reference to Judeo-Christian values. It meant to create an antipathy toward Judeo-Christian ideals and those that espouse these values in their decisions about dealing with modern life.

Gramsci's blueprint for action, Martin explained, called for a stealthy attack on Christianity, one that

> . . . had to be pursued by means of a quiet and anonymous revolution . . . everything must be done in the name of man's dignity and rights, and in the name of his autonomy and freedom from outside constraint. From the claims and constraints of Christianity, above all. Accomplish that, said Gramsci, and you will have established a true and freely adopted hegemony over the civil and political thinking of every formerly Christian country. Do that, he promised, and in essence you will have Marxized the West. The final step—the Marxization of the

politics itself—will then follow. All classes will be one class. All minds will be proletarian minds. The earthly Paradise will be achieved.[47]

Gramsci's formula for replacing traditional Judeo-Christian culture with a new Marxist culture applied two main tactics: repeat the same arguments over and over, changing only the literary style, and, secondly, create new secular intellectuals by reaching into the masses and elevating a unique anti-Christian type of Marxist intellectual. Because these new intellectuals are drawn from the population, rather than the elite, they will become the "spearheads of the new socialist order." Their secular mentality will reject the Judeo-Christian theology of history and of man's origin and his end.[48]

How does the Marxist revolutionary go about developing this "new type of intellectual" from hallowed academic towers that will spearhead the transformation of American culture? While education is not the only factor to take into account, Alberto M. Piedra observes, "a cultural revolution can *only* be successful if the educational system is firmly committed to the transmission of the new forms of behavior that the revolutionaries endorse."[49] Hence, anti-Christianity and education in the hands of the Gramsci Marxists are mutually supportive.

Direct attacks on the family can boomerang and trigger defensive actions that could slow progress toward realization of Gramsci's goals. Hence, America's radical Left chose to attack indirectly by ridiculing the family and questioning its underlying value system. In place of the family, relationships of all kinds are promoted as being normal options, including homosexuality, same-sex marriage, abortion as birth control, and unending propaganda of permissiveness through multiple channels, including Hollywood's entertainment sewer lines, advertising, television, radio, and the Internet. Then-Cardinal Joseph Ratzinger and now Pope Benedict

XVI summarized in 2005, "we are moving [toward] a dictatorship of relativism . . . that recognizes nothing definite and leaves only one's own ego and one's own desires as the final measure."[50]

On the other hand, more than three quarters of the American people identified themselves as Christian and some 42 percent in the forty-eight continuous states attended religious services weekly or almost every week. The South, less Florida, was highest with 50 to 59 percent reporting weekly religious attendance. The Northeast was lowest with a third or so attending services, and especially low in Vermont and New Hampshire.[51]

Secular humanism is a political philosophy that rejects all forms of religious faith and worship, except the worship of man. When this philosophy of worldly things is placed into the hands of dedicated Marxists, it becomes an intellectual cudgel to smash the underpinnings of Christianity in American culture. University professors and other intellectual elites, the news media, and politicians, often in cooperation with the homosexual and feminist (pro-abortion) lobby groups, lead the charge against Judeo-Christian values. By pulling new Marxist intellectuals from the population, the Left also capitalizes on any number of dupes, dopes, and useful idiots to pick-up the arguments and repeat them over and over in a variety of communication channels.

Four organizations lead the anti-Christian secularization of American culture: American Civil Liberties Union (ACLU), American United for Separation of Church and State, People for the American Way, and Freedom From Religion Foundation. Each of the four anti-Christian groups apply the "Establishment Clause"— "Congress shall make no law respecting an establishment of religion"—of the First Amendment to the Constitution as a cover for their attacks against the "Free Exercise Clause"—"or prohibiting the free exercise thereof."

The anti-Christian groups are experts on the use of legal challenges to bludgeon communities and social groups into submission. Local government leaders often find it far less expensive to eliminate a Christian cross, no matter its historical accuracy, or eliminate a Christmas creche on public property than to defend their community-supported actions in legal battles. Together, the secular-Marxist warriors, many of whom are from the ACLU, leave no stone unturned as they scour the countryside for even the slightest reference to Christianity on public signs, flags and banners, or use of the people's property. When the ACLU obtained a photograph of massed U.S. Marines with their heads bowed in personal prayers during a ceremony honoring the birthday of the Marine Corps, for example, a spokesman stated: "For them to pray is clearly an establishment of religion, and we must nip this in the bud immediately."[52]

The ACLU has collected millions of dollars in awards from federal judges. Who pays? The cities, towns, and counties across the nation. Ultimately, of course, the ACLU is picking the pockets of the American people to build their coffers to pay their legal staff and for more assaults against the traditions of Americanism.[53] Perhaps the award-winning TV writer Burt Prelutsky best expressed the reality of the ACLU: "The problem with the ACLU is that it is composed in equal measure of self-righteous fools and fascistic bullies."[54]

For the Gramsci-motivated radical Leftists, erasing Christmas from the public domain is mandatory. Christmas (and Easter, to a lesser degree) is particularly troublesome for the Marxist humanists. These two most significant days of Christian worship rub salt into the wounds that the New Left cut into American culture. John Gibson of Fox News began his book, *The War on Christmas*, with one of the most inane *true* stories of modern America. A father accompanied his son to grammar school only to find banners and drawings celebrating "Happy Hanukkah" and the "Miracle of Kwanzaa," but without the slightest reference to "Christmas." However, a small undecorated tree that was called a "Friendship Tree," was sitting on a table. When the father asked the principal why it was not called a "Christmas Tree," the chief educator replied:

"Oh, we're trying to make sure we don't offend people."[55] The war on Christmas is a major battle between traditional American culture and the future envisioned by the radical Left.

"Traditional Christian beliefs have always been counter-cultural," Michael Novak at the American Enterprise Institute explained. "It was so in the days of Ancient Rome, through the Middle Ages, in the early period of the Enlightenment, and it is so today."[56]

Score one for the Marxist humanists. And then read Gibson's book and score several more points for the progressive-socialist-marxist ultra-Left that shreds the religious meaning of Christmas. John Gibson selected several telling case studies that underline the successful efforts by the Left to make Christmas politically incorrect. This "war on Christmas" has many American uncertain: should I say "Merry Christmas?" Or, would saying "Happy Holidays" be safer, since the individuals may be of other faiths? Or should I say nothing at all?

On another level, images related to Christmas presented in public can be troublesome—not just crosses and nativity scenes, but also Christmas trees, Santa Claus, and even Rudolph's red nose. Christmas Carols? Forget it. Christmas may be Macy's busy season and so it is for the ACLU and its three major anti-God consorts. The ACLU's actions reveal that they harbor a secret desire to lead the charge against celebrations of the birth of Christ as a way of supporting Antonio Gramsci. Oh, yes, they whine and explain that their actions are based on the "Establishment Clause" that prohibits any government support for religion, no matter how slight or popular it might be. But the fundamental issue is this—Gramsci's blueprint cannot be satisfied until Christianity's back is broken and erased from American culture. Only then will the mind-control techniques of Marxism in the hands of the progressives-socialists-marxists be used in guiding society into a liberty-busting socialist fantasy world. Hence, anything the ACLU, People for the American

Way, and other anti-religion organizations can do to hasten that day may explain their Gramscian anti-God activities.

The stakes raised by the progressive-socialist-marxist anti-Christian crusade are enormous. Reform Rabbi Joshua O. Haberman explained the importance of having a culture based on Judeo-Christian values in his article "The Bible Belt Is America's Safety Belt": "It's what keeps us [Jews and Christians] from careening into a moral abyss of death-on-demand, sex divorced from values, a Roman orgy and demolition derby passing as entertainment, drugs used to fill lives devoid of meaning, and a generation of strutting savages in Calvin Kleins."[57]

The Family

Pope Benedict XVI delivered a traditional New Year's prayer on January 1, 2008 that criticized "those who are hostile, even unknowingly, to the institution of the family . . . [and who] make peace fragile for the entire national and international community." The pontiff's focus on defending the traditional family has been a constant concern since he was elected in 2005. He said the traditional family led by a husband and a wife instilled values that promote peace and was an "irreplacable institution." Pope Benedict's comments focused on a slide in several European countries toward granting unwed and homosexual couples legal recognition, such as same-sex marriages.[58]

For the Marxist Left, discrediting the traditional family is an essential aspect of the culture war. The family is under persistent attack and ridicule in an effort to alienate it "from a system of values based on natural law and an objective moral order." These assaults, Alberto Piedra writes, pave "the way for a permissiveness that can only be harmful to the integral development of man," and he warns that "a new concept of the family is being propagated."[59] Children are specifically targeted by the progressives-socialists-marxists for separation from their parents moral teaching. Only by opening a door of independence from parental guidance at a young age can the radical Left block a continuation of traditional culture. This much was recognized by Lenin, Stalin, Hitler, Mao, and Castro in creating their respective new communist countries. "That's the blueprint," Bill O'Reilly of Fox News says. "If you want to change a country's culture and traditions, children must first abandon them and embrace a new vision."[60]

Permissive relationships of all kinds that are considered immoral by Judeo-Christian standards are now being accepted by increasing numbers of Americans accommodating themselves to the Marxist intellectuals in academia, the media, and in a clandestine army of agents operating under Gramsci's influence. Moral permissiveness is "in" and traditional values are "out." The feminist and homosexual agendas, for instance, clash with traditional family values directly and indirectly.

Feminism

Tammy Bruce, a clear-thinking feminist and former Leftist, and David Horowitz, a former hard core communist and New Leftist, tell the story of the radical policies, myths, and activities of the feminist movement. *The Femine Mystique*, a bestseller written in 1963 by Betty Friedan, is the generally accepted platform that launched the modern feminist movement. But in the fairytale that Friedan wove, she portrayed herself as a "typical suburban housewife," politically inactive and, according to Horowitz, not "even conscious of the woman question." Actually, Betty Friedan had been a clever communist propagandist for nearly three decades before her best product, *The Femine Mystique*, exploded onto the American scene.

Friedan had been a Stalinist Marxist from her college days through her mid-thirties. She served as a "political intimate of leaders of America's Cold War fifth column" and a lover of J. Robert Oppenheimer, a young communist physicist working on

America's atomic bomb. She attended communist front meetings and generally operated quietly behind the scenes.

The truth be told, by 1963 Friedan was already well-steeped in the "woman question" and had written about it from the angle of Engels, Lenin, and Stalin in a publication for the United Electrical Workers Union. By 1966 she had created the national Organization for Women and set the women's movement on its way. Give the lady due recognition. Mixed among her lies and denials about her communist past she introduced the idea that the U.S. national security containment policy vis-a-vis the Soviet Union put a damper on women's aspirations at home. American communists posing as feminists began to inflict a madcap picture of reality on young women. Friedan betrayed her deep hatred for America and shared her Stalinist mentality when she described America's typical family household as a "comfortable concentration camp."[61]

The consequences of radical Leftists creating and directing the feminist movement are hidden behind a shadowy string of communist fronts that do not give a hoot about women's issues, except insofar as they advance Gramsci's agenda. "Hiding behind 'progressive' and 'liberal,' the Left insists that certain steps . . . are necessary to stop racism, homophobia, and sexism," Tammy Bruce writes. "What we fail to recognize is that today's 'progressives' are not actually interested in dealing with those issues; they're simply exploiting them to further their much more complex and menacing agenda, which is all about power and control."[62]

Feminists denounce "patriarchy," a blend of religion, family, and capitalism that is said to allow men to keep women down. American culture is especially singled out as the villain of patriarchy.[63] Feminism, by its focus on marriage as the source of inequities between men and women, came to the conclusion as early as 1969 that marriage had to be destroyed. Twenty textbooks used in 8,000 college courses across the country in the mid-1990s expressed the view that "marriage is more a problem than a solution."[64]

Many still believe that the best hope for women's liberation in the twenty-first century is by taking a Marxist path. "For gender inequality to be abolished," Australian Lisa MacDonald opined, "not only must women be brought fully into social production, but private domestic labor must be replaced by socialized services, and there must be a thorough-going, conscious struggle against bourgeois culture and social psychology sexism."[65]

In moments of candor, feminists from the ultra-Left will admit that the movement is all about destroying the traditional American nuclear family. Led by sloganeering feminists that seem to be persuaded by their own anti-American propaganda, a kettle of nasty, angry women has been spawned. The Vatican charged the feminist movement in 2004 with trying to blur the boundary between men and women and in the process threatening the family, which is based on a mother and a father. The nuclear family introduces Christianity to American youth, which helps to shape future culture. When the "lethal effects" of feminism undermine "the natural two-parent structure" of the family, a Vatican letter to the Bishops explained, it makes "homosexuality and heterosexuality virtually equivalent."[66]

Such a commentary from the Vatican is hardly surprising given the harshness and success of the feminist assault on the natural relations between women and men. The cultural consequences of these attacks, Midge Decter explained, includes assault on "the traditional relations between the sexes, on courtship and marriage, and perhaps above all on the family that has made the deepest inroads into millions of ordinary American lives."[67]

Since women were excluded from the 1964 Civil Rights Act, the National Organization for Women (NOW) was created to give women a seat at the national political table. Forever mired in a Marxist swamp, NOW operates on the premise that women are "victims of repression and discrimination." Its political agenda includes a woman's right to abortion, gay and lesbian rights, and opposition to sexism, racism, violence against women, and sexual harassment. At the same time, NOW attacks Christianity and traditional values and sees men's behavior as oppressive. NOW also pursues an agenda of sideshows, including a project on sadomasochism and lesbianism. The organization refuses to oppose worldwide legislation against prostitution; it also advocates unrestricted access to pornography in public libraries.[68]

NOW's dark side is exposed in detail by Tammy Bruce in her books—*The New Thought Police* (2001) and *The Death of Right and Wrong* (2003). NOW's leadership betrayed the women's movement by diluting efforts with the broader Marxist concerns of "social justice," including the cultural transformation issue areas of race, homosexuality and other sex issues, immigration, and social subject areas.

Gloria Steinem, top feminist leader of NOW, "is a socialist," Tammy Bruce says, "so her primary concern is not with the quality of women's lives at all. She apparently is still awash in how awful this country and 'patriarchy' really are."[69] Steinem holds an honorary chair at the Democratic Socialists of America, the largest socialist organization in the United States and an affiliate of the Socialist International.

Patricia Ireland's support for the Communist Party is discussed in her autobiography. Her pro-socialist views and participation in pro-communist rallies in Miami exposed her political perspective. Ireland's friend and lover, Pat Silverthorn, was an activist in the Socialist Worker's Party, a radical Left-wing group "identified with the revolutionary Marxist, Bolshevik-Leninist perspectives of Leon Trotsky." In the 1980s the Socialist Workers Party began identifying itself closely with the Communist party of Cuba.[70]

The National Organization for Women and other national groups are all about using women's issues as social leverage to advance Antonio Gramsci's anti-family agenda. "The feminist groups that have most influence on Capitol Hill and Wall Street do not represent most American women," Kimberly Schuld explains.

"They may be savvy in politics and public relations, but they don't know or care about what most women and girls think or the problems they face in their homes, schools, and communities."[71]

Abortion

The National Abortion and Reproductive Rights Action League (NARAL) is the major political activist group supporting abortion, including access for everyone and federal funding. NARAL pursues a three-pronged approach as a non-profit lobbyist, a charitable education and research group, and a political action committee for pro-abortion rights candidates. NARAL receives corporate and major foundation grants, including those from the Buffett, Packard, Soros, and Turner entities. Jane Fonda also is a NARAL cash cow.

Fonda's Leftist credential are solidly pro-Marxist and Marxist-Leninist and anti-American. Her father, actor Henry Fonda, said that he began to worry about Jane after she "had "Angela Davis over to the house."[72] He had reason for concern. In November 1969, Jane Fonda told her audience at Michigan State University that "I would think that if you understood what communism was, you would hope, you would pray on your knees that we would someday become communist."[73]

Kate O'Beirne calls abortion on demand the "Holy Grail" of feminism. Since most Americans oppose the majority of abortions, feminists work hard to keep human fetus-killing issues in the courts. By using the courts to insulate abortion from public opinion through an array of euphemisms and lies, feminists have been successful in misdirecting criticism of their radical agenda. Demonizing their opponents an "mysogynistic religious zealots" also contributed to their defensive posture. "Feminist fundamentalism," Kate O'Beirne observed, "holds that the battle of the sexes can't be won unless women make war on the tiniest enemies of their independence."[74]

Homosexuality

Similar to the case of women, homosexual groups are typically strong advocates of abortion rights. Many homosexuals possess a philosophy of "sex without restrictions or consequences," the same sexual license agenda held by abortion advocates. This "absolute sexual license" unites those who advocate abortion and same-sex marriage.[75] According to their drum-beat, homosexuals are oppressed by whites, males, Christians, the wealthy, and even those pesky heterosexuals—or "breeders" in homosexual slang—who seem to be everywhere. Multiculturalism, therefore, accommodates homosexuals in the Left-wing's name-calling political tactics: "racist," "sexist," "homophobe," and other labels from their cheap-shot hit list.[76]

The ultra-Left wants a new society with "no rules" or ideas about morality that might compete with their vision of a socialist world. For the progressive-socialist-marxist, "decency," "virtue," and other values of traditional America mean "oppression." In order to manipulate more people to support their envisioned Gramsci-based culture, a stepping-stone on the societal space to obtaining power, the hard Left will say and go just about anything to present itself as possessing great concern and empathy for homosexuals who are "oppressed" by American culture.[77]

Homosexual groups claim that their cause is to bring about "the normalization of homosexuality in Western culture." For more than three decades homosexual advocates, many from the radical Left, have become a powerful political force on the American landscape, especially in getting their message out in the schools, media, television, films, and Christian churches. Homosexual activists won many victories along the way, which were spread to a larger audience through the echo chambers of television, movies, and the broader "social justice" message of the radical Left.[78]

When Nigerian Cardinal Francis Arinze, a Vatican official, said in a commencement address at Georgetown University in May 2003 that "the family is under siege" in many parts of the world and that the family is "mocked by homosexuality," he triggered angry responses from several students and professors. Georgetown University, a one-time admired Jesuit institution reflecting Roman Catholic values, revealed the depth of its contemporary gutter secularism when theology professor Theresa Sanders, who was seated on the commencement platform, arose and stomped off the stage to protest Cardinal Arinze's "incredibly offensive" remarks about the family being "mocked by homosexuality." Catholic teaching and good manners be damned was the message Georgetown University sent to the world.[79]

The National Educational Association (NEA) has promoted the homosexual agenda for many years. In 2001, for instance, at the NEA convention, conferees ". . . considered a resolution to implement promotion of full-scale indoctrination of children to accept and affirm homosexual behavior."[80] Bob Chase, NEA President, is quoted by Alan Sears and Craig Osten as saying: "Let me make it clear. . . . Some critics want the public schools to be an agent of moral doctrine, condemning children and adults when they are not in accord with Biblical precepts."[81] Actually, it was the NEA, Sears and Osten explain, that was "condemning parents who object to homosexual behavior and believe that it should not be taught in public schools, accusing them of forcing their 'moral doctrine' on children." Sears and Osten continued, "they are trying to push a doctrine of homosexual behavior on young children while condemning and ridiculing those, including parents, who hold to biblical principles and to undermine the beliefs they are trying to instill in their children."[82]

Same-sex unions is another tool Marxist activists use in fostering a revolutionary cultural change. Gay and lesbian "marriage," one activist says, "will dethrone the traditional family." Another homosexual leader told activists that their goal was "to fight for same-sex marriage and its benefits, and then, once granted, redefine the institution of marriage completely . . . to transform the notion of 'family' entirely." "Gay activists are sexual Marxists," Alan Sears and Craig Osten quoted one homosexual activist as saying. "Legitimizing same-sex unions is a warm-up act. Ultimately, activists want to eliminate any barriers, any signposts, that limit or channel the exercise of human sexuality."[83]

Stanley Kurtz, a fellow at the Hoover Institution found that "fragile families"—such as the Scandinavian model of domestic partnerships and unwed childbearing—were two or three times more likely to break up than married ones.[84] The incipient logic from the experience in Sweden, Denmark, and Norway—where same-sex couples have enjoyed the same rights as heterosexual couples for more than a decade—heterosexual marriage has been declining steadily. The main reasons, according to Stanley Kurtz, are, first, marriage is no longer seen as a prerequisite for parenthood, and secondly, marriage has become just another choice on a menu of alternative adult relationships. This framework leads to a perception that all forms of "family" are equal: married, non-married, and same-sex unions. Hence, same-sex relationships accelerate the contemporary trend away from marriage. The separation of marriage from parenthood has a devastating impact on children and opens them up to proselytizing by Gramsci-motivated members of the far Left.[85]

With Italian legislation pending in May 2007 that would give greater rights to unmarried couples and homosexuals, which perhaps could open the door for same-sex marriage, more than 500,000 Italians took to the streets to protest. They were met by a "secular courage" counter-demonstration whose advocates were waving and banners that read "Family Day—No Thanks, Family Gay."[86]

Another conspiracy of silence in America covers up the rampant number of sexually transmitted diseases within the homosexual and bisexual communities. Syphilis, for example, was close to being eradicated in 2000, when the rate was 2.1 cases per 100,000 population. But, as a result of men having sex with men, the national syphilis rate has made a vengeful comeback. After seven straight years of increases, the rate in 2007 had leaped to 3.7 cases per 100,000 people or a total of 11,181 cases.

According to Dr. Kevin Fenton of the Centers on Disease Control and Prevention's (CDC), "STDs [sexually transmitted diseases] remain a major threat to the gay and bisexual men, in part because having an STD other than HIV can increase the risk of transmitting or acquiring HIV."[87] Since homosexuality, especially in men, is a high risk action, it seems that if state officials are going to compel someone, especially uninformed children, to support homosexual behavior, they should first be educated on the dangers involved. Pre- "Day of Silence" lectures by qualified medical professionals, and supported with appropriate medical slides or photos might best inform these hapless schoolchildren who are being set-up by adults to make uninformed judgments. Let "informed" kids and their parents decide.

Sexualization of Children

"Control the children and you control the future," wrote that infamous, well-known Irish-American from China, "O'Reilly Tzu" in *Culture Warrior*.[88]

Dr. Judith Levine, a member of the ultra-Left elite and highly regarded in academia and the homosexual establishment, soft-peddled child molesters—"pedophiles are not generally violent"—in a candid snapshot of what the radical Left plans for the sexualization of American children.

Sex is not harmful to children. It is a vehicle to self-knowledge, love, healing, creativity, adventure, and intense feelings of aliveness. There are many ways even the smallest of children can partake in it. Our moral obligation to the next generation is to make a world in which every child—for accomplishment, connection, meaning, and pleasure—can be marvelously fulfilled.[89]

Harmful to Minors: The Perils of Protecting Children from Sex is another progressive-socialist-marxist political propaganda "hit" against mainstream American culture. Levine argues that American parents are responsible for creating "wellsprings of danger" that "are the very ignorance and terror we're instilling in kids, whereas the means of their self-defense are knowledge and courage. . . . Sexual peril is real, just as terrorism is real," Levine said. "But the kind of 'protection' that is mobilized by fear, the kind that purports to keep the young safe by locking them in their rooms, ignorant and scared to death—policies like abstinence-only education—will not protect them."[90]

This is not a headline story; after all, academics have been promoting pedophilia since 1981. Professor Gilbert Herdt at San Francisco State University, for example, argued the category of "child" is a simple "rhetorical device for inflaming what is really an irrational set of attitudes against sex with children." John Money, a professor of Pediatrics and Medical Psychology at John Hopkins University, says that those who oppose pedophilia "do so because of 'self-imposed moralistic ignorance.' " An article published by the Institute for the Advanced Study of Human Sexuality, "Sexual Rights of Children," stated that there is considerable evidence to support the position that there is no "inherent harm in sexual expression in childhood."[91] Moreover, the federal Ninth Circuit Court of Appeals in San Francisco ruled, as quoted by Bill O'Reilly, that "parents are possessed of no constitutional right to prevent the public schools from providing information on that subject [sexual information] to their students in *any forum or (manner)*."[92]

Tammy Bruce's outrage over such arguments roars off the pages of her writings: ". . . the *idea* of normalizing the sexualization of children in the minds of the public is of great importance of leftist thinkers," she says. The only way these "malignant narcissists will ever feel normal, healthy, and acceptable," Bruce continues, is to remake "society—children—in their image."[93] The radical Left's alternative press, however, expressed many laudatory statements about Levine's screed, *Harmful to Minors*: "Levine's research . . . is a trenchant look at America's failure to extol the erotic"—*The Progressive*; "Levine's" work recounts ". . . how the right wing, through sham social science, media sensationalism and self-righteous congressional inquiries, convinced the mainstream that sex is by nature dangerous to children. . . ."—*In these Times*; and "the greatest virtue in Levine's book is its hope that children might learn to find joy in the realm of the senses. . . ."—*The Nation*.[94]

Re-Education

Lenin moved swiftly in 1918 to consolidate power over the Soviet Union. At a special conference for Soviet educators, they were told that "we must remove the children from the crude influence of their families . . . from the first days of their lives they will be under the healthy influence of Communist children's nurseries and schools."[95] Antonio Gramsci did not give up on Lenin's efforts to create a "New Soviet Man," at least insofar as Western schooling was concerned. During his scribbling in prison, Gramsci realized that the whole field of Western culture, as "elaborated and diffused" as it was, could not be protected. Hence, he chose those targets that appeared most vulnerable to stealthy penetration and conversion. Three main culture targets were selected by Gramsci: the family unit (as a component of the larger anti-Christianity objective), education from grade school through high schools to university; and the media and political parties. These targets, Malachi Martin, explained were all wide open to "systematic and professional Marxist penetration."[96]

Education is essential to cultural transformation, first to destroy the vestiges of the previously existing values structure and social system and secondly for the inculcation of the new set of prescribed norms. Especially for the young, the education system is a key for the transmission of new sets of ideas and attitudes. Cultural revolution becomes natural and possible when the radical secularists control "the family, the school, and the media," Alberto Piedra counseled. By these means, the new society, Gramscian one, will be given birth.

"Gramsci in most of his writings insists that the first and almost exclusive role of the Marxist intellectual lies in education," Piedra explained. "The revolution, he believed, must be prepared with time, patience, and a calculating mind. This involves dismantling or destroying the values of the past by slowly infiltrating the 'old' institutions and changing the mentality of the masses."[97]

America's radical Left is guided by Marxist intellectuals ensconced in America's universities and high schools. These "teachers of destruction" emulate Lenin's use of the education to build a wall of separation between parents and their children, one so effective as to allow a reshaping of America's young minds. It is difficult to avoid concluding that by conducting a stealthy progressive-socialist-marxist assault against American culture through the education system, the United States has already moved well down the path toward establishing Little Red Gramsci Schoolhouses across the country, from pre-school through university.

By converting American schools and universities into progressive-socialist-marxist re-education camps, the radical Left anticipates that it will be able to trigger a cultural transformation within the next generation. The curricula would no longer include Western civilization, civic education, and other courses essential to understanding one's linkage with traditional American institutions and values.[98] If this malignant cultural tumor continues to mestastisize, it will eliminate individual liberty as it exists, even in its abbreviated form, in the early twenty-first century. In the place of traditional values would be, at minimum, a fascist, jack-booted civil order and at worst a totalitarian socialist elite trampling freedom and liberal democracy. Overstatement? David Horowitz, a former communist and New Leftist, has been combating the malicious Left-wing indoctrination on American campuses for several years. He is quoted by Tammy Bruce as saying:

> Beginning in the mid-1960s, the left made a concerted effort to take over our colleges and universities. . . . As they've taken control, they've trampled free speech, virtually banished conservative professors, and turned our schools into little more that huge megaphones for anti-American rhetoric from coast to coast.[99]

Progressive-socialist-marxist professors proclaim expertise in "cultural studies" and focus on "social constructs" rather than the realities of daily life. By assuming this intellectual "high" ground, they are allowed to practice Marxist politics from the shadows of Plato's cave by inflicting their students with their hate-filled explanations of American society.

New "Teachers of Destruction"

The Marxist professors and other members of the radical Left scored enormous achievements on the underside of American society with carefully planned and executed political warfare. Masking itself behind "political correctness" extremism, the radical Left convinced many Americans than an extreme social and cultural transformation is needed to cleanse the United States for a better future. Through use of massive propaganda in the nation's schools, colleges and universities, Hollywood films and television, the workplace, and a thousand other information outlets, the hard Left turned the United States into a massive re-education camp. The Frankfurt School and Antonio Gramsci provided the right strategy to American Leftists who, like coyotes smelling blood, sense a great victory for Marxism.

Today's Left has no Soviet Union as a beacon, former American communist Ronald Radosh observed in *Commies*, "but its reflexive hatred of the American system is intact, and its devotees have no qualms about running off to join with the young, self-proclaimed 'anarchists' who trash Starbucks and picket the World Bank and International Monetary Fund, the institutions that for them symbolize the abiding evil of big corporations and international capitalism."[100] To be certain, the links between the 1960s radicals and the New Left are at the core—the driving force—of the contemporary drive to revolutionize American culture.

Many radical Leftists said that the United States "deserved" the murderous September 11, 2001 terrorist attacks against the World Trade Center and the Pentagon. One protest letter signed by Left-wing actors, writers, and academics suggested that the terrorist attack resulted from "past U.S. military *aggression*" (emphasis added). Actors Ed Asner and the late Ossie Davis, feminist Gloria Steinem, and many others urged "all Americans to resist war and repression that had been loosed on the world by the Bush administration. It is unjust, immoral, and illegitimate."[101]

Two professors, Peter Drier and Dick Flacks, writing in the long-time progressive-socialist-marxist mouthpiece, *The Nation*, rightly observed that "'progressive' and 'patriotism' have rarely been used in the same sentence." These university educators expressed concern that the "patriotic fervor" triggered by the terrorist attacks on September 11 could be used to "undermine dissent and progressive initiatives." They concluded that the Left-wing needed to remember its forgotten legacy. "We need to ask, once again," Drier and Flacks wrote, "what is America to us?"[102]

3

THE ANDROPOV PLAN

RUSSIA LOOMS AS A major global geopolitical competitor to establish a one-world government system sometime in the second half of the twenty-first century. Unless the United States allows its deterrent posture to erode over time or a strike by militant Islamists so weakens the country that Americans drop their guard, a Russian nuclear attack will remain unlikely. It is important to remember, however, that not much has changed between yesterday's strategic objectives of the Soviet Union and those of Russia today. One former Soviet KGB officer was quoted by J. R. Nyquist as saying his training identified Soviet geopolitical goals as being ". . . the vast infiltration of agents all over the globe. The communist plan, based on Lenin's teachings, was to take over the world without physical struggle." Nyquist quoted Cold War defectors as saying Soviet objectives were to extinguish capitalism and "socialize" [Marxize] the United States, separate Europe from America, defeat the U.S.

with a superior strategy backed by propaganda and disinformation, and reconcile with China to develop a "scissors strategy."[1]

The Andropov Plan put into motion by Mikhail Gorbachev in 1988 maintained these goals but flipped the Soviet-Russian geopolitical strategy from open Marxism-Leninism and confrontation against the West to Antonio Gramsci's stealthy approach of cooperation and promotion of a quiet cultural transformation of capitalist countries. Moreover, reconciliation with China, close relations with Iran and Cuba/Brazil/Venezuela, and engaging "progressive" supporters inside the United States, have collectively positioned Russia for long-term geopolitical competition with the capitalist West and militant Islam.

Hidden deeply in the darkness of Russia's shadow world is a strategy that some in the West have called "The Andropov Plan," named after Yuri Andropov, KGB chief from 1967 to 1982 and General Secretary of the Communist Party from1982 until his death in February 1984. Many in the West remain skeptical about the Plan's existence and label it a "legend." But there is a funny thing about hindsight, especially when seeing the whole of events from the tumultuous 1980s leading to the death of twentieth century Marxism-Leninism, followed by the chaos and mayhem of the 1990s, and finally stumbling into President Vladimir Putin's regressive years in the new millennium. A multitude of new facts have become evident from the writings of numerous journalists, researchers, and commentators of the world scene since the implosion of the Soviet Union. Collectively, when their perspectives are integrated with the *Glasnost* ("openness") and *Perestroika* ("restructuring") initiatives of Communist Party chairman Mikhail Gorbachev in the late 1980s, it becomes quite evident that some kind of a plan was in place and that the KGB played a key political role in executing a wide-range of covert operations necessary to implement it.

Since the Andropov Plan was born under the cover of great secrecy, the covert actions that put it into motion were shrouded in a shadow world of deception and disinformation. The sheer enormity of the shift in the Soviet Russian long-range deception strategy makes it a difficult story to tell. Yet, by comparing the Andropov Plan's strategic framework with key points of an alleged new disinformation strategy, old facts, as seen through the light of new evidence, make an informed historical interpretation possible.

Former KGB officer Anatoliy Golitsyn's Memoranda for the CIA in the 1980s detailed the bold transformation of Soviet Russia's grand strategy that was designed to bring about a ". . . convergence of the capitalist West with the Communist East on Soviet terms and the creation of a socialist World Government as a solution to the arms race and nuclear confrontation."[2] Golitsyn's warnings, however, were largely ignored by CIA analysts and swept under the rug as being useless disinformation.

The evolution of the initial ideas rooted in today's Russian grand strategy to achieve global power and influence began as long ago as the late 1950s and 1960s. While striving to put the Stalin years behind them, it had become obvious to Soviet leaders that, despite their substantial industrial and military advances, Western economies would eventually outstrip their troubled economy and frustrate the attainment of the Kremlin's global goals. Something had to give. A new grand strategy was needed. With a boldness characteristic of the Russian character, the strategy developed through the Khrushchev and Brezhnev years in the 1960s and 1970s outlined an approach entailing an enormous realignment of the political and economic systems inside the Soviet Union to strengthen its long-term competition with the West.

Yuri Andropov had a powerful voice in Soviet domestic and foreign policies. A master of duplicity and dedicated Marxist-Leninist, he was obsessed with suppression of dissidence inside the U.S.S.R. and Eastern Europe. The speed with which the Communist government in Budapest was toppled in the 1956 Hungarian Uprising haunted him all of his life. His lesson learned was that the response to such

situations had to be quick and hard through the use of military force.[3]
Many experts on the Cold War Soviet Union regarded Andropov as
the toughest and "shrewdest Soviet politician since Stalin." He spoke
reasonably good English with an American accent and was well-
educated, sophisticated, and preferred scotch to vodka.

Andropov climbed to the top over several decades through the
support of several powerful Party political figures. He exerted a
considerable influence over the governing system during that period
and was a long-time trusted advisor to Leonid Brezhnev during the
"period of stagnation" in the 1960s and 1970s. Andropov was the
KGB chief from 1967 to November 1982 when, upon Brezhnev's
death, he became General Secretary of the Communist Party.
Brezhnev bequeathed two major problems to the new Party leader:
an economy in shambles that was forever falling further behind the
West and systemic corruption throughout the Soviet socialist
governing system. These weaknesses had compelled the Eastern
Bloc to turn repeatedly to Western banks for assistance. At the end
of 1981, the East owed some $80.7 billion to Western banks,
including $9.5 billion by the Soviet Union alone. At the same time,
the East disguised rampant unemployment, since ideologically the
socialist system ostensibly operated at full-employment. Out-of-
work individuals were seen to be personally at fault of "social
parasitism," and many were assigned to forced labor camps (more
than 23,000 in Poland alone in 1983).[4]

One of Andropov's first moves as KGB chief was to restore the
Committee for State Security (KGB) to its status as the world's most
feared intelligence service and notoriously effective internal control
agency. Harold "Kim" Philby, the head of the British Soviet section
and a KGB agent, sought safety in Moscow in 1963 after some three
decades of successful spying for the Kremlin. Philby and Andropov
hit it off well and worked together to strengthen the KGB. At Philby's
urging, Andropov made great efforts to improve the education and
quality of KGB officers, a move that would pay off handsomely in

subsequent years. Together the Englishman and Russian developed
KGB operatives who were socially comfortable at the highest level
of diplomacy, business, and society throughout the world.[5]

Andropov's health failed him soon after he took the reins of
power from Brezhnev, yet his focus remained on the struggling
economy and corruption by Party and government officials. Without
ready answers to the problems ailing the socialist economic system
in place, Andropov turned to Mikhail Gorbachev, and a long-time
friend and protege, Georgi Arbatov, director of the then-new U.S.A.
Institute. Arbatov was regarded as the top Soviet expert on the
United States and Andropov had nurtured Gorbachev since 1971 to
become a rising star in the Party hierarchy. Like Andropov,
Gorbachev was a dedicated Marxist-Leninist and embraced Lenin's
slogan "one step forward, two steps back," or retreat temporarily
while pursuing long-term objectives that provided ideological
direction for development of what was to become known among
some as "The Andropov Plan."

Gorbachev was tasked to develop plans for the re-structuring and
re-invigorating of the economic and political systems to assure that
the Kremlin stayed on the pathway toward the long-range goal of
establishing a Party-State directed socialist world government.
Gorbachev organized a host of task forces from the country's
intellectual institutes and think tanks, commissioned 110 different
policy studies, and integrated economists, scientists, technologists,
computer scientists, educators, and labor and agriculture specialists.
At the same, due to Andropov's ill health, Gorbachev was serving
as his de facto deputy in running the Party. Although Gorbachev
was groomed to become Andropov's replacement, an aging and sick
Konstantin Chernenko was next in line. After eleven months in
office, however, he died, and Gorbachev ascended to General
Secretary of the Communist Party in March 1985.[6]

Gorbachev's reform efforts confronted three bulwarks of power
that were flourishing in Soviet society: the Communist Party; the

nomenklatura or privileged elite in the Party and those occupying senior positions in government and the enterprises; and the KGB. A fourth, but far weaker power center, public opinion, was growing harsher it its condemnation of the corruption evident among three most powerful societal centers. Gorbachev's strategy addressed each of these power centers in a different way. Since successful reform of the existing socialist system would require popular support, Gorbachev tapped into the Soviet people by giving them a greater voice, albeit a well-monitored one, and freedom to speak-out about their grievances with the current system in place. Hence, Gorbachev's *Glasnost* policy was the key to giving the people an opportunity to let off steam and let their leaders know what they wanted. *Glasnost* was a long way from freedom of speech as known in Western liberal democracies, but it offered an essential opening that would garner popular support for the coming restructuring of the country's economic and political systems.

Secondly, the Communist Party was persuaded to give up its monopoly of power and permit the formation of opposition parties. This was a big step since the Party had guided everything and kept the Soviet people in a perpetual state of passivity, except for a few dissidents, religious believers, and Jews wanting to emigrate.[7] Thirdly, the approximately 1.5 million *nomenklatura* had to be guaranteed that they would continue to receive the resources necessary to sustain their life-style in the new order. And, lastly, the KGB was given substantial political and economic power inside the new Russia and in its intelligence-gathering and special tasks worldwide.

The resulting strategy, *perestroika*, which had been under consideration, planning, and rehearsals since 1958–60, was larded with strong doses of deception and disinformation to mask the measures taken to satisfy the demands of the Communist Party, the *nomenklatura*, and the KGB.[8] The Communist Party did not renounce its long-term objective of marching toward a convergence with capitalism in establishing socialist world governance. While the world was focused on Gorbachev's acquiescence to the collapse of Communist regimes in Eastern Europe, the tearing down of the Berlin Wall, and other monumental events, "poof," the Soviet Communist Party turned invisible. Was Communism dead as many in the West presumed or did something else happen?[9] Did the world witness another example of Lenin's dictum of "one step forward, two steps back?" If so, where is the Party located in its post-Soviet Russian structure and how does it operate? These questions were not really addressed in any serious way as the Soviet Union imploded and the Russian Federation was born. Bits and pieces of information, events, and testimony that have emerged over the years beg answers to the open issues.

Nearly twenty years have passed since the new Russia emerged from the rubble of the Soviet socialist system. The historical interpretation presented in this strategic analysis addresses open questions about the three pillars of the Soviet system—the Communist Party, *nomenklatura*, and KGB—in an effort to penetrate the deception and disinformation that were contrived to mask the whole truth. Propaganda and disinformation are best when they are founded on selected aspects of truth, but not the whole truth, since even a scrap of veracity can ascribe credibility to the fictional tale. Nonetheless, when contradictory evidence begins to mount over the years, one may be able to grasp greater insight into what really occurred in Soviet Russia twenty years ago and during the two decades since. It is a tortuous path, but one worth taking.

Deception and Disinformation

Former KGB Major Anatoliy Golitsyn defected to the West in December 1961 and began to tell Central Intelligence Agency de-briefers the details of a new Soviet long-range, global deception strategy. At the time, he said that the plan was in the initial stages of development. The goal of the strategy was the creation of the conditions necessary for convergence of the East and West in establishing a socialist world government. Deception and disinformation were to be the primary measures used to reach these objectives. In Soviet eyes, disinformation is a far-reaching tool that creates images in the minds of others that will guide their behavior toward Soviet Russia. Like the shadows on the wall of Plato's cave, these images become reality to beholders who will resist changing their manipulated perceptions. Disinformation is more than simply disseminating false data through the media and agents of influence (propaganda). For Soviet Russia, influence operations were more about mind-control, borrowed from the revisionist Marxist writings of Italian Communist Antonio Gramsci, than simply reshaping public opinion:

> KGB disinformation operations are progressive; they are designed to mislead not the working people but their enemies—the ruling circles of capitalism—in order to induce them to act in a certain way, or abstain from actions contrary to the interests of the USSR; they promote peace and social progress; they serve international detente; they are humane, creating the conditions for the noble struggle for humanity's bright future.[10]

The new Soviet strategy, identified by Golitsyn, which later became known by a few in the West as "The Andropov Plan," drew heavily from the experience of the Lenin's New Economic Policy or NEP in the 1920s. With the Soviet Union facing a full societal collapse in 1921, Vladimir Lenin and his cohorts used deception on a massive scale to encourage the West to come to the aid of the ailing U.S.S.R. The New Economic Policy had a different meaning for the West than Soviet Russia. To bait the "profit" hook, the Kremlin offered Western firms concessions in Soviet industry, reorganized its industries into trusts that operated on a for-profit basis, and invited Westerners to open new businesses in Soviet Russia. For the Soviets, the New Economic Policy meant economic recovery, expansion of foreign trade, attraction of foreign capital and expertise, diplomatic recognition by Western governments, and, at the same time, promotion of a worldwide Communist revolution. Lenin believed that this aggressive policy could be effective only if it was accompanied by a well-conceived and executed deception and disinformation program.[11]

With Soviet industry in ruins, agriculture in crisis, peasant uprisings, separatist movements, and the Russian people on the brink of revolt, disinformation was essential for concealing from the West a full dimension of the internal crises. By the time Stalin brought the New Economic Policy to an end in 1929, Soviet Russia had garnered a fist full of gains, including industry, agriculture, and trade that had all improved dramatically. Russia also had attracted large credits from the West and new technology and equipment were brought into the country. Western firms had built essential factories, and, with American, British, German, and Czech assistance, the foundations for Soviet heavy and military industries had been put into place. In addition, the peasants were pacified, political parties liquidated, the independence of churches eliminated, and national movements crushed. The Security Service clamped-down with effective societal controls, communist parties around the world increased their influence in unions and parliaments, and twelve new communist parties joined the Communist International (Comintern) for a total of forty-six.[12]

In ending the New Economic Policy and calling for "a socialist offensive on all fronts," Stalin cancelled concessions for foreign industries and private enterprise in Soviet Russia, confiscated private property, collectivized agriculture, and intensified political repression.[13] Through deception and disinformation, the Soviets fulfilled Lenin's promise to create the conditions necessary for the capitalist West to become its own "gravedigger."

Despite the fact that Golitsyn had placed the skeletal structure of "The Andropov Plan" into the hands of Western intelligence, mostly at the CIA and British intelligence, his claims were heavily discounted. He was believed to have spun wild conspiracy theories about the Kremlin's future actions. He said the Sino-Soviet split in the 1960s, for instance, was disinformation designed to deceive the West and that the 1968 Prague Spring was a KGB deception. Golitsyn's greatest supporter at the CIA was James Angleton, the legendary head of the CIA counterintelligence staff. But Golitsyn persisted in spinning wild tales, such as the British Prime Minister Harold Wilson was a KGB agent. Later, we discovered that he was not far wrong about a Soviet mole positioned in the top ranks of the British government, only it was not Wilson but Kim Philby who served as a KGB agent at the top level of London's intelligence branch. By damaging his own credibility, Golitsyn tarnished his own reports to the CIA on the development of a massive Soviet global deception strategy. The CIA's Soviet analysis division, for instance, simply rejected Golitsyn's claims. This writer was told by one analyst that "Golitsyn is nuts, don't believe a word he has to say." It was bad advice, for history over the past two decades has validated Golitsyn's warning.

By failing to separate fact from fiction and allowing emotional responses to Golitsyn's irritating personality, the FBI was equally unimpressed with Golitsyn's demeanor. Sam Papich, Golitsyn's FBI de-briefer, is quoted by Mark Reibling as having said that the defector ". . . was a bright, arrogant bastard; he even tried to ask *us* questions to improve his knowledge base."[14]

The problem with this CIA and FBI grand trashing of all that Golitsyn had to say is that his many predictions had a curious way of proving correct over time. They missed it. In 1994, Mark Reibling assessed Golitsyn's predictions in his 1984 book *New Lies For Old*. He found that out of Golitsyn's 194 predictions expressed in his book, 139 were fulfilled by 1993, forty-six were "not falsifiable at this time," and nine were "clearly wrong." Yet critics piled-on, focusing on the hand-full of Golitsyn's false predictions and not giving him credit for a ninety-four percent accuracy rate. Some went to far as to say his analysis "strained credulity" and accused him of being a "demented" proponent of "cosmic theories." Wild theories or not, it seems that no one took the time to separate fact from chaff in Golitsyn's memoranda to the CIA. Golitsyn had provided the CIA a top secret analysis in 1982 that alleged a tidal wave of changes would soon be forthcoming from the Kremlin that would set the new strategy [The Andropov Plan] into motion.[15]

By placing Golitsyn on an official assassination list, the Soviets may well have tipped their hand that much of his testimony to the Western intelligence community was valid. First, in an obvious effort to smear Golitsyn, the KGB alleged he was a smuggler and defected because they were on to his criminal actions. Secondly, Soviet "damage assessment after his defection concluded that he had been able to betray a wide range of intelligence to the CIA." Third, the KGB issued instructions in early 1962 to fifty-four overseas agents of influence of the actions they should take to limit the damage incurred from Golitsyn's defection.[16] Fourth, given that Kim Philby, KGB agent, was still the chief of the Soviet section at British intelligence early in Golitsyn's defection, one should suspect that character assassination of Golitsyn was also on Philby's agenda. And, fifth the KGB chief Vladimir Semichastny approved a plan for "special actions" against a group of "particularly dangerous traitors," including the assassination of Anatoliy Golitsyn.[17] If Golitsyn was such an unbelievable flake, why would the KGB stretch so far as to silence him? Were the details of Golitsyn's early CIA de-briefings shared with the British MI-6? If so, with Kim Philby in the Kremlin's pocket, the KGB had an open feedback channel about everything Golitsyn said.

The Plan

The Soviet Russian grand design governed the Kremlin's internal and international initiatives over an extended period toward winning its strategic objectives in the geopolitical competition with the capitalist West and Islamic Salafism/Wahhabi. "The Andropov Plan" was set into motion in the late 1970s or early 1980s by shifting gears from confrontation to cooperation with the West. Russia later would orchestrate operations with its strategic partners—China, Iran, and Cuba/Brazil/Venezuela.

Perestroika, the penultimate phase of the Gorbachev's "reforms," unleashed a flood of covert special actions by the Central Committee of the Communist Party. These main tools were used to flip the political-economic system from Soviet Marxism-Leninism to Russia's "democratic" and "Bolshevik market" reforms. The Party mounted a massive strategic disinformation program to mask its grand design, while continuing a clandestine political role by the Federal Security Bureau, a happy-face mask for the KGB. The deception also included use of a "controlled political opposition" to give Russia a more liberal image in order to convince the West that Russia was moving rapidly toward a democratic, non-communist government.[18]

An initial problem with moving toward democracy under the *perestroika* was the absence of political opposition parties to compete for power. Alexandr Yakovlev, Gorbachev's *perestroika* mastermind, was clear about how they solved the problem: "We created our own opposition."[19] Since no one was standing in the wings ready to enter the political fray, the contrived origin of the Gorbachev-era opposition was created by the Communist Party. American scholars Peter Reddaway and Dmitri Glinski found that "an indispensable role in this process was assigned to the Moscow party machine (from December 1985, presided over by Boris Yeltsin)."[20]

Golitsyn argued that *perestroika* would include the deployment of a "controlled political opposition" dressed up in democratic and anti-communist garb. "No other truly independent candidates exist," he said.[21] Golitsyn also contended that the emergence of Vladimir Zhirinovskiy as a vocal Russian nationalist was "not a spontaneous political development." Rather, Zhirinovskiy, as a hard-hitting ultra-nationalist, was invented to forestall the emergence of legitimate right-wingers and to allow Russian leaders to play the "Zhirinovskiy card" in discussions with Western officials.[22]

The idea of a "controlled political opposition" was certainly a logical aspect of Andropov's long-range deception plan. It was also consistent with KGB contingency plans readied during the "period of emergency" to keep a lid on the political turmoil anticipated during the transition to democratic government and a free market economy.

Christopher Story, British editor of Golitsyn's *The Perestroika Deception*, explained how a key Russian stratagem to re-shape the way in which the West viewed Russia was based on the ideas expressed by Italian Communist Antonio Gramsci in the 1930s. The "Marxist renewal and re-emergence" process that emerged in the West following the ostensible death of Communism in Russia is consistent with Story's "Foreword" written in the mid-1990s.

> Ambition to control the Western mind is a long-standing objective of Soviet policy, embracing the ideas of the Italian Communist Antonio Gramsci, who argued that mastery of human consciousness should be a paramount political objective . . . control of the Western mind is to be achieved not only by the dishonest use of language, but also to demoralize the West through corrosive attacks on society's institutions, the active promotion of drug abuse, and the spiral of agnosticism, nihilism, permissiveness and concerted attacks on the family in order to destabilize society. Religion and the traditional cultural and moral hegemony must first be destroyed, before the revolution can be successful. . . .[23]

When Benito Mussolini seized power in Italy in 1922, ending the rule of the king, Victor Emmanuel III, Antonio Gramsci, then-chairman of the Italian Communist Party, was surprised that the "exploited" Italian workers did not take advantage of the situation by rising up against their capitalist exploiters in a massive proletarian revolution. Later, while imprisoned by Mussolini in the 1930s, Gramsci wrote his thoughts of this and other societal issues in his "notebooks." He asserted that the Roman Catholic Church had inculcated the Italian people with an unassailable values structure, allowing the Church to exercise mind control over the people's political actions. Gramsci concluded that, because workers followed the values learned from the Catholic Church, "religion must be destroyed" and the Church's mind control approach must be emulated by communist leaders. The Andropov Plan, based on mind control techniques in its deception and disinformation strategy, shifted the dominant ideology from Marxism-Leninism to the revisionist Marxism of Antonio Gramsci.[24] Communism in Russia did not disappear, it simply converted to a more subtle and, for the West, more dangerous form: cultural Marxism.

The critical assumption that the ongoing "culture war" in the United States somehow just happened does not standup when placed under scrutiny. The radical Left successfully de-constructed American society by undermining moral values and traditional institutions, thereby opening the door to the Gramcians who would move into positions of political authority and begin a process of convergence with Russia.

With the collapse of Marxist-Leninist communism in Russia in 1991, the Western parties and other ultra-Leftists began the implementation of Gramsci's revisionist Marxism as the basis for new strategies to culturally transform the Western democracies. The Gramsci madness began almost simultaneously among the hard Left in Europe, the United States, Australia, New Zealand, and Latin America, suggesting a coordination of a new anti-Western doctrine.

In light of the events surrounding *perestroika* and the possibility of the Gorbachev Foundation serving as a cover for activities of the former International Department of the Soviet Communist Party, can one legitimately infer that Soviet Russia traded Marxism-Leninism and confrontation with the West for Gramcian Marxism and ostensible cooperation with Western democracies? Are Russian clandestine activities in deception and disinformation, Federal Security Bureau covert political operations, and extensive use of agents of influence in Western countries moving forward as predicted by Anatoliy Golitsyn?

Implementing Perestroika

In a March 1990 memorandum to the Central Intelligence Agency, Golitsyn was adamant: "Western blindness to the strategy behind *'perestroika,'* is rooted in Western ignorance, ignorance and *ignorance.*"[25]

Perestroika operations took place at two levels: one in the open and a second in the underworld. The first actions were a series of events, a grand theatrical display, that stunned the world: the release of the Kremlin's hold on East European and Central Asian client-regimes, the tearing down of the Berlin Wall, the withdrawal of Soviet forces from Eastern Europe, the re-unification of Germany, opening Russia to Western visitors and businesses, and the dissolution of the Soviet empire itself. Momentous events inside Russia rushed forward, including formation of political parties, democratic elections, a free press, and a mad-cap rush to convert Russia to a market-driven economy. All of the bells and whistles of a modern democracy and free enterprise economy were soon in place, albeit with considerable chaos and mayhem. Europeans and Americans were stunned, giddy with delight. We, a generation of "Cold Warriors," finally had pulled the Communists down. These were heady times.

The combatants in the Cold War standoff could look forward to peace and prosperity. The West turned to helping Russia make its transition as smooth as possible with aid, training, advice, and encouragement. For seven decades the essential entrepreneurial skills needed by Russia had been painstakingly mined out of the Soviet people by the Communist system. Meetings between American and Russian scientists, educators, military officers, and cultural groups began building a new bridge of cooperation and mutual understanding. The good humor and camaraderie often experienced between Americans and Russians could very well have led one to conclude that they actually liked each other on a personal level.

A second level of *perestroika* activities took place in the shadows, invisible to those of us still celebrating the easing of tensions in the Soviet-American nuclear standoff. One reason for missing the clues about what was going on is that we simply were not looking. Like hungry fish, we took the *perestroika* bait, accepting the "gift" without serious examination or debate. Our experts told us "communism" was dead and Russia reborn was on a pathway to modernize humankind's standard of democratic government and free market economies. Francis Fukuyama went so far as to say it was the "end of history." But some of us had an "itch"—there was something too pat about the whole transformation and the sudden lurch from communism to democracy/free markets. Pieces to the puzzle were missing and others did not quite fit. Finally, we set our suspicions aside as being a paranoia hangover from the Cold War and quietly accepted the portrait of the re-invention of Russia painted for us by the Party's disinformation image-makers.

In Russia's *perestroika* underworld, however, the KGB operated at a fast pace to move the Party's treasury, and whatever could be looted from the Soviet state, out of the country and into the West where financial resources could be invested for use by residual elements of the International Department of the now invisible Communist Party. While some KGB men were slipping out the backdoor into the West, others marched through the front door into top positions in major

Soviet industries in order to take advantage of privatization called for by the Andropov Plan.

Yuri Andropov had made provisions for these strategic clandestine moves during *perestroika* by sending several KGB officers to the West in the late 1970s to learn the secrets of capitalism and for-profit operations. According to the Maldon Institute, the highly trusted KGB officers were expected to garner new experiences and develop new skills. Upon their return, the KGB men reported on their investments and helped develop a new "tool kit of skills" for use by intelligence officers in making future investments in the West.[26] This preparation for what was to occur later under the rubric of "*perestroika*," as guided by Mikhail Gorbachev, was almost certainly on the Andropov's initial agenda, as well as a "democratic" leader, such as the role filled by Boris Yeltsin in the 1990s. The results would be a decade-long flow of funds from the West, transfer of economic skills, cooperative arrangements, direct investments, and new technologies transfer that took the Soviet economy off life-support.[27] It seems quite clear from twenty years of hindsight that the model for the Andropov Plan was drawn from Lenin's New Economic Policy that successfully boosted Russia's economy in the 1920s, only to be followed by the harsh years of Josef Stalin's totalitarian rule—or an example of Lenin's strategy of "one step forward, two steps back."

During the late 1980s, the Communist Party dipped into the Soviet state's financial resources and used them as if they were its own. The Party also controlled billions of dollars worth of property and investments. All of these assets were available to protect the some 1.5 million *nomenklatura* or Party elite as they passed through the revolving door leading to the death of the Soviet Union and birth of the Russian Federation and Commonwealth of Independent States (CIS). According to Stephen Handelman, a veteran foreign correspondent and former Moscow bureau chief for the *Toronto Star*, the Central Committee prepared a secret list of names of the "most worthy Party members." Their place on the list was their personal passport for special appointments, including top government officials, ambassadors, and other senior positions. "The nomenklatura constituted a private club of individuals whose loyalty to the Party transcended any other obligation," Handelman explained.[28]

A key step in implementing the Andropov Plan was taken at a plenary session of the Central Committee of the Communist Party. At the urging of Mikhail Gorbachev, General Secretary of the Central Committee, at a February 5, 1990 meeting, the Party voted to revoke Article Six of the Soviet constitution. The major impact, Handelman explained, was elimination of the Party's right to appropriate government monies to fund overseas operations by the Party and the KGB. According to documents from the Party archives that Handelman was able to review, this decision appears to have been the trigger that led to the quiet transfer of Party funds to secret bank accounts and enterprises outside of Russia.

Several of the Party banks also served as money laundries for huge dollar deposits from Colombian and Panamanian drug dealers. The drug money was converted from dollars to rubles and then reconverted to dollars again in return for sizable commissions. Another currency shenanigan took the money resulting from the sell-off of Soviet military property in East Germany in Soviet rubles, which were converted to East German marks. Later, they were exchanged for West German deutchmarks at the time of re-unification of the two Germanies. The Party, Handelman discovered, reaped enormous profits.[29]

In the months just prior to and during *perestroika*, Moscow's foreign trade bank transferred billions of dollars to fake banks and commercial enterprises in the West. Most of the money went to Greece, Cyprus, Italy, and Portugal. Another aspect of the KGB's money-making tool kit was exercised through shipments of oil, metal, and timber to KGB-sponsored overseas enterprises. The raw materials were purchased at a fraction of their sales value. When the resources were sold at world market prices, the resulting profit went into the Party's black treasury.[30]

Soviet gold reserves amounted to 1,300 tons (about $30 billion) in the early 1980s. Once *perestroika* was set into motion about 1,000 tons were sold. Meanwhile, the Soviet Union's foreign exchange reserves tumbled from about $15 billion when Gorbachev entered office in 1985 to just $1 billion.[31]

Further evidence of the Andropov Plan is shown in a memo uncovered by Paul Klebnikov. KGB Colonel Leonid Veselovsky, First Chief Directorate, sent a secret memorandum to Nikolai Kruchina, who was in charge of property for the Central Committee of the Communist Party. Veselovsky's "memo urged Kruchina's support in creating a network of captive banks and trading companies, both in Russia and abroad, to collect billions of dollars of government funds during the 'period of emergency,'" Klebnikov reported, "and keep them for the communist nomenklatura until a more propitious time arrived."

Additional insight to the Plan is in Klebnikov's quotation of the Veselovsky's memo:

'The earnings which are accumulated in the Party treasury and are not reflected in the financial reports can be used to purchase the shares of various companies, enterprises, and banks. On the one hand, this will create a stable source of revenue, irrespective of what may happen to the Party. On the other hand, these shares can be sold on the security exchanges at any time and the capital transferred to other spheres, allowing the Party to keep its participation anonymous and still retain control. . . . In order to avoid mistakes in the course of this operation during the 'period of emergency,' it is essential to organize, both in the U.S.S.R. and abroad, special rapid response groups, staffed by specially trained instructors from the active reserve of the KGB of the U.S.S.R., as well as by trusted individuals volunteering their cooperation and by individuals who, for one reason or another, have lost their job in the field units or administrative departments of the KGB of the U.S.S.R.'[32]

The privatization of Soviet state property was also an insider's game. Nearly, 47,000 state companies had been placed mostly into the hands of company managers and the *nomenklatura* by the end of 1992—90,000 enterprises a year later. These transfers from public to private ownership at minimal cost set the foundation for fabulously wealthy oligarchs during the 1990s. Chaos and hardship often marked the economic reform of the 1990s but the privileged elite benefitted greatly by the "back-door" privatization process.[33]

The oligarchic culture that emerged during the 1990s was hardly new. Russia's ruling elite, going back to the days of the tsars, were often alienated from the Russian people. "This oligarchic culture," Reddaway and Glinski observed, "accentuated in the Soviet period by the Bolsheviks' paranoia and their constant need to combat 'enemies of the revolution' provided fertile soil for the rapid decay and mutation of the Bolshevik revolutionary elite into the nomenklatura—a conservative and privileged ruling class isolated from society."[34]

For nearly a year leading up to August 19, 1991 the possibility of a KGB-coup against Gorbachev, staged or otherwise, was an "open secret." Peter Reddaway and Dmitri Glinski examined the August coup in their 2001 book, *The Tragedy of Russia's Reforms*, for the United States Peace Institute. They called the coup a "riddle" and asked three questions: (1) "To what degree was President Gorbachev involved in the preparation of the coup?; (2) To what extent was he denied communications during the coup?; and (3) Why did the plotters want so badly to meet him after the coup's collapse?"[35]

In a 1991 "Memorandum to the CIA," Anatoliy Golitsyn asserted that "the Soviet 'coup' and its 'failure' constituted a grandiose display of deception."[36] On the other hand, Major General Oleg Kalugin, once the KGB's top spy against the United States and now retired in the Maryland suburbs of Washington, D.C., told this writer in a 2005 discussion that the coup was legitimate, though an ill-founded one and the result of insider positioning for power. Nevertheless, the evidence simply did not fit in the explanations given to Westerners.

According to Golitsyn, the activities surrounding the coup "were calculated displays intended primarily for the West."[37] It was used for a spectacular display of the influence of Russian democrats and Boris Yeltsin's "courage" in defending the Soviet parliament. This event, combined with "tear[ing] down that wall" in Berlin and removal of the statues of Vladimir Lenin and Feliks Dzerzhinskiy— the "Knight of the Revolution" who headed the Cheka, the first Soviet security and intelligence agency—were staged to underline the ostensible death of communism and the end of the U.S.S.R. Golitsyn explained these symbolic changes as being essential for erasing the image of Soviet repression and terrorism from the Western mind, as well as fostering the convergence of the capitalist West and democratic free-market Russia in a socialist world government.[38]

Reddaway and Glinski cited factual evidence that may well validate Golitsyn's assertions. Gorbachev, a day before he left Moscow for a vacation in the Ukrainian Crimean Peninsula, observed that "emergency measures are needed. . . . [In] emergency situations, all states act and will act accordingly. . . . Tomorrow I will leave for vacation, with your permission, [so as] not to impede your work."[39] Insofar as the second question, Gorbachev twice telephoned Arkady Volsky, Chairman of the Scientific Industrial Union, while he was supposedly being held incommunicado by the coup plotters. And a Ukrainian KGB officer denied reports that Gorbachev had been "held in isolation." Even without Reddaway and Glinski's factual accounts, it is difficult to see how the President of the Soviet Union could say one day that "emergency measures were needed" and walk out the door and go on vacation the next day.

But if it was a staged coup, what was in it for the Kremlin? Reddaway and Glinski believe that since Gorbachev's primary objective in 1990–91 was to somehow find a way to secure Western financial assistance, presenting the specter of an unstable nuclear armed Soviet Union could be so frightening to the West that aid would be forthcoming quickly to stabilize the country.

The coup, real or contrived, was followed by four months of rapid deterioration and, finally, the disintegration of the U.S.S.R. The anti-Western, anti-democratic, and anti-market forces, as well as the Soviet institutions underwriting these ideas, collapsed. The Soviet Communist Party disappeared. And, the "power ministries"—the KGB, army, and Ministry of Interior (internal security)—were dismantled. The Soviet Union was terminated on December 31, 1991.

The KGB was tasked to maintain some sense of control during the instability created by the political and economic reforms—a robust KGB served as a "guardian" that bridged the transition from old to new. A document recovered from the KGB archives, as reported by Handelman, provides keen insight into the political role played by the KGB in the Andropov Plan. KGB Document No. 174033, dated January 5, 1991, relayed coded instructions from KGB Chairman Vladimir Kryuchkov. He directed the creation of private firms to sell military technology overseas. In light of the domestic turmoil surrounding the shift from a communist system to a Western style capitalist one, Kryuchkov also outlined three strategic objectives:

- Private companies, he ordered, would "serve as 'reliable covers' for [KGB] leaders and the most valuable [KGB] operatives, in case the domestic . . . situation develops along East German lines;"

- "Provide financial means for the organization of underground work if 'destructive elements' came to power;" and
- "Create conditions for the effective use of foreign and domestic agent networks during [a period of] increased political instability."[40]

Klebnikov described how the KGB, neither an organ of the Soviet state nor an operation of the Communist Party, operated on its own, ignoring for the moment whether an invisible International Department of the former Soviet Communist Party was parked at the Gorbachev Foundation. Not only was the KGB busy squirreling-away Communist Party funds, but it controlled the privatization of Soviet state property and "infiltrated and sponsored leading organized crime groups."[41]

"The KGB was an important secret player—perhaps the most important—in bridging the criminality of the old regime with the criminality of the post-Communist era," Stephen Handelman concluded. The privatization program during the final days of the U.S.S.R., which was controlled by the KGB, witnessed the transfer of some three billion rubles (about $120 million) for creation of some 600 newly established commercial firms and banks around the country.

Once implemented, the Andropov Plan surprised many of the Party elite, including Gorbachev, that invoking public opinion would give such a strong impetus toward economic reform and political restructuring. Tens of millions of Russians participated in the first Soviet elections, raising their expectations sky high. Gorbachev noted that *perestroika* had ". . . become a truly nationwide movement."[42]

For Russia, the 1990s was a decade of painful transition. Stumbling through these years of economic turmoil, chaos, and gangland violence, the new Russia carried out privatization, stabilized the ruble, developed a balanced budget, and strengthened important government institutions. By the end of the 1990s, Russia had laid the groundwork for the free market, including the civil tax and land codes, pension legislation, and deregulation, loosening the government choke-hold on business activities. The net result was a tumbling gross domestic product and an economy that hit rock bottom in 1998.

Russia had collected a basket full of problems. Foremost among them were the machinations of the oligarchs who dominated economic life and strongly influenced political activities. The Russian government, for instance, could not function without the oligarchs buying treasury bills.

These problems in the years of President Boris Yeltsin provide a backdrop for the "hired gun" brought into town at the end of his tenure. Vladimir Putin's meteoric rise to the presidency was engineered by the security and intelligence heavies in the Kremlin. First, Putin was appointed in 1998 as head of the Federal Security Service (FSB). In September 1999, a series of bombings destroyed four apartment buildings, killing more than 300 people. The bloody results were broadcast across the country, inflaming a popular sense of outrage. Self-defense groups were formed in various parts of the country and the people demanded personal safety.[43] From the beginning, the Putin-led FSB blamed the Chechens for the two bombings in Moscow and two other cities. The man who would become president promised retribution. "They will," Putin said, "be wiped out in their sh–houses."[44] These were words the Russian people could understand and Putin's popularity rocketed through the roof. Yet, questions remain unanswered as to whether the bombings were a result of FSB efforts to open the political leadership door for one of their own.

Appointed Russian prime minister by Yeltsin in 1999, Vladimir Putin was elected president in March 2000 with 54 percent of the vote. In power, Putin was confronted with an increasingly corrupt government, oligarchs in control of large sectors of the economy, and regional governors who wielded immense personal power. His task was to put the Andropov Plan back on track and complete the final stage of the long-range deception and disinformation strategy: convergence with the capitalist West and creation of a socialist world governance.

Vladimir Putin

From the start, Putin set a course for Russia to establish itself as a major geopolitical competitor against the economic globalization designs by the capitalist West and restoration of a world caliphate by militant Islam. Putin moved quickly to prepare for the long-term geopolitical competition that lay ahead by developing a number of political tools.

The Andropov Plan unfolded in two phases: the first, the Gorbachev reforms so reminiscent of the 1921–29 New Economic Policy and, secondly, a retrenchment, though somewhat constrained, to promote the discipline and focus required to compete for world power. For nine years in Russia, the 1990s looked a lot like the 1920s. While the economies of the capitalist West and post-Soviet Russia converged, Moscow reaped great benefits through investment, transfer of skills, training, finished consumer goods, and assistance for democracy-building and creation of a free market. The privatization of state owned property, however, placed a wild card in the deck. The plundering of Russia's riches converted the "chosen ones" of the *nomenklatura* into millionaires overnight. A few took their consumption at the public trough to astounding heights and became billionaires in a very short period, then turned their resources into political voices with monied muscle behind them. The oligarch "family" supporting President Boris Yeltsin, through their uncoordinated gluttony for wealth and power, were hijacking the Andropov Plan mid-way through its execution.

The risks associated with the Andropov Plan included the chance that, once the Soviet controlled economy was unleashed and political controls were relaxed, the Plan would be taken off-track. The order by KGB chief Kryuchkov in January 1991 (Document No. 174033) that called for the creation of underground agent networks to be used "during increased political instability" reflected an awareness that just such events might occur. The road from Soviet socialist economic and political systems to a "managed" economy and "managed democracy" appears to have been a bit rockier road than predicted by Gorbachev and his *perestroika* gurus in the 1980s.

The free-booting oligarchs and others of the super-wealthy elite were sending the Andropov Plan spinning out of control. These activities triggered a response, unsurprisingly, by the conservative pro-discipline advocates who had been or still were members of the traditional "power ministries"—KGB, military, and internal security—in the Soviet system. In a face-off at the end of Yeltsin's presidency, they reached an agreement on who would be the next "democratically-elected" president. A seemingly rather pedestrian former KGB lieutenant colonel with a modest record of success, Vladimir Putin, was their agreed upon compromise. The oligarchs would come to rue the day that they cut this deal. They soon discovered that they had greatly underestimated Putin's political skills and hard-nosed dedication to instilling discipline in Russian society and restoring the country to a position of world power.

President Putin instituted governmental "adjustments" by bringing a small horde of former KGB officers into key positions. As the succession of events that ushered Putin into the presidency in 2000 unfolded at an ever greater pace, he moved quickly by bringing into government hundreds of people experienced in Soviet security measures, eliminating powerful regional governors and replacing them with his own appointees who reported directly to him, and taking preparatory moves for the coming political assault against the oligarchs.[45] Under Putin, the final phase of the Andropov Plan under Putin was put back on track.

The power of the former politicians, bureaucrats, military leaders, intelligence officers, internal security men—known as the *Siloviki*—was greatly increased. Peter Reddaway, a professor the George Washington University, notes that *chekistry* (the *Cheka* were the first Soviet secret police) is sometimes used synonymously for *Siloviki,* since the latter is dominated by former KGB officers.[46]

More than 6,000 *chekists* (former KGB and Foreign Security Bureau officers) followed Putin into office. By 2004, Anna Politkovskaya reported that they were occupying the highest offices in the key ministries.[47] Even before Putin was elected president on March 26, 2000, he ordered a monument and plaque commemorating Yuri Andropov be returned to their former places of honor at the headquarters of the Foreign Security Bureau.

Olga Kryshtanovskaya of the Russian Academy of Sciences in 2004 exposed the extent of the *Siloviki* penetration of the Russian government. As reported by John B. Dunlop at the Stanford Institute on International Studies, Kryshtanovskaya's "convincing" analysis revealed that about 34 percent of Russian top officials were *Siloviki* as well as some 18 percent in the Duma or parliament. "Putin," she said, "in essence has structurally recreated the Politburo of the Central Committee of the Communist Party of the Soviet Union," where the governing core was 58 percent *Siloviki.* The heads of the Foreign Security Bureau, Foreign Intelligence, Defense Ministry, and Ministry of Internal Affairs under Putin were all *Siloviki.*[48]

Kryshtanovskaya's analysis also showed that 78 percent of Russia's political and business elite were *Siloviki.* The impact of their presence was being felt in the restrictions on the media, censorship of school textbooks that strayed from historical facts and that could "provide grounds for new political infighting," and an assessment that democracy tends to be seen as a potential source of instability. Russia's contemporary ideology is statist. In the eyes of President Putin and his *Siloviki* supporters, Russia needs less debate in the parliament, media, and elsewhere in the country. State interests are judged as being far more important than individual interests.[49]

With his presidency packed with men with guns, Putin turned to the oligarchs, focusing sharply on the billionaire big three: Boris Berezovsky, Vladimir Gusinsky (MediaMost), and Mikhail Khodorkovsky (Yukos Oil). Each of the them presented Putin's rule with an independent political force, the first two used their control of television and radio to underwrite their political activities, while the latter applied his riches from oil, natural gas, and metals to win political muscle. It did not take Putin long to chase the Russian billionaires Berezovsky and Gusinsky out of the country and jail Khodorkovsky for fraud and tax evasion. According to Michael McFaul at the Hoover Institution, Khodorkovsky may have drawn Putin's ire in the spring of 2003 when he had the temerity to suggest that "Russia needed a parliamentary democracy rather than a presidential republic." The eight-year jailing of Khodrokovsky, McFaul says, "was the execution of the latest change for regime change in Russia—autocratic regime change."[50] Russian prosecutors opened an additional investigation of Khodrokovsky in February 2007 for money laundering and embezzlement. Fresh charges were leveled in June 2008, facing the once free-wheeling oil tycoon with up to an additional fifteen years imprisonment.[51] Boris Berezovsky, one of the tycoons exiled in London, accused Putin of plotting to murder him and called for the nonviolent overthrow of the Russian government. Russian prosecutors in April 2007 were filing criminal charges against Berezovsky allegedly for looting $50 million from Aeroflot and said they would ask Britain to eliminate his political asylum status and extradite him to Moscow.[52]

Another step deemed necessary by Putin to consolidate his control of Russia was the suppression of dissent by those most harsh in their criticism of the new president. Thirteen journalists and writers critical of Putin were killed under mysterious circumstances and others left the country in a self-imposed exile.[53]

American journalist Paul Klebnikov, editor of *Forbes Russia*, was murdered as he left work in Moscow on July 9, 2004. He was gunned-down in a gang-style execution. As he lay dying after being shot four times, he could name no one who might have wanted to kill him. Some speculated he may have made few friends in Chechnya because of his published appeals to Europeans to protect the "Christian civilization against Islamic extremism." Others thought that Russia's security services could have believed that he "knew too much."[54] His book, *Godfather of the Kremlin,* published in 2000, provided many details about the KGB's covert activities during *perestroika*—that may have been enough to order his assassination.

Before she was murdered in her apartment in October 2006, Anna Politkovskaya sincerely lamented what she believed was a return to the old Soviet ways:

> As the chekists have become entrenched in power, we have let them see our fear, and thereby have only intensified their urge to treat us like cattle. The KGB respects only the strong. The weak it devours. We of all people ought to know that.
>
> Like cancer, bad history tends to recur, and there is only one radical treatment: invasive therapy to destroy the deadly cells. We have not done this. We dragged ourselves out of the Soviet Union and into the New Russia still infected with our Soviet disease.[55]

Ultimately, Anna Politkovskaya fell prey to Russia's new governance—gunned down in Moscow.

As negative images of Putin's Russia began to grow in the West, Russia's chief prosecutor Yuri Chaika announced in August 2007 that ten people had been arrested for the murder of Anna Politkovskaya. He insisted that the contract-killing was ordered by someone outside of Russia, intimating oligarchs in exile were responsible. Chaika's announcement occurred before the charges were prepared and the names of the accused were leaked to the press. Among those charged were three former police officers and a police major of the FSB (successor to the KGB). Some believed government officials were taking extraordinary measures to ruin the case, especially against the police officers, and propaganda began to flow like sour wine. Chaika insisted that Polkovskaya's murder was an attempt to "destabilize the country, change its constitutional order, . . . return to the old system where money and oligarchs decided everything, discredit the national leadership and provoke external pressure on our country."[56]

The voice of another Putin critic, and collaborator of Politkovskaya, Alexander Litvinenko was poisoned to death in London a month later. Similar to a Hollywood espionage thriller, London police and Scotland Yard discovered traces of a mysterious radioactive substance at a restaurant where Alexander Litvinenko had dined. Later, it was discovered that he had been poisoned with a difficult to obtain substance called polonium-210, which is used to reduce static electricity in many industries. Ninety-seven percent of the world's Polonium-210 is produced at the Avangard nuclear reactor located 450 miles outside Moscow.* Like hounds, British law enforcement traced polonium-210 traces to aircraft that had visited Moscow and Germany. The tangle of numerous factual threads were brought together by a steadfast British law enforcement.

Conspiracy theories galore were spun about the assassination by polonium-210. Some argued that rogue agents inside the FSB did it; others say no, the killers were former KGB. A few thought billionaire Boris Beresovsky did it. A couple believe Litvinenko poisoned himself. Most observers, however, assumed that Litvinenko had gone too far in his criticism of the Russian president

---

*The amount of Polonium-210 that entered Litvenenko's body was of a microscopic size. He died after twenty-two agonizing says in the hospital, Peter Finn, "Poisoning of Ex-Agent Sets Off Alarm Bells", *Washington Post* (January 7, 2007), p. A16.

and Putin ordered his killing to shut Litvinenko up and to deter others.[57]

The Litvinenko murder threw a pail of cold water on the Western image of the new Russia. President Putin is widely assumed to have had a hand in the poisoning. Regardless of whether this is a fair or unfair judgment, the dreaded picture of a KGB-controlled Russia has been dredged from the wreckage of the Soviet Union. The Politnovskaya and Litvinenko murders, plus the killing of American journalist Paul Klepnikov in Moscow, reflects a creeping coup of the democratic and free market Russia that the West had been celebrating. The West's wake-up call was long in coming.

In the end, the British accused Andrei Lugovoy, a former KGB officer, of poisoning Litvinenko and sought his extradition from Russia to stand trial for murder in Britain. Russia refused London's request, citing its constitution which prohibits extraditing Russian citizens to other countries. The British responded by expelling three Russian diplomats, and Russia answered by ordering the return of three British diplomats from Moscow. The London-Moscow row left the Litvinenko matter standing without a resolution.[58] Andrei Lugovoy was elected to the States Duma (Russian parliament) in December 2007 on the platform of a radical nationalist party that generally supports the Kremlin's policies.[59]

In retrospect, these events should not be surprising. The Andropov Plan disassembled the Soviet Union, turned the Communist Party invisible, and left the KGB standing with a new political role. KGB Document No. 174033 (January 1991), an order issued by KGB chief Vladimir Kryuchkov, a protege of Yuri Andropov, directed the agency to "create conditions for the effective use of foreign and domestic agent networks during increased political instability."[60]

Already at a high level, Russian espionage, especially against Europe and North America, surged under the presidency of Vladimir Putin. The Russian Foreign Intelligence Service (SVR) replaced the foreign spying tasks of the First Directorate of the Soviet KGB. Michael Kozakavich, who characterizes the SVR as being a "leaner, if not meaner, successor to the KGB's First Directorate," found the Service to reflect "several interesting tendencies in Russian thinking." He noted that SVR activities demonstrated a "strong gloss of Russian nationalism," especially in the areas relating to the "multipolar" objective, preserving and enhancing Russia's international status, and protecting Russia from intervention from the outside.[61]

These highlights of an effective and professional corps of Russian foreign intelligence officers should not be surprising. Gorbachev had a close interaction with Yuri Andropov and the KGB during his political ascent and the run-up to *perestroika*. Soviet KGB defector Oleg Gordievsky was quoted by Waller as saying that "Gorbachev's new thinking was . . . powerfully influenced by his many briefings by the KGB."[62] Throughout the ups and downs of *perestroika* the KGB delivered successful results and remained "unscathed." The KGB was a coveted wild card during *perestroika*, for it was entrusted to serve as a bulwark against the processes of change tumbling into anarchy. And Gorbachev smartly "never used his immense political capital to touch the chekists."[63] Thanks to a still robust KGB hiding behind the names of *Federalnaya Sluzba Bezopastnosti* (Federal Security Bureau) or FSB and *Sluzba Vneshnei Razvedka* (SVR), President Putin entered office with sharpened and familiar tools to help with his governance.

It did not take long for President Putin to wield the "sword" of the SVR. Britain's *Jane's Intelligence Service* reported in November 2002 that Russia was engaged in a "massive stepping-up of espionage activities in Europe and North America." The SVR intensified its recruitment of members of Russian emigres living abroad. Coercive techniques to win emigre agents in foreign lands included threats to fabricate prosecution cases against them prior to leaving Russia. If the target would refuse, extradition charges were immediately initiated.

Putin and the SVR also preyed on Russian entrepreneurs who were operating successfully in the West. The Russian president, for instance, is said to have ordered the investigation of the owner of a successful metallurgical factory in Switzerland. Meanwhile, the Czech Republic, a country of ten million people, plays host to a Russian embassy staff numbering more than four hundred "diplomats." The Czech Republic is a target rich country for the SVR and its coercive recruitment, since tens of thousands of Russian businessmen live and work in the country. In North America, the SVR has stepped-up its intelligence operations in large Russian emigre communities in New York, Miami, and Toronto.[64]

In March 2004, President Putin was re-elected with a stunning 70 percent of the vote. And this confidence expressed by Russian voters was after Putin had already made some extraordinary moves to impose some "discipline" on the democratic and economic systems—always Yuri Andropov's answer for dealing with social unrest and economic weakness. The Russian people expressed the belief that Putin would establish a more honest government and secure society.[65]

By the summer of 2005, however, a significant erosion of support for Putin's government was evident. The late Yuri Levada, director of the Moscow Center for the Study of Public Opinion, said that two-thirds of those polled affirmed their support for democracy but "strong pluralities" rejected the concentration of power in the hands of the president.

"The economy [under Putin] . . . is a curious hybrid of the free market, ideological dogma, and other features," Russian investigative journalist Anna Politkovskaya wrote shortly before her murder in 2006. "It is a model that puts Soviet ideology at the service of big-time private capital."[66] She also described "Putin's new-old *nomenklatura*," saying that they had "taken corruption to heights undreamed of under the Communists." In 2004, she said, they were "devouring small and middle-size businesses and with them the middle class" in favor of the "*nomenklatura's* preferred source of bribes"—"big and super-big businesses, the monopolies and quasi-state enterprises."[67] The middle class, of course, is an essential aspect of free market democracies. Anna Poltkovskaya took her knock-out swing at the Putin presidency by summing up: "Their hankering [Putin and his cronies] after the old times is increasingly reminiscent of the thinking in the Soviet Union during the height of the period of stagnation in the late Brezhnev years— the late 1970s and 1980s."[68] "How does this iron-fisted one-time KGB agent [Putin]," columnist Arnold Beichman asked after Politkovskaya's murder, "differ from the bloody days of Josef Stalin?"[69] Gorbachev had an answer: The system "was not working" when Putin came to power. He had to move to "stop disintegration."[70]

Russia 2008 presented two faces: one looking forward and another back. The push and pull between these separate forces deep inside the Russian psyche leaves many in the West quizzical. Is the Russian government democratic or non-democratic, liberal or authoritarian? As is often the case with Russia, unambiguous answers prove elusive. People living in Moscow and other urban areas are doing quite well with an economy growing at an average of six percent annually and real income jumping by about ten percent a year. People have money in their pockets and they are spending it on a wide array of consumer goods that only a few years ago were but an unattainable dream. But the backward face of the Russian Janus shows nearly a third of the population living on just $350 a month, the country's health care system in shambles, and other critical human needs unmet. Both faces represent the real Russia. Meanwhile, the KGB, which was given critical political roles to play in during the implementation of the Andropov Plan, performs important functions in assuring state security. Yevgenia Albats, a Russian investigative journalist quoted by Fred Weir in *The Christian Science Monitor,* described the contemporary situation this way: "The Kremlin has built a system in which one man, Putin, is responsible for everything. . . . The KGB is in power in this country, their man is president, and they conduct their affairs as in Soviet times."[71]

In a series of steps reminiscent of Stalin's shutting down the New Economic Policy in 1929, President Putin moved to crush all independent challengers to his one-man rule. With the big-three oligarchs out of the picture and the remaining super-wealthy cowed into obedience, Putin turned his sights towards any independent areas still remaining in Russian society. The political parties were gelded, businessmen learned how to play ball by Putin's "I always win" rules, and most civic society groups modified their behavior to satisfy the model demanded by the Kremlin. The final stage of the Andropov Plan seemed well underway in 2008.

The business community adapted to the reality of quietly paying their taxes to keep the *Siloviki*-bloated government running and contributed "soft dollars" in protection rackets run by the Putin power-men. Firms that cooperated were protected from overseas competition and strict regulations. While the Putin government works to root out corruption, the favored companies, such as Gazprom, an energy giant run by Putin cronies who siphoned some $20 billion from the company during the first term of the Putin presidency, get special treatment.[73]

President Putin's promise to "manage democracy" also produced authoritarian fruit. Following the star of his hero Yuri Andropov, Putin believes most problems can be resolved through discipline at the knee of a dictator. When Garry Kasparov, the legendary Russian chess champion, tried to apply his strategy skills to organizing an integrated opposition to *Siloviki* rule, the Kremlin took strong action. Kasparov attempted to bring Russia's fractured opposition groups together to speak with a single voice. When about 4,000 members of "The Other Russia" gathered at Moscow's Triumph Square, just a short walk from the Kremlin, to voice their concerns with Putin's policies, they were met by police and military forces that heavily outnumbered the demonstrators. Several skirmishes occurred and as many as 600 were arrested. The police also had raided Kasparov's offices a few days before the demonstration, seizing what they called "extremist literature."[73] "This is not the geopolitical monster of Soviet times," Kasparov said. "This is all about money. The government is business. It's about Gazprom, it's about Rosneft. Putin leads a ruling elite that has very different dreams than in Soviet times. They're all thinking about their great life in the Cote d'Azur."[74]

In July 2007, President Putin signed into law an expansion of the definition of criminal activity to include such action as "public slander of public officials" and "humiliating national pride." Andrei Piontkovsky, a brave critic of Russia's President Vladimir Putin and a resident scholar at the Hudson Institute in Washington, D.C., found himself in a Moscow court in September 2007 accused of inciting violence against Russia. Piontkovsky, a mathematician and creative thinker, denounced the charges as "absurd" and "primitive."[75]

The two government manuals are used as a basis for development of textbooks that foster a national ideology and vision of the Russian people with their own national identity—a kind of reverse Gramsci formula. At the same time, Americans are blamed for creating new international tensions. "From the beginning of the 1990s, the U.S. tried to realize a global empire," the new teacher's manual explains, "one of the U.S. strategies was to isolate Russia from all other former Soviet republics."[76]

In addition to the education manuals, ten thousand 14–28 year-old Russian "commissars" (the old Soviet word) gathered at a youth camp in July 2007 to prepare to eliminate challenges from opposition groups to the Putin government. The pro-Kremlin "Nashi" organization cheers President Putin and is dedicated to restoring Russia to superpower status. The vision ahead foresees a vast network with virtually all Russian youth being members of

Nashi. The slogan of the new commissars is "Let There Be Sovereign Democracy," or a democracy without Western influence. The organization already has grown quickly, extending branches to most of Russia's eighty-five regions.

At the summer camp, Russian youth combine patriotism with self-improvement, all of which is very similar to the Soviet Komsomol. The idea is to channel the energy and enthusiasm of Russian youth in the service of the state. Kremlin officials often speak at some of the Nashi functions, including President Putin in July 2007.[77]

The Kremlin's efforts in turning back the clock, such as Putin's comparison of the United States with the Third Reich, are paying off. A summer 2007 survey of 1,802 Russians, ages sixteen to twenty-nine, is telling because this "Putin generation" represent Russia's "political and economic future." The majority of Russian youth viewed the United States as public enemy Number One. Nearly 80 percent believed the U.S. is trying to impose its standards on other countries, 75 percent thought Washington offered aid to interfere in other countries, and 70 percent agreed that the United States does more harm than good. The top words selected from five in the survey that best describe the United States were "enemy" or "rival" (64 percent). This same cohort agreed that Stalin did more good than bad (54 percent) and 63 percent agreed with the proposition that the Soviet collapse was the "greatest geopolitical catastrophe of the twentieth century."[78] The Putin government has already prepared the next generation of Russians to carry on the Andropov Plan to a successful geopolitical conclusion. The Kremlin has drawn the lines in the sand demarcating the struggle for the coming one-world government. The propaganda message is clear: "Hey, West, don't complain. Putin will prevent a return to the old ways."[79]

These opinions, plus the political murders of Paul Klepnikov and Anna Politkovskaya in Moscow and Alexander Litvinenko in

London, make the years 2006–2007 appear as a turning point back
to the life in the days of the Soviet Union. The major difference in
2008, thanks to rising energy prices, found Russia floating in money.
The Deutshe Bank in Russia estimated that the country will have the
fifth largest economy in the world in 2020, with a $2 trillion
economy in 2010.[80] The ordinary Russian, however, was growing
increasingly restless about the turn of events, so much so that many
yearned for the hard but predictable days of the Soviet Union. In
December 2006, celebrations of Soviet leader Leonid Brezhnev's
eighteen-year rule were widely attended and included a flurry of
exhibitions, films, and television documentaries. While most
Russians spoke approvingly of Brezhnev's rule, one sensed that
something was missing in the new Russia—his was a time "when
the rest of the world treated the Kremlin with respect."[81]

A 2006 Levada Center poll showed that a staggering 61 percent
of the respondents regretted the fall of the Soviet Union. They
missed the religious-like comfort of Marxism-Leninism or an
ideology that could help make their hardships more bearable. In the
absence of an ideology to provide a code of conduct to live by, the
people were left uncertain and restless.[82]

The 64 million ruble question in 2007 was over who would
succeed President Putin, or, would he be succeeded at all. Having
served the constitutionally allowed two terms in office, Putin
announced he would not run for a third term. Then the search for
political wiggle-room began. From Western news reports, most
Russians would be very happy to have Vladimir Putin as a
permanent president. A variety of alternatives were sent up as trial
balloons—Putin could serve as prime minister with power over a
presidential puppet, he could go fishing and possibly return in
2012, or the constitution could be changed. Masha Lipman, a keen
observe of Russian political affairs, noted that "the Russian public
isn't any more concerned about adherence to the constitution than
is Russia's ruling elite."[84]

The succession of Putin to Putin occurred in two steps. First, the United Russia Party, listing President Vladimir Putin as its candidate, won 64 percent of the vote, or 315 of the 450-seat State Duma (parliament) on December 2, 2007. This sizable majority is more than enough to pass any legislation or amendment to the Russian constitution. Second, in the presidential election held on March 2, 2008, Putin's deputy prime minister Dmitry Medvedev won with about 68 percent of the vote. This step opened the door for President Medvedev to transfer all significant decision-making powers to the office of the prime minister, Vladimir Putin's new office. In the process, these steps transformed the country into a parliamentary republic. While none of this finagling resembled democracy in action, from all indications the Russian people do not care. They want Vladimir Putin in charge. He is the one who rescued them from the hardships and deprivations of a 1990s associated with capitalist plundering and gangland violence. Putin is the one credited with improving the lives of millions of Russians. After the March elections, president-elect Medvedev said the "'we will [now] be able to preserve the course of President Putin.' "[84]

Russian political analyst Dmitry Oreshkin is quoted as having put the facts-of-life in Russia this way: "The parliament is loyal to Putin. The security services are loyal to Putin. The mass media is Putin's. Any independent step by Medvedev will be considered a declaration of war on the current elite, and they will strike back."[85]

Energy Superpower

Russia has about 1,700 trillion cubic feet of natural gas reserves, more than any other country, and it is the world's largest exporter of the resource. The country's proven oil reserves number 60–74 billion barrels, most of which are located in Western Siberia. Gazprom, a Russian government-controlled oil firm, outlined plans to quadruple its $251 billion market value to become the world's first trillion-dollar firm by 2011.[86]

In order to prosecute its geopolitical competition against the capitalist West and Salafism/Wahhabi, President Putin took advantage of Russia's plentiful natural gas and oil resources and its transcontinental size and central position in Eurasia by crisscrossing the country with pipelines to fuel an energy-hungry world. When oil and natural gas prices rose shortly after President Putin's accession to power, the Kremlin had more cash to fund its worldwide geopolitical operations.

In addition to the normal conduct of the business of foreign sales of gas and oil (some $200 billion a year), Gazprom serves as a domestic stick to end free speech in Russia and a foreign policy tool to be used as leverage to compel the convergence of Europe and Russia from the Atlantic to the Ural Mountains. Gazprom Media assumed control of Russia's last independent television station after Putin had closed its operations. The Gazprom media firm also bought two once-independent newspapers. Meanwhile, Gazprominvest Holdings, the company's financial arm, purchased another newspaper and fired the editor. The newspaper's military correspondent had a fatal fall from a third story window.[87]

The convergence of Europe and Russia remains a key driving force to restoring Russia to its "natural home" as a European power. Nevertheless, Europe still looks toward North America in its transatlantic identity rather than toward the Urals. The convergence project dreamed-up by the Kremlin's geopolitical competitors should be recognized as a calculated assault against the capitalist West. Russia supplies about half of the European Union's natural gas, which gives Moscow considerable economic clout. Past energy supply cut-offs to Ukraine and Belarus, as well as the Baltic countries, placed Europe on notice of is vulnerability. "Cruise missiles and a nuclear a nuclear umbrella might have prevented the Red Army from rolling across Europe," Irwin M. Selzer concludes, "but they are no match for supply cutoffs that can throw the West into economic recession and freeze consumers."[88]

As the storm clouds rise once again to the east of Europe, the capitalist West is floundering. The refusal by Americans and Europeans to recognize that the post-Cold War party is over and their failure to develop a common strategy vis-a-vis an energy-muscular Russia is self-defeating. The Kremlin recognizes that its energy resources place it in a position to peel Europe away from the Atlantic Alliance, which would put the United States into a substantially weakened competitive position. Top Russian and Belorussian officials have been discussing the possible merger of Russia and Belarus since they signed a union agreement in 1996 that envisioned a close political, economic, and military convergence. With the transition of Mr. Putin to prime minister completed, the time may be ripe for Russia to offer Belarus President Alexander Lukashenko an offer he cannot refuse.[89]

While Russia plays a game of economic warfare against them, the Europeans do little more than wring their hands. The Kremlin's game is replete with energy blackmail and financial arrangements hidden deeply the world's shadows. By 2008, Moscow had scored victories in influencing the energy infrastructures in Lithuania, Latvia, and Estonia, as well as in Georgia, Ukraine, Moldova, Bulgaria, Armenia, and Greece. At the same time, Turkey, holding important supply routes, was drawing its energy policies closer to Moscow. Meanwhile, Europe, which has no enforceable common energy policy, "should not expect to compete effectively with a Russia that plays by a different rule book," Ambassador Keith C. Smith at the Center for Strategic and International Studies, concluded. "Europe seems mesmerized by the energy warfare swirling around them," Smith added. "The Russians are world-class chess players, while the European and American competitors play gentlemanly amateur croquet."[90]

Shadow Play or Reality?

The more one examines the main events that took place in the Soviet Union and Russia over the past two decades, the more they look like a re-play of the New Economic Policy of the 1920s. By drawing on the structure of KGB defector Anatoliy Golitsyn's warnings that the Kremlin was developing a new grand strategy based on propaganda and disinformation, the analysis reveals that some kind of plan or an organized set of ideas guided Mikhail Gorbachev's "restructuring" of Soviet foreign and domestic policies. By taking account of Yuri Andropov's iron-fisted control of the Soviet Union at the beginning and Vladimir Putin's authoritarian rule of Russia at the end of the story, one obtains a sense that little in Soviet Russia has changed. As for the years between the two leaders, the picture presents more of a grand shadow play cast on the wall of Plato's cave to support a Russian strategic objective of establishing a one-world governing system over the long-term.

Similar to Alexis de Toqueville in his study of *Democracy in America*, another Frenchman, the Marquis de Custine, following a five-month tour of Russia, wrote *Russia in 1839*.

In Russia secrecy presides over everything . . . the Russians' Byzantine policy, working in the shadow, carefully conceals from us all that is thought, done, and feared in their country. We proceed in broad daylight; they advance under cover: the game is one-sided. The ignorance in which they leave us blinds us; our sincerity enlightens them; we have the weakness of loquacity; they have the strength of secrecy. There, above all, is the cause of their cleverness.[91]

4

GLOBAL STRATEGIC QUADRANGLE

A **FEW MONTHS AFTER** the Soviet Union crumbled, a small group of us met in Washington, D.C. for what is known as a "bogsat" (bunch of guys sitting around a table) for an evaluation of alternative U.S. ballistic missile defense strategies. When the agenda items were exhausted, the ten or twelve of us turned to an issue we all had on our minds: the stunning collapse of the Soviet Union and the end of the Cold War that had shaped all of our lives for more than four decades. A basket-full of ideas was expressed by the scientists, engineers, diplomats, and military officers present about what these events meant for peace and cooperation with the new Russia and the U.S. role in the world. The late Paul Nitze, principal author of the American Cold War containment policy in the early 1950s, listened quietly, taking it all in. When everyone's ideas had been shared, Nitze quieted the room when he offered his own perspective (paraphrase): "We face a world in which the United States will be left standing as the only superpower with enormous

military, economic, and political influence. No one likes the big kid
on the block and no one country will be strong enough to confront
the United States for some time. In the future, we will face a world
competitor made up of a coalition that includes Russia, China,
maybe India, and a major Islamic country."

At the time, if anyone else had made such a statement, I would
have thought they were a bit balmy, for there were no discernible
indications to support Nitze's picture of the world ahead. But I had
had the opportunity to work with Paul on a few national security
problems in the 1970s and 1980s and had a pretty good idea of
how his mind worked. I felt compelled to take him seriously.

Ambassador Nitze had not lost his touch. Through the 1990s
and into the Putin era, we witnessed Nitze's geopolitical insight fall
into place, piece by piece. By 2008, the United States and its allies
were confronted by Russia as a new geopolitical competitor, backed
by a Moscow-led global strategic quadrangle consisting of Russia-
China-Iran-Cuba/Brazil. India remained in a "maybe" category, but
New Delhi had played an excellent geopolitical hand itself by
simultaneously maintaining good relations with Moscow and
Washington.

Using Antonio Gramsci's revisionist Marxism as a guide book, the
Kremlin created four strategic hubs, with itself as the coordinator
(and driving force) that makes up a quadrangle of international
influence in the creation of a new world order. Moscow is able to
compete with the United States through this system of proxies and
sub-proxies whose activities are hidden deeply inside a shadow world
dedicated to diminishing U.S. power and influence. Numerous
political, economic, military, and ideological cross-connections
highlight the relationships between the four strategic hubs or corners
of the quadrangle. The Latin American hub was modified later with
the addition of Venezuela, when Hugo Chavez, dictator-president of
Venezuela, muscled his way into a coalition with Cuba and Brazil by
virtue of his plentiful oil resources.

It is important to recognize the global strategic quadrangle for the geopolitical and doctrinal purposes it serves. From the beginning of *perestroika*, a one-world socialist ("Leninism Marxism") order was envisioned in the eyes of Moscow's ruling elite. By elevating Antonio Gramsci's formula to an international level that fosters a transformation of Western culture to one more amenable to being "Marxized," the Kremlin believes it has the right doctrinal tool to win the geopolitical competition against the capitalist West and militant Salafism/Wahhabi. The global strategic quadrangle of proxies and sub-proxies is a vital operational tool for Moscow's initiatives in the three-way geopolitical competition to define the future world order. Malachi Martin explained the strategic bridge that the quadrangle serves in linking the Kremlin's contemporary foreign policies and its long-term objective of promoting socialist world governance.

> At the geopolitical level, the Gorbachevist design for a new world order envisages a condition in which all national governments as we now know the will cease to exist. There is to be one central governing hub located in Moscow and dominated exclusively by the Communist Party of the World (CFW). . . . All military and security matters will be in the hands of the CPW and its surrogates throughout the nations. The geo-economy of the new world, meanwhile, will incorporate all the practical lessons Communists have learned from the market economies of the Western democracies; but it will preserve the centralizing principle of Leninist Marxism.[1]

Russia

Vladimir Putin considered China, India, and Iran as "strategic partners" right from the beginning of his presidency. The Cuban/Brazilian leadership of the Latin American communist and terrorist organizations was solidified in the 1990s and, in Putin's eyes, were potential proxies and sub-proxies for countering the United States in its own backyard. Russia's prodigious oil and natural gas supplies presented a potential opportunity to make the country an energy superpower. Satisfying the ever-increasing global energy demand could also open the door to the exercise of enormous political muscle. Pragmatic geopolitics also led Russia to sign agreements to construct nuclear power plants in China, India, and Iran. With two Russian nuclear reactors already under construction in India in early 2007, for example, Moscow and New Delhi signed agreements for four additional reactors to help satisfy India's compelling need for assured energy supply. "Energy security is the most important of the emerging dimensions of our strategic partnership," Indian Prime Minister Manmohan Singh said. "We look forward to a long-term partnership with Russia in this vital field."[2]

As the principal driving force of the anti-U.S. and anti-Salafism global strategic quadrangle, Russia's promotion of a multipolar world would put the brake on Washington's economic globalization policies. This Kremlin move resonated well in Asia. Voices around the world grew louder about America's ostensible "imperialist ambitions." International journalist Sultan Shahin, for instance, wrote in the *Asia Times Online* that favoring a multipolar world "obviously doesn't suit the United States, the lord and master of the present unipolar system in which it even threatened . . . to make the United Nations obsolete."[3]

Iraq War

Yevgeny Primakov, a tough-minded Soviet cold warrior, asserted in 2006 that "a multi-polar world [had] started taking shape. That's the new reality." He stressed that Russia was playing it straight and was not making anti-American statements, citing the Kremlin's silence about U.S. operations in Iraq.[4]

As is always the case with Mr. Primakov, one must decode his words in reverse to penetrate the disinformation imbedded in his message. The Kremlin had been able to stand above the global criticism of American foreign policies in Iraq through the use of proxies and sub-proxies drawn from its global strategic quadrangle and the ubiquitous anti-American far Left agents of influence inside the United States and in Europe, Canada, Australia, New Zealand, and elsewhere in the world. These proxies serve as the Kremlin's global anti-American megaphone. The strategic quadrangle and Western agents of influence represent important parts of Russia's second-rail foreign policy operating in the shadows. The Kremlin's propaganda and disinformation strategy masks the implementation of the Gramsci formula to undermine America's traditional Judeo-Christian, values-based culture. Moscow's in-the-shadows drum beat is insidious, all-encompassing, and constant. American far-Leftists, the progressives-socialists-marxists, are the major drummers. Their collective, mutual-reinforcing hate for the American way of life and dedication to creating a massive cultural transformation toward socialist governance has driven them into Moscow's waiting arms.

Yevgeny Primakov was the guy that President Putin sent to Iraq for discussions with Saddam Hussein during the run-up to the American assault in March 2003. Although the discussions remain cloaked in mystery, it is clear that Russian companies, in violation of UN sanctions, had been helping to arm Iraq and train Iraqi forces in using advanced military weapons.[5] Among the Russian military equipment sold to Iraq were night-vision goggles, anti-tank weapons, missiles, and jamming devices to counter the U.S. global positioning system and precision-strike weapons. Stephen Blank observed that such arms transfers were hardly unique and noted that Yevgeny Primakov, during a stint as President Yeltsin's prime minister in the 1990s, had assisted Iraq in stonewalling the UN arms inspection teams. Primakov was even believed by British and American intelligence agencies to have been on Saddam Hussein's payroll. Meanwhile, Blank noted, Russian newspapers reported repeatedly that the Kremlin and arms dealers had established linkages with defense industries in former Soviet republics, such as Belarus, to sell arms to foreign buyers that Moscow did not want to be associated with.[6] In a word, such arrangements were necessary to preserve Moscow's carefully cultivated image as being a respectable "friend" of the West. It is also a part of Antonio Gramsci's blueprint to smile at the capitalists, while one is carefully cutting their throats.

The Kremlin's arms sales in Iraq were accompanied by an extensive disinformation campaign conducted in the back alleys of the Middle East. According to one Arab report, Moscow warned several countries, including Iran and Syria, that they could become targets in a U.S. war against Iraq. Washington's coming campaign against Baghdad would lead to the toppling of any regime that was connected with terrorism, the Russians warned. The warnings were accompanied by fictitious attack scenarios of lightening air strikes against terrorist sites in Lebanon's Bekka Valley, Damascus, and the Afghan-Iranian border. Another Russian scenario discussed a hypothetical U.S., British, and Turkish assault against Iran's nuclear reactor at Bushehr and Shihab-3 missile facilities.[7]

Russian intelligence services had no comment on a report in April 2003 that the Foreign Intelligence Service (SVR) had urged Baghdad to destroy any weapons of mass destruction in its possession to undermine a key U.S. argument for toppling the Saddam Hussein regime. The report was based on documents found during the ransacking of government offices in Baghdad by the Western press in the immediate aftermath of the American assault. Other documents also showed a direct Baghdad-Russian SVR connection.[8] The *Sunday Telegraph* (London) obtained top secret documents retrieved from the heavily bombed intelligence service building in Baghdad that showed Russia provided a wide-range of assistance to Iraqi spies and the military during the months leading up to the U.S. attack. Among the documents recovered, according to columnist David Harrison, was an intelligence report that one Iraqi agent said a Russian colleague had passed to him—it detailed a private conversation between British Prime Minister Tony Blair and Italian Prime Minister Silvio Berlusconi at a meeting in Rome on February 15, 2002. Blair confided that he had refused to engage in any military action in Iraq because British forces were engaged in Afghanistan and nothing could happen until a new government in Kabul had been set up. "Another document, dated March 12, 2002, appears to confirm that Saddam had developed, or was developing nuclear weapons," Mr. Harrison wrote. "The Russians warned Baghdad that if it refused to comply with the United Nations then that would give the United States 'a cause to destroy any nuclear weapons.' "[9] This report should be given some degree of credibility, since the 1991 UN inspection reports on Iraqi weapons of mass destruction found that the Hussein government had built at least two workable nuclear triggers, whose alleged destruction could not be confirmed by UN inspectors. Western experts estimated at that time that Saddam Hussein was just eighteen months away from having a usable nuclear weapon. As this writer observed in 1996, "the Iraqi case, both in terms of pre-war intelligence and post-war on-site inspections, demonstrates that there will *always* be great uncertainties about nuclear weapons programs."[10]

Based on foreign intelligence released to the public by a senior Pentagon official without permission (he was fired), the United States was well aware that Russian special forces had helped in the removal of Saddam Hussein's WMD weeks before the attack in March 2003. The Russian covert arms removal was caught in a satellite image released by the Pentagon that showed trucks lined-up to move the materials. In addition, two Russian generals were given awards by Saddam Hussein shortly before the U.S. attack for undisclosed services.[11]

An analysis by the Institute for Defense Analyses, a federally-funded think tank, of 600,000 documents captured in Iraq, reported in March 2008 that "Saddam supported groups that either associated directly with al Qaeda (such as the Egyptian Islamic Jihad, led at one time by bin Laden's deputy, Ayman al-Zawahiri) or that generally shared al Qaeda's stated goals and objectives." The government analysis also found numerous connections between Saddam Hussein's Iraq and various organization associated with al Qaeda and other terrorist groups. As quoted in the government-funded, 1,600 page study entitled *Iraqi Perspectives Project: Saddam and Terrorism: Emerging Insights from Captured Iraqi Documents*, the "captured documents reveal that the regime was willing to co-opt or support organizations it knew to be part of al Qaeda—as long as that organization's near-term goals supported Saddam's long-term vision."[12] In 1993, for instance, Saddam Hussein personally ordered the formation of an Iraqi terrorist group to join Osama bin Laden's fighters battling Americans in Somalia. Saddam's regime also hosted a series of thirteen conferences for non-Iraqi jihadist groups in 2002, just a few months before the U.S. invasion.[13]

Russian Military

The once mighty Red Army was allowed to tumble into a state of disrepair, aging and outdated equipment, and poor morale after the disintegration of the Soviet Union. By 1994, 70 percent of the military commanders said that "their units were unable to fight properly," and, according to a German report, they were unable to fight outside the Commonwealth of Independent States. Out of Russia's eighty-one ground divisions, fifty-one were not combat ready. Similar faults weakened the air forces—fuel shortages left training far below standard and more than a third of Russia's helicopters were grounded.[14]

The state of armed forces nagged at Vladimir Putin and the Russian people who, together with their president, viewed the disrepair of the military as a principal reason for the West's disrespect for Russia's security. Other priorities seem to nudge military reform onto the back-burner, especially since Putin's "nice guy offensive" against the West delivered him a lengthy in-office honeymoon. By the summer of 2007, however, Putin declared the "'one of the unconditional priorities is the reinforcement of all aspects of our Armed Forces.'"[15]

Jacques Fontand in the annual French Yearbook of International Relations offered the right appraisal: "'Intent on regaining for the country a part of the luster of the past even as its strategic position is weakening by the enlargement of NATO and the military initiatives of the United States, the Russian President proposes to re-concentrate the defence apparatus on priorities, meaning domestic threats, the borders, reinforcing nuclear arms and developing the means of cooperation and diplomacy.'"[16]

President Putin drove another stake into the ground, indicating a return to a Party-State rule as Russia neared final political recovery from the rigorous implementation of the Andropov Plan. The successful theatrical production of *perestroika*, like Lenin's New Economic Policy, had pretty well run its course. The final steps in building a "new" Russia are focused on restoring the armed forces and combining their authority with the growing energy-clout enjoyed by the Kremlin. Together they will be used to satisfy Putin's major objective of winning international recognition that a multi-polar word had replaced the United States' two decades long unipolar global dominance. Russia is back, and Putin and the Russian people demand that their country be recognized as one of the major players on the world scene.

Two days before the December 2, 2007 parliamentary election President Putin signed into law a resolution passed by the Duma in November that called for scrapping the Conventional Armed Forces in Europe (CFE) treaty. This was a capstone on the harsh, anti-Western rhetoric and promises to restore Russia to greatness by Putin's supporters in the run-up to the elections. The CFE had been signed during the last days of the Cold War to limit the number of heavy weapons (such as tanks, artillery pieces, armored personnel carriers) and combat aircraft and helicopters that could be positioned in Western Europe and the western part of Russia. NATO considered the CFE to be a cornerstone of stability and security in Europe.[17]

It seems that right from the beginning of Putin's presidency, the CFE bothered the Russians. In the military doctrine approved in 2000, Putin made it quite clear that Russia might use nuclear weapons to protect Russia and its allies from a large-scale ground attack. In January 2008, the nuclear ante against the West was increased, when the Chief of General Staff Yuri Baluyevsky said that nuclear weapons, *including preemptive strikes*, would be used to protect Russia and its allies.[18]

In January 2008, the Russian Navy held its first major maritime exercise in fifteen years. Ships participating included an aircraft carrier, a guided missile cruiser, destroyers, and support vessels. Russian air forces joined the simulated defense against attacks by exercising the air forces in support of the maritime exercise: Backfire and Blackjack strategic bombers, aerial tankers, and Fox Hound long-range interceptors and Flanker fighter-attack aircraft).[19]

In February 2008, with presidential voting just ahead, Putin lashed out at the West, claiming Russia had been taken advantage of during its period of weakness after the Soviet Union imploded. " 'It is clear after a new arms race has been unleashed on the world,' " Putin said. " 'It is not our fault, because we did not start it.' " The Russian president added that " 'we have returned to the world arena as a state which is taken into consideration, a state that can stand up for itself.' "[20]

A month later, fuming over Kosovo's independence from Serbia, Putin accused the West of trying to replace the United Nations with NATO. The Russian president claimed NATO had mounted "an endless expansion . . . when there is no confrontation between two hostile systems."[21]

Arms Exports

In pursuit of a larger share of the international arms market, Russia has signed multi-billion dollar contracts with China, India, and Iran; Venezuela was added later for everything from submarines and super-sonic jets to tanks and other battlefield weapons. "Our allies expect from Russia a clear and consistent policy on issues of military-technical cooperation," Putin said. He also revived military cooperation agreements in key regions of the world, placing the United States on notice of Moscow's intention to compete on the geopolitical chess board.[22] In a reversal from the Cold War, Putin was constructing a containment strategy against the United States.

Russian arms manufacturers rely on foreign sales for about 90 percent of their revenue. Russia's military exports in 2006 amounted to $8 billion, plus $30 billion in contracts under negotiation (though not all were signed). The Middle East accounted for 17 percent of these exports.[23] Aircraft accounted for 57 percent of the exports. These companies are on a constant hunt for new clients worldwide. A sizable proportion of Russian overseas military sales have gone to China and India. As these markets began to stagnate, the Russians turned increasingly to arms sales to Arab states, especially in the resource-rich Middle East and North Africa. Russia has been particularly aggressive in pursuing the growing air defense and satellite market in these regions. Belarus served as a front for Russian military sales in the Middle East and other developing countries—$1.1 billion in annual exports from Minsk indicate a steady pipeline of arms from Russia.[24] Some of the arms transfers appear to be quite sensitive. Ivan Safranov, a military correspondent for *Kommersant*, a business newspaper, was killed on March 2, 2007, when he fell or was thrown from a third floor window (suicide was deemed unlikely). Safranov was investigating Russian arms sales to Syria and Iran via Belarus. Victor Bout, a notorious former-KGB arms dealer who was finally arrested in Thailand in March 2008, may have been involved.[25]

Syria and Iran were sold weapons that the Russians said were "defensive" and would not upset the regional balance of power. In early 2007, Syria ordered advanced MIG-31E fighter jets from Russia, giving Damascus a significant leap in combat capability. Iran financed the Syrian purchase and most of the top of the line aircraft would be shared with the Iranian air force. Sources also said that Iranian Air Force and intelligence officers had been deployed to Syrian military bases and were operating strategic radar and missile batteries. "Iran's strength is Syria's strength," Syrian Defense Minister Hassan Turkmani said.[26] Despite Russia's claims of selling only "defensive" weapons, during the July–August 2006 conflict between the Syrian- and Iranian-supported Hezbollah terrorists, Israel found itself facing an array of advanced military weapons made in Russia: RPG-29 Vampire anti-tank grenade launchers and anti-tank missiles for use against low flying helicopters. Russia denied being the source and explained that Hezbollah could have obtained the RPG-29 grenade launchers from any number of its buyers. In 2007, Russia provided Iran with highly secret advanced technology, rocket powered torpedoes. The high-speed torpedo is said to be able to move underwater at speeds up to 100 meters per second.[27]

The Algeria-Morocco rivalry over the Western Sahara opened another door for Russia's arms suppliers. It had made a $7.5 billion arms package deal with Algeria, with an option for another $2—$3 billion in follow-on contracts. Algeria ranks third, behind China and India, in terms of volume of Russian military imports. Russia has delivered hundreds of advanced warplanes to the Algerians, plus 300 top-line T-90S main battle tanks, eight battalions of surface-to-air missiles, and other weapons systems.

Russian energy-driven interests often were at the center of these arms sales. Moscow was concerned about losing revenue, if the European Union opted to become a major consumer of Algerian natural gas. To block such an event, the Russians persuaded the

Algerian government to agree to productivity sharing agreements with Gazprom and other Russian energy firms.

Russian military sales, energy geopolitics, and commercial boldness have coalesced to give the Kremlin greater influence in countries far beyond its borders. Beneath the surface of the well-polished veneer of international cooperation and understanding, Russia is firm in its rejection of Western criticism concerning to whom Russia sells arms: "I often hear criticism that one must not sell to certain states," Sergei Ivanov, Minister of Defense, said. He further lamented, "according to this logic we cannot sell anything."[28]

Meanwhile, covert Russian, North Korean, and Chinese assistance to Burma's nuclear reactor facilities raised the specter of a new nuclear proliferator on the horizon. North Korea's aid to the Burma project is in line with threats it has made to proliferate its nuclear weapon technology abroad. Chinese nuclear assistance raises fears that it will proliferate nuclear technology like it did with Pakistan in the 1980s.[29]

By January 2007, the United States finally had had its fill of the Kremlin's and Beijing's tactic of saying one thing and doing another. Sanctions were slapped on twenty-three Russian and Chinese companies. Both countries blasted the U.S. action, with Moscow claiming that "the U.S. has tried to extrapolate its domestic laws to foreign companies, to make them work under U.S. rules." China complained that it was "unreasonable" for the United States "to sanction . . . Chinese companies without providing any evidence," and strongly urged "the U.S. to correct its wrong practice."[30]

The curtain drawn across Russia's transformation from a Marxist-Leninist totalitarian state to a secret Leninist-Marxist follower of Gramsci's formula, began to let in small beams of light, raising questions about the Kremlin's strategic goals and operations in the years ahead. President George W. Bush expressed his disillusionment with Russian President Vladimir Putin in late 2006. "We have lost Putin," he said. "Putin fears democracy more than anything else."[31]

Putin's Geopolitical Offensive

President Putin began a public whining campaign in early 2007 about U.S. international activities at the 43rd Munich Conference of Security Policy. Putin blasted the United States before an audience of major world leaders: "one single center of power. One single center of decision-making. This is a world of one master, one sovereign." He added that "today we are witnessing an almost unconstrained hyper use of force in international relations—military force." Mr. Putin continued that "primarily the United States has overstepped its national borders, and in every area." He went on about U.S. military actions as being "unilateral" and "illegitimate" and saying that "they bring us to the abyss of one conflict after another. . . . Political solutions are becoming impossible."[32]

In addition to wielding an energy geopolitical hammer in Europe and a verbal attack against U.S. security policies, President Putin and his generals resorted to dark Cold War rhetoric over a U.S. initiative to provide an anti-ballistic missile defense for Europe against Iranian long-range rockets, possibly nuclear-tipped, and other future threats from the Middle East. Washington explained that the interceptor missiles would be based in Poland and the acquisition radar in the Czech Republic and that the system was not intended to threaten Russia. The American explanation was summarily dismissed by the Kremlin whose strategic analysts saw the defensive system as "offensive" in so far as they viewed the *ten* interceptor missiles magically threatening the regional balance in Europe. If the truth was to be told, this flap was more about Russia's hurt feelings for not having been consulted ahead of time as a legitimate European power.[33] "If the governments of Poland and the Czech Republic take such a step," General Nikolai Solovtsov, commander of Russian missile forces warned, "the [Russian] strategic missiles forces will be capable of targeting these facilities if a relevant decision is made."[34] Putin went so far as to compare the ten planned air defense rockets with the Cuba missile crisis in 1962. He called the proposed U.S. defense shield a needless provocation, noting that Russia had liquidated everything in Cuba.[35]

President Putin moved quickly by launching several additional initiatives with geopolitical implications. Not only promising to strengthen Russia's military with new weapons, Putin also moved to increase foreign intelligence collection. He made no bones about it—expanding Russia's espionage network was important in countering the United States in the Middle East. These Russian intelligence operations would also use disinformation to spread dissent against U.S. policies in Saudi Arabia and the Gulf states.[36]

A third geopolitical initiative was taken when Russia announced that it would expand the country's Black Sea naval base by establishing a permanent presence in the Mediterranean. Most speculation centered on possible ports in Syria at Tartus and Latakia where Russian engineers have been busy in dredging operations. A presence in Syria would place Russian naval vessels near U.S. operations in Iraq, Israel, and Turkish ports with their new oil pipeline facilities. The port of Tartus would be especially useful for intelligence collection against the U.S. Sixth Fleet and Israel. Admiral Vladimir Masorin, Russia's naval commander, said that "the Mediterranean is very important strategically for the Black Sea Fleet." Military analyst Pavel Felgenhauer added that "it has been the dream of our admirals for a long time to restore our naval greatness and keep the task force we had under the Soviet Union."[37]

Another Russian geopolitical move in August 2007 occurred when long-range bombers were sent to Guam to challenge the U.S. naval base located on the island. Russian Major General Pavel Androsov asserted that U.S. interceptors scrambled to track the bombers. A week later, Russia launched twenty bombers to establish its broader sovereign presence; the aircraft completed twenty-hour military patrols. Russian bombers, President Putin explained, would continue to conduct long-range air patrols regularly. In September, a Russian military exercise included a strategic cruise missile attack on the United States.[38]

The Russian bombers supported a combined eight-day military exercise, "Peace Mission 2007," in China's northwestern Xinjiang Uighur Autonomous Region, which included China and other members of the Shanghai Cooperative Organization. A primary focus was placed on countering terrorism, separatism, and drug and arms trafficking. China and Russia remain wary of each other, especially in Central Asia, despite their cooperation on strictly focused security issues. According to some American analysts, this move and others answer an emotional Russian need to restore some of the Cold War stature that the Soviet Union had enjoyed.[39]

China and Iran joined Russia in August 2007 by warning the United States that its interference in the resource-rich Central Asia would not be welcome. The warning coincided with the beginning of a war-game in the region. Washington had already cut back its presence in Central Asia, leaving only its NATO-support base for Afghanistan at Manas Air Base in Kyrgyzstan.[40]

Another geopolitical chess move was staking a claim to the seabed under the North Pole. According to the Kremlin, the continental shelf extending from Russia's shores covers an area the size of Western Europe. Billions of barrels of oil and trillions of cubic feet of natural gas could be at stake. Moscow went so far as to dispatch a mini-submarine to place a Russian flag under the Pole. Other potential claimants to the northern seabed—the United States, Canada, Norway, and Denmark—were taken by surprise.[41] Russia remained dismissive of some claims that the Russians had started an "Ice War" with the West. Rather, President Putin was clear that the polar move "should become a core of Russia's stance on ownership of part of the Arctic shelf."[42] This series of events revealed President Putin tipping his hand about the continuing socialist competition in the shadow world of implementing Antonio Gramsci's formula for sapping the West's will to resist.

China

China is Russia's most important strategic partner in the global strategic quadrangle and the "scissors strategy" against the United States. The cautious relationship between Moscow and Beijing serves as a counter-balance to the power and influence of the American superpower. Despite this joint posture, many issues remain outstanding between the two countries, not the least of which is neither fully trusts the other. Russia is well aware that it runs the risk that by underwriting China's military strength it may be contributing to the emergence of a future rival Eurasian superpower. The Chinese People's Liberation Army conducted a ten-day military training exercise in September 2006 in its Shenyang and Beijing Military Districts opposite the armed forces of Russia across the border. Some units deployed 1,000 kilometers into the Beijing Military District, demonstrating its strategic movement capabilities. The exercise scenario was based on attack rather than defense.[43]

A key aspect of the Russia-China coalition is its loose structure. The partnership with China is no guarantee that Beijing will support all of Russia's policies and vice versa. Each has many relationships with different countries around the world; the glue that binds them is their common interest in undermining the U.S. superpower position in favor of a multipolar world order governed by socialist ("Leninist-Marxist" or geopolitical Gramscian) principles.

Russia and China signed a Treaty for Good Neighborliness, Friendship and Cooperation in July 2001 that joins forces in opposing the unipolar world structure that emerged at the end of the Cold War. In a joint statement when unveiling the Russia-China strategic pact, Presidents Jiang Zemin and Vladimir Putin said that their mutual agreement was created with the hope for a "just and rational new international order," emphasizing their merger was "not directed toward third countries." In addition, the Treaty settled the long simmering border disputes between the two countries and set the stage for arms and technology transfers, energy and raw materials supply, and mutual concerns about the rise of militant Islam in Central Asia.[44]

While the two presidents downplayed their new "partnership" as little more than a few general principles for establishing a new international order, Russia experts viewed the pact, according to former Soviet Colonel Stanislav Lunev, "to actually be the practical formalization of the military alliance between Moscow and Beijing." Colonel Lunev said that the new "partners" were interested in confronting the United States and undermining world stability, citing Russian assistance to China's conversion of their silo-based missiles to road-mobile missile launchers, the Russian made Topol/Poplar/ICBMs.[45]

The Shanghai Cooperation Organization was founded in June 2001, building on a series of border agreements, confidence-building measures, and other security guarantees by Russia, China, Kazakhstan, Kyrgyzstan, and Tajikistan. Uzbekistan joined the original five members later. The Shanghai agreement addressed a very broad array of issues concerning regional security and politics in Central Asia. Anti-terrorism is a primary concern and exchanges of information about terrorist threats and joint studies helped to keep all members informed. Although "the Shanghai Cooperation Organization lacks the internal cohesion and capabilities found in multilateral security institutions such as NATO," the Hudson Institute's Richard Weitz observed, "the SCO members collectively share (to varying degrees) a desire to prevent external intervention in their own affairs."[46]

The Shanghai Cooperation Organization serves as China's primary tool for implementing its anti-U.S. policies in Central Asia. Fearful of strategic encirclement, the Chinese remain very antagonistic toward the United States military presence in the region. The Shanghai Cooperation Organization gives China a multilateral mechanism to engage countries in Central Asia and encourage them to oust the Americans. Meanwhile, the Russians and Chinese, behind the facade provided by the Shanghai Cooperation Organization, remain bitter rivals for contracts that tap the region's energy resources and, especially for the Chinese, rail and road access rights to the energy fields.

China benefits from the Aterlao-Kenjiyaker-Atasu-Alashankou oil pipeline from Kazakhstan that opened in December 2005. The pipeline can handle about twenty million tons per year, a major increase over the half-a-million tons shipped by rail. Beijing has spoken about building additional pipelines from Central Asian countries to secure the oil and gas necessary to fuel its expanding economy. Iran remains the most important Caspian producer for China, supplying up to 17 percent of Chinese oil imports in 2005 and 25 percent in the first quarter of 2006.[47]

In addition to Central Asia as a center for Russian-Chinese cooperation, Beijing looks to Moscow and Middle Eastern energy sources as well. China's global energy search also extends across North Africa and into the sub-Sahara, including Nigeria, Kenya, and Angola. Thanks to some shrewd bargaining and deep pockets, China has built an energy partnership in Angola, as well as engaging Chinese companies in the construction of schools, clinics, hospitals, and low-cost housing.[48] Sinopec, one of China's three large state-owned oil firms, offered Angola more than $2 billion for the right to explore for oil in three parcels of Angola's territorial waters.[49] China's President Hu Jintao toured eight Africa countries in February 2007 scouring the continent for oil and trade. Hu presented some $100 million in gifts and wrote off debts owed by thirty-three African countries to China. Beijing's trade with Africa grew to $45 billion in the final ten months of 2006. In the absence of any moral concern, China won 60 percent of Sudan's oil output in return for arms supplies that overlooked a UN arms embargo in place to deal with the genocide in Darfur that numbered more than 300,000 black Christians killed. China also provided trade and infrastructure support that helped Sudan's economy to grow by 13 percent in 2006, while the slaughter in Darfur continued.[50]

In an energy-related area, China has launched a major drive "to gain control of strategically positioned ports that could support worldwide military and economic actions against the United States," warned security analyst Charles R. Smith. The Chinese-owned Hutchison Whampoa Ltd. is the world's largest cargo terminal operator and port owner. Hutchison controls numerous possible choke-points to assure seaborne shipping to and from its 169 berths at 41 ports worldwide, which accounts for about 15 percent of global maritime container traffic.[51]

China's energy strategy includes development of a national tanker fleet sufficient to transport up to half of its yearly oil imports, up to 750 million barrels, by 2010. In order to do so, China will have to build as many as 40 very large crude oil transports, each can carry 1.5 million or more barrels of oil. Three-quarters of the country's oil imports come from the Middle East and Africa. Oil pipelines from Kazakhstan and Russia will satisfy up to a quarter of China's needs. Beijing calculated that land transport would remain an important aspect of its imports but would be insufficient to relieve its dependence on seaborne oil. Closure of the Straits of Hormuz and Malacca constitute one of China's nightmare scenarios—the "Malacca Dilemma." The potential crisis offers Beijing motivation for continuing arms transfers to Iran to keep the Persian Gulf open to oil transit. The inability to keep the straits open against U.S. naval interdiction would make military action against Taiwan more problematic. Nonetheless, the reality is that seaborne oil imports are most cost effective, although such action is inherent with risks of interdiction at sea during emergencies.[52]

With cash in its pocket from its fast-growing economy, the Beijing government moved to modernize and increase the size of its military forces. Behind a screen of Chinese secrecy, expert Western observers say that annual defense spending ranges between $130 billion and $200 billion when foreign arms purchases, the military-run space program, and other costs are accounted for. The Chinese explained that it had to increase military spending for "protecting national security [primarily against the United States] and promoting the reunification of the motherland" [Taiwan].[53]

In 2007, China pushed the United States aside from it decades of reigning as the primary engine of global economic growth. According to the International Monetary Fund, China would drive the global economy to expand by 5.2 percent, which was expected to be the largest part of the increase in global growth.[54] China is North Korea's most important trading partner ($1.7 billion in 2006), including 70 percent of Pyongyang's grain imports. Trade with Burma is about $1.2 billion, and China is believed to have supplied the military government with more than $2 billion in weapons since the 1980s. Trade with Iran is expected to top $15 billion in 2007, much of it natural gas and oil. In Africa, bilateral trade with the troubled Zimbabwe government amounted to some $200 million, while China's trade and investment alone keeps the government of Sudan afloat, not to mention its sizable weapon sales since the 1990s. In Latin America, China's trade and support have been crucial in Cuba after assistance from the Soviet Union stopped flowing. Trade between Cuba and China was $1.8 billion in 2006, or about twice the amount in 2005. Trade also doubled in Venezuela in 2006 to $4.3 billion. The two countries have a declared "strategic partnership," with Beijing having a closer eye on Venezuela's oil.

China also launched aggressive investments in Latin America, a fourth hub of the strategic quadrangle. According to a poll conducted in late 2007, 83 percent of Americans perceive China's expansion of economic and political influence in Latin America as a threat. In Cuba, China was instrumental in upgrading the country's air defense system and has two intelligence stations on the island collecting U.S. electronic and communications data.

Chinese-Brazilian cooperation in satellite technology, which could be used for collecting high resolution imagery, is troublesome from a U.S. perspective. Moreover, Brazil accounts for 45 percent of China's soybean imports. China plans to build a steel plant in Brazil, a deal has been signed for a gas pipeline, and Brazil has opened its economy to Chinese imports.

Venezuela-China military cooperation is extensive. President Hugo Chavez has visited China four times leading to the signing of $11 billion in energy and transportation agreements. China will participate in the construction of three oil refineries in Venezuela, and Chavez promised uninterrupted deliveries of oil to China, increasing oil imports through 2011.

China has been busy in other Latin American countries as well. In Panama, for instance, it holds a fifty-year lease on the management of ports on each side of the Panama Canal. El Salvador has a deal for purchase of Chinese automobiles, Sinopec put up $800 million to acquire a 50 percent share of a large Colombia oil company, and Costa Rica, Ecuador, Peru, Chile, Mexico, Bolivia, Paraguay, and Argentina have all profited from the market sales with China. The growing commercial juggernaut in North America's backyard has not gone unnoticed in Washington.[55]

A key aspect of the build-up is focused on development of a balanced ballistic missile force, both qualitatively and quantitatively, sufficient to reach the United States as well as increased operational capabilities for regional warfare. By 2010, the Chinese are expected to have up to sixty missiles capable of striking the United States. New medium-range missiles capable of striking Taiwan also are being fielded.[56]

China is arming itself to wage war against the United States, its worst-case planning scenario. Hence, Beijing's military build-up extends across the board for purchasing Russian jet fighters and submarines to blockade Taiwan and challenge U.S. naval power in the region. The British and French have sold China long-range airborne radars for its naval aircraft, and the British and Germans have sold Beijing satellite technology for use in military reconnaissance. The Chinese government remains dedicated to modernizing its armed forces and increasing its ability to project power. The latter objective compels Beijing to emphasize advanced technology to allow its military to reach far beyond its shores.[57]

A major security concern for China is the U.S. efforts to build an anti-ballistic missile shield for Japan. A spokeswoman for China's Foreign Ministry said in June 2007 that a U.S.-Japan missile defense system would "impact stability and the strategic balance" and asserted that "it is not conducive to mutual trust of major nations and the strategic balance."[58] Nevertheless, the Chinese expect to "lay a solid foundation" for its military build-up by 2010 and make "major progress" by 2020. In addition, Beijing expects to "reach the strategic goal of . . . being capable of winning informationalized wars by the mid-21st century."[59] These capabilities and a superior strategy should provide Beijing the security comfort zone that it was missing in 2008.

China's military sales to Iran, one of its partners in the Russian-led global strategic quadrangle, has drawn considerable U.S. attention. The Chinese decried U.S. sanctions in 2002 resulting from its supplying Iran with materials to produce chemical and biological weapons. Sanctions were also imposed by the United States for China's sale of modified Silkworm anti-ship missiles and high-speed catamaran missile patrol boats to Iran.[60]

China's missile and nuclear transfers to North Korea and Pakistan can potentially trigger a nuclear arms races between India and Pakistan, as well as North Korea and Japan, and in South Korea and Taiwan. Chinese assistance to Pakistan's nuclear program was passed on to North Korea at least with the tacit approval of Beijing. Pyongyang's nuclear program drew a great deal of Chinese expertise through its Pakistan proxy, including large numbers of centrifuge machines to produce weapons-grade plutonium. This should be hardly surprising since China and North Korea share the Sinic culture and have had long historical ties, as well as, at least in their eyes, common threats from Japan and the United States.

Both Chinese and North Korean missile technicians were dispatched to Iran in 1997 to assist Tehran in its long-range missile development. Iran's subsequent missile tests provided useful data for North Korea in its own missile program. Intelligence sources in the United States as early as 2002 suspected that Russia, both its companies and government bodies, had been transferring missile and nuclear weapons components technology to Iran through China and North Korea to avoid being detected. China had used North Korea since the early 1990s as a conduit for export of missile and nuclear weapon components.[61] By assisting Pakistan and North Korea nuclear and ballistic missile programs, China "has opened the Pandora's box of a regional nuclear arms race," Thomas Woodrow observed in an analysis for the Jamestown Foundation. "By spreading WMD technology throughout Asia, Beijing is only helping to create the regional instability it claims it wants to avoid."[62]

Is China's relaxed WMD proliferation policies indicative of a major mistake or of an element of its proclaimed "superior strategy" that includes the use of proxies? After all, North Korea's nuclear-missile capabilities check Japan, and Pakistan's nuclear-missile arms check India. The Korean Peninsula is a traditional Japanese invasion route into China, and outstanding territorial issues and traditional enmity between India and China could also rationalize its WMD proliferation.

The China-Iran alliance, an important cross-connection in the global strategic quadrangle, is based on a shared mistrust of the United States and its role as the last remaining superpower trying to retard both countries' march toward WMD and missile proliferation. In the eyes of Beijing and Tehran leaders, the world is being shaped into an "unbalanced post-Cold War world" by the United States. The two countries tend to see the U.S. as a hegemonist that weakens peace and stability in the world. Hence, as predicted by Paul Nitze in the early 1990s, they have joined forces whereby China provides Tehran arms and technological expertise and Iran delivers vital energy resources. This nukes-for-oil relationship is wrapped in more than commercial dealings. Iran's ruling elite favor deeper relations with China and the hardliners in the Islamic republic have gone so far as to advocate copying the "Chinese Model." As described by David R. Sands, the Chinese Model is seen by the Iranians as being a combination of "major economic growth and exports with continuing authoritarian controls."[63]

Energy and Iran

China and Iran signed a $70 to $100 billion energy agreement in 2006. China's oil giant Sinopec agreed to buy $250 million worth of liquefied natural gas over thirty years from Iran (or nearly 10,000 tons yearly). Sinopec also agreed to develop Yadovaran, one of Iran's largest on-shore oil fields. A second phase of the Iran-China deal involves construction of a pipeline in Iran to transfer oil some 386 kilometers to the Caspian Sea and from there the oil would be transported east via the China-Kazakhstan pipeline. Sinopec holds a 51 percent stake in the Yadovaran project, with India subscribed to 29 percent of the oil output, and the remainder split among Iranian companies.[64]

In January 2006, Iran replaced Saudi Arabia as China's primary source of imported oil. The Yadovaran oil field deal promises to increase Iran's position as China's first supplier of oil. The Chinese and Iranians also signed an agreement for China's purchase of 110 million tons of Iranian liquified natural gas over a twenty-five year period. The Yadovaran oil field agreement further binds the two countries' cooperative relationship. China was also the second leading supplier of conventional arms to Iran after Russia from 1995 to 2005. The transfer of Chinese scientific expertise and dual-use technologies were important in Tehran's own arms manufacturing capacity.

American University Professor John Calabrese characterized the China-Iran cross-connections in terms of potential UN sanctions and U.S. military action as providing Beijing a possible policy dilemma.

> . . . Sinopec [China's oil giant] is not willing to sink billions of dollars into a project that could be destroyed in a potential military confrontation between the United States and Iran. That is why, oddly enough, China should have a stronger interest in supporting nuclear diplomacy rather than in subverting it. At some point this might require that Beijing choose to side either with Washington or Tehran—a choice that until now Beijing has managed to avoid in the interest of cementing a less than perfect but nonetheless fruitful relationship with Iran.[65]

Ignoring the UN Security Council's ultimatum to cease uranium enrichment—producing the plutonium necessary to make nuclear bombs—Iran expanded its program and was assembling some 700 centrifuges of a planned 3,000 by May 2007. Iran's goal is to build some 54,000 centrifuges, or enough to produce several nuclear weapons annually. Tehran also was building a heavy water reactor, which could foster its nuclear weapons program. The United States positioned two aircraft carrier battle groups within reach on Iran's nuclear facilities in early 2007. After Tehran ignored a Security Council demand that it had sixty days to cease uranium enrichment and construction of heavy water reactors or face UN sanctions, the world body moved closer to crisis. Since both Russia and China held veto power over Security Council actions, the face-off between East and West was the most serious to occur in the post-Cold War era.[66]

According to investigative journalist Bill Gertz, new intelligence reports revealed in mid-2007 that "China is covertly supplying large quantities of small arms and weapons to insurgents in Iraq and the Taliban militia in Afghanistan, through Iran." This stunning revelation was hidden for years behind the "willful blindness" of the Clinton and Bush Administrations, said John Tkacik, a former State Department official. Among the items shipped to Iran for distribution to Iraqi anti-U.S. militias and the Taliban in Afghanistan were large-caliber sniper rifles, millions of rounds of ammunition, rocket-propelled grenades, and components for assembling roadside bombs. Other small arms were also supplied by China, which has full knowledge to whom they were being shipped.

"The Bush Administration has been trying to hide or downplay the intelligence reports to protect its pro-business policies toward China, and to continue to claim that China is helping the United States in the war on terrorism," Bill Gertz explained. "U.S. officials have openly criticized Iran for the arms transfers but so far there has been no mention that China is a main supplier."[67]

John J. Tkacik traced large-caliber sniper rifles shipped from China to Iran for arming Islamic fighters in Iraq where at least 170 U.S. and British soldiers had been killed by well-equipped and trained snipers. The source of the sniper rifles was China South Industries. Based on an Austrian-made armor piercing .50 caliber weapons whose patent had expired long ago, China South produced its own version. Iran's Revolutionary Guards placed large orders for Chinese sniper rifles, as well as other arms and ammunition. The Chinese shipped the rifles, whose serial numbers had been removed, directly to Iran by large cargo aircraft.[68]

Iran

The third hub of the Russian-led global strategic quadrangle is represented by Iran. The Tehran government brings several strengths to the table: oil resources, potential for nuclear weapons and the ballistic missiles necessary to deliver them accurately across great distances, transnational terrorism, and leadership of the Shia religious revival in the Middle East. These assets give the Tehran government greater influence in regional affairs and, through the Moscow-coordinated global quadrangle, worldwide influence as well.

The Tehran government's race to produce nuclear weapons is an important geopolitical development in the post-Cold War era. Threading the strategic needle in efforts to persuade Iran to cease its march toward nuclear weapons was engulfed in uncertainty, given the secrecy surrounding Iran's program and the accompanying disinformation designed to throw the international community off track. Suspending uranium enrichment would be sufficient to stop the program. A second step would involve the creation of a global system of enrichment under strict international controls. These measures would lead to a crucial third step of allowing the International Atomic Energy Agency verification of Iran's declared compliance with existing nonproliferation regimes. Yet, Iran's strategic objectives in South Asia, the Middle East, and the world at large account for much of the drive toward nuclear weapons. Henry Kissinger counseled that "Iran simply cannot be permitted to fulfill a dream of [a Shia] imperial rule in a region of such importance to the rest of the world."[69]

A second important objective is Iran's "centuries-old quest for respect," explained Yale history professor Abbas Amanat. Noting that this emotional drive to gain "respect," a key element of the country's race to field nuclear weapons and a cornerstone for independence rests deeply inside the Persian psyche. Iran's insistence on its sovereign right to field nuclear weapons is driven in large part by the country's last two centuries of confronting aggression, domestic interference by outsiders, and the West withholding technologies that retarded Iran's development. For half a century, from the 1870s to the 1920s, Russia and Britain deprived

Iran of the railroad that was essential for the country's economic progress. Both big powers opposed a trans-Iranian railroad, Professor Amanat explained, because they thought a it would imperil their respective imperial frontiers. Once a railroad was finally built in the 1920s and 1930s, the United States, Britain, and Russia seized control of it in World War Two, calling the railroad a "bridge of victory" over Nazi Germany. Western interference did not stop there. When the Iranian leader Mossadegh moved to nationalize oil in 1951–53, the West moved quickly to deny Tehran economic sovereignty. Mohammad Reza Shah was installed to protect American interests.

These historical events are widely known among Iranians and remain the subject of common discussion. As a result, when the West comes forward through the UN to deny Iran nuclear technology, one can better understand Iranian rage concerning the prospect of the West once again trying to deny Iran modern technology, in this case nuclear weapons. The problem of stopping Iran's uranium enrichment is as much, and maybe more, a "nationalism" issue as it is a rational evaluation of Iran's geopolitical and Shia revival interests. Moreover, this "Persian complex overhangs its imperial ambitions in Iraq, Syria, and Lebanon, as well as the greater Middle East."[70]

While the United States is going through Russia's front door with a ten-year $20 billion package to help dismantle the former Soviet Union's huge military arsenal, especially nuclear weapons and related facilities, the Russians are going out their back door to support Iran's nuclear weapons program. Russia released a ten-year plan in 2002 to complete the $800 million civilian reactor at Bushehr in addition to five other reactors. The deal could be worth another $6 billion to $10 billion to Russia's nuclear industry.[71] Despite the Kremlin's tap dance about refusing to complete the Bushehr nuclear complex for lack of payment, the unfinished plant stands ready for rapid completion.

President Vladimir Putin had insisted that its agreement to assist Iran's nuclear development was "watertight" in terms of International Atomic Energy Agency standards. The Bushehr nuclear facility would receive 100 tons of enriched uranium from Russia and Iran would return used fuel to Russia. There were two problems, Pavel K. Baev observed, with the "strictly commercial" exchange. First, Baev explained, "there are few doubts that . . . [Iran] aspires to develop a nuclear capability." Secondly, the Russian "pretense of being a part of the solution actually makes Russia the second part of the problem." While Russia tries to explain away its nuclear assistance to Iran as being economically motivated, more serious geopolitical calculations also are involved. "Ultimately," Baev concluded, "Iran armed with a few nuclear missiles would make Russia's dwindling strategic forces all the more impressive and could give a boost to the nuclear-political power play that some politicians in Moscow have been missing since the end of the Cold War."[72]

Iran is a perfect proxy for Russia and China for underwriting their joint anti-American, socialist world order agenda. It offers the benefit of helping to create a significant Islamic Shiite presence in the heretofore Sunni-dominated Middle East and places at risk Saudi Arabia whose oil production promises to remain America's Achilles Heel. At a meeting with President George Bush in New York, Putin said that Iran's President Mahmoud Ahmadinejad assured him that Tehran did not want nuclear weapons. "We, of course, are against Iran becoming a nuclear power," Putin said.[73]

Yet, the CIA had been consistently reporting for several years, despite Russian and Iranian denials, that the Kremlin's scientists were in fact helping the Iranians acquire the technology, expertise, and material to strengthen all aspect of Iran's drive to build nuclear weapons. In 2005, Russia accelerated its training program for more than a thousand Iranian technicians to operate the Bushehr nuclear reactor. The different levels of training would take from three months to a year.[74]

Others also assisted Iran's march toward nuclear power status. Abdul Qadeer Khan, the father of Pakistan's nuclear weapons program, met with officials of Iranian intelligence and nuclear establishment at minimum six times in Dubai. On at least one of those visits, he was accompanied by Lieutenant General Ehsan-ul-Haq, the director of Pakistan's Inter-Service Intelligence (ISI). After reports that the IAEA inspections discovered traces of enriched uranium in the second-hand centrifuges being used by Iran, the Pakistani's panicked. According to a very reliable source, A. Q. Khan pleaded with the Iranians to return the copies of the drawings of a uranium enrichment plant in Holland that he had given them. He implored the Iranians to remain silent about the Pakistani origin of the centrifuges.

Pakistani sources claim that A. Q. Khan had met with Saddam Hussein-era intelligence officials who sought his help in airlifting Iraqi nuclear material from Syria to Pakistan for safe custody to prevent them from falling into the hands of the IAEA. Khan is said to have agreed. According to Pakistani sources, in October 2002 Khan directed a Pakistani aircraft that had flown to Iran to deliver equipment to swing by a Syrian airport on its way back. It picked up the "WMD material" and brought it to Pakistan for safekeeping.

German businessmen were linked with a covert supplier network headed by A. Q. Khan that provided goods to Iran's nuclear program. Germany's Custom Crimes Office identified eight people, including Russian nationals, in 2005 involved in the illicit trade of such items as semi-conductor modules for nuclear arms and a loading crane for changing fuel elements. German investigators identified ten Iranian organizations involved in procurement of nuclear production equipment.[75] Britain's MI6 uncovered a network of Iranian fronts engaged in obtaining dual-use material for Tehran's nuclear program. One British company was found to have been trying to procure uranium from the Russian black market for shipment to Iran via Sudan. British authorities broke the plot in early 2006.[76]

A confidential report in June 2004 by the IAEA revealed Iran's deception concerning its clandestine nuclear weapons program. Iran had failed to disclose its possession of P-2 centrifuge "design drawings and to associated research, manufacturing, and mechanical testing activities." The report detailed Iran's initial plans for building 2,000 to 4,000 centrifuges, which are used to convert uranium gas into highly-enriched uranium for use in nuclear weapons. Iran admitted that it had imported some magnets relative to P-2 centrifuges from Asian suppliers, which remained unidentified. China had provided similar magnets to Pakistan for its centrifuge program, which was also designed around a P-2 centrifuge cascade.[77]

By late 2007, the nuclear picture in Iran changed dramatically after it installed thousands of uranium centrifuges at its Natanz nuclear facility. This initial phase of some 3,000 centrifuges was reached in September and expected to increase to some 54,000 over the years ahead. These machines, which spin uranium gas into sufficiently highly-enriched radioactive material, should be sufficient to produce several nuclear warheads yearly. A senior State Department official said that it would be a "major miscalculation" for Iran to carry out the reported plan.[78]

Iran has long collaborated with North Korea on its nuclear weapons program. Iran built two secret plants with North Korean assistance, one of them underground. North Korea is also said to have sent experts to Iran for joint development of nuclear warheads. The North Korean nuclear test in October 2006 had an impact on Tehran. Since Tehran is believed to have financed much of the North Korean's nuclear and missile programs, Western officials expected that North Korea would soon transfer the details of its nuclear experiment to Iran.[79]

In what was believed to be an Iranian warning against any military action to destroy its nuclear program, Tehran unveiled six Shihab intermediate-range ballistic missiles at a military parade in

September 2003. The Shihab-3 has a range of 1,380 kilometers and an extended version Shihab-4 can reach out to 3,500 to 4,000 kilometers. China, Belarus, North Korea, and Russia are assisting the Iranian fielded Shihab-4, which by some accounts could hit Paris and London as early as 2009. An extended range missile, the Shihab-3ER, with a 2,000 kilometers striking range, was already being fielded in 2007.[80]

The Iranian missiles have received continued attention and have entered serial production. In 2004, Iran began to integrate its missiles with a Chinese navigation system based on the Global Positioning System. This added capability promised to improve missile accuracy so significantly that they could reach Saudi Arabia, Israel, Europe, and, perhaps after a few years of further development, the United States. Iran and North Korea have cooperated on development of a "space launch vehicle" that could be designed for use as an ICBM capable of reaching the all of Europe and the U.S. before 2015. In a reassessment announced in late 2007, the U.S. intelligence community estimated that Iran could deploy a strategic missile capable of striking the United States within five years. The North Koreans test fired a Taepodong-2 missile in July 2006 that failed after forty seconds from launch. This two stage version has a range of 6,200 miles and a three-stage version under development would be able to reach out 9,300 miles.[81]

In December 2000, nine months following President Putin's inauguration, Russia and Iran announced a "new chapter" in military cooperation in all fields. A month prior to the announcements, Moscow said it was removing a secret 1995 deal agreed to by President Boris Yeltsin that would have blocked conventional military sales to Iran. Russia's move irked the White House, but the Putin government promised to sell only defensive weapons and to avoid violating international agreements. The Iranians were ready immediately to order S-300 anti-aircraft missiles, MI-17 combat helicopters, and SU-25 jet fighters. By summer 2007, the Iranians were considering the purchase of at least fifty SU-30 multi-role fighters comparable to the U.S. F-15E. India has been a major buyer of the SU-30 and would co-produce the Russian aircraft.[82]

During a three-day visit to Iran, Russian Defense Minister Igor Sergeyev met with President Mohammad Khatami, Foreign Minister Kamal Kharazi, and top commanders from the armed forces and the Revolutionary Guards. President Khatami made a return state visit in Russia for further discussions. Some Russians held reservations about the "dangerous deal" made with Iran, especially in provision of dual-use nuclear technology. Once the Russia-Iran strategic partnership was underway, Tehran played an increasingly vital role in the global strategic quadrangle. By 2005, Iran had purchased as many as twenty-nine TOR-M1 short-range mobile anti-aircraft missiles and ordered additional batteries in a contract estimated to be $1.4 billion. Some batteries had already been deployed to defend Iran's nuclear facilities. The U.S. imposed sanctions on the Russian export firm Rosboronexport in 2006 for the TOR-M1 sales to Iran.[83]

President Putin's view was expressed in 2001 at the beginning of the Russia-Iran arms sales relationship: "Economically, Russia is interested in cooperation," Putin explained. "And politically, Iran should be a self-sufficient, independent state that is ready to protect its national interests."[84] In 2007, Russia upped the ante by selling Iran 250 advanced Su-30 fighter bombers. These aircraft gave Iran an unprecedented power projection capability, including a nuclear delivery vehicle, other than missiles. The arms sale also included advanced S-300 air defense missiles that upgraded Iran's aging defenses. The Chinese version of the Russian aircraft, the J-11, would include new precision guided missiles and munitions. The Il-78 refueling tanker aircraft could also be on the list of purchases, which would buttress a long-range aerial assault capability.[85]

The U.S. invasion in Iraq triggered Russian actions to strengthen Moscow's ties with China, Iran, and Syria. In addition to a significant military relationship and arms sales, Russia's effort to supply Tehran with dual-use nuclear technology and conventional weapons has strengthened the Kremlin's hand in the Middle East.[86] The Moscow-Beijing-Tehran axis is designed to counter U.S. foreign policies in the Middle East and Asia. The creation of a multi-polar new world order stands out as a mutual interest of these three countries, each occupying its own corner of the global strategic quadrangle. Such a multipolar international system is an essential step toward establishing one-world socialist governance sometime after 2050.

Since Iran was tagged by President Bush in 2002 as being part of the "axis of evil," Tehran feared it might be on a list for U.S. military intervention. Supreme Leader Ali Khamenei, for instance, rejected U.S. claims that it acted against Iraq because of weapons of mass destruction, calling them "big lies." The U.S. objectives, Khameini argued, included the intention of placing increased pressure on Iran and Syria and changing the "political map of the Middle East." President Putin said that Russia sees no evidence of Iran developing a clandestine nuclear weapons program and urged the United States not to attack Iran. Meanwhile, U.S. targeteers were developing attack plans in event President Bush gave the "go" order. To minimize future risks of a U.S. strike, Iran began constructing a new bomb-proof underground nuclear site inside a mountain.[87]

Iranian leaders expressed several major concerns about the U.S. presence in Iraq. Iranians fear the loss of control over Shiite spiritual centers in Iraq's holy cities of Karbala and Najaf—"holier than even Mecca for the Shi'ites." Another concern is that the real American goal of U.S. occupation of Iraq was focused on the oil fields in the Middle East and control of OPEC. Former Iranian President Ali Akbar Hashemi Rafsanjani, speaking as the chief of Iran's Expediency Council, commented on the American "play" in Iraq.

Speaking to thousands of worshipers during Friday sermons, Rafsanjani said that "the U.S. presence in the Middle East is worse than Saddam's weapons of mass destruction," adding that the American presence in the Persian Gulf region revealed its "sinister" intentions.

Iran also postured to deter the U.S. from attacking its nuclear facilities. Insofar as the strategic linkage and proximity of Iran and Iraq is concerned, Supreme Leader Ali Khameini warned the U.S. that it would get bogged down, if it launched a military strike against Iran and if it stayed in Iraq. Khameni declared that Iran would not permit

> American highway robbers and savages in civilized clothing to rule our country again . . . they have disclosed a plan to install an American as the ruler for Iraq and to channel all Iraqi resources into the pockets of American and Zionist companies. Such a plan, of course, will not materialize. Even if the U.S. might get control of Iraq in the short term, the Iraqi nation will ultimately drive the Americans out of the country.[88]

The Supreme Leader's remarks were about as close to a declaration of war that one can make without saying so. Rumors abounded in 2007 that Ali Khameini was seeking an alliance with Russia to help block U.S. hegemony in the region. Meanwhile, the United States signaled its allies in the Gulf Cooperation Council that a strike against Iran was possible in the short term.[89]

The suspected Iran relationship with al-Qaeda was clearly established in June 2004 when former CIA analyst Douglas MacEachin, a member of the 9/11 Commission staff, linked Iran to two of the hijackers. Nawaf al-Hazmi and Khalid al-Mihdhar, who were aboard the airliner that struck the Pentagon, had stayed at the Iranian ambassador's residence in Kuala Lumpur, Malaysia, before entering the United States in 2001. MacEachin also disclosed strong but indirect evidence that al-Qaeda was also involved in the 1996 bombing the American Khobar Towers residence in Saudi Arabia that killed nineteen Americans and wounded hundreds more.[90]

Iranian documents captured in December 2006 during the arrest of suspected Iranian commandoes in Baghdad revealed that Iran had helped train and equip al-Qaeda members in Iraq as well as both Shia and Sunni insurgents. The documents included the names and cell phone numbers of the Sunni liaisons with the Iran's Islamic Revolutionary Guard Corps.[91] In the following month, U.S. forces subdued five Iranian members of the special warfare al Quds brigade. A U.S. military statement explained that the al Quds was an Iranian "organization known for providing funds, weapons, improvised explosive devices technology and training to extremist groups attempting to destabilize the Government of Iraq and attack coalition forces." Most of the sophisticated roadside bombs, including those with shaped-charges and explosive-formed projectiles, were made in Iran.[92] A significant number of U.S. casualties were inflicted by the weapons, while the top U.S. officials turned a blind eye to the perpetrators and let the American blood-letting go on. At the same time, Iranian killers of American troops were captured and then released from late 2005 and throughout 2006 "to avoid escalating tensions with Iran and yet intimidate its emissaries." In 2007 President Bush at last authorized U.S. "troops to kill Iranian operatives in Iraq" as a part of the change in strategy.[93]

Syria's President Assad found his support slowly eroding among political and military elites. Over the period from 2003 through 2007, Assad imported about 100,000 Iranian mercenaries to keep him in power. He settled the mercenaries around strategic centers, particularly in the urban areas of Aleppo, Damascus, Homs, and Latakia. During the same period, the Iranians have built Shiite mosques throughout Syria and paid Alawites and Christians to convert to Islam.

Many of the Iranian mercenaries have jobs in the security services, and Assad's presidential protective force is made up of Iran's Islamic Guards and members of the Iran-sponsored Hezbollah. Meanwhile, Assad has lost the backing of key family members, including his uncle, Rifat, who has been stirring unrest among the Syrian military.[94]

Iran's relationship with Russia and China in the context of the Kremlin-led global strategic quadrangle is well established. Iran has also been busy cultivating political support for its anti-U.S. policies among Latin American countries, the fourth hub of the quadrangle. On a tour of shanty-towns in one of Latin America's poorest countries, Nicaragua, Iran's leader Mahmoud Ahmadinejad hailed the growing number of Leftist leaders in Latin America. "We have to give each other a hand," Mr. Ahmadinejad told reporters. "We have common interests, common enemies and common goals."[95] For the followers of Antonio Gramsci in Latin America, Ahmadinejad's tour of the region was a very important event, for it demonstrated solidarity of the anti-U.S. global strategic quadrangle.

Opposition to the United States has brought Iran and Venezuela closer together. Their alliance embraces economic, political, and military interests, and possibly a nuclear alliance that could strengthen Russia's hand in dealing through proxies and sub-proxies in Latin America. Representing 20 percent of the Organization for Petroleum Exporting countries or OPEC, Iran and Venezuela have formed a strategic alliance inside the cartel in favor of higher crude oil prices. Saudi Arabia, on the other hand, generally favors more moderate prices through greater output. Venezuela insists on higher prices for greater resources to be used in neutralizing traditional U.S. political influence in Latin America.

Iran promised to help Venezuela develop nuclear technology, an initiative that Caracas insists is for peaceful purposes. In 2005, Venezuela asked Tehran to sell it a medium-sized nuclear reactor. The sale has not yet taken place, while the Iran-Venezuela relationship turned to areas of more realistic cooperation, such as Iranian specialists advising the Caracas government about development of a plant for explosives and propellants. Perhaps Iran will help Venezuela refurbish its U.S.-made F-5 fighter jets. Since the U.S. banned arms sales to the Chavez government in 2006, the spare parts pipeline from the United States for Venezuela's F-5 jets has been shut down.

Joint financial projects are expanding Iran-Venezuela cooperation from $17 billion to $20 billion. In October 2006, a joint investment project brought Tehran and Caracas together to build an oil refinery in Syria that would be capable of processing 150,000 barrels per day.[96]

Latin America

Lenin died in 1924 convinced that the developing or "third world" would one day turn against capitalism and imperialism, triggering the decisive battle of the proletarian revolution. A succession of Soviet leaders from Joseph Stalin to Yuri Andropov supported KGB operations in this global Marxist-Leninist struggle. Andropov said in 1967 that "a heightening of the class struggle" was being decided "within the framework of the whole world system, in a global struggle between two world systems."[97] The KGB penetration of Latin America in the 1970s through the wars in the region during the 1980s pivoted off Cuba, the single Marxist-Leninist regime in the Western Hemisphere and sole survivor following the disintegration of the Soviet Union in 1991.

In Latin America, the 1990s was a decade of doctrinal shifting from Marxism-Leninism to the blueprint designed by Antonio Gramsci. The first pragmatic action of the new formula was shown in Mexico's Zapatistas direct action against "neoliberalism," a specially defined word to capture the Gramscian opposition to the profit-making culture of free trade. The Zapatista leader, Subcommandante Marcos, was a Cuban trained Marxist and active among Gramsci activists in the United States. This first stone tossed into the pond of political change triggered an anti-free trade slide to the Gramscian Left across Latin America. In the early 2000s, behind the voice and activities of Venezuela's President Hugo Chavez, one country after another slipped into a fledgling anti-U.S., anti-free trade bloc. By 2008, seven countries had elected left-wing governments, three others were on the brink of slipping to the Left, and another was under pressure by a sizable number of Marxist guerrillas.

By late 2007, it had become evident that the global strategic quadrangle had provided a framework for Iran to extend a presence into South and Central America. Such a presence would be designed to counter any U.S. military action against Iran by sending waves of terrorists into the United States. Iran's National Council of Resistance details plans to infiltrate several countries south of the U.S. border within a stone-throw's distance of Arizona, New Mexico, and Texas. According to the plans, these elite military units would be drawn from Iran's Revolutionary Guard Corps. The Revolutionary Guard would also infiltrate Mexico's arms and drug trafficking and immigrant smuggling networks.

Tehran's plans also call for establishing a terrorist presence in Bolivia, Colombia, Nicaragua, Uruguay, and Venezuela. Unsurprisingly, all five countries have established revolutionary Marxist groups or what might be called a "Gramscian Marxist" presence. The Iranian Revolutionary Guards plan on building a very large strategic reserve of resources in the region. Reportedly, Iranian President Ahmandinjad and Venezuelan President Chavez have already discussed this initiative and are moving forward.[98]

5

LATIN AMERICA'S SLIDE TO THE LEFT

LATIN AMERICA'S SLIDE leftward since the implosion of the Soviet Union sparked the attention of Russia, China, and Iran. Through a series of political and economic arrangements, Latin America was drawn into the Kremlin-led global strategic quadrangle in opposition to the capitalist West, the United States in particular. Russia became a major arms supplier in the region. China established a presence in Panama and is a major purchaser of the region's commodities. Additionally, Iran has expressed solidarity with the leftist regimes and may one day become a supplier and source of expertise for Brazil's once-dormant nuclear power and missile capabilities and also a partner with Venezuela on various trade and military projects.

In a very brief period, the Gramsci formula was used to penetrate Latin American politics and with a success far beyond the Soviet KGB's modest gains during the Cold War.[1] But the shift in Latin America's orientation did not just happen—two people were primarily responsible: Cuba's Fidel Castro and Brazil's Luis Inacio "Lula" da Silva.

Forum of Sao Paulo

In July 1990, "Lula" da Silva, then leader of Brazil's Marxist Workers Party, with the encouragement of Fidel Castro and the Cuban Communist Party, created the Sao Paulo Forum. From the beginning, the Forum was about building socialism and restructuring U.S. influence in Latin America. Cuba's Fidel Castro, following the implosion of the Soviet Union and the death of Marxism-Leninism, joined Lula in his Marxist renewal and re-emergence program.

The Forum of Sao Paulo had more than one hundred members of the Latin American left in the mid-1990s and held regular meetings. The first five sessions of the Forum were hosted by Brazil's Workers Party, the Revolutionary Democratic Party of Mexico, the Sandinista Front in Nicaragua, the Cuban Communist Party, and Uruguay's left-wing Broad Front. The Leftist participants at the Forum's meetings sought to find viable alternatives to the "neo-liberal ideology"—a euphemism for free trade—that was said by the Left to have weakened many government social services and created massive unemployment throughout Latin America.

Delegates from Maoist, Trotskyist, Marxist-Leninist, Marxist, and Social Democrat parties, as well as several terrorist and guerrilla organizations, attended the 1995 meeting of the Sao Paulo Forum in Montevideo. The Forum organizers proposed a model "with real economic, social and participatory democracy which . . . [included] everybody in national and regional production and where the state . . . [had] a role in guaranteeing social welfare, just distribution and economic regulation."[2] This was not a prescribed strategy for Latin America, but a batch of Leftist alternatives for improving social development, achieving social justice, stability and peace.[3]

The Forum's ninth meeting was held in Managua, Nicaragua, in February 2000 where the debate over the "alternative to neoliberalism" continued. During this session, the Forum members recognized that "through 'democracy,' the voters and their representatives will be able to ward off the pressures of the great powers, neutralize the damaging actions of the transnational corporations, counteract the power of traditional ruling elites and advance towards sustainable economic and social development, in justice and equality."[4]

The tenth meeting of the Sao Paulo Forum was held in Havana in December 2001. Participants numbered 518 delegates from eighty-one countries in Latin America and the Caribbean, Europe, Asia, Africa, the Middle East, and Australia. Seventy-four member parties and political movements were represented, plus 127 invited parties and organizations. Among the attendees were several active terrorist organizations, including the FARC and ELN from Colombia, Tupac Amaru from Peru, MIR of Chile, the Basque ETA from Spain, and others.

The main axes of the alternatives discussed emphasized the priority of social objectives in the "recovery of development and sovereignty; impulses to regional integration as a form of insertion into the world economy; the construction of authentic participatory democracies, by taking into account the increasing role of women and young people; the ongoing profound struggle of the indigenous peoples; and the fight against every form of exploitation, economic oppression and alienation of the rights of citizens." The Final Declaration closed with: "Our struggle is for political, economic and social transformation. It is a battle of ideas for a better world."[5] Absent was the Marxist-Leninist rhetoric of the past about "class struggle," violent clashes with capitalism, and "world revolution." The twenty-first century battle for ideas was about "transformation" and "participatory democracy" (Leftist-speak for engaging the self-disenfranchised poor) and outing the ruling elite through the ballot box. This is Antonio Gramsci's formula for "passive revolution." The ideological die had been cast for Latin

America's transformation into socialist states, while working in concert with each other against economic globalization through an idealized regional entity, the South America Community of Nations.

When Luis Inacio "Lula" da Silva ran for Brazil's presidency with the strong backing of the Marxist Workers Party (PT)—*Partido de los Trabajadores*—and much of the peasantry, he played down his role as a radical worker's leader and supporter of land reform. Immediately upon being elected to the presidency in 2003, Lula began casting new images on the wall of Plato's cave presenting his orthodox economic politics to northern financial circles. "Lula is a free trader," gushed bankers in North America. Brazil's huge foreign debt would be serviced but nationalization of major industries and land reform were not on Lula's expressed agenda. Lula's foreign policy advisor, a hard-line Marxist, Marco Aurilio Garcia, spilled the beans when he commented on Lula's effort to fool the world about the true nature of Brazil's Marxist regime: "We have to first give the impression that we are democratic, initially, we have to accept certain things. But that won't last."[6] This is a perfect example of Antonio Gramsci's formula for gaining power through the ballot box, consolidating control while implanting Marxism in the "inner man," and finally moving to a socialist "Worker's Paradise."

Venezuelan President Hugo Chavez joined Fidel Castro and Lula da Silva in their joint leadership of the Sao Paulo Forum by virtue of his huge oil wealth and a mouth to match in excoriating the United States. When Castro's secret intelligence services helped engineer Chavez's return to power after a short-lived coup in 2002, Chavez returned the favor by giving Cuba billions of dollars in free and heavily subsidized oil. Moreover, Castro became a revolutionary mentor to the brash chieftain from Caracas. Chavez appeared to have seized the inside track on becoming Latin America's next Fidel. In the absence of Castro, it would fall to Lula to keep Chavez on the Gramscian track and save him from his penchant to overplay his cards.

These "Big Three" each brought something special to the revolutionary table in Latin America. Fidel Castro contributed decades of experience in neutralizing the hostility of a succession of U.S. presidents. Moreover, Castro's image as a guiding-light of Marxism looms bright across Latin America. In addition, thanks to Soviet assistance during the Cold War, Castro had trained more than 10,000 intelligence agents whose networks extend across the world and even into the most secret warrens of the U.S. government.

Lula da Silva brought long experience in leading a Marxist workers union in Brazil, and for years he maintained under-cover close relations with communists and revolutionaries throughout Latin America. Brazil's previous nuclear and ballistic missile technology programs could provide a credible starting point for development of weapons of mass destruction, especially if Hugo Chavez funded such an effort.[7] This is more than a theoretical "what if" possibility. In a letter to President George W. Bush from thirteen members of Congress in October 2002, the Representatives expressed their concern with Lula da Silva's remarks concerning adherence to the Treaty on Non-Proliferation of Nuclear Weapons. Lula is quoted in the letter as having said that compliance with the NPT "would make sense only if all countries that already have [clear] weapons all gave them up." He continued, "if someone asks me to disarm and keep a slingshot and he comes at me with a cannon, what good does that do?" And, concluding, "all of us developing countries are left holding a slingshot while they have atomic bombs."[8]

Hugo Chavez walked a carefully scripted line in a slow-rolling "passive revolution" by first winning election through the democratic process, consolidating his presidency with active Cuban support, de-fanging the military and police, neutralizing opposition forces, assuring his electoral base through land redistribution, obtaining expanded political powers for a national assembly he controlled, silencing the independent news media, rewriting selected portions of the nation's constitution beginning the nationalization of strategic economic entities, and setting new profit-sharing rules for foreign corporations. He built, with the aid and counsel of Fidel Castro and Lula da Silva, a Latin American version of the Gramsci blueprint of "passive revolution" for export to neighboring countries.

The Gramsci blueprint used by Fidel Castro, Lula da Silva, and Hugo Chavez in development of the Venezuelan socialist model exerts a continued influence on at least five other Latin American countries impelling their respective slide to the Left. Some appear to be following the Gramsci-Chavez populism script for the "Bolivarian Revolution," while others seem to pick and choose in their choice of political salsa for developing their new socialist orientation.

Social inequality is Latin America's central problem, a reality that has not been lost on Fidel Castro, Lula da Silva, or Hugo Chavez. Like the "Three Musketeers," this socialist trio wields the sword of radical populism, or Gramsci Marxism, throughout Latin America. They provide the frustrated masses charismatic leadership, messianic impulses (revolutionary socialism), and the increasing ability, thanks to Venezuela's prodigious oil resources and rising prices, to provide grants to the poor. Their Gramscian program is based on reducing social inequalities through income supplements and government promises of more to come as a tool for garnering votes. In a word, democracy is being used to secure power for socialist governance under the guidance of charismatic leaders, who, in time, will destroy their own liberal democracies. Constitutional reform in Venezuela, for instance, is not about simply re-writing principles to govern society. Rather, the new constitution embodied Hugo Chavez's philosophy for revolutionary change and a new strategic vision of the role of the state in people's lives, anti-imperialism (the United States), and a shift in Latin America's geopolitical balance of power.[9]

Cuba

Fidel Castro laid out a severe indictment against capitalism in an address at the Group of 77 meeting in September 1999.[10] Castro's themes would be repeated over and over by Western progressives-socialists-marxists in the subsequent anti-globalization protests in North America and Europe.

> . . . the world is still very far from materialising the potential of globalisation. It develops today under the aegis of neo-liberal policies that impose unregulated markets and unbridled privatisation. Far from promoting the expansion of development throughout an increasingly interdependent world badly in need of sharing the progresses achieved, neo-liberal globalisation has aggravated existing inequalities and raised to inordinate heights social inequities and the most disturbing contrasts between extreme wealth and extreme poverty.[11]

Less than three months following the 1999 G-77 session, more than 50,000 anti-globalization protesters poured into the streets of Seattle and shut down meetings of the World Trade Organization meetings. Peter Boyle of the Australian Socialist Party put it succinctly: "This movement is fundamentally against capitalism. . . . Ideologically, it is a ragtag army whose leading detachments include communists, anarchists, feminists, environmentalists, anti-racists, neo-hippies and alternate lifestylists." Boyle added that "these currents are united in opposition to corporate tyranny."[12]

Four months after the "Battle for Seattle," Castro honed the "corporate tyranny" and other key anti-globalization themes in an address at the opening session of the South Summit. "Globalization has been held tight by the patterns of neoliberalism; thus it is not development that goes global but poverty; it is not respect for the national sovereignty of our states but the violation of that respect;

it is not solidarity amongst our peoples but 'suave-qui petit' in the unequal competition prevailing in the marketplace," Castro told his audience. "At this Summit of the Third World countries we would have to say: 'We either unite and establish close cooperation, or we die!' "[13]

With the anti-globalization movement underway and socialism strengthened at home, Castro celebrated his seventy-fifth birthday with his Marxist protege Hugo Chavez in August 2001. A key aspect of Chavez's "social revolution" in Venezuela was close collaboration with his mentor, Fidel Castro. One must strongly suspect that Chavez learned the ABCs of the Gramcian blueprint from Castro as well as at the meetings of the Forum of Sao Paulo during the 1990s.[14]

More than 3,000 Cuban trainers and 450 medical personnel were sent to Venezuela to assist Chavez in consolidating his control and garnering support among the country's most needy. The Cuba-Venezuela links were also strengthened at the mid-level through the exchange of governors and civil society politicians, youth delegates, and trade unionists. The latter are especially important in the Gramsci formula for consolidating support among the people. Castro was helping Chavez build the foundation necessary for a transition to a totalitarian communist state, albeit one based on Antonio Gramsci's cultural Marxism.[15]

In 2001 the Venezuela-Cuban relationship was just the beginning. By the end of 2005, Cuba had dispatched 30,000 doctors, dentists, teachers, and sports trainers to Venezuela to work mainly in the pro-Chavez slums of Caracas. Such measures are essential in the Gramsci blueprint to consolidate support among the people in preparation for the neutering the coercive authority of the police and military.[16]

Also in 2005, Venezuelan President Hugo Chavez invited hundreds of Cuban intelligence agents to Caracas where they took up positions in key security positions throughout the government. Cubans have been noted in the main civilian intelligence and preventive investigations agency, military intelligence, the central bank, interior ministry, and immigration department. Cubans also moved into key administrative positions in all states of Venezuela, and Cubans dominated Chavez's security entourage. Meanwhile, Venezuela was providing money for Gramscian opposition voices in several Latin American countries with the aim of enabling Marxist regimes to emerge across the continent.[17]

Cuba trained personnel and Venezuelan oil resources coalesced in pushing Latin American countries to the Left. The key ingredient in making this possible was the implementation of Gramsci's cultural Marxism, a blueprint that is producing significant results against tepid opposition.

During a visit of a Chinese military delegation in July 2001, Raul Castro took the opportunity to reiterate Cuba's full support to Beijing's efforts to achieve national unity by incorporating Taiwan. Members of the Chinese delegation said that their visit was a part of continuing efforts to strengthen "the ties of friendship and cooperation between the two peoples and their armed forces."[18] In April 2005, China increased its military sales to Cuba, although Castro said it did not include weapons. Nevertheless, U.S. intelligence agencies had detected shipments of arms to Cuba in 2000, including dual-use, civilian-military explosives.[19]

Fidel Castro visited Iran, the third hub in the strategic quadrangle, in May 2001. He praised Tehran for its struggle against imperialism. "My visit to Iran for me and my nation is a great privilege," Castro said on Iran's state-run television. "I truly believe the relations of the two countries will be stronger after this trip."[20] At Tehran University, Castro told his audience that "Iran and Cuba, in cooperation with each other, can bring America to its knees. The U.S. regime is very weak, and we are witnessing this weakness from close up."[21] By 2003, Tehran and Havana joined forces, with Cuba jamming U.S. satellite broadcasts to Iran. The Telestar-12 commercial communications satellite orbits at fifteen degrees west, 22,000 miles above the Atlantic. The satellite was positioned too far from Iran to jam it effectively, but it was within range of Cuba. With Havana's help, TV-news broadcasts by the Voice of America in the Persian language never reached their intended audience.[22]

Brazil

Luis Inacio "Lula" da Silva was swept into the presidency on January 1, 2003, with 62 percent of the vote. A Marxist, Lula tapped into the public frustrations over the government's inability to deliver prosperity after a decade of free market reforms and a public debt mounting to a whopping $260 billion. Throughout his campaign Lula portrayed the United States as the main enemy and he remained steadfast in his opposition to the proposed Free Trade Area of the Americas agreement. He also promised to use Brazil's high-tech industry to boost the economy by producing and selling nuclear weapons.[23]

Lula da Silva created and convened annual meetings of the Forum of Sao Paulo in 1990. These early conferences were attended by all of the communist and radical Left parties in Latin America, as well as the region's terrorist organizations, Irish Republican Army, Spain's ETA terrorists, Popular Front for the Liberation of Palestine General Command, and representatives of state sponsors of terrorism (Iraq, Libya, Cuba, and others). The Sao Paulo Forum meetings served as the successor to Fidel Castro's Tricontinental Congress established in 1966 to help terrorist groups better coordinate their attacks against the United States and its allies. From this modest beginning the Forum grew into a major coordinator for an increasing number of international members. The Forum also served as a major source of disinformation against the West. Working papers from the Forum's December 2002 meeting, for example, claimed that "NATO troops perpetrated genocide in Kosovo, U.S. and British forces massacred the population in Afghanistan . . . and Israel continues to carry out a systematic policy of murdering Palestinians."[24]

From the first day of his presidency, Lula made it clear that he would operate in partnership with his ideological allies, Fidel Castro in Cuba and President Hugo Chavez in Venezuela. On his first day in office, Lula had breakfast with Chavez and dinner with Castro.[25] Given Lula's close relationship with Castro in bringing radical Leftists and terrorists together at the Forum of Sao Paulo's meetings and his hard-nosed leadership of Brazil's Leftist Worker's Party, it is not a surprise that he embraced Castro and his protege, Hugo Chavez. Moreover, given Lula's position on North America's alleged exploitation of Latin America, he certainly was a partner in Castro's guidance of the anti-globalization campaign against neoliberalism and the United States in particular. The Forum of Sao Paulo, including all of its communist and radical Left members, appears to have been the "board of directors" for the anti-globalization campaign against the International Monetary Fund, World Bank, World Trade Organization, and other international financial institutions and free trade fora.

In spite of his rhetoric and anti-U.S. activities in the shadows, Lula has had a long running campaign trying to convince officials in the lending agencies and the U.S. foreign policy community that he is a politician they can deal with. The Washington D.C.-based Institute for Policy Studies, a radical Left think tank with many connections among the so-called "progressives" in the U.S. government and the Congress, helped Lula make his case.[26]

President Lula da Silva's support in the Worker's Party, according to the Maldon Institute, was drawn from "the radical Roman Catholic Church liberation theology adherents . . . and the Church's Labor Pastorate, leftist and Castroite students and intellectuals . . . Trotskyist communist factions and radical peasant organizations including the militant *Movimento dos Sem Terra* (MST) [Movement of Landless Rural Workers]. "[27] The MST is a founder of the People's Global Action (PGA) anti-globalization direct action network.

Lula's pragmatism in implementing Gramsci's revisionist Marxist model created a cross-current of perceptions in the industrialized North. While he gagged on the necessity of free trade to service and reduce Brazil's huge foreign debt, he also met regularly through the Sao Paulo Forum with revolutionary Leftists such as the Cuban Communist Party, Brazil's Marxist Worker's Party, Nicaraguan Sandinistas, El Salvador's communist FMLN, terrorists of the Irish Republican Army, Basque ETA, Colombia's FARC, and some of the most blood-drenched terrorists in the Middle East.[28] In a word, President Lula da Silva is a Marxist with the goal of eliminating U.S. power and influence in Latin America, but only when the time is right. He remained a disgruntled free trader out of necessity, even when he hugged President George W. Bush during his visit to Brazil in March 2007. The open question is what might be his policy course when he deems the "time to be right."

Lula's strategy is to deal with the United States while he assists South American countries in their slide to the left and to promote a new unity through the South American Community of Nations, an envisioned continent-wide community similar to the European Union. Twelve countries have signed an agreement to create the new trading bloc representing 361 million people with a gross domestic product of $973 billion, exporting $181 billion of goods and services. The Community of Nations provides a means of maintaining good relations with the U.S., while building a continental unity of socialist states and exploring economic and political connections with emerging powers, such as China and Iran.[29]

When President Lula da Silva was elected to the presidency, he found his troubled country with longstanding problems that defied quick fixes. Organized crime had plundered the nation for years, and assassins had been hired by merchants to eliminate the very poor and street people. An analysis conducted by the MST revealed in 2004 that the government under Lula had settled less than 30,000 rural families as compared to 115,000 families called for by the National Agrarian Reform Plan. As a consequence, the MST promised landless peasant invasions of land and buildings as well as public demonstrations to call attention to the need for agrarian reform.[30]

President Lula da Silva's *Bolsa Familia* cash assistance program, amounting to more than $11 million, paid $40 per month to poor families so long as their children attended school regularly and had regular health check-ups and vaccinations. Many believed the *Bolsa Familia* program to be one of the most successful social programs in Brazil, and it was the key to Lula's landslide reelection in October 2006 (60 percent).[31]

But right from the beginning of his first term, Lula faced a dilemma. While his foremost desire was to transform Brazil into a "fair trade" socialist state, the country's large government debt, underwritten mostly by U.S. banks and contracts, led him to dance with the capitalist devil enroute to reaching his Marxist revolutionary goals. To calm his nervous creditors in the North, Lula promised to service the debt and to fulfill existing free trade contracts. While acknowledging that the Brazilian people voted for "another economic model" (socialism), Lula held his nose and toed-the-line in accommodating free trade talks with President George W. Bush and U.S. trade officials in March 2007.[32]

Pledging to use his second term in office, which began on January 1, 2007, to craft policies that would produce five percent growth annually, President Lula da Silva faced an enormous economic task. Brazil was being torn down by a huge debt with a benchmark interest rate of 13.25 percent (down from a high of 19.75 percent). These are the highest interest rates in the world and promise to keep Brazil in a condition of perennial economic depression.[33]

President Lula da Silva successfully put off the day for the inevitable confrontation with the United States. First, at the outset of his first term, Lula had to find a way to smooth ruffled feathers among his followers for taking a "tactical" free trade path. The opportunity to achieve this came in January 2003, when Lula used the podium at the World Economic Forum at Davos, Switzerland, to make a case for helping the world's poor. The Davos meeting was attended by hundreds of the world's top financial shakers and movers and important political leaders from around the globe. Lula called for Northern governments and big investors to create a global fund to fight poverty and hunger around worldwide. Lula, the son of a poor farmer, said that "countries are spending billions and billions of dollars in an arms race and spending money on things that are not priorities." At the same time, he said, "we look at the Third World countries and millions and millions of women and children die because they don't manage to eat the calories they need."[34]

Lula is not without potential leverage in dealing with the North and its creditors. He has openly declared that Brazil should re-start its nuclear weapons and ballistic missile programs. President da Silva is adamant that its nuclear facility at Resende, not far from Rio de Janeiro, will be used to produce low-enriched uranium for use in power plants, not highly enriched material for use in nuclear weapons. In addition, Brazil has one of the largest uranium deposits in the world. If it masters the complete fuel cycle, it could sell low-enriched uranium to others, netting Brazil billions of dollars annually. One problem with this scenario is that Brazil has a long record of restricting the UN's International Atomic Energy Agency (IAEA) inspections. During past IAEA inspections, critical machinery was covered to prevent disclosure of Brazil's "technological breakthroughs." The IAEA insists that full disclosure of all equipment is necessary to ensure uranium is not being enriched to a level where they could be used in the development of nuclear weapons. In addition, the IAEA wants to know the sources of Brazil's equipment.[35] According to reports in

1975, Brazil transferred technology from its power plants to a nuclear weapons program.[36]

Brazil is China's largest trading partner in Latin America, while China is Brazil's third largest trading partner after the United States and Argentina. In a visit to China in early 2004, President Lula da Silva told his hosts that "Brazil and China share the vision of an international order that is more just and equitable, based on multipolarity and on respect for international law." China's leader Hu Jintao replied that he believed Lula's visit would "push forward the strategic partnership between China and Brazil." Several agreements were signed during the visit to promote greater cooperation between the two countries.[37]

During a two-week tour of Argentina, Chile, Cuba, and Brazil, Chinese President Hu Jintao told the Brazilian National Assembly that China was determined to force "unprecedented" ties with Latin American and Caribbean countries. Brazil proclaimed China as a "strategic partner."[38]

About ten million Arabs live in Brazil, the largest Arab population outside the Middle East. Some 25,000 of the country's Muslim population live in the southwestern city of Foz de Iguacu, which is Brazil's portion of the Triple Border Area where its borders converge with those of Paraguay and Argentina. It is an area widely known for arms and drug smuggling, document and currency fraud, money laundering, and any number of other illegal activities. Estimates report $10–$12 billion pass through the tri-border area annually. Some of the money is diverted to Islamic militants in the Middle East. Brazil denies the presence of Islamic jihadists in the triple border area.[39]

In September 2007, President Lula da Silva launched a one-year, cabinet-level effort to develop a new security and national defense strategy. The ostensible goal is to make Brazil a military power in the twenty-first century. "We can't be subordinate, Lula said. "We have to be bold."[40]

Venezuela

President Hugo Chavez controls the world's fifth largest oil-producing country, which places an enormous amount of money at his disposal. A Marxist protege of Fidel Castro, he proved to be an effusive firebrand that attracted a bevy of best friends in Russia, China, and Iran. President Chavez has shaped his government to serve as a model for the practical application of the Gramsci formula in Latin America and the Caribbean, and has given Colombia's narco-trafficking Marxist guerrillas, the FARC, privileged sanctuary in Venezuela. Many poor Latinos respect him highly for the programs he put into place to help those at the bottom of the economic ladder. Journalist Arnaud de Borchgrave calls Chavez a "Robin Hood in Che Guevara clothing, robbing from the rich to give to the poor, including free hospitals staffed by 17,000 Cuban doctors and dentists."[41]

Despite Venezuela's billions of dollars in oil revenue, Hugo Chavez's socialism has brought high inflation, chronic food shortages and riots, growing crime, and long lines filled with hundreds of Venezuelans waiting to buy scare supplies of milk, chicken, and sugar at state run outdoor markets staffed by the military. Support for Chavez's "Bolivarian socialism" began to slip, even among the poorest of the poor.[42]

President Chavez remains fixated on his vision of emulating Simon Bolivar, a Caracas-born leader of rebel armies that freed a large area from Spanish rule in the early nineteenth century. Bolivar died in 1830. According to Chavez, Bolivar, like himself, was a socialist whose vision of a united Latin American was based on his determination to oppose the United States in building a classless society in opposition to an array of oligarchs and imperialists.[43]

Chavez is surrounded by extreme poverty in his own country, including sizable slums on the margins of Caracas. In 2007, 74 percent of Venezuelans were living under the poverty line. Chavez moved quickly following his election to the presidency, expropriating land and turning it over to small farmers and began nationalizing major industries. "I represent a nation," Chavez declared in 2003. "The revolutionary hurricane has been unleashed in Venezuela and will not stop until we have a true and beautiful homeland."[44]

President Chavez ordered the creation of 17,000 communal council's across the country and assigned $2 billion to fund their operation. The official slogan of these councils is "Build Power from Below." The purpose is said to build grass-roots democracy and give "power to the people," but the real purpose seems to be strengthening central control. Urban poor were singled out for special attention, those most fervent supporters of Hugo Chavez. The members of these "social councils" also constitute the core of the nationwide militia being developed. The central core of these militias are trained in "Cuban-style guerrilla warfare and counterinsurgency" and armed with guns, grenades, and knives to defend Venezuela. These communal councils fall under Chavez's direct control. Plans are to expand Venezuela's reserve from about 200,000 to one million. In addition to building a controllable martial spirit in the Venezuelan people, the militias are focused away from their own hardships toward the "gringos" in the United States.[45]

Chavez's quest to end poverty in Venezuela led him to bring thousands of Cuban medics and education advisers into the country, as well as the Cuban secret police. Among the lessons Chavez learned from Castro was how best to tighten control over domestic politics through control of public institutions and enhancing his international stature by challenging the United States.[46]

Chavez, following Fidel Castro's advice, took a hard line in consolidating his position, especially after surviving a misfired military coup against him in April 2002. Two of the top plotters, the heads Venezuela's largest business and labor federations, were hunted down by police and charged with treason.[47] Chavez did not

miss a step in the conduct of his "revolutionary hurricane." In the
summer 2007, Chavez, boasting the region's most powerful
military, replaced his defense minister, General Raul Baduel, with
General Gustavo Rangel who had commanded Venezuela's
100,000-member national militia. This was an important move,
since it eliminated General Baduel who said in his farewell speech
that "we must separate ourselves from Marxist orthodoxy" and
strengthened the integration of the armed forces and the militias
(each would keep an eye on the other).[48]

By 2005, he moved to restrict freedom of the press or as President
Chavez put it, "we can say that the Venezuelan people have began
to free themselves from . . . the dictatorship of the private media."[49]
Chavez engineered a law giving him the power to suspend the
licenses of radio and television stations when their broadcasts were
deemed to be "contrary to the security of the nation." He also sent
thousands of young Venezuelans to Cuba for indoctrination and
rewrote the constitution to broaden his powers in several areas.[50]
For the "Chavistas" any criticism of the president is an attack on
the nation. President Chavez proclaimed that he could "take away
the concession of any media outlet that practices media terrorism."[51]

Major storm clouds hung over press freedoms in Venezuela after
the Chavez government refused to renew the broadcast license of
Radio Caracas Television, known simply as RCTV in mid-2007.
Since much of its wildly popular, racy soap operas drew a large
audience, the Chavez government cited children as being affected
by the sex and violence as being the reason for refusing to renew
RCTV's license. Chavez had accused RCTV of "poisoning the souls
of children with irresponsible sex." But RCTV's programming also
included daily reports that harshly criticized Chavez and the
government, which in Chavez's terms made them "media
terrorists."

Tens of thousands gathered in the streets of Caracas to protest
the closure of the RCTV network. University students blocked a

major highway for hours after the Radio Caracas Television ceased broadcasting. President Chavez would not budge, accusing RCTV of "subversive" activities. Rubber bullets and tear gas were fired by police in efforts to break up the demonstrations. The protesters chanted "freedom, freedom" to protest Hugo Chavez's refusal to renew RCTV's broadcast license.[52]

In the end, President Chavez won the day by silencing RCTV, one of the last sources of criticism of his increasingly totalitarian socialist (Marxist) regime. Chavez and his guidance counselor Fidel Castro fulfilled the requirement in Gramsci's formula that requires shutting down independent media voices. Such an action is a prerequisite for success in the follow-up steps in the Gramscian blueprint for cultural revolution. Meanwhile, Bolivia and Ecuador took copycat initiatives to subdue the independent media. Bolivia's Evo Morales explained that "the main adversaries of my presidency, of my government are certain communications media."[53]

President Chavez's rush toward building socialism in Venezuela was slowed by the people's refusal to validate his thirty-three major constitutional changes proposed in August 2007 that would have allowed him to be re-elected indefinitely and to move forward on his "Bolivarian Revolution."[54] With President Chavez's political supporters in firm control of the National Assembly, 160 supported the proposed constitutional revisions and seven abstained. Thousands of events were scheduled to explain the sixty-nine amendments requiring popular vote in order to secure approval through a referendum in December. University students began protests against the constitutional changes and were met by police firing tear gas and rubber bullets and other Chavez supporter firing pistols into the massed demonstrators. The confrontation led to the government challenging the autonomy of Venezuela's public universities whose rectors were aligned with those opposing Hugo Chavez and his moves toward socialism.[55]

On December 1, 2007, Venezuelans rejected President Chavez's proposed amendments to the constitution by a margin of nearly ten percent. Many simply said they were opposed to socialism in Venezuela. Others believed the changes would have given Chavez too much power. Many dissatisfied Chavistas did not come out to vote. Among their grievances was Chavez's earlier insistence that the four political parties making up his governing coalition merge into a single "United Socialist Party." Another smoldering anger center was based on Chavez's earlier heavy-handed refusal to renew the broadcasting license of a popular television station. Some in the military dragged their feet because of Chavez's effort to turn the military into a tool of his socialist project. And many Chavista politicians were unenthusiastic about the reforms, especially since their approval would allow Chavez to run for office indefinitely while other posts would still be functioning under the pre-socialist constitutional rules.[56]

President Chavez took his electoral defeat gingerly by saying that "the motor seized up, so we'll have to go by donkey instead."[57] He admitted that he had moved too fast and too far ahead of the Venezuelan people. Chavez said that his five years remaining on his current term in office would be focused on "the three Rs"—the "revision, rectification and relaunching" of the socialist revolution. From this platform, Chavez moved forward to address the outstanding issues and problems that led to the withholding of support for the proposed constitutional amendments in December 2007.[58]

By 2007, freedom of the press in Venezuela was in jeopardy as the country was moved another step toward "21st-century socialism." Many journalists and media owners believe Chavez will control or eliminate all independent media voices by 2012.[59]

In the Gramsci blueprint, the Roman Catholic Church was public enemy number one. For the success of Marxism, the Church must be destroyed. Hence, it was not surprising when Chavez took aim at the Roman Catholic Church, calling it a "tumor on Venezuelan society."[60] Chavez also told Archbishop Roberto Luckert Leon that he would "see him in hell."[61]

After his 2006 reelection, Chavez faced a problem that Antonio Gramsci had warned about in achieving an indirect route to a Marxist government: the autonomy of the Roman Catholic Church, which served as a major source of contrary values to guide ordinary citizens in their daily lives. Ninety-six percent of the Venezuelans were Roman Catholic in 2006 and 74 percent had expressed their trust in the Church in a 2005 public opinion poll. The Church stayed mostly to its ministries and serving the Venezuelan people. Cardinal Urosa Savino, however, placed President Chavez on notice that the Venezuelan Church would continue to speak against the slide toward socialist dictatorship, since it challenges liberty under the guise of helping the poor. The church in Latin America should maintain a clear separation between itself and the state, Father Robert A. Sirico counsels, but it also has an interest in preserving freedom and pluralism.[62]

President Chavez's response was interesting because it reflected Gramsci's teaching, and it became a key point in the Venezuelan model of the practicality of the Gramsci formula. Avoiding confrontation with Cardinal Savino, Chavez turned to "self-immersion in Christian imagery." He used "Messianism" as a means of trying to convince the Venezuelan people that "socialism is Christianity" and referred to the Christ as "the greatest socialist in history." Chavez said that "the Kingdom of Christ is the kingdom of socialism." The Church, however, was having none of it. Many Church documents condemned socialism in theory and in practice. Taking measure of how Chavez deals with the Roman Catholic Church will be a central aspect of the Gramscian model exported to other Latin American countries. Marxists like Chavez must neutralize the Church's influence, for Christian values by their very existence challenge dictatorial rule. Gramsci was clear: the

Roman Catholic Church must be destroyed. The first casualty resulting from the quashing of religious freedom has always been individual liberty.[63]

Gramsci counseled that "any formation of a national-popular collective will is impossible unless the great mass of peasant farmers bursts *simultaneously* into political life."[64] Following the Italian thinker's formula, Hugo Chavez promised an "agrarian revolution" when he came to power in 1998. As elsewhere in Latin America, most of the country's agricultural lands were concentrated in a few hands. Chavez was especially harsh with cattlemen and owners of large estates, which made him very popular with Venezuela's numerous poor who made up the base of his political support. The elite were outraged, especially after the Chavez government handed out titles to about 9,000 acres to poor farmers in 2001. One cattleman who lost 360 acres of his family's 7,400-acre ranch said: "I believe it is the beginning of the Cubanization of Venezuela."[65]

President Chavez's vision of a "passive revolution" by redistributing large land holdings picked up speed in 2005. Venezuela's poor were ecstatic as more titles to land were given to the rural farmers. Hailing Hugo Chavez, Carlos Julia Roja, who was awarded thirty-seven acres, said that "he [Chavez] is a man of the poor, the only one who has fought for the poor." He asked, "how many peasants would be able to eat off this land?" The land-holding loser in this case was a British-owned 32,000 acre tract that had been expropriated by the government.[66]

By 2007, Chavez, after winning a third term in a landslide election in 2006, revved his proletarian engines: "We're heading toward socialism, and nothing and no one can prevent it." He requested the National Assembly to grant him special powers, "a revolutionary enabling law," that would permit him to approve economic laws by decree. Railing about the privatization that had preceded his presidency, Chavez spoke of the need to bring the country's most important oil fields under state control.[67]

Pocketing his new economic powers, Chavez quickly nationalized by decree Venezuela's electrical and telecommunications companies. The firms initially affected were the AES Corporation and C.A. National Telefonos de Venezuela (CANTV), the country's largest publicly traded company. "The nation should recover its ownership of strategic sectors," Chavez declared."[68]

President Chavez spent billions of dollars to create the idea a "Bolivarian Revolution" across Latin America and the Caribbean. In August 2007, Chavez urged the Caribbean nations "to seek greater independence from the United States." Pledging to share Venezuela's oil wealth, Chavez promised to provide fuel supplies under preferential conditions. Insinuating himself into the affairs in other countries, he created a backlash of varying intensity from country by country against his meddling. Yet, the score-sheet includes several countries sliding leftward, with a few becoming ideological allies of Hugo Chavez. The fact that he has billions of dollars at his finger tips doubtlessly has not been lost in some of these strategic reorientations. Socialists of varying solidarities with Chavez ruled over 300 million people in early 2008: Venezuela, Brazil, Uruguay, Argentina, Chile, Bolivia, Ecuador, and Nicaragua. Chavez had been helpful to some of the candidates. In July 2003, for instance, Chavez purchased as much as $3 billion in Argentine bonds, allowing the new socialist leader in Buenos Aires to pay off and cut ties with the "neoliberal" International Monetary Fund. Chavez also bought $25 million of Ecuador's debt and offered to buy $25 million more. In addition, Peru and Mexico in their respective 2006 national elections reflected sizable numbers of socialists voting, just missing defeat of conservative candidates.[69]

By 2006, Chavez was arming his soldiers with Russian weapons, having signed $3.5 billion worth of contracts with the Kremlin for more than thirty military fighter jets, fifty-three assault helicopters, and 100,000 AK-47 assault rifles. The United States delivered a formal protest to Russia over the sale of assault rifles, since Chavez was known to be working secretly with Marxist revolutionary guerrillas in the region. In mid-2007, Venezuela explored the possible purchase of nine diesel-powered submarines from Russia as a cost of $3 billion—the 636 and 677E Amur-class submarines carry medium range missiles. Russia asserted that it operated within the framework of international rules for arms exports, and contended that "the cooperation between Russia and Venezuela isn't aimed against anyone."[70]

China agreed to invest $100 billion in Latin America in a wide-range of energy-related and commodity partnerships. The idea was to "try to lessen . . . [Latin America's] trade dependence on the U.S."[71] China's aggressive policy in Latin American bore fruit by cutting trade deals with Cuba, Argentina, Brazil, and Venezuela. From 1997 to 2005, China invested $700 million in Venezuela, and trade between the two countries amounted to $3 billion in 2005. Beijing also invested $3 billion in Venezuela's petro-chemical sector. Trade agreements between China and Venezuela include energy, agriculture, transportation, mining, housing, tourism, telecommunications, and information technology. President Chavez called it a new "strategic alliance" that was designed to foster multilateralism.[72]

President Chavez was warmly welcomed by President Hu Jintao in an August 2006 trip to China. Chavez expressed the hope that Venezuela could export 500,000 barrels of oil per day by 2009 and a million barrels a day in the coming decade. President Chavez also mentioned his willingness to buy jet fighters from China to supplement those he bought from Russia. In September 2006, China delivered the first of three advanced long-range air defense radars purchased by Venezuela; seven more of the JYL-1 radars were in the pipeline.[73]

Visiting Iran for talks with President Mohammad Khatami in 2001, Chavez called for a "strategic alliance" to work for "peace and stability." Both countries were members of OPEC and had been advocating higher oil prices. Five years later, Hugo Chavez was riding high on a wave of soaring gas prices, and he teamed up with Russia, Iran, and China as a major oil consumer, in an "Axis of Oil." The new oil club challenged U.S. foreign policies as the "Axis" members pushed for an end to the unipolar world led by the United States to a multi-polar international system in which Russia would have a strong voice.

Another key aspect of Hugo Chavez's anti-U.S. program includes building close relationships with al-Qaeda and other terrorist groups. Seeing himself as the new Castro, a long-time collaborator with international terrorists, Chavez, according to a Venezuelan defector, rewarded al-Qaeda with $900,000 in cash and $100,000 in humanitarian aid to the Taliban after September 11. He continued to follow his Cuban mentor's steps by collaborating with and assisting anti-U.S. international terrorists.[74]

Hugo Chavez is widely known to be sympathetic with the Marxist rebels, the *Fuerzas Armadas Revolucionarias de Colombia-Ejercito del Pueblo* (Revolutionary Armed Forces of Colombia—People's Army or FARC-EP). When one of the FARC's leaders was "snatched" by bounty hunters in Caracas while attending a Leftist conference, Chavez was outraged at the violation of Venezuela's sovereignty. When Colombian military force began bombarding a FARC camp just inside a remote area of Ecuador at the end of February 2008, killing twenty-one guerrillas, including one of its top commanders, Paul Reyes, Chavez treated this as a cause for war. He ordered troops to the border with Colombia, broke of diplomatic relations with Bogota, and warned Colombia's President Alvaro Uribe not to try such an action against Venezuela. Meanwhile, Ecuador's President Rafael Correa, a socialist confidant of Chavez's, felt compelled to follow suit by dispatching troops to the border with Venezuela. Little more than torrents of insults were exchanged by the three leaders, but the military confrontation was the first in

South America for more than a decade. After a week-long intervention of the Organization of American States, the crisis was calmed by a softly nuanced compromise.[75] The greatest danger exposed in this scrap with Colombia was President Chavez's hair-trigger response to a quite minor Colombian cross-border operation. Chavez showed extraordinary immaturity. He bears watching.

According to one report, Chavez is following the blueprint Fidel Castro drafted for Chile's Salvador Allende, who imported thousands of Cuban paramilitaries to overthrow the constitution in Chile in order to establish a Communist regime. Chavez is continually facing domestic unrest and challenges to the revolutionary road of Antonio Gramsci. In an effort to ensure that his "passive revolution" takes place, Chavez is replicating parts of Cuba's experience by "plugging international terrorist networks into the country's security services, financial system and state corporations as part of his plans."[76]

Islamic terrorists have been operating out of Venezuela's resort island of Margarita, located about twenty-three miles off the northeast coast of Venezuela. The island serves as a stop-off for terrorists en route to the tri-border region or "Triple Frontier," a no-man's land where the borders of Argentina, Brazil, and Paraguay converge. Margarita has been identified as a center of terrorist financing along with the Cayman Islands and Panama. Hezbollah was also suspected of using Margarita Island as a part of its financial network.[77]

Other Socialist Countries

Six countries with socialist governments—Bolivia, Ecuador, Uruguay, Nicaragua, Argentina, and Chile—are primary candidates to join the Chavez-led "Bolivarian Revolution." Two additional countries are of interest because of the sizable proportion of their voters leaning toward the Left: Peru and Mexico. And Colombia is of concern because of the sizable number of Marxist guerrillas engaged in a Leninist-style armed revolution through violence and terrorism.

Bolivia

Following several years of violence and turmoil in Bolivia, a socialist understudy of Hugo Chavez was elected president in January 2006. Evo Morales, of Aymara Indian origin, was a Marxist deputy in the National Congress where he headed the leftist caucus. He was better known as head of the *cocoleros*, about 30,000 coca-growing farmers and peasants in the Chapare region of the country. He blamed the United States for the poverty in Bolivia owing to the "geopolitical and economic interests of multinational corporations." He declared, "peasants resort to illegal crops as the only alternative to poverty."[78]

Strikes by workers and peasants were almost continuous in 2001, demanding an end to U.S.-sponsored drug eradication. One Marxist, Oscar Olivera, was leader of riots in Cochabamba, where he led members of the Federation of Factory Workers against foreign control of water resources. He showed-up in Washington, D.C., in April 2000 when the Institute for Policy Studies, "the think tank of the left," presented him its Orlando Letelier-Ronni Moffitt Award for his leadership in the union insurrection against privatization of public water supplies.

Bolivia remained a political powder keg through 2001 with protests by miners and workers in other economic sectors. With three-quarters of Bolivia's people living below the poverty line, many analysts at the time referred to the country's "pre-revolutionary condition." President Gonzalo Sanchez de Lozada held on until October 2003, following six weeks of massive protests, he fled to Miami. By this time Evo Morales was riding a crest of popularity, while leading the Movement Toward Socialism political party and serving as the head of the coca-growing union. "I dream of boosting this anti-imperialist message with a great summit including Fidel, Lula and Chavez, to show that we are

united, and to make the North American imperialists think twice,"
Evo Morales declared.[79]

After chasing President Sanchez de Lozada out of the country,
Bolivia's indigenous majority had, for the first time, found its
political voice. Ten percent of the population owned 90 percent of
Bolivia's wealth. Many of the indigenous Indian majority were
homeless and lived on less than $2 a day. Dependent on outside
assistance, South America's poorest country relied on the World
Bank and International Monetary Fund. The government had
traditionally served the white and Mestizo minority, largely
ignoring the majority indigenous Indian population. When
Bolivia's hydrocarbons were assessed between 1997 and 2002,
Bolivia's proven reserves of gas increased by 362 percent to an
estimated fifty-five trillion cubic feet. A dream had come true. But
Bolivia's civil society feared the government would favor foreign
investors over the people. The "water war" in Cochabamba also
had generated a combative mood in the country's social
movements.[80]

The issue of who should profit from Bolivia's resources
continued to hound new President Carlos Mesa. But continuing
anti-government protests, violence, and the rage of the people drove
him from office in June 2005. Mesa's departure was a victory for
the cocoleros who had already profited by expanding their crops
during the prolonged period of instability. The Morales-directed
"Movement to Socialism" organized the final round of protests
that toppled President Mesa.

Evo Morales was elected president of Bolivia in December 2005,
the country's first indigenous chief executive. At his first news
conference, Morales explained that he believed the United States
used the fight against drug trafficking as a "false pretext" to install
military bases. Saying that his government would fight drugs,
Morales said that "neither cocaine or drug trafficking are part of
the Bolivian culture."[81]

Comfortable in the warm embrace of Venezuela's Hugo Chavez and Cuba's Fidel Castro, President Morales moved quickly down a socialist path laid out by the Gramsci-Chavez model. First, Morales promised to emulate Hugo Chavez. Morales declared: "I guarantee you the presence of comrade Chavez, who will teach us how he brought forward a new constitution in Venezuela and fought with the gringos and oligarchy."[82] A national assembly set up in August 2006 had one year to write a new constitution that would "deliver a second liberation to the Bolivian people."[83]

Shortly after his inauguration, Evo Morales confronted the country's Roman Catholic bishops over the teaching of religion in the schools. Many were surprised by his action since the Church had a close relationship with the grass-roots groups that brought him to power. But the Roman Catholic Church remained Antonio Gramsci's enemy number one. Morales apparently found that the time was not right to challenge the Church directly and backed-off the idea of confronting the country's bishops. But his time would come.[84]

In January 2006, Morales moved to tighten his control of the security services by expelling twenty-eight generals from the police and armed forces for alleged complicity with a U.S. planned covert operation to remove Bolivia's air defenses. The new president brought in Cuban and Venezuelan intelligence teams to clear government offices of hidden microphones. He sent about 10,000 of the Movement to Socialism party cadre to Cuba with medical scholarships for education in needed specializations.[85]

Morales announced plans to redistribute 77,000 square miles—an area about the size of Nebraska—among Bolivia's Indian majority from 2007–2011. The land that Morales promised to redistribute included acreage and private holdings deemed unproductive or fraudulently obtained. The government will also help the farmers by providing technical support, equipment, schools, and safe drinking water.[86]

Mr. Morales proposed legislation that would allow the government to tighten control of the media. The legislation was said to be necessary to take measures against television for content deemed to be "harmful to society." Meanwhile, Venezuela provided $2 million to finance a new state-owned television channel and more than 100 provincial radio stations (propaganda transmitters) throughout Bolivia, and President Morales was given $30 million to subsidize some of the country's municipalities.[87]

Six members of Spain's Basque ETA terrorist group traveled to Bolivia and met with high officials of the Morales government in 2006. They bought homes in Cochabamba, Bolivia's narco-trafficking center and stronghold of Evo Morales' Movement Toward Socialism that was instrumental in bringing him to power. The Basque political organization Batasuna issued a communique praising the Morales government, calling Bolivia's Movement Toward Socialism a model for the Basque region.[88]

Hugo Chavez promised to dispatch 400 accountants from Venezuela's state oil company to Bolivia to audit the books of foreign energy companies. Supposedly the auditors searched for evidence to support renegotiation of existing contracts under the threat of expropriation.[89]

President Morales nationalized Bolivia's energy resources on May 1, 2006. Foreign firms operating at Bolivia's oil and natural gas fields were given a choice to either cede control of their operations or leave the country. Seven companies signed new contracts with the Bolivian government, the caretaker of the country's energy resources. In a demonstration for the Bolivian people, Morales sent soldiers to occupy fields that he said had plundered the country's energy riches for years. It was a wildly popular move for most Bolivians. The new deals compelled the foreign energy companies to give at least 50 percent of their revenue to the state energy company. The percentages surrendered could range as high as 82 percent of revenues for large producers.[90]

In a visit to China in February 2006, President Morales was counseled to avoid taking actions that could prompt the U.S. to organize a coup among disaffected military officers. "You have to be nice to the United States," he was told, reflecting China's own long-term strategy to undermine U.S. influence in Latin America. Playing "nice" is a key to Gramsci's formula for "passive revolution."

The Chinese offered Morales thirty-eight Chinese-made HN-5 MANPAD surface-to-air missiles to replace those taken by the CIA in a covert operation in December 2005—the Agency had been helped by Bolivian security officers who feared the missiles would find their way into the hands of terrorists. The man-portable air defense missile is a shoulder-fired, low-altitude missile, which, in terrorist hands, could be used against commercial airliners.[91]

Morales celebrated his first year in office in January 2007 with nearly a 50 percent approval rating. The partial nationalization of the country's energy sector promised more revenue for Bolivia's socialist pathway. By drastically altering the tax structure, the Bolivian government received 82 percent of the profits generated by the foreign energy countries. This percentage was exactly the reverse of profit-sharing before the renegotiation of the company's contracts. Next on Morales' nationalization agenda was overhauling the mining industry.[92]

Accusing the justice system of constraining the nationalization of key economic sectors in Bolivia's march toward socialism, Morales demanded the resignation of four Supreme Court justices. He accused the judicial system of stealing $300 million and releasing delinquents, thieves, and narco-traffickers. Mr. Morales was supported by key members of the Movement Toward Socialism.[93]

Morales's success rate began to decline in late 2007 when the Indian coalition that brought him to power was split by rivalries. Strikes, riots, and threats occurred in six of Bolivia's nine provinces.

The chief complaints were the drift toward dictatorship and militant socialism. Informal alliances were formed to protect people's "democratic rights."[94]

While Morales and government soldiers were dealing with the uprisings, Hugo Chavez made it clear that he was not amused. He declared that he would wage war against Bolivia if the opposition tried to topple Morales. Then, perhaps with the ghost of Chile's Marxist president Salvador Allende, who was overthrown and killed on September 11, 1973, whispering in his ear, Hugo Chavez said: "I warn the oligarchy of Bolivia that if they overthrow or assassinate Evo, Venezuela will not remain with its arms crossed."[95]

Ecuador

Leftist Lucio Gutierrez won over Ecuador's poor and indigenous Indian workers and, from that political base, defeated banana magnate Alvaro Noboa for the presidency in November 2002. Noboa was the country's richest man, heading more than 110 companies.

The country's leftist alignment was shown when an estimated 10,000 to 12,000 local and foreign protesters marched in Quito against thirty-three trade representatives from the Organization of American States who had arrived in Ecuador's capital to discuss the ramifications of the proposed Free Trade Area of the America's agreement. The nationalities of Ecuador asserted that the proposed easing of trade restrictions would "put an end to life, natural resources, national production, and employment." Shouting "*Los Excluidos—por Trabajo, Justicia y Vida*" (Excluded Ones—for Jobs, Justice and Life), left-wing nationalities of Ecuador registered its opposition.

President Gutierrez's missteps in governance led to allegations of corruption and charges of making backroom deals. The 100-seat unicameral Congress removed him from office, and Ecuador's military withdrew its support for Gutierrez.[96] After the fumbles by an interim president for more than a year, the Ecuadoran electorate was overwhelmingly supportive of left-wing economist Rafael Correa for president in November 2006.

With a doctorate in economics from the University of Illinois, President Correa spoke sharply against globalization, neoliberal and orthodox economic policies, and multilateral financial organizations, especially the International Monetary Fund and the World Bank. A Roman Catholic, he embraced the people's church idea of Latin American liberation theology. When opponents cast him as a Chavez clone, Correa responded sharply: "We are not copying Lula, Chavez or Kirchner. . . . We are not waiting for a prescription from abroad."[97]

President Correa won by making it clear that he was against market reforms, the Bush Administration, a free trade agreement with the United States, and transnational corporations that did not obey the law. He also threatened to default in Ecuador's $10 billion foreign debt, if social needs were greater than the imperative to service the debt.

He promised the long-abused Ecuadoran people that the government would construct low cost homes and double the $36 "poverty bonus" to 1.2 million poor Ecuadorans. Correa said that Ecuador would rejoin OPEC to assist in seeking the best price for the 555,000 barrels of oil it pumps per day. He said that he would seek closer ties with leftist presidents such as Michelle Bachelet in Chile, Nestor Kirchner in Argentina, and Luis Inacio "Lula" da Silva in Brazil. Hugo Chavez is "a friend of mine," he explained to his critics. Correa's doctoral thesis at the University of Illinois reflected a deep-seated concern with the distribution of income. His thesis dealt with the "impact of globalization on development and poverty." President Correa said that "we are looking for a united Latin America that can confront a globalization that is inhumane and cruel."[98] A close ally of Hugo Chavez, Ecuador's president asserted in late 2007 that he thought his Venezuelan friend was "a very honest person—a clear leader, a very democratic president."[99]

Iranian President Mahmoud Ahmadinejad attended Rafael Correa's inauguration and said that "any nation seeking to defend itself can count on Iranian aid." He added that "we are partisans of peace. It is the Americans who are at war with the entire world."[100]

Uruguay

The leader of the neo-Marxist Broad Front, Tabare Ramon Vazquez-Rosas, was sworn in as president on March 1, 2005. Thousands of supporters celebrated in the streets of Montevideo in support of Vazquez-Rosas who promised to "work tirelessly" for the people. Except for Fidel Castro who had to cancel for health reasons, the Latin American Marxist gang were all there: Brazil's Lula da Silva, Venezuela's Hugo Chavez, Argentina's Nestor Kirchner, and Chile's Richard Lagos, plus Paraguay's centrist Nicanor Duarte Fritos.

One of President Vazquez's first acts was restoration of diplomatic ties with Cuba. He also announced a $100 million emergency social welfare plan to provide basic health care and food for the country's neediest. The Gramsci formula had helped bring another Leftist to power in Latin America.

The Broad Front had entered the political scene in 1971, a loose coalition of Communist and Socialist parties, the Christian Democratic Party, and others attracted from small left-wing parties, including the then-urban guerrilla Marxist Tupamaros whose loyalty was to Fidel Castro. Surviving an iron-fist response from Uruguay's government, the Broad Front's membership added and dropped various leftist groups over time. However, after the restoration of democracy, the Front steadily increased its membership. Voter support for the Front remained stable over the years, gaining strength since 2002 when austerity measures were put into place to service the country's foreign debt. Vazquez rode the crest of the misery wave right into the presidency.

The Vazquez campaign promised to apply "a new and more equitable development model [Gramsci], one that will benefit the workers, the middle classes, the most vulnerable sectors of society, and sectors involved in the various areas of national production." He had plenty counsel from his Marxist compatriots in Latin America.

Uruguayan parliamentary investigators discovered an attempt to smuggle 15,000 rounds of Iranian-made 5.56 millimeter ammunition aboard one of its naval vessels. The shipment was picked up in Venezuela and was part of a larger deal involving the purchase of 18,000 Iranian-made automatic rifles. The deal would have violated the UN Security Council restrictions imposed on Iran for failing to halt its uranium enrichment program. The Iran-Venezuela-Uruguay triangulation appeared to be a part of the $2 billion "strategic fund" announced by Iranian President Mahmoud Ahmadinejad and President Chavez in their September 2007 meeting in Caracas. The fund was to be used to help Latin American governments "liberate themselves from Imperialism."[101] One the Uruguayan Broad Front's coalition members, the Tupamaros Liberation Front, supports the Chavez brand of socialism.

Nicaragua

The Sandinista National Liberation Front (FSLN) seized power from dictator Anastasio Somoza in 1979. The Sandinistas were a pro-Soviet, pro-Castro revolutionary group that pledged a broad, all-inclusive democracy. However, it was not long before the FSLN took the Nicaraguan people down a pathway toward a Soviet model of totalitarianism. The slaughter of indigenous Indians and the heavy footprint of Marxism-Leninism soon snuffed the flicker of the people's democratic aspirations and hope for an end to human rights abuses. The principal architect of the Sandinistas brutal rule was Daniel Ortega.

The Sandinistas stumbled, however, by believing their own propaganda in the 1980s that they had consolidated their rule and enjoyed widespread popular support. Hence, they consented to national elections in 1990. The surprise of surprises occurred when Violeta Chamorro of the Liberal Constitutional Party won 51 percent of the popular vote in the presidential elections, defeating the bloody rule of Daniel Ortega.[102]

Mr. Ortega ran for president three more times in the 1990s and 2000s, losing each time. Behind the scenes, however, the FSLN (Sandinistas) were busy working with terrorists from the Middle East, Europe, and Latin America, including such state-sponsors as Iraq and Libya, and transnational groups like Colombia's FARC, the Basque ETA, and others. Five Nicaraguan passports were found in the apartments of suspected terrorists in the 1993 World Trade Center bombing in New York.[103]

Nicaragua's political system struggled through the 1990s with a long list of economic and corruption problems. The FSLN, which put its weapons down in 1992 and joined the political mainstream, did not lose its Marxist revolutionary edge. It was not lost on the Sandinistas that Nicaragua was a poor country with two-thirds of its population living in poverty. Confronted with these intractable realities, Nicaragua's democracy remained on a shaky life-support system. Unable to deliver relief to the majority of people, the central government's position eroded over time while the Sandinista's position improved.

The Sandinistas were among the initial members of the Forum of Sao Paulo organized by Lula da Silva and Fidel Castro in 1990. The da Silva-Castro idea was to help radical political leaders win control of their countries through successful campaigns in national elections. Following the Gramsci blueprint, Marxists would present themselves as populists opposed to corruption in government and as being dedicated to helping the poor by providing health programs, education, and workable anti-poverty measures.[104]

The Sandinistas rebounded in 2004 by winning the mayoral office in Managua and several other municipalities. Sandinista leader Daniel Ortega described the election results as a new "revolution without guns or bloodshed," which seems to be a direct reference to the "passive revolution" formula designed by Antonio Gramsci. The die was cast for Daniel Ortega's return, not as an ardent Marxist-Leninist but as a "man of the people," a follower of Marxist revisionist Antonio Gramsci. For instance, he joined forces with Arnoldo Aleman's Liberal Party (a Gramcian move) that would have ended the existing administration by gutting the powers of the presidency. It would seem that Ortega had learned his lessons well about the Gramsci formula for success at the school house of the Sao Paulo Forum.[105]

Gone during Nicaragua's 2006 presidential campaign was Ortega's fiery Marxist-Leninist rhetoric. His new message conformed with Gramsci's counsel to say or do whatever was necessary to achieve power through the electoral process. Only then should measures be taken to shape societal values in a way to support a consolidation of power sufficiently to impose Marxist principles on society and its political system.

During his presidential campaign, Ortega gave everyone a peek into how he would rule in the initial days of his new presidency. The challenges he faced were great. Nicaragua's 5.5 million people were the second poorest in the Western Hemisphere, only Haiti ranked lower. Annual per capita income was about $910. Ortega's answer was to partner with Fidel Castro, Lula da Silva, Hugo Chavez, and other socialist leaders in rejecting what he called "savage capitalism." "We are victims of a savage neo-liberalism," a street vendor supporter of Ortega said. "But united, we will keep fighting this neo-liberal system that lets our children die of hunger."

The street vendor spilled the beans about Ortega's true position, while Ortega began his tenure as president of Nicaragua with an engaging smile. He emphasized peace, reconciliation, stability, close ties with the United States, and free trade. He also presented socialist images of free education, medical care, wage supplements to the poor, and land redistribution. In actuality, Ortega basked in the warm welcome to the world of Gramsci from Lula da Silva, Fidel Castro, and Hugo Chavez. Subsidized oil and gas deliveries from Venezuela would help the new regime consolidate its power, and Iranian President Mahmoud Ahmadinejad's visit in January 2007 promised additional assistance to help Daniel Ortega consolidate his position before the next revolutionary steps were taken.[106]

Argentina

Argentine President Nestor Kirchner burst onto the political scene in May 2003 and combined an assault on entrenched domestic interests with an aggressive foreign policy. Signaling his socialist, if not Marxist, propensities Kirchner quickly established warm relations with Fidel Castro, Luis Inacio "Lula" da Silva, and Hugo Chavez, the trio representing Latin America's Leftist brain trust and primary funder. Kirchner also reached out to other leaders estranged from the United States, including Bolivia's Evo Morales. In a January 2004 meeting of the Special Summit of the America's, Kirchner boasted that he would "win by a knockout" in an upcoming meeting scheduled with President George W. Bush.[107]

Kirchner successfully restructured $120 billion in total debt of the $190 billion Argentina owed, which included past interest due that covered 150 bond issues and 600,000 investors. As a result of these moves, Argentina's total debt fell from $190 billion to $125 billion in one month without assistance from the International Monetary Fund. This step forward gave Argentina a small space for tackling other debt issues serving as a drag on the country's economy.[108]

While President Bush met with thirty-three presidents attending the November 2005 Summit of the Americas, thousands of protesters rallied against the United States and capitalism. One protester from Honduras put the demonstrations very simply: "We're a people united against free trade, because free trade is a policy of death for our countries."[109]

In October 2007, Christina Fernandez de Kirchner, Argentina's first lady, won the presidency with more than 40 percent of the votes. She replaced her husband, Nestor, in December and became Argentina's first woman elected president. Her popularity was based largely on her husband's success in pulling the country back from the threshold of economic collapse since 2001. President Fernandez de Kirchner is a street-smart lawyer who worked ably by her husband's side. While political continuity is assured to some degree in the Fernandez de Kirchner presidency, a number of dicey economic issues continue to plague the country, including high inflation, price controls, and surging energy demand.[110] One merchant is quoted as exclaiming: "I'm so excited. Christina is going to pull us out of poverty."[111]

Chile

The country's first chief executive, Michelle Bachelet, was sworn into office on March 11, 2006. President Bachelet became the fourth consecutive leader of the socialist coalition that had ruled Chile since 1990. While a socialist, Miss Bachelet sits at the pragmatic end of the Leftists ruling in Latin America. The region's socialist-Marxist ruling elite were on their best behavior at Bachelet's swearing-in ceremony, including Kirchner, Vazquez, Lula da Silva, and Morales. One can be certain that their collective most ardent desire was to guide President Bachelet on to the path of following the Gramsci formula in Chile and to oppose free trade or what they call "U.S. imperialism."

Time will tell if Bachelet takes the bait. Venezuela's Hugo Chavez could not help himself from saying: "In Latin America, you have a laborer becoming president, that's Lula; an Indian, Evo, has arrived; a socialist woman; and a soldier—that's me, a revolutionary soldier—building a new South American project that is vital for the salvation of our people."[112]

"Bolivarian Revolution"

The combined effect of the Forum of Sao Paulo setting the stage for implementation of Antonio Gramsci's cultural blueprint for action and Hugo Chavez's "Bolivarian Revolution" has set several Latin American countries on a pathway toward socialism (Marxism). President Chavez provided the model for others to follow and the inspiration of Simon Bolivar as a liberator in class warfare.

Hugo Chavez was overwhelmingly elected to office in 1998 by the 80 percent of Venezuelans who were mired in poverty and with little hope for their world to change. By winning the popular elections, Chavez changed the rules of society against the wealthy elite businessmen, holders of large tracts of land, the armed forces and mass media, and others enjoying privileged positions.

President Chavez continued to restructure society as he moved toward creation of a model socialist state built on the cooperation of masses. His paradigm underwriting the "Bolivarian Revolution" was designed for export through emulation, first by Bolivia and Ecuador, Uruguay and Argentina, Nicaragua, and, perhaps in the future, Chile.[113]

The efforts by Fidel Castro and Lula da Silva in the 1990s to slow-roll the United States toward limiting free trade helped to provide a formula for the successes already won by the Forum of Sao Paulo, South America's Gramscian version of socialism.

6

SAMUEL RUBIN IMPERIUM

FROM A HOLES-IN-THE-POCKET communist in the mid-1930s to a creator of a new universe of radical Left-wing activists and organizations in the 1960s and 1970s, Samuel Rubin gave birth to a twenty-first century global-girdling imperium that dominates America's revolutionary progressive-socialist-marxist movement and remains a *force majeure* internationally. Samuel Rubin, a lifelong communist, and Philip Stern, whose uncle Alfred was indicted in 1958 for spying on behalf of the Soviet Union before fleeing to Czechoslovakia, provided most of the start-up money in 1963 for the Institute for Policy Studies (IPS) based in Washington, D.C. Rubin and Stern joined forces again a decade later to create an overseas star in the IPS solar system, the Transnational Institute (TNI) in Amsterdam.[1]

Rubin and Stern shared an abiding hatred of capitalism and, one may assume by logical extension, America itself. Yet, each benefitted enormously from capitalist success. The Samuel Rubin Foundation that contributed most of the funds for IPS and TNI was endowed by the $25 million that Rubin realized when he sold A. C. Faberge, a cosmetics firm, in1963. In Philip Stern's case, the original endowment of the Stern Fund came from the estate of Julius Rosenwald, the Sears, Roebuck magnate.[2] The firms of Faberge and Sears, Roebuck were as American as apple pie in the 1940s and 1950s. In the hands of Rubin and Stern, however, their assets were turned toward the radical goals of destroying American liberties and enslaving its people into the service of the foreign doctrines of Marx and Lenin.

The secret to the longevity of Samuel Rubin's organizational creation is rooted in assured funding from the Samuel Rubin Foundation that he established before his death, and the investment strategy and portfolio managerial acumen shown by his daughter, Cora, over the years. A third vital ingredient of the successes won by IPS and TNI was drawn from an unrelenting criticism of the "Establishment" by the IPS co-founders, Marcus Raskin and the late Richard J. Barnet, whose driving force was fueled by a bottomless pit of hatred for American culture and government. And, fourth, the IPS and TNI successes were drawn from the idea of "social justice," which has long served as a guiding light for the radical Left. It serves to silence anyone disagreeing with them and draws large numbers of dupes, dopes, and useful idiots attracted to its fantasy of creating a socially-conscious world guided by socialist governance. David Horowitz, a former communist, shares his special personal insights about the real meaning of "social justice."

> Far from being progressive, the left's demands for 'social justice,' if realized, would destroy the very basis of social wealth. . . . In the modern world, competition is not the contrary of cooperation, but the form that cooperation must take in order to coordinate the activities of millions of people unknown to each other, pursuing goals that are not common and cannot be shared. The profit motive is the engine of wealth not only for the rich but

for the poor as well. In the real world, the attempt to plan economic systems produces inefficiency and waste; the attempt to redistribute wealth diminishes well-being and individual liberty; the attempt to unify society crushes its freedom; the ambition to make people equal establishes new forms of tyranny and submerges human individuality in totalitarian designs.[3]

Together, daughter Cora, Raskin, and Barnet, plus Cora's husband, Peter Weiss, continued the creation of new strategic partners in Samuel Rubin's radical imperium. They were supported by an array of hard Leftists, including radical labor unions, the religious Left, radical litigators, a news media heavily tilted to the Left, Marxist university professors, Left-wing politicians, and an unending cacophony of propaganda voices from Hollywood bubble-heads. Together, these extremists who created and supported the Institute for Policy Studies developed broadly-based policies and programs designed to transform America into a progressive-socialist-marxist society and government.

The IPS-TNI network attracts billionaire radicals like George Soros, Peter Lewis (Progressive Insurance Company), Ted Turner, and others; Left-wing extremists in politics, labor, and social issues like Ramsey Clark, George Sweeney, and Jesse Jackson; radical litigation centers such as the National Lawyers Guild, Center for Constitutional Rights, and American Civil Liberties Union; the religious Left, including the World Council of Churches (Protestant and Orthodox), Pax Christi (Roman Catholic), and Tikkun (mostly Jewish); and foreign supporters in Russia, the European Union, and United Nations. These strategic partners contribute to, participate in, or lead radical programs orchestrated by IPS and TNI.

The thinkers and tinkerers at IPS and TNI reflect a fluid mind set, one that defies easy definition. IPS and TNI have gone to extensive effort to avoid being labeled as "communist," or "Marxist-Leninist," and any other "-ists" or "-isms" from the Left. Their creators play too smart a hand to show their ideological cards. At their base, the Institute for Policy Studies and the Transnational Institute are revolutionary "idea houses." They adopt what works against the United States within their constipated progressive-socialist-marxist world view. Their perspectives are broadly based anti-capitalist and pro-socialist. The IPS-TNI vision of American socialism, according to the expert judgment of the Maldon Institute's John Rees, is focused on which economic and social planning and control model would be best in carrying out the progressive-socialist-marxist message at the lowest political unit, such as a city, community, or neighborhood. The economy would be dominated by small businesses. Public control would be exercised over major economic decisions, especially those taming the profit-margin of large corporations in order to ensure human priorities are served first.[4]

From the beginning, John Rees counsels, "IPS . . . has been more interested in power through influence than in building an empire under its direct control."[5] Yet, trying to define an agreed upon IPS-TNI ideology is a bit like interpreting the shadows on the walls of Plato's cave. Just when one thinks he or she has it, the images change and a new form is presented. By flashing multiple images of themselves to outsiders, the IPS and TNI ideologues may have us believe they are open-minded, fair, and balanced in their thinking, projects, and reports. But, as always, the proof is in the pudding: the only pudding served at the dining tables in these two radical think tanks is a revolutionary blend of progressivism-socialism-marxism. In IPS- and TNI-speak, "progressive" is a cover word for "socialist" and "socialist" is the same as "Marxist." Give them credit when it is due. IPS-TNI radicals have made "progressive" an accepted American euphemism for socialism and Marxism, both enemies of individual liberty and liberal democracy. For them, this is a great victory, for it is the first step toward reshaping the U.S. culture in a way that will accept a draconian shift toward socialism that will make Americans "poor beyond their wildest dreams."

Samuel Rubin

Born in 1901 in Bialystok, then a part of Czarist Russia and now in Poland, Samuel Rubin migrated at age four with his mother and father to the United States. His parents opened a small "dry goods" store in a poor Jewish neighborhood in Brooklyn. According to contemporary propaganda, "Rubin never forgot where he came from . . . and throughout his life carried memories of poverty, discrimination and abrogation of human rights."[6] Big words for a little man who plundered the dead and less fortunate in Spain during the mid-1930s.

Samuel Rubin was the primary communist sugar-daddy for the Washington D.C.-based IPS and TNI in Amsterdam.[7] In the hands of his daughter and son, Cora and Reed, the money Samuel made from his dirty deals in Spain was multiplied through smart investments, which provided more blood-money funding available to the Samuel Rubin Foundation, which, in turn, kept both the IPS and TNI in operation as well as partner radical centers. In this way, Samuel Rubin's social vision has been extended beyond his death in 1978. Or, as he put it at the founding of the Transnational Institute in 1972, "all you can have from me is perhaps a humanist approach to the problems that concern the people of the world."[8] Rubin's "humanist approach" was to push the first blood-stained domino in Spain that set into motion a cascade of revenue for use by the Left-wing centers in Washington, D.C., and Amsterdam.

By assisting those guilty of crimes against humanity in Spain during the Civil War, including the Soviet Union's Communist International (Comintern), its intelligence service NKVD (forerunner of the notorious KGB), and by the Spanish Communist Party, Samuel Rubin immersed himself in a cesspool of dirty money. Stalin provided the Spanish Republic with arms, ammunition, and other war supplies, including aircraft and tanks, but in the process the Soviets defrauded the hapless buyers out of hundreds of millions of dollars. Exchange rates were secretly manipulated, prices arbitrarily hiked, account books cooked, and similar swindles in order to draw every possible shred of wealth out of the Republic. "The Soviets forced the Spanish to pay for every aspect of their involvement, including the cost of transporting, feeding, and maintaining the Soviet advisers in Spain," historian Ronald Radosh and his colleagues recount. "Meanwhile, they played with exchange rates and the cost of weapons to ensure that they spent every bit of the Republican gold—and more."[9]

The Spanish Civil War was marked by atrocities on both sides, which does not speak well of either. However, the secret torture and killings by the Soviet Comintern, NKVD, and GRU (military intelligence under the cover of "advisers" to Spain's Republican Army), however, has gone largely unnoticed and under-reported over the years. The NKVD built a secret crematorium in Spain in order to dispose of their victims without leaving a trace. Many of the "enemies of the people" selected for liquidation were lured into the building housing the crematorium and "killed on the spot."[10] Stephane Courtois and five other European scholars joined forces in using documents briefly available in 1991–92 from the Soviet archives to tell much of the story:

> In 1936–39 the country [Spain] became a sort of laboratory where the Soviet authorities not only applied new political strategies and tactics but also tried out techniques that would be used during and after World War II. Their aims were manifold, but their primary goal was to ensure that the Spanish Communist Party (by now run entirely by the Comintern and the NKVD) seized power and established a state that would become another Soviet satellite. To achieve their goal, they used traditional Soviet methods, such as establishing an omnipresent police force and liquidating all non-Communist forces.[11]

The "killing fields" in Spain were filled with corpses of those slain by covert Soviet assassins. Spanish Communists supplemented the Kremlin's strategy of liquidating all non-communists. Torture, rape, and horrendous depravity frequently preceded death for many. Summary executions were common. Two special prisons held members of the International Brigades (Horta district of Barcelona and Castellon de la Plana). The number of foreign fighters liquidated is difficult to estimate, but one executioner is reported to have killed about 500 "undisciplined members" or those having "oppositional" tendencies.[12]

Thousands of Spanish children, ages five to twelve, had been sent to the U.S.S.R. where they were raised under the guidance of Soviet officials. When the Republic was defeated in 1939, most of the children's teachers were imprisoned for Trotskyism and others were sent to work in factories. The conditions in their colonies became increasingly severe. By 1941, about half of the children had contracted tuberculosis and about 750 of them had died before their trek to the Ural mountains and central Siberia. Some committed suicide, others formed criminal gangs, and, when they matured, women entered prostitution. All told, some 2,000 of 5,000 Spanish children died. In 1956, the first 534 of the survivors were allowed to return to Spain. In the end, only 1,500 would be repatriated.[13]

The scene presented above is the one Samuel Rubin walked into in the 1930s to join his friends in the Soviet Comintern. Having emerged from the Comintern underground, Rubin surveyed the already plundered wealth of Spain's Republican Government for an opportunity to enrich himself and the Communist Party.[14] What he found was rather peculiar, although his earlier experience with a French perfumery enabled him to choreograph an uncommon means of war-profiteering. The Republican Government held a sizable stock of ambergris, a key raw ingredient used in the production of exquisite perfumes.[15] Desperate for revenue for the purchase of arms and maintaining Soviet specialists in Spain, the cash-strapped Republican Government decided to sell its large stock of this valuable commodity below market prices. With the undercover assistance of Spanish Communists, who at the time were under Stalin's total control, Samuel Rubin purchased the ambergris. Communist ships ran the Italian and German naval blockades to deliver the Rubin's ambergris consignment to the United States.[16]

Needless to say, Rubin's profit margin on his initial offering of new perfumes and cosmetics in the American market was enormous. The perfume sales price also increased as a result of a suggestion by his friend Armand Hammer—according to some reports Hammer had bankrolled and brokered the ambergris deal—that Rubin call the new firm "A. C. Faberge." Hammer had already stolen the Faberge name, with Lenin's blessing, many years before when he was dealing in Russian jewelry that had been confiscated by the Bolshevik regime. The "Jeweler of the Imperial Russian Romanov Court" was Carl G. Faberge. He was famous for creating some of the most exquisite jewelry the world has ever known, especially the renowned Faberge eggs. Soviet archives, open for a brief period in the early 1990s, confirmed what many in the West had believed for some time: Armand Hammer "and his father were actually an official part of the Comintern's covert financial network."[17]

Rubin was no slouch in business either. Labeling his scents with dreamy names like "Aphrodesia" and "Tigress," he soon turned A. C. Faberge into a multi-million dollar business. Through the 1940s and 1950s, Faberge, in effect, had become a laundry for the blood of innocents spilled years before in Spain. Yet, once blood it is on your hands it never goes away. In Rubin's case, he had pulled a major business coup, but at the expense of Spain's Republican Government whose wealth was based on countless Spanish victims who had been tortured and murdered by Moscow's killing-machine.

The open question, since Rubin was a communist working with Armand Hammer, who was an official of the Comintern's financial network, is whether the International Department of the Soviet

Communist Party (after the Comintern was disbanded in 1943) was an off-the-books partner with A. C. Faberge. If so, how much of its profits went to Rubin's benefactors who arranged the purchase and delivered the ambergris for him at the beginning? If the Soviets were silent partners of A. C. Faberge, what role may they have had with the formation and operation of IPS and TNI over the years? S. Steven Powell's book *Covert Cadre* (1987) presents several photographs of Soviet officials attending IPS functions in Washington, D.C.[18] Why was IPS so cozy with the Soviets? Do IPS and TNI have similar with relations with Russia today?

The CIA was curious about the IPS-Soviet relationship, sharing with the FBI that "IPS potentially presents an excellent source of information for foreign intelligence services concerning U.S. foreign policy developments."[19] In a March 1969 file, the FBI noted that "individuals who have been identified as CP [Communist Party] members or sympathizers of CP activities, have participated in IPS functions. IPS representatives have also affiliated with known communists."[20] Four months later the FBI sent a letter to the U.S. Attorney General and Director, FBI: "A confidential source . . . reported that on June 21, 1969, [name redacted] . . . she had accepted a position with the Institute for Policy Studies . . . [name redacted] described 'Marxist-Leninists' [text redacted] was also working at the Institute for Policy Studies and 'being radicalized' by the Institute."[21]

Carl Faberge's family fled Russia in 1920 and eventually opened a small jewelry house in Paris and a craft shop in Geneva. Members of the Faberge family were dismayed after World War Two when they discovered their trade name had been stolen by Samuel Rubin and used to make millions of dollars. They obtained a court-ordered injunction against Rubin. Afterward, it had become quite clear that Rubin's wealth enabled him to influence the legal proceedings. The injunction against Rubin was lifted in 1951, and eventually he paid the Faberge family $25,000 for the right to use their trade name for perfumes and toiletries. Although the Faberge family's financial condition influenced their decision to accept Rubin's payoff, they were upset that Rubin later used the fortune he had amassed to help set up the Institute for Policy Studies and Transnational Institute. The Faberges had fought against the Bolshevik takeover of Russia in 1917, only to be imprisoned, impoverished, and exiled. Rubin inflicted one final indignity by stealing their renowned name and using it to aid their tormentors.[22]

Samuel Rubin sold A. C. Faberge in 1963 for $25 million, the same year that the Institute for Policy Studies was created, and a year later he put a sizable portion of his personal wealth into the newly created Samuel Rubin Foundation. The Foundation's boilerplate simply stated: "The purpose of this foundation is to carry on the work of its founder, who pursued peace and justice and sought an equitable reallocation of the world's resources."[23] The officers of the Foundation included Rubin's son-in-law, Peter Weiss, vice president, who was active in the National Lawyer's Guild, a communist front according to Congressional sources; Cora Weiss, Samuel Rubin's daughter, as secretary, who was active in several Leftist causes; and Reed Rubin, treasurer, Samuel Rubin's son who was named after John Reed, the first American Communist representative to the Soviet Comintern (1919–20).[24]

In a puff-piece interview for the *Washington Post* shortly before his death, Samuel Rubin was in a self-congratulatory mood in sharing his thoughts about how a communist becomes a successful capitalist. Slamming "the lust for . . . the last dollar of profit," Rubin said that "there's something else out there to life besides accumulating more wealth. The average businessman suffer diseases of tension and competition which rob him of the beauty of life."[25] Yet, Rubin ignored that the "beauty of life" was taken from tens of thousands Spaniards in the 1930s by his Soviet cohorts. He built A. C. Faberge on a foundation of corpses of simple people desiring to create a federally structured democracy to pursue their lives in peace and freedom. Many were betrayed and died shocking deaths at the hands of Rubin's friends, the Soviet and Spanish communists.

Cora Rubin-Weiss

Samuel's daughter, Cora, took over family control and day-to-day management of the Samuel Rubin Foundation following his death in 1978. Her husband, Peter Weiss, served on the board at the Institute for Policy Studies and pursued a long agenda of Left-wing initiatives through the National Lawyers Guild. There is little personal information in the public domain about Cora, and even less about her brother Reed.

Cora and Reed were "red diaper babies," meaning they were the offspring of active American communists. The term was coined by communists during the 1920s as a criticism of comrades who appeared to use their "birthright" rather than their deeds to move up the ranks of the clandestine movement.

Autobiographical profiles of forty-six red diaper babies, particularly the children of Jewish immigrants from Russia and Central Europe from the late nineteenth century to about 1920, are contained in a 1998 book edited by Judy Kaplan and Linn Shapiro, entitled *Red Diapers: Growing Up in the Communist Left*.[26] By carefully sifting forty-six childhood stories in the book for common themes, this writer found it possible to create a composite profile that characterized this first cohort of "red diaper babies." We have no way of knowing how closely these themes, when integrated into a common profile, may reflect Cora Weiss' experience as a "red diaper" youth nor her attitude about today's world. But several stories that recur in the brief autobiographies are so strong and repeated so many times by those sharing their individual experiences that they may come very close to helping us understand Cora's contemporary world view and penchant for radicalism.

Many of the "red diaper" children remember their parent's passion for Marxism-Leninism and their dedication to restructure

American society to be more like what they believed existed in the Soviet Union. Their mothers and fathers were seen as working for "a better world," and they tended to keep their children close in order to protect them from American culture as much as possible. As children, the "red diapers" remembered the secrecy and need to ensure they did not reveal their parents' life on the Left. Many were conflicted by trying to present a "normal" front, while always being fearful of being discovered and ostracized by friends and teachers. Parents were often too busy with their fierce devotion to the communist cause to deal with the insecurities their children experienced at public schools. Many "red diapers" were lonely and learned to lie at an early age about their parents' activities. Some remained seated during the recitation of the Pledge of Allegiance in school, while others stood and remained mute. They withstood pressures from their peers and teachers. When their teachers said the Soviet Union wanted to destroy the United States, many of the "red diapers" learned to bite their tongues to avoid a response that could expose or endanger their parents. Many found the FBI to be very scary, especially when arrests of people known to them occurred. They were aware of government surveillance and feared most an inadvertent betrayal of their parents.

The experiences of the "red diapers" were not always gloomy and grim. "As children," the "Red Diaper" editors Judy Kaplan and Linn Shapiro pointed out, "most red diaper babies learned that millions of people around the globe shared our aspirations for socialism, for a more participatory democracy and a more just distribution of societal resources."[27] Indeed, in testimonial after testimonial, the forty-six writers in *Red Diapers* expressed the "privilege" of growing up as members of the communist movement. The political values of their mothers and fathers were passed on through an informal process of listening to what was going on around them as their parents supported the communist cause. Many played with their friends at Communist Party functions. Most participated in some aspect of the formal process of being a member of the Pioneers, Youth Communist League, and the Communist Party, USA.

Typically, the "red diapers" were proud of their parents and the devotion they showed toward a cause much greater than themselves. In adulthood, several "red diapers" said that they felt lucky to have been raised in communist families. Others said that they would not trade the experience for anything. Most were well aware that they were imbued with the same passion and social vision about ending the class system that had motivated their parents.

With this broad composite of the "red diapers," it should not be surprising that one of their number, Cora Weiss, has been railing against the United States and its policies all of her life. When her father died in 1978, Cora stepped in and carried the family's red banner to ever greater heights of radical causes and activities. The Rubin Foundation became the "sun" dominating an ever expanding solar system of individuals and organizations under the radical Left influence of progressivism-socialism-marxism.

Cora exploded onto the American public scene when she and husband Peter visited Hanoi in 1969 during the height of the war in Vietnam. Cora Weiss was an active leader of the Women's Strike for Peace, a pro-Hanoi organization, according to a congressional panel, and it enjoyed full support of the Communist Party, USA.[28] Upon her return from North Vietnam, she denied that Americans held as prisoners-of-war were mistreated. On one of her visits to Hanoi, Mrs. Weiss met with American POWs and reported their personal comments that they had shared with her to their North Vietnamese captors. So informed, the prisoners were tortured after she had left for their "wayward attitude."[29]

Cora Weiss was very busy in subsequent days with frequent meetings with communist officials in Hanoi and Paris. As an anti-Vietnam War leader, she directed the People's Coalition for Peace and Justice and the Committee for Liaison With Families of

Servicemen Detained in North Vietnam. The latter group was approved by the communist government in North Vietnam to serve as a conduit for contacts between American POWs and their families. "Weiss attempted to coerce POW families to make pro-communist propaganda by promising them contact with their loved ones in Hanoi," Michael Tremoglie reminded us. "None of the families accepted the arrangement."[30]

In addition, Cora did her very best to convince Americans that the prisoners-of-war were not being abused or tortured. But the POW's testimonies following their release, together with the visible scars on their bodies from the teeth-grinding torture by their North Vietnamese captors, belied Cora Weiss' plaintive bleats.[31] In addition, the victorious North Vietnamese later executed more than 100,000 political prisoners, created more than a million and a half refugees, and imprisoned more than a million people in the former Republic of Vietnam.

The North Vietnamese were admitted to the UN in September 1977, which became a forum for Cora's giddy display of her lack of humanity. Ignoring Hanoi's trampling of human rights, Hanoi's blatant torture of American POWs it held captive, summary executions, and re-education camps in South Vietnam for millions of southerners (often incarcerated for more than a decade), Cora Weiss shouted to the Vietnamese delegation "Welcome in the name of the American people." Cheering by the assembled radical Leftists continued while the four-member North Vietnamese delegation moved to the stage. One of them, Ngo Dien, read a speech which excoriated what he called U.S. "imperialism." Always careful to make a distinction between the American people (good) and American government (bad), Dien said: "From such a long distance the American imperialists send [sic] a half a million troops to wage a bloody colonial war," he declared in English. "Yet no enmity exists between the Vietnamese and American people."[32]

Cora continued her support for the North Vietnamese communists through the end of the war in 1975 and afterward. She was active through the end of the 1970s in channeling material aid to Hanoi through the Church World Service of the Left-wing National Council of Churches. Once the North Vietnamese conquered South Vietnam, Weiss founded and served on the Interim Committee of Friendshipment, an organization established to send material aid to Hanoi and raise the issue of opposition to the U.S. embargo. After several years with Church World Service, Cora Weiss moved her focus to the Riverside Church—whose senior minister Reverend William Sloan Coffin was an anti-Vietnam War activist—where she had been selected to direct the Riverside's newly established Disarmament Program.[33]

William Sloan Coffin, under what can be termed only as being questionable circumstances, was elected senior minister in the summer of 1977. A long-time good friend of Cora Weiss, Coffin may have benefitted from some of Cora's behind the scene influence. Whether by chance or design, a Soviet front group, the World Peace Council, was just beginning its peace campaign in the West. As soon as Coffin placed his new nameplate on his desk, he invited Cora into the Christian sanctuary.

Officially launched in May 1978, the keys to the Riverside Church World Disarmament Program were handed to Cora Weiss. Rather than a celebration of Judeo-Christian partnership, the arrangement was more a pact with the devil. Coffin and Weiss had a close bond, owing to their activism against the Vietnam War, travels to North Vietnam, and work together at major activist organizations. For Coffin, one sin that preoccupied him most was anti-communism. This position was consistent with Coffin's view that "communism is a page torn out of the Bible." Three IPS guests attended the World Disarmament Program inaugural at Riverside Church: Peter Weiss, Marcus Raskin, and Richard Barnet. Raskin, in good form, emphasized that "relating morality to politics" as being a good agenda for churches to lead the way.

Coffin and Cora Weiss also invited two members of the Soviet Embassy—Yuri Karpralov and Sergy Paramonov. Both men were identified as being KGB officers. Karpralov, according to well known expert John Barron, was always seeking Americans who would communicate Soviet foreign policies and views as their own.[34] The December 1978 soiree at Riverside Church must have gone well for the Soviets, since they became regulars at public events to cultivate their support. Soon, Soviet correspondents began to show up, many of whom doubtlessly had important espionage and disinformation agendas. This became a cozy arrangement for the Soviets. In September 1983, a Soviet delegation—Sergey Plekhov and Vasiliy Vlanikhin—that had entered the United States to attend a UN conference was picked up by a man and a woman in a car registered to Peter Weiss. Both men were under FBI surveillance.[35]

In between playing footsy with the Soviets, Cora took on the task of destroying the common American perceptions of the Soviet threat. Her position at Riverside Church gave her an open forum for making the case that the alleged Soviet threat was little more than a "hereditary disease." By the end of 1979, some 156 Left-wing disarmament conferences had been held across the country. But trends have a way of triggering counter-trends, even in the halls of faith-based institutions like the Riverside Church. Those members of the church who were committed against the arms race reported back to their congregations. IPS and Riverside shared "vanguard" responsibilities, while the disarmament program had begun to draw a lot of attention, especially since Cora Weiss' office budget went from $15,000 in 1978 to $148,000 in 1984. Some long-time members of the church began to question Coffin's and Weiss' activities. The deacons of the church backed Coffin and Weiss against charges raised against them.[36]

Meanwhile, the disarmament program began to bring in prominent speakers, such as Prime Minister Olaf Palme of Sweden, Archbishop Helder Camara of Brazil, and former communist party member, E. P. Thompson. European and American peace movements also participated in the program. Celebrities followed in 1983, including Bianca Jagger and the ambassadors from the Soviet Union and Nicaragua.[37]

Cora Weiss was a member of a U.S. delegation that were the guests of the Sandinista government in Nicaragua in 1984. Meanwhile, Coffin was banging the pulpit to "Love your enemies. . . . Love means positive Christianity, not negative anticommunism."[38] A Moravian bishop from Nicaragua, supposedly a Miskito Indian warring against the Sandinistas but in reality one of their supporters, also addressed the activists gathered at the Riverside Church.

Solidarity with progressivism-socialism-marxism has been an important part of the IPS culture since its inception. This became quite clear in 1985. Alexandra (Sandy) Pollack, a member of the Communist Party, USA, and U.S. Peace Council, an arm of an important Soviet front, the World Peace Council, met a tragic death on January 19, 1985, when her Cubana Airline flight crashed enroute to Managua. Although she was an avowed atheist, a memorial service was held for her at Riverside Church two weeks later. Gathered were some 600 party members, foreign diplomats, and others. Reverend Coffin said "she may not have believed in God, but God believed in Sandy." Isabel Letelier, wife of Orlando Letelier who had met his death by a car bomb in Washington, D.C., said "as Latin Americanists we know she will always be alive in our struggles." Henry Winton, Communist Party, USA, national chairman, said "Sandy . . . drank from the fountain of Marxism-Leninism, and was able to apply this science to everything she did." Johnetta Cole, a member of Moscow's World Peace Council said that Sandy "as an internationalist, so it shouldn't surprise us that her life reached beyond us." A number of Soviets were present, though adopting a low profile.[39]

The Sandinista head-of-state Daniel Ortega visited New York to address the UN in November 1985 and took time to visit the Riverside Church where Coffin and Weiss had organized a reception for him. Addressing the assembled group, Ortega said that "Ronald Reagan's U.N.-day speech yesterday was incompatible with the principles of International law." The audience registered its full approval. Ortega concluded by shouting "we cannot afford to forget about what happened in Chile." This topic—the military coup against Chile's communist president Salvadore Allende on September 11, 1973—is close to the heart of IPS, a theme returned to time and again.[40]

Cora Weiss maintained close alliances with religious groups working on peace issues and Nicaragua, including the World Council of Churches and the Interfaith Council; she integrated these interests with women's issues, including the August 1995 conference on women in Beijing. In May 1999, Cora, with the able assistance of husband Peter Weiss, created a multinational non-governmental organization, the Hague Appeal of Peace. More than 10,000 activists, government officials, and community leaders from more than a hundred countries attended the five day conference at the Hague. This new transnational organization, born amidst a great deal of hoopla, included some four hundred panels, workshops, and roundtables that focused on identifying the best mechanisms for abolishing war and creating a culture of peace in the twenty-first century.

Since many of the initiatives credited to the Hague Appeal of Peace are integrated with the United Nations, they will be discussed in Chapter 11—A World Without Borders. Suffice it to say for the present, Cora had launched a massive project that has already made tell-tale inroads into international institutions. In an address to peace educators in Hamburg, Germany, in June 2003, Cora Weiss defined the challenge ahead for the listeners and the Hague Appeal for Peace itself: "Now we must *educate people* [a codeword for propaganda and disinformation] to put the institution of war on the table for de-legitimation, for abolition, because the lethality of today's weapons, of nuclear weapons, is such that this precious little planet and its mostly wonderful people can not afford war any more."[41]

Peter Weiss

Officer of the Samuel Rubin Foundation, chairman of the board of the Institute for Policy Studies, and board member at the Transnational Institute, Peter has been a principal architect of the Rubin imperium and leader of its constellation of radical litigation strategic partners for more than four decades.[42]

Born in Vienna, Austria in 1925, Peter Weiss, a lawyer, specializes in international law. In the 1960s, he became a cooperating lawyer and vice president of the Center for Constitutional Rights (CCR). For years in the 1960s and early 1970s, he was an officer of the New York chapter of the National Lawyers Guild (NLG), an organization of Communist and leftist lawyers originally set up in the 1938 with the assistance of the Comintern and which remains to this day affiliated with a former Soviet and now Russian front—the International Association of Democratic Lawyers (IADL) whose Soviet roots go back to 1946. Weiss' other international work included an attempt to assist the radical West German lawyer Kurt Grönewold, who was arrested in 1974 and eventually convicted of running a communications network between jailed terrorists of the Red Army Faction and their comrades who were still at large. In 1977, Weiss led a delegation to the Philippines to publicize reports of government torture of political prisoners that was sponsored by two fronts for the Communist Party of the Philippines, Friends of the Filipino People, and the Anti-Martial Law Coalition.

Peter Weiss has a long public record of Left-wing activism. In 1974, he became a member of the advisory committee of the Center for National Security Studies (CNSS), an organization whose founders were drawn from IPS, the National Lawyers Guild, and the self-proclaimed pro-Castro "intelligence arm of the New Left," the North American Congress on Latin America (NACLA).

In addition to the National Lawyers Guild, Peter served in the 1960s and early 1970s as a member of the national council of another Communist-controlled organization, the National Emergency Civil Liberties Committee (NECLC).[43] I. F. Stone decided to create an activist committee that would prod the American Civil Liberties Union and liberal lawyers to take on cases involving current or former communists. He named the group the National Emergency Civil Liberties Committee. Irving Kristol of the American Committee for Cultural Freedom immediately exposed NECLC as a communist front.[44] Members of NLG that directed the NECLC, included William Kuntsler, Peter Weiss, and Leonard Boudin and his partner Victor Rabinowitz.

During the late 1960s and through the 1970s, Peter Weiss was also active with the American Committee on Africa (ACOA), then the principal support organization for the communist-controlled African National Congress, which was waging a campaign of sabotage and terrorism to overthrow the whites-only government of South Africa. In 1979, he signed a letter from the Southern Africa Working Group urging the Carter administration to withhold recognizing the moderate black-majority government of Bishop Abel Muzorewa. ACOA was the first group to send ANC members to the United States to meet with black activists. IPS sponsored Ruth First in 1980, a communist party member of the ANC, to take part in one of its seminars. Ruth First was also the spouse of the ANC military's Joseph Slovo, second in charge of Soviet KGB operations aimed at destabilizing the South African government.[45]

In 1976, at the time of his assassination by car bomb in Washington, D.C., the director of TNI, Orlando Letelier, a former high official of the *Unidad Popular* [Popular Unity] Marxist coalition government of Chile, was transformed into a martyr of the Left. Peter Weiss continued his solidarity work for the Chilean left. Peter Weiss also was a "hidden hand" behind the international campaign to bring former Chilean president, General Augusto Pinochet, to trial as a war criminal. In the *Covert Action Quarterly*, Weiss contributed a full-page article entitled "Punishing Pinochet," which outlined how Spanish judges were persuaded that they had jurisdiction over events that had occurred over some twenty-three years earlier in Chile. The *Covert Action* reports noted that Peter Weiss was vice president of the Center for Constitutional Rights, which represented the family of Charles Horman, a young American who died in Chile during the coup. The Horman family's lawsuit against Henry Kissinger and other high officials of the U.S. government was used primarily by the Center to obtain, through the discovery process, classified U.S. government documents on Chile, U.S. policy, and diplomatic and intelligence reports on events in the country's political leaders, anti-Marxist Chilean parties, and Chile's military. The CCR charged that Washington's anti-Communist foreign policies regarding the *Unidad Popular* government made the United States responsible for the deaths of Allende supporters during the coup.

Weiss and other prominent and influential members of the NLG, including Martin Popper, a member of the Communist Party, USA, who helped found both the National Lawyers Guild in 1938 and the International Association of Democratic Lawyers in 1946, founded the Lawyers Committee on Nuclear Policy (LCNP) in 1981. The LCNP's officers and "consultative council" were packed with IADL and NLG activists, including IPS's Richard Barnet. In August 1987, in association with the Soviet Lawyers Association, the LCNP hosted the founding of the International Lawyers Against Nuclear Arms (ILANA), at a conference financed in part by the Samuel Rubin Foundation.[46] The organization was created specifically to be in direct parallel with the International Physicians for the Prevention of Nuclear War (IPPNW), which had been co-founded by Soviet officials and hard-left U.S. physicians active in disarmament campaigns since the early 1960s.[47]

The organizations Peter Weiss was affiliated with also made up an interlocking directorate of an anti-intelligence lobby, which included the NLG, Center for Constitutional Rights (led by William Kuntsler), NECLC, the ACLU, and Committee for Public Justice. Although labeled a Communist Party front in the early 1950s, the full extent of NECLC's role was unknown to the public until the VENONA project was released in the 1990s. Out of public sight, the top-secret VENONA Project conducted by American intelligence was decoding Soviet espionage cables. As early as 1948, the deciphered cables revealed that "the Soviets had recruited spies in virtually every major American government agency of military or diplomatic importance." Hundreds of Americans, many of whom were members of the American Communist Party, were targeted by Soviet espionage officers. In all, the decoded cables by VENONA revealed "349 citizens, immigrants, and permanent residents of the United States who had had a covert relationship with Soviet intelligence agencies."[48]

Marcus Raskin and Richard Barnet

IPS was founded in 1963 by Marcus Raskin and Richard Barnet, former White House and State Department aides.[49] In order to make a case for shifting national priorities from the military-industrial complex to social programs, Richard Barnet grossly understated the Cold War nuclear and conventional threats posed against the United States and its allies and peddled paper-thin ideas for arms control that would entail taking great risks. Barnet's wishful-thinking and under-the-table manipulations were combined in his disassembly of the defense budget. In the end, based on his false assumptions, Barnet discovered the "Economy of Death" could be substantially cut back to provide for the "Economy of Life." All that was missing from his analysis about the real Soviet nuclear threat was some kind of reasoned assurance that enough Americans would still alive to enjoy his balmy predictions.[50] Nevertheless, as Richard Barnet put it in 1970, "the central task of American society is to free ourselves from the Economy of Death."[51] Missing, however, was a rational blueprint for dealing with the nuclear threat posed by the Soviet Union against the United States and its allies.

With the formation of the IPS, Raskin and Barnet set about organizing networks of progressive contacts not only in the U.S., including Capitol Hill and state and local governments, but also worldwide in many governments, executive branch agencies, and among leading academics. IPS placed its contacts in seminars with disarmament leaders and revolutionary activists who supported Fidel Castro's government in Cuba and various Third World national liberation movements backed by the Soviet Union. Together, they worked out alternative governmental policies for disarmament, termination of military alliances, and nonintervention against Soviet aggression carried out through surrogates. By 1978, the IPS had so penetrated Washington's circles of Left-wing legislators, congressional aides, government agencies, academics, and the media that the IPS not only won stunning victories but also attracted fresh recruits.

The FBI produced thousands of documents on IPS's activities. Some are available to the public through the Freedom of Information Act. The FBI withheld hundreds of documents. The documents collected by the FBI described IPS as a Washington-based "Think Factory," which "helped train extremists who incite violence in the United States and whose educational research serves as a cover for intrigue and political agitation" (FBI file 175-398) or "the Rand Corporation of the Left," and "IPS apparently exercises considerable influence in the New Left Movement and may have as its goal the destruction of the United States Government." In this context, the mainstream media described the IPS in the 1970s and 1980s as follows: *Wall Street Journal*—"A funnel for disinformation," *Forbes*—"A radical Washington propaganda mill," *National Review*—"The perfect intellectual front for Soviet activities which would be resisted if they were to originate openly from the KGB."

From the beginning, IPS targeted NATO, the Defense Department, defense contractors, arms manufacturing companies, and the intelligence agencies for its propaganda and agitation. One of the first Rubin Imperium projects was to undermine and hollow out organizations that could expose their double agenda, namely the intelligence agencies. The Rubin network did not mind being a powerful tool for the Soviet KGB, East German Stasi, and Cuban DGI. Phillip Agee, a turncoat CIA intelligence officer, was a paid agent for Cuba's intelligence agency, the DGI. Another case was Klaas de Jonge, a Dutch communist and anti-apartheid activist who carried land mines for the African National Congress, turned out to be trained by the notorious East German Stasi. The most well known case is Orlando Letelier, former head of the Transnational Institute in Amsterdam. At the time of his murder in 1976 he carried documents showing that he was being paid by the Soviet-controlled Cuban intelligence. The DGI money was brought clandestinely to Washington, D.C., from Havana via the Cuban diplomatic pouch.

"Act Globally, Learn Locally" opens the catalogue to the IPS school house in Washington, D.C. The Social Action and Leadership School for Activists (SALSA) serves as a Left-wing center with "a skills training program that strengthens community activism and fosters engaged citizenship, a forum for discussion and development of progressive issues and agendas, [and] a unique networking opportunity to social change activists." The winter 2001 schedule, for example, offered courses in the ABCs for creating non-profit organizations, leadership and management, developing a media strategy, grant writing, accounting and internal controls, "cultivating major donors," lobbying, grassroots organizing, and a few policy issues. The idea is to equip the student with new skills and assist in refining their thinking in advancing the progressive cause.[52]

Marcus G. Raskin, co-founder of the Institute for Policy Studies, is the intellectual leader of those dedicated to restructuring American life and institutions in preparation for the global civil society that lies ahead. Raskin tells us that he began his "political and intellectual life as a liberal," which was reinforced during his growing years by what he called the "sewer socialism" of Milwaukee, Wisconsin. An advisor to Congressman Robert Kastenmeier in 1959, Raskin prepared a political screed for twelve "ultra-liberal" members of the U.S. House of Representatives. *The Liberal Papers* were to be used to move the Democratic Party back on a track that would simultaneously finish the New Deal program which had been left undone by President Truman. At the same time, the Papers would correct the turn taken by liberals to support national security initiatives during the Cold War of the 1950s. The latter area was centered on a host of unilateral disarmament and diplomatic disengagement areas that would leave the United States and its allies exposed to Soviet nuclear forces, while protected by the Raskin's "liberal dream" that the Kremlin would respond in pacific ways.[53]

The Liberal Papers, published in 1962, argued that U.S. Cold War foreign policies were responsible for destroying the domestic political tasks defined by the New Deal program. In order to get back to the liberal pathway laid out by the New Deal program, therefore, the U.S. had to modify its Cold War foreign policies significantly. Raskin's problem, however, is that there was no indication that the Kremlin had any other objective, as Soviet chief Nikita Khrushchev said at the time, than "to bury" the United States—and he had the nuclear weapons to do so. Hence, the U.S. needed to maintain a strong nuclear deterrent and the sweet dreams

of the New Deal program became just that: a dream held by
pathetic, baggy-pants liberals who looked at reality and said in a
childlike manner: "I don't want it [their socialist fantasy] to be
over." Marcus Raskin would have been well advised to "gird up his
loins" as President Teddy Roosevelt was fond of saying, or playing
children's games in what he called the "sewer socialism" of
Milwaukee. He did neither. He got angry. He refused to support the
U.S. government's fight for survival during the Cold War. "The
Papers," Francis X. Gannon observed in 1969, "were devoted
exclusively to foreign policy and reflected abject appeasement with
Communist powers, extravagant extensions of foreign 'aid'
programs, reckless disarmament proposals and groveling obeisance
to the United Nations."[54] It was "capitalist" interests growing in
the "national security state" as he and his ilk would define the
United States. Two decades later, when journalist John Train asked
a well-known columnist about what motivated Marcus Raskin, he
responded: "I know him well, but I don't know the answer to that
question. I guess he just hates America."[55]

In 1961, Raskin met another malcontent, Richard Barnet, at a
White House-Department of State meeting in preparation for a
disarmament conference in Geneva. Both men said that from the
time their eyes first met, they knew they were kindred spirits.
Raskin was at the meeting representing McGeorge Bundy, a
member of a special staff of the National Security Council. Barnet
was supporting John J. McCloy, head of the State Department's
disarmament office. According to stories attributed to Barnet and
Raskin over the years, they recognized each other's alienation and
hostility toward the American brain trust gathered for the meeting:
Dean Rusk, Paul Nitze, John McCloy, and a "long row of
generals." These two "aides," given the honor to serve their
country in protecting itself against hostile, dangerous powers, were
not up to the task. In the end, they saw themselves superior to the
senior officials for whom they worked and held them "in

contempt." A wise investigative journalist for many years, John Rees, noted that "the ancient Chinese military strategist Sun Tzu made note of such arrogant junior officials almost 2,500 years ago, and suggested that those chafing with resentment are good prospects for recruitment as agents."[56] Those of us having had the privileged to serve the U.S. government during the Cold War were well aware that those of our countrymen who positioned their intellect above others and felt superior to their peers were among the most dangerous people in Washington, D.C. By putting themselves above all others, these ego-driven self-lovers could be enticed to make the wrong decisions for the wrong reasons. In a world of nuclear weapons, such persons posed a threat to all Americans.

Raskin and Barnet stayed with the Kennedy Administration until 1962. By that time they had pretty well lined up the resources need for creation of a "think tank of the Left" to be launched in 1963. Rooted in the unfulfilled program of the New Deal as expressed in the Liberal Papers and a strong dosage of socialism, the IPS core philosophy was centered on two ideas: first, that the bureaucratic process of government smothered fresh political ideas and moral truths to the degree that government became unresponsive and destructive; and, secondly, that universities insisted on keeping social action and social theory distinct, which resulted in false ideals. Hence, IPS was to become a place where no government funds would be taken and where "social theory must be informed by, as well as inform, social action."[57]

Raskin and Barnet brought their own unique world views to the IPS table where they were integrated into cohesive social theory and social action programs. Raskin described the United States as an "imperialist country" made up of four colonies that the poor and young had come to see as their primary enemy. The four colonies imagined by Raskin included the *Violence Colony,* which was most important, for it was the central element that used the university as a terrorizing element of the state. The *Plantation Colony* was said to produce unreal work that fed human wants but did not satisfy needs. Meanwhile, the *Channeling Colony* was really the education system that promoted the passive acceptance of other colonies by the *Dream Colony*. Finally, *Decolonization* was a major goal pursued by Marcus Raskin, Richard Barnet, and their colleagues at IPS. The key to understanding the Institute for Policy Studies has been for many years and remains the dismantling of the national security state, including pulling down America's "militarist economy" and "threats and provocations" posed against other countries. In Raskin's world view, all decisions in a *reconstructed society* will be made face-to-face in local meetings. "In short, the 'Reconstructed Society,'" as Rael Jean Isaac summarizes Raskin's outlook, "is an anarchist-syndicalist federation of autonomous cooperatives. Since present human imperfection is wholly attributable to the colonizing agents, in Raskin's utopia there will be no hierarchy, no coercion, no real organization beyond the local level."[58]

The Institute for Policy Studies uses international subsidiaries, strategic partners and cooperative arrangements to extend its reach directly overseas. The most prominent research centers abroad, however, is its sister organization, the Amsterdam-based Transnational Institute. This close relative is also a "think tank on the Left." Together with IPS, TNI brings together radical labor organizers; leaders of support networks Left-wing activists operating from non-governmental organizations; revolutionary terrorist groups; leaders of the peace and disarmament movements; and radical and "liberal" academics, journalists, foreign officials, politicians, diplomats, intelligence officers, and representatives of parliaments.

Eqbal Ahmad and Susan George

One of the Transnational Institute's most important tasks, from the first day of its creation, was protecting "IPS's respectability by providing a cover for IPS's relations with the international communist movement."[59] Susan George, a long-time fellow of TNI and its director in 2008, organized an IPS dinner in Paris on October 9, 1972, to discuss ideas shared by several European intellectuals about TNI's potential activist agenda. The foremost item on the agenda was the creation of TNI as an overseas extension of IPS. Peter Weiss, Marcus Raskin, and Richard Barnet were present. Among the prominent members of Europe's radical Left was Roland Barthes, Simone de Beauvoir, Claude Bourdet, Michael de Foucault, Andre Gorz, Claude Julien, and Jean Paul Sarte (who wrote an extensive preface for the terrorist Frantz Fanon in his book, *The Wretched of the Earth*). A similar meeting was held at the Café de Paris on London's Regent Street.

TNI was to become one of the Rubin Imperium's most powerful tools. Samuel Rubin pledged $4 million in start-up funding for TNI. Philip Stern, a millionaire Maoist and a trader in real estate, also was a donor. Ed Janss, a philanthropist and underwater photographer in California, sold TNI a large building at the Paulus Potterstraat 20 in Amsterdam. TNI was established there in 1973 and has served ever since as the international arm of IPS.[60] Amsterdam was not only chosen because of its central location in Europe but also because it has an aura of tolerance. In addition, the Dutch government had been closely aligned with Chile's Allende regime and social movement. For the Left, TNI began as an Allende backlash.

Samuel Rubin and the other powers at IPS chose the right person when they tapped Eqbal Ahmad to serve as TNI's first director in 1973. Ahmad combined a superior intellect and record of scholarship in support of Arab extremism with the practical matters of revolutionary warfare and terrorism in the Third World. He held a Ph.D. from Princeton University and had taught at the University of Illinois in Chicago and Cornell University. From 1960 to 1963 he worked with Frantz Fanon, leader of the Algerian

National Liberation Front (NLF), who was known in many circles as the "Che Guevara of the Middle East." Fanon, a self-described "creative extremist," became Ahmad's mentor in the business of revolutionary terrorism or waging an intense killing campaign against ethnic French and Algerians opposed to the Front's terrorist war.[61] Eqbal Ahmad, one can assert with confidence, got a considerable amount of blood on his hands from Fanon's murderous campaign before he served as a member of the Algerian delegation to the peace talks with France at Paris and secured Algeria's independence in 1962.

Eqbal Ahmad's TNI was developed with a strong dedication to the extremist goals and actions of the Palestine Liberation Organization (PLO) and its leader Yassir Arafat. Since some potential funding sources might take exception to the IPS relationship with the PLO and other terror groups, the Middle East Research and Information Project (MERIP) was founded in 1971 as a cover for the Institute's shadow world activities. By 2004, MERIP's *Middle East Report* was being published four times a year from the editorial office in Washington, D.C. It is a "clean" publication with no easily discernable linkage to IPS or TNI. MERIP's "Media Outreach Program" extends progressive-socialist-marxist thinking on the Middle East through a variety of print, radio, and television resources. Fred Halliday, a TNI adviser, is one of the MERIP report's contributing editors.[62] During the Soviet-Afghan War, Fred Halliday was one of the rare Western journalists allowed to enter Afghanistan to report on the war. It was for good reasons that the IPS-TNI fellow Halliday received such special treatment. Following the Soviet's December 1979 invasion, Halliday wrote several articles in MERIP's reports and magazines, *The Nation*, and *New York Times* that rationalized the Kremlin's actions.[63]

Samuel Rubin, daughter Cora Weiss and her husband Peter, and IPS founders Marcus Raskin and Richard Barnet gave Ahmad a full mandate to set up TNI. In early 1973, Ahmad was sent across Europe by IPS on a five week trip to discuss the TNI project with some 200 European thinkers and activists drawn from a wide spectrum of the Left. His discussions included those involved in peace and disarmament issues, solidarity in the Third World between terrorists and "national liberation" movements, women's rights, minority rights, and combating transnational corporations that exploit the resources of Third World countries. The message was clear that TNI's door was open and would stay open to all those involved in the fight against imperialism and for social and economic justice. In a interview in a Dutch newspaper in 1973, Ahmad mentioned that "the new institute will not be comparable with any other Dutch institution. It will concentrate on scientific research and social action. Left. Clear. Internationally known left intellectuals will walk in and out. Everybody," Ahmad said, "who is against imperialism and for social justice, is welcome with us. Communists, Trotskyists. We are not sectarian."[64]

TNI's first major conference on Chile was organized in 1974, following the overthrow of Marxist President Salvador Allende. In the wake of the September 11, 1973 military coup, TNI and IPS built close working relationships with concerned progressives-socialists-marxists. The big issue in the eyes of the extreme Left then and today is that Allende gained the presidency through the ballot box, but, because of his Marxist ideas and programs and friendship with the Soviet Union, he was turned out by the military, allegedly with outside (U.S.) assistance. The 1973 military coup in Chile is seen by IPS extremists as a rehearsal by the ruling corporate capitalism system in the event progressives-socialists-marxists accede to power in the future. Since the radical Left generally follows Antonio Gramsci's counsel to set up a transformational revolution by changing a target society's values over time, the specter of a violent response is very bothersome to them. Hence, the IPS-TNI elite have grasped the coup against Allende for more than thirty years as if the events were a powerful "worry stone" for the radical Left.

By the time Helen Hopps, Marcus Raskin, and Eqbal Ahmad went to the Netherlands in July 1973 to initiate TNI's operations, IPS already had found research fellows in the Netherlands, including Dr. Ernst Utrecht, publicist and Indonesian specialist, and Gerrit Huizer, who taught at the University of Nijmegen on Third World problems. Huizer took care of the IPS people from Washington and coordinated the contacts with several other organizations.

Ahmad organized TNI to serve as a bridge between IPS and revolutionary communists in the Third World. In the end, his bridge-building may have also included those who were to become al-Qaeda Islamists. Ahmad "first met" Osama bin Laden in 1986. Eqbal Ahmad used the phrase "first met" bin Laden—clearly inferring there were meetings with Osama after 1986—in a presentation at the University of Colorado in October 1998. At the time, he was explaining in his unique low-key manner why Osama bin Laden felt "betrayed" by the United States for retaining military forces in Saudi Arabia to patrol the no-fly zones over Iraq *after* the 1991 Gulf War. Ahmad grossly ignored bin Laden's attacks against Americans in a feckless effort to retain some coherence to his faulty line-of-argument. Eqbal Ahmad died on May 11, 1999.

Susan George has been a fellow and intellectual guide of the Transnational Institute since its founding in 1973. She is "one of the intellectual superstars of the antiglobalization movement in Europe and the United States." She also plays a key role as a "thought leader" and activist in the "global days of action" called for by the People's Global Action, the primary coordinator of the Left-wing movement against international financial and trade institutions (e.g., World Bank, World Trade Organization). She also compares the market economy to a "malignant tumor."[65]

In an April 2007 speech to graduates of Spain's *Universidad Nacional de Educacion a Distincia*, a distance learning institution with 180,000 students, she explained TNI's world view and action programs for the future. Since we are "progressives," she said, "our views are usually ahead of their time" and are "necessarily unpopular with many political adversaries." She cited as an example the "far right forces" in the United States encouraging students "to monitor professors they consider too far to the left." She cited David Horowitz's book *The Professors* that unveils the activities of the 101 most dangerous professors in America. "I do not need to remind you," George continued, "that obscurantist forces, often religious, are also at work in Europe."

Susan George explained that at TNI they believe "action is an integral part of our lives as intellectuals"—we call ourselves "scholar-activists." TNI intellectuals research, write, and publish but we also "intervene in public debates," she explained. "We are active in the social movements of our own countries and often internationally as well."[66]

From the start, disarmament was one of TNI's main programs in cooperation with its TNI fellows heading Britain's major anti-nuclear Campaign for Nuclear Disarmament (CND) and European Nuclear Disarmament Organization (END), in Washington, including Michael Klare and Richard Barnett, and an extreme European network. Researchers from the Netherlands, West Germany, England, France, Italy, Spain and Denmark met regularly in Amsterdam at international conferences on such topics as NATO and the Soviet threat. The Swedish research center SIPRI participated in the conferences.

The Transnationals Information Exchange (TIE), established in 1978, is a network of research organizations working on better understanding the strengths and weaknesses of transnational corporations in several European countries. Initially, TIE was created to simply exchange information between research entities. Over time, however, its work became focused more sharply on the discussion between transnational corporations in Europe and the rest of the world, including dialogue between trade unions and other workers' organizations. The main objective was to encourage development of positive and practical alternative strategies within the labor movement in dealing with cross-border industries. The first consultations, for instance, were focused on the auto industry (1979) and telecommunications (1980).

As early as the 1980s, IPS and its Europe-based sister entity, TNI, were beating the drums of Left-wing dogma about transnational corporations and their "vast wealth, power and ability to cross national borders." The TIE's definition of transnational corporation issues expressed twenty-five years ago and the years of data collection and analysis on specific industries are being echoed in the radical Left's anti-globalization campaign early in the twenty-first century. The following mid-1980s quotation, for instance, could have been heard at the 2008 anti-globalization protests in Europe and North America.

The global corporations have devastated communities in the developed countries by shutting down dozens of plants when more profitable investment opportunities appeared elsewhere. As unions have increasingly learned in recent years, strikes against large corporation by workers in one country alone can be rapidly undermined by corporate shifts of capital to workplaces abroad where workers labour at similar levels of productivity for substantially less pay. For the Third World, the growth of global corporations has meant more consumer goods for the rich, but deepening poverty for the majority of people. Nor have the hundreds of billions of dollars lent by large banks translated into development. Instead, many developing countries are suffering the horrors of austerity that accompany massive debts.[67]

Among those credited for their contributions to the above-referenced TIE report were John Cavanagh, then a TNI fellow and now director of IPS, and Susan George, now Director of TNI. Anti-globalization certainly is not a new phenomenon; it has served at the core of international socialism for many years. The TIE, with the active support of TNI and the World Council of Churches and other faith-based organizations, remains at the forefront of the renewal and re-emergence of Marxism in the post-Cold War world.[68]

From the beginning the World Council of Churches has collaborated with TIE and TNI on gaining a better understanding of the advent of transnational corporations and their creation of a global marketplace. From the perspective of the World Council of Churches, a hard Left entity with a Soviet KGB agent on its governing Board, TIE "was a group of European centers of Christian inspiration who look attentively at what TNC's [transnational corporations] are doing in Western Europe, and the consequences of this action."[69] In a letter to the World Council of Churches supporting organizations in March 1982, Julio de Santa Ana wrote: "TIE has given evidence of being in solidarity with victims of TNCs." Based on that premise, de Santa Ana argued that European churches "should be given the opportunity" to support the TIE program of investigating the actions of the transnational corporations.[70]

The Transnational Institute adapted to the post-Cold War world by reorganizing its study and activist agendas in the Third World. Three strands of thought, when taken together, were expected to identify obstacles to social and economic justice; uncover causes of insecurity, conflict, and war; and develop new ideas of political economy that will change the terms of debate on the interaction of the natural environment and the economy.[71] These three strands of thought and action at TNI became central aspects on the international radical Left's agenda guiding the anti-globalization movement that began with the Zapatista challenge to the government of Mexico on January 1, 1994, the first day of the North American Free Trade Agreement. The international Left drew a line in Mexico and then burst into the headlines in Seattle during the December 1999 protest against the World Trade Organization.

While TNI was reorienting itself for future challenges in the post-Cold War, one of its longstanding fellows, Joel Rocamora, faced a different kind of problem. He had guided TNI's support for radical leftists in the Philippines for many years. But he sent a letter to "Dear Friends" on TNI letterhead on October 8, 1992, explaining a dilemma he faced. "Yesterday . . . I received my walking papers. After having devoted over twenty years of my life to the revolutionary struggle as a member of the Communist Party of the Philippines, I have just been expelled from the organization. . . . My expulsion appears to be part of a wide-scale Stalinist purge that the Party leadership has decided to launch under its so-called 'rectification' campaign. . . ."[72] Incidentally, TNI's Philippine Project received a core grant of $130,000 annually from the Samuel Rubin Foundation for many years and grants from the European Community of around $40,000 to $50,000.

IPS and TNI assumed central roles in the large anti-globalization protests in 1999. Protests in Europe and North America against "neoliberalism" grew in size and scope over time and eventually the radical organizers found themselves intertwined with the anti-war movement against the post-September 11 U.S. military operations in Afghanistan and Iraq.

The fellows of the Transnational Institute are among the best and brightest of those on the revolutionary Left. One of those persons is Susan George. She is deeply involved in the "movement for global justice," the anti-globalization project, and George previously served as the vice president of ATTAC-France, a Paris-based "Association for the Taxation of Financial Transactions to Aid Citizens," that still serves as a thought center for the World Social Forum.[73] During the latter days of the Soviet Union, Susan George reportedly met with Mikhail Gorbachev several times in Moscow. Together with other

Left-wing organizations under TNI's guidance, the Western participants strongly urged the Soviet leader to focus on environmental issues as a means of slowing U.S. armament programs and economic growth. The idea was to help Moscow during its economic and political restructuring in the days just ahead.

Other Core IPS and TNI Players

John Cavanagh

He has been one of Cora Weiss' most important field soldiers for many years. While working as an international economist with the UN Conference on Trade and Development (UNCTAD) and the World Health Organization in Geneva in the early 1980s, he kept close contact with the Weiss network. In a January 1982 letter to Jeroen Pijnenburg of TNI's Transnationals Information Exchange (TIE), Cavanagh feathered his future employment nest by volunteering his services in gathering UNCTAD documents needed for TIE's radical economic research and shipping them to Pijnenburg. A year later, John Cavanagh was an IPS fellow and a member of the board of advisers for *CounterSpy*, CIA defector Philip Agee's magazine that exposed American and British undercover agents. At least one U.S. intelligence officer was murdered, possibly from the Agee-Cavanagh exposure, and many others were placed in jeopardy.[74]

Cavanagh's talents were recognized early and he moved quickly up the IPS ladder to become Director of the Institute. John Cavanagh's single most important activity as Director was the caring for and feeding of seventy-plus members of the Congressional Progressive Caucus. The Caucus, whose members served in important positions in the U.S. House of Representatives, pursued an agenda that fit quite comfortably with the IPS goal of restructuring U.S. society along progressive-socialist-marxist lines. All but Senator Bernard Sanders, a declared socialist from Vermont, are Democrats.

John Cavanagh performed many other high profile projects and tasks serving as Director of IPS, but his first love for many years has been the "rise of corporate global power." Here he could get his teeth into the anti-people monster he sees as having been unleashed upon the world by greedy capitalists. Cavanagh's primary concern has been in producing propaganda campaigns against transnational corporations. As is the case with many progressives-socialists-marxists, truth is the first casualty in their heavily slanted "analyses" specifically designed to promote key propaganda points.

Nowhere is Cavanagh's hatred of corporations more evident than in *Meeting the Corporate Challenge*, a 1985 ideologically-motivated, progressive-socialist-marxist handbook against these capitalist profit-makers. The Transnational Information Exchange published the book and John Cavanagh served as the lead editor of the project. The Institute for Policy Studies, said by many to be the international driving force of the anti-corporate movement, combines the resources of its own Transnational Resource and Action Center (TRAC) with its overseas arm, the Transnational Institute.[75]

The IPS propaganda factories concerning the operations of trans-national corporations include Corporate Watch (CorpWatch), a subsidiary of TRAC. The Data Center—a spin-off from the Students for a Democratic Society—is listed as a Corporate Watch affiliate. Ralph Nader's *Multinational Monitor* is also listed. Other progressive-socialist-marxist organizations with links to TRAC and CorpWatch include the Rainforest Action Network, Sweatshop Watch, and the Sierra Club.[76] For Cavanagh and others at TRAC and CorpWatch, the root of all evil lies in the capitalist world, which is driven by profit-salivating multinational corporations. The "corporate encirclement of the planet is the inevitable result of the ongoing globalization process: transnational corporations weave global girdling webs of production, commerce, profit-driven culture, and finance." These economic units face little or no opposition as wealth is concentrated in fewer and fewer hands.

Cavanagh and his merry band of like-minded progressives-socialists-marxists argue that the transnational corporations are following a "neoliberal" economic pathway that exploits the absence of democratic systems of global governance.[77]

Saul Landau

"Saul Landau has always been a passionate patriot of the highest order," or at least former senator and presidential candidate George McGovern says so.[78] On the other hand, former communist Ronald Radosh believes that after the 1959 Cuba Revolution "Saul would become perhaps America's most ardent Castro admirer."[79] David Horowitz says that "Landau had volunteered himself as an agent of the Castro regime."[80]

Saul Landau has been rumbling around IPS and TNI for decades. It seems that others have worked hard to keep him occupied and employed. He has a flashy temper, judging from some of his interchanges with IPS-TNI insiders. His connection is perhaps solidified by the fact that he and Cora Weiss attended the University of Wisconsin—Madison at the same time. He filled in as head of TNI after Orlando Letelier was assassinated in 1976.[81]

Saul Landau had a bad day on September 21, 1976. Not only did he lose his colleagues Orlando Letelier and his aide Ronni Karpen Moffitt who were assassinated by car-bomb in downtown Washington, D.C., but the blast and fire from the explosion that killed them instantly did not destroy Letelier's briefcase. The briefcase was stuffed with documents linking Letelier at the height of the Cold War with the Soviet clandestine intelligence service, KGB, and the KGB-controlled Cuban intelligence, the DGI. Orlando Letelier, head of the IPS overseas arm TNI had been working for the KGB and DGI for more than a decade. In addition, Letelier was hand-carrying a letter from Saul Landau for Pablo Armando Fernandez, head of Cuba's intelligence service, the DGI.[82] Landau's letter to Fidel's intelligence chief discussed his "Jamaica work" and was accompanied with articles and a film supporting the pro-Castro Manley government. Landau also wrote:

> I think . . . that the time has come to dedicate myself to . . . making propaganda for American socialism. It is still a forbidden word here, but eventually someone, or some group of people will have to put it together with a serious political movement. We cannot any longer just help out third world movements and revolutions, although obviously we shouldn't turn our backs on them, but get down to the more difficult job of bringing the message home.[83]

In 2008, co-directors Robert Borosage and Roger Hickey did just that: they turned the progressive-socialist-marxist Campaign for America's Future into "a serious political movement" guiding Barack Obama's run for the White House. This is also Saul Landau's propaganda dream come true.

Orlando Letelier

Chilean President Salvador Allende fell into popular disfavor almost immediately after his election in 1970 (he received only 36 percent of the vote). Price fixing, nationalization of industry, and other socialist measures threatened to destroy the country's economic base and triggered a severe recession and inflation. Allende's efforts to gag the opposition press in 1973 was declared illegal by the Chilean Supreme Court, while the country's Chamber of Deputies condemned Allende's effort to impose a totalitarian governing order on the Chile. During his tenure, President Allende welcomed Cuban assistance to establish a Soviet-style intelligence apparatus, including informers on each block. When the regime was toppled by the military forces on September 11, 1973, Letelier had become the Minister of Defense and was arrested. Released after a year, Letelier went to Caracas where Saul Landau telephoned and offered him a fellowship at IPS.

The IPS-TNI connection with Fidel Castro's intelligence service, the DGI, is most fully exposed by S. Steven Powell in his 1987 book *Covert Cadre* and secondarily by James L. Tyson in *Target America*. The documentation of this long suspected linkage, and other important intelligence relationships, entered the public domain in a rather peculiar way. Orlando Letelier, a member of the Chilean Socialist Party in exile and director of TNI, was assassinated in Washington, D.C., by a car bomb that exploded while he was en route to the Institute for Policy Studies on the morning of September 21, 1976. The explosion killed Letelier and an aide, Ronni Karpen Moffitt, and injured her husband. Letelier's briefcase, however, was recovered from the damaged vehicle. The papers in the briefcase were photocopied by the FBI as a part of their investigation before the originals were returned to his wife, Isabel Letelier. Meanwhile, Saul Landau and others cleaned out Orlando's files at his IPS office ostensibly to eliminate the chance that they could be used to compromise the resistance inside Chile.[84]

S. Steven Powell's *Covert Cadre* provided his countrymen a needed insight into the operations and methods of the Institute for Policy Studies. He concluded his case study of Orlando Letelier with a telling Statement: "The Case of Orlando Letelier provided hard evidence of the connection between Cuba and the IPS . . . Letelier worked as an agent of influence under the Cuban DGI while directing IPS's Transnational Institute."[85]

Philip Agee

Forced to resign from the CIA in1968 for boozing and making boorish moves on the wives of American embassy personnel, Philip Agee refused a return ticket from Latin America to the United States. His whereabouts for the next five years remained ambiguous, but he did make five trips to Cuba, one of which lasted for six months, to conduct research for his expose of the CIA. Vassily Semenov, chief KGB offer who held oversight responsibility over the Cuban intelligence service, the DGI, took a great interest in Agee's book, *Inside the Company: A CIA Diary*. In the book, Agee recognized the Cuban Communist Party, Michael Locker of the North American Congress on Latin America (NACLA), Nichole Szulc, and John Gerassi.

As S. Stephen Powell tells the story in *Covert Cadre*, Agee racked-up an impressive score of disinformation successes by spoon-feeding U.S. journalists. In February 1981, Agee issued a critique of a State Department white paper on El Salvador, especially its exposure of arms transfers from the Soviet Union and its East European allies. Step one of the disinformation plan was placing Agee's "independent analysis" in *CounterSpy* and the *Covert Action Information Bulletin* to attract the attention of Western journalists. Step two was use of the "alternative media" (Left-wing), including such propaganda organs as *Mother Jones, Village Voice, The Nation,* and *The Progressive.* This technique is similar to running a "chum line" to give the fish just enough to trigger their taste buds. Third, the big time "trolling" began and for Agee it was not long before he started landing some very big fish. The first was the *Wall Street Journal*'s Jonathan Kwitney followed by Robert Kaiser at the *Washington Post.* Both ran as page-one stories. The "jail break was on" as America's journalists stormed to gates to gather more disinformation from other Agee outlets.[86] Rael Jean Isaac and Erich Isaac state the case very simply: "Journalists are ready to believe the most improbable charges against institutions they distrust."[87] As Agee said, "*Washington Post* reporters are among the large number of working journalists from virtually all the major print and electronic media in the country who call upon us daily for help, research, information, and of all things, names of intelligence operators in connection with articles they are writing."[88] Agee died in Havana on January 7, 2008.

7

RUBIN IMPERIUM—
CENTERS OF GRAVITY

THE LEADERS OF THE Institute for Policy Studies and Transnational Institute have taken bold steps toward turning intellectuals, journalists, and politicians into supporters of cultural Marxism. Together, these Leftist professors, reporters, and elected officials have stolen the nation's history and other important elements of culture from the American people. American public schools and universities, the nuclear family, and God remain on their collective hit list.

Meanwhile, taking their guidance from the Institute for Policy Studies and its spin-offs and strategic partners, far-Left intellectuals, journalists, and politicians work together fostering a stealthy program following Antonio Gramsci's formula for cultural transformation. New "teachers of destruction" fill their student's heads with the supposed evils of "corporate America" and offer socialism as if is was some sort of anti-acid to temper capitalism. Journalists tilt their reporting ever so quietly to the strategic goals of the IPS-inspired cultural revolution, manipulating public opinion rather than serving as the eyes and ears of the people on important national and international issues. Meanwhile, Leftist politicians shape contemporary legislation in ways that will erode the substructure of Congress and the Constitution, as well as state and local governments, and support the radical progressive-socialist-marxist agenda.

Gramsci's message that "a communist society is best achieved through cultural transformation" has not been lost on the Institute for Policy Studies. IPS has played a major role in the cultural transformation in America by promoting a gradual process of radicalization of the societal superstructure of bourgeois institutions. The process would transform values and morals of society, which, once they are weakened, would open the country's political and economic foundations to destruction and restructuring. According to S. Steven Powell in his landmark book *Covert Cadre*, exposing the inner-workings of the Institute for Policy Studies, the Institute has been a leader of the radical Left prosecuting Antonio Gramsci's cultural war plan for many years.

> As a relatively unknown force, IPS has been working tirelessly to change the American political culture and bend public policy. While IPS finds no enemies on the Left, it considers anticommunism a dangerous ideology. . . . *There is a consistency between the way IPS operates and the revolutionary activity advocated by the Italian communist Antonio Gramsci.* For both it is important to infiltrate autonomous institutions—schools, media, churches, public interest groups—so as radically to transform the culture, which determines the environment in which political and economic policies are played out.[1] [emphasis added]

Carl Boggs counseled his readers in 1976 to heed "Gramsci's creative and dialectical philosophy, his innovative concept of ideological hegemony and his sensitivity to the hidden dimension of mass consciousness . . . his totalistic conception of the revolutionary process—all this constitutes an expansive theory of cultural revolution."[2] Gramsci's formula for stealthy penetration of society with progressive-socialist-marxist revolutionary dogma and multiple actions that will lead to the transformation of existing U.S. culture is what IPS and TNI are all about. Their actions over the past four decades have made significant gains and they may soon lead to the capture of the American presidency. They were successful in getting several of their agents of influence into high positions in the Clinton Administrations, including Tony Lake, Samuel Berger, and Morton Halperin, and their man John Kerry just missed defeating President George H. Bush in the 2004 presidential election. Undeterred, the IPS progressive-socialist-marxist Left began their campaign for the 2008 election on January 20, 2005, the day President Bush took the oath of office for his second term.

Boggs also counseled his Left-wing readers in 1976 that "what Gramsci anticipated, and what has become the reality of contemporary capitalism, is the importance of the struggle for ideological hegemony [cultural strength and domination by the existing political-social order] as the precondition for socialist transformation." He also outlined the pervasiveness of the dominance of the existing order in capitalist societies, most clearly present in the United States but also evident in Western Europe, Canada, and Japan. Quoting Franz Schurmann—whose affiliation with the Institute for Policy Studies was through its West Coast mouthpiece, the Pacific News Service—Boggs underlines his main point.

Revolutions do not begin with the thunderclap of a seizure of power—that is their culmination. They start with attacks on the moral-political order and the traditional hierarchy of class statuses. They succeed when the power structure, beset by its own irresolvable contradictions, can no longer perform legitimately and effectively. It is often forgotten that the state has often in the past been rescued by the moral-political order and the class hierarchy (authority) that the people still accepted.[3]

If there is one grinding purpose that drives the Institute for Policy Studies and its overseas sister organization, the Transnational Institute, it is the total, top-to-bottom, remaking of the United States, including its social norms, cultural traditions, economic engine, and political system according to socialist principles. Those persons attracted to IPS and TNI find themselves on the outside of conventional society and life in America. Their lives are based on "anti-" something: they always seem to be "against" and rarely for corrective social action unless it falls under one of the Left's oft-mouthed palliatives for "social justice" or stealthy cultural revolution.

Who Are the Progressives-Socialists-Marxists?

The struggle to apply Antonio Gramsci's formula for a gradual, stealthy cultural transformation that will bring America's progressive-socialist-marxist radicals to power has been underway for some time. Gramsci was adamant that a socialist revolution would have to be built through human action in order "to sweep away every component of the old order—the *cultural* as well as the economic and political," Boggs explained. "If socialism is to assert its ideological hegemony, it must create its own culture . . . as an integral part of a total revolutionary process; in doing so it must build upon embryonic currents of cultural protest and revolt."[4] That means human actors must take "counter-hegemonic" action against the bourgeois mind-control exercised over the existing working class through "a monopoly of the press and other levers of influence." In order to carry out the "counter-hegemonic" action required for cultural revolution, Gramsci said, it would be necessary to "educate" the popular masses through a range of structures and activities, such as labor unions, media, schools, churches, and the family. Only in this way could the "class interests dominating" the existing system of values, beliefs, and morals be overturned.[5] This is what the Institute for Policy Studies and the contemporary "embryonic currents of cultural protest and revolt" are all about.

For Gramsci, the mass media played a crucial role in "educating" (read: "propagandizing") the masses. Gramsci founded the newspaper *Ordine Nuovo* in 1919, which declared that "the aspect of the class struggle in Italy is characterised at the present time by the fact that the industrial and agricultural workers are unswervingly determined, throughout the nation, to bring forward the question of the ownership of the means of production in an explicit and violent way."[6] Recruiting new members and voices to the progressive-socialist-marxist action plan for Americans are also vital Gramscian goals. "A new culture is created not only by individual 'original' discoveries, but also by the wide propaganda of those truths which have already been discovered," Carl Marzani explained in *The Open Marxism of Antonio Gramsci*. "These truths must be socialized . . . so they can give use to action and be woven into the growing structure of a new moral and intellectual order."[7] For Gramsci, it was crucial over the long-run to broadcast a socialist world view through education of the masses and use of the media, "including a broadly critical understanding of the existing society, a vision of the future, and a strategic sense of how to get there," Carl Boggs writes. "Gramsci sought to incorporate theory into a new popular language, which is where the linkage between politics and philosophy is ultimately grounded."[8] He explained that

In Gramsci's view, class domination is exercised as much through physical coercion (or threat of it) by the state apparatus, especially in advanced capitalist societies where education, the media, law, mass culture, etc. take on a new role. To the extent, therefore, that 'superstructural' phenomena such as beliefs, values, cultural traditions and myths function on a mass level to perpetuate the existing order, it follows that the struggle for liberation must stress the task of creating a 'counter-hegemonic' world-view, or what Gramsci called a new 'integrated culture.'[9]

"Progressives" label themselves as such to differentiate themselves from "liberals." At the same time, however, true liberals are recruited by progressives who downplay their Gramscian orientation or their affinity for critical aspects of socialism and Marxism. So, who are the American "progressives"? According to the Virginia-based Culture and Media Institute, "progressives" make up just 17 percent of the public, and they advocate a humanist or secularized approach to life. For the progressives-socialists-marxists, deeply held religious beliefs are unnecessary "for living a good and moral life." Their secular humanism is founded on the belief that man should worship man and "live their lives according to their own personal principles, even when those principles contradict God's teachings." Morality falls into a situational gray area—it is not an absolute. The individual is the final authority for actions taken, *not* God or the law. Surprisingly, 53 percent of the progressives-socialists-marxists "say" they believe in God. But one-third say they do not believe in God, which is four times greater than the 8 percent of non-believers nationwide.[10]

Progressives-socialists-marxists also are differentiated from the 31 percent of America's most religiously observant, the "orthodox," and the 46 percent (the "independents") who do not fully subscribe to either the "progressive" or "orthodox" value systems. When the three groups were compared, the Culture and Media Institute's survey of 2,000 American respondents to its telephone and Internet inquiry found that a substantially higher number of progressives-socialists-marxists admit that they are willing to act dishonestly in everyday life. Only about two-fifths, half as many as the religiously observant, think "it is always wrong to break the law," 45 percent think it is permissible to break laws that "they" deem outdated or believe breaking them would not "really hurt anyone." Ten percent of "progressives" say people should not obey laws they judge to be "unnecessary and stupid." And 45 percent of progressives-socialists-marxists think it is okay to cheat on a restaurant bill when the waiter did not list all of the items; nearly half would take a job paid in cash to avoid paying taxes; and 17 percent believe adults should be allowed to use any drugs, even if they are illegal. In addition, only 10 percent of the progressives-socialists-marxists responding to the values survey identified themselves as pro-life, just 15 percent thought homosexuality was wrong, and only 20 percent were against same-sex "marriage."[11]

Centers of Gravity

The Institute for Policy Studies, operating under the guidance of the Rubin Imperium, has grown for more than four decades by bringing a wide range of key societal players under its protective wings. Three centers of gravity provide the Imperium's main strengths for use in guiding its supporters—intellectuals, mostly America's Marxist professors at universities and colleges across the country; journalists in the mainstream and "alternative" news media; and elected officials at the federal, state, and local levels. These centers of gravity are integrated and mutually supportive in the Institute's ideological drive for America's cultural transformation and eventual progressive-socialist-marxist governance.

An iron triangle of radical intellectuals, fellow traveler journalists, and Left-leaning politicians provide an essential foundation to spawn a cultural revolution that would make individual liberty conditional and democracy re-structured to satisfy the social and political goals of the progressive-socialist-marxist movement. These three cornerstones are partially hidden in a shadow world of denial and deception. Bringing them wholly into the sunlight is a prerequisite to understanding how the shadow world operates by thousands of Left-wing activists. They are busy everyday, gnawing away at America's cultural strengths in an effort to implant their radical Left ideas in the body politic.

Today's Left is unimpressed that their brothers and sisters who carried the banners of Karl Marx, Vladimir Lenin, Mao Tse-tung, Fidel Castro, and others in the last century were, in the final analysis, responsible for the murder of 100 million innocent people worldwide. These killings came at the hands of those wielding the sword of communism in one hand and a hammer and sickle in the other. "After all," the hard left says, "twentieth century Communism was not a fair test of socialism." The Leftists add that "by applying Antonio Gramsci's culture transformation formula, we have been able to create a movement toward 'Marxist renewal and re-emergence' in the twenty-first century." The open hypothetical question is, after the contemporary Left successfully accedes to power in key Western countries, how many more people will have to die in miserable gulags to satisfy their "idea" of progressivism-socialism-marxism.

Intellectuals

For Antonio Gramsci, "revolutionary intellectuals," or the properly educated masses, must ultimately create socialism. Gramsci's grassroots perspective argued for a bottom-up cultural transformation over time that would shape a "counter-hegemonic" political order. Hence, Gramsci's "philosophy of praxis" seeks to meld intellectuals and masses in what he called "organic unity." And Gramsci argued, Carl Boggs writes, that "to be effective, intellectuals must be an 'organic' part of the community; they must articulate new values within the shared language and symbols of the larger culture."[12]

The revolutionary intellectuals would carry the new modes of thinking developed by the Left into bourgeois society and provide "theoretical" guidance to the mass struggles that lie ahead. The "organic" intellectuals—those who are inherently a part of the working class—and who are in community with the masses serve as a safeguard against creeping "elitism and political isolation." It is through this mechanism, Carl Boggs explained in *Gramsci's Marxism*, that "new ideas . . . would be integrated into the very fabric of proletarian culture, life-styles, language, traditions, etc. by the revolutionaries who themselves worked and lived within the same environment." In other words, "organic" intellectuals would both lead and represent the "everyday social existence of the working class."[13]

In *Radical Son*, David Horowitz described the hard Left's infiltration of American colleges and universities after the 1991 implosion of the Soviet Union. They became agents of influence for "Marxist renewal and re-emergence" in the United States and beyond.

> The situation in the universities was appalling. The Marxists and socialists who had been refuted by historical events were now tenured establishment of the academic world. Marxism had produced the bloodiest and most oppressive regimes in human history—but after the fall, as one wit commented, more Marxists could be found on the faculties of American colleges than in the entire former Communist bloc.[14]

Hiding behind academic masks, these progressive-socialist-marxist professors—modern "organic" intellectuals—have poisoned the minds of millions of students with America-hating, Gramscian Marxist advocacy. Out of some 617,000 college and university professors in the United States in 2006, David Horowitz estimated, some 25,000 to 30,000 of them were radical Leftists. When one tallies the number of university students passing through the classrooms of these "teachers of destruction" each year and the number influenced by their radical writings, Horowitz found that on the order of three million potential brainwashees could have been influenced annually.[15]

The Leftist bias on America's campuses is also shown by political party enrollments of professors in departments most important to American democratic culture: economics, history, English, political science, sociology, psychology, and anthropology. Professors at Brown University in 2002, for example, numbered fifty-four on the Left to three on the right. The Left-right disparity was obvious at other universities as well: Stanford University—151 to 17, Cornell University—166 to 6, and the University of California at San Diego—99 to 6. A similar lack of diversity and pro-Left bias was apparent at Penn State, University of Maryland, University of Colorado at Boulder, and many other colleges and universities across the country.[16]

Marxists running professional associations reflected the shift of focus in academe to "a kind of pseudosociology of race-gender-class oppression," Horowitz explained. "The mission of the university . . . was now of 'social transformation.'" Not only had "radical politics . . . become the intellectual currency of academic thought," Horowitz continued, but the "faculties, administrations, and departments . . . tried to recruit students to their political agendas."[17] Testifying before a Kansas House of Representatives hearing on academic freedom, Horowitz explained that "entire academic departments and fields are no longer devoted to scholarly pursuits, but have become ideological training and recruitment centers for radical causes."[18] Adopting the role of "revolutionary intellectuals," these radical professors are working like Gramsci's fellow travelers in the promotion of actions to destroy the values supporting the American identity.

Turning political correctness into a tool for oppressive speech and mind control, the radical Left threatens to destroy individual liberty by imposing draconian restrictions on freedom of speech. Children are being encouraged from grade school by their teachers to respond emotionally rather than to analyze logically on a wide range of issues, extending from the environment to homelessness: "our children are being trained to be sheep and to respond automatically to words that strike an emotional chord," Thomas Sowell observed. "We are being set up to be played for suckers by anyone who wants to take up where the totalitarian movements of the 20th century left off."[19] Dare anyone express an opinion that violates the radical Left's speech code about certain ethnic and social groups, thereby tacitly challenging the Left's cultural orthodoxy, they can expect to have their reputations dragged through the mud and to be publicly humiliated by being called "racists," "homophobes," or worse.[20]

Yet, one of the most egregious "hate crimes" practiced in America, a hate crime by omission, is the radical Left's distortions of the historical record of American Communism and Soviet espionage in the United States during the Cold War. Such writings as *The Black Book of Communism* that documented one hundred million people slaughtered at the hands of Communist governments and revolutionaries, twenty million persons by the Soviet Union alone, have hardly seen the light of day on American university campuses. American revisionists, most of whom are Marxists perched at universities and colleges across the country, ignore or reject the book's commentary and conclusions. Why? Bad scholarship by the authors? No, that is hardly the case, since much of the *Black Book*'s well-documented research is drawn from the Soviet Union's own archives and top European scholars chronicled the crimes of twentieth century Communism.[21]

American Professors John Earl Haynes and Harvey Klehr made a solid case in their 2003 book *In Denial* that those who "hold distinguished positions in American higher education and cultural life" openly applaud and apologize for the murderous Communist regimes. These "revisionists," as Haynes and Klehr call them, see America as using democracy to mask its "capitalist oppression and aggressive imperialism." The revisionists tend to see Marxism-Leninism as an embodiment of humankind's utopian fantasies, and American communists, according to the revisionists, ". . . were among the most heroic fighters for social justice in the nation's history."[22]

As a consequence of the horrific intellectual dishonesty rampant in American academic culture, revisionist gatekeepers of professional journals ensure that published writings either reflect or do not contradict the "Big Lie" that the radical professors have concocted. Rather than confront and debate new information available about American communism and Soviet espionage in the past, the academic revisionists ignore new evidence drawn from the archives of Moscow's Institute of Marxism-Leninism and code-breaking of Soviet diplomatic cables during World War Two. The latter reveal numerous Americans at the highest levels of the federal government serving as espionage agents for the Soviet Union.[23]

Historians of American communism are among the most blatant revisionists. Despite the facts gleaned from Russian archives since 1992 and corroborating information released by the Federal Bureau of Investigation, many revisionists refuse to acknowledge that the Soviet Union secretly funded the Communist Party, USA, and individuals and front organizations.[24]

John Barron chronicled the $28 million transferred to the American Communist Party by the Soviet Communist Party in his book *Operation Solo: The FBI's Man in the Kremlin*. This gripping account of intrigue, espionage, counter-intelligence, and human emotions certainly should be a candidate for an award-winning film. Yet, Hollywood producers seem reluctant to expand American awareness of Soviet espionage in the United States and the dangers it presented. Or, perhaps, they just cannot bring themselves to say anything nice about the FBI. After all, to salute the FBI's penetration of the Soviet leadership and its espionage program could burst some of the giant, self-serving myths about the House Committee on Un-American Activities that led to the blacklisting of those involved with integrating Soviet propaganda into American films.[25]

Revisionists remain resistant to new evidence documenting extreme measures taken by the new American communists—those of the Gramsci strain—in its support of Soviet espionage. This shameless deception of American students and the people at large has no excuse. It is the worst kind of treason—treason by omission. The sweeping generalizations, inaccurate declarations, indoctrinating rather than educating students, denials, evasions, averted eyes, and impossible scenarios all point toward academic betrayal of the United States.[26] The military confrontation between NATO and the Soviet Union may be over, but the war of ideas between Marxism, Leninism, and Gramscism on one side and Americanism on the other goes on.

John Earl Haynes and Harvey Klehr, two of America's foremost historians of American communism, linked the contemporary progressive-socialist-marxist movement with the Cold War communism of the past. They characterized their own intellectual search for truth ". . . as an illustration of how an alienated and politicized academic culture misunderstands and distorts America's past, and the crucial role played by historical gatekeepers such as professional journals in misshaping cultural memories to fit the ideological biases of the academic establishment." They state flatly: "This book [*In Denial*] takes a step back to see how contemporary scholars and intellectuals have failed to confront new evidence about the history of American communism and Soviet espionage."

Communism as a social fact is dead. But communism as a pleasant figment of the 'progressive' worldview lives on, giving a phantom life to the illusions and historical distortions that sustained that murderous and oppressive ideology. The intellectual Cold War, alas, is not over. Academic revisionists who color the history of American communism in benign hues see their teaching and writing as the preparation of a new crop of radicals for the task of overthrowing capitalism and its democratic constitutional order in the name of social justice and peace. Continuing to fight the Cold War in history, they intend to reverse the victory of the West and convince the next generation that the wrong side won, and to prepare the way for a new struggle.[27]

Journalists

Many in the American news media aide and abet the radical Left's silent cultural revolution. Some of these acolytes are faceless; others are not. A few operate so deeply in the shadows that their propaganda passes undetected or they are mistakenly labeled "liberals" by mindless commentators who are so frightened—or perhaps are stealthy supporters themselves—of the hammer of political correctness that they tumble into a mental gulch of sweeping generalizations. Consequently, Robert Lechter, the director of the Center for Media Affairs, notes "the public thinks the media is biased and arrogant—trying to tell them not facts, but what to think as well."[28]

Some of the progressive-socialist-marxist voices emanate from such Leftist-oriented magazines as *Mother Jones*, *The Nation*, *Progressive*, and *In These Times*. Others, often more deceptive propaganda sources, are found in the mainstream media where slanted news help shape opinions in support of the Left's revolutionary agenda. Some of the candidates that might be given an award for "lack of objectivity" might include the major television networks and CNN cable news, *Washington Post* and *New York Times*, National Public Radio, and the Left-wing dominated public television. These propaganda voices can be seen as legitimate efforts to satisfy two main tasks of Gramsci's "philosophy of praxis"— combating modern ideologies and educating the popular masses.[29] This warping of the news is supplemented by a "progressive" Hollywood that churns out an unending assault against America's traditional values. According to a survey of 2,000 adults by the Culture and Media Institute, 73 percent of Americans blame Hollywood and 54 percent blame the media for eroding values.[30]

Robert Knight, the director of the Culture and Media Institute, reported that research reveals that the more American's watch Hollywood's television fare, the more likely they will hold "permissive attitudes toward abortion and sexuality," and the more they will think their problems are "someone else's responsibility."[31] Meanwhile, a bevy of progressive-socialist-marxist Hollywood celebrities are joined by a less informed group of their peers in supporting the ongoing social struggle to create a massive cultural transformation in America.

Most Americans believe, as reflected by the respondents to the National Cultural Values Survey, the media undermines core moral values and influence people to avoid taking responsibility for their own decisions and actions. Among the Survey's major findings were (1) 74 percent of Americans believe moral values declined in the United States over the past twenty years, and a large majority holds the media responsible for contributing to that decline; and (2) 54 percent of the respondents agreed that the news media has had a negative impact on moral values. "Despite the denials of the media elite, most Americans believe the news is politically biased," Brian Fitzpatrick, senior editor at the Culture and Media Institute says, and "44 percent of Americans say the news media favor the left, and 17 percent say the news media favor the right. Only 27 percent say the news is balanced."[32]

It is no wonder that the British leader Tony Blair likened the news media to a "feral beast" that has largely abandoned balanced reporting in favor of sensation, shock, and controversy that poorly serves the public.[33] In the United States one could add the increasing "trash" journalism of television news in the seemingly unending coverage of foibles by the so-called Hollywood "celebrities," such as Anna Nicole Smith, Paris Hilton, Britney Spears, O. J. Simpson, and an unending cast of others. This is also lazy journalism, since it is easy to bring in small hordes of "esquires" for hours of babble that takes away time for coverage of issues important to keeping the public informed about real issues that shape their lives.

Mainstream Media

A growing threat to American liberty and democracy festers and spreads every day as a result of the "arrogance, power, and lack of accountability" of people calling themselves "journalists."[34] American journalists have entered a dark world of deceit and deception that support the progressive-socialist-marxist revolutionaries.

Bernard Goldberg, for instance, explains that left-leaning bias expressed in stories from major news outlets are more a result of shared views than any kind of shadowy conspiracy. These "shared views" occur within a cavern of liberal bias that echo the progressive-socialist-marxist world view. A one-time insider at CBS News, Bernard Goldberg writes that the television news of the major networks permit their journalists to (1) "slant the news in a leftward direction," (2) "deny their bias while . . . saying their critics are really the ones who are biased," (3) adopt a position that "in their opinion, liberalism . . . from abortion to affirmative action to the death penalty and gay rights is not really liberal at all, but merely reasonable and civilized," and (4) foster bigotry against conservatives by dividing "Americans into two groups—moderates and right-wing nuts."[35]

ABC News Political Director Mark Halperin, a "red-diaper baby" of one of the collaborating "shining stars" in the Institute for Policy Studies solar system, Morton Halperin, tripped over his own bias. This is not to rest the sins of a father on his son, but it does reveal, as Lowell Ponte writes, "an entire Left-spin universe in which Mark grew up exposed to his father's comrades and radical ideas." Halperin "wrote a memo that to many . . . [seemed] to direct ABC reporters, anchors, and producers to slant its coverage by downplaying the misstatements of Democratic presidential candidate Senator John Kerry and viewing negatively any misstatements by Republican candidate Bush."[36] Senator Kerry was the candidate of choice for the IPS and its left-wing network of stars.

L. Brent Bozell III concluded that the liberal media has become "weapons of mass distortion," and he cited "overwhelming evidence . . . that liberal bias in the mainstream news media continues unchecked." He found that the counterattack against public criticism of the media's liberal bias resulted in the "turning their guns" on Republicans over the Bill Clinton-Monica Lewinsky story or dropping other stories altogether as in the case of Gennifer Flowers. Bozell concluded that the chief problem is that "many media figures are less than pleased with the mounting assaults on their credibility and trustworthiness."[37]

The elite media, Bozell explained, cannot "accept or tolerate . . . the Christianity practiced by most Americans. . . . Popular culture, whether in television, film, or art, constantly derides and attacks faith. . . . Christianity has become an institution to be exposed, denounced, attacked, and ridiculed whenever possible."[38] This ideological orientation shows the American news media, by aligning themselves with the teaching of Antonio Gramsci advocating a cultural revolution, in a seeming slavish support for the progressive-socialist-marxist agenda. "The anti-Christian bias in the media is so pervasive," Bozell writes, "that a network can insult Christians on national television in front of millions—with impunity."[39] Christians pose no threat to anyone, except for those who would foster a culture revolution en route to bringing about socialist governance that would assure an equality of poorness for all Americans. What would happen to the "free press" with the progressives-socialists-marxists in power?

Sometimes the news media are not satisfied with simply serving up a "daily diet of bias," and they try to steer the course of events. When the U.S. government seized a six-year old child at gunpoint—Elian Gonzalez—and sent him back to a communist hell in Cuba, the liberal media did all it could do to obscure, deny, and cover-up the truth. The Left-oriented news became a part of the story as they demonized "the staunchly anticommunist Cuban exiles who so vocally supported Elian's right to remain in America."[40]

William McGowan writes that "political correctness has corrupted American journalism." Political correctness is the tip of the spear of the Gramsci Left's cultural revolution, an example of Gramsci's "philosophy of praxis" and how the news media are used in support of the Left in America's culture war. Diversity and multi-culturalism are cornerstones of the Left's support for Gramsci's formula. William McGowan explains in *Coloring the News*, the journalism shakers and movers declared that "diversity was crucial if the news industry was to realize its mission of 'service to democracy.'" Hence, diversity became the new religion in journalism—it "opened the door to ethnic, racial and gender cheerleading."[41]

McGowan sweeps up the journalistic mess in observing that "by siding so openly with the cultural left on controversial diversity issues, the press has compounded the estrangement and anger of much of the electorate, unintentionally feeding the cultural and political backlash against that agenda."[42]

When the news reflects the editorial room opinion rather than the facts underlying the story, Bob Kohn says, the distortion is a problem of extreme dishonesty.[43] Kohn's research revealed a mind-set at the *New York Times* that makes it one of the leading polluters of straight news with editorial opinion. The "news bias" at the *Times* has simply turned the front page into carefully crafted stories that support the political agenda usually reserved for the editorial page. This reckless mixing of fact and opinion, Bob Kohn says, is "journalistic fraud."

The *New York Times* has accepted the task, either wittingly or unwittingly, of shaping public opinion to support the progressive-socialist-marxist agenda of undermining and destroying American values, moral beliefs, and traditional institutions. In so doing, the *Times* emulates the propaganda tactics of Dr. Joseph Goebbels, minister of information in Nazi Germany. This rather "big" statement is supported by the *Times*' style-book on deception unearthed by Bob Kohn.[44] Mallard Fillmore, a cartoon duck speaking for the *New York Times* through his creator, Bruce Tinsley, sums up the double standard guiding the *Times*: "When a story affirms our liberal biases, its front page! When it doesn't, we bury that sucker on 'B-34'."[45]

The *New York Times* is not alone in such "journalistic fraud." The *Washington Post* seems to be a willing voice for an unending stream of slanted and warped "news" stories that feed the secular-seeking, progressive-socialist-marxist fifth column. Cross-connections between the Institute for Policy Studies and the *Post* are longstanding. The *Post* began subscribing to the IPS-connected Pacific News Service in 1983. Blending Left-wing propaganda mixed with facts from legitimate news services in the *Post*'s stories, from the front page to the last, leads one wonder whether or to what extent all of its articles are tilted toward the Left.

In a December 1978 article, for instance, the *Post* ran a story about the National Lawyers Guild's (NLG) charge that Israel was using torture and violating Palestinian rights. The story failed to tell the reader that the Congress had cited the NLG to be a communist front and that the Palestinian Liberation Organization paid the expenses of the NLG "fact-finding" delegates when they visited the Middle East. Only one word fully describes the *Post*'s omission of critical facts such as the political orientation of the NLG: "propaganda."[46]

The *Post* uses many of the same deception tools the *New York Times* applies to editing stories in order to have them serve its political bent. The *Post*'s information pollution passed to its readers is as dangerous to American liberties and democratic system as that spawned from the *Times*.

The Institute for Policy Studies has long maintained good relations with the *Washington Post*. Karen DeYoung, a senior editor at the *Post*, previously taught at the IPS Washington School. She told the class of radical Left activists that liberal media tends to see "no enemies on the Left." "Most journalists now," she told the class, "most Western journalists at least, are very eager to seek out guerrilla groups, leftist groups, because you assume they must be the good guys." Those words boomeranged in public and the *Post* compelled her to cease participation in IPS programs.[47]

After visiting the Sandinista's in 1978 during the assault on the government in Nicaragua, she denied that they were Marxists at a time when accurate information was in short supply on Capitol Hill in making decisions on funding for the Somoza government. She said that Daniel Ortega, leader of the anti-Somoza forces was not a Marxist and described him as a member of "the most moderate faction which advocates pluralistic democracy." She painted the Sandinistas as "romantic revolutionaries" and ignored the fact that Daniel Ortega worshiped Fidel Castro. According to a senior defector from the Sandinistas, the leaders in the 1980s considered DeYoung "as one of their most important allies in the American media."[48]

William Arkin, a long-time radical Leftist, had worked to undermine U.S. national security for many years, including publication of national secrets and a continuing information pollution of disinformation designed to poison popular support for protecting Americans from harm. Michael Tremoglie of the *Philadelphia* Bulletin, after quoting liberally from Arkin's sophomoric writings, concluded that Arkin's ideas "should tell you all you need to know about the reportage of the mainstream liberal media of the Iraq war. Their reportage is biased, it is firmly in the camp of the antiwar groups, and worst of all, it is packaged as if it is impartial. The liberal mainstream media have an innate hatred and contempt for those in the military."[49]

None of this is new for IPS fellow William Arkin who began his anti-U.S. government career at the Center for Defense Information. The Center is interlocked financially and bureaucratically with the Institute for Policy Studies. In the 1980s, Arkin helped create Greenpeace International's "Nuclear Free Seas" campaign, which included revealing locations of naval nuclear weapons around the world. As a nine year fellow of the Institute for Policy Studies, he exposed the classified nuclear defense contingency plans to Leslie Gelb for publication in the *New York Times*. He also passed parts of the plan to Iceland, Canada, and other U.S. allies in 1984, which provided grist for anti-American propaganda. In January 1982, he warned those present at the Riverside Church Disarmament Program—headed by Cora Rubin-Weiss—of the "aggressive nuclear 'theology' of the Reagan Administration." Arkin was also a member of the April 1982 IPS-Soviet bilateral exchange in Moscow along with Marcus Raskin, then-IPS director Robert Borosage, and Roger Wilkins. The revelations offered by Arkin may have contributed to Soviet Communist Party General Secretary Yuri Andropov's well-documented paranoia of the potential for a U.S. nuclear first strike.

Anti-Soviet rhetoric was quite high during Ronald Reagan's presidential campaign in 1980. Contrary to expectations, it was not relaxed after the election, and, in fact, intensified. President Reagan's strong rhetoric was founded on his belief that the American deterrent had been placed into question by the Soviet military buildup during the Carter Administration. President Carter had suspended work on the intercontinental MX ballistic missile and B-1 bomber—both were reinstated by Reagan.

From Soviet Party Chief Andropov's perspective, Reagan's rhetoric and reinstatement of strategic military weapons programs could well have been parts of a program to deliver a successful first strike against the U.S.S.R. The American rhetoric and military upgrades, combined with Andropov's paranoia, made the early 1980s, according to Christopher Andrew and former KGB officer Oleg Gordievsky, "the most dangerous period of East-West tension since the Cuban missile crisis."[50] In the middle of this quiet but very real tension, William Arkin ran around like a "Mad Hatter" pouring gasoline on the dangerous fires raging between Washington and Moscow.

In response to the deteriorating situation, General Secretary Andropov reportedly initiated a joint KGB-GRU (military intelligence) worldwide intelligence operation code-named RYAN— an acronym for Raketno Yadermoye Napadenie—Nuclear Missile Attack. In March 1982, top-gun Vasili Krivokhizhia, a KGB officer (First Department, North America), was assigned responsibility for taking personal charge of RYAN intelligence collection in the United States. Soviet intelligence operations were also intensified in Europe, especially its protest efforts to prevent deployment of nuclear-tipped cruise missiles and Pershing ballistic missiles scheduled for late 1983.

NATO conducted a command post exercise "Able Archer 83" from November 2–11, 1983, to practice nuclear release procedures. Soviet contingency plans for a surprise attack against the West envisaged the use of a training exercise to mask their preparations for attack. Thus, the Soviets were "haunted by the fear that Western plans for a surprise attack on the Soviet Union might be the mirror image of its own." The atmosphere remained tense as nuclear attack indicators multiplied during the NATO exercise.[51] While all of this was going on between the two superpowers and their European allies, William Arkin and the Institute for Policy Studies continued to throw fuel on the fires between NATO and the U.S.S.R. The Riverside Church Disarmament Program provided a venue in January 1982 for Arkin "sounding a dark warning about the aggressive 'nuclear theology' of the Reagan administration. . . . 'Let there be no illusion about it, the Soviet Union and its defensive plan will not stand for an attack upon the motherland and it will respond in kind.'"[52]

William Arkin's 2005 book *Code Names: Deciphering U.S. Military Plans, Programs and Operations in the 9/11 World* includes some 3,000 U.S. national security code names, some of which are still classified.[53]

Dana Priest, a *Washington Post* reporter, swapped a series of undocumented stories about the CIA and the war on terrorism for a Pulitzer Prize in 2006. Her sources, if any, were unnamed. One of those "unnamed" is believed to have been Priest's "friend," Mary O. McCarthy, a CIA officer, whose childish hatred for President George W. Bush, allegedly prompted her to betray the trust that her country had placed in her. Some of Dana Priest's accounts of CIA-operated prisons for terrorists overseas—whose existence was confirmed by President George W. Bush in 2006—sounded as though they were ghost stories made up around a Girl Scout campfire, especially a whispered story about the "Salt Pit" and mysterious terrorist "ghost detainees."[54] These stories about "secret prisons" leave the reader with no facts and no corroboration. So how in the world did Dana Priest win the once prestigious Pulitzer Prize? Awards for rumors and fictional accounts, especially those perhaps copied from anonymous notes scribbled on the wall of the ladies room, fall into another literary category.

Priest's scary stories might not be bothersome until one realizes the damage inflicted on America's ability to protect its citizens in a time of terrorist war. Apparently, some of Dana Priest's raw material came from Mary O. McCarthy, a rather pedestrian CIA officer in her own right. If Priest was able to collect a few nuggets of information through her convenient friendship with McCarthy, they could well have become grist for instant ghost stories from Madam Priest's stubby pencil.

But the story worsens. It turns out McCarthy was a Democratic partisan while working at the CIA—partisanship is always a very bad idea for anyone serving in a sensitive national security position. According to Jennifer Verner, writing for Accuracy in Media, McCarthy worked closely with the IPS-penetrated Clinton Administration, and John Kerry's campaign foreign policy team, including Sandy Berger, Richard Clarke, Rand Beers, and anti-Bush fact-twister Joe Wilson. Dana Priest's Pulitzer Prize looks more and more like a payoff for a Bush political "hit" team.

Wait. The real story gets worse. Dana Priest is a graduate of the University of California at Santa Cruz, which is appropriate labeled by David Horowitz and Jacob Laskin as "The Worst School in America."[55] With the likes of Communist Professor and recipient of the Lenin "Peace Prize" from East Germany Angela Davis, revolutionary professor William Domhoff, and supporting hard Left acolytes on the faculty, it is surprising that Dana Priest was not one of Mary McCarthy's "reportable contacts" to the CIA security division.[56]

And the true story turns ugly. The next series of events take us into the caverns of deceit and disinformation at the *Washington Post*. Jennifer Verner "walked the dog backward," as the saying goes, and uncovered more about Dana Priest, proud recipient of a 2006 Pulitzer Prize. Ms. Verner discovered that Priest's "matrimonial ties . . . leaves a strong appearance of conflict of interest." Priest, it so happens, is married to William Goodfellow, a far-Left political activist and long-time executive director of the Center for International Policy. The Center is a progressive-socialist-marxist spin-off of the Institute for Policy Studies. One of its sister organizations is the radical Left's Center for Defense Information; another is the anti-intelligence Center for National Security Studies, which was headed by Morton Halperin who, in preparation for the 2008 presidential election, joined George Soros in his financial takeover of the Democratic Party.

A curious fact about Mr. Goodfellow's Center for Information Policy is that it was created with the assistance of Orlando

Letelier while he was working with the Institute for Policy Studies. The contents of Letelier's briefcase, which was not destroyed in the bomb blast that killed him on September 21, 1976, revealed his close contacts with the Cuban intelligence service. The briefcase also contained a personal letter from Saul Landau, a long-time fellow at IPS who remains active in its operations, to the head of Cuban intelligence. We are now left with more open questions than we began with. The story of anonymous sources, bias, and propaganda spun by Dana Priest now turns to possible Cuban espionage and hostile disinformation operations. Successful covert operations have occurred on a lot fewer links between the players than the ones in this vignette of intrigue, betrayal, and anonymous sources.

Jennifer Verner is adamant in her assessment of Dana Priest.

> Dana Priest should not be allowed to hide behind the tattered veil of 'anonymous sources.' . . . Priest's Pulitzer Prize-winning story not only lacks evidence, it looks like a carefully designed and planted effort to sabotage the war or terror, a move that has put Americans at increased risk of terrorist attack.[57]

The McCarthy-Priest-Goodman-maybe Saul Landau (Fidel Castro's friend) cabal raises open questions about a possible role having been played by the Cuban intelligence. Have U.S. espionage laws been violated? Is this another story about a Cuban "mole" burrowed inside U.S. intelligence?

The *Washington Post*'s top wordsmith, Robert Kaiser, knows a thing or two about traitors, disinformation, and espionage, and perhaps even assassination. In February 1981, Mr. Kaiser relied on Philip Agee, a notorious CIA turncoat who joined the Institute for Policy Studies and whose exposure of CIA field officers may well have resulted in the murder of Richard Welch who was gunned-down outside his home in Athens after his identity and residence appeared in Agee's *Counterspy* magazine.[58] The Kaiser-Agee collaboration focused on a U.S. government White Paper on "Communist Interference in El Salvador." Drawing on captured documents and other hard intelligence, the White Paper revealed the extent of Soviet and Cuban arms sent to guerrillas in 1979. But Jeffrey Stein, a former fellow of IPS, telephoned Peter Osnos, the *Washington Post* national editor, and said that he could not believe the *Post* would leave the U.S. White Paper without a critical examination.

Meanwhile, Philip Agee, assisted by his new "Cuban friends," in April 1981 provided a forty-six page attack on the White Paper and distributed it through the IPS-sponsored *Covert Action Information Bulletin.*[59] Robert Kaiser used Agee's critique in his own anti-U.S. attack article, citing Agee as a source. An editor at the *Washington Post*, however, said the citation was unnecessary. Thus, Agee became an unacknowledged source and an inconvenient clipping left on the editorial floor.

Given Kaiser's past complicity with the hard Left and IPS, it seems to have made sense to *Washington Post* editors to spike the truth that was beginning to ooze out of the Dana Priest's unnamed sources about secret prisons. On June 11, 2007, Robert Kaiser's article "Public Secrets" was published in the *Post*'s Sunday edition. He explained the "contest between press and government" with "facts" qualified by "apparently"—that is to say, he offered no facts. Kaiser writes that he knew Dana Priest had many sources, but "I don't know who they were." He sloppily tipped his hand, however, by quoting that the *Washington Post*'s executive editor, Leonard Downie Jr., as having said: "It [the Dana Priest story] raised important issues for American voters about how their country was treating prisoners, and it raised significant civil liberties issues." Voters? Why voters, unless the *Post*'s eye was on influencing anti-Bush, pro-Democrat voters? Were American secrets divulged with the expressed purpose of influencing elections? Could it be that the *Post*'s "news" reports were not "fair and balanced?"

Kaiser goes on by presenting a selective history lesson on the First Amendment to the Constitution. He writes that the "government overclassifies with abandon" (source?) and that acting "as though revealing any classified information threatens our nation's security . . . seems preposterous." Yet, earlier Kaiser, in explaining how journalists like Dana Priest and himself operate, said her article "was assembled like a Lego skyscraper, brick by brick. Often the sources who help reporters . . . don't even realize they have contributed a brick or two to the construction." If the latter statement is true, then the wall of official secrets needs to be sturdy and high to keep the "brick builders" at bay. Kaiser does not tell the reader that espionage agents from hostile countries are building their own "Lego skyscrapers, brick by brick." Hence, the government builds high walls to protect official secrets. What happens when members of the press build a "Lego skyscraper" that aids and abets the espionage tasks of hostile intelligence services?

The Dana Priest stories, for instance, included a "Lego brick provider," knowingly or unknowingly (Mary O. McCarthy), members of the hard Left (Priest's husband William Goodfellow), and potential links with the Cuban Intelligence Service through connections at the Institute for Policy Studies and Robert Kaiser's personal collaboration with CIA turncoat Philip Agee. Were the Priest's articles used as a cover to build an espionage front? Dana Priest did not cite a single source for her "ghost stories." Were some of her sources hostile intelligence officers manipulating facts for her use? Disinformation is most effective when hostile intelligence officers can find ways to influence native journalists to use their carefully shaped "bricks" in their stories. The readers of her stories cannot make a judgment because she cited no sources. Can one be certain some of her sources were not friends of Philip Agee?

At minimum, one can safely assume, that Priest's musings were clipped and will be used by those who would do Americans harm. She has become an unacknowledged source, similar to Robert Kaiser many years ago when he plundered Philip Agee's critique of a U.S. government White Paper on Soviet-Cuban arms supplies to Communist guerillas in El Salvador. America-hating propaganda and disinformation used by those who would destroy the United States may well draw upon Priest's writings.

One of the most damning critiques of the biased American news media came from the lips of an unlikely source in October 2007. Retired Army Lieutenant General Ricardo Sanchez, commander of U.S. troops in Iraq in 2003–04, delivered a speech to military journalists by first blasting the Bush Administration and the State Department for their lack of a workable strategy in Iraq and a long string of errors. General Sanchez seemingly lulled the assembled news reporters into their collective anti-Bush comfort zone. The second part of his speech, however, suddenly shifted gears and accelerated into a well-deserved roasting of the press corps that apparently left the journalists in silence and unable to scribble an account of what General Sanchez had to say. Neither the *New York Times* nor the Hearst Newspapers mentioned the story at all. The United Press International and the Associated Press followed suit. A reporter from the *Washington Post* wrote a long story about the first part of Sanchez's speech and a trace amount of his critique of the media at the end. Perhaps it was something the General said:

Over the course of this war, tactically insignificant events have become strategic defeats for America because of the tremendous power and impact of the media. Your measure of worth is how many front page stories you have written and unfortunately some of you will compromise your integrity. It seems that as long as you get a front page story there is little or no regard for the collateral damage you will cause. The death knell of your ethics has been enabled by your parent organizations who have chosen to align themselves with political agendas. What is clear to me is that you are perpetuating the corrosive partisan politics that is destroying our country and killing our service members who are at war. Your profession has . . . allowed external agendas to manipulate what the American public sees on TV, what they read in our newspapers, and what they see of the Web. For some of you . . . the truth is of little or no value if it does not fit your own preconceived notions, biases and agendas. . . . As I assess various media entities, some are unquestionably engaged in political propaganda that is uncontrolled. . . . This is the worst display of journalism imaginable. . . . Our military must embrace you for the sake of our democracy. But you owe them ethical journalism.[60]

The "political propaganda" referred to by General Sanchez is an example of how the progressive-socialist-marxist movement uses the mainstream media to help "Marxize the inner American" and carefully transform the country's cultural values and traditions to those that will accept Gramsci's socialist world view.

"Alternative" Media

When IPS co-founders Marcus Raskin and Richard Barnet concluded in the early 1970s that revolutionary change was not in America's immediate future, they realized that their strategy had to be modified. Raskin and Barnet realized, while they developed a strategy in the early 1970s for the longer term, that they had to dissociate themselves from the "underground press" and replace these essential propaganda and disinformation voices with communications that would be held in higher credibility by the governing "bourgeois superstructure." "Alternative Media" became an acceptable camouflage phase by the Left-wing following a consensus reached by members of the Underground Press Syndicate in 1972 and general usage over the years.[61]

The radical Left boasts of a basket full of magazines, newspapers, radio broadcasts, and blogs that supplement the progressive-socialist-marxist elite's message to the masses. David

Horowitz points out that "a standard operating principle of the Left: [is] the responsibility of progressive journalists . . . to suppress facts that hurt the progressive cause, and to print only those truths that support it."[62]

The Nation is the largest and most popular Left-wing magazine. Publisher Victor Navasky[63] has deep roots in the radical Left movement trying to bring down the United States government. This journal caters to members of the progressive-socialist-marxist movement with articles expressing harsh criticism of "corporate lobbyists," "oil drillers," and "fat-cat executives." Hate-filled articles targeting those who allegedly "trash civil liberties," as well as "war-profiteers," human rights abusers, and politicians whose tax cuts wreck "real world devastation" on the less fortunate.[64] The alleged under-reported "Secret Air War in Iraq" and use of cluster-bomb units, and "A New Stance Toward Havana" (Cuba After Fidel) round out some prominent national security issues in 2007. A special issue May 2007 addressed "Surviving the Climate Crisis: What Must Be Done."[65]

One example of the *The Nation's* toxic pollution of American society *The Nation*'s stooping to name-calling. Al Franken, for instance, called conservative radio commentator Rush Limbaugh a "Big Fat Idiot" and said he once was "morbidly obese."[66] Advertisements in *The Nation* also reflects the "anything goes" attitude of the editorial board. From *The Nation*'s pages one can purchase the *Anarchist Cookbook*, a magazine with the headline "Fuck the Corporate Media," an erotic adult telephone conversation, or a trip to Havana that will break American laws.[67]

The publisher and editor of the *Progressive*, Matthew Rothschild, places the magazine in perspective: "The United States does not have clean hands in the world. The history of the last fifty years is that history of U.S. war and repression in one Third World country after another."[68] Another propaganda spit-ball was fired by Barbara Ehrenreich (also an IPS member): "We have a choice:

Either raise all wages to a 'living wage' level or greatly expand the government programs that make life a little easier for low-wage families." Howard Zinn adds a supporting propaganda line: "We should recognize the greatness of this generation for launching a world movement against corporate domination."[69] The cover of the June 2007 issue denigrates those who choose military service in a cartoon depicting a recruiter with a vicious dog-in-tow stepping over half-naked college students on spring break and urging them to "look up from their beer guzzling, beanbag tossing, and football throwing for a moment and contemplate a thrilling tour of duty or two in a military uniform."[70]

The Institute for Policy Studies established *In These Times* as a propaganda mouthpiece for the Left's agenda in 1976. This bi-weekly publication billed itself as "The Independent Socialist Newspaper." The idea behind this IPS propaganda organ was the "creation of a 'mass movement for socialism,'" one that could be sustained over the long-term. The activities to be unleashed, S. Steven Power recounts in *Covert Cadre*, would embrace the spirit of the "old socialist movement of 1900–19, the Communist movement inspired by the example of the Russian Revolution, and the 'New Left' of the 1960s."[71]

Since *In These Times* articles were aimed at "forging unity against capitalism," they were filled with articles praising revolutionary figures in the Third World, Marxist liberation movements, European Communists, and radical Left-wing leaders in the United States. Several American labor unions endorsed *In These Times*, including the United Auto Workers (UAW) and the American Federation of State, County, and Municipal Employees (AFSCME).[72]

IPS published *In These Times* until June 1982, when it handed operations over to the Mid-Atlantic Publishing Company. In 2003–08 the Leftist magazine included articles on the U.S. corporate media that frustrate smaller progressive and socialist mouthpieces. Norman Soloman, for instance, argued that "the degradation of journalism and mass entertainment is entwined with pervasive corporate power that chokes virtually every facet of this country's political and social life."[73]

The Institute for Policy Studies created several Left-wing organizations in the 1970s. Some were far more successful that others. The magazine *Mother Jones*, for example, was an instant success in furthering the Left's agenda with articles on feminism, environmentalism, problems in the Third World, dangers of nuclear power, and ridicule of political conservatism. S. Steven Powell further recounts how IPS masked its relationship with the magazine in an article entitled "Who's Behind *Mother Jones?*" In spite of the editor's "virtuously asserted" statement that the magazine did not speak for banks or corporations, no mention was made of its longstanding connection with IPS. The Foundation for National Progress, publisher of *Mother Jones*, described its purpose in 1975 as one "to carry out on the West Coast the charitable and educational activities of the Institute for Policy Studies." Powell also noted that *Mother Jones* had very subtly advocated "a creeping socialism."[74]

Articles in *Mother Jones* fostered the New Left, conducted smear campaigns against the Reagan Administration, and spread doubts about the free markets and corporations. Among the 2002–08 subjects of the magazine's articles were "it's time for the left to reclaim the term 'anarchy,'" "smashing windows for a better world?," "Blaming America First," and "Goodbye, New World Order: Keep the Global Idea Alive."[75]

Members of the Communist Party, USA, find their way to many IPS gatherings, including those co-hosted by the Congressional Progressive Caucus in Capitol Hill meeting rooms. The Communist Party usually sets up a table with free literature, sign up sheets for later contacts and more propaganda, and distributes their weekly newspaper, *People's Weekly World*. In many cases, the newspaper is given away. This writer was given a copy at an IPS-Congressional

Progressive Caucus meeting in January 2001, when a strategy was being developed to make the claim stick that the Republicans stole the November 2000 election. Free copies of *People's Weekly World* also were picked up at Robert Borosage's (former director of IPS) conference on "Campaign for America's Future" in June 2004 and 2007. The usual anti-American mud was dripping from this communist propaganda rag: "100,000 Strikers of the Communications Workers of America," "Bush Speech 'Defends the Indefensible,'" "Stop the Torture! Fire Rumsfeld! Dump Bush!," "Travel Groups Defy Bush's Cuba Policies," "Owners of Gay Bars Say 'No' to Coors—Again," and "U.S. Companies Employ Blackmail in 'Free Trade' with Central America."[76] By 2007, subscription information was provided in Spanish and English—"A National, Bilingual Newspaper with a Grassroots Reach" and "News and Analysis from the Communist Party USA and Communist and Workers Parties from Around the World." The Young Communist League, USA, says "we struggle together for a socialist USA, for jobs, for youth, against racism and oppression, and for peace . . . and more."

A wide-range of other Left-wing propaganda channels routinely bombard American society from their shadow nooks and crannies in the communications world. The Pacific News Service, for example, enjoys nationwide distribution of its tilted-left news and analysis into the mainstream news. Founded in 1969 by Franz Schurmann, who was quoted liberally in Carl Bogg's *Gramsci's Marxism*, the original fare spewed by the Pacific News Service was stridently radical. The Institute for Policy Study's West coast affiliate, the Bay Area Institute, began to tone down its revolutionary Marxist message in the 1970s while Raskin and Barnet turned to masking its earlier counter-cultural message.[77]

The propaganda organs of the radical Left also feed into the mainstream media, perverting the objectivity in many print and electronic news outlets. John Cavanagh, Director of IPS, told supporters in a November 2004 letter of the Institute's success in "reaching a larger and larger audience with messages that help shift public opinion." The IPS annual reports on CEO pay have become mainstays for CNN, *Time*, *New York Times*, and *Los Angeles Times*, plus more than 350 other newspapers. "IPS scholars" [propagandists], Cavanagh bragged, "are also using radio, film, video, and electronic media to reach new people in new ways."[78]

The United States National Public Radio (NPR) accepts a large amount of taxpayer money and then denies objective reporting and aligns its programming strongly with the progressive-socialist-marxist Left-wing. Richard Rahn notes how NPR seemingly has a never ending number of stories about failures in the private sector but rare reports on socialist schemes, let alone any weaknesses. "Many NPR stations," Rahn points out, "are now airing the BBC in part to further propagandize Americans in the socialist way of thinking."[79] On other occasions, NPR tries to smother their guests in efforts to persuade them to mouth the radio producers' views of the Iraq war, only to become upset when truth is enunciated over the public's airwaves.

Bill Moyers, a long-time certified member of the Left, used the Public Broadcasting Service to peddle his rather nasty brand of propaganda against private wealth and corporations, and government policies. Moyers accused President George W. Bush, for instance, of pursuing "a radical-right agenda" that included "a crony capitalist corruption devoid of shame."[80] In the process, Moyers has become a multi-millionaire by pillaging the public money trough.

Politicians

Progressives-socialists-marxists are using America's democracy to destroy America's democracy. That is to say, for the Left, political activity, as counseled by Antonio Gramsci, is all about "the struggle for socialist transformation."[81] Populist messages about loss of societal programs filling "human needs," a corporate-controlled government, corporations breaking the "social contract" with working people (health care, fair wages, pensions), and greed by corporate leaders all underline the process of "Marxizing the masses." Progressives-socialists-marxists are using the democratic process to educate Americans in ways that will lead to the transformation of the culture and open the door to socialist governance. For Gramsci, Carl Boggs explained, revolution rests on an "*active* political knowledge incorporating an awareness of human needs, objectives, and consciousness."[82] For the Left, education and cultural transformation are crucial to acceding to political power. Socialist governance in America is deemed necessary to block the continuation of economic globalization, which is essential to the United States position in the geopolitical competition with Russia and its strategic partners and militant Islam.

Democracy in America centers around some 513,000 elected offices in the United States.[83] Like a giant boa constrictor, American progressives-socialists-marxists have been slowly squeezing the very life out of the once liberal-dominated Democratic Party by replacing its big government agenda with a series of harsh progressive-socialist-marxist policies and programs.

Despite the disputed election of George W. Bush, the Institute for Policy Studies retained considerable influence on Capitol Hill through its association with the Congressional Progressive Caucus. In a December 4, 2000, memo, IPS director John Cavanagh wrote that at a meeting with Congressional allies "we found progressive unity and optimism on five crucial issues: transformation of the electoral system and financing elections; universal health care, starting with children (Cavanagh added that "this should be winnable with a strong, consolidated push"); drug policy and sentencing reform; closing the wage and wealth gap; and ending corporate-led globalization." Cavanagh continued that "IPS is committed to playing a central role in research, mobilization, and citizen activism in two major areas where our major political parties have no answers: reining in corporate power and ending the war system." On all of these issues the Institute's director wrote, "IPS has helped put together coalitions to build unity and focus the efforts of activists on every level from communities to Capitol Hill."

Four years later, Cavanagh wrote a sheepish letter on November 3rd to "Dear Friends" mourning John Kerry's loss and the re-election of President Bush. "I want you to know," he lamented, "that we at IPS share the profound disappointment that the progressive goals of achieving equality and fairness here and around the world appear much farther away." It was not long, however, before IPS and its allies were back on the attack. "It is time for progressives to launch a comprehensive challenge to America's extreme concentration of wealth," former IPS fellow Gar Alperovitz wailed in early 2005. "This is not only morally and economic [sic] right; a number of developments suggest it is also one of the areas where progressives can aggressively take the political offensive."[84]

By mid-2008, the outlook of progressives-socialists-marxists appeared to have improved significantly. Lance Selfa wrote in the *International Socialist Review*, for instance, that "increased public support for the social safety net, signs of growing public concern about income inequality, and a diminished appetite for assertive national security policies have improved the political landscape for the Democrats as the 2008 presidential campaign gets underway."[85]

A major player in the politics of the progressive-socialist-marxist movement is Robert Borosage, a former IPS director and in 2008 a co-director of the Campaign for America's Future, which is locked at the hip with IPS. In Borosage's view, "IPS is engaged in the struggle over the underlying principles and future direction of the political culture itself." He has turned all of his energies, as he outlined in an interview with S. Steven Powell in 1983, to "move the Democratic party's debate internally to the left by creating an invisible [IPS] presence in the party."[86]

The 2008 presidential election campaign became the culmination of Robert Borosage's efforts to infiltrate an "invisible" progressive-socialist-marxist presence inside the Democratic Party. At the same time, the synergism of the intellectual and journalist centers of gravity with the Rubin Imperium at the state and national levels provided a solid operational base to win political power by subverting the democratic process.

Congressional Progressive Caucus

Boasting a base of seventy-two members in early 2008, the Caucus represented almost a third of the 232-member Democratic majority in the U.S. House of Representatives. Buoyed by their new-found influence inside the Democratic Party and the House, Caucus members pushed to extend their influence into new arenas. The Caucus has long followed its "Progressive Caucus" agenda, including affordable health care, fair trade, civil rights and liberties, global peace, and environmental protections. In 2007, the Caucus, with the assistance of the Institute for Policy Studies, began developing specific policy proposals in the areas of immigration, trade, Iraq-war spending, and other topics vulnerable to progressive-socialist-marxist exploitation. U.S. Representative Lynn Woolsey, a Caucus co-director along with Representative Barbara Lee, bragged a bit in commenting on the clout enjoyed by the progressive-socialist-marxist Caucus concerning the Iraq war: "We're a force to be reckoned with and we know it."[87]

The Congressional Progressive Caucus is appropriately nestled comfortably under the wing of the Democratic Socialists of America, the U.S. representative to the Socialist International, which assures solidarity with the world socialist movement. Senator Bernie Sanders, a declared socialist and the only Senate member of the Caucus, provides an important connecting link between the Congressional Caucus and the Democratic Socialists.

Operational support for the Caucus has been provided by the Institute for Policy Studies since its inception in 1990. "The IPS provides members with bold policy approaches to national and international issues with research showing how skewed federal budget priorities [from a Gramscian communist perspective] cause economic, political and racial inequalities," the editors at *The Nation* explained. "IPS also takes caucus members to vulnerable communities to see the effects of these inequities firsthand."[88] The IPS-sponsored bus trips, walk-throughs, and on-the-scene discussions are key tools in its Gramsci toolbox for garnering support for socialist governance. Hugo Chavez used the same populist approach in garnering votes in the slums of Caracas that helped bring him to power; Evo Morales followed a similar approach with the indigenous peoples in Bolivia.

In the final analysis, the Congressional Progressive Caucus, Institute for Policy Studies, Democratic Socialists of America, and the Socialist International are working in solidarity to change the cultural outlook in America. Step one is to substitute the phrase "progressive" for "socialism and Marxism," when in fact they are one in the same. That means, Malachi Martin explains in *The Keys of This Blood,* dropping all references to Lenin, Marx, revolution, dictatorship of the proletarian and Workers' Paradise in favor of such ideas as national consensus and national unity. This means that Gramscian Marxists, labeled "progressives-socialists-marxists" in this book to highlight their common philosophical grounding, must participate in the normal and accepted democratic process in the United States. Lobbying, exerting clout, voting, and playing by the full gamut of congressional processes are prerequisites for the members of the Congressional Progressive [and socialist-marxist] Caucus. Gramsci went further, Malachi Martin writes, in saying that Marxists around the world "would have to behave in every respect the way Western democrats behave—not only accepting the existence of many political parties but forging alliances with some and friendships with others. They would have to defend pluralism, in fact."[89]

The Institute for Policy Studies serves as the idea house and puppeteer of the Congressional Progressive Caucus. It provides Caucus members a coherent socialist agenda and "bold, workable solutions to the country's most vexing problems."

In its 2004 Annual Report, the Institute for Policy Studies described its implementation of "new ways to organize our resources to maximize their impact on creating a country and world where democracy, human rights, justice, ecological balance, diversity, and peace can spread." or these activities can be legitimately be labeled as examples of Gramsci's "philosophy of praxis." The Institute laid out its grand strategy for encouraging a quiet cultural revolution inside the United States that would bring the progressives-socialists-marxists to power: "IPS public scholars [researcher-activists] continue to work closely with dozens of other groups to strengthen the progressive infrastructure in this country, in particular through" (1) " a new Cities for Progress network that links local elected officials with activists to build national campaigns," (2) "a revitalized link between the . . . Congressional Progressive Caucus and progressives across the country," and (3) "mechanism to link thousands of progressive academics into the public debate."[90]

Campaign for America's Future

Leaders of the American Left were giddy when they believed in June 2007 that the "worm had turned"—the last quarter century of conservative dominance had crashed and burned. The time for the progressive-socialist-marxist movement had arrived. No one was more delighted by this turn of events nor more dedicated to take advantage of this perceived downfall than Robert L. Borosage, once the organizing director of the anti-intelligence Center for National Security Studies, director of the Institute for Policy

Studies, issues director for the Reverend Jesse Jackson's run for president, and the president of the Institute for America's Future and co-director of the Campaign for America's Future.

A Yale Law School graduate, Borosage helped the Institute for Policy Studies in 1972 create the Project on National Security, which prepared critical studies on U.S. government intelligence agencies (the CIA, FBI, and National Security Agency) and collected information on corporate and private security programs, which alarmed transnational corporations whose employees were often the target of kidnapping in various parts of the world. In 1974, IPS moved the anti-intelligence initiative outside of its direct purview. A new legal entity was created, the Center for National Security Studies, under the direction of Robert Borosage. The new Center operated under the Fund for Peace umbrella, which was closely linked with the Institute for Policy Studies and its funders. Peter Weiss, for instance, was at the same time Chairman of the Board of IPS and also served on the Executive Committee of the Board of Trustees of the Fund for Peace.[91]

By 2004, while Borosage was still fully engaged in the "struggle over the underlying principles and future direction of the political culture itself" by pouring his efforts into the Campaign for America's Future, he still had time to serve the Rubin Imperium as a member of the IPS Board of Directors.[92] In more than three decades of trying to transform American culture en route to bringing progressives-socialists-marxists to political power, Borosage never strayed far from the Institute for Policy Studies. As his words betrayed in June 2007, Borosage is one of the radical Left's "true believers."

Robert Borosage delivered "Straight Talk 2007" on June 18, 2007, to the 3,000-plus attendees at the Campaign for America's Future conference "Take Back America 2007." He pitched this near-perfect political propaganda to a wildly enthusiastic Left-wing audience. It demonized "conservatives," while offering an up-lifting soaring of the "progressive" eagles who would save "working" Americans from those devils that profit from corporate success—the Left would drive a spike into the heart of those who have broken the "public social contract." Never mind that the world had changed and the American economy was accommodating globalization. Rather than enlighten by explaining the transition from a national to an integrated world economy, Borosage and his progressive-socialist-marxist acolytes would hide behind the truth by casting images on the wall of Plato's cave that do not equate with reality in the world of sunlight. Insofar as political propaganda is concerned, "Straight Talk 2007" selects just enough of the truths, which are ballyhooed by incessant Left-wing propaganda to make Borosage's sweeping generalizations attractive to the unknowing. Instead of leading all Americans, including those labeled "working people" by the Left, to a better life and economy and security for themselves and their children into the future, the real progressive promise is to lead the American people down a yellow brick road filled with magic stories, which, eventually, would produce collective poverty beyond most people's wildest imagination.

Straight Talk 2007

Our time has come. Progressives are on the move. We are driving the political debate. . . . The 2006 election exposed the collapse of conservatism. . . . In 2006, Americans had had enough. They voted for change—from the U.S. Senate down to the local city councils. . . . Conservatives now scramble to divorce themselves from the Bush debacle. The circular firing squad has formed. . . . Conservatism has failed because it gets the world wrong. Its foreign policy misconceptions have left us less secure and more vilified across the world. . . . Its social and political strategies drive us apart rather than bring us together. . . . Large majorities of

American now understand that we are on the wrong track. They are looking for a new direction. They want bold leadership, with real solutions that address real challenges. . . . Progressives now drive the debate. Americans increasingly want the debacle in Iraq brought to an end. . . . On clean energy, on health care, on trade, on affordable college, a growing majority of Americans are looking for action. . . . But while Americans are moving our way, conservative ideas still shackle our imaginations and the conservative message machine backed by power corporate lobbies still stifles our progress. . . . We need a new public contract that the corporations are now shredding. We need to give workers power and hold executives accountable to law. We need a global economic strategy in trade and investment that works for the nation, not simply stateless multinationals. Americans are demanding an end to the costly big oil energy policies. . . . Health care is once more on the agenda. . . . It is time to take on the insurance and drug industries, to insist that this country join every other industrial nation in providing affordable, high-quality health care to everyone. For over a quarter of a century, conservatives have dominated our politics. They have created a society in which we grow apart, rather than together, an economy in which working and middle-class Americans work harder and longer simply to stay afloat. They have left our nation less secure abroad and our citizens with less shared prosperity at home. It's time for change. We can build a more just and more prosperous nation. . . . Conservatives have failed. The struggle for the next era has begun.

—*Robert L. Borosage, Co-Director,*
Campaign for America's Future, June 2007

8

NATIONAL SECURITY

We must create a whole solar system of organizations and smaller committees around the Communist Party, so to speak, smaller organizations working actually under the influence of our Party (not under mechanical leadership).

—Otto Kuusinen, a top official of the
Soviet Union's Communist International, 1926[1]

The genius of the Samuel Rubin Imperium is founded on keeping its central hub, the Institute for Policy Studies, small—twenty-five to thirty researcher-activists—while extending its outreach by building and nurturing a vast Left-wing network of what might be called a "solar system of organizations." Secondly, the Institute's "collaborator 'shining stars,'" as IPS calls its strategic partners that make up the Left's solar system, do not function under the Institute's direct or "mechanical leadership." Rather, IPS serves like a "sun," exercising its influence through leadership and continuity of effort by its researcher-activists on wide-ranging cultural, societal, and political agendas. Other organizations and groups are drawn to its orbit in small clusters or constellations that collaborate in the greater progressive-socialist-marxist movement.

"IPS is an independent, alternative voice on key issues that shape our world," the Institute explained in its 2004 annual report, "with links to the social movements that are the engines of change."[2] The IPS "voice on key issues," however, is a bit stronger than simple "links" to the "social movements." While IPS eschews direct or "mechanical leadership" over its collaborator "shining stars," its influence is an essential behind-the-scenes driving force for those "engines of change."

When one appraises the Institute for Policy Studies over its more than four decades in operation, there is no denying its organizational genius as being similar to the vision expressed by Otto Kuusinen in 1926. But that is not to say IPS had somehow been tied to international communism over the years. It is to say, however, that the "test-bed for radical organizing" underlying the Rubin Imperium appears very much like the image presented by Mr. Kuusinen some eighty years ago. Moreover, Kuusinen's structure provides a useful framework for analyzing the inner workings of the Rubin Imperium's strategic partnership with hundreds of Left-wing organizations, communist and non-communist alike.

The "solar system" comes to operational life through IPS guidance, which is often expressed as a vision for others to follow. In 2007, for example, IPS expressed several broad proposals for action based on a beginning premise: "Current U.S. foreign policy is unjust and breeds insecurity for all. . . . We must focus instead on a just security, because there can be no real security without justice." Among the items on its normative wish list, IPS calls for cutting the U.S. defense budget by one-third, reducing U.S. and Russian nuclear arsenals dramatically as a first step toward nuclear disarmament, and advancing toward a "latticework of international institutions and laws."[3]

S. Steven Powell described the Left's spinoff organizations as being "a wilderness of mirrors. . . . The proliferation of spinoffs has given IPS influence a multiplier effect. Its themes are reinforced by ostensibly separate groups, but in fact little diversity exists. The spinoff strategy has also helped to diversify funding sources and to build networks. This gives IPS a central role in coalition-building, which is increasingly important in this era of special-interest politics."[4]

One well-traveled pathway for IPS to multiply its influence on the progressive-socialist-marxist movement is through its Washington, D.C.-based Social Action Leadership School for Activists (SALSA). The School provides training to enhance the effectiveness of activists or "nonprofit professionals." IPS explains: "SALSA's curriculum includes 'nuts and bolts' classes on organizing, management, and activism, as well as seminars on policy issues from the local to the international level."[5] This hands-on training helps to preserve and enhance IPS's central position in the progressive-socialist-marxist solar system of organizations.

The ostensible "core philosophy" of IPS is founded on the notion that independent centers of thought outside government are needed to develop social theory, as distinct from social action, while sharing a vital learning interaction. "In practice," John Rees observed, "Institute fellows sought to become political organizers, the idea-people behind a broad range of campaigns of the Left." IPS skillfully selects words to create a light smokescreen about its intentions. This half in the shadows and half in the world of light approach has delivered benefits over the years—it keeps observers guessing about its goals and ideological orientation. The mainstream media, dominated by those with liberal world views, has been reticent in coverage of IPS and its members. Rather than refer to the Institute as being "radical," or "progressive," its own self-description, the news media often remains silent. When IPS is addressed by the media, it is usually in neutral terms, such as being a "Washington think tank" or "liberal think tank."[6]

IPS is hardly "liberal." It is a training center for progressive-socialist-marxist organizations, a center for production and dissemination of propaganda against U.S. foreign and domestic policies, and a forum for ideas to redesign America culture, society, and government. At the same time, IPS is not static. Rather, it evolves with the world and operates through what it calls a "transnational network of scholars and activists." IPS manages its public exposure through its network of contacts with current and former policymakers, generals and admirals, academics, journalists, members of Congress, and spinoff organizations adopted, created, or encouraged by the Institute. IPS fellows also use their ready access to the editorial pages of the *Washington Post* and *New York Times*, two of the country's leading newspapers. Writers affiliated with IPS also publish their views in *Foreign Policy, Village Voice, New Statesman*, and in the "alternative" media—*The Nation, Progressive, In These Times*, and others.

The IPS self-image is based on its record of "transforming ideas into action for peace, justice and the environment."[7] The leadership sees the Institute as a "multi-issue think tank" serving as "an independent, alternative voice on key issues." "Throughout this work," IPS writes in its 2004 annual report, "we have collaborated with, supported, built, and linked activists, elected officials, organizations, and social movements across issues, race, geography, and other traditional divisions."[8] This is a bit tame when compared to the IPS anniversary report in 1983 when Americans were referred to as having been "hostages" or "prisoners" by co-founder Marcus Raskin and the IPS mission was defined as being "to 'liberate' people from their colonized status and to 'reconstruct' society."[9] While the rhetoric was tamed in 2008, IPS goals were no less radical than they were a quarter of a century ago.

According to an IPS overview, "the Institute for Policy Studies strengthens social movements with independent research, visionary thinking, and links to the grass roots, scholars and selected officials.

Since 1963, we have empowered people to build healthy and democratic societies in communities, the U.S., and the world." IPS is also very clear in its disclaimer on taking positions: "IPS works with but is independent of political parties and movements. We embrace internal diversity of thought, and believe that discussion and debate are crucial in forging solid, practical public scholarship." Secondly, its disclaimer states that "in order to give our scholars and projects the widest freedom to explore and express their own views, IPS as an institution does not take positions on issues."[10]

IPS has also described itself as a "source of radical scholarship." Then-IPS director Robert Borosage explained in the Institute's 1979–80 Annual Report that "public scholarship" is "not academic" and "does not adhere to academic disciplines." As IPS uses "public scholarship," it refers to academics that are actively supporting radical goals of remaking American society and government. This perspective slides smoothly into an adaptation of Antonio Gramsci's view that for intellectuals to be effective they "must be an organic part of a community [and] they must articulate new values within the shared language and symbols of the larger culture." Carl Boggs, himself an IPS collaborator, added that Gramsci took the view that "during the long struggle for ideological hegemony, the revolutionary intellectuals would have to take the initiative on many fronts: raising new questions and introducing new modes of thinking about reality, attacking the accepted wisdom of established intellectual authorities, and providing theoretical guidance to the emerging mass struggles."[11]

IPS-affiliated scholars are expected to be researchers and activists. Writing a tome on a particular issue with a string of recommendations and leaving it on the table for someone in government to pick up and implement is insufficient. IPS people are expected to be activists and to push their ideas and writings through books, films, articles, and demonstrative experiments that put into practice radical alternative policy options. S. Steven Powell, in his chapter on "Revolutionary Think Tank" in *Covert Cadre*, for example, quoted then-IPS director Robert Borosage in 1983 (and a member of the IPS Board of Directors in 2007) as asserting: "Our job is to expose the moral and political bankruptcy of the ideas and assumptions governing America."[12] "The concrete meaning of politics in Gramsci's Marxism," Carl Boggs added to this revolutionary perspective, "was its role in enlisting mass energies in the struggle for ideological hegemony and in establishing a new socialist 'national-popular' community out of the cleavages and crises of the old society."[13]

Revolutionary Left

Bubbling in the shadows of world affairs following the Soviet Union's demise are several Marxist-Leninist, Maoist, and other communist and socialist parties. Contrary to popular belief, the Old Left survived the death of Soviet Marxism-Leninism. Some of their ideas have been re-shaped to accommodate Gramsci's stealthy, long-term cultural transformation formula for defeating the capitalist West. But, by and large, for the revolutionary Left, the worker's struggle is still all about class war, the proletariat versus the bourgeoisie. For the Institute for Policy Studies, which never has had enemies on the left, nothing changed.

When the Soviet Union passed from the world scene, Gramsci's political philosophy of penetrating existing cultures to transform society and its institutions through direct action and propaganda intensified its efforts underwriting the IPS-guided progressive-socialist-marxist faceless international. Perhaps Norman Thomas, a founder of the American Civil Liberties Union and a six time Socialist Party presidential candidate, said it best: "The American people will never knowingly adopt socialism, but under the name of liberalism they will adopt every fragment of the socialist program until one day America will be a socialist nation without ever knowing how it happened." Now substitute the euphemism "progressive" for "socialism" and remember Vladimir Lenin's words: "the goal of socialism is communism."

Communist Party of the United States

The Communist Party of the United States did not disappear with the disintegration of the Soviet Union on December 31, 1991. Rather, the Party adapted with a new revolutionary warfare doctrine to carry out the "workers struggle" against capitalism. The Communist Party's past role as an important link in the Kremlin's worldwide espionage efforts during the Cold War has been exposed. The KGB (Soviet Communist Party-directed) and GRU (military) intelligence spent millions of dollars year after year funding the U.S. Communist Party's espionage. Much of this relationship is documented in John Barron's book, *Operation Solo* (1996); additional details about the Party's interaction with the Kremlin are anticipated after the thousands of documents and other records donated by the Communist Party, USA, to New York University in 2007 are catalogued and opened to the public.[14]

Sounding like an echo chamber from the Cold War, Communist Party national board member John Bachtell said in 2003 that "the Bush Doctrine flows from the political dominance of government by the extreme right wing sections of monopoly capital (finance capital, the oil, energy and military transnationals) and their ideologues, including religious fundamentalism of all sorts." Bachtell added that "US imperialism has always sought world domination."[15]

Communist Party, USA, leaders continue to refer to the Old Left entity as a "leader of the class struggle" and a "labor-led people's coalition against right-wing domination of our nation's political structures."[16] The brochure with these points and other materials from the Communist Party, USA, were distributed at the June 2007 conference on the Campaign for America's Future, a function hosted by IPS collaborators Robert Borosage and Roger Hickey.

Committees of Correspondence for Democracy and Socialism

The Committees of Correspondence for Democracy and Socialism is a splinter group of the Communist Party, USA. Angela Davis, a tenured professor at the University of California at Santa Cruz, exited the Communist Party, USA, in 1991. She believes that "the only path of liberation for black people is that which leads toward complete and radical overthrow of the capitalist class"—it was on the basis of this viewpoint that Davis established the Committees of Correspondence.[17] Others joining at the Committees include Bettina Aptheker and Conn Hallinan, also teaching in the "Big Red School House" at Santa Cruz, Purdue's radical "peace" professor Garry Targ, and long-time Communist Leslie Cagan, an ardent supporter of Fidel Castro.

Radical professor Harry Targ, director of Purdue University's Peace Studies Program, in 2003 called for "opposition to U.S. imperialism" and a clarification of the links between "U.S. capitalism, global conquest, and visions of empire." A longtime Castro backer, Targ's Peace Studies course at Purdue includes a university trip to Cuba where students are indoctrinated and visit farms and factories to learn about socialist means of production.[18]

Leslie Cagan, a communist since the 1960s, is an original founder of the Committees of Correspondence and a strong supporter of Fidel Castro. She is co-chair of United for Peace and Justice, a virulent anti-war coalition. In 2004, she co-founded Global Exchange with Medea Benjamin who has gained notoriety with Code Pink. Benjamin and her acolytes established a major presence at the IPS-surrogate Campaign for America's Future in June 2007.[19]

Workers World Party

A third cabal on America's revolutionary Left is the Workers World Party. This Marxist-Leninist working-class party fights against what its adherents believe are "evils of capitalism." At the same time, "Workers World fights for a socialist society—where the wealth is socially owned and production is planned to satisfy human needs."[20] Party members claim to be "independent Marxists" whose "goal is solidarity of all the workers and oppressed against . . . [the] criminal imperialist system."[21] Similar themes were echoed by "progressives" at the 2007 Campaign for America's Future conference. The World Workers Party has stated that "we know that nothing is secure—not our jobs, our homes, our health care, our pensions, our civil rights and liberties—as long as capitalism exists. So our goal is a society run by the workers, not just as pawns in a capitalist political game but as collective owners of the social wealth."[22] The International Action Center's propaganda library is loaded with lies, half-truths, and sometimes crazy inventions of U.S. wrongdoing in the world, especially regarding North Korea, Cuba, and Palestine. In 2008, the Workers World Party operated under the banner of the International Action Center, led by Ramsey Clark, in New York.

The relationship between IPS (Peter and Cora Weiss) and the International Action Center (Ramsey Clark) and its supporting Workers World Party has been enriched by the anti-war movement following the September 11, 2001, terrorist attack. One reason is that the Texas-reared Ramsey Clark seems to see himself as the new gun in town: he labels American officials "international outlaws," accuses them of murdering "innocent people because we don't like their leader," and makes them out to be inhumane monsters— "They're like the neutron bomb, which is the most 'inspired' of all weapons, because it kills the people and preserves the property, the wealth. So you get the wealth and you don't have the baggage of the hungry, clamoring poor."[23]

Clark built a law practice by representing a host of societies' worst violators.[24] In December 2004, Clark, a former U.S. Attorney General, joined Saddam Hussein's legal team, defending him in Baghdad. Clark explained his action as being a result of the U.S. intention to secure a conviction of "the former leader in an unfair trial . . . [that] would corrupt justice."[25]

The Revolutionary Communist Party, the premier Maoist Party in the United States, has been a regular participant in the anti-globalization and anti-war protests since late 1999. The radicals that formed the Party's ancestor, the Progressive Labor Movement, in 1962 did so to favor Chinese Communism over Soviet Marxism-Leninism. Several members joined forces with the Students for a Democratic Society in 1966, which split into the Revolutionary Youth Movement that, in turn, broke into two factions—the notorious terrorist group Weatherman and another that eventually became the Revolutionary Communist Party. In 2007, many of the Party's members were teachers and professors, and journalists and writers, as well as the San Francisco and California Poet Laureates.[26] H. Bruce Franklin, for instance, an English professor at the Bay Area Revolutionary Union in 1969 was also a founder of Cuba's *Venceremos* Brigade. Franklin's group argued for armed struggle in the hope of establishing a "dictatorship of the proletariat" in the United States. In 2003, Professor Franklin, then at Rutger's University, was a signatory to the "Historians Against the Iraq War," a denunciation of the U.S. invasion.[27]

Robert Avakian was the Party's founder and former "Chairman-in-Exile." Criminal indictments in 1981 for breaking into the White House grounds during a presidential ceremony prompted Avakian to flee to Paris, a location from which he agitated for the overthrow of the U.S. government. The following quotation offers a sample of the Revolutionary Party's radical program:

Of all the tyrants and oppressors in the world, there is none that has caused more untold misery and committed more screaming injustices against the people of the world than the ruler of the U.S. This is a country founded on genocide and slavery. . . . The rulers of the U.S. have plundered and slaughtered their way to the top position within the worldwide system of capitalist-imperialism—a system of global exploitation, of political and military domination, and of murderous rivalry among the imperialist powers themselves.[28]

Democratic Socialists of America (DSA)

A fourth example of the hard Left's efforts to disassemble America and rebuild it in their image is the Democratic Socialists of America (DSA). For the Democratic Socialists, "building progressive movements for social change while establishing an openly socialist presence in American communities and politics" is the base of their three-phased vision for the future. First, restructuring society will be necessary through Democratic Socialists advocating their version of democracy as a means of giving the people "a real voice" in the issues that affect them. Secondly, the DSA, as the largest socialist organization in the United States, will serve as the American affiliate of the Socialist International, a worldwide organization of more 140 socialist, social democratic, and labor parties, plus selected radical terrorist groups as observers. And, third, the DSA will prosecute a broad global anti-capitalism agenda in support of the IPS-inspired progressive-socialist-marxist movement. The DSA-sponsored activist group "Mobilization for Global Justice," for instance, grew out of the anti-globalization protests in Seattle in 1999 and subsequent ones in Washington, D.C.[29]

The Congressional Progressive Caucus of more than seventy members of the House of Representatives (and one senator) is directly supported by the Democratic Socialists of America and the Institute for Policy Studies. For these three radical political centers, the march toward a socialist restructuring of American society is the goal. Since the Caucus was established in 1992, it has attracted members of the Democratic Party. Since 1994, the Congressional Progressive Caucus, for example, has favored sizable reductions in military and intelligence funding, the centerpiece of efforts by the "peace" movement to disarm the United States unilaterally.[30]

Several links between individuals and organizations make up the socialist network in America. The fact that the DSA and IPS are closely allied gives Cora Weiss and the other leaders of the Rubin Imperium access to and an inner presence in the Socialist International.

Barbara Ehrenreich is the Honorary Chairwoman of the Democratic Socialists of America, and she is a member of the IPS board of trustees, ensuring a continuing linkage. Rather than seeking to increase its political influence by establishing its own political party, the DSA has chosen to work closely with the Democratic Party to promote its Leftist agendas, which include opposition to the U.S. war on terror. It also is a member of Communist Leslie Cagan's United for Peace and Justice anti-war organization.[31] Ehrenreich is also an Institute for Policy Studies "shining star."

A "Just" National Security

From the beginning, the Institute for Policy Studies has held a devil theory of the United States, saying it was necessary to tear down the "national security state" and replace it with a "just security state." IPS co-founder Marcus Raskin explained in his 1979 book *The Politics of National Security* that what America's liberal democracy called the national security state was "a conglomerate of great corporations, police and military agencies, and technical and labor elites tied [to] their world empire, making and preparing for war, and transforming nature into material processes for domination while parading these processes as social development."[32] In an earlier writing, *Being and Doing*, Raskin also likened corporations as being "colonizers" of American society that secretly controlled the U.S. government. Raskin said the United States was "the most crucial and dangerous colony is the Violence colony . . . [that] grew out of technology, anticommunist paranoia and a subsidized socialist system of corporate entities."[33] "Parts of the *Federalist Papers*," Raskin wrote, "made it clear that the United States was to be an empire with imperial designs."[34] This quotation is IPS's Rosetta Stone—it provides the secret to translating the bulk of IPS hate propaganda directed toward the United States. The powerful in society have led Americans to a point where "political and social problems are getting worse." He added that "other ways of thought are picking up the slack," noting that "such positive social philosophies as Marxism are beginning to have a larger following in an underground way." Raskin writes a stunning insight to his thinking: "We are all Marxists—either by using that analysis or playing out, as actions, the tragic role Marx foresaw."[35]

This picture of corporations serving as ogres suppressing the United States and colonizing its people remains a cornerstone of the contemporary progressive-socialist-marxist movement. Whatever a particular national security issue might be, the Institute for Policy Studies and its constellations of "shining stars" preserve this anti-corporate core. Images cast onto the walls of Plato's cave always return to corporation devils controlling the United States government and its defining national security in ways to foster their interests. True believers in the IPS philosophy are converted or have their perceptions strengthened by the constant anti-corporate propaganda emanating from the Institute and its "shining stars." The sunlight of reality blinds those who have been converted to support the progressive-socialist-marxist cultural revolution, which advances step-by-step every day. In the final analysis, this pathway aligns broadly with Gramsci's formula of cultural revolution in advanced capitalist societies.

Not only does such propaganda erode popular support for national defense, but it confuses America's friends and allies while encouraging its enemies. A June 2007 IPS monograph, for instance, says that "current U.S. foreign policy is unjust and breeds insecurity for all. . . . We must focus instead on just security, because there can be no real security without justice."[36] According to the Institute for Policy Studies, security includes not only "freedom from military conflict and terrorist attack" but also sufficient access to food and shelter, good health care, good jobs, a clean environment, and "well-functioning, accountable political structures."[37]

The broad view of national security as cast by the Institute for Policy Studies is good propaganda. It interweaves just enough truth to be believable, it is sufficiently logical to withstand frontal alternatives, and it drags its nets through shallow waters to catch as many fish as possible, as small as they might be. It also implies that Americans are being shortchanged on many of their personal security needs that should be fulfilled by government, which may not be fully accountable due to its role of serving corporations and global imperialism. Finally, the IPS corporate devil theory and design for "just security" by government in some kind of socialist world view provides the basis for constant attacks on the existing national security structure in the United States.

Additional propaganda and disinformation pour into American society through four main Institute for Policy Studies spinoffs that supported its devil theory of a corporate-controlled U.S. government. The Samuel Rubin Foundation and numerous other money sources on the Left donated tens of millions of dollars to support this cornerstone anti-American project.

Center for National Security Studies (CNSS)

The Center for National Security Studies (CNSS) has long served as the radical Left's primary political mouthpiece in the 1970s by railing against the CIA, FBI, and other federal intelligence and law enforcement agencies. Against a background of questionable actions by the CIA and FBI to confront threats to U.S. security during the Cold War, the IPS and its spinoff front, the CNSS, and its extremist allies slandered and attacked the CIA and FBI to the point that political pressure from the Congress mandated changes to operational procedures that in the end gravely endangered the United States by opening gaps in the nation's security.

A "Congressional vendetta" was unleashed against the CIA and FBI in the mid-1970s with the care-and-feeding of the House and Senate select committees on intelligence in the hands of radical Leftists associated with IPS. So effective were these assaults against the country's national security agencies that operational changes created a "wall" between intelligence and law enforcement. Islamic terrorists exploited this illogical barrier in the 1993 attack World Trade Center in New York, and, in the absence of corrective action by the Clinton administration, again on September 11, 2001. S. Steven Powell warned Americans in his 1987 book, *Covert Cadre*, of the internal dangers to the United States:

> . . . IPS, with its entourage of National Lawyers Guild [identified as a communist front by a congressional committee] activists and friends in the media, attempted to scandalize and discredit the U.S. intelligence agencies. Henceforth, a great portion of IPS energies would be devoted to an antiintelligence campaign, the power of which was fully felt some years later. . . .[38]

This Center for National Security Studies was established at a two-day conference on Capitol Hill at the Russell Senate Office Building in September 1974 that addressed "The CIA and Covert Action." Powell characterized the proceedings as being "a trial of the CIA, which was assumed guilty of various crimes; the embattled CIA director, William Colby, faced nearly two dozen accusers, critics, and witnesses."[39] About 300 participants took part, many of them legislative aides to U.S. representatives and senators. Four members of Congress—Senators Edward Brook (R-Mass.), Phillip Hart (D-Mich.), James Abourezk (D-S. Dak.), a senior advisor to Barack Obama in 2008 (though hidden in the shadows), and Representative

Michael Harrington (D-Mass.)—gave credibility to the assembled Left-wing America-haters. The news media were enlisted to make public real or alleged abuses and wrongdoing by the intelligence agencies. CIA Director William Colby attended the conference to defend the Agency, but he miscalculated the goodwill of the cabal of anti-Americans and was pounded by false allegations, lies, and distortions by his inquisitors. IPS co-chairman Richard Barnet, for instance, made it clear, that he believed " 'national security' . . . [was] the holy oil that converts felonious acts into patriotic exploits."[40] He went on by slandering the CIA and its dedicated operations officers:

'It is not possible to maintain a bureaucracy of hired killers, thieves, and con men for use against foreigners who get in our way without soon feeling the effects at home. . . . The fundamental reason why the secret war bureaucracy threatens the rule of law is that by all democratic norms it is inherently a criminal enterprise.'[41]

In an act of infamy, Congressman Michael Harrington (D-Mass.) filed suit, in collusion with the radical Left's National Emergency Civil Liberties Committee, a communist front, which triggered the House Intelligence Committee to compel Colby to testify in closed session. Harrington then demanded and received a copy of Colby's classified closed-session testimony, quickly leaking the transcript to Seymour Hersh at the *New York Times*. Hersh's article alleged that the CIA conducted large-scale covert activities against the Marxist, Soviet-leaning Salvador Allende, president of Chile. The news piece helped trigger political support for the creation of the Church Committee (Senate) and Pike Committee (House) that began radical investigations into the CIA, FBI, NSA, and military intelligence agencies. Many sensitive documents were released to the press. The strict congressional oversight procedures over the intelligence agencies exercised by the Senate and House in place in 2008 are rooted in these events that occurred in the 1970s.[42]

Robert Borosage, a former IPS fellow and head of the National Lawyer's Guild's Washington Office, became the first director of CNSS.[43] The Center, organized "in 1974 to work for control of the FBI and CIA and to prevent violations of civil liberties in the United States," drew heavily on the best and brightest of IPS thinkers for direction and developing propaganda attacks against these government institutions.[44] Among the brain power skimmed from IPS were Robert Borosage, Morton Halperin, Anthony Lake, and Michael Klare. Klare, a revolutionary activist, had been very helpful to Philip Agee, the CIA turncoat turned communist, in writing his screed against the CIA, *Inside the Company*. Klare also gave speeches at places like the University of Havana, the Oslo Peace Research Institute, and IPS's very own Leftist indoctrination center, The Washington School.[45] In 2008, Mr. Klare operated as one of Cora Weiss's discreet soldiers by scheming behind the scenes on a variety of issues, including international control of small arms. He operated out of Amherst, Massachusetts, where he was a Professor of Peace and World Security for five universities.

W. Anthony Lake had been railing about abolishing the CIA for years. A long-time IPS operative, Lake served as National Security Advisor to President Clinton. He was also among the IPS radicals receiving government appointments during the Carter Administration. In Lake's case, he was head of the State Department Policy Planning Staff. Earlier he had served on the National Security staff under Henry Kissinger; he resigned to express his disagreement with the U.S. incursion into Cambodia.[46] Lake also had a close association with Orlando Letelier, a Chilean Marxist with warm relations with top Cuban officials.[47] He was said to be an inside advisor for Barack Obama's 2008 presidential campaign.[48]

In a 1976 "search and destroy" book, *The CIA File*, Robert Borosage and his co-editor, John Marks, stated their basic premise: "Covert action violates some of the basic principles of our constitutional order, international law, and of values generally shared by American citizens." Borosage was plugged-in to the Clinton Administration by means of personal relationships. He and Hillary Rodham Clinton knew each other and shared an intense interest in student activism at the Yale Law School in the early 1970s, especially in helping members of the Black Panther Party. Borosage enjoyed contacts with Strobe Talbot, State Department; Robert Reich, Secretary of Labor; and Mickey Kantor, political operative. In April 1982, IPS Director Borosage was one of those traveling to Moscow who signed a joint statement on arms limitations and reductions and on how best to create the conditions necessary for a stable peace. During the Clinton Administration, Borosage headed the Campaign on Demilitarization and Democracy and advocated cutting the Defense budget in half or more.[49]

Morton Halperin was at the center of the CNSS campaign to destroy the CIA's ability to conduct covert actions and the FBI's capacity to carry out effective counterintelligence activities. He was a partner of Robert Borosage and Anthony Lake in the launching of CNSS in 1974. Halperin, a staff member at Harvard's Center for International Affairs, 1960–65, also served on the Nixon-Kissinger National Security Council in 1969. Suspected of leaking the story of secret bombing of Cambodia sanctuaries (an action that may have saved this writer's life), Halperin resigned. He joined CNSS in 1974 and joined in the far Left's slander of the CIA. With the backing of the National Lawyers Guild, a communist front, Halperin founded the Campaign to Stop Government Spying. He was a regular on Capitol Hill, spewing scorn against the intelligence collection and counter-intelligence activities of the CIA and FBI. As writer James L. Tyson put it so gently about Halperin's activities: he has "*No* record of any writings or statements that might be against the Communist line."[50] S. Stephen Powell added that "a balance sheet analysis of Halperin's writings and testimonies reveals a continuing advocacy of weakening U.S. intelligence capabilities and ignoring the vast intelligence espionage, and intrigues of the KGB." "For Halperin," Powell said, there are "no enemies on the Left."[51] In 2006, Halperin joined George Soros at the Open Society Institute in Washington, D.C., as director of U.S. advocacy, and participated as controlling presence inside the Democratic Party.[52]

Center for Defense Information (CDI)

Since its inception in 1969, the Center for Defense Information—calling itself an "independent monitor of the Pentagon"—has been a critical voice dedicated to undermining public support for the armed forces and their armament programs, supporting Soviet Cold War propaganda and disinformation (William Arkin who leaked nuclear defense plans in the early 1980s began his activist career at CDI), and unleashing constant criticism of American defense policies, strategy, and counter-terrorism operations. Admiral Gene R. LaRoque for many years gave military credence to CDI's propaganda. Rather than support the Kremlin directly, CDI published articles favorable to the Soviet point of view. The Soviets, in turn, would use the CDI pronouncements to buttress its arguments against U.S. policies. In this way, CDI could support Moscow indirectly. "Even though the president and his ambassador to Moscow have difficulty in communicating with the Kremlin," S. Steven Powell wrote in 1987, "Adm. Gene LaRoque (ret.), director of CDI, has no problem." He added that "whenever the Soviets need American help to buttress their position, they can count on LaRoque, on whom they call frequently."[53]

The World Security Institute (WRI), another IPS collaborator, was established in 2005 as an umbrella organization for the Center of Defense Information. The CDI was joined by three propaganda divisions that were designed to educate foreign audiences about political, social, and cultural issues in the United States; deliver television programs, documentaries, and new media investigations of international issues; and provide travel grants for journalists, photographers, and film makers to deliver selected coverage of international crises to the American media. The CDI's *Defense Monitor* pumps-out propaganda against weapons programs, unilateral use of military force, and a full range of measures designed to weaken support for national security programs.

In the spring of 2004, when a lot of national security issues were outstanding and Americans were looking down an al-Qaeda gun barrel at home, General Anthony Zinni became the latest senior military officer to unleash a load of CDI propaganda. He had retired from the Marine Corps in July 2000 after nearly forty years in uniform to become a "Distinguished Military Fellow" at CDI. He did lend credence to a constant stream of anti-war, anti-American propaganda pouring forth from the radical Left. The worst of it is, as J. R. Dunn put it, Zinni's time at CDI undoubtedly encouraged "a half dozen other officers to join him." He concluded that "a group of veteran officers are being effectively used as fronts for a powerful secretive Leftist organization during a time of war."[54]

There is something very curious about CDI's recruitment of retired senior military officers to generate and give credibility to its anti-defense propaganda. During the final decades of the Cold War, East Germany's intelligence arm, Stasi, organized (under Soviet KGB guidance) "Generals for Peace and Disarmament." Operating out of an office in Ittervoort, the Netherlands, the members were made up of retired senior officers from NATO European countries, including the Netherlands, Germany, France, Norway, Canada, United Kingdom, Greece, Portugal, and Italy. Their task was to generate support for the Western "peace" movement and undermine NATO militaries. Some of the members retired early when they discovered they might be ordered to use nuclear weapons against Soviet and other Warsaw Pact forces. The generals (and admirals and air commodores) prepared a series of memoranda and reports on NATO nuclear policy, creation of nuclear free zones, and deployment of cruise and ballistic missiles (whose on the ground presence was demanded by the European governments). The Transnational Institute, IPS's sister organization in Amsterdam, was at the center of the European "peace" movement and is reported to have had a close rapport with the Generals for Peace and Disarmament.[55] Suffice it to say, the CDI operates very closely to the European-based anti-military model.

The Center for International Policy (CIP)

The Center for International Policy (CIP) is still funded in part by the Samuel Rubin Foundation. It remains a key IPS collaborator. A number of people from CIP were placed on the Church committee investigations of intelligence organizations in the mid-1970s, including the committee's staff director, William Miller, and task force leader, David Aaron. The late Orlando Letelier helped establish the center. Susan Weber, an early staff member, was formerly a copy editor for *Soviet Life* and was an employee of the Soviet Embassy; she was a registrant under the Foreign Agents Registration Act. Sidney Harman, an IPS trustee and husband of Congresswoman Jane Harman (D-Calif.), was a consultant to the Center for International Policy.[56]

William Goodfellow, husband of *Washington Post* reporter Dana Priest served at the beginning as deputy director.[57] Goodfellow conducted research on policy issues in post-Allende Chile and received admiring comments about his good work in a letter from Elizabeth Farnsworth of the North American Congress on Latin America, a pro-Communist lobbying group. Farnsworth's letter was found in the "Letelier Papers" published in the Congressional Record.[58]

Mel Goodman serves as a CIP senior fellow and director of the National Security Program. He was division chief and senior analyst at the Office of Soviet Affairs at the CIA from 1976 to 1986, which makes him one of those who failed to take KGB defector Anatoliy Golitsyn seriously. Goodman and his colleagues at the CIA had a chance to warn U.S. policymakers of the on-coming Soviet disinformation strategy triggered by Mikhail Gorbachev in the 1980s and the ideological flip from Marxism-Leninism to the stealthy Gramsci or cultural Marxism. Goodman presented a rather profane series of loosely connected thoughts in a series of sweeping generalizations about U.S. national security policies and weapons programs at the Borosage-Hickey June 2007 conference on the Campaign for America's Future.

National Security Archives

The National Security Archives, an IPS franchise operation that operates behind the cover of George Washington University, has served IPS and TNI well over the years. Among its donors are the Samuel Rubin Foundation and Philip M. Stern Family Fund, traditional IPS supporters, the [Barbara] Streisand Foundation and Open Society Fund (George Soros), and the Washington Post Company. The Archives exploit the Freedom of Information Act by "mining" U.S. government documents for secrets. The archive's mainframe computer hosts major databases of released documents (more than 90,000 records) another 15,000 records in files of individuals and organizations.[59]

These resources are sufficient to allow an efficient intelligence analyst to piece together a mosaic of major U.S. defense programs. Missing pieces can be filled by extrapolating data or focusing intelligence collection assets to fill the gaps to provide a more complete picture. Hence, it is not surprising that, according to David Chang of the National Security Archives in the late 1980s, an IPS collaborator ran a courier service for the Soviet intelligence by taking declassified documents processed by the National Security Archives to Moscow.[60]

Peter Kornbluh, a special soldier partner with Michael Klare in support of Cora Weiss, has one great goal in life: to expose the CIA's alleged role in the 1973 coup that toppled Chile's Marxist leader Salvador Allende and brought General Augusto Pinochet to power. Kornbluh is in charge of the Archive's Cuba Documentation Project, a position he uses with great effect in dunning the U.S. government with all kinds of policy prescriptions.

Kornbluh, along with Cora Weiss, Richard Barnet, Saul Landau, and Robert Borosage, visited Nicaragua in 1983, 1984, and 1985. The IPS entourage was warmly greeted by top Sandinista leaders, including Tomas Borge, Daniel Ortega, and Sergio Ramirez. Later, Borosage and Landau explained their visit in terms of helping the Sandinistas organize various projects in ways that would attract European support. Meanwhile, media activists at the U.S. National Public Radio (NPR) maintained close ties with Peter Kornbluh and other operatives to ensure that the right propaganda line flooded American airways.

The IPS gang, including its affable Peter Kornbluh, needs to account for their relationship with the Nicaraguan Sandinistas. *Covert Cadre* author S. Steven Powell wrote in 1987 that, "Tomas Borge, who works hand in glove with the Cuban DGI intelligence and is responsible for the execution of hundreds of political prisoners, has personally received IPS fellows, such as Richard Barnet and Peter Kornbluh, in his home in Managua."[61]

"The Peace Racket"

Writer Bruce Brawer coined the right phrase in characterizing such progressive-socialist-marxist "peace" disinformation campaign as "The Peace Racket."[62] The hate-filled speech by many "peace" advocates betrayed the underlying disdain for America's culture and government. Truth is often the first casualty in the "peace racket." Hollywood's Tim Robbins, for instance, presented to American viewers in an anti-Iraq war scream on HBO's "Real Time" with Bill Maher in 2007 that included a blatant lie and a slander of American troops: "we've killed over 400,000 Iraqis," Robbins howled.[63] Not even close—extraordinary tactical measures are taken to minimize non-combatant injuries. Saddam Hussein and his sons were the genocidal maniacs, rapists, and torturers, not U.S. troops. American soldiers are not war criminals, despite the Hollywood star's hard Left bombast. Maher, a world-class blame America-firster himself, let Robbins' hate speech pass.

"Peace" for the radical Left is more than simply anti-war. It is also about destroying what they denounce as the American "war system," which they assert is at the basis of U.S. foreign policy. The "peace racket" has been a hallmark activity at the Institute for Policy Studies for more than four decades. IPS co-founder Marcus Raskin has been consistent for many years in arguing that it is crucial to destroy the "U.S. national security state" and its "taxation, bureaucratic, technical, and military power to support the U.S. imperial system."[64]

IPS director John Cavanagh and board chair Ethelbert Miller reported in 2005, for instance, that "over the past year, we made great strides in linking our work on the rising costs of war to an expanding peace movement here and abroad, and we continue to strengthen our work to end the Iraq War and to prevent future wars with bold alternatives for the United States and the world."[65] These anti-U.S. goals are typical of the "popular front" technique used to mask the fires of the Left's deep loathing of American culture and government.

Popular front organizations were used during the Cold War, and as early 1921 in Lenin's hands, to attract supporters for Soviet anti-American propaganda and disinformation. These non-governmental organizations in the United States served as transmission belts to serve up a full course menu of Marxism-Leninism. These popular front techniques did not change in the hands of the Western progressives-socialists-marxists during the 1990s and early 2000s.

The popular fronts are still based on denial, deceit, and deception, but the goals of these activities are now defined in terms of Antonio Gramsci's formula for cultural transformation and accession to political power. The shift took place so passively that most in the West, whose images were shaped in Plato's cave about the "end of communism," screened out the contrary indicators in a mass cognitive dissonance.

Selected case examples illustrate how five of the most prominent "peace racketeers" quietly shifted from supporting Soviet goals to underwriting Russia's Gramsci's formula for U.S. cultural transformation: War Resister's League, American Friends Service Committee, Women's International League for Peace and Freedom, Fellowship for Reconciliation, and Vietnam Veterans Against the War, plus latter-day hard Left veterans groups.

War Resisters League

The War Resisters League is an example of the cross-connections existing between Marxists, progressives, socialists, churches, unions, and an array of other activist groups. The War Resisters League was founded in 1923 by the socialist suffragettes Jessie W. Hughan, Tracy D. Mygatt, Frances Witherspoon, and others. The League's membership pledge, which has remained essentially unchanged since its inception, reads: "The War Resisters League affirms that war is a crime against humanity. We therefore are determined not to support any kind of war, international or civil, and to strive non violently for the removal of all causes of war."

The War Resisters League is affiliated with War Resisters International and throughout its activist history, it has worked closely with many other peace organizations, including the International Peace Bureau, Fellowship of Reconciliation, American Friends Service Committee, and American Civil Liberties Union. The League was perhaps the first blame Washington for the terrorist attacks on September 11, 2001. This "peace racketeer" released a statement on the same day "that the policies of militarism pursued by the United States resulted in millions of deaths. . . . May these profound tragedies remind us of the impact U.S. policies have had on other civilians in other lands."[66]

American Friends Service Committee (AFSC)

A second group of "peace racketeers," the socialist Quakers, founded the American Friends Service Committee (AFSC) in 1917. Committed to non-violence and justice, AFSC members believe in the worth of every person and faith in love to overcome injustice. The Quakers were penetrated by communists in the early 1920s, when Committee programs were carried out in Russia to relieve famine and disease. Hungry children also were fed by the Quakers in Poland, Serbia, Germany, and Austria, both sides of the Spanish Civil War; by 1947, the Quaker mission took them to India and then the Gaza Strip.

In March 2003, the AFSC was a signatory to a letter exhorting members of Congress "to oppose . . . [the] Patriot [Act] II" that could severely dilute and possibly undermine basic constitutional rights.[67] Given the Committee's history of support on the radical Left and disdain for the United States government, it is no wonder that AFSC is one of IPS's collaborating "shining stars." The AFSC's members are trusted agents of progressive-socialist-marxist movement.

Women's International League for Peace and Freedom (WILPF)

A third conclave of "peace racketeers," the Women's International League for Peace and Freedom (WILPF), which was founded by socialists to protest World War One and over the years found itself penetrated by the Communist Party, USA. The theme "Woman" has always been a valuable and strong instrument in Weiss NGO network, with Cora Weiss in the lead. Her predecessors have been Jane Addams, Tracy Mygatt, and Frances Witherspoon who, beginning in the 1920s, worked with the Women's Peace Union.

The League was an enthusiastic supporter of the world disarmament movement in the 1930s and following World War Two placed all of its faith in the United Nations as a tool for universal disarmament. This sharp focus on the United Nations has not waned in the intervening years. Along the way, WILPF found time to condemn U.S. actions against the Cuban government; found the Soviet invasion of neighboring Afghanistan to be "regrettable," albeit "understandable;" condemned U.S. anti-communist efforts in Central America during the 1980s; and called for an end to all nuclear testing in the 1990s. The League denounced the 2003 invasion of Iraq, calling it an "illegal war" and asserted that "the Bush administration created the so-called 'War on Terrorism' to instill fear as the premise for U.S. foreign policy."

In May 2007, WILPF put all of its cards on the table, showing the world that it is dedicated to supporting a pro-Gramsci "passive revolution" in the United States and a leader in the progressive-socialist-marxist movement striving for culture transformation and a Left-wing attainment of political power. At the League's 14th Congress held in Caracas, Venezuela, more than a thousand delegates representing 165 organizations from eighty countries issued the following statement that touches many bases of progressive-socialist-marxist propaganda and disinformation:

We are women . . . working to bring down the unjust economic social and patriarchal order that rules the world today imposed by Neo-liberal globalization. Because we want a peaceful world, we denounce the imperialist military escalation across the planet, in particular the war of aggression sustained by the US government and its allies against Afghanistan, Iraq, Lebanon, Palestine. . . . We will not have peace so long as there exist the exploited, the hungry, the excluded, and the marginalized. For this reason *it is necessary to change the capitalist system*. It is also necessary to change the patriarchal system in order to eliminate the imbalance of power between men and women. . . . *We condemn the undeclared war that transnational corporations have imposed with their neoliberal policies* giving way to world hunger, poor nutrition, misery, illiteracy, inequality, which particularly and powerfully affect women.[68] [emphasis added]

Fellowship of Reconciliation (FOR)

A fourth "peace racketeer" cabal is centered on the Fellowship of Reconciliation (FOR), an interfaith and international movement established in 1915 to combine love with active nonviolence against militarism, war, racism, and injustice. The religious pacifist organization's membership consists of Jews, Christians, Buddhists, Muslims, and those of other religious affiliations or none at all. An interfaith and international movement, the Fellowship has branches and groups in forty countries and on all continents.

A socialist pacifist group that worked on disarmament campaigns initiated by the Soviet Union, Iran, Iraq, and North Korea over the years, the Fellowship also supported Marxist-Leninist terrorists movements in South East Asia.[69] Yet, in its own words, FOR "seeks to replace violence, war, racism, and economic justice with nonviolence, peace, and justice." The Fellowship "is committed to active nonviolence alternatives to conflict, and the rights of conscience." In the final analysis, say FOR's adherents, they "envision a world of justice, peace, and freedom. It is a revolutionary vision of a beloved community where differences are respected."[70]

The U.S.-based Fellowship and its overseas arm, the International Fellowship of Reconciliation (IFOR), perform important work for the leadership inside the Samuel Rubin Imperium. Fellowship members are interweaved with the American Friends Service Committee, War Resisters League, and Women's International League for Peace and Freedom, plus working relationships with the majority of disarmament groups and numerous other "peace racketeers."

Vietnam Veterans Against the War (VVAW)

The *Daily Worker*, official newspaper of the Communist Party, USA, announced in September 1967 that another radical Left "peace racketeer," the Vietnam Veterans Against the War (VVAW) had been created. The Vietnam Veterans first flew their organizational banner at an April 15, 1967, New York City peace parade. Some of the protestors wore their jackets inside-out to symbolize the "Turncoat Contingent" mixed among the marchers.[71]

John Kerry testified before the Senate Foreign Affairs Committee in April, 1971. He began by saying that "several months ago in Detroit honorably discharged, and many very highly decorated, veterans testified [to] war crimes committed in South East Asia." Then he unloaded a string of lies, half-truths, inventions, and slander of Americans serving, fighting and dying in Vietnam. The stories spun in Detroit triggered some of those testifying to relive "the absolute horror of what this country, in a sense, made them do. They told stories that at times they had personally raped, cut off ears, cut off heads, taped wires from portable telephones to human genitals and turned up the power, cut off limbs."[72]

The *Winter Soldier Investigation* was organized through the efforts and about $50,000 put together by Jane Fonda, Tom Hayden, Donald Sutherland, Dick Gregory, Phil Ochs, and others. About a hundred of the supposed veterans told their "personal" tales of war crimes and atrocities, including those they had ostensibly participated in. Later, it was found that several of those testifying had never served in the armed forces, let alone Vietnam, and that they had never been in the war zone. John Kerry knew about these imposters before he addressed the Senate but, unable to identify the liars and slanderers nor separate the actual veterans from the play actors for follow-up questioning and verification, Kerry went along with the charade.[73]

Arthur Knight, a known member of Communist Party, USA, was deeply involved in the formation of the Vietnam Veterans Against the War. Analysts at the Maldon Institute found that "it is possible to unravel something of the Communist intrigue that resulted in establishment of VVAW."

The Vietnam Veterans Against the War were well represented as a group and in terms of individual members at the 2003–08 anti-Iraq war demonstrations in Washington, D.C., and other cities across the country. The Vietnam anti-war protesters formed a coalition with the Iraq Veterans Against the War (IVAW) and military families for "peace" organizations. The Iraq Veterans group served on the steering committee of the hard Left's United for Peace and Justice coalition led by long-time Communist Leslie Cagan whose politics are aligned with Fidel Castro's Communist Cuba.[74]

With the Gramsci-driven culture war underway, progressives-socialists-marxists took advantage of the "gains" derived from the indoctrination base of thirty years of inculcating students with anti-military, anti-U.S. disinformation. In 2008, peace studies professors, latter-day "teachers of destruction," generally depicted the United States as being founded on militarism, colonialism, oppression, racism, sexism, and class conflict. Their focus is on transforming American culture and anti-war organizing. Many college-age protesters at rallies in Washington, D.C. reflected an astounding ignorance of the reasons for the policies guiding government decisions, the stakes involved, or possible realistic outcomes, especially a total obliviousness of the geopolitical factors involved. Rather, they answered questions with bumper-sticker statements and did so in an almost robotic way. These students were not informed; they had been programmed to respond unthinkingly.

The progressive-socialist-marxist collaborators use college students as "street workers" to carry their message to the media and the American people. The Institute for Policy Studies serves as the *"Don"* of the "peace racket." IPS alleged in 2007 that "the United States has taken on the role of the world's policeman, but the world is not calling 911 for our services." It continued that "ending U.S. military intervention will require a full-scale reversal of the imperial trajectory embedded so deeply in U.S. foreign policy."[75]

Radical Litigators

Among the Institute for Policy Studies most critical constellations of the American way of life are the radical litigator collaborator "shining stars"—the National Lawyers Guild, Center for Constitutional Rights, and American Civil Liberties Union, plus, by extension, the former Soviet and now Russian front: the International Association of Democratic Lawyers. These hard Left radical litigators supplement IPS's efforts to diminish the U.S. government in the eyes of the American people by keeping federal activities under the cold eye of a high-powered microscope for bits and pieces of information that can be used in propaganda and disinformation. Secondly, radical lawyers keep up the Left's unending drumbeat to erase American sovereignty in favor of redistribution wealth among citizens of the world. Thirdly, hard Left litigators build bridges of cooperation with Islamic jihadists that help to undermine law enforcement efforts to protect Americans from terrorist attacks. And, fourth, hard core Leftist lawyers find no aspect of civil society as being exempt from their efforts to undermine the American way of life and promote a cultural transformation that would result in dominant progressive-socialist-marxist leaders political power at the community-state, and national levels.

National Lawyers Guild (NLG)

No radical Left-wing issue is too small for members of the National Lawyers Guild (NLG). The Guild was established in 1937 by mostly liberal and communist lawyers who were concerned about the American Bar Association's conservative bent. With the advent of the Nazi-Soviet Pact, however, most of the liberal lawyers resigned. By the 1950s, only a few non-communist lawyers remained, and by the end of the decade the NLG found its membership tumbling to about 600.

The civil rights struggle in the 1960s gave the NLG an opportunity that resulted in attracting a younger group of radicals and revolutionaries. The NLG embraced the Palestine Liberation Organization (PLO) and worked with the IPS-inspired Center for National Security Studies in its propaganda and disinformation attacks against the FBI, CIA, and other intelligence agencies. In support of the NLG's avowed goal of helping to nurture the creation of an "organized revolutionary working class" to serve as "the main component of the socialist revolution in the United States," the Guild promised to provide assistance to the Left-wing. Harvey Klehr, one of America's foremost experts on communist activities within the United States, quoted William Kunstler as having said that "the thing I'm most interested in is keeping people on the street who will forever alter the character of that society: the revolutionaries."[76]

The terrorist attacks on September 11, 2001 and the resulting Patriot Act that facilitated more effective use of intelligence and law enforcement, changed the rules of the game. The National Lawyers Guild cozied-up to its friends of the Workers World Party—pro-North Korea and pro-Cuba communists—by posing as advocates for peace. The Guild also sent e-mails to U.S.-based Muslim organizations in November 2001 urging them to inform their members: "If police or FBI or INS or anyone else tries to question you or tries to enter your home without a warrant, just say No! Anything you say to the police, FBI, INS, etc. will be used against you and others."[77] The NLG's scare tactics were designed to dissuade American-Muslims from identifying the terrorists hiding in their communities.

It seems natural enough for radical attorneys to provide support for America's enemies tried in U.S. courts. Ramsey Clark, for instance, persuaded Leftist attorney Lynne Stewart to take the case of Egyptian sheikh Omar Abdel Rahman who was recognized as the "spiritual leader" of the Muslim terrorists that bombed the World Trade Center on February 26, 1993. Later, Stewart was indicted for assisting the relay of messages from the sheikh to his followers. Despite her bluster designed to mislead, it is quite clear that Lynne Stewart stands as another example of the merger between Marxists and Islamic jihadists. In a speech before the NLG in 2003, Stewart cited her modern heroes as being Ho Chi Minh, Mao, Lenin, Castro, Nelson Mandela, and Che Guevara. She asked for NLG members to help defend her so that she could continue to defend "the people" [including Islamic jihadists] against America's "poisonous government."[78]

The NLG's roots in America are well-established by its key members. Peter Weiss, chairman of the board of trustees at IPS, and long-time prominent member of the NLG, helped in defending the Baader-Meihoff terrorists in West Germany who were on trial for bombing and kidnapping. At the same time, he was vice president of the Rubin Foundation and the Center for Constitutional Rights and served on the executive committee of the board of trustees of the Fund for Peace, which included the Center for National Security Studies. The NLG was cited by the U.S. Congress is the early 1950s as a front and "the chief legal bulwark of the Communist Party."[79]

The Guild's constitution explains what it is all about: "The National Lawyers Guild is an association dedicated to the need for basic change in the structure of our political and economic system." Or, as Robert Benson says, a leading Guild attorney, it is about "corporate power subverting our democracy" by being "routinely engaged in the mechanics of the civil governing of the state."[80]

The National Lawyers Guild remains an IPS collaborator "shining star" in the 2000s. Members of the hard Left are still among the Guild's principal members, including Peter Weiss and Robert Borosage. It still pursues its founding commitment of "putting human rights before property rights," and is made up of some thirty national committees, a hundred lawyers chapters, and offices in all fifty states and Washington, D.C.[81] While international relations have changed substantially over the years, the Guild still maintains its connection with the Soviet-Russian front, the International Association of Democratic Lawyers (IADL). In a December 1983 interview with S. Steven Powell, author of *Covert Cadre*, Robert L. Borosage became "particularly riled" when Powell asked him "how he, as a member of the National Lawyers Guild, felt about the guild's affiliation with the International Association of Democratic Lawyers, a Soviet front."[82] In the absence of an answer, perhaps it is appropriate to ask Mr. Borosage the same question again, now that IADL is a Russian front.

Center for Constitutional Rights (CCR)

The Center for Constitutional Rights (CCR) was founded in 1966 with the announced goals of protecting and advancing U.S. constitutional rights and Universal Declaration of Human Rights, the CCR is ostensibly a non-profit legal and educational organization. The Center was created in response to the unrest in the 1960s associated with African-American civil rights and human rights activists in the southern United States. William Kunstler, Ben Smith, Arthur Kinoy, and Morton Davis concluded from their legal work in the South that a need existed for a privately funded legal center to undertake litigation in support of the "popular movements for social justice" (Kinoy and Kuntsler were also well known for their pro-Castro politics).[83]

One of the Center's key propaganda themes alleges that government at all levels disregards the "Constitutional obligations" to the "poor and oppressed." Hence, the CCR says that it tries to craft litigation about racial injustice, which they believe is the root cause for both discrimination and oppression in capitalist countries. In striving to achieve corporate accountability, the Center for Constitutional Rights' anti-capitalist premise shapes its perspective that "the new face of human rights violation is too often the multinational corporation looking for an easy way to increase profits."[84]

The Center's education and outreach programs focus in particular on its dear friend Fidel Castro. Asserting that it believes the ban on travel to foreign countries is unconstitutional, the "CCR's Cuba Travel Project was formed to defend the First Amendment right to travel."[85] The Center is very careful, however, to inform those it encourages travel to Cuba that it is illegal for most Americans to spend dollars in Cuba without a license from the Treasury Department.

The Center also supports American killers who have found safe haven in Cuba. Joanne Chesimard adopted the name Assata Shakur when she became a militant in the Black Panthers. She was a leader of the Black Liberation Army in the 1970s. In May 1973, a simple traffic stop on the New Jersey Turnpike turned into a wild shootout in which she was badly wounded and the State Trooper who had stopped her and a passenger in Shakur's car were killed. Tried and convicted in 1979, Shakur called the proceedings a "legal lynching." With the assistance of her revolutionary comrades, Shakur escaped from prison and turned up in Cuba where she was granted asylum.[86]

New York radical attorney Lynne Stewart was convicted in February 2005 on charges of illegally facilitating and concealing communications between her terrorist client—the "blind sheik" Omar Abdel Rahman—and members of his terrorist organization, the Islamic Group that had ties with al-Qaeda. Her attorney, Michael Tigar, has close ties with the Institute for Policy Studies. A jury had convicted Rahman in 1995 of conspiracy to blow up several New York landmarks, including the headquarters of the United Nations. Stewart acknowledged that she had passed notes from Rahman to his terrorist colleagues that called for a return to violence and killing Jews wherever they might be found. The sixty-five year old Stewart was found guilty and faced at least twenty-six years in prison. She cried when the jury's verdict was announced but offered no apologies for her illegal behavior. "I know I committed no crime," she said. David Cole, an IPS-affiliated law professor at the Georgetown University said that the verdict would have ". . . a chilling effect on lawyers who might represent an unpopular client."[87]

The Center for Constitutional Rights was an outspoken supporter of Lynne Stewart during her trial. Yet, Stewart was adamant that terrorists are simply misunderstood freedom fighters. She viewed Muslim fundamentalists as "basically forces of national liberation." Stewart said that "we, as persons who are committed to the liberation of oppressed people, should fasten on the need for self-determination, and allow people . . . to do what they need to do to throw off oppression."[88]

This explanation drives to the core of the red-green alliance between progressives-socialists-marxists (red) and militant Islam (green). The assistance given to militant Islamists in the United States by the radical Left is clearly shown. If one's world view on the Left perceives Muslim terrorists as simple freedom fighters striving to throw off the yoke of oppression, it is easy to rationalize support for them and to encourage their behavior. The progressives-socialists-marxists not only aid and abet Russia and its strategic partners in their global competition with the capitalist West, but they also assist Islamic Salafists/Wahabbis in their drive toward establishing a world caliphate.

John Perazzo correctly labels the Center for Constitutional Rights as a "Fifth Column Law Factory." For decades, the Center, along with its America-hating litigation partners, have portrayed the

United States as "a racist, corrupt, arrogant violator of human rights both at home and abroad." The Center for Constitutional Rights remains cocked and ready to launch verbal assaults against the federal government for alleged wrongdoing, real and imagined.[89]

Michael Ratner, CCR president and a man who never saw a communist cause he did not like, suggested that the U.S. would do better to " 'make fundamental changes in its foreign policies.' " "In other words," John Perazzo said, "America brought about the terrorism. . . . It is difficult to identify any American action of which CCR publicly approves."[90]

The American Civil Liberties Union (ACLU) files more than 6,000 court cases annually, and uses legal terrorism to further its agenda of molding society in ways that will make Americans more amenable to accepting progressive-socialist-marxist governance. It claimed more than half a million members in late 2006; many of these members were newly recruited after September 11. This cultural Marxist group asked for donations to combat the anticipated homeland security measures likely to emerge as a result of the terrorist attacks.

Filing law suits against the weak, often small municipal governments, the ACLU also intimidates those whose financial resources are limited to accept its dictates or be compelled to spend thousands of dollars in court costs. Such abusive tactics are more reminiscent of organized crime shakedowns than a freedom loving protector of civil liberties. In the end, the democratic wishes of the majority are trampled upon and their civil liberties are denied. Perhaps the ACLU in the twenty-first century still reflects founder Roger Baldwin's 1935 dictum: "Communism is the goal." The ACLU's many activities over the past seven decades, Ralph de Toledano chronicles, reflect Baldwin's words as well as those of other ACLU founders, such as Socialist Party leader Norman Thomas, U.S. Communist Party executive Elizabeth Gurley Flynn, and Soviet espionage agent Agnes Smedley.[91]

The ACLU bills itself as America's "guardian of liberty" and says that "our job is to conserve America's original civic values."[92] By and large, it has been quite successful in selling this self-serving image to a shockingly uncritical U.S. journalistic cadre, and, as a consequence, the American people whose discretion has been left at the mercy of Left-wing propagandists.

Just days after the September 11 terrorist attacks, the ACLU swung into action. At a time when a premium was given to national unity, the ACLU had put into place a program to "resist . . . [a] radical reshaping of our own nation." Unleashing a massive disinformation campaign designed to alarm and mislead the American people, the ACLU set up a "Keep America Safe and Free Campaign" that it contended would stop the government "anti-civil liberties" activities, "violations of due process," and "unwarranted spying on political and religious activities." For the ACLU, the enemy was not Osama bin Laden but the U.S. government.[93] In 2003 the Union opposed the Patriot Act designed to protect Americans against terrorism and, despite it allegations of government abuse, the ACLU could provide no evidence, and it stood against the Real ID Act that would require every American to have a federal identification document to fly on commercial airplanes, enter government buildings, or open a bank account.[94]

The hard Left's magazine, *The Nation*, jumped on the ACLU's bandwagon by blasting what it called "the Bush Administration's war-fevered assault on civil liberties" and "constitutional power grab." They also lambasted the Administration's readiness to sell American values 'down the river.' "[95]

Another campaign on the agitation and propaganda fronts found the ACLU partnered with the Council on American-Islamic Relations (CAIR) in distributing brochures in Arabic, English, and Spanish. The ACLU provided free legal representation for Muslims facing FBI questioning. Some 5,000 young Middle Eastern men were being asked to consent to interviews in December 2001 for the purpose of garnering assistance in the Bureau's post-September 11 terror investigations.[96] The ACLU believed that these respectful requests for help from the FBI violated "the spirit of the American criminal justice system." Instead of cooperating, the ACLU unleashed its own "jihad" against the FBI by counseling those receiving invitations not to cooperate.[97]

The Supreme Court wisely rejected the ACLU's emerging challenge to the government's anti-terrorist practices, including the ACLU's shrill and hysterical argument about wiretapping and surveillance.[98] The ACLU's hysteria over the Patriot Act was parroted by progressives-socialists-marxists across the country. As shown in September 2003, some 158 towns and cities and twenty-eight states had passed critical resolutions against at least portions of the Patriot Act. Despite the hype and anti-government and anti-Christian bigotry, one could find little to chew on that even hinted bad behavior by Justice Department personnel and least of all violations in the area of civil liberties.[99] A telling cartoon by Stayskal at the Tribune Media Services was shown with a *Washington Times* article by Michelle Malkin. "The Leftist War on the FBI" depicted three characters with weapons, maps, and explosives as they prepare for a terror attack. The leader asks: "Got everything Abdul . . . maps to the targets, detonators and, in case you get caught, the ACLU's phone number?"[100] Bill O'Reilly asks: "Is the ACLU bin Laden's best ally?"[101]

Master propagandists, the ACLU has created a self-image of itself as a great protector of the civil liberties enjoyed by all Americans, which is a gobbled up by the mass media without looking behind the headlines. The reality is far different. For the ACLU, civil liberties stand in the way of the Left seizing political power. Roger Baldwin's advice to a friend in 1917 still guides the ACLU in the twenty-first century:

'Do steer away from making it look like a Socialist enterprise. . . . We want also to look like patriots in everything we do. We want to get a good lot of flags, talk a good deal about the Constitution and what our forefathers wanted to make of this country, and show that we are really the folks that really stand for the spirit of our institutions.'[102]

International Association of Democratic Lawyers (IADL)

The Soviet-Russia International Association of Democratic Lawyers (IADL) was founded in Paris in 1946 IADL had long been recognized by the U.S. Central Intelligence Agency (CIA) as a front for the Soviet Union and today as a foreign policy tool of the Russian government. More specifically, IADL provided cover and deception for KGB (and now, FSB) espionage and disinformation. A 1978 CIA study described the IADL as "'one of the most useful communist front organizations at the service of the Soviet Communist Party.'"[103]

A decade and more after the demise of the Soviet Union, IADL served Russian interests by serving as a front for Moscow's support of the international anti-globalization movement. IADL held its fifteenth Congress in Havana, Cuba, in October 2000. Representatives from fifty-six countries attended, including Robert L. Borosage from the United States. The theme of the Congress was "Establishing A Just International Legal Order." The clear implication is the existing legal order was somehow "unjust" and there was a perpetrator benefitting from this discrepancy.

Based on the 163 papers presented at four IADL commissions and the discussions of the participants, a final declaration "that summarizes the consensus reached in the debates" centered on neoliberalism (global capitalism) and a long list of alleged political, economic, and ecological sins by the United States and other "imperialist powers."

The topics addressed in Havana are the core mainstays of the anti-globalization movement of the radical Left. Russia's shadow world support for anti-globalization reveals the Kremlin as a key supporting member of the anti-American Left and its agent of influence, the Institute for Policy Studies. It also reveals continuing connections between the Kremlin and Havana and the European Left that has been particularly violent in its anti-globalization protests. The competition between Russia and its strategic partners and the capitalist West goes on in the world's shadows while respective national diplomats smile and act as if everything is hunky-dory.

The National Lawyers Guild for many years was the only U.S. member of IADL. By the 1980s, however, the National Conference of Black Lawyers and La Raza Legal Alliance had become affiliated with the IADL. The interlocking directorate of these legal radical services gives the hard Left a useful tool in advancing it progressive-socialist-marxist cause. Lennox Hinds, for example, has served as a member of the National Lawyers Guild, Director of the National Conference of Black Lawyers,[104] and the permanent representative to the UN for IADL.[105] Peter Weiss of IPS has also been active in IADL while serving as vice president for the National Lawyers Guild and an officer of the Center for Constitutional Rights.

Socialist Governance

The Rubin Imperium's national security "counter-hegemony" strategy includes a cooperative relationship with the hard-core revolutionary Left and guiding relationships with three constellations—Just Security, "The Peace Racket," and Radical Litigators—of "shining stars." Each of these radical clusters rip at American culture, societal norms, and democratic traditions in different ways. They are among the most effective progressive-socialist-marxist puppet-masters casting false images in order to instill mind-control over the American people. These two-faced, conniving, and treacherous agents of Antonio Gramsci pledge to bring socialist governance to the United States and the world, no matter what obstacles stand before them.

9

PROGRESSIVE-SOCIALIST-MARXIST POLITICS

FROM ITS BIRTH IN 1963, the Institute for Policy Studies has operated on the basis of an image of the United States as being a "national security state" that is controlled by greedy corporations supporting a militarized regime that pursues a global imperialist agenda. The U.S., therefore, is seen as the world's greatest threat to peace and a pillager of the economies and environments of developing countries. The Institute for Policy Studies has carried out wide-ranging propaganda and disinformation attacks against U.S. power and its global network of alliances and cooperators including commentary aimed at the destruction of the public consensus supporting defense spending, NATO and other military alliances, the CIA, FBI, and military intelligence agencies.

The Heritage Foundation writes that "the Institute's founders hoped to have an impact upon governmental policy and . . . hoped that this impact would be a radical one." This unbending hate of America and dedication to tearing down the government, not reform, lies at the base of the Institute for Policy Studies radicalism. The rhetoric of IPS publications is always couched in radical terms, bespeaking a fundamental dissatisfaction with the very bases of American society and government. The rhetoric of IPS leaders reveals an essentially revolutionary perspective of American society, "an outright rejection if one prefers, of our society, our government and our economic system."[1]

This IPS radicalism sets the foundation for focusing sharply on a question left open by S. Steven Powell in *Covert Cadre* (1987). As previously quoted, Powell wrote that "there is a consistency between the way IPS operates and the revolutionary activity advocated by . . . Antonio Gramsci. For both it is important to infiltrate autonomous institutions—schools, media, churches, public-interest groups—so as radically to transform the culture, which determines the environment in which political and economic policies are played out."[2] Or, as Carl Boggs, one of IPS's "shining stars" and author of *Gramsci's Marxism* wrote, "the role of revolutionary theory is to create the foundation of a new socialist order precisely through the negation and transcendence of bourgeois society."[3] This "transcendence of bourgeois society," Boggs explains, was the basis for "Gramsci's first priority . . . the multi-dimensional transformation of civil society."[4]

The key to Gramsci's formula for revolution centered on the idea of breaking what he called the "hegemony" or mind control exercised by the ruling capitalists over the masses. Bourgeois societies were ruled, Gramsci believed, by educating the citizenry that their accommodation of the moral, political, and cultural values defined by the governing system was in their best interests.[5] Hence, Gramsci designed a "reversal strategy" that would silently challenge the existing culture and value-systems that dominated bourgeois governance. That is to say, his formula was based on an ideological struggle that would transform a whole range of activities in civil society, including Judeo-Christian values, the family, schools, unions, and politics and popular trust in the existing government. It followed, according to Carl Boggs, that "the main political task of a socialist movement then is to create a 'counter-hegemony' to break the ideological bond between the ruling class and various sectors of the general population."[6]

The radical political program prosecuted by the Institute for Policy Studies since its inception has been a solar system of progressive-socialist-marxist organizations that are conducting a "counter-hegemony" campaign against the American culture, economy, and government through the use of its multiple collaborator "shining stars." Triggering a cultural revolution that re-wires American values and transforms the political system could assure the Left sufficient mind control to accede to power. "In Gramsci's view, class domination is exercised as much through popular 'consensus' achieved in civil society as through physical coercion (or threat of it) by the state apparatus, where education, the media, law, mass culture, etc. take on a new role."[7] Or, to put it another way, there are ten steps toward an American progressive-socialist-marxist civil society: change the popular consensus by destroying Christianity, the traditional family, and existing social mores; transform the culture by installing a radical Left mind control; attain political power by imposing strict control of the military and law enforcement; restrict freedom by socializing the economy; erase American sovereignty by embracing a world without borders; attain political power by winning democratic elections; dominate both Houses of Congress; impose strict control of the military and law enforcement; restrict freedom of the press and expression; enforce a massive redistribution of wealth from the private and public sector; limit freedom of speech, religion, right to bear arms, and state's rights; socialize the economy; and erase American sovereignty to make way for a world without borders.

Four political arenas have been constructed by the progressive-socialist-marxist Left to "format" or erase America's collective brain and install a mind control program that will produce a compliant robotic America of theological radicalism, socialist unionism or syndicalism, radical community-state politics, and the "Shadow Party" owned and operated by billionaires and millionaires inside the Democrat Party.

Theological Radicalism

Antonio Gramsci's formula for socialist revolution in capitalist countries is focused on "corruption of their Christian cultural basis," Martin writes. Neither political penetration nor military superiority, Martin says, will bring the capitalist West to its knees. The Christian cultures of these countries are the ties that bind the people in all aspects of society. Hence, Gramsci counsels his followers, Martin says, to join the capitalists in all aspects of life, from "their profession of ethical and religious goals" to their family needs and all social issues affecting their lives. But Gramsci had a catch, Malachi Martin explains: Gramsci admonished his followers to "let the entire effort be solely by man for man's sake. . . . Make sure man never repeats the famous cry of German philosopher Martin Heidegger: I know that only God can save us."[8]

Gramsci's writings also reflected his sensitivity to the intimacy between what is known as "common sense" and religion.[9] Hence, Gramsci realized that Christian culture had to be undone quietly, carefully, and over time. Stealth and passivity would serve as key principles of the war on Christian culture and open the door for progressive-socialist-marxist mind control.

The late Richard Barnet, an IPS co-founder, reached out to tap Christian compassion and moral authority as a force for political change. His focus was on how man, not God, could influence the "wicked world" created by man, and, in particular "the principal source of evil," the United States.[10] Addressing the dangers of mankind's arms race and the need for man to create "a world community of caring interdependence," Barnet warned that "humankind is entering a period of unique opportunity and unprecedented danger." Barnet's work with the faith-based group, World Peacemakers, led them to distribute 40,000 copies of his scripture about nuclear-dangers, *A Time to Stop*, and why readers should join the anti-nuclear movement. Later, with other religious entities, the World Peacemakers adopted the covenant: "In the name of God let us [humankind] abolish nuclear weapons."[11] Four main faith-based, theological radicals have longstanding strategic alliances with the Institute for Policy Studies.

The World Council of Churches (WCC) promotes Christian unity as its primary mission, and has long been involved in global disarmament activism. The WCC is not a church but an organization that promotes the fellowship of churches and common statements and actions around the world and maintains a UN Liaison Office in New York. The effort to curb the proliferation of arms is seen by members of the Council to be a part of their ecumenical commitment to overcome violence and to build a culture of peace. The membership is made up of roughly 550 million Christians represented through some 350 churches of at least 25,000 members, denominations and fellowships, except the Roman Catholic Church, in 120 countries and territories throughout the world. Among those churches are Anglican, Lutheran, Methodist, Orthodox, Baptist, Evangelical, Presbyterian, Episcopal, Moravian, Mennonite, Pentecostal, and several others. The World Council of Churches and the Roman Catholic Church maintain a close relationship; a joint working group meets annually.[12]

The Russian Orthodox Church was penetrated by the Soviet KGB and used "ecumenicism" to promote Soviet policies during the Cold War. The Soviets also set up a "church front" called the Christian Peace Conference, which included church members from the Eastern bloc along with Protestant clergy in the West that supported Soviet aims. The controlling KGB officer was Alexei S. Bujevsky. He also served on the WCC Executive Committee. When the Russian Orthodox Church and Eastern bloc churches joined the WCC in 1961, the Kremlin took control of the World Council.[13]

These events explain why so much of the WCC's disarmament program during the Cold War was directed against the West, while the Soviet Union was depicted as a hapless victim of aggression. In November 1981, the WCC held an international hearing on nuclear weapons in Amsterdam, where Cora Weiss, then holding the disarmament chair at the Riverside Church in New York, offered some specific recommendations that would use the WCC as a Left-wing political front to collect money for the peace movement from "unsuspecting churchgoers."[14]

The Transnational Institute and the WCC founded the Transnational Information Exchange (TIE) in 1978. By the mid-1980s, TIE had some 130 affiliates worldwide, from Europe to Latin American and Asia. These partners addressed what they described as a "transnational corporation problem." Among the cutting-edge anti-corporate groups in the TIE were research entities, workers organizations, trade unions, labor research centers, shop stewards' committees, third world groups, church organizations, and local government and economic planning centers.[15] Corporate workers often spied on their employer, providing inside information to TIE analysts. The WCC's links with the Socialist International and the radical anti-corporate network is reflected by its periodic contributions to the TIE through its Christian Medical Commission to the Transnational Institute, which often fed corporate information to the Institute for Policy Studies.

The National Council of Churches of Christ in the USA (NCC), founded in 1950, is a community of thirty-six Protestant, Anglican, and Orthodox communions, as well as black and historic Christian denominations. The Council represents forty-five million members through its subscriber churches. The General Assembly, which brings together nearly 300 representatives, is the NCC's highest policy-making body. A smaller executive board meets several times a year to act on behalf of the General Assembly. The NCC's members conduct humanitarian actions in more than eighty countries, including the United States. The NCC building in New York is right across from the Riverside Church and connected by a tunnel and maze of underground pathways.[16] The NCC works with many ecumenical and interfaith organizations, including working relationships with the Roman Catholic Church, Evangelical, and Pentecostal communities and other Christian bodies.[17]

The NCC's traditional political focus has been placed on poverty and war. The U.S. NCC adopts a double standard of taking a position that it can only influence and resolve in its own society. Thus, the United States is placed under the glare of being seen as an oppressor, while others countries get a free pass for often terrible, murderous actions. "In the NCC view," Rael Jean and Erich Isaac write in *The Coercive Utopians*, "social determinism applies only to the poor and minorities. Those higher on the social scale possess freedom, responsibility, culpability—and should go to jail."[18]

The NCC adopted a similar peculiar twist on U.S. arms sales in that it does not blame Arab and other countries with oil revenue sufficient to buy them. Rather, the NCC joins its progressive-socialist-marxist allies in blaming the United States and transnational corporations for selling the weapons. In the final analysis, Rael Jean and Erich Isaac's 2001 conclusion remains valid: "The NCC looks upon the United States as an oppressor, both at home and abroad."[19]

The NCC joined the Institute for Policy Studies in efforts to shape U.S. foreign and defense policies, especially in Latin America. The North American Congress on Latin America (NACLA), for instance, enjoyed funding from the NCC while coordinating its political activities with IPS. Originally conceived in 1966 by the Students for a Democratic Society (SDS) as the "intelligence-gathering arm of the New Left," NACLA soon became a primary source of information on revolutionary guerrilla movements in Latin America. Thanks to NCC support and its provision of office space, the NACLA research group "proudly described itself as an intelligence operation for revolutionary movements in Latin America.[20]

The defeat of Nazi Germany and Japan in 1945, combined with the subsequent threat of the Soviet Union, demanded new foreign policies by the Roman Catholic Church. By and large the pontiffs over the next four decades or so were "cold warriors" insofar as they supported the Western powers against the godless Soviet communists, though an intense concern was reflected on human rights, economic justice, and international order. Pope John Paul II differed from previous papal policies by engaging world leaders directly, discussing power of the state and how it should be used.[21] It almost got him killed when a Turk, Mehmet Ali Hagca, shot him four times in Rome on May 13, 1981. According to Polish journalist John O. Kohler, a KGB contract-killing warrant on John Paul II was signed by Mikhail Gorbachev in November 1979.[22] Pope John Paul II, though despising communism, did not fully embrace the free market. He subscribed to capitalism only so long as democracies and market economies were disciplined sufficiently for "humanity to flourish."

Pax Christi was inspired during World War Two by Pierre-Marie Theas, Bishop of Montauban in the south of France. He preached about the need to "Love your enemies," and in the process found how truly difficult and demanding it was to find true reconciliation between enemies. Mathe Dortel-Claudot, who also lived in southern France, prayed that Germany would be healed of the moral and spiritual wounds inflicted upon it by Nazism. At the end of the war, bishops in Germany and France supported the healing power of prayer, calling it "Pax Christi."

Pax Christi spread to other European countries in the 1950s, and Pope Pius XII in 1952 recognized Pax Christi's mission as being the Catholic peace movement. The spirituality core of Pax Christi moved toward social and political action. Soon the peace movement accommodated the problems of poverty in under-development countries struggling within the context of U.S.-Soviet confrontation.

Pax Christi's political agenda grew substantially over time. In 2005, Pax Christi's member organizations numbered more that sixty with a total of some 60,000 members located in some fifty countries.[23]

Pax Christi is a principal member of the radical Left's anti-globalization campaign: "The World Trade Organization has become the most powerful international institution in the world," the *Catholic Peace Voice* declared. "Its power over governments is undermining peace and human rights, and promoting military spending and the arms trade."[24]

Michael Lerner, a 1960s Berkeley radical, identifies himself as an ordained rabbi. Others question his claim, since he ostensibly was given a private rabbinic ordination by "Jewish Renewal" rabbis whose own ordinations were only recognized within the confines of the Jewish Renewal community and Reconstructionist Judaism. All such ordinations are regarded as invalid by Orthodox Judaism, the Central Conference of American Rabbis of the Reform movement, and the Conservative movement's Rabbinical Assembly.[25]

Lerner's philosophy is a blend of medieval cabala mysticism, Old Testament teachings, and 1960s campus Marxism that he defined for David Horowitz. Upon learning that Mr. Horowitz had never taken LSD, Michael Lerner admonished him: "'You *have* to take LSD. Until you've dropped acid, you don't know what socialism is.'"[26] [emphasis in original]

Michael Lerner founded *Tikkun*—"A Jewish Magazine, an Interfaith Movement"—and based it on his counterculture mind-set nourished at Berkeley, California, nearly four decades ago. Concerning the long-running Israel-Palestinian conflict, Lerner comes out on the side of the American Left, that is on the side of Palestine. For Lerner, Israel is "repressive" and its "fascistic" leadership uses "disproportionate force to repress an essentially unarmed population."[27]

Sojourners is a Christian evangelical ministry founded by Jim Wallis in Chicago in 1971 under the name People's Christian Coalition. In

1975, Wallis was coaxed to bring his "social justice" ministry to Washington, D.C., by IPS co-founder Richard Barnet. The ministry changed its name to the "Sojourners" at its new location. Richard Barnet was listed as a "contributing editor" to the *Sojourners Magazine*. "Sojourners" is an allusion to Biblical pilgrims, signifying a commitment to a "radical social order."

The key political tenet that guides the Sojourners' pilgrimage toward "biblical faith" is "radical social renewal." Sojourners believe violence and war will not provide answers to conflicts between people and nations; they refuse to accept structures and assumptions that would normalize poverty and segregate people by class; and they believe that their gospel faith provides a vision for social revolution that will transform economics, gives the power to share bread and resources, and "welcomes all to the table of God's provision."[28]

IPS co-founder Richard Barnet believed faith could be a powerful tool in moving emotion against and arms race and a fuel for disarmament. He wrote several articles published in the *Sojourners Magazine* over the years about the nuclear arms race, the "no first use doctrine," outlawing nuclear weapons, and related issues. Barnet claimed that "the Soviet threat is the big lie of the arms race." He said "to be obsessed by the Soviet threat . . . is . . . to be blinded by hate."[29]

Over the years, Jim Wallis has not been bashful about criticizing American "imperialism" nor in extolling the virtues he believed existed in Marxism and in the third world revolutionary movements. As a religious community, the Sojourners embraced liberation theology in the 1980s, as well as the freeze movement, "hatred of the war," and blasting the lack of welfare reform as being "mean spirited."[30]

Revolutionary Unionism (Syndicalism)

Antonio Gramsci foresaw an increase in the complexity of civil society that would occur over time in the most advanced capitalist countries. This situation would raise the complications between the

Left, or progressives-socialists-marxists, and those governing the state to a greater level, he said. Confronted by a growing tension with the Left, the capitalists, or democratic America in this case, would increasingly rest their authority on "hegemony" extending into every civil society sector, including the schools, the media, culture, the family, and, importantly, labor unions and the workplace.

Carl Boggs explains Gramsci's view that this hegemony or "socialization process" extends throughout society and is the means through which people internalize the dominant free market, democratic values. It follows that the progressive-socialist-marxist Left's struggle against the dominant liberal democracy is a "precondition for socialist transformation."[31] This requires a confrontation at all levels of society to undermine, weaken, and replace traditional American values in the schools, media, family, and unions with Gramsci's socialist ideals. "To conduct this universalized hegemony," IPS member Boggs writes, "means to transform repressive consciousness into a liberating one that makes socialist politics at a *mass* level possible—the central focus of any thorough-going cultural revolution."[32]

Major elements of American organized labor have not only imported the alien doctrine of Antonio Gramsci as a guiding light for its socialist ideological struggle against the traditional American way of life, but also imported another foreign doctrine— syndicalism—most popular historically in France and Spain. In its shirt sleeves, syndicalism is a socialist doctrine dedicated to transforming capitalist societies through working class political action on the labor front, including through strikes, sabotage, and terrorism. For American progressive-socialist-marxist syndicalists, labor unions are a tool for use in transforming capitalism into a society run by working people who are guided secretly by agents among the leadership. Labor federations, according to their plan, would run industry and the workplace as well as government in a socialist society.

It should not be suprising, therefore, that organized labor in the United States has shifted its main focus from the worker and his/her needs to progressive-socialist-marxist politics. For union leadership, their efforts are all about power—power for themselves, social power, and political power. Five U.S. labor unions stand out from their efforts of making socialist politics possible at the *mass* level by applying the imported ideals of Italy's Marxist Antonio Gramsci and France's and Spain's socialist syndicalism: AFL-CIO, Service Employees International Union (SEIU), American Federation of State, County and Municipal Employees (AFSCME), National Education Association (NEA), and American Federation of Teachers (AFT).

Of these five leading unions, only the members of the AFL-CIO operate primarily in the private sector. The other four are centered more on government employees, insulating themselves from the vagaries of the free market. The safety of operating on the taxpayers nickel gives the public-service unions freedom to pursue progressive-socialist-marxist politics to transform America's liberal democracy, while taking a free-ride on the productive economy.

The move toward embracing Gramsci's formula and union syndicalism is a result of the 1960s radicals having come of age. The late Michael Harrington gave intellectual and organizational leadership to labor unions and other societal elements that preserved an alliance with the remnants of the New Left in the Democrat Party and Democratic Socialists of America.[33] SDS's Paul Booth, for instance, coordinated student support for a United Auto Workers slate and marshaled some two thousand students in the Chicago region in support of the union. Booth, like other Leftists, highlighted General Motors "nastiness."[34] One can track members of the 1960s radicals, Students for a Democratic Society, and the New Left into key leadership positions in several labor and teachers union positions. These aging radicals have not given up on remaking America. "A new politics must include a revitalized labor movement; a movement which sees itself, and is regarded by others, as a major leader of the breakthrough to a politics of hope and vision," explains the 1962 Port Huron statement of the Students for a Democratic Society. "Labor's role is no less unique or important in the needs of the potential political strength, its natural interest in the abolition of exploitation, its reach to the grass-roots of American society, combine to make it the best candidate for the synthesis of the civil rights, peace, and economic reform movements."[35] Yesterday's socialist-marxist revolutionaries may wear suits and ties and pantsuits four decades later, but these ideologues who were thoroughly immersed in Germany's Critical Theory, Italy's revisionist Marxism (Antonio Gramsci), and France's and Spain's syndicalism have not given up. Their power in the 2000s is political power drawn from organized labor.[36]

The *American Federation of Labor and Congress of Industrial Organizations (AFL-CIO)* is affiliated with more than fifty unions representing some ten million people. John Sweeney is president of the AFL-CIO. His labor organization background began in 1960 when he was hired as a contract director for a New York City Local of the Service Employees Union International (SEIU).

Right from the beginning at the top post in the AFL-CIO, Sweeney made no secret of his desire to advocate European-style democratic socialism. He also opened the union's doors to the Communist Party, USA. Following the AFL-CIO's 1996 convention, the late American Communist leader Gus Hall said that "the radical shift in both leadership and policy is a very positive, even historic change."[37]

Sweeney is a card-carrying member of the Democratic Socialists of America (DSA), which is the principal American affiliate of the Socialist International. "In the Sweeney era, the same Marxist notions that characterize the DSA have come to define Big Labor," former federal labor official Linda Chavez says. "John Sweeney and other union bosses have tried to portray American capitalism as a nightmare for workers, despite the real-world evidence to the contrary."[38]

The AFL-CIO's triumvirate, in addition to Sweeney, includes Richard L. Trumka and Linda Chavez-Thompson. Trumka, the union's second in command, rose from the ranks as a coal miner in the United Mine Workers of America. Chavez-Thompson serves as the AFL-CIO's executive vice president and is third in command. She is also a member of the Democratic National Committee that controls the Democrat Party. She rose from the ranks of the American Federal, State, County, and Municipal Employees (AFSCME) to vice president before assuming her current position in the AFL-CIO triumvirate. She invited Communist Party members to join the AFL-CIO, while purging anti-communists inside the union. The granddaughter of Mexican immigrants and daughter of sharecropper parents, Chavez-Thompson is adamant: "We want to defend their right as workers, whether they're documented or undocumented."[39]

The AFL-CIO's top troika call themselves a "New Voice." Their unrelenting focus on the socialist aspects of the Democratic Party are matched only by their viciousness in sweeping away the plea by the 40 percent of the union's members who are Republican to target how their union dues are spent for political candidates.

John Sweeney, the dominant ruler of the "New Voice," has guided the policy to turn away from the union member's needs, such as higher wages and better working conditions, to the political agenda of socialized health care, abortion rights, homosexual rights, same-sex marriage, welfare rights, opposition to English as an official language of the United States, anti-Christianity, and racial and gender preferences in the workplace.

Another aspect of the "New Voice" centers on recruiting and training hundreds of young people as organizers and political activists. Through an AFL-CIO program called "Union Summer," youth are indoctrinated with class warfare rhetoric, including the idea that only the working class can end "capitalist oppression." These street workers are then turned loose on society as cannon fodder challenging America's democratic traditions and culture.

Heather Booth, a radical organizer and activist since the early 1960s, helped develop the methods adopted by the AFL-CIO's "Union Summer" program. In addition to being a guiding force of the extremist Association of Community Organizations for Reform Now (ACORN), she and her husband, Paul Booth, a founder and former national secretary of the Students for a Democratic Society, created the Midwest Academy in 1973. The academy, until it was supplanted by the AFL-CIO's "Union Summer," served as a "little red schoolhouse" for the far Left activists by teaching radical techniques to win local community issues—a focus prescribed by Antonio Gramsci. One of the Academy's graduates, Andrew Stern is president of the SEIU. The Midwest Academy prepared a 425-page manual, *Organizing for Social Change*, which is a widely used by radical activists as a textbook for direct action. John Sweeney and the Reverend Jesse Jackson have encouraged the supporters to read and take heed of its tactics and other prescriptions for successful activism.[40]

The Service Employee International Union (SEIU) boasts nearly two million members across the United States and Canada, as well as in Puerto Rico. It is the largest and fastest growing union in North America. It has more than 300 local affiliates and twenty-five state councils. Voicing the progressive-socialist-marxist call to transform the United States radically, the SEIU's mission is to create a more just and humane society, and to improve the lives of their worker and their families. Its members make up a diverse cross-section of working America: long-term care employees (500,000), public services (850,000 government workers, public school employees, bus drivers, and care providers), property services (225,000 workers who clean, maintain, and protect commercial and residential buildings), and hospital employees (900,000 of which 40,000 are doctors and 110,000 are nurses).

Former New Left radical Andrew Stern told his members at the outset of his days in office that he expected "every leader at every

level . . . to devote five working days this year to political action."
As a consequence of this edict, Stern has a seat in the so-called
"Shadow Democratic Party" that is seizing control from legitimate
Party liberals on behalf of the progressive-socialist-marxist
movement.[41]

Of special concern to Andrew Stern is what he sees as the coming
end of employer-based health insurance and "defined benefit
pensions." Presumably, the fixes to these problems are to transfer
the costs to the taxpayers. Stern's tickle list of political "wants" also
includes "job security, better schools, affordable energy, an end to
global warming, and less environmental impact of a growing world
population."[42]

One of SEIU's agenda items is "to win complete amnesty for
illegal aliens," William R. Hawkins writes, "to pave the way for
their recruitment as left-wing voters."[43] To translate this perspective
into terms with Gramsci's formula for cultural transformation, it is
to say "illegal immigration is being used as a progressive-socialist-
marxist tool to transform American society and traditions in ways
that will foster the radical Left's accession to power." This
viewpoint has been suspected for some time, but Mr. Hawkins
helps to bring all of the puzzle pieces together in a poignant picture
of what Americans might anticipate.

> Those who want to radically transform the United States need to
> create a new proletariat, one that is as alienated from American
> society on class, ethnic and cultural grounds as leftist intellectuals
> are alienated on ideological grounds. Drawing more illegal aliens
> into the country is the strategy for creating such a movement. In
> an evenly divided electorate, the influx of millions of foreign-
> born voters skewed towards the political Left could be decisive.
> *Thus, behind the unionization of more janitors, kitchen helpers,
> and day laborers lurks the far more ambitious project of
> importing revolution.*[44] [emphasis added]

The American Federation of the State, County, and Municipal Employees (AFSCME) represents more than 1.4 million government workers, ranging from child care providers to corrections officers; it is the second largest government employees union. Led by its president Gerald McEntee and secretary-treasurer William Lucy, the union is comfortably in the pocket of the Democrat Party. Its political reach is extended through 3,500 local unions in forty-six states, the District of Columbia, and Puerto Rico. These outlying entities are at the end of money pipelines to help Democrat Party candidate positions with regard to issues important to government workers. Linda Chavez wrote in her tell-all book, *Betrayal: How Union Bosses Shake Down Their Members and Corrupt American Politics*:

> Alas, this is what happens in the world of modern unionism: The government-employee union puts its own power ahead of everything else—the public good, the community's health and safety, even its own members' welfare. Nearly fifty years ago, Big Labor threw out the idea of primarily looking after its members' interests in favor of expanding its own political power. It was at this time that private sector union membership began declining, and union leaders suddenly looked to government-employee unions as a means of expansion.[45]

AFSCME held a Democratic Presidential Forum in Las Vegas in June 2007. More than 2,000 union leaders and members attended the meeting. Democrat candidates for president were all summoned by the caretakers of AFSCME's vast money tree. If the AFSCME spent a few million dollars less on politicians, they could raise member take-home-pay by reducing union dues. But, since the real issue is ego-enhancing political power for the union elite, the workers and taxpayers alike pay for contributions to Democrat Party candidates. To enhance their chances for success, the

AFSCME provides its members with "how to" coaching: "How to Develop Support for Lobbying," ". . . Convince Elected Officials Through Lobbying," and ". . . Get the Message Through to the Media."

None of this political prostituting is surprising. The AFSCME has long been a player in progressive-socialist-marxist politics. It was an early supporter of the nation's largest "independent" socialist news weekly, *In These Times*, a 1980s mouthpiece for the Institute for Policy Studies, which is now published "independently." AFSCME promoted *In These Times* to its members as a part of its agenda to foster closer links between union leaders and the Democrat Party.[46]

Gerald McEntee has been a long-term influence at the upper levels of the AFSCME. He was elected president in 1981 and again in 2004. Between these top positions McEntee was vice president of the AFL-CIO and a key leader in its political program. He is a co-founder and board chairman of the Economic Policy Institute based in Washington, D.C.—another co-founder is Roger Hickey who, along with Robert Borosage, is a co-founder of the Campaign for America's Future. In late 2003 leading up to the 2004 reelection of President George W. Bush, McEntee declared that the AFSCME ". . . is going to mobilize the largest and most aggressive grassroots campaign this nation has ever seen."[47] Brenda Stokely, another AFSCME official, explained the union's political participation more candidly: "the first thing we have to do is remind ourselves that we are fighting for socialism."[48]

The National Education Association (NEA) and American Federation of Teachers (AFT) occupy a central role in the progressive-socialist-marxist application of Gramsci's formula for cultural transformation of America. For Gramsci, penetration of education and weakening student understanding of traditional cultural and societal norms were especially important. S. Steven Powell reported in his book *Covert Cadre* in the late 1980s that the Institute for Policy Studies enjoyed close relations with the National

Education Association.[49]

The National Education Association promotes itself as being "committed to advancing the cause of public education." In reality, the NEA controls the education system from pre-school to university and a major political player on behalf of the progressive-socialist-marxist movement and Democrat Party. With authority to do nearly whatever it wants with the dues of its hapless 3.2 million members, the NEA is high on political power. Its affiliates are present in every state in some 14,000 communities, which allows the NEA to control public schools, taxpayers, parents, families, communities, and other stakeholders in quality public education nationwide. The slogan of the NEA is "Great Public Schools for Every Child." But such a public relations bumper sticker does not make up for the reality that the NEA, like the other progressive-socialist-marxist oriented unions, "habitually regard employers as enemies rather than as partners."[50] This NEA orientation should not be surprising since the teachers union is a member of the AFL-CIO's activist group Jobs with Justice, a national coalition of unions that support anti-corporate "worker justice" campaigns through a variety of pressure tactics, demonstrations, and negative media attention.[51]

By July 2004, the NEA had already transferred $3.6 million in the current election cycle and a fund raising drive had collected another $1.57 million. Meanwhile, NEA aligned itself with an ultra-Left organization, MoveOn.org, to coordinate Democrat money-collection house parties across the nation.[52] This partnership with the MoveOn political attack dog gives the NEA an insider's seat at the central committees of the George Soros-controlled Shadow Party ensconced inside the Democrat Party.

The National Education Association is also partnered with the American Federation of Teachers (AFT), an affiliate union of the AFL-CIO; its roots in the progressive movement reach back to the 1920s. The AFT was founded in 1916 and had several communist members during its early years. The Federation brings 1.4

million members to the combined 4.6 million educators in NEA-AFT. Owing to its early communist orientation, the AFT has a strong tradition of prosecuting "social justice" issues. The American Federation of Teachers collectively pursue social values of "advancing human rights, opportunity, [and] social and economic justice." Other socialist values and principles are centered on "building a society" where all people have fair and decent working conditions, quality healthcare regardless of income, dignified work and retirement, decent housing, responsive public services, a clean environment, and a government that "protects against discrimination and exploitation, and evens the playing field in curbing abuses of concentrated power and privilege."[53]

The NEA and AFT, like other unions in the government services conclave, are more concerned with supporting the politics of the Democrat Party and the progressive-socialist-marxist movement than they are about caring for their members. Linda Chavez and her co-author Daniel Gray described union leaders' lust for power at the expense of their members, taxpayers, and students. "Despite the platitudes the NEA spouts about commitment to 'improving the quality of our schools and the education that America's children receive,'" Linda Chavez observes, "the truth is the NEA cares far more about increasing its political power and promoting a liberal, social, and economic agenda than it does about quality education."[54]

Politics loom over organized labor. Supposedly the worker can be better represented through political power to shift the playing field to their advantage. NEA's annual revenue is in excess of $350 million. The American Federation of Teachers collected another $150 million or so. Most of the money goes for the fat-cat salaries and benefits for union officials. Sandra Feldman, former president of the AFT, for instance, garnered a total salary and benefits package of $525,735. Hundreds of other union officials at the NEA and AFT earn six-figure incomes.

"The NEA has one of the largest checkbooks in American politics," Linda Chavez reports. The teachers' unions maintain a monopoly of power over government schools by controlling the Democrat Party. This political machine is fed year-after-year by millions of dollars siphoned from the union dues paid by the members. This influence money is not intended to benefit teachers in the workplace directly. Rather, the money paves a pathway to corruption. Ultimately, the NEA's efforts are aimed at achieving enough influence in the Congress via members it helped win seats "to reorder the priorities of the United States of America."[55]

The NEA's executive director, Terry Herndon, tipped his hand in the 1970s when he described the union's primary strategic objective:

'The ultimate goal of the NEA is to tap the legal, political and economic powers of the U.S. Congress. We want leaders and staff with sufficient clout that they may roam the halls of Congress and collect votes to reorder the priorities of the United States of America.'[56]

American Syndicalism

Once upon a time in the darkness of deadly nuclear threats during the Cold War, AFL-CIO leaders George Meany and Lane Kirkland supported the U.S. deterrence and defense posture. The AFL-CIO in 2008, lead by John Sweeney, a member of the Democratic Socialists of America, is working to create a progressive-socialist-marxist America within an overall international socialist labor movement. According to Lowell Ponte, Sweeney is no communist, but he is aligned ideologically with the AFL-CIO's "Working Class Commitment" pledge "that we produce the world's wealth, that we belong to the only class with a future that our class will end all oppression." The deal is that the NEA and AFT will help Democrats get elected to Congress but payback is expected in the form of support for the greater progressive-socialist-marxist agenda.

Syndicalism is a set of ideas, movements, and tendencies that share the stated aim of transforming capitalist society by means of action by the working class in the industrial arena. Syndicalists use labor unions as their primary means of both overcoming capitalism and ordering society towards the interests of the majority.

The United States has already entered a syndicalism shadow world.

Radical Community-State Politics

For the Institute for Policy Studies, politics is the common denominator of all activities underwriting its "solar system of organizations." Gramsci understood that a revolutionary undertaking in a bourgeois society like the United States could proceed only from a sound "philosophical base" and an "ongoing political involvement."[57] The unique progressive-socialist-marxist blend provides the "philosophical base," while IPS and its far Left acolytes assure an "ongoing political involvement" at the community, state, and national levels. According to editor Bernie Horn's commentary in the "Progressive Agenda for the State 2008," which was prepared by the radical Left's Center for Policy Alternatives, "most Americans are progressive on most issues." But, Mr. Horne adds, "most Americans also support traditional conservative principles—limited government, lower taxes, free markets, and personal responsibility." The way out of this conundrum, he suggests, is to alter the balance of power by espousing "an attractive progressive philosophy."[58] That is to say, a "socialist philosophy." Since "progressive" is but a euphemism for "socialism," the Left once again promises a full blast of political denial and deception, propaganda and disinformation in "framing the future." By presenting "progressive" shadows on the wall of Plato's cave, radical Leftists hope to deceive Americans and lead them to vote unwittingly for socialist candidates at all levels of government.

The Institute for Policy Studies, while not driven by a single philosophical doctrine, has from its inception set into motion a variety of initiatives that would create a "decentralized socialist United States." The IPS brand of socialism pushes economic and social planning to the lowest practicable political unit level—the community and perhaps the city. This translates to an economy that serves human needs first and property second. According to the radical Left, large corporations—since they control so many jobs, community welfare, and health and retirement benefits—need to be placed under public control.[59]

Two major influences have helped shape IPS socialism policies over the years: Antonio Gramsci's cultural transformation formula and Saul D. Alinsky's radical community organizing methods. Gramsci has been an important influence due to his emphasis on politics, as explained by Carl Boggs, being concerned with "arousing popular passions" and as being essential to creating a "cohesion to the process of socialist transformation." Politics at the community and state level would help transform "fundamental conflicts of class society . . . into revolutionary ones . . ." at the national level.[60]

Politics of Community

Saul Alinsky's method of community organizing was initially shaped in the worker neighborhoods in Chicago and continued to evolve over three decades to include broader geographic areas and the middle-class until his death in 1972. His method was based on three principles: (1) develop a "trade union in the social factory"— that is to say, use of bargaining, strikes, and struggle to advance community interests, (2) create a confrontational, power-oriented community organization that is willing to use militant tactics, and (3) build a grassroots democracy in which indigenous leaders are developed and the people exercise their own self-determination (*not* the organizers).[61]

Some criticized Alinsky's model as being limited to mobilize only about two percent of a targeted community. But Hillary Rodham-Clinton dismissed such criticism. In a rather elitist opinion about the people at the grassroots, she stated in her 1969 senior thesis at Wellesley College: "The point is valid but of little significance since in any organization the leaders are among the most active members, and decision-making necessarily excludes some elements at times."[62]

By 1970, Alinsky mused about how much the United States had changed since his early years of radical organizing neighborhoods proximate to the Chicago stockyard neighborhoods. Since about 80 percent of Americans were middle class, he said, that is where the power is located. In order to tap the middle-class to fight for the poor, Alinsky asserted that trained organizers, different from the past, were needed. He recognized that economic and social problems are no longer local issues but regional and national ones. To put together a national power organization, one must assemble the local pieces and orient their resolution to higher political action tiers. In a country with a corporate economy, Alinsky asserted, one needs ". . . to find the strength to make corporations use that power for the things that need to be done."

The poor and minorities need allies. This means finding supporters among the more than four-fifths of Americans who are middle class. "You find out what they [the middle class] is worried about, and you organize them around these issues," he said. Alinsky added that "people are drawn together by common interests, not because they live near each other."[63] Thirty-eight years later, Alinsky's observations provided much of the framework for the 2008 presidential campaign of Barack Obama.

The Institute for Policy Studies created the National Conference on Alternative State and Local Public Policies (NCASLPP) in 1974 to spearhead its grassroots politics of community organizing toward a socialism program. The activists recruited included a variety of

Leftists, identified communists, and other revolutionaries. At the organization's 1975 conference, Sam Brown, a prominent member of the often violent anti-Vietnam war demonstrations in the 1960s, "urged radical state officials to press for regulations limiting the size of bank holdings and assets, putting state funds only in banks which agree to make loans 'to particularly socially desirable goals,' and setting up 'public enterprises,' using taxpayers' funds as capital to drive private enterprise out of certain, selected areas."[64] As this example shows, the conference provided a means for satisfying Alinsky's revolutionary approach, while at the same time following Gramsci's counsel to generate an "arousing of popular passions."[65]

Derek Shearer explained at a NCASLPP conference co-sponsored by Ralph Nader in September 1981 that the title of his recently released book *Economic Democracy* was meant to hide the reality that local activists would take over local government in order to use "the power of the city to control the wealth of the city." He added that it was essential to conceal the true socialist-marxist nature of their program.

> I particularly like the phrase 'economic democracy' . . . because it has been referred to by some of my friends as the 'great euphemism.' And while we can't use the 'S' word [Socialism] too effectively in American politics, we have found that in the greatest tradition of American advertising, the word 'economic democracy' sells. You can take it door to door like Fuller brushes and the doors will not be slammed in your face. . . .[66]

Apparently "economic democracy" had a shorter shelf-life than Shearer had predicted, for within a few years Stalin's 1930s popular front phrase, "progressive," was rehabilitated and became the new codeword for "socialism." It is often peddled as meaning general progress, not telling Americans it is a shadow puppet from the wall of Plato's cave.

In 1984, IPS members Gar Alperovitz and Jeff Faux published *Rebuilding American,* a "blueprint for the new [socialist] economy." The central question addressed was: "What kind of economic policies meet the needs of the new economic era *while reinforcing certain values—especially community and fairness—essential to support the kind of economic policies we need?*[67] Consistent with both Gramsci's people's revolution formula and Alinsky's grassroots activism, Alperovitz and Faux presented ". . . a dual vision of the principles on which a new political consensus could be grounded: strategic planning for national economic stability, combined with an emphasis on radical decentralization and local development." For the authors, "the differences between liberals and conservatives lies less in their view of the appropriate size of government than in whom government serves."[68] But they missed the real question: How will Americans be best served? By central planning similar to the old Soviet Union's recipe for economic disaster or through a dynamic life of liberty-enjoying marketeers where free enterprise thrives? S. Steven Powell writes in *Covert Cadre*:

> In economic policy, IPS has launched a many-tiered campaign to foster socialism in the United States, headed by Lee Webb, Gar Alperovitz, Derek Shearer, and Chester Hartman. Since socialism is anathema to Americans, the campaign speaks instead of 'economic democracy'—stage one in IPS's revolution.[69]

Twenty years later Gar Alperovitz sounded off again. He offered a new set of numbers but the same old, stale solutions for ensuring wealth will "benefit the vast majority directly."[70] Professor Alperowitz and his close friends at IPS and the Samuel Rubin Foundation just do not get it: re-engineering the American economy from an open, dynamic free enterprise system tempered by law to a closed, centrally-planned public ownership system will lead to a suffocating oppression that will impoverish all Americans. The radical Left's grand progressive-socialist-marxist system was tried and tested in the Soviet Union and ended up bankrupting the country and driving ordinary people into the ground. As David Horowitz is quoted in the anagram to this book: "Socialism makes men poor beyond their wildest dreams."[71]

Several radical Leftist groups are dedicated to bringing the progressive-socialist-marxist message to prepare Americans for socialist governance. One of the most important radical organizations dedicated to peddling socialism to Americans at the community and municipal level is the *Association of Community Organizations for Reform Now (ACORN)*, and it has close relations with organized labor. ACORN was founded by Wade Rathke who organized draft resistance for the Students for a Democratic Society in the 1960s.

Michelle Malkin reported in June 2008 that ACORN ". . . has leveraged nearly four decades of government subsidies to fund affiliates that promote the welfare state and self reliance. . . ." She added that a whistleblower ". . . claims that Chicago-based ACORN has commingled public tax dollars with political projects."[72]

ACORN members have often bullied social workers violently in pursuing its mandate on behalf of low-income and working class people. In the 2004 elections, ACORN members were implicated in numerous reports of fraudulent voter registration, vote rigging, voter intimidation, and vote-for-pay scams. In October 2006, for instance, the chair of the St. Louis Board of Election Commissioners reported at least 1,500 "potentially fraudulent" registration cards had been submitted by ACORN's workers. Similar irregularities occurred in Florida, Missouri, Ohio, New Mexico, and Minnesota.[73] ACORN hit the "Jack Pot" of fraud in Washington state when seven ACORN community organizers submitted nearly 2000 bogus voter registration forms.[74] In recent years, ACORN has received 40 percent of its funding from the U.S. Department of Housing and Urban Development and several foundations, including the George Soros's Left-leaning Open Society Institute. Barack Obama was a community organizer for the progressive-socialist-marxist ACORN before becoming a practicing lawyer, entering politics, and running for President.[75]

The Cities for Progress is one of fifteen major projects of the Institute for Policy Studies. A initiative to bring the progressive-socialist-marxist message to local governments across the country, this IPS program offers a toolkit—Big Box Reform: Wal-Mart—for use in countering superstores displacing smaller "mom and pop" outlets; a how-to guideline on getting a resolution passed by a local community government; sample resolutions on "no war in Iran" and "bring the troops home;" propaganda "fact sheets" with selected data on education, national health, and poverty; and, a Cora Weiss favorite, a United Nations information packet on cutting poverty in half by 2015.[76]

Founded in 1968, the Center for Community Change follows Saul Alinsky's grassroots agitation and social change training programs for preparing activists to spearhead Leftist political issue campaigns, promote increased funding for social welfare programs, and bring attention to major national issues relating to poverty. Deepak Bhargava, who worked in several positions at ACORN, is president. Among the Center's board members are Heather Booth, co-founder and president of the radical Midwest Academy and close associate of ACORN, and Paul Booth (Heather's husband) who is a founder and former national secretary of the Students for a Democratic Society.[77]

Social Policy is a quarterly journal published by the American Institute for Social Justice and the ACORN Institute. It offers its radical social activist readers insight to ". . . what is to be done to secure basic structural changes in American society." This translates to strategies for radical reconstruction of American institutions. Wade Rathke, president of ACORN, is editor-in-chief.

Another radical Leftist activist group is the Planners Network that offers planning tools to resolve the "great inequalities of wealth and power in our society." These resource allocation tools are said to be necessary "because the private market has proven incapable of doing so." Chester Hartman, a former IPS fellow, serves as chair of the Network's advisory committee. Hartman is a long-time advocate of socialist change, not reform. In 1978, Hartman proposed—in an IPS budget priorities analysis that was prepared for fifty-six members of Congress—to replace the country's private real estate business with a massive public housing program. He estimated that at least $150 billion would have to be added to the budget deficit and "further undermine the existing economic system." This would trigger an investment fall-off, he said, raising "the broader issues of public enterprise, economic planning, and control of the economy inevitably would have to be confronted."[78]

Founded in 1954, the New World Foundation offers grants for radical progressive-socialist-marxist movements. Among its more notorious recipients have been the Peace Action Network (Cora Weiss), Center for Constitutional Rights (Peter Weiss), National Lawyers Guild (Robert Borosage), the Nation Institute (friend of IPS), American Civil Liberties Union Foundation (friend of IPS), and a variety of union, legal defense, and community action organizations. Hillary Clinton chaired the foundation from 1982 to 1988—during her tenure, grants were delivered to the National Lawyers Guild (a congressionally designated communist front), the Committees in Solidarity with the People of El Salvador (communist revolutionary insurgents), and Grassroots International (ties to the Palestinian Liberation Organization).[79]

These selected progressive-socialist-marxist players in the community politics are indicative of the broad range of organizations and individuals striving to do all they can do to transform American culture as a first step in transforming the U.S. political and economic systems. These are Gramsci's mind control guerrillas using every propaganda and disinformation trick in the book to transform America's communities by convincing middle-class Americans that their lives and livelihoods are being placed at risk by corporate giants and a federal government that serves property first and people second. Through unending deceit and deception, these community guerrillas are linked with other mind control insurgents at the state legislatures and federal government. Their aims remain unchanged: transform American culture to one consistent with the mind control goals of the progressive-socialist-marxist movement, convert the U.S. economy to public ownership and control, and eliminate U.S. sovereignty to facilitate a reform of the United Nations toward a borderless world of socialist governance.

Radical Politics of the State

Progressives-socialists-marxists consider the state legislatures as being "a testing ground for the newest political debates" and assert that "legislators are now the vanguard of the progressive movement." In a sense, state legislators serve as a bridge between middle-class Americans and the issues affecting their lives at the community level and the national political arena. The state legislatures pass far more laws than the U.S. Congress and many of their actions directly affect the lives and livelihoods of the middle-class, the power center in America, as Saul Alinsky referred to the American people more than three decades ago.

The Center for Policy Alternatives serves as the radical Left's support center and idea factory for state legislators. The Center provides leadership and training on important progressive-socialist-marxist issues, including those that further cultural transformation in preparation for socialist governance. A one-stop radical idea supermarket, the Center also serves as a place where state legislators can participate in leadership programs, gain assistance to polish their skills, and gather information on specific progressive-socialist-marxist issues. The Center for Policy Alternatives also makes its unique State Action Network available to "progressive" legislators, bringing together a means for exchanges between lawmakers from all fifty states. The Center's "Leadership Circles" bring legislators together in sharing information and strategies from state to state. More than 200 major victories were racked-up by progressive-socialist-marxist state legislators in 2007. Tim McFeely, the Center for Policy Alternatives executive director contends that state "legislators are now at the forefront of the progressive movement, enacting the nation's most far-reaching, visionary measures."[80]

The Shadow Party

Operating from the triple impact of the Frankfurt School's Critical Theory (Marxist), Antonio Gramsci's revisionist Marxism of cultural transformation as a precondition to achieving political power, and the radicalism of the New Left's continuing focus on the politics of neighborhoods and state legislatures and union political power at the national level, IPS has created an infrastructure, or a "solar system of organizations," that promises to bring socialist governance to America. For more than four decades, the Institute for Policy Studies has applied the image-shaping tools of denial and deception, propaganda and disinformation in casting shadows on the wall of Plato's cave. These mind control efforts have been designed to create a false reality for the American people. Pounded incessantly by propaganda tricks, false images, and denial of truth, many Americans, blinded by the sunlight outside Plato's cave, understandably see only the contrived negative images of traditional culture, societal norms, and contrived historical "truths" that were spoon fed to them so carefully by progressives-socialists-marxists.

The main plot behind the IPS theatrical production of shadows cast on the walls of Plato's cave was finally given away by Carl Boggs' discussion of *Gramsci's Marxism*: The *"ideological-cultural struggle and political action . . . as a part of . . . long-range political strategy: a thoroughgoing cultural revolution that sets out to transform all dimensions of everyday life and establish the social-psychological underpinnings of socialism before the question of state power is resolved."*[81] [emphasis added] The plotting and conspiracies were already being hatched by the radical Left, while it took advantage of its hen-house of billionaires and millionaires laying golden eggs for use in creating an effective movement for the 2008 presidential election.

The progressives-socialists-marxists are counting on their community and state level victories to win the "key cultural battles," as IPS director John Cavanagh put it: "Environmentalism, feminism, and multiculturalism have become mainstream values, and progressive movements have brought attention to myriad injustices." Cavanagh brags that "IPS has been a convener of progressives for years," and that it ". . . strengthens social movements with independent research, visionary thinking, and links to the grassroots, scholars and elected officials."[82] The open question is whether it will be enough to bring them to power in order to socialize and Marxize America.

George Soros

Said to be the world's thirty-eighth richest man, George Soros possesses about $7 billion in net worth, $11 billion in investments, and his foundations disperse more than $400 million a year for a variety of causes ranging from euthanasia and abortion to legalization of recreational drugs and Left-wing political power building. His political philosophy is drawn from some rather balmy ideas about "open societies" expressed by Karl Popper, under whom Soros studied in 1948 at the notorious left-wing London School of

Economics. For Professor Popper, an atheist, nothing was "self-evident." Drawing on Popper's teaching, Soros concluded that the U.S. Declaration of Independence, rather than based on so-called "self-evident truths," is but a statement of "our imperfect understanding" of the world around us. Hence, America's founding documents are disposable in what Soros believes is our godless society.[83]

Moreover, for Soros, "the state can be an instrument of oppression." Soros argues for development of an interdependent world based on the principles of open society. This requires fostering "open society within individual countries and international laws, rules of conduct, and institutions to implement these norms." But, since nation-states contradict a development of international, open society, the impulse for change must come from "citizens living in open societies" who "recognize a global open society as something worth sacrifice."[84] To create the "Age of Open Society," Soros's vision would require terminating U.S. sovereignty, disposing the Declaration of Independence, U.S. Constitution, and Bill of Rights, or at least significant amendments to make them square with open society norms, and reforming the United Nations to facilitate a world socialist governance with the new social-political institutions to enforce its principles, such as the International Criminal Court, and civil society organizations, such as Cora Weiss's Hague Appeal for Peace

It should not be surprising that Soros's Open Society Institute lavishes huge sums of cash on U.S. progressive-socialist-marxist civil society entities. By fastening himself like a leech to the IPS's progressive-socialist-movement, Soros's open society dream sucks the life-giving blood from the Gramsci-IPS advances toward America's cultural transformation. By his infusion of large sums of money, and persuading other plutocrats to contribute as well, Soros is moving toward a take-down of the United States through control of the Democrat Party and its progressive-socialist-marxist candidate whose hidden pay back agenda is foreordained: move forward on the open society initiative.[85]

Soros made his political move to ally himself with the IPS and their collaborators in forming "Shadow Party" as the control-center inside the Democrat Party.[86] A secret meeting was held on July 17, 2003, at Soros' Southhampton beach house on Long Island. Morton H. Halperin, a long-time IPS collaborator, was present. He had been hired by Soros a year earlier to head the Washington office of the Open Society Institute, a part of the global network of institutes and foundations located in fifty countries around the world. Halperin made a name for himself by waging open war against the U.S. national intelligence agencies, while director of the IPS-oriented Center for National Security Studies in 1974 and the American Civil Liberties Union from 1984 to 1992.

A complete list of the wealthy donors present in Southhampton, Left-wing union leaders, and Democrat Party activists remains unavailable, but among those present were John Podesta and a bevy of other Clintonites, including Jeremy Rosner, Madeline Albright, Robert Borstin, Steven Rosenthal (union advisor), Carl Pope (Sierra Club), Ellen Malcolm (pro-abortion lobby Emily's List), and prominent Democrat donors: Peter Lewis (Progressive Insurance), Rob Glaser (RealNetworks), Rob McKay (Taco Bell), and Lewis and Dorothy Cullman (Benson & Hedges tobacco). When the cabal went public in November 2003 about the creation of the Shadow Party, Soros assumed the position as spokesman: "America under Bush is a danger to the world," Soros declared. "The 2004 presidential race," he said, "is a matter of life and death. . . . And I'm willing to put my money where my mouth is."[87] In the final tally, Soros poured some $27 million into the campaign to win the presidency for John Kerry. He lost.

After licking his wounds and completing a damage assessment of what went wrong in 2004, Soros turned to winning the 2008 presidential election through his clandestine Shadow Party tucked away inside the Democrat Party. Another secret meeting, this one in Scottsdale, Arizona, was held in the spring of 2005. Seventy well-heeled potential donors listened intently while George Soros laid out a five-year plan to create a network of think tanks, media outlets, and training centers to promote his own special blend of progressive-socialist-marxist politics. Those at the secret meeting, calling themselves the "Phoenix Group," focused initially on three main goals: creating progressive-socialist-marxist think tanks, training centers for the young progressives, and media centers.[88]

Progressive-Socialist-Marxist Political Power

Thanks to an analysis shared by Bill O'Reilly at *FoxNews*, the American people can have a clearer idea in 2008 as to how their perceptions are being shaped through a combination of propaganda, disinformation, denial and deceit by the radical left, which has seized control of the Democrat Party. The model is based on Antonio Gramsci's ideas to first prepare the "masses" for a change in political power by transforming American culture and, as John Cavanagh at IPS explained, the Left has won many battles in the culture war. What makes 2008 ripe for the Left's passive seizure of power through the ballot box is the enormous infusion of millions of dollars from George Soros and his tight clique of Left-wing billionaires and millionaires who are pooling their loose change to buy the 2008 election on behalf of the progressives-socialists-marxists. The big losers in this deal are the legitimate American liberals who favor a larger role of government in solving societal needs. Instead of competing through a fair democratic election, the Left has imposed a "dictatorship of the plutocrats," brushing Democrat liberals aside in order to win the election by whatever it takes. In this case, both liberals and conservatives lose, while the complexion of American politics becomes forever changed through the progressive, socialist, and Marxist politics of the non-democratic Democrat Party.

Center for American Progress

This is a progressive-socialist-marxist think tank that operates under the guidance of former Clinton Chief of Staff John Podesta. The Center was said to be "the official Hillary Clinton think tank," a "Clinton White House-in-exile," or "a White House staff in readiness for President Hillary Clinton." Persistent leaks make it clear that Senator Hillary Clinton is in charge of the Center's policy direction and its links with Media Matters to counter conservative views. The Center's headlines "a progressive think tank dedicated to improving the lives of everyday Americans." It satisfies this challenge, according to the Center's annual report, by asking "what if" and then "answering in ways that define, defend, and advance a progressive vision for America."

Democracy Alliance

Founded by Rob Stein, a long-time Clintonite and Democrat Party insider, the Democracy Alliance is all about funding the operations of the Shadow Party, not only for the 2008 elections but to realign U.S. politics over the long-term. The Alliance consists of a loose-knit group of wealthy business and philanthropic leaders who have been hooked by the progressive-socialist-marxist message. One may join by invitation only. The "partners" agree to pay an initial fee of $25,000 and $30,000 in annual dues. They also pledge to give at least $200,000 yearly to progressive groups identified by the Democracy Alliance. When the partners met in October 2005, for example, they decided to distribute $28 million to nine grantees— most of the money went to the Center for American Progress and Media Matters for America. In May 2006, the Alliance partners gave another $22 million to sixteen groups, including important players in the November local and state elections.[89]

Tides Foundation

The Tides Foundation and its legal firewall partner, the Tides Center, work in tandem as a money laundry for those who wish to donate money to the extremist Left-wing and other causes. Since some people would like to remain anonymous in their giving to contentious programs, the Tides Foundation will pass the donor money through to the designated recipient, less an eight percent fee. It is connected to the Shadow Party, since George Soros's Open Society Institute gave more than $13 million to the Tides Foundation/Center from 1997 to 2003. In addition, Foundation grants have been made to the Center for American Progress and Media Matters. More broadly, the list of Tides Foundation and Center grant recipients include numerous progressive-socialist-marxist groups supporting the Institute for Policy Studies strategy for the cultural transformation of America.[90]

MoveOn.org

Funded by George Soros, Peter Lewis (Progressive Insurance), and Stephen Bing (Hollywood producer) in its early days, MoveOn.org contributes to the Shadow Party by drawing "real Americans into politics to fight for a more progressive America and elect progressive candidates."[91] In 2006, for instance, the Web-based pressure group poured an enormous amount of resources into defeating Senator Joseph Lieberman, a Democrat who apparently was insufficiently progressive. The political pressure group even reached into the depths of Stalinist viciousness in an effort to defeat the Connecticut Senator by referring to him as "the Jew Lieberman."[92] In 2007, MoveOn.org drew a great amount of criticism for its ad in the *New York Times* that mocked General David Petraeus as being "General Betray Us." MoveOn.org's main contribution to the Shadow Party is its ability to draw into the progressive-socialist-marxist political process an ever-growing number of young, Internet activists who contribute to political causes and turn out for protest rallies in large numbers.[93] These are cyber-street thugs who swarm designated "hate" targets and exert significant political pressure to squash all those in their path.

Media Matters for America

This is a Web-based, propaganda and disinformation center dedicated to immediate political counterfire. Media Matters monitors, analyzes, and corrects what it calls "misinformation in the U.S. media." "Misinformation" is defined as anything that does not conform to the progressive-socialist-marxist propaganda line. In many cases it provides information to cooperating activists, journalists, pundits, and the general public to rebut what it considers to be false claims and "to take direct action against offending media institutions."[94] Media Matters, however, faces a significant credibility issue. As David Horowitz and Richard Poe explain, "Media Matters quickly acquired a reputation for lock-step partisanship and reckless disregard for the truth." The trouble is that the so-called media watchdog perceives ". . . virtually every conservative utterance that finds its way into the major media as a 'lie,' a 'smear,' a 'slander,' or a 'falsehood.' "[95] Another problem is the personal credibility of Media Matters president David Brock, a self-confessed liar and gossip peddler in the past. As Rondi Adamson writes for *Human Events.com*, "Brock's own past casts a shadow over his current self-proclaimed dedication to truth-telling."[96]

Barack Obama

The campaign for Barack Obama's run for president began with enigmatic shadows on the walls of Plato's cave. The image-making included carefully crafted words and brilliant oratory that left many Americans gasping with delight. As the campaign wore on, however, the Barack Obama that was presented to the public was found to be in a significant contradiction to the real Obama. The "real" Obama is the "chosen one" for the far Left progressives-socialists-marxists. Disciples of the Gramsci Left supported Obama's campaign with millions of dollars to fund a massive propaganda and disinformation campaign—in the end, Barack Obama was exposed as a puppet of the far Left, an agent of influence for the Gramsci formula of transforming American culture and leading hard working Americans toward a comfortable embrace with socialism-marxism. A solution that would make "men poor beyond their wildest dreams" (David Horowitz).

Barack Obama speaks in elliptical words when discussing his background, values, ideals, and general world outlook. He has yet to reveal his real self to assist Americans in deciding whether he would be a good president. He remains a mystery man similar to the "stranger" that rides into town in Hollywood Westerns— Obama would be the man to "change" the political construct in Washington, a system, in the constipated view of progressives-socialists-marxists, that is controlled by capitalism, or "corporate America." Obama promises a cultural revolution based on socialist principles—he is the man chosen to "Marxize" America.

The mosaic of Barack Obama that follows is in three parts: communist influence during his high school years in Hawaii and at college; communist, terrorist, and socialist-marxist ties in Chicago that fueled his rise to political prominence; and black liberation theology rooted in socialism and Marxism. The slivers of information making up a mosaic of the real Barack Obama reveal a common thread that yields insight to his values, ideals, and plans for changing America.

Hawaii and College

Barack Obama has been under the influence of Communists and socialist-marxists (or what may be called Gramscists) since 1975 and perhaps even earlier. The warm words Obama wrote in his autobiography, *Dreams from My Father*, about an older black poet identified simply as "Frank" turns out to have been Frank Marshall Davis, a long-time member of the Soviet-controlled Communist Party, USA, and a writer for the Party newspaper, the *Honolulu Record*. He was also a close friend of Obama's maternal grandfather and served as a confidante and role model for Barack during his teens.

Cliff Kincaid, a fact-finding researcher, uncovered "Frank's" true identity in discussions with Dr. Kathryn Takara at the University of Hawaii. She had known and interviewed Frank Marshall Davis as a part of her own research for a Ph.D. dissertation. She confirmed that from 1975 to 1979 Davis had "a significant influence over Obama during the three or four years that he attended the Punahou prep school in Hawaii" (actually, Obama attended Punahou from the fifth grade through high school). Dr. Takara explained that she had been introduced to Davis by Obama's Caucasian grandfather, Stanley Dunham, who considered Frank Marshall Davis to be a "strong black male figure," a man who exerted a "positive" influence over the young man during his high school years. "His [Obama's] grandfather was one of Frank's closest friends," Takara said. "They played chess or cards together."[97]

Following his prep schooling and values-shaping by Frank Marshall Davis, Obama in 1979 attended Occidental College in Los Angeles for his freshman and sophomore years (he later graduated from Columbia University and Harvard Law School). Occidental College has had a long-time affinity for radical Left politics. The California Senate, for instance, linked Occidental to the Communist Party, USA, as far back as the late 1940s.[98] In recent years, the College has had several far Left students and professors supporting the progressive-socialist-marxist movement. One time student Eqbal Ahmad, for instance, was a Pakistani terrorist with French blood on his hands from his days in Algeria with the notorious terrorist Frantz Fanon and had met with Osama bin Laden on more than one occasion. Ahmad served as the first director of the Institute for Policy Studies overseas arm, the Transnational Institute in Amsterdam. In the early 2000s, two far Left professors, Derek Shearer and Saul Landau, both boasted close ties with the Institute for Policy Studies. Shearer is an expert in trying to use cover words for socialism so as not to alarm American voters. He recommends using "economic democracy" rather than "socialism." Landau fancies himself as a propagandist for socialism, and he has close personal ties with senior members of Cuba's intelligence service that is very active in the United States.

The socialist-marxist environment at Occidental College was ready-made for Obama after his warm relationship with Frank Marshall Davis. It was here that he was involved in the beginning of the hard Left's anti-corporation movement. Unsurprisingly, Obama was very comfortable with his Marxist professors, and he participated in many intense discussions with "politically active black students," as well as Chicanos, feminists, and punk rock performance poets. "To avoid being mistaken as a sellout, I chose my friends carefully," Obama writes in *Dreams from My Father*.[99] "Sellout" to what?

Given his soaring rhetoric in 2008 calling for "Change in Washington," it is reasonable to believe Obama meant a "sellout" to the traditional American system of commerce, free market economics, or, if one wishes, capitalism. It remains a mystery as to how and why Obama jumped from Occidental College to the more prestigious Columbia University in New York and on to Harvard Law School. Was he being groomed for future service to the radical Left?

Chicago and the Rise to Political Prominence

Barack Obama moved to Chicago and worked for Wade Rathke, a former SDS member and organizer of the National Welfare Rights Organization, who had established ACORN, the Association of Community Organizations for Reform Now.[100] Rathke developed "A People's Platform" calling for nationalization and "neighborhood control." ACORN's early "Platform" stated "Enough is enough. We will wait no longer for the crumbs at America's door. . . . We will not starve on past promises, but feast on future dreams." And, according to ACORN's handbook, it would accomplish its goals "by grabbing hold of the reins of political power."[101]

ACORN in 2008 was a progressive-socialist-marxist "shining star" of the Institute for Policy Studies "solar system of organizations." ACORN was also the radical center chosen by Barack Obama for his $1,000 a month street activist experience, a building block for a future in elective office, first in the State of Illinois Senate and then the U.S. Senate. Obama was cultivated and preened for many years to become a stealth candidate for the hard Left progressives-socialists-marxists "to grab hold of the reins of political power" in 2008. According to Hank De Zutter of the *Chicago Reader*, Obama believes that "elected officials could do much to overcome the political paralysis of the nation's black communities." Obama also thinks that government officials "can play a critical catalytic role . . . rebuilding bottom-up democracies that create their hard won strategies, programs, and campaigns and that forge alliances with other disaffected Americans."[102] Obama's run for the presidency is to become not just the commander-in-chief of the armed forces but the "Community Organizer-in-Chief" for affected black communities and its hard Left supporters.

Wade Rathke, one of ACORN's founders, is a former SDS member and a protege of George Alvin Wiley who in August 1967 created the National Welfare Rights Organization. An antecedent of ACORN, the National Welfare Rights group presented a deceptive front while attacking the viability of the U.S. economy. It's agenda was all about "grabbing" political power, with the poor being used as unwitting shock troops against the "system." The National Welfare Rights Organization served as the model adopted by ACORN. It was at ACORN during Obama's 1983–1987 community organizing that he was steeped in the Left's operational activist program of co-opting the disadvantaged; it was at ACORN that Barack Obama was trained and groomed for future political office by former New Left members, including the extremist Students for a Democratic Society, and he was trained how to implement the Cloward-Piven strategy.

Developed by Columbia University sociologists Andrew Cloward and Frances Fox Piven, "the 'Cloward-Piven strategy' seeks to hasten the fall of capitalism by overloading the government bureaucracy with a flood of impossible demands, thus pushing society into crisis and economic collapse."[103] As a direct result of orchestrating a welfare spending crisis in New York City in 1975, just eight years before Obama joined ACORN, the City was forced to declare bankruptcy and almost pulled down the entire state of New York with it.

In 1983, ACORN was a leader in the Cloward-Piven "voting rights" strategy designed to overwhelm America's poorly policed political electoral system. This is the ACORN of Barack Obama's time with the radical Left organization. ACORN's political assaults against "the system" over the years evolved to include election fraud in enrolling underage, dead, and non-existent people—Mary Poppins, Dick Tracy, Jive Turkey, and others—on the election rolls. In some cases, crack cocaine was exchanged for fraudulent registrations.[104]

William Ayers—Obama's neighbor, friend, and co-board member—and his wife Bernardine Dorhn were both high profile Weathermen as a result of their terrorist bombing activities, including dynamite explosions at the Pentagon, Capitol Hill, several banks, and a New York police station. For a time, Bernardine, who called herself a "Communist revolutionary," was one of the FBI's "Ten Most Wanted" fugitives from justice. In 1981, Ayers and Dorhn turned themselves in to the authorities but their charges were dropped because of "prosecutorial misconduct." It seems law enforcement overlooked administrative details in its efforts to capture these America-haters before someone else was killed. Neither Ayers nor Dorhn apologized for their destructive tactics and placing lives in danger with their explosives. The Weatherman Underground's terrorist tactics may have occurred some thirty or forty years ago, as Obama plaintively explains, but a photograph of William Ayers stomping on a U.S. flag in August 2001 is depicted in Susan Braudy's *Family Circle*—it offers clear evidence that William

Ayers remains very much a vicious and untrustworthy America-hater.[105] Obama tried to wiggle out of his "friendly" relationship with Ayers during a debate with Hillary Clinton in Pennsylvania on April 17, 2008, by saying that what Ayers did forty years ago when he was eight years-old makes it difficult for him to reject their friendliness.[106] Yet, Obama was forty-one years old when Ayers was jumping up and down on the American flag just six years after supporting Obama's 1995 run for the Illinois Senate.

William Ayers said in an interview with the *New York Times* in September 2001, just before the September 11 attacks, that it might become necessary to again bomb government buildings.[107] The Obama campaign insists that William Ayers and Bernardine Dohrn did not injure or kill anyone. Yet, an informant in the Weatherman terrorist group, Larry Grathwohl, testified before the U.S. Senate Internal Security Subcommittee on October 18, 1974, that Dohrn had planned and carried out a 1970 bombing that killed a policeman. He also explained how William Ayers described Dohrn's actions to his compatriots reflected detailed knowledge of the bombing at a San Francisco police station. A pipe bomb was designed to kill—it was stuffed with heavy metal staples and lead bullets and, according to Grathwohl's testimony, Dohrn placed it on a window ledge outside the police station. Sergeant Brian V. McDonnell died from shrapnel wounds and several other policemen were hit by the shrapnel of pipe pieces, heavy staples, and lead bullets.[108]

Ayers and Dohrn are members of the string of hate-America Communist terrorists whose hatred is drawn from Critical Theory, Antonio Gramsci, and the New Left of the 1960s and 1970s to the present day. They are part of an aging clan in search of disciples to pass on the torch of "tear down this government." The aging radical Left has anointed Obama as a disciple of the successor generation that will bring progressives-socialists-marxists into the White House and political power.

"Social justice," as defined by the progressive-socialist-marxist Left, can be achieved only through confrontation with bourgeois society (including those with free market economies, a bill of rights specifying individual freedoms, and democratic governments). A monumental piece of who Barack Obama really is was shown in a private meeting with potential donors in San Francisco. Addressing the challenges he faced in securing the support of working-class voters, Obama told the well-heeled liberals gathered that "it's not surprising . . . that they get bitter, they cling to guns or religion or antipathy to people who aren't like them or anti-immigrant sentiment or anti-trade sentiment as a way to explain their frustrations." William Kristol, a leading intellectual of our time, quickly recognized the historical and dogmatic root of Obama's "cling to religion" as a reflection of Marx's famous statement on religion: "Religious suffering is at the same time an expression of real suffering and a protest against real suffering. Religion is the sigh of the oppressed creature, the sentiment of a heartless world, and the soul of a soulless condition. *It is the opium of the people*" (emphasis added). Kristol says that Obama let "the mask slip," asking "what has Barack Obama accomplished that entitles him to look down on his fellow Americans?"[109] Obama's comments in San Francisco allowed us to peer into his soul for just a moment. Many were surprised to find that Barack Obama—an elitist, latter-day apostle of the Students for a Democratic Society, the Cloward-Piven strategy, and ACORN's voter rights tactics—had been chosen to preach the gospel of Antonio Gramsci's revisionist Marxism. The hard Left supports Obama for president in order to create a cultural revolution in America that will enable progressives-socialists-marxists to "grab" political power.

Obama gained considerable political notoriety in Chicago from his community-organizing, or what might be more accurate to call "community-Marxizing," and his relationship with the Communist terrorists, William Ayers and Bernardine Dohrn. Illinois State Senator Alice Palmer, a Communist, chose Barack Obama in 1995 as her successor. Senator Palmer has been a prominent member of the U.S. Peace Council, a front for the Communist Party, USA, and the World Peace Council, a Soviet front that was operated by the International Department of the Central Committee of the Communist Party.[110] Senator Palmer was hailed in 1986 by the U.S. Communist Party newspaper, *People's Daily World*, as being "the only Afro-American to cover the 27th Congress of the Communist Party of the Soviet Union."[111] Barack Obama never explained to the American people why the Illinois Senator, a dedicated Communist, chose him to be her successor.

The Communist connection, however, spilled over into the Illinois Senate and the U.S. Senate where Obama boasted of having the most Liberal (that is to say "very, very far Left") voting record in 2007. Following Obama's win in the Iowa Democrat Party caucuses in early 2008, Frank Chapman, another leading member of the Communist U.S. Peace Council, wrote a curious letter to the *People's Weekly World,* the Communist Party, USA newspaper.

Obama's victory was more than a progressive move; it was a dialectical leap ushering in a qualitatively new era of struggle [Antonio Gramsci's formula for cultural revolution]. Marx once compared revolutionary struggle with the work of the mole, who sometimes burrows so far beneath the ground that he leaves no trace of his movement on the surface. This is the old revolutionary 'mole,' not only showing his traces on the surface but also breaking through. The old pattern of politics as usual has been broken. It may not have happened as we expected it to happen [violent uprising of the workers to set up a socialist state] but what matters is that it happened [a socialist-marxist ballot-box cultural coup d'etat].[112]

For the prospective First Lady's part, Mrs. Obama said in her 1985 thesis at Princeton University that she was greatly influenced by Stokely Carmichael. IPS brought the firebrand black nationalist Carmichael to Washington in 1964 for a conference series. A short time later, he turned up in Havana and declared "we are moving toward urban guerrilla warfare within the United States." He added that "we have to fight in the United States in order to change the structure of that capitalist society," insisting that "we have no alternative but to use aggressive armed violence."[113] Later, Carmichael was named "Honorary Prime Minister of the Black Panther Party." Michelle Obama has yet to clarify just what aspects of Carmichael's radicalism influenced her.

The so-called "godfather" of the Obama campaign is said to be James George Abourezk, a former Democrat congressman and senator from South Dakota and the first Arab-American to serve in the U.S. Senate. Tom Daschle, another former South Dakota senator and Obama's messenger to Abourezk, is busying himself putting together Obama's transition team to facilitate a smooth transfer of presidential power after his election.[114] During his Washington years, Abourezk often associated himself with the Institute for Policy Studies.

Black Liberation Theology

Another peek inside Obama's radical Left (beyond liberal) proclivities is reflected by his being steeped in black liberation theology from his twenty years of listening to the hate-filled, anti-White, anti-American sermons by his pastor, the Reverend Jeremiah A. Wright, Jr. Instead of "God Bless America," the Reverend Wright, Obama's spiritual counselor, preaches "God Damn America." He said that September 11 was America's fault, that it was the country's "chickens coming home to roost." More vile anti-America disinformation poured from Wright's mouth about AIDS being invented by the government to keep the black community down. Obama's church had ties with the Nation of Islam and the radical ideas of Louis Farrakhan; the church bulletin has an open space for propaganda by the violently anti-American and anti-Israel Palestinian terrorist group Hamas.[115]

Stanley Kurtz's analysis reveals that "a scarcely concealed, Marxist-inspired indictment of American capitalism pervades contemporary 'black-liberation theology,'" the same theology that provided the foundation for Reverend Wright's sermons at the Trinity United Church of Christ in Chicago.[116] Author Kathy Shaidle explains that black liberation theology "combines warmed-over 1960s vintage Marxism with carefully distorted biblical passages." She says that "in contrast to traditional Marxism, it emphasizes race rather than class," and it substitutes "the Christian notion of 'salvation' in the afterlife . . . [with] 'liberation' on earth, courtesy of the establishment of a socialist utopia." James Cone, the leading theorist of Black Liberation Theology, posits a Black Jesus and sees whites as "the devil."[117] In the final analysis, this framework underlies the rants from the pulpit at Chicago's Trinity United Church of Christ that led Reverend Wright's African-American parishioners to a socialist fantasy land.

James H. Cone is the founder of Black Liberation Theology, and Reverend Wright has acknowledged Cone as being the basis for Trinity's perspective. These are the views that Barack Obama and his family internalized for nearly twenty years, and it is reasonable to conclude that their perspectives of America and their frameworks for future policies may well have been shaped in part by Cone's thought. Cone's radicalism, Stanley Kurtz explains, rejects "anything short of total social revolution." Since Cone believes "white society cannot improve, and blacks are enduring a perpetual de facto holocaust as long as they stay inside it, revolution is the only answer." Capitalism, Cone believes, must be replaced by some sort of "democratic socialism." Cone says, "I do not think that racism can be eliminated as long as capitalism remains intact." He adds that "together black religion and Marxist philosophy may show us the way to build a completely new society."[118]

Cone's perspectives on black theology are rooted in Reverend Wright's speeches arguing that "white America's corporate dollars" turn middle-class blacks into "slaves." Attacks on capitalism are normal fare at Reverend Wright's sermons and are found in many of his messages. The fact of the matter is that "Wright believes that American capitalism is both the underlying cause of the poverty and suffering of black people abroad, and the sinfully tempting apple that lures deluded middle-class blacks to enslave themselves to corporate white America."[119]

Obama joined the Trinity United Church of Christ in 1992, steeping himself and his family in "a polarizing but undeniably popular combination of black-power fulminating, racial separatism, and community outreach."[120] Under the guidance of the Reverend Jeremiah Wright, the Trinity Church adopted a "black value system" that emphasized "black community," the "black family," a "black work ethic," and urged support for an "all black leadership." Jacob Laskin explains that this led to another element in the "black value system" calling for ceasing pursuit toward "middleclassness." Laskin reported that this view depicted American society as an enemy of black people and it stood accused of "killing them off directly, and/or fostering a social system that encourages them to kill off one another," and "placing them in concentration camps, and/or structuring an economic environment that induces captive youth to fill the jails and prisons."[121]

Reverend Wright's voice in his sermons and speeches became one of "political extremism and racial separatism." When examining the disturbing core assumptions of black liberation theology one can clearly see the echo of the radical socialist "Black Manifesto" that was adopted in April 1969 during the National Black Economic Development Conference and presented a month later to the congregation of the Riverside Church in New York City. It states in part: *"Our fight is against racism, capitalism and imperialism, and we are dedicated to building a socialist society inside the United States where the total means of production and distribution are in the hands of the State, and that must be led by black people, by revolutionary blacks who are concerned about the total humanity of this world.*"[122] [emphasis added]

The reality is that Obama has been a member of Chicago's Trinity United Church of Christ for twenty years; regardless of whether he sat in the pew with his family every Sunday taking in the lies and distortions pouring from Reverend Wright's pulpit, Obama's values and views certainly were shaped partially by Reverend Wright's poisonous anti-White rants. "It is impossible," Thomas Cushman, professor of sociology at Wellesley College, says, "to imagine that he could not have known about them. In church everyone knows what the pastor says, either by direct observation or word-of-mouth." Professor Cushman concludes from this reality that "a man who chooses someone like Reverend Jeremiah Wright to be his spiritual mentor simply lacks the good judgment necessary for high office . . . because it suggests a close relationship to a kind of self-serving and coarse black liberation theology." Moreover, Fred Siegel adds that the "presidential candidate Barack Obama never apologized for his own failings in never having chastised Wright."[123]

Obama, for instance, told the Soujourners religious group, a far Left conclave closely associated with the Institute for Policy Studies, that "I . . . believe in the power of the African-American religious tradition to spur social change." "Because of its past," he said, "the black church understands in an intimate way the biblical call to feed the hungry and clothe the naked and challenge powers and principalities" (or, replacing Christian "salvation" with "'liberation' on earth"). He continued by explaining that "in its [the African-American church's] historical struggles for freedom and human rights, I was able to see faith as more than a comfort for the weary or a hedge against death, but rather as an active, palpable agent in the world, as a source of hope."[124] Obama's strained Christianity reflects more of a belief in finding "liberation on earth" than a transcendental belief in God. Christianity in the hands of the radical Left is one that embraces Antonio Gramsci's formula for a massive cultural revolution in America, one leading to socialism-marxism—it is a diluted Christianity whose transcendent beliefs are replaced by immanent ones.

The Institute for Policy Studies and its "solar system of organizations" have a major influence on policy-making in the Congress, many state legislatures, and municipalities. With its international reach to Europe and Russia through the Gorbachev Foundation, constellations of the Institute's "shining stars" also influence U.S. foreign policy. With the exception of President Jimmy Carter and, to some degree, Bill Clinton the progressive-socialist-marxist movement has been shut out of the White House. The IPS directors and members of their network are drooling to once again have one of their acolytes as President of the United States. With the assistance of George Soros and his gang of fellow plutocrats, the far Left has taken over the Democrat Party by developing fronts inside a "shadow party" secreted within the Democrat Party. It was from here that the radical Left placed all its chips on Barack Obama.

Obama promises a vague image of "real change" when he is elected president. But "real change" is defined through his long relationship with Communists and progressives-socialists-marxists and peddlers of Black Liberation Theology. Senator Obama is a shadow puppet for the Institute for Policy Studies drive toward creating a new social construct that embraces Antonio Gramsci's formula for a socialist-marxist economy and a government exerting mind control over the American people through a comprehensive cultural revolution.

In the real world, Barack Obama is the progressive-socialist-marxist soldier hiding inside a Trojan Horse cast onto the walls of Plato's cave. He is the one who, when elected, will slip out of the radical Left's wooden horse to open America's gates to a horde of socialists, Marxists, and assorted Communists intent on swarming the federal government and carrying out a family-destroying, religion-busting, freedom-infringing cultural revolution and an extended political dominance over the entire country. They will seek to "Marxize" America.

10

ANTI-CAPITALISM AND ANTI-WAR STREET WORKERS

THE INSTITUTE FOR POLICY STUDIES and its hard Left collaborators have centered their progressive-socialist-marxist goals and strategies on a theory of the United States being ruled by a corporate-controlled government that is dedicated to an imperialist world military domination. While the rhetoric is nauseatingly familiar, the radical Left's pivot points of attack are now aimed at fostering a transformation of American culture as a first step in bringing a "progressive" government to political power.

In the 1990s, when the world economy began shifting toward economic globalization and the U.S. stood as the sole military superpower, the Left went to work in North America, Europe, and Oceana (Australia and New Zealand) to counter American economic and military influence. The IPS director, John Cavanagh, and Transnational Institute director, Susan George, assumed key roles in curbing U.S. global influence. Cavanagh took responsibility for the North American radical Left, while, George, who was not yet the TNI director, worked with western European socialists and Marxists. In addition to her role at TNI, Susan George was on the board of Greenpeace International from 1990 to 1994, and vice-president of ATTAC France (Association for Taxation of Financial Transactions to Aid Citizens) from 1999 to 2006, which promotes taxation of international financial transactions for revenue for developmental projects in Southern Hemisphere countries.

As was the case in North America, the hardline European Left, as well as Leftists in Oceana, turned to Antonio Gramsci to help pave the way on the path to "Marxist renewal and re-emergence." The anti-globalization and anti-war movements coalesced in confronting the twin devils of transnational corporations and the U.S. war on terrorism.

Susan George presented the IPS/TNI and the hard Left's anti-globalization (anti-capitalism) baseline perspective in November 1999. During the 50,000 strong Left-wing "Battle for Seattle," an effort to block economic ministers from around the globe from holding discussions at the World Trade Organization (WTO) meeting, Dr. George stated that she thought "we are really at war."

> We've got an enemy which is the whole corporate system. The objective of that corporate system, whether financial or industrial, is to be able to go where it wants, and produce what it wants, when it wants, for as long as it wants, to make as much money . . . as it can, and damn the costs. The goal is profit and anything that enhances that goal is good and anything that goes against that goal is bad.
>
> If the enemy is transnational and is going for total control, then I think it's obvious that the response has also got to be transnational and it's got to be a mix of people. . . . We want international democracy. But if we're to get it we've got to fight for each other. The threat is to all of us. If we're not fighting each-for-all, all-for-each, we're going to be picked off one-by-one.[1]

John Cavanagh, IPS director, took a similarly harsh position on the U.S. war on terrorism: "The United States has taken on the role of the world's policeman, but the world is not calling 911." He argued that "the United States spends way too much on the military," proposing a $213 billion cut in the 2008 military budget, including $145 billion from the "world policeman" accounts, and $68 billion through unilateral nuclear weapons cuts and trimming Pentagon bureaucracy. The IPS view is that some of these savings can go to Homeland Security and "human needs," a codeword for progressive-socialist marxist programs designed to help transform American culture and bring the radical Left to power.

Ending U.S. military interventions will require a full-scale reversal of the imperial trajectory embedded so deeply in U.S. foreign policy. . . . A just counter-terrorism policy would shift the focus away from military solutions . . . [and] focus on strengthening homeland security and the international mechanisms that hold terrorists accountable. . . . Fear is the greatest weapon of terrorists. When it becomes our greatest weapon, too, what does that make us?[2]

By late 2002, the anti-capitalist and anti-war movements persuaded thousands of unsuspecting Americans to support the hard Left activists conducting civil disobedience protests in the streets of North America and Europe. Following the IPS/TNI position that terrorist action was a law-breaking event that required a law enforcement response rather than a military one, radical Leftist organizations built influential anti-globalization and anti-war quasi-realities. All of this was about the Gramsci's insistence upon "raising issues necessary to *destroy* bourgeois society." IPS member Carl Boggs writes in *Gramsci's Marxism* that the transition to socialism would not follow a fixed path, but would respond to the "socialist politics and place human actors at the centre of the revolutionary process." Gramsci was adamant "that socialist revolution would not come mechanically from the breakdown of the capitalist economy but would have to be *built*, that is won through purposive human action within a wide range of historical settings."[3]

Street workers ranged all the way from bored college students seeking a little excitement to hard-bitten anarchists, socialists, and Marxists hiding under the "progressive" label. Direct action included peaceful demonstrations, property damage against capitalist businesses, and physical challenges against public safety officers. Propaganda reinforcing the impact of violence and property destruction were often accompanied by puppets, large banners, signs, buttons, handbills, posters, newspapers, and other written materials. Chants by protestors—"Whose streets? Our streets!"— provided a sense of solidarity in "sticking it to the man." In the final analysis, anti-capitalism and anti-war were two sides of the same coin, only the propaganda themes differed. The protests were all about political power: building a viable anti-capitalist movement and fostering "Marxist renewal and re-emergence."

Each anti-globalization and anti-war protest from 1999 through 2008 developed its own personality as derived from the mix of radical Left groups and street workers on the scene. These protests, in the main, were propaganda and disinformation events staged by the Institute for Policy Studies and Transnational Institute and their "shining stars" in the "whole solar system of organizations." The torrent of deceit and deception used by the radical Left savaged the Bush administration, whose response, one must admit, was pitiful. The anti-capitalist and anti-war campaigns were always about undermining the U.S. government and Americans leaders, while calling for "change" in time for the 2008 presidential election. Operating under close ties with the "Shadow Party" inside the Democrat Party, the Institute for Policy Studies "prepared the political battlefield" for the 2008 presidential candidate Barack

Obama by sponsoring and preparing the anti-capitalism and anti-Iraq War street protests.

Anti-Capitalism

The coin of the realm for anti-capitalists is direct action and propaganda, or agitprop. Drawn from the parlance of the former Soviet Union, "direct action" is designed to stir up emotions at major demonstrations against the "imperialists," the United States in particular, while propaganda, selected truth, works on the minds of the capitalists. The aim is to combine language to stimulate emotional and intellectual reactions in order to motivate and guide "direct action" against capitalism. The political messages are designed to build an ever stronger movement against the free market and sovereignty itself. Direct action and propaganda promote the radical Left's utopian revolutionary vision of world socialist governance.

The People's Global Action (PGA) was established in Geneva in February 1998, to carry red (socialist-Marxist), red and black (anarcho-communist), and green (environmental/anti-corporate) banners forward in the twenty-first century. Three of the most important PGA creators in Geneva were Mexico's Marxist Zapatistas, Brazil's Landless Peasants Movement (*Movimento Sem Terra*), and India's Karnataka State Farmers Union. These three groups became members of the first PGA conveners, or leadership committee. Among the 300 delegates from seventy-one countries meeting in Geneva to give birth to the PGA were the Canadian Postal Workers Union, Earth First!, Korean Trade Union, Reclaim the Streets (Britain), and the Women's Network of North America. Others present included representatives of radical anti-nuclear groups, French farmers, and indigenous peoples' organizations from around the world.[4]

The People's Global Action decided at its second conference, held in Bangalore, India in August 1999, to broaden the scope of its direct action and propaganda from an almost exclusive opposition to capitalist institutions and treaties—especially the World Trade Organization, World Bank, and International Monetary Fund—to the social and environmental issues created by global corporate activities. At the same time, the PGA extended its reach to the South, through links between indigenous people's movements and other groups alleged to have had their lives worsened by transnational corporations and their enabling institutions in the North.[5]

At its core, the international People's Global Action is made up of anti-globalization socialists, communists, anarchists, and Gramscian Marxists, including a strong syndicalist or union cadre. Its outreach extends to countries in the Southern Hemisphere (the South), consisting of numerous social and cultural groups. Another strong cadre within the PGA provides a core of urban street fighters dedicated to "revolutionary change and worker control." "Anarcho-syndicalism fights private enterprise and state control alike," Albert Meltzer, a leading anarchist-syndicalist, explained in 1996. "Its aim is to abolish both."[6] Some in these groups describe themselves as anarcho-communists.

The PGA's conference at Cochabamba, Bolivia, in late September 2001 went off track from the beginning. Because of the disruption of air traffic following the September 11 terrorist attacks, only one American and three Canadian delegates were able to reach Cochabamba; Bolivia refused visas to all African delegates, except those from South Africa; activists from Asia arrived days late or were refused entry; and forty Latin American delegates in a bus caravan that passed through Colombia, Ecuador, and Peru were prevented from entering Bolivia at the border. In the end, some 150–200 foreign delegates did not make the meeting. Nonetheless, about 175 foreign delegates managed to join more than a hundred Bolivian militants for the PGA session. The PGA conclave was hosted by the *Cinco Federaciones del Tropico de Cochabamba*

(Five Federations of Cocoa Growers of the Tropic of Cochabamba). This farmer's union, later with six federations, served as a powerful voice and action group for the *cocoleros* or coca-bush growers that fueled the cocaine traffic.[7]

PGA propaganda frequently used a *cocolera* named "Leonida," a Bolivian farmer, who wailed a well-rehearsed tune of a Bolivian tradition of coca-leaf chewing to ward-off hunger and how U.S.-funded spraying of coca crops also damaged the gardens planted along side coca fields by "peaceful" peasants. The coca spray turned bananas black, she told me.

Among the groups participating from the South in the fall of 2001 PGA conference in Cochabamba were India's National Alliance of People's Movements, Mexico's National Liberation Army (Zapatistas), Colombia's *Processo de Comunidades Negras* (Black Communities Process), Brazil's *Movimento Sem Terra* (Landless Peasants Movements), Indian groups located in Latin American countries, and new urban movements in Argentina and Brazil.[8]

The international Marxist renewal and re-emergence represented by the People's Global Action declared its revolutionary "hallmarks" or philosophy at the Cochabamba conference. These "hallmarks" declared war against the capitalist West:

1. A very clear rejection of capitalism, imperialism and feudalism; all trade agreements, institutions and governments that promote destructive globalization.
2. We reject all forms and systems of domination and discrimination including, but not limited to, patriarchy, racism and religious fundamentalism of all creeds. We embrace the full dignity of all human beings.
3. A confrontational attitude, since we do not think that lobbying can have a major impact in such biased and undemocratic organizations, in which transnational capital is the only real policy-maker.

4. A call to direct action and civil disobedience, support for social movements' struggles, advocating forms of resistance which maximize respect for life and oppressed peoples' rights, as well as the construction of local alternatives to global capitalism.

5. An organizational philosophy based on decentralization and autonomy.[9]

Meanwhile, some anti-war groups, such as Britain's Committee for Nuclear Disarmament, were retooling their anti-globalization focus to merge it with their opposition to a possible United States response to the September 11, 2001 terrorist attacks.

Protest Target—World Trade Organization (WTO)

Organized and guided by the ultra-Left, some 50,000 people—from apple-cheeked college students dressed in turtle costumes to grizzled, no-nonsense union workers—gathered in Seattle in late 1999 with one clear objective: to stop some 5,000 trade ministers and delegates from the 135 member countries and thirty-five observer states from conducting business at the World Trade Organization conference.[10] International Leftists based their protest on the premise that the WTO was atop a structure of global governance in which transnational corporations exerted influence over sovereign governments. The key assumption holding up this shaky action plank was that transnational corporations were preventing governments of industrialized countries from exercising "democratic control over their economies." In this way, the ultra-Left claimed, the "sovereign right and authority of the people" to shape their own lives was "being hijacked by giant corporations through the WTO."[11] "Power to the People," the protestors screamed in Seattle, echoing Jane Fonda's anti-American shouts in the early 1970s.[12]

The IPS-spinoff, International Forum on Globalization (IFG), set the stage of the anti-WTO violence and protests in Seattle in a 1999 report that described the World Trade Organization as an *Invisible Government* in clear radical Left terms.

The central operating principle of the WTO is that global commercial interests—actually, the interests of global corporations—should always supersede all others. Any obstacles to the smooth operation and rapid expansion of global corporate activity should be suppressed. In practice, however, these 'obstacles' are national, provincial, and state and community laws and standards that are made on behalf of labor rights, environmental protection, human rights, consumer rights, local culture, social justice, national sovereignty, and democracy. Such standards of nations are viewed by the WTO and global corporations as impediments to 'free trade,' when they are actually national expressions of democratic processes within individual countries that reflect local values, cultures, and interests. . . .[13]

The IFG, representing more than sixty organizations in twenty-five countries in 1999, became the steel teeth in the jaws of the anti-globalization movement. An IPS spin-off, the IFG masked its board of directors from direct public view. Collectively, however, the Board and Associate Directors shrouded by the world's shadows provided the driving force behind the anti-globalization movement.

IFG Board of Directors
  Maude Barlow, *Council of Canadians*
  John Cavanagh, *Institute for Policy Studies*
  Tony Clarke, *Polaris Institute (Canada)*
  Edward Goldsmith, *The Ecologist (UK)*
  Martin Khor, *Third World Network (Malaysia)*
  Andrew Kimbrell, *International Center for Technology Assessment*
  Jerry Mander, *Public Media Center*
  Helena Norberg-Hodge, *International Society for Ecology and Culture (UK)*
  Mark Ritchie, *Institute for Agriculture and Trade Policy*

Vandana Shiva, *Research Foundation for Science, Technology and Ecology (India)*

Lori Wallach, *Public Citizen*

Associate Directors (Selected)

Walden Bello, *Focus on Global South (Thailand)*

Brent Blackwelder, *Friends of the Earth*

Kevin Danaher, *Global Exchange*

Randall Hayes, *Rainforest Action Network*

David Korten, *People-Centered Development Forum*

The ultra-Left's direct action-propaganda campaign against the WTO in Seattle was divided into four steps: (1) *Strategic Preparation*—identify corporation-government collusion that denies the people's democratic rights; (2) *Strategic Focus*—establish campaign priorities and objectives by exposing how the target corporation is undermining the people's democratic rights; (3) *Strategic Action*—take direct action (such as boycotts, labor strikes, protests) to mobilize public pressure on the government to withdraw its support for the target corporation; and (4) *Strategic Change*—participate actively in global movements to create new mechanisms for governments to exercise control over transnational corporations in ways that will preserve the people's democratic rights.[14]

Despite public statements to the contrary by protest leaders, street disorder, property damage, and violence were key aspects of their anti-WTO direct action tactics. Many of the radical Left, environmental, and labor chieftains had worked together previously in opposing free trade initiatives. Among the top planners were labor unions affiliated with the AFL-CIO.[15]

Organization and planning from non-governmental organizations were provided by the "think tank of the left," the Institute for Policy Studies, its European sister organization the Transnational Institute, and the International Forum on Globalization (IFG), another IPS-spawned entity. Other NGO's included the Ralph Nader's Public Citizen and Global Trade Watch, plus the World Development Movement (WDM), a British-based, non-governmental organization that helped to organize the raucous protests in London on June 18, 1999. The Direct Action Network (DAN) served as an umbrella group in Seattle to make on-the-scene suggestions to protestors on redirecting their illegal marches en route to blocking key intersections that would prevent WTO delegates from reaching the conference center. While the Seattle police broke up large crowds, Direct Action Network organizers stepped in and redirected the protestors to blockade other cross-streets, sometimes in four or five different directions, and then recombining to provide multiple human barriers.[16]

The Ruckus Society trained thousands of activists prior to anti-WTO protests in Seattle. Funded in part by CNN founder Ted Turner and the Ben and Jerry's Foundation, the Ruckus Society became "the nation's boot camp for civil disobedience."[17] Opening a college spring break training camp in Arcadia, Florida in March 2000, Ruckus offered civil disobedience training. Eighty persons paid their own way and participated in the "Peace River Campground." The camp's sponsors included the radical leftist group Rainforest Action Network (RAN), Free the Planet (a student group), and Ozone Action, a global warming activist group.

The "peace camp" was another tool in the Ruckus Society's rucksack of lessons on how to the break the law. Established in 1995, Ruckus is also one of the most flagrant abusers of U.S. nonprofit, tax-exempt groups. The Senate Finance Committee as late as mid-2005 had adopted a "hear no evil, see no evil, speak no evil" position, while the Ruckus Society and other radical Left tax-exempt non-governmental groups ran amok trying to undermine the U.S. government. The Rainforest Action Network and Ruckus Society, according to non-governmental organization expert David

Hogberg, "are two of the biggest practitioners of so-called civil disobedience."[18] Among the key street workers driving the Seattle protests were radical environmentalists and opposition to biotechnology, eco-terrorists, and the Animal Liberation Front, corporate media critics, and college-based activists against sweatshops in the developing world. Another band of rogues included a variety of communist leftovers from the Cold War and "renewed" Marxists. Legal services were offered to the protestors by the National Lawyers Guild and the American Civil Liberties Union (ACLU). The Seattle chapter of the National Lawyer's Guild provided a tell-all handbook that offered the protestors guidance on the do's and don'ts of confronting police, and on behavior after arrest for civil disobedience (or violence, property destruction, and other illegal acts).[19]

In Seattle, the resistance to the World Trade Organization led by the ultra-Left tied the trade organization to global environmental abuse and "social justice." Many protestors were dressed as sea turtles to draw attention to the alleged damage inflicted on turtles by WTO policies. The Left's message in Seattle was quite clear: "Trade policy must have an environmental dimension because the environment is a global collective resource."[20]

According to one estimate, some 4,000 non-governmental organizations are active in environmental issues. Many are not focused exclusively on the environment, but include broader agendas, such as women's issues, human rights, labor problems, and others.[21]

The larger non-governmental organizations like the Rainforest Action Network (RAN) and Greenpeace also peddle the radical Left's "progressive" message. RAN activists take great pride in their radicalism and eagerness to resort to "direct action." The latter boils down to an array of innovative stunts that shake down companies by painting them with bad public images. First, target companies receive a letter notifying that they have been selected as a target of

RAN's "rainforest protection campaign." Second, companies make the evening news reporting the screaming antics of RAN protestors and their intimidation of employees and customers. Third, while still trying to deal with the bad publicity and anxiety of what comes next, a telephone call comes for an appointment with Randall Hayes, president of RAN. Fourth, Hayes makes an "offer you can't refuse"—the "peaceable solution" he places on the table is strict obeisance to RAN's demands. And, finally, the target company agrees not to order from suppliers of rainforest products.[22]

Greenpeace, to borrow a phrase from Holland's investigative journalist Peter Siebelt, is a prominent member of the global "Econostra."[23] Patrick Moore, a Greenpeace co-founder, described his former creation as being made up of "a band of scientific illiterates who use Gestapo tactics."[24] Susan George, director of the Transnational Institute, was on the board of Greenpeace International, 1990 to 1994. The secret to the success in making Greenpeace the largest environmental organization in the world—five million members and offices in more than twenty countries—is good management, creative direct mail, and keen image manipulation. After all, if one is concerned, at the very minimum, about the air he/she breathes, water he/she drinks, and the gas and oil he/she consumes, which is everyone, Greenpeace is a wonderful organization. Direct mail propaganda sets up its members and prospective members with mindless, patently untrue claims, such as: "Don't believe it when President Bush and his administration suggest that, in the name of fighting terrorism, we have to tolerate the devastation of our environment or the elimination of our environmental laws. . . . Your generous contribution to Greenpeace."[25]

Earth First! is a radical environmental coalition of neo-Marxists, anarchists, and other extremists that support anti-neoliberal objectives of the international revolutionary socialists. The group's logo is a green, clenched left fist, which is a recognized international communist symbol of solidarity. Earth First! claims to be a "warrior society," much in the same way that radical members of the Sioux Lakota nation more realistically claim. Earth First members, in a grand romantic sweep, say that they will use "any means necessary" in "defending mother earth." Rather than participate in the democratic process, Earth First! prefers to commit assault, arson, sabotage, and other crimes of violence against farmers, ranchers, loggers, and others on their enemies list.

The Mexico Solidarity Network is one of the most dedicated anti-capitalist groups, with members in North America and Europe. This ultra-Left group stated its anti-capitalist agenda clearly in 2003 while protesting against the World Trade Organization's conference in Cancun: "The corporate agenda implemented by the WTO pits worker against worker and nation against nation in a race to the bottom."[26]

On the opening day of the WTO ministerial meeting in Cancun, street workers challenged police lines, meeting batons and tear gas, while a fifty-six year old South Korean farmer activist died from a self-inflicted stabbing. Soon after, the WTO trade talks abruptly collapsed. The world's poorest nations erupted against the United States, European Unions countries, and other wealthy nations. The deep fissure separating the wealthy from the poorest members of the WTO rocked the international trade group. The poorest countries were adamant that global trade was tilted too heavily against them, which was driving some of the most vulnerable deeper into poverty.[27]

Ten months later, trade leaders met in Geneva to address the differences expressed at Cancun between rich and poor nations. There was no way during the four-day meeting to ignore the dark clouds threatening the World Trade Organization's viability. Since the WTO operates on consensus, the breakdown in Cancun was a major wrench in the trade group's machinery.

The ultra-Left was exhilarated by this turn of events. John Cavanagh and Robin Broad of IPS, for example, celebrated by noting that "India, Brazil, China, and nearly two dozen other poor nations, representing more than half of the globe's population, negotiated as a bloc . . . they rejected the meeting's final text, which . . . was crafted to address the corporate interests of richer nations."[28]

Protest Target—International Monetary Fund and World Bank

Flush with a victory in Seattle against the World Trade Organization, the ultra-Left turned its attention to Washington, D.C. for demonstrations in April 2000 against the International Monetary Fund (IMF) and World Bank. The Mobilization for Global Justice (MGJ) served as the primary coordinator of the protests, teach-ins, lobbying, and other direct actions. For the ultra-Left, the IMF and World Bank "global rule makers" are akin to the World Trade Organization and international free trade agreements. The IMF and World Bank "policies ensure open market access for corporations," the hard Left's Global Exchange rails, "while cutting social spending on programs such as education, health care and production credits for poor farmers."[29] If one can be persuaded through a constant din of radical Left direct action and propaganda that transnational corporations, globalization, and capitalism are the root of all evil, one might believe such tripe. As is the case in all good propaganda, one can always find a bit of truth selected out of a mass of information that is molded by the clever Goebbelists on the Left to fool us and take advantage of our lack of insight. Ralph Nader's April 2000 *Multinational Monitor*, for instance, depicted a skull atop the Lincoln Memorial on its front page, with "World Bank" and "IMF" in its eye sockets, and the headline "Resist Corporate Dictatorship." Inside the cover "Defund the Fund! Dump the Debt! Bankrupt the Bank!" headlined the journal's April issue dedicated to "The IMF on The Run."[30]

A masterpiece of "renewed" Marxist propaganda and direct action, the Mobilization for Global Justice, April 2000 protest was drawn from the core of the ultra-Leftists—Marxists, anarcho-communists, and anarcho-syndicalists. The new movement included the Institute for Policy Studies, Ruckus Society, Direct Action Network, 50 Years Is Enough, Global Exchange, Rainforest Action Network, Friends of the Earth, Transnational Institute, Greenpeace, International Forum of Globalization, National Lawyers Guild, Public Citizen's Global Trade Watch, and anarchists Chuck Munson and Luke Kuhn. Others would be added to this list over time.

The major demand of those on the radical Left was elimination of the debt amassed by developing countries in the South. "Beside the debt forgiveness and IMF issues," analysts at the Maldon Institute observed, "Marxist groups are active in the protest, blasting capitalist institutions for seeking to create a world of *landless laborers ripe for exploitation by the profit-hungry multinational corporations.*"[31]

The protestors gathered in Washington, D.C., intent on directing a reprise of their staggering victory in Seattle just five months previously. A similar result against the IMF and World Bank would have given a strong impetus to the ultra-Left's worldwide movement against the growing global market economy ("neoliberalism" in the ultra-Left's propaganda parlance).

In an effort to capture the spirit of Seattle in the protests against the IMF and World Bank, top leaders of the new movement were often the principal speakers at organizational meetings and press conferences. Among the lead speakers were Roger Newell, International Brotherhood of Teamsters; Kevin Danaher, Global Exchange (former IPS fellow) and pro-Castro activist; Robert Neiman, Center for Economic and Policy Research and identified as having thrown a pie into the face of Robert Camdessus, IMF managing director, at a February 2000 UN meeting in Bangkok; Robert Weissman of Ralph Nader's Essential Action; Nadine Bloch, known for creative protest tactics; and Soren Ambrose, 50 Years is Enough.[32]

More than 400 U.S. and international direct action organizations supported the anti-IMF protests. Among the groups were the Communist Party of the United States and of India, "progressive" entities serving as fronts for "Marxist renewal and re-emergence," and other left-wing organizations. Some of the main concerns were social justice, broadly defined, and economic justice issues, like "Fair Trade Coffee." This twenty-something-year-old campaign promised benefits for low-income farmers and local businesses in the developing world. By 2005, the campaign boasted support from the hard-Left Marxist Zapatistas in Mexico—"Zapatista Coffee . . . building direct markets at fair prices for the products from the indigenous communities in resistance in Chiapas, Mexico," and the Catholic Relief Services in the United States—"We know the people who sell us our coffee. We know the farmers who grow it. And we know our decision to buy Fair Trade coffee ensures they will earn a fair price and live with dignity." Neither organization provides the details on the large sums of money from the "fair trade programs" accruing to Dutch churches for their support of the longstanding Max Havalaar "fair coffee" program.[33]

"Environmental Justice" was a hot topic in the late 1999 anti-WTO protest in Seattle, and again in Washington, D.C. in April 2000. Friends of the Earth (FoE) supported the anti-IMF and World Bank street action by alleging the two financial institutions failed to integrate environmental assessments in their policies prescribed for some of the world's poorest countries. Consequently, FoE alleged, countries were often coerced to over-exploit their natural resource base in efforts to earn foreign exchange that leads to pollution, environmental destruction, and non-sustainable exploitation of forestry and mining.[34]

Global Exchange, a well-funded, IPS-connected, anti-globalization mouthpiece declared: "We must make our demands for economic justice heard. . . . Finance ministers from around the world will be in Washington to ratify their plans for the expansion of elite, corporate power."[35]

The anarcho-communist bloc was unhappy with the Mobilization for Global Justice's planned "peaceful militant direct action" and its promise to avoid attacking property. The anti-authoritarian and anti-capitalist revolutionaries, including autonomists, anarchists, anti-state libertarian Marxists, and other radical groups, created the Revolutionary Anti-Capitalist Bloc. Despite their chest thumping, menacing costumes, and chanting "Whose streets?, Our streets!," the Black Bloc was no match in confrontations with police. In the end, they coughed, sputtered, and mumbled something about the pepper spray used in Washington, D.C. being stronger than that sprayed in Seattle five months previously.[36]

The D.C. Metropolitan Police, U.S. Park Police, and a variety of other federal law enforcement agencies stunned the some 20,000 protestors in Washington by adopting what was essentially a small-scale version of Roman strategy. With the Roman Empire surrounded by hostile barbarian tribes, there was no way Rome could provide a perimeter defense of standing forces in the depth necessary to hold them at bay. Instead, the Rome built roads to facilitate rapid response by its army to meet challenges on its borders, engage and defeat the barbarians, and then use the roads to return quickly to the Empire's center in order to deter the other barbarians before they became aware that major units of Rome's army were out of position.

The D.C. Metropolitan Police and their federal supporters did much the same thing. First, a large number of city blocks around the IMF/World Bank meeting site were barricaded (metal fences and a thin line of police officers). Within the multi-street area blocked off was the law enforcement nerve center and a large number of mobile police. Once demonstrators surged on 17th Street, they were met with overwhelming force of horse-mounted police, motorcycle police, and police cars as far as one could see to the rear. Meanwhile, the thin blue line along the crowd-control fence was thickened. The protestors, who had been in the process of working themselves into a rebellious lather, muttered and whined while they backed off. That became the main story of the April 2000 protest. The police outwitted and out-maneuvered the protestors at every corner. One could almost hear the heavy sound of wind going out of the demonstrators sails. Later, one could hear anti-war marchers moaning about having nothing to do and being bored sitting around for hours on end waiting for the combat to begin; the rousing call to arms never came.

In the end, the D.C. police had protestors milling about and muttering to themselves about law enforcement moves that neutralized their strategy and tactics. A big problem loomed for the demonstrators: how to get arrested. Such an arrest was a big battle star or "merit badge," for being taken in by the police would give the protestors bragging rights, a demonstration of their resolve, and popularity with the opposite sex. The police would not cooperate and arrest them. In the end, the street workers negotiated their "arrest" by agreeing to cross police lines in an orderly manner. More than 400 protestors were accommodated by the D.C.'s finest.[37]

Propaganda disseminated during the D.C. protests (agitprop) included the use of hand carried signs, puppets (large and small), banners, handbills, newspapers, magazines, pamphlets, books, Internet reports and photos of events on the scene, and topless women with propaganda messages scrawled on their breasts, a rather novel means of communication. Anti-capitalism, neo-Marxist, and international socialist revolution stood out as the predominant messages. Supporting themes included labor, farm, environmental, and anti-media ("corporate media is mind control") propaganda.

Largely because of the violent protest of an estimated 20,000 persons against the North America Free Trade Agreement in Quebec the week before, only about 150 protestors showed up for the protests against the IMF and World Bank on April 29–29, 2001. Though few in number, the protestors on hand, including a handful of anarchists, picked up where the assembly left off the year before. The main theme was repeated: write-off the debt of the poorest countries. World Bank President James Wolfensohn pointed out that $34 billion in debt relief for twenty-two countries had already been eliminated, with another $16 billion in the pipeline for another seventeen countries.[38]

Marxism, a revisionist version first expressed by Italian communist Antonio Gramsci in the 1930s, dominated the September 27–29, 2002 Anti-IMF and World Bank protests in Washington, D.C. Through their anti-capitalist convergences, the anarcho-communist groups played strong roles in the planning and conduct of the direct action and propaganda that took place in the streets of the nation's capital.

Influenced by the violent direct action tactics in Europe and Canada, and no doubt their burning resentment over the Left's resounding defeat at the hands of law enforcement during the 2001 protests, planning included more widespread violence and mayhem in than had been seen since the "Battle for Seattle" three years previously. A key to the success of these tactics was having a sufficient number of protestors to provide "cover" for the anarcho-communist blocs prior to the confrontation, and to "melt" into the mass of demonstrators. An important aspect of disappearing into the mass was to "ditch your black clothes completely," or place them in a bag or backpack to avoid the police, while heading for rendezvous points and safe houses. Rumors were persistent that the international direct action network of the People's Global Action (PGA) might dispatch key urban guerrilla units to Washington to lead challenges against law enforcement authorities.

In the days leading up to the September 27 confrontation between urban guerrillas determined to shut down Washington, D.C. and the Metropolitan Police equally dedicated to frustrating the anarcho-communists, both sides prepared. Commuters were advised to avoid driving into the city on September 27, and a fenced perimeter was established around the IMF and World Bank How many protestors, with embedded anarcho-communists, would show up remained an open question, although the police prepared for up to 20,000 by augmenting their ranks of 3,200 officers from nearby and some distant jurisdictions.

Commuters largely heeded the D.C. Metropolitan Police entreaties to avoid going to work or driving into the city on Friday, September 27. A brief delay occurred at about 8 A.M. on a major access bridge from northern Virginia, and other interruptions occurred as a result of roving gangs of protestors blocking city streets. Windows were broken at a Citibank branch, and "class war" was painted on a Bank of America branch. The anarcho-communist promise to "shut down the city" collapsed with timely counter-actions by law enforcement. Police arrested 649 protestors, including forty at Citibank, twenty at the Verizon Building, and 200 were gathered up at Pershing Park, which was located inside the secured perimeter around the White House, IMF headquarters, and the World Bank main building after the protestors were encircled by police and herded into a tighter mass in order to isolate and ensure immediate quelling of any violence.[39]

Bleats from the Anti-Capitalist Convergence were quick to come. In a press release calling the police arrest an 'unprecedented attack of civil liberties," the Anti-Capitalist Convergence quoted its member Ray Valentine: "These are frightening abuses of power, and signal the intent of police departments and the Bush Administration to criminalize dissent, political activism, and public assembly."[40] An editorial in the *Washington Times* the day after the attempt to "shut-down the city" perhaps best put the September 27 madness in perspective: "What all this ruckus has to [do] with expressing sympathy for the world's poor—and the alleged complicitous role of the World Bank and the IMF—is hard to discern."[41]

The Mobilization for Global Justice's center piece protest march on September 28, 2002, fizzled when only about 3,000 to 5,000 demonstrators attended. The size of the central stage and audio system near the Washington Monument betrayed the Left's expectations of a much larger crowd. Their numbers were no where near the 15,000 to 20,000 that had showed up April 2000. Many who may otherwise have been inclined to join the march were dissuaded by the confrontations and violence that had taken place the day before.[42]

The Mobilization for Global Justice issued a press release announcing that "thousands descend on DC to prevent massive outbreak of social and environmental devastation led by the World Bank/IMF."[43] The demonstrations were modest, with several anarcho-communists in mufti without their black garb, as well as communist labor organizers and other modern-day revisionist communists at the core of the march. Ralph Nader, for instance, accustomed to hiding behind Lori Wallach of the Global Trade Center, and Robert Weissman of Essential Action, gave a rousing speech about the great evils of corporatism, especially transnational companies. Laced with muted Marxism to maintain his progressive cover, Nader's words were in line with mainstream ultra-Left propaganda. Nader' colleague, Robert Weissman, who serves as a co-director of Essential Action and an editor of Nader's *Multinational Monitor* magazine, pounded home the notion of international corporate exploitation.

The protest on Saturday, September 28 was replete with black and red anarchist flags, legal observers with the National Lawyers Guild, and a wide range of propaganda messages. One of the most unique tools was a fifteen-foot long Trojan horse, indicating that World Bank aid was responsible for exploitation in the global South; it had signs at its mid-section to indicate the responsible powers: Citibank, Exxon, Halliburton, human rights abuse, global warming, and others. Handbills distributed at the protests covered a wide spectrum of issues.

Following a long series of often violent protests against capitalism by the People's Global Action in Seattle, Prague, Ottawa, Genoa, and other locations, the international G-8 meeting in Heiligedamm on the Baltic Coast of Germany took place on June 5–7, 2007. The politics of the eight richest and most powerful countries in the world (Britain, Canada, France, Germany, Italy, Japan, Russia, and the United States) triggered massive protests.

A big part for the G-8s drawing power for the radical Left protests is that the eight members represented only 13 percent of the world's population, but they nevertheless addressed questions concerning the world economy, the environment, economic development, war and peace, and other issues of concern affecting all humankind. The People's Global Action resent the wealthy benefactors in the G-8 countries as opposed to poverty elsewhere on the planet, the destruction of the environment in the name of profit, and the constant warfare on the earth either directly or indirectly involving the G-8 countries.

About 16,000 German police took on 100,000 G-8 protesters who had assembled in Rostock, a city adjacent to Heiligendamm. More than 500 people were injured, many hospitalized, and a large number of arrests were made. Meanwhile, warships patrolled access from the sea. The communist and anarcho-communists turned out in large numbers with their red flags, some emblazoned with the hammer and sickle. "Death to Capitalism," "Capitalism Kills," "I Hate War. I Hate Capitalism" were among the propaganda placards and banners.

The summit leaders themselves addressed climate change and means to achieve a global reduction of emissions; international problems in Kosovo, Iran, and Darfur; and Africa and AIDS, malaria, and tuberculosis. As for the anti-capitalists protesters, they were little more than a side-show. True, they expressed their opposition to the G-8 as an expression of globalization, but in the end they had little, if any, impact. Gary Smith, director of the

American Academy think tank in Berlin got it right—"What does it mean to be anti-globalization? It borders on nonsense."[44]

Ira Straus, U.S. Coordinator of the Committee on Eastern Europe and Russia in NATO, presented an excellent analysis of those who protest against the activities of the G-8 and other free market fora. He was quite clear—"they're against us . . . for being 'capitalist.'" The protesters are delighted to break the law and disrupt government actions since "they are opposed to our law and society to the very core."[45]

World Social Forum

"Another World Is Possible" exclaimed the World Social Forum's rallying cry against the policies of the North's free market democracies. On a second dimension, the Forum's motto rallies the peoples in the developing world or the South who do not participate in the decisions of the World Trade Organization, International Monetary Fund, World Bank, and G-8, as well as regional economic pacts such as the European Union and Free Trade Area of the Americas.

The World Social Forum began as a protest to serve as a counterweight to the World Economic Forum, a meeting of capitalist shakers and movers from the industrialized countries, including chief executives of the largest and most influential transnational corporations, academic supporters (or "mercenaries" in the eyes of the Left), and government leaders of the free market democracies. Since 1971, the World Economic Forum has been called to order annually every January at the Swiss resort town of Davos, or occasionally at alternative sites. These conclaves typically would include discussion about major commercial issues associated with the global free market and the development of an economic agenda for the coming year.

The first World Social Forum, also known as the "anti-Davos conference," was held in January 2001 at Porto Alegre, Brazil, a city enjoying a robust Left-wing government. The organizational spark for the birth of the Forum was provided by Bernard Cassen, editor of *Le Monde Diplomatic* and the leader of ATTAC, a French anti-globalization group, and Brazilian grassroots organizations, ranging from civil society groups and NGOs to political parties, churches, and unions. The idea for creation of the Forum began in 1998 and accelerated when the protests in Seattle brought many more voices into a broad social movement opposing globalization. Cassen took advantage of the strategic moment by suggesting that a meeting at Porto Alegre would offer symbolic and direct opposition to global capitalism.

While some 3,000 activists were invited to the 2001 World Social Forum, another 12,000 militants showed up for the plenary sessions, marches, informal meetings, seminars, and some 400 workshops on various topics. The overwhelming support for the World Social Forum at its maiden session was not accidental. Progressives-socialists-marxists and communists—including parties, groups, and individuals—rushed to the World Social Forum to assert their leadership of the anti-globalist and anti-capitalist protest movement. The ultra-Left's goals were twofold: promote Marxist analysis and discipline, and to contribute to building an anti-capitalist movement deeply inside the People's Global Action.[46]

Any doubts about the meaning of the anti-capitalist rhetoric pouring forth from the 2001 Forum should have been swept away during the larger and more tightly organized second meeting a year later. Some 51,000 activists from 161 countries gathered in Porto Alegre in January–February 2002, about three times more than just a year before. The opening march by the those attending was marked by a tumultuous sea of red flags, many emblazoned with the image of Cuban revolutionary Che Guevara. Thousands of red flags were carried by Marxist and communist parties and labor unions, sending a clear message: "Marxist renewal and re-emergence" was far more than a global slogan, especially in Latin America. The red flags were swelled in numbers by the home-grown Brazilian radical Left, especially the *Partido dos Trabalhadores* (PT) (Workers Party) and the *Movimento dos Trabalhadores Rurais Sem Terra* (MST) (Movement of Landless Rural Workers). The MST became notable for its direct action in support of four million landless families in Brazil, especially its seizing and working farmland held by absentee owners. Unsurprisingly, land reform through the redistribution of farmland was a central issue at the Forum.[47]

The Institute for Policy Studies played a significant role at the 2002 Forum meeting. Among the IPS officers, fellows, and associates were the IPS director, John Cavanagh; Martha Honey and Sarah Anderson, IPS; Joshua Karliner, executive director of Corporate Watch (an IPS spin-off); Susan George, a founder of World Social Forum through France's ATTAC and director of TNI in Amsterdam; Martin Khor, Third World Network; Lori Wallach, head of Ralph Nader's Public Citizen; Njoki Njoroge Njehu, executive director of 50 Years Is Enough; and Maude Barlow, a long-time Canadian radical Left activist and leader of the International Forum on Globalization (IFG). According to Canadian activist Naomi Klein, the IFG was created by IPS to serve as "the brain trust of the North American side of the [anti-globalist] movement."[48]

Susan George, a long-time senior fellow and thinker-activist of the Institute for Policy Studies and the Transnational Institute, placed the utopian goals of the World Social Forum into a distinctive anti-capitalist Western perspective: " 'What we are doing at Porto Alegre is not building a new society for governments, nor a new society of nations. *What we are building is a new society of societies.*' "[49] [emphasis added] Walden Bello, a long-time anti-corporate campaigner working with IPS and Focus on the Global South, described the Forum succinctly: "There is no blueprint. We've had two blueprint disasters in the past fifty years: centralized socialism and corporate capitalism. We need something different."[50]

Fidel Castro's DGI (intelligence service) and *Organizacion Continental Latino Americano de Estudiantes* were active throughout the World Social Forum conclave, recruiting young activists from a number of countries. There were some 10,000 hard-knuckled militants, up from 1,000 the year before, for the Cubans to choose from. Among these attendees, including a large number from Latin America, were various brands of anarchists, Marxists, and communists, including veteran street fighters from Europe and a few from North America. Many of those at the Forum's "Youth Camp" also were dedicated anti-capitalist activists from the People's Global Action.

At the 2003 World Social Forum, about 100,000 radical leftists from 126 countries participated in the discussions, seminars, and other activities. About 5,000 anti-capitalist organizations attended, many from communist parties in Europe and Latin America. Some 200 of these communist contingents were from Cuba alone. French and Italian communists, anarcho-communists, and anarcho-syndicalists also were heavily represented. The "Youth Camp" numbered about 25,000 in a boiling caldron of communists, Marxists, and anarchists. Street fighters from Britain, France, Germany, Italy, Spain, Greece, Switzerland, Canada, and the United States mingled with representatives of Cuba's Young Communist League.

The Transnational Institute exerted a strong influence on the third World Social Forum, including a workshop on "New Politics: Actors, Strategies and Alternatives." The major topics addressed by TNI included a critique of democracies in Brazil, South Africa, and the United States; "Progressive National Governments in the South: Possibilities and Limitations;" and "Alternatives and New Political Thinking." Among the TNI leaders present at the 2003 World Social Forum gathering were the ever-present Susan George, "the Marxist grandmother of WSF;" Martin Khor, Third World Network; Walden Bello, Focus on the Global South; Tariq Ali, historian; Arundhati Roy, dissident from India; and Roger Burbach and Candido Grzyowski of the Brazilian IBASE group.[51]

The 2004 World Social Forum broke the mold of annual meetings in Porto Alegre by holding its fourth conclave in Mumbai, India. Incredibly, more than 150,000 participants from 130 countries supported the WSF's expansion into Asia. The self-appointed coordinators of the social movement emerged from the multitude of participants as peer-approved spokespersons for common points of view. While most subscribed to some form of Marxism and socialism, they were neither doctrinaire nor dogmatic about their position. This approach is basically consistent with Antonio Gramsci's revisionist Marxism, which emphasizes culture and filling open social spaces as steps leading toward a community-directed economy and government.[52]

In reality, it would seem that the direct action advocates gravitate toward the People's Global Action, while the World Social Forum appears more in line with "people power" as expressed in Mumbai by former president of India, K. R. Narayanan:

> This movement is one of the most significant in history. To fight globalization, you need to fight the way Mahatma Gandhi fought with the strength of the masses. He was the first to show the way to non-violence and this has also been the method of this new movement. People's power is a new factor in international politics.[53]

Some 155,000 activists participated in the 2005 World Social Forum at Porto Alegre, Brazil, of whom 35,000 were crammed into the "Youth Camp." Most of the 2,000 odd militants from the United States were associated with the World Social Forum movement or the People's Global Action. Four highlights of the 2005 Forum underline the social movement's radical Left-wing orientation and anti-American hatred.

Venezuelan President Hugo Chavez played the Forum participants like a fine violin before, during, and after his address. When he arrived at the Porto Alegre airport, Chavez went directly to a 2,000-person settlement occupied by the Landless Workers Movement, which provides work for thirty-seven families. He was dressed like a peasant farmer and wore a farm hat. Chavez, always the unabashed thespian, unbuttoned his shirt, exposing to the assembled farmers his tee-shirt with the image of Che Guevara next to his heart. He was embraced and cheered: "Hugo, campesino and soldier!"

At the World Social Forum, Chavez spoke to a jammed-packed audience in a local gymnasium. Participants had already been cheering whenever his named was mentioned: "Beware, beware, beware imperialist, the entire Latin America will become socialist." Chavez's words enthralled the activists. " 'It is time to take a step and this fifth WSF could be the beginning of a new phase, and the next five years should be accompanied by a world socialist agenda,' " Chavez said. " 'To that agenda we must add a strategy of power.' "[54]

Another notable event was the presence of representatives from the United Nations. This was not the first time that the U.N. had been deeply involved in the activities of the hard Left, anti-U.S. World Social Forum conferences. In 2004, eight U.N. agencies were listed as providing funding for the World Social Forum's anti-U.S. and pro-ultra-Left conclaves that fanned hatred of America, its president, and the American people. Members of the Socialist International also participated in a debate on reform of the U.N. and engaged activists and others present in discussion of outstanding issues.[55]

Some 60,000–70,000 people attended the 2006 World Social Forum held at Caracas, Venezuela. The gathering under the banner "Another World Is Possible" attendees included liberals, progressives, socialists, neo-Marxists, communists, anarchists, unionists or syndicalists, and activists in support of various causes. Around 1,800 events were scheduled for the attendees by the some 2,000 non-governmental organizations representing various issues on the Left-wing's menu for direct action and propaganda.[56] Thematic issues addressed at the Forum included "power, politics and social emancipation; imperial strategies and peoples' resistance; diversity, identities and cosmo-visions [world views]; work, exploitation and reproduction of life; and communication, culture and education."[57] Additional WSF meetings were held in Pakistan and Mali, with each of the three sessions focused on their particular economic, political, social, and cultural issues. The World Social Forum conference in Caracas was centered on the prospective integration in Latin America made possible by several countries moving toward the ultra-Left.

A summary perspective of the World Social Forum shows an "open space" concept that allows participants to organize their own activities. It is a horizontally structured network. This approach minimizes disputes and facilitates a dynamism of dialogue and collaboration. The Forum's first principle, for example, interlinks groups and civil society movements that are opposed to capitalism and imperialism. The Forum offers "an open meeting place for reflective thinking, democratic debate of ideas . . . and interlinking for effective action."[58]

Anti-War

The Institute for Policy Studies has been a key player at the center of the radical Left's anti-war campaign since September 2001. IPS refers to its opposition to the conflicts in Afghanistan and Iraq as being support for the "peace movement" in the service of "justice." The Institute was co-covener of the session that created United for Peace and Justice (UFPJ) in October 2002, which was to become one of the leading anti-war activist organizers of street protests. Amy Quinn, a veteran and excellent organizer, worked full-time on IPS anti-war activities and served on the board of the United for Peace and Justice steering committee. Before leaving for graduate school in 2005, she was especially helpful in coordinating the anti-war work of "Military Families Speak Out" and "Iraq Veterans Against the War" that operated within the broader IPS anti-war coalition.[59]

IPS tapped its long history in conducting such "peace and justice" campaigns, such as the Vietnam war, in seeking guidance for its contemporary anti-war leadership. But, for the people at IPS, the war itself was less interesting than the opportunity it offered to denigrate the political and economic systems of the United States. The war opened an opportunity to advance IPS's progressive-socialist-marxist revolutionary program for the transformation of American culture—it was not about the war on terrorism, but on political power. Former Marxist Ronald Radosh was very clear that even though the Vietnam war "galvanized us and gave our lives meaning," in reality "*our intention was never so much to end the war as to use antiwar sentiment to create a new revolutionary socialist movement at home.*"[60] The same is true for the progressives-socialists-marxists in their intense post-9/11 anti-war protests—for them, the war against terrorism is a godsend, an opportunity to advance the agenda to transform American culture. The core of the street workers at the sometimes numberous (150,000 people) anti-war protests in Washington, D.C., for instance, was made up of a tight knot of two mutually supporting Left-wing coalitions: progressives-socialists-marxists and the old Left communists and anarcho-communists. Thousands of "civilians," or non-ideological protestors, swelled the ranks of the hard Left, who regarded them as being little more than dupes, dopes, and useful idiots. Many of the non-ideological street workers were simply people who, for one reason or another, were against the war. They did not know or, if they did, they did not care that they were participating in radical Left protests against the American way of life and government. The dupes multiplied the number of Leftist street workers, and they became soft targets for harsh anti-U.S. propaganda and disinformation to reinforce their support.

Two primary coalitions were formed to provide overlapping support for the anti-war movement. Not in Our Name (NION) sponsored anti-war protests in the fall of 2002 and in several cities around the country. Some seventy members of the ultra-Left signed the initial statement calling on "the people of the U.S. to resist the policies and overall political direction that have emerged since September 11, 2001." Among the first to sign up were IPS associates and pro-Communist Cuba advocate Medea Benjamin; Kevin Danaher of Global Exchange; Leslie Cagan, a founder of the Committees of Correspondence (a splinter of the Communist Party, USA), who also served as a co-chair of the IPS-sponsored United for Peace and Justice; and Noam Chomsky of the Committees of Correspondence, as well as a grab bag of Hollywood actors and ultra-Left attorneys from the National Lawyers Guild, the Center for Constitutional Rights, and other radical litigation fronts.[61]

The International ANSWER[62] coalition included anti-war ("peace") groups, faith-based communities, environmentalists, communists (Socialist Workers Party; Communist Party, USA; Committees of Correspondence; Maoists; and Marxist-Leninists), a network of Arab and Arab-American groups; and it cooperated closely with IPS's progressive-socialist-marxist coalition. Medea Benjamin and Leslie Cagan created cross-walks between the two coalitions. Benjamin was a co-founder of the anti-war group "Code Pink," or "Women for Peace," that had been pushing a Marxist agenda since the 1980s. The women-run, anti-war group works the halls of Congress and has handed out "pink slips" to those disagreeing with their calls for the ousting of President Bush. Gael Murphy, a Code Pink co-founder, explains that "we're trying to change the culture and say, 'Listen, these are not your hallowed halls of seclusion.' "[63] Cagan, a long-time Communist Party activist provided a bridge between the old Left and the Gramsci Marxists promoting a stealthy culture transformation and accession to power by Leftists.[64]

The birth of the Iraq anti-war movement began in January 2003, three months prior to U.S. military action against the bloody Saddam Hussein regime. Conception of the movement occurred at the Congress Against American Aggression on Iraq, which was held in Cairo, Egypt, on December 18–19, 2002. More than 400 activists, thought leaders, journalists, and agitprop organizers attended the Congress. Participants included those from twenty Islamic countries, and several non-Arab countries, including Brazil, Cuba, Canada, France, Germany, Italy, Russia, the United States, and Britain. Saad K. Hammoundy, Iraq's ambassador to the Arab League, said that U.S. aggression was inter-linked with the globalization of capital investments.[65] More "Marx to Allah"[66] themes were included in the "Cairo Declaration Against U.S. Hegemony and War on Iraq and in Solidarity with Palestine."

Cairo Declaration

The Cairo meeting is not an isolated event, but an extension of a protracted international struggle against imperialism, from Seattle and Genoa to Lisbon and Florence, and Cordoba and Cairo. The U.S. provides unlimited support . . . to the Zionist perpetrators of genocidal crimes against the Palestinian people. The suffering of the Iraqi people under a regime of genocidal sanctions lasting over a decade, and the aggressive militarism which they face today is but a logical outcome of the structures of power asymmetry of the existing world order:

- The U.S. monopolizes political, economic and military power within the framework of capitalist globalization, to the detriment of the lives of the majority of the world's people.
- The U.S. imposes control through naked aggression and militarized globalization in pursuit of its rulers' interests, all

while reinstating the characteristic direct occupation of classical colonialism.

- The U.S. global strategy, which was formulated prior to September 11, 2001, aims to maintain the existing uni-polar world order, and to prevent the emergence of forces that would shift the balance of power towards multi-polarity. The U.S. administration has exploited the tragic events of September 11, under the pretext of fighting terrorism, to implement the pre-existing strategy.[67]

The Cairo Declaration is a rather stunning document. Not only did it denounce the United States in no uncertain terms, but its commentary reveals a fusion between the anti-globalization and anti-war activism. Secondly, it shows a fusion between international Communism and Islamic extremism. And, thirdly, it exposes a "Marx to Allah" linkage with Russia in its criticism of the "uni-polar world order" and the need for "multi-polarity." This latter statement is straight out of Russia's Vladimir Putin's foreign policy commentary.

The IPS-led anti-capitalist campaign that "big business bought the government," reducing the average citizen to having a small voice in foreign policy, was intertwined with the anti-war message. Allegations of corporate war-profiteering, creating a new national security state, and building a war economy to feed the corporate machine were at the center of much of the anti-war propaganda. This anti-war movement became a stunning progressive-socialist-marxist schoolhouse to educate the non-ideological protesters. They might have been dupes, dopes, and useful idiots to the Left, but they also represented tomorrow's voters who, when educated with appropriate anti-government propaganda, could be called upon to bring the Left to power.

IPS and its acolytes lost no time in seizing what they call the "strategic moment" to advance their Gramscian strategy toward political power. Robert Stacy McCain, an assistant national editor at the *Washington Times,* summed-up the post-September 11 protest events well In an article entitled "Communists, Go Home." He pointed out the communist roots of the International Action Center and its anti-war front, ANSWER, as well as protest support from the Communist Party, USA, and the Maoist group, the Revolutionary Communist Party, as well as the ultra-Left Institute for Policy Studies and the National Lawyers Guild. McCain rightly concluded that ". . . if all the communists were purged, there wouldn't be any movement left."[68]

Three protest groups showed up in Washington, D.C. on September 29, 2001, including the Anti-Capitalist Convergence (anarcho-communists), "peace" advocates from Oberlin University, and International ANSWER (Act Now to Stop War & End Racism). The latter group was created after September 11 behind the curtains of the International Action Center, itself a front for the Workers World Party (self-described as Marxist-Leninist).

The Washington, D.C.-based Anti-Capitalist Convergence began in late morning, first assembling near the Capitol building at Freedom Plaza and then parading their "Anti-Capitalist March Against Hate" toward the White House. Claiming that "we are a movement devoted to social justice," the Anti-Capitalist Convergence announced, "There is no justice to be found in retribution, war, racism, corporate globalization or capitalism itself."[69]

Some fifty students from Oberlin College (Ohio), who had been recruited to attend the protest by their professors, arrived in Washington, D.C. to demonstrate for peace. They carried paper-mache human bodies like shields in front of them to symbolize the dead that would result from a U.S. attack against the Taliban and al-Qaeda in Afghanistan. The students intermingled with the communist and anarchist protestors, swelling their numbers. When asked why the Oberlin students fell in with the hard Left, one young woman replied, "Oh, we aren't political. We are for peace."

The third group protesting on September 29 was International ANSWER—"Stop War & End Racism." Announcing for a mid-day rally in Washington, D.C., the International Action Center's call to action stated: "While at this moment thousands of families are in mourning for the death and injuries of loved ones, the Bush administration is taking advantage of the tragic human toll to strengthen the forces of repression while intensifying the Pentagon's war drive, especially in the Middle East."[70]

John J. Tierney, faculty chairman and professor at the Institute of World Politics in Washington, D.C. best characterized the post-9/11 creation of the anti-war ANSWER as being "but the latest creation in a series of ruses that stretch back decades."[71]

ANSWER sponsored a large preemptive anti-war protest on January 18, 2003 in Washington, D.C., along with nineteen other countries, most of them in Europe. Few Americans appeared to be aware that Communist organizations were the ones supporting Saddam Hussein and opposing U.S. action against Iraq. The swarm of protestors in the nation's capital were primarily non-communists, and many brought their children to teach them the ways of democracy in action. Unwittingly, these demonstrators gave aid and support to the Communist cause against the United States. An estimated 150,000 people showed up in Washington, D.C., and a similar number in San Francisco. Anti-war demonstrations in other U.S. cities were smaller but nonetheless sizable. An "even greater anti-American enthusiasm . . . [surged] in some forty foreign cities."[72]

Neither the October 2002 nor January 2003 Washington, D.C. protests had anything to do with peace—they were all about tearing down the United States government and replacing its liberal democracy with an autocratic Party-State arrangement similar to that in the former Soviet Union. It is not that these leftist agents of change did not learn from history they are confident that they can step over the Kremlin's ideological errors and lead the United States to a borderless world of socialist governance.

As the U.S. Congress prepared to debate the proposed 21,500 troop increase in Iraq (the "Surge") in January 2007, tens of thousands of people demonstrated across the country. In Washington, D.C. the hard Left was present in great numbers, and they were joined by celebrities, including re-treads Jane Fonda, Tim Robbins, Susan Sarandon, and Sean Penn, plus the Reverend Jesse Jackson and Representative Maxine Walters. Meanwhile, the co-chairs of the Congressional Progressive Caucus held a press conference on January 17 to announce the introduction of bills proposing a cutoff of funding and that would also compel military withdrawal from Iraq within six months.[73]

The core of the anti-war protests makes three points: (1) communism is not dead after all; (2) communism in America has some degree of re-born political traction; and (3) by operating together with the progressive-socialist-marxist coalition led by IPS's United for Peace and Justice, the ultra-Left has exerted strong anti-war voices from the world's shadows. The non-ideological protesters allowed themselves to be used as cannon fodder for the extreme Left. Not only were they used like so many street walkers, but the were betrayed by the far Left and progressive-socialist-marxist coalitions.

For the "Allah" side of the "Marx to Allah" connection at the Iraq anti-war protest was the Progressive Muslims Network. Tarek Fatah explained that the members describe themselves as "Progressive" because they "envision a society where wealth and its acquisition are not the sole and primary factors determining relationships between human beings and Muslims in particular."[74] The Muslim American Society's Freedom Foundation describes its focus as being "engagement of . . . American institutions and organizations in order to build a broad based coalition that will enhance the religious, political and social viability of the American

Muslim community."[75] The "Marx to Allah" brigade also served as speakers at the Washington, D.C. rally, including Mahdi Bray, executive director, Muslim American Society Freedom Foundation; Ashraf al-Bayoumi representing the December 2002 Cairo Congress; Ihab Darwish, Free Palestine Alliance; Ismail Kamal, Muslim Student Association; Ghazi Khankan, Council on American-Islamic Relations (CAIR); Professor Hani Abdullah; and *Imam* Johan, chaplain of Howard University. An Islamic literature table was open to those who might be interested.

From the speaker's platform, U.S. Representative John Conyers, Jr., saluted his close associates, IPS co-founders Marcus Raskin and the now late Richard Barnet, who were unable to attend. Conyers also hailed supporters of Palestine and other Muslim groups and the Workers World Party.[76]

On March 20, 2003, after President Bush announced the assault against the Saddam Hussein regime, tens of thousands of anti-war protestors were on the streets or at noon rallies in cities and college campuses or candle light vigils in the evening. The most violent protests took place in San Francisco, where thousands blocked traffic at the entrance to the San Francisco-Oakland Bay Bridge and financial district. Some 300 protesters at one of San Francisco's Federal Buildings staged "vomit in" by drinking a nauseating liquid and then barfing onto the sidewalks and plaza areas as commuters arrived. "War Makes Us Sick" was the slogan in this rather innovative direct action and propaganda event.[77]

Nearly 200,000 anti-war protesters took to the streets in Manhattan on March 22. The march in New York, organized by long-time communists associated with United for Peace and Justice, stretched twenty abreast and forty blocks long. Ultra-Left groups, such as the Trotskyite Spartacist League, were also on hand pushing their particular brands of revolutionary socialism.[78]

While U.S. protests were underway, thousands more demonstrated across Europe, Asia, and Oceana. Many of the organizing groups were Marxists and revolutionary socialists, as well as people who for one reason or more held anti-American sentiments. European protests in sizable numbers were held in London, Paris, Madrid, Barcelona, Berlin, Lisbon, Stockholm, Dublin, Naples, Vienna, and Brussels. Demonstrations against the war took place in Afghanistan, India, Bangladesh, South Korea, and Japan. In Oceania, protesters took to the streets in Indonesia, Malaysia, Australia, and New Zealand.[79]

Having failed to prevent the Iraq war, the ultra-Left turned to direct action (agitation) and propaganda to end the occupation of Iraq. The first major anti-war protest following the U.S. victory over Saddam Hussein occurred on October 25, 2003 in Washington, D.C., San Francisco, and some 140 other cities across the United States and Canada. International ANSWER and United for Peace and Justice were once again the major mobilizers of hundreds of coalition partners who took to the streets. Their primary protest banners demanded an "End to the Occupation [in Iraq]," "Bring the Troops Home Now!," and "The World Unites Against U.S. Militarism." ANSWER made a major effort to encourage "people of African descent" to march on October 25th. In addition, numerous Muslim organizations had joint International ANSWER's coalition against the war and "racism," including American Muslims for Global Peace, Muslims Against Racism and War, Muslim Student & Faculty Association, al-Awda Palestine Right of Return, Muslim Women's Political Action Committee, editor of *Arab Journal*, Muslim Student Union, and others. The coalition partnership between the World Workers Party behind ANSWER and numerous Muslim associations suggest once again that a strong "Marx to Allah" bond has been formed inside the United States.

Direct action (agitation) and propaganda was quite coarse in many cases, and developed new themes. A major spin-off of the Institute for Policy Studies, the Institute for Southern Studies, carried the IPS propaganda line: "a second invasion has begun of powerful corporations who seek to reap billions in profits from the devastation of war, and who aim to seize the wealth and resources of the Iraqi people." Southern Studies continued its anti-corporation diatribe be alleging, without a shred of evidence or a single supporting anecdote, that "through multi-billion-dollar 'reconstruction' contracts, a handful of well-connected, mostly U.S. corporations—many with scandal-ridden business records—are making hundreds of millions in war profits."

The next large turnout for a communist organized antiwar protest occurred on April 24, 2005. Express metro trains from northern Virginia were packed with demonstrators, many of whom were oblivious to the ultra-Left's agenda. Their ages were from teenagers to seniors, and many protesters brought their children. The Federal Triangle metro stop was the destination for most, referred to as the "Federal Crime Center" by several protesters. In addition to sizable numbers of locals attending the protest, large numbers of anti-war demonstrators poured into Washington, D.C. from locations the east of the Mississippi River. Meanwhile, protests were also taking place in San Francisco, Seattle, and other cities. Anti-war demonstrators adopted a new propaganda line as a rallying cry following the devastation along the Gulf coast by Hurricane Katrina: "From Iraq to New Orleans, fund human needs, not the war machine."

Once again the communist International ANSWER and United for Peace and Justice took the lead in organizing the protest. Other ultra-Left groups joined the Marxist cabal, including Code Pink, MoveOn.org, and Veterans for Peace. The Mobilization for Global Justice conducted a small protest against the International Monetary Fund and World Bank. Bill Dobbs, spokesman for United for Peace and Justice, told journalists that the message was simple: "End the war in Iraq. Bring them home now."[80]

The hard Left's "queen of the antiwar protest" was Cindy Sheehan, mother of a soldier killed in Iraq. For whatever personal reasons, she buried her son and then became a communist-supporting hater of America, performing her role well whether she was hugging Venezuela's Hugo Chavez or camping out in front of President George Bush's home in Texas. The radical Left's Code Pink raised money for her anti-war propaganda and the communist led MoveOn.org used her in its anti-American ads.[81]

The anti-war coalition organized by ANSWER held a series of protest events, September 22–28, 2007 to demand that Congress cut off all war funding. A preemptive move against the expected testimony of General David H. Petraeus on the "surge" strategy revealed the extreme Left's strategic purpose to work with its partner, the progressive-socialist-marxist coalition led by the IPS-sponsored United for Peace and Justice. Some 100,000 protesters marched from Lafayette Park across from the White House to the Capitol lawn where they attempted to hold a "die in." Numerous protesters, about 165, were arrested for jumping over police barriers. The U.S. Marxist-Leninist Organization was very pessimistic: "The failed U.S. state . . . refuses to meet the people's just demands to end the war now and bring all the troops home. On every front, it has abandoned all social responsibility."[82]

The sad part about the radical Left's lies and deceit over the Iraq War was that it led good, patriotic Americans to false conclusions. Not only that, but the Left turned them into anti-democratic activists against the United States way of life. As Americans, we are supposed to collect all of the facts, decide on the appropriate direction for the government leading us, and take actions through the ballot box, letter writing, or even protests to make our will be known. We must be clearly informed. Many of the non-ideological Iraq war protestors were lied to, manipulated, and turned into dupes, dopes and useful idiots by the Institute for Policy Studies and its progressive-socialist-marxist "shining stars" in its "solar system of organizations." Betrayal of people's goodwill is a vile political action and that is exactly the path taken by the radical Left. Blinded by the sunlight outside of Plato's cave, these hapless Americans became street workers for the Left—they simply could not see the truth.

"We have long warned . . . that the peace movement is not about peace," former Marxist-Leninist and New Leftist David Horowitz intoned in March 2003, "that it is a fifth column communist movement to destroy America and give victory to our totalitarian enemies."[83]

11

A WORLD WITHOUT BORDERS

"THE UNITED NATIONS ONCE dealt only with governments," UN Secretary General Kofi A. Annan mused in 2005. "By now we know that peace and prosperity cannot be achieved without partnerships involving governments, international organizations, the business community and civil society. In today's world, we depend on each other." Annan went a step further by concluding that "in the age of interdependence, global citizenship is a crucial pillar of progress."[1] But "progress" in Secretary General Annan's perspective would demand the destruction of national sovereignty to make room for the creation of a borderless global civil society. World governance would be doled out by a massive, faceless international bureaucracy, which would disrespect liberty and relegate individuals to the status of worker ants in a socialist authoritarian universe.

In Annan's utopia, world citizenship, or democracy from the bottom up, and regional and global supranational institutions would be added to a witches brew of Leftist propaganda and direct action designed to make people believe that the 500-year-old concept of national sovereignty is hopelessly outmoded and the underlying cause of war. The hard Left creates a false image that depicts sovereignty, the nation-state, and peace and war through the selective use of truth. The fragments of truth used today to make a paste of sovereignty is the ultra-Left's argument that the inability of nation-states to establish a lasting peace and protect human rights illustrates a failure of mankind. If the sovereign state is the cause of war, the advocates of a UN-oriented global governance say, then one should eliminate sovereignty and replace it with a world without borders, supplant national citizenship with global citizenship, and create international institutions, such as the International Criminal Court, to deal with violations of a world code of justice.

H. G. Wells, among those of his time in the early 1920s who were shattered by the carnage of the Great War, closed his renowned work *The Outline of History* with a speculation about the world government evolving over time. A major weakness he found in the League of Nations was its structural deference to sovereignty and emphasis on nationality, when just the opposite focus was needed. "The world perishes unless sovereignty is merged and nationality subordinated," Mr. Wells opined. "And for that the minds of men must first be prepared by experience and knowledge and thought," he said. "The supreme task before men at the present time is political education."[2] Hitler, Stalin, Mao, and lesser demons of the twentieth century tried to re-educate the people to embrace their own versions of a socialist fantasy world, enforcing political education by the power of the gun. Individual liberty and the thirst for freedom, however, withstood the best of the Fascist and Communist efforts to create new citizens, despite their killing of millions.

The United Nations under Kofi Annan and his acolytes brushed this recent history aside in a program of agitation and propaganda masked as an "education" project. The UN's "Teaching Toward a Culture of Peace" program was organized and is directed by the ultra-Left that would destroy sovereignty of the nation-state to make way for a global governance through a authoritarian socialist world without borders.

The revisionist Marxist ideas of Antonio Gramsci from the 1930s were picked up and rolled around in the United States and Western Europe during the 1960s and 1970s, when traditional values and appreciation of heritage were challenged and reexamined by the New Left. Gramsci's ideas did not disappear. Many of his exponents found their way into the academy where they toiled at political education in order to change the values of society and the people's understanding of their heritage, both of which served as guide posts for contemporary life. Hence, we discover in the early twenty-first century that the seeds of change that would destroy sovereignty in favor of socialist authoritarianism are upon us once again. The challenge against sovereignty and for a world without borders is manifested largely through the United Nations.

As "Marxist renewal and re-emergence" evolved from the pit through the 1990s, the hard Left visionaries drove home their key propaganda points—the global environment, human rights, and world peace—as a part of their overall message of global justice and citizenship.

The United Nations Behind the United Nations

Dore Gold's 2004 report *Tower of Babble* and Joseph A Klein's 2005 *Global Deception* together do an excellent job of exposing some of the UN's most monumental failings and persistent weaknesses, especially those cropping-up since the early 1990s. Former Israeli ambassador to the United Nations Dore Gold finds the world body to be an "abject failure" and "dominated by anti-Western forces, dictatorships, state sponsors of terrorism, and America's worst enemies." Betraying the noble ideals of the UN's founders, Gold argues, the organization lost its *moral clarity* and had proven unable to confront aggression effectively, preserve international peace, and defend human rights.

As supporting evidence, Ambassador Gold notes that barely an eyebrow was raised at the UN during the 1970s when millions were slaughtered in Cambodia and Uganda; in 1994 United Nations peacekeeping forces maintained "strict impartiality" while 980,000 Rwandan Tutsis were slaughtered; in 1995 when 7,000 Bosnian Muslims were murdered by Serb military forces after having been lured into a UN "safe haven" and another 40,000 "deported" to other areas of Bosnia; and in 1998, when five African countries invaded the Democratic Republic of the Congo to plunder its plentiful natural resources wealth, the UN sent a small observer force while 2.5 million people were being killed over the next three years. The end of the Cold War brought the world a new UN majority consisting of dictatorships, terrorist supporting countries, and those controlled or advised by America-hating revolutionary socialist states. Secretary General Kofi Annan used the confusion of transition at the UN to undermine nation-state sovereignty in favor of using key advisers and NGOs as tools to advance his global governance agenda. In the process, the UN was "emptied" of moral clarity.[3] By 2008, the world's focus shifted to Darfur, Sudan's troubled region, where more than 300,000 people had been killed (mostly Black Christians) and another two or three million driven from their homes over a five year period. The UN once again showed itself unable and/or unwilling to respond to the needs, in columnist Nat Hentoff's words, of the "innocent people in Darfur."[4]

Gold's indictment was peppered with "value neutral," "diplomatic neutralism," "moral equivalence," "moral relativism," and similar words and phrases. But his well-grounded argument uses words as lashes in what can best be described in his observations that the "UN ethos has shifted" and that it uses "impartiality as a guiding principle," which is then stood on its head by misapplying it to mean "make no moral judgments." To be impartial means not to take sides while protecting both antagonists. By doing nothing to stop aggression, the UN puts itself on the side of genocidal violence.[5] Ambassador Gold concludes that

> The UN is protected by a very high wall of political correctness that makes criticism of it tantamount to an attack on all mankind. But it is time to recognize that it has utterly failed to achieve its founders' goals: to halt aggression and assure world order. The UN has proven itself to be singularly unsuited to preserving global order. The organization's record over the past half century reflects one shocking failure after another. The 1990s brought the UN's flaws into sharper focus, and they have only grown more glaring in recent years.[6]

Joseph Klein's critique of the contemporary UN takes a different tack, but is no less realistic and demanding in its appraisal. For Klein the "*real* threat" posed by the UN was spawned from its "globalist ideology that has corrupted its founders' original intentions." The globalists' goal, Klein explains, is "to neuter the United States Constitution and the nation it defines." To those ends "powerful, pervasive, and 'progressive' ideologies . . . have led it [the UN] astray."[7]

In January 2008, Joseph Klein said that UN Secretary General Ban Ki-moon was "certainly a big improvement over his predecessor, Kofi Annan, noting his quiet diplomacy on issues associated with the Israeli-Palestinian conflict. But, insofar as the institution is concerned," Klein writes, "the United Nations continues to spiral downward." Klein cited the lack of progress in Darfur, where mass killings of non-Arabs were continuing at genocidal rates. These events unfolding before the world's eyes continued because a UN and African Union peacekeeping force large enough to stop the killing could not be put into place. Secretary General Ban Ki-moon has been reduced to begging Sudanese leaders to stop the killing, but to no avail.[8]

Having lost the initial battle for creation of a world government structure during the debates leading up to the founding of the UN in 1945, the globalists created the World Federalist Movement in 1947 at the "Conference of the World Movement for World Federal Government." The World Federalist ideologues set for themselves the task of penetrating the bureaucratic structures of the UN, coopting the UN's internal processes toward global governance, and transforming the international body into a centerpiece cluster of international institutions that would lead to a world without borders, world citizenship, global taxes, universal gun control, global economic redistribution, and an International Criminal Court that could place individuals as subjects under its jurisdiction.

Standing in the way of the globalist's plans is the U.S. Constitution that makes some 300 million Americans the sovereigns of the state and enthrones the idea of individual liberty as the ultimate purpose of the United States. Hence, the first victim—if the globalists' fantasies were realized—would be American liberty and the sovereignty of the state. Americans and others in the world would become slaves to an alien, faceless bureaucracy forever narrowing the boundaries of individual freedom.

Non-Governmental Organizations (NGOs)

The foot soldiers supporting world government ideologues are thousands of non-governmental organizations, most of which burst onto the world during the 1990s. These are the cutting edge essential to carrying out the Left's strategy of penetration, co-optation, and transformation of the UN into a center of world governance. Certainly the UN is blessed by the large majority of NGO's that help to provide basic humanitarian services, from poverty programs to health assistance in troubled areas of the world, but these "good" NGOs are being trampled by those already having penetrated and coopted many UN programs, and which are being used to transform the United Nations into a global citadel of world governance.

A largely unreported phenomenon on the reform measures taken under the guidance of Secretary General Kofi Annan was the explosion in the number of NGOs, or "civil society organizations" as they like to be called, and their direct participation in all areas of the United Nations.[9] The Economic and Social Council (ECOSOC) granted consultative status to forty-one NGOs in 1946, which reached 377 in 1968 and 700 in 1992. In January 2008, 3,052 NGOs enjoyed such standing, and 145 others were awaiting validation, which offers unprecedented access throughout the UN system to peddle their ideas. Once a UN office bites on a particular concept or project, the NGO can shop its UN-interest item among thousands of funding sources in the philanthropic community. In a word, being a UN-approved non-governmental organization is a license to do business. It costs the UN nothing, and nation-state sovereignty is diluted a little bit with each UN-NGO action. This phenomenon is sometimes characterized by glittering generalities as the "global associational revolution" and is cited as being a part of a universal movement of greater citizen action. In reality, it is all about lining the pockets of ostensible do-gooders.

Senior UN officials offer lavish praise for the non-governmental organizations. Secretary General Kofi Annan, for example, addressed a UN-sponsored non-governmental organizations conference commemorating the Universal Declaration of Human Rights in September 1998. Describing the growth of the NGO as "heartening," he noted that the UN is "opening up, training our staff to work with NGOs and providing funding and other

assistance to NGOs, particularly in the developing world."
Secretary-General Annan closed by saying that "there is no turning
back from the global NGO revolution. So let us move ahead in
partnership."[10] Louise Frechette, the Deputy Secretary-General,
gave a further elaboration of the view from the top echelons of the
United Nations:

> . . . There is a widening gap between what citizens demand and
> what governments can deliver. Our challenge is to bridge that
> gap. . . . NGOs are the leading edge of civil society . . . who are
> bringing new life and meaning to the idea of an international
> community. With goodwill and reason, you are serving as the
> global conscience.[11]

The UN's strategic partnership with the NGOs is drawn from the
mandate in the UN Charter to work with "civil society." The
international peace movement, led by the extreme Left, has
perverted the UN Charter by infringing upon, and sometimes
supplanting, the role of national governments. Increasingly, the
Left-wing NGOs are hijacking the UN agenda and actively
subverting the role and authority of sovereign nation-states. With
their hands firmly on the throttles of the UN information system,
the radical Leftist leadership has built a global propaganda forum
to prosecute its goal for world social transformation from the
"bottom-up."

When Antonio Gramsci's revisionist Marxism became popular
among the Left in the 1990s, the term "civil society organization,"
which had used to portray the activities of political-cultural centers
against capitalist tyranny, mushroomed in popularity. Civil society
came to be seen as a means of "Marxist renewal and re-emergence"
after the Berlin Wall came down and citizens were empowered in
Eastern Europe. Or, as Thomas Carothers put it, "civil society
became a key element of the post-cold war *Zeitgeist*."[12]

The hard Left began equating "civil society organizations" with non-governmental organizations. The "civil society movement" served as the engine of change in the United Nations and the point-of-the-spear in undermining the place of sovereign nation-states. More than 3,000 NGOs enjoyed UN "consultative status" in 2008, most of which were dedicated to humanitarian relief, medical, faith-based, societal, educational, and other projects. Swimming among them like sharks, however, are strategic members of the Weiss Imperium and the broader global socialist community. Among these "friends of the Weiss Imperium" were the World Federation of Democratic Youth (Soviet Union-Russia), World Council of Churches, World Federation of Trade Unions (Soviet Union-Russia), Socialist International, Institute for Policy Studies and the Transnational Institute, Human Rights Watch, Global Exchange, American Civil Liberties Union, International Association of Lawyers Against Nuclear Arms (Peter Weiss), Peace Action (Cora Weiss), International Peace Bureau (Cora Weiss), World Federalist Movement (Peter Weiss), Open Society Institute (George Soros), and a lengthy list of others.[13]

These NGO's claim to represent "civil society" and use this propaganda device to help rationalize and shroud their activities inside the United Nations. Robert Huberty and David Riggs explain in a report for the Capital Research Center how these NGO's "increasingly monopolize international meetings about the global future." They routinely reject the U.S. and other democratic governments and their activities in the "free markets, free trade and economic development," Huberty and Riggs explain. The Left's NGOs peddle environmentalism, multiculturism, wealth redistribution, disarmament, the abolition of nuclear weapons, elimination of trade in small arms, and a wealth of other social reconstruction topics.[14]

UN Secretary General Kofi Annan actively promoted the Left's "civil society organizations" as a tool to undermine the role of the nation-state in UN activities. Annan asserted in 2000 that ". . . global affairs are no longer the exclusive province of foreign ministries, nor are states the sole source of solutions for our small planet's many problems," and added that "many diverse and increasingly influential non-state actors have joined with national decision-makers to improvise new forms of global governance."[15] Annan, in essence, raised the voice of the Left's NGOs to the level of sovereign nation-states, and, from their inside positions given to them by Annan and the UN General Assembly, their voices may be louder on global policy that the sovereign nation-states themselves. A 1998 General Assembly statement on "Strengthening of the United Nations System," for example, asserted that "NGOs are the clearest manifestation of what is referred to as 'civil society,'" and opened the UN's inner doors to these external, unaccountable organizations: "If NGOs are to continue making a meaningful contribution to the work of the United Nations, it is crucial that their access to information and documentation be secured in a timely and appropriate manner."[16] In a word, members of the General Assembly desire larger voices by NGOs inside the UN to help counter the sovereign authority of permanent members of the Security Council. And one may be certain that NGOs were behind the position taken by the General Assembly, guiding its members to support positions that would help the "civil society organizations" attract funding that would foster the UN sliding toward world governance.

This course of events within the UN did not just happen willy-nilly. Rather, the World Federalist Movement, a front for the Left, has been leading a campaign on behalf of strengthening the role of NGOs at the UN, noting that the General Assembly has established a working group on extending NGO and citizen rights to "all areas of the UN." The World Federalist Movement contends that these activities will help to democratize, reform, and strengthen the General Assembly, Women's Caucus, World Wildlife Fund,

Greenpeace, Amnesty International, World Council of Churches, and other NGOs supporting the revised UN process.

Reforming the UN from the inside to promote greater involvement of civil society (read: NGOs) is only one of World Federalist Movement's activities. Its Left-wing vision includes a commitment to a genuine world community where governments kow-tow to global cooperation, democratic world institutions of law, a balance of the right to national self-determination with the collective rights of the global community, individuals as the rightful source and subject of the authority of world law, an end to the arms race and elimination of all weapons of mass destruction, termination of the use and threat of use of military force, a respect for universal human rights, and common environmental actions. For the World Federalist Movement, the "a global ethos and a consciousness of humanity as one community and of every person as a citizen of one world" is an all embracing theme.[17] This vision envelops Federalist Movement's work inside the UN system and was instrumental in successfully setting the stage for the May 1999 emergence of the Hague Appeal for Peace as a mammoth NGO, suitable for striking alliances with the moderate Leftist non-governmental organizations. As a matter of fact, the Hague Appeal for Peace used the offices and network of the World Federalist Movement to advance socialist, Marxist, and peace causes within the UN system and worldwide.

UN Power Brokers

Controlling the UN's powerful NGO activists are insiders, or "power brokers," operating within the Secretary General's inner circle. Three "senior advisers," shrouded in the shadows of the UN during Secretary General Kofi Annan's tenure, pushed the global governance transformation agenda. The points of the ultra-Left's spear in penetrating, co-opting, and transforming the United Nations were Maurice Strong, Jeffrey Sachs, and Cora Weiss.

Maurice Strong cashed his chips from the UN's environmental program to its "global governance" transformation of the UN into a tool for undermining sovereignty and subverting the original intentions of the UN founders. Jeffrey Sachs promoted the "scientific-based" Millennium Project, which is said to promise an end world poverty over two decades through a huge redistribution of wealth from the rich countries of the North to the impoverished states in the South. Cora Weiss created a huge international peace corporation to promote world government and citizenship, transfer sovereignty from nation-states to non-governmental organizations, and teach peace to children (read: "propaganda") worldwide. Each of these world government advocates used NGO's as their cutting tools to carry out the anti-nation-state programs. Their efforts are underwritten by drawing resources from the UN and foundations that are open to funding approved United Nations initiatives.

Maurice Strong, sometimes called "an international man of mystery," preferred to work in the shadows of the UN. Strong was a senior advisor to the UN Secretary General. Kofi Annan appointed him to transform the UN's sprawling worldwide structure toward a system of global governance. As a result of Strong's efforts the sovereignty of the nation-state members have been slowly squeezed to make room for the socialist power of "civil society organizations." A wealthy Canadian, Maurice Strong had been the "indispensable man," journalist Ronald Baily observed, "at the center of this creeping UN power grab."[18]

Strong's first gig in the UN spotlight came when UN Secretary General U Thant appointed him to organize and conduct the "first Earth Summit, the Stockholm Conference on the Human Environment." A year later Strong was appointed director of the UN Environment Program. Strong's methodological march toward UN global governance had begun. At the 1992 Earth Summit in Rio de Janeiro—UN Conference on the Environment and Development—Strong presented his perspective at the opening session:

> The concept of national sovereignty has been an immutable,
> indeed sacred, principle of international relations. It is a principle
> which will yield only slowly and reluctantly to the new
> imperative of global environmental cooperation. It is simply not
> feasible for sovereignty to be exercised unilaterally by individual
> nation states, however powerful. The global community must be
> assured of environmental security.[19]

Strong has also been quoted as saying, "I am a socialist in
ideology, a capitalist in methodology."[20] Many members of
Strong's family have been associated with communists and
socialists, including a cousin who was a member of the Comintern.
Strong was a confidant of former Soviet Communist Party head
and leader of the Soviet Union Mikhail Gorbachev. They have been
closely aligned for many years through solidarity of Strong's Earth
Council and Gorbachev's Green Cross International. One would
be wise to remember Strong's comments at the Rio meeting:
"national sovereignty . . . will yield only slowly . . . to
environmental security."

On the capitalist side of the Maurice Strong hydra-head, one
finds him to be a very successful businessman. He manipulated
various areas of the energy sector to amass an ample fortune. He
used a network of energy companies to gain sufficient control of
activities to attract political notice, and then converted this
attention into influencing political appointments. Strong took this
basic model with him to the UN, where, using his own NGO as a
hub, he could control the activities of several other NGOs that were
favorably committed to UN global governance. Strong made
certain that the "right" NGOs were funded by the UN or by the
private foundations supporting the global governance agenda.

Strong also served on the UN-funded Commission of
Governance. In order to mask the underhanded transformation of

the UN from an institution of nation-states dedicated to preserving human rights and peace to a world government of individuals, the phrase "global governance reforms" has been used. These "reforms" set into motion a slow-rolling of the UN toward elimination of the veto power of the five permanent members of the Security Council, an independent menu of UN global taxation schemes, and the International Criminal Court whereby the UN assumed direct control over individuals rather than follow its charter making it an organ created by nation-states and for nation-states.

Maurice Strong should be known as "the great manipulator." His genius was found in creating networks of networks of progressive and other Left-wing oriented individuals, UN offices and programs, and non-governmental organizations into a subtle mesh of political activity. The Janus-faced Maurice Strong applied his technique successfully in the capitalist arena to millions of dollars in wealth, and on the socialist side to moving the UN toward a position of global governance.

The Volcker report on oil-for-food transfers between the UN and Saddam Hussein's Iraq turned up a mid-1997 check in Maurice Strong's name for $988,885. Drawn on a Jordanian bank, funded by Saddam Hussein, and delivered by a known UN back-channel go-between with Saddam, Strong endorsed the check to invest in Cordex Petroleum, a Strong-family controlled business. Strong left the UN in the spring of 2005.[21]

Jeffrey Sachs, a professor at Columbia University, is another behind-the-curtains UN power broker. Sachs was appointed head of an independent advisory body, the Millennium Project, commissioned in 2002. The UN's flagship anti-poverty program, the Millennium Project, charged Sachs and his advisory body to develop an action-plan that would lift the world's poor out of poverty, hunger, disease, and lack of shelter by 2015 (and extreme poverty by 2025). More than a billion people live in poverty worldwide. In order to achieve the Millennium Project goals, an annual investment of about $110 per poor person would be needed. Sachs's final report was presented in January 2005 and, after review, was accepted. The Millennium Project's work was incorporated into the UN bureaucracy in 2007 to implement the recommended development strategies.[22]

According to Professor Sachs and members of his hand-selected advisory committee, the key to lifting impoverished areas out of poverty, disease, and hunger is through the creation of thousands of "Millennium Villages," sixty of which were underway by early 2006 with private and corporate funding. The advisory body defined Millennium Development Goals as time-bound, quantified targets to aid in focusing resources and actions on major poverty factors. Most of the work is carried out by ten thematic Task Forces, which are composed of more than 250 experts from around the world, NGO representatives, the private sector, the UN, International Monetary Fund, and World Bank.[23]

Sachs's central, non-governmental organization for spreading United Nations resources to a multitude of non-governmental organizations in support of the Millennium Project is the Earth Institute at Columbia University. These UN resources, if the Millennium Project estimates are correct, would amount to contributions to the Project on the order of 0.7 percent of gross domestic product annually through 2015. For the United States, this massive redistribution of wealth would range from about $70 billion in 2003 to $140 billion in 2015. In the absence of good governance, it is unclear how these funds would be prevented from being diverted into the pockets of dictators and their supporters.[24]

The steep rise in food and energy prices in mid-2008, however, rocked the momentum of progress toward the Millennium Project goals. The dramatic price increases threatened to erase the seven years of progress toward reducing poverty in thousands of Millennium Villages.[25] Joseph Klein, in *Global Deception*, placed his finger on the pulse of the UN's "stealth assault on America's freedom." Labeling the Secretary General's special advisers Maurice Strong and Jeffrey Sachs as "Leaders of the Globalist Brigade," Klein explains how NGOs, accountable to no one, are being used to trample and subvert the concept of state sovereignty inside the UN and in ways that supersede the U.S. Constitution.[26] The International Criminal Court, for instance, is postured above the American Constitution and individual freedom. Meanwhile, Sachs is using NGOs in much the same way to subvert sovereignty through a massive redistribution of wealth, which reaches UN targets through NGOs.

A third coat hanger in the UN's shadowy deep closet is reserved for the international peace movement, with special wings extended to the human rights and global governance agendas as well.

Cora Weiss, "a grandmother in the shadows," and her husband, Peter Weiss, are the creators of the Hague Appeal for Peace. They serve as president and chief executive officer of this large, Left-wing, multinational enterprise. Cora Weiss is both a principal organizer and strategist for radical and moderate socialists, Marxists, and peace and human rights activists, operating behind the facade of the Hague Appeal for Peace and other front organizations. She shows a multitude of public faces.

From the 1960s until the end of the 1980s, many publications indicated that Cora Weiss participated actively in several ultra-Left front activities. She headed and co-founded Women's Strike for Peace, helped bring about the end of atmospheric nuclear testing, and served as a delegate to the World Congress of Women held in Prague, Czechoslovakia, in 1981. She played a pivotal role in getting a host of front organizations and allied non-socialist NGOs to protest the war in Vietnam, helping organize anti-war demonstrations, including the largest one on November 15, 1969, in Washington, D.C. Cora Weiss served as co-chair and director of the Committee of Liaison with the Families of Prisoners Detained in

Vietnam. The FBI investigated the Committee from 1970 to 1973, which was "alleged to be a vehicle of North Vietnamese propaganda whose activities were believed to be detrimental to the health and welfare of the prisoners held in North Vietnam."[27] David Horowitz placed this particular front organization and Cora Weiss's activities into a proper perspective:

> Joan Baez took out a full-page ad in the *New York Times* for an 'Appeal to the Conscience of North Vietnam.' She enlisted a number of former 'anti-war' activists to sign her call to the Communists to show more humanity in their treatment of their opponents. As soon as her statement appeared, however, Baez was attacked by Tom Hayden and Jane Fonda as a tool of the CIA. A counter-ad was organized by Cora Weiss, who had traveled to Hanoi and collaborated with the regime in its torture of American POWs. The Weiss ad praised the Communists for their moderation in administering the peace.[28]

Cora Weiss has a long record of support for the United Nations, starting in the 1950s when she hosted petitioners seeking their independence in colonial Africa. Weiss was the co-initiator of the Women's Peace Petition to the UN General Assembly calling for a transfer of five percent of all military budgets a year for five years to support sustainable development and programs for women's empowerment.

Cora Weiss and the late Richard Barnet, also a Council on Foreign Relations member, were among the principal IPS associates who made the Jane Fonda-Tom Hayden pilgrimage to Hanoi, to confer with the North Vietnamese Communist government. Mrs. Weiss also was a prominent figure in the People's Coalition for Peace and Justice (PCPJ), leading demonstrations and lobbying efforts for PCPJ on specific peace campaigns, including People's Peace Treaty, Citizen's Action Pledge, and Nixon Eviction Campaign. She was one of the brains behind resolutions pertaining to the Assembly for Peace and Independence of the People of Indochina held at Versailles, France, in February 1972.

Weiss has maintained close alliances with religious groups working on peace issues, such as Clergy and Laity Concerned About Vietnam, the World Council of Churches, and the Interfaith Council. In 1985 she was a delegate of the World Council of Churches to the Third International Conference on Women, Decade of Women in Nairobi, and as a delegate to the Beijing conference on women in August 1995. At these fora, she often spoke on war, conflicts and prevention, and alternatives to violence.

As President of the 1999 Hague Appeal for Peace, Cora Weiss launched a large "civil society" (NGO) movement, which she has helped build during her many years of dedication to radical socialist, Marxist, and peace activist causes. Cora Weiss is also a principal officer of the International Peace Bureau, vice president of the steering committee in the International Peace Brigade 1997 to 2000, and other front organizations of the Left.

Just like his wife, Peter Weiss presents a chameleon-like profile. With the dissolution of the Soviet Union, he adopted a new image as a "progressive" fighting for human rights, disarmament, and world peace. His associations with like-minded persons extend worldwide, from the Socialist Democratic Party in the United States to the African National Congress in South Africa, and from the liberation movement in Burma to the National Congress in the Netherlands.

Peter Weiss has a long association with the National Lawyers Guild, a radical lawyer's association organized in 1936 with the assistance of lawyers from the Communist Party, USA, and he served on the Board of Trustees. The National Lawyers Guild has handled important cases against the U.S. intelligence agencies, represented the late CIA deserter Philip Agee's interests, and often supported groups involved with foreign terrorist and resistance movements, ranging from members of the Baadar-Meinhoff gang to the Puerto

Rican Socialist Party. The National Lawyers Guild is the U.S. section of the Soviet-Russian International Association of Democratic Lawyers (IADL).

For some 15 years, Peter Weiss has been a leader of the Center for Constitutional Rights (CCR). The Center was founded in 1966 by three leaders of the National Lawyer's Guild: William Kunstler, Morton Stavis, and Arthur Kinoy. Also giving a hand were the late Ben Smith, a registered agent of the Cuban government, and Peter Weiss. The CCR represented the family of Charles Horman, who was murdered in Chile shortly after the Pinochet coup, in their suit against Henry Kissinger and other high officials of the U.S. government. When the Center defended Puerto Rican Socialist Party member Delfin Ramos, who was charged with possession of stolen explosives, the Center defense team stated that they were "representing Ramos in such a way as to not only expose the government's political motivations for the prosecution, but to reveal the oppressive nature of the colonial relationship." The Center also instituted legal suits designed to help the guerrillas of El Salvador and the Cuban government and published material from the Sandinistas of Nicaragua. One of the articles published in the Center's newsletter, *Fight The Right*, in May 1981, was titled "Reagan's Reign of Terror."

A Socialist Manifesto for the Early 21st Century

When the Berlin Wall fell in 1989, the extremist Left-wing was left stranded like a small boat on a Marxist sand bar as the Soviet Union was swept away with the receding tide. Left-wing activists occupied themselves with continued agitation and propaganda against the West, including anti-nuclear, anti-apartheid, anti-arms trade (licit and illicit), anti-U.S. bases in the Philippines, anti-Gulf War, and anti-U.S. activities in Central America. They also critiqued NATO's new strategic concept, drew dire fictitious scenarios about the U.S. military concept of "low intensity warfare," and pursued similar themes that would lead to abolishing war. Yet, the Left in the early

1990s, both leadership and rank and file alike, seemed to lack the fire in the belly quality that had marked their "anti" heyday during the Cold War. For them, the first half of the 1990s was spent mostly in the wilderness, trying first to come to grips with the realization that the promised communist revolution would not occur, or at not in the manner that the leadership had promised, and secondly, to determine the course of their future activism on behalf of Marxist renewal and re-emergence through the international peace movement.

The Left-wing, especially the radical socialists, Marxists, and peace activists, faced an identity crisis. Among themselves they wailed like an off-key choir about how to distinguish themselves from liberals—their natural allies, but always at some distance— and conservatives. Since calling themselves "socialists" is regarded as counterproductive in the United States because of McCarthyist hyperbole in the 1950s against Communism and the international socialist movement, some Leftists began calling themselves "social democrats," others "progressives," and for many "social progressives." They unabashedly used "McCarthy's Ghost" to their advantage by shutting off debate on their support for radical causes, often attacking critics as being guilty of McCarthyism.[29]

Within this search for identity, however, there occurred new thinking about reorienting the socialist culture of political activism worldwide. While the collapse of the Soviet Union and socialism in several other countries seemed to negate most of what the radical Left had believed, they dismissed the idea that these events had any real meaning for the revolutionary future. For the extreme Leftists, "it was only 'actually existing socialism' that had failed;" David Horowitz explains. " 'Real socialism' had not yet been tried. . . . *Socialism:* It was still the name of their desire."[30] Horowitz continues that, since the Leftists are "revolutionaries," in their drive toward creating a "dreamed of future" that remains unaffected by current events, they can live comfortably in a reality that has been rejected by new objective conditions. Meanwhile, the radical politics of "social transformation" created by Marxist and socialist professors at American universities flew in the face of recent history that documented the repressive and bloody actions of regimes of the Soviet-led communist world.[31]

The international peace movement's search for new issues in the mainline of global human events first bore fruit in the highly successful Campaign Against Land Mines. Organized into non-governmental organizations worldwide, their political activism hit national governments unprepared for the resulting sustained public support for a global land mine ban. Combining centralized control by an elite NGO "Board of Directors" dominated by the Left and decentralized execution by supporting NGOs, this action team was joined by a wide range of government officials from the United Nations, the European Union (EU), and national governments, as well as by persons of world stature such as the late, beloved Princess Diana and others.

The Campaign Against Land Mines also served as a pilot project for a new NGO multinational enterprise—one that would drive the Left-wing bandwagon into the new millennium. By 1999, the Left-wing could be seen as having emerged from their years in the wilderness and actively going about the business of restoring or strengthening the international peace movement. Likewise, coalitions were reinforced with labor unions, national liberation movements, faith-based organizations, and a host of specialized activist organizations on issues of human rights, refugees and displaced persons, economic development, conventional and nuclear weapons disarmament, conflict prevention, peacekeeping, humanitarian aid, minority programs, women's and children's issues, and others involved in non-violent conflict resolution.

Peter Weiss is a regular visitor to the UN and participates in many of its panel discussions. These can be seen as "nurturing" sessions, a presence to ensure continued radical Leftist penetration at the world body.

In cooperation with UN Secretary General Kofi Annan, Cora Weiss took the lead on the formation of the Hague Appeal for Peace, which combines and integrates UN global governance, world citizenship, and human rights, and international peace. In response to an appeal by four NGOs of the radical Left— International Peace Bureau, International Physicians for the Prevention of Nuclear War, International Association of Lawyers Against Nuclear Arms (IALANA), and the World Federalist Movement—nearly 10,000 activists, government representatives, and community leaders from more than 100 countries attended a May 11–15, 1999, conference at The Hague. In reality, the Hague Appeal for Peace was a celebration and launching pad for a new multinational corporation for hundreds of non-governmental organizations. Some 400 panels, workshops, and round tables served as forums for conference attendees to discuss and debate mechanisms for abolishing war and creating a culture of peace in the 21st century. The Hague Appeal—dominated by radical Leftists masquerading as "social progressives"—advocated the creation of new partnerships between citizens, governments, and international organizations that will help make as progress toward peace. In reality, it is old wine in new bottles as the traditional anti-West, anti-U.S. rhetoric espoused by the Left has been dressed for respectability in the post-Cold War order. Growing clout inside the UN and EU with regard to a range of Left-wing policies and advocacy programs provide the proponents an air of social acceptance in their use of UN, EU, and national government monies, mostly provided by North America and Western Europe.

Peter Weiss clearly stated the purpose of the international peace movement. The "sole purpose" of the Hague Appeal is "to send a clear message to the world's policy makers" on "how to eliminate the causes of war, including racism, colonialism, poverty and other human rights violations, the limitation of arsenals to a reasonable level for territorial defense, the elimination of all weapons of mass destruction including nuclear ones, the establishment and utilization of conflict resolution mechanisms (as an interim measure on the way to abolish war), improvements in humanitarian law, and most importantly, the creation of a culture of peace for the world's war-oppressed people."[32]

Among the speakers at the Hague gathering in May 1999 were Kofi Annan, Secretary-General of the UN; Noeleen Heyzer, Executive Director of the UN Development Fund for Women; Carol Bellamy, Executive Director of the UN Children's Fund; Judge Christopher Weermantry, Vice President of the International Court of Justice; Jody Williams, International Ambassador for the International Campaign to Ban Landmines; Jozias van Aarten, Minister of Foreign Affairs, The Netherlands; Pierre Schori, Deputy Minister for Foreign Affairs, Sweden; David Andrews, T. D., Minister for Foreign Affairs, Ireland; Archbishop Desmond Tutu; and H.M. Queen Noor of Jordan. Jimmy Carter, Nelson Mandela, and other notables sent messages of support.

The Hague Appeal for Peace, the name of the new NGO multinational corporation, was heralded by its organizers as "a great success." This new activist enterprise is organized into seven major product or operating departments. These corporate directorates are mutually supporting and responsible to the President/Chief Executive Office and a Board of Directors for all operations. Decentralized execution by "independent" NGOs participating in alliances and caucuses on specific regions or issues is emphasized along policy lines prescribed by the Hague Appeal for Peace. Since the Hague Appeal is often the direct source, pass-through source, or approving authority for donors contributing funds to the participating "independents," centralized control over the multitude of NGOs is assured.

"The Hague Agenda for Peace and Justice for the 21st Century," a document distributed during the May 1999 conference, represents what should be called "A Socialist Manifesto for the Early 21st

Century." This manifesto, which is also distributed as a UN document, represents what the NGOs and individuals associated with the international peace movement consider to be some of the most important challenges facing humankind. Its basic premise underwrites a socialist action plan to undermine and destroy the sovereign nation-state as the source of the UN's international legitimacy that is astonishingly candid:

> In a great many cases, the world's governments have manifestly failed to fulfill their responsibility to prevent conflict, protect civilians, end war, eradicate colonialism, guarantee human rights and create the conditions of permanent peace. Therefore, this historic mission and responsibility cannot be trusted to governments.[33]

A key proposition in the contemporary socialist manifesto is making human security a centerpiece in its action plan. By drawing on international humanitarian and human rights law to reinforce the basic premise that governments cannot be trusted to prevent war, Leftists redefine security in terms of human needs. Finally, they pose small arms as a threat to human security, which makes it an acceptable subject for concentrated attention by the UN and its civil society partners (NGOs) as well as the European Union. Extending an olive branch to faith-based NGOs and international labor ensures a unity of effort under the guiding hands of Cora and Peter Weiss, the creators of the Hague Appeal for Peace.

The Hague Appeal for Peace, as an umbrella multinational enterprise, conducts its day-to-day operations through four activist NGOs: World Federalist Movement, International Peace Bureau, International Physicians for the Prevention of Nuclear War, and International Association of Lawyers Against Nuclear Arms. These action centers maintain alliances with numerous international front NGOs, supporting the international socialist manifesto.

As a co-sponsor of the 1999 Hague Appeal for Peace, the World Federalist Movement (WFM) focused on its longstanding goals of creating lasting peace, preventing conflicts, and protecting civilians. The purpose of the WFM from its 1947 founding has been "to transfer the Charter and the UN into a democratic legal order capable of . . . preventing war and enforcing peace." The resulting world federalism would make it possible to reduce the size of armed forces and promote a transfer of political power and responsibilities to the most appropriate levels of government. The world federalists also "support the creation of global structures that are accountable to the citizens of the world."[34]

The World Federalist Movement's William R. Pace served as secretary-general of the Hague Appeal for Peace at its May 1999 founding. He spoke eloquently, saying that "one of our main goals" was to "*prevent*" future wars. He said, "global civil society is demanding new approaches, citizen-based 'bottom-up' alternative strategies for peace, early-warning and conflict-prevention."[35]

Another co-convener of the Hague Appeal for Peace was the International Peace Bureau. This NGO was founded in 1892 and has always been critical of the way in which both the League of Nations and the United Nations have been manipulated by the most powerful states and interests. It has 170 member organizations and groups in more than forty countries. The IPB focuses on supporting the peace and disarmament initiatives taken by the UN, and devotes most of its resources to informing and assisting grassroots peace campaigns. Cora Weiss served as a vice president and member of the IPB steering committee. The Cora Weiss-led Samuel Rubin Foundation has also been an institutional donor. The IPB plays a central role in the Geneva-based Special NGO Committee for Disarmament.[36] "Governments are far too much in the pockets of the military," Colin Archer, secretary general of the International Peace Bureau in Geneva is quoted as having said at the Hague Appeal for Peace inaugural. "They're not necessarily accountable to the people. Millions of people around the world don't have drinking water [but] in many countries where military spending is up."[37]

The International Physicians for the Prevention of Nuclear War (IPPNW), a third action center for the socialist manifesto, is a federation of national medical organizations in fifty-eight countries, representing tens of thousands of doctors, medical students, other health workers, and concerned citizens who share a common goal of creating a more peaceful and secure world freed from the threat of nuclear annihilation. To that end, IPPNW members educate the public and organize demonstrations against government policies.[38]

A fourth activist group, the International Association of Lawyers Against Nuclear Arms (IALANA), was created in 1988 with the aim of preventing nuclear war through international disarmament and conflict resolution mechanisms. As a co-initiator of the Hague Appeal for Peace, IALANA has been deeply involved in its efforts to define mechanisms for abolishing war and creating a culture of peace. IALANA continues its pivotal role in this peace campaign and successful coalition of hundreds of supporting NGOs.[39]

Seven main actions initiated by the Hague Appeal for Peace in support of the United Nations included measures to restrict possession and trade of small arms, establish an International Criminal Court (entered into force on July 1, 2002), ban landmines, abolish nuclear weapons, eliminate social and economic injustice to prevent war, stop the use of child soldiers, and conduct a global campaign for peace education, which in reality is socialist propaganda and disinformation.

Peace Movement

Like warriors in the mist of a rain forest, the "reinvented" Left-wing international peace movement in 1999 began launching new volleys of poisonous arrows at Western policy-makers from the shadows of a mammoth multinational front, the Hague Appeal for Peace. This

NGO multinational launched in May 1999 masks permanent political activism inside the United Nations to fashion political actions against the capitalist West. The Hague Appeal's plan-of-action, due largely to vigorous Left-wing activism inside the UN system, has been aligned with the UN agenda and has crosswalks to the progressive-socialist-marxist movements in North America and Europe and the Japanese peace movement.

Yoko Furuyama, representing Peace Boat Japan at the 1999 Hague Appeal for Peace committed the Japanese to making two around the world cruises to "spread the word" about the Hague Appeal's discussions and identification of peace and human rights issues for all humankind. When an ocean-going peace ship travels to a troubled place, people gather on land or on board to discuss issues of peace and local initiatives. The Peace Boat tries to bring these voices to meetings with international institutions to help activists better understand the issue at hand. It is important for the Japanese peacemakers to take the initiative before a war starts in order to prevent war. Japan has been organizing such peace cruises since 1983. As a collateral effort, the Japanese say that since they have a big ship, they also carry relief goods. They also carry handicrafts and sell them at the follow-on ports of call to support the sustainable development of the people.[40]

More than sixty peace voyages had been made by January 2008. The Peace Boat traveled to more than 100 ports in over eighty countries. Chartered passenger ships provide open spaces that are used to accommodate peace discussions with about fifty guest educators aboard ship from across the globe. Educational activities include peace education workshops and lectures, plus language and cultural programs. The peace program is oriented to contemporary issues affecting the countries visited as well as expert discussion of global issues.[41]

The Japanese also offered open forums on Peace Boat voyages around the world. The Peace Boat offers a neutral space for networking between groups that share common concerns, especially those civil society groups that are unable to convene or participate in major international conferences.

In September 2007, Peace Boat began collaborating with "Mayors for Peace Campaign" to call on city executives around the world for their solidarity for and participation in global action toward the abolition of nuclear weapons. The 59th Global Voyage for Peace in September 2007 collaborated with mayor's offices all along the voyage route. This program began in 1982 when the mayors of Hiroshima and Nagasaki called upon municipal leaders around the world to join them in their anti-nuclear efforts. In January 2008, more than 2,000 mayors in nearly 200 cities worldwide had supported the peace program. Organizers announced their 7th General Conference of Mayor for peace in 2009 would be held in Nagasaki where they hope to strengthen their relationship with other non-governmental organizations and raise the public demand for nuclear abolition.[42]

Cora Weiss's Global Campaign for Peace Education is in the process of creating a Peace Boat-US similar to Peace Boat, Japan. She has tied the Hague Appeal's propaganda and disinformation to Article 9 of Japan's Constitution. Written by America at the end of World War Two, Article 9 simply "renounces the right to wage war and to maintain armed forces for that purpose." Hence, the Peace Boat-US, dedicated "to building a culture of peace around the world" has adopted a "Global Article 9 Campaign to Abolish War."

Peace Boat-US is a tax-free organization founded in 2006. Its purpose is to extend the Peace Boat experience developed by Japan to English-speaking individuals. Peace Boat-US is a floating peace education campaign. Much like the Japanese peace program, people of all ages at ports of call will be brought on board to receive the hot-bed propaganda drawn from the bowels of the Hague Appeal for Peace. The Peace Boat-US people depict pleasant propaganda pictures of activists simply standing with their fingers interlaced, smiling, and with imaginary halos over their heads. "Peace Boat-US is . . . working to promote peace, human rights, equitable and sustainable development, and respect from the environment throughout the United States and the world." Who can stand opposed to such a simple statement of purpose.[43]

The Hague Appeal for Peace also set into motion a "Global Campaign for Peace Education." The initiative "insists that peace education be made compulsory at all levels of the education system," and "demands that education ministries systematically implement peace education initiatives at a local and national level." The campaign is being carried out through a global network of educational associations and regional, national, and local task forces of citizens and educators."[44]

Cora Weiss, President of the Hague Appeal for Peace, in a June 1999 speech at Saint Petersburg, Russia, billed the meeting at The Hague as "the biggest peace conference of its kind." This "civil society initiative," she said, brought together nearly 10,000 people from national governments, international governmental organizations, NGOs, and leaders of other civic entities. Noting that "small arms are a big problem," Mrs. Weiss added that eliminating small arms, from pistols to rifles, is "just as the first step toward the abolition of slavery was the abolition of the slave trade, so the first step toward the abolition of excessive national arsenals should be abolition of the arms trade."[45]

The traditional far Left "peace" propaganda continued to pour forth from the Hague Appeal for Peace on Behalf of the United Nations. Cora Weiss addressed the 4th European Congress for Peace Education in Hamburg, Germany in June 2003, ostensibly to talk "education" but in reality took a tried-and-true anti-United States propaganda line. She saluted the assembled "peace educators," emphasizing the importance of their ". . . help to shape the minds and the direction of every future inhabitant on earth." Mrs. Weiss asked rhetorically, "why are British and American soldiers in Iraq?

Why did the US and UK invade Iraq if the Security Council didn't say it was ok? . . . Where are the weapons of mass destruction that posed an 'imminent threat' to warrant war?" She advocated that "we need to teach the importance of a strengthened United Nations. . . . We need human security, not national security."[46] This theme underlies the anti-nation-state agenda of the radical Left to lead the world toward socialist governance.

The Hague Appeal for Peace also offers a peace educators kit, *Learning to Abolish War: Teaching Toward a Culture of Peace*, underscoring the key propaganda and disinformation points to be used in addressing elementary, middle grade, and secondary schools in the United States and throughout the world.

- Elementary grades 4–6 should be ". . . guided to understand that peace is, and a culture of peace will be, the consequence of efforts of individuals and groups committed to making peace by personal actions and cooperative efforts. Civil society [read: NGOs] . . . is made up such individuals and groups."[47]
- The middle grades 6–9, a violence survey is called for to give an overview of the state of the world: "To begin learning the ways peace and what is needed to develop a culture of peace, students need to understand the culture of violence and how it affects our lives."
- And, for the secondary grades 8–12, "Cora's Vision" explains: "Peace educators have long understood the need to cultivate the 'moral imagination' of learners, so as to enable them to see peace as an actual condition of a preferred and possible future. The educational task then becomes the designing and imparting of the learning required to bring about the changes that can make the possible a probable one."[48]

French Professor Jacques Ellul' s central thesis in *Propaganda: The Formation of Men's Attitudes* was that modern propaganda could not work without "education" or, more accurately, "pre-propaganda." According to Professor Ellul, education conditions the mind with vast mounts of incoherent information.[49] Follow-up propaganda and disinformation give coherence to the collective of "incoherent information" in ways that are consistent with the communicator's intentions.

When reviewing the "Global Campaign for Peace Education" by the Hague Appeal for Peace, it is quite evident that "Learning to Abolish War: Teaching a Culture of Peace" is about neither. Rather, the education program is but a pre-propaganda campaign for a flood of selected truths and blatant lies (disinformation). Hundreds of non-governmental organizations are involved in multiple aspects of the Hague Appeal have endorsed the global Campaign for Peace Education. War is bad. Peace us good. Everyone agrees. But when these statements are placed into selected local contexts, they become tools for propaganda and disinformation.

While propaganda and education are obviously related in terms of the general process of opinion formation, Professor Terence H. Qualter argued persuasively that "the very essence of the distinction between propaganda and education is the deliberate nature of propaganda." To put it in a simple direct sentence: *The purpose of propaganda is to control actions by influencing attitudes.*[50] The "deliberate attempt" by Cora Weiss, and the global network of peace educators supporting her are taking advantage of students by helping to form, control, or alter their attitudes and take the actions desired by the UN culture of peace program. This is evidence of propaganda, *not* education.

Cora Weiss, a longstanding icon of the radical Left, has keenly used the common ground between "education" and "propaganda" to hide in plain sight a universal UN-sponsored peace propaganda campaign.

The UN peace propaganda program is not only run by a coalition of anti-war activists, but it is sharply focused against the United

States. As shown in Cora Weiss's comments in Hamburg, Germany, the "educational" materials served up by the Hague Appeal for Peace on behalf of the UN do not address the concepts of sovereignty, individual freedom, democracies being answerable to their own citizens, and other topics essential explain to a real "culture of peace." Readers are not told that the first casualty of a "culture of peace" would be individual liberty. Nor are readers informed about how a "culture of peace" would open "social spaces" in terms of Gramsci's revisionist Marxism to be filled by revolutionary socialists.

Secretary General Kofi A. Annan found a way to work around the grand ideals of the United Nations founders, and perhaps even the letter of the UN founding documents, to put the UN on a path of global governance. Using a shadowy clique of back-channel of "advisers," the Secretary General placed the UN in opposition to the sovereign authority of nation-states, not only the five permanent members of the Security Council, but those in General Assembly as well. These advisers, Maurice Strong, Jeffrey Sachs, and Cora Weiss, not only drew upon UN resources to advance the global governance agenda, but they successfully obtained money for UN efforts from progressive governments, foundations, and the business community. The key to opening the treasure chest of donor dollars was through a pipeline created by so-called "civil society organizations," or more accurately non-governmental organizations.

Like voracious Formosan termites, these ultra-Left NGOs were enabled by the UN back-channel by seeking donor funds for the UN projects they were associated with. There could be no global governance, millennium anti-poverty, or anti-war propaganda campaign without external funding. The goal is to engage more and more of the so-called civil society organizations to dilute the authority of sovereign nation-states inside the UN. These Gramscian grand tactics of subversion have set the UN on a pathway to creating a world without borders, global citizenship, and a faceless international bureaucracy towering over the very countries responsible for its creation.

Death of the Nation-State

The slippage from state sovereignty to a world socialist governance will happen quietly and without fanfare. One day Americans may well awaken to find the Declaration of Independence has been amended to delete any transcendental reference of "being endowed by their Creator," the Bill of Rights restructured to accommodate multi-cultural changes, and the Constitution cast aside as being outdated and irrelevant. All of this will occur to make room for the United Nations, or some such global entity, to guide us through socialist world governance, a world without borders.

It is just such a conspiracy against the American electorate and government that the progressives-socialists-marxists have in mind. Follow Gramsci's formula: change the culture, destroy Christianity, undermine popular appreciation of American heritage, slip into power through the ballot box, consolidate their political position, and begin the slide toward world socialist governance through a co-opted United Nations. The latter becomes facilitated by world-embracing peace, human rights, and environmental, human rights, and peace movements headed by the Hague Appeal for Peace, the "grandmother of the Institute for Policy Studies."

12

RESTORATION OF A WORLD ISLAMIC CALIPHATE

THE CALIPH OR SUCCESSOR OF Muhammad is the title for a religious and civil head of a Muslim state. The caliphate represents the political unity (jurisdiction of a caliph) and leadership under a single caliph—the "Commander of the Faithful"—in the Muslim world. When the Turks took control of most Arab lands in 1517, the Ottoman rulers adopted the title "Caliph" symbolically. Four hundred years later, the first President of the Turkish Republics, Gazi Mustafa Kemal Ataturk, abolished the institution of the caliphate on March 3, 1924. Since the 1920s, despite a growing interest to reestablishing the caliphate, the tight restrictions on political activity in most Muslim-ruled countries frustrated process toward restoring Islamic political unity and leadership.

Osama bin Laden, leader of al-Qaeda, called upon the Islamic people to restore the caliphate, and Hassan al-Banna, the twentieth century founder of the Muslim Brotherhood, also wrote about resurrecting political unity. Bin Laden deeply resented the "historic rupture" of the caliphate following the break-up of the Ottoman empire. He found the Muslim regimes left behind by Western colonizers to be godless, allowing foreigners to meddle in Muslim affairs, and allowed the creation of Israel on Muslim lands. Bin Laden's anger, burning like molten lava pouring from a volcano, was clearly apparent in a video released after the September 11, 2001, attacks. "What the United States tastes today is insignificant compared to what we have tasted for tens of years," Osama bin Laden lamented on the video. "Our nation has been tasting this humiliation and contempt for more than 80 years. Its sons are being killed, its blood is being shed, its holy places are being attacked, and it is not being ruled according to what God has decreed."[1]

It is not surprising that a principal goal of the al-Qaeda jihadi terrorists is to create a world that is dominated by Muslims, Islam, and Islamic law (the Sharia). Daniel Pipes cited the *Daily Telegraph*'s analysis of al-Qaeda: "Their 'real project is the extension of the Islamic territory across the globe, and the establishment of a worldwide 'caliphate' founded on Shari'a law.' "[2] As one major al-Qaeda leader put it: " 'Due to the blessings of jihad, America's countdown has begun. It will declare defeat soon,' to be followed by the creation of a caliphate."[3]

Resurgent Islam has emerged as a mortal threat to the capitalist West in the twenty-first century, and over time it will become an increasingly dangerous georeligious competitor for world dominance. The world Islamic community stands in opposition to Russia and the United States and their respective strategic partners in its effort to dominate the world. This is a holy war, "jihad," whose strengths are drawn from deeply held from religious convictions and passions. George Weigel of the Ethics and Public Policy Center states the simple reality of the ongoing global geopolitical competition: "Jihadism is the enemy in the multifront war that has been declared upon us." And " 'Jihadism,' Weigel quotes Richard John Neuhaus as writing, " 'is the religiously inspired ideology [which teaches] that it is the moral obligation of all Muslims to employ whatever means [are] necessary to compel the world's submission to Islam.' "[4]

There are certain things about the 9/11 attacks that "we cannot *not* understand," George Weigel writes. "For unless we grasp the character of this new kind of war, its religious and ideological roots, the passions that have grown from those roots, and our current vulnerabilities to those passions, our chances of prevailing against an adversary with a radically different view of the human future—and a willingness, even eagerness, to die for the sake of hastening that future—are weakened."[5]

Islamic identity in the early twenty-first century has been shaped from what is seen as the success of jihad in defeating the Soviet Union in Afghanistan during the 1980s and in taking advantage of America's shocking unpreparedness in preventing the 9/11 hijackings/ aerial suicide bombings and the anthrax attacks that followed. None of this should be surprising. "Islam has been almost continuously at war with Christendom since the seventh century," George Weigel reminds us, and it has placed the survival of the West in jeopardy at least twice over a thousand years of history until its devastating defeat at the battle of Vienna in 1683. This event triggered a 500 year decline of the Islamic world, lasting until the 1990s. The contemporary jihad is not unlike Islam's historically continuous war against the West.[6] Noting that American education has not done its job of informing Americans of the teachings of the world's religions, George Weigel writes that "a West that does not take religious ideas seriously as a dynamic force in the world's unfolding history is a West that will have disarmed itself, conceptually and unimaginatively, in the midst of war."[7]

It is difficult for Americans to come to terms with the idea of being at war with the politics of a religion, Islam. It is even more complex, since not all Muslims are at war against the capitalist West. One must be careful of making unfair generalizations. The truth of the matter is the United States is at war with a highly dangerous, influential doctrinal school of Islam—Saudi Arabia's Salafism as well as other Islamist groups that have joined the international jihad against the capitalist West. Americans and Europeans must remain clear that the enemy is not all Muslims, but only those conducting jihad against us and those that may be supporting them. Since the jihadists do not wear uniforms nor badges giving their affiliation, Europeans and Americans are placed at a severe disadvantage. One can never be certain just who is and who is not a jihadist at war with the West. This dilemma is not lost on the jihadists and their clandestine supporters.

Regardless of the mixed picture of Islamist hostility toward the West, it remains a fact. Weigel reminds us, that we are facing an "obligatory holy war of conquest, [which is] to be waged until Allah's sovereignty is acknowledged by the entire world."[8] The West did not start terrorist attacks, poverty is not the cause of jihadism, and Israel is not responsible for jihadism. "It is not 'Islamophobic' to note the historical connection between conquest and Muslim expansion, or between contemporary jihadism and terrorism."[9]

Akbar Ahmed, a highly respected professor of Islamic Studies at American University, makes a point about the difficulty facing Westerners confronting jihad. Professor Ahmed opened his 2007 book, *Journey Into Islam,* with a quotation by "the politest of young men" who said to him during a visit to South Asia: " 'The actions of Osama bin Laden, Hezbollah, Hamas, and the Taliban, *even if* they kill women and children, are perfectly justified by Islam.' "[10] (emphasis in original)

In light of such anti-Western hatred and willingness of Islamists to kill, often indiscriminately, the one thing that Americans and Europeans can do, as recommended by Robert Spencer, is to "stop insisting that Islam is a religion of peace."[11] Islam was not a religion of peace in Muhammad's time, Islam is not today. Islam in the early twenty-first century is not of one piece: many Islamic interpretations support jihad and death to the Western world, while many sit in the grandstands cheering on the killers and offering a sweet face of peace to Westerners. Most Muslims are content to worship Islam in a world of religious freedom.

But the reality remains: Islam does not teach the Golden Rule to help its adherents guide their lives. "Jesus's dictum that 'whatever you wish men would do to you, do so to them;'" (Matthew 7:12) appears in virtually every religious tradition on the planet—except Islam," Robert Spencer explains. The Qur'an and Hadith make such a sharp distinction between believers and unbelievers that there is no room for any commandment of beneficence."[12]

Walid Phares offers another piece of the jihad puzzle: "The United States was not attacked randomly," Phares writes, "but as a part of a planned offensive war." The 9/11 attacks were not an action by a small group of deranged, out-of-control extremists, Phares explains, they were ". . . a prelude of future attacks to come, in pursuit of clearly defined goals."[13]

Religious Passion

A brief excursion into the historical and theological roots of jihadism is necessary to gain at least a sense of the past world power and religious passions motivating the jihadists to oppose the West. Such sensings offer insight into the specific nature of the jihadi threat posed against Western culture today.

In a hundred years of warfare, A.D. 632–732, Arab conquest extended like the body of a huge eagle-like caliphate with its body resting in Iraq, with one wing reaching across Iran, Afghanistan, Pakistan, and India to the Chinese border and the other across Palestine, north Africa, and the Iberian peninsula and into southern France. It was from this central position in Iraq and Palestine that the Arabs won victory after victory over the Byzantines and Persians. Arabs enjoyed high morale, superior mobility, support of the native populations, and the crumbling weaknesses of the existing empires. The Arabs lost momentum after 732 as a result of Byzantine resurgence that allowed it to take the battle to the Arabs and the combat strength of the Uigher Turks that blocked Arab expansion into the Chinese empire. The efforts by Charlemagne in the west provided a barrier to the fourth Arab expansion into Europe. At the same time, Arab disunity drained the caliphate's fighting capacity.

Taymiyya, Wahhabism, Salafism, and the Muslim Brotherhood are complementary in their eight hundred year common goal of restoring Islam's golden era under a world caliphate and their willingness to follow a path of violent jihad to win this profoundly religious objective.

The idea that violent jihad was necessary to assure the survival of Islam was first expressed in the late thirteenth and early fourteenth centuries by Ahmed ibn Abd al-Halim ibn Taymiyya (1263–1328). He taught that the political power could be restored over the lands and Muslim communities conquered by the Mongols through the power of the sword wielded with the religious passion of jihad. This passion for jihad included "'absolute hatred'" for heretics, apostates, hypocrites, sinners, and unbelievers (including Christians and Jews).[14]

Wahhabism and Salafism began as two distinct trains of thought. Saudi King Faisal embraced Salafi pan-Islamism, which resulted in an integrated doctrine based on ibn Abd al-Wahhab's teachings and Salafi interpretations of the sayings of Muhammad. King Faisal's main objective was one of blocking those who were leaning toward pan-Arabism in favor of pan-Islamism. It also created, however, radicalized Salafi constituency elements, which were funded by the Saudis through the Muslim World League in 1962.[15] The West needs to be aware of the fact that "Saudi students in the 1970s learned engineering and administration alongside an ideology of xenophobic alienation," Trevor Stanley warned. "In the long run, the battle against violent Salafism will be fought not only on the battlefields of Afghanistan and Iraq, but also in the universities of the Middle East."[16] As in all wars, the battle of ideas reigns supreme over the sword.

The Salafis believe that the first generation of Muslims during Muhammad's time and the two generations following offer an example of how Islam should be practiced. Current day Salafis believe that materialist and cultural influences have distorted the purity of Islam as it was practiced during the days of Muhammad. They believe that an Islamic revival will purge religious innovation that has weakened Islam. By cleansing Islam of changes made to its doctrine over time, the Salafis believe they can restore Islam to the three generations during Muhammad's time.

Many current-day Salafi point to Muhammad ibn Abd al-Wahhab (1703–1792) as being the first modern era figure to advocate a return to the religious practices of the "righteous predecessors." His evangelizing in the eighteenth century called upon Saudi Arabia for a return to the religious practices of the early generations. His works are read by Salafis today.

Osama bin Laden and his followers think and operate in the tradition of the Salafists, whose main goal was to return Islam to its "Golden Age" under the Prophet Muhammad and the first caliphs. "The Salafi ideology, called *al Aqida al Islamiya al salafiya*," Walid Phares explains, "is grounded in the works of many clerics, chronicles, imams, and a panoply of leaders."[17] The emergence of the contemporary salafi (Sunni) jihadi is focused on the specific strategic objective of restoration of the caliphate.[18] The Saudis and Wahhabism claim to be the leader of all Sunni Muslims (slightly more than one billion people worldwide). In the Salafi tradition, the Saudis/Wahhabists reject all innovations in Islam after the third Islamic century, or about 950 A.D., and their main focus is on maintaining the purity of Islam as it existed at that time. Other Muslim groups, however, deny the Wahhabi/Salafi claim to represent "pure" Islam.[19]

Wahhabism evolved from the teachings of Muhhamad ibn Abd al-Wahhab, a Sunni cleric, who in the mid to late eighteenth century, established the Salafist movement in the remote desert areas of the Arabian Peninsula. Islam, Wahhab taught, must be preserved in ways that are consistent with and supportive of the Prophet Muhammad's teachings. Since the Salafi after Muhammad established a caliphate to continue His ways, so too should the Muslim governments opposing Ottoman power. Wahhab joined with the bandit al Saud who wielded the cutting edge of the sword against the Turks, whose power had been extended across the Arabian Peninsula. Al Saud's ancestors and followers of Wahhab kept up the fight into the twentieth century. In the end, with the help of World War One that crushed remaining Ottoman power, the Peninsula was freed and Saudi Arabia became an Islamic state.[20] Wahhabism . . . since has become a pillar of legitimacy for the Saudi Arabian monarchy."[21]

The "Muslim Brotherhood" is a second movement of Salafi jihadists, began to come together in Egypt during the 1920s. Guided by Salafism and jihadism, the Brotherhood was an urban group whose long-term objective was to takeover the government. Hassan al-Banna, strongly influenced by his mentor Muhammad Rashid Rida, emerged as the major organizer behind Egyptian fundamentalism. When he organized the Brotherhood, its credo was: "God is our objective; the Quran is our constitution; the Prophet is our leader; struggle is our way; and death for the sake of God is the highest of our aspirations."[22]

An Egyptian schoolteacher, Hassan al-Banna founded the Muslim Brotherhood, or "The Society of Muslim Brothers," in 1928 to promote implementing the Koran's *sharia* law and social renewal. Al-Banna was opposed to the political and social injustices he witnessed and encouraged an Islamic ethos of altruism and civic duty. By the 1940s, the Brotherhood had about 500,000 members. Sayyid Qutb visited the United States as a student between 1948 to 1951. " 'Appalled by the racism and sexual permissiveness' " he encountered, Qutb returned to Egypt with a burning hatred of the West and its society. He joined the Islamist Muslim Brotherhood and would become one of its most outspoken jihadists. Qutb has an extensive influence on jihadist groups in Egypt in showing his hatred of the West. Since the Muslim Brotherhood was also connected with jihadists in Saudi Arabia, there can be little doubt about his influence on Osama bin Laden.[23]

During the 1950s, the Muslim Brotherhood was a leader of political opposition to Egyptian strong-man and socialist Gamal Abdel Nasser, which included assassination attempts. Many Brotherhood members were driven out of the country and found refuge in Saudi Arabia. Wahhabism had long been a mentor for al-Banna—the relationship coalesced during the Egyptian exile in Saudi Arabia when many similarities, as well as differences with Wahhabi, were discovered and often resolved. Over time the two fundamentalist approaches began to meld, and the Wahhabis spread its message through the Muslim Brotherhood.[24]

Sayyid Qutb (1903–1966), an Egyptian, became a leading ideologue of Muslim fundamentalism and he was also a member of the Muslim Brotherhood. Sent to the United States in late 1949 to mid 1950, Qutb apparently was shocked, as Bernard Lewis explains, by the strong support for Israel he found in America. His outlook doubtlessly was partially shaped by the formation of the Israeli state and diplomatic recognition by Washington. But Qutb, Lewis recounts, saw events as a "Jewish onslaught on Islam, with Christian complicity."[25]

Qutb taught that "Islam is a religion of peace," Robert Spencer observes. But to Qutb, Spencer continues, ". . . Islam is a religion of the peace that will come when everyone is Muslim or at least subject to the Islamic state. And to establish that peace, Muslims must wage war."[26] The United States and Israel are first in line.

In the 2000s, al-Qaeda and the Muslim Brotherhood remained united by strategy but divided by tactics. According to Lydia Khalil, al-Qaeda's number two leader Aymann al-Zawahiri denounced the Muslim Brotherhood for what he believed was a misguided direction toward political Islam. The issue was over the Brotherhood's participation in Egypt's parliamentary elections. Al-Zawahiri's criticism was drawn from his militant Salafist perception that participation in the elections put the Brotherhood in position for pursuing the goal of Islamic governance at the expense of jihad.[27]

For Wahhabis the ideal world occurred at the time of the Prophet Muhammad when he shared the teachings of the Koran with the tribes of the Arabian Peninsula. The task of contemporary Wahhabists and their Salafist brothers is to resurrect those earliest days with a restored caliphate that ruled the Islamic world after the Prophet's death in 632 A.D.[28] At the acme of its power, the caliphate's hegemony stretched across the territories of northern Africa, Portugal into France and across to northern India, through the Balkans and into Poland, Hungary, and Austria. The caliphate's governance held strictly to Islam's religious code prescribed by Allah: the *sharia*. But for the Wahhabis/Salafists, fundamentalism is not just about imposing the *sharia*. Seeing the world through a novel Islamic lens permits them to see Islam as being not just a religion, France's Olivier Roy explains, but it is also a political ideology encompassing all aspects of society, including politics, law, economy, social justice, foreign policy, and other major areas of contemporary society. "Islamism," Roy says, "is the brand of modern political Islamic fundamentalism which claims to *recreate a true Islamic society. . .*." [emphasis added][29] The new world envisioned would convert all people around the globe to Islam. Those who refused to convert would be relegated to an existence of extreme harshness. Many would be slain.

From these early influences of Taymiyya and al-Wahhab, Al-Banna and Qutb, and Salafism emerged as the current-day jihad. Ayman al-

Zawahiri and Osama bin Laden, and Egyptian and a Saudi, joined forces in the creation of al-Qaeda and the global jihad.[30]

Islamic Caliphate

Muhammad (570–632) was a man of war turned Prophet. When he ordered his followers to fight for the new religion he had delivered to them, some of the tribes rejected his entreaties in favor of worshiping their own gods. Shouting invectives, Muhammad picked up the sword and attacked the recalcitrant until they succumbed to his rule and Islam. Forcible conversions were not made, although those who did not willingly subscribe to Islam were compelled to live as non-Muslims in an Islamic system that gave all support to Muslims and oppressed those who would not convert.

Once his base was assured, Muhammad turned to using the sword to spread the word of Islam. According to the Koran, the "'surest path to Paradise'" would be found by those who "'slay and are slain for Allah.'" Over time, Christian lands fell quickly to the massive Islamic armies that pounced upon them, wielding the sword for Allah: Christian North Africa, Portugal, Spain into France, across to Armenia, Cyprus, Rhodes, Crete, and Sicily. Muslim leaders encouraged obedience to the rule of the Caliph by reaching into the Koran to echo the words of God: "'When you meet the unbelievers in the battlefield, strike off their heads and, when you have laid them low, bind your captives firmly'" (47:4).[31]

Islam has no moral code similar to the Ten Commandments. Hence, just about anything can be justified, if it contributes to the spread of Islam. Muslims are required to speak the truth with other believers, but not unbelievers. Muslims can be friendly with non-Muslims but they cannot be friends. To step across this boundary, Muslims would risk falling afoul of the Koran's (3:28) admonishment to "'guard yourselves from them [non-believers].'"[32]

Many contemporary Islamists want to restore the caliphate in order to unify the Muslim peoples against the West. By reimposing the *sharia*, they believe, the historical caliphate can be restored. From this centralized base, Wahhabism (Sunni) can underwrite jihad to suppress and convert the people of non-Muslim states until Islamic rule is imposed worldwide.[33]

Restoring the caliphate by turning the clock back to the seventh century is an interesting vision. But today's instant global communications, especially travel, television, and the Internet, provide an alternative perspective. "Both its [the United States] low form of girly magazines and punk rock as well as its impressive literature, art, commerce and technology now saturate the world. And why not?," Victor Davis Hanson asks. "American radical individualism appeals to the innate human desires for freedom and unbridled expression." "Westernization," he says, "subverts most hierarchs, especially in the reactionary world of Islamic fundamentalism, where the mullah, family patriarch or state autocrat can't keep a lid on it."[34] Americans must remain solid in their belief that an intense yearning for individual liberty beats inside all people everywhere. A part of realization of that liberty is given expression in a profound respect for people of all religions and those who do not believe. Every opportunity should be taken to invite Muslims to join in this fundamental expression of human liberty.

The Islamists' nightmare is fear of change—fear of a secular world that would disconnect the political state from religious law. They fear democracy and equal rights for women. They fear liberty. Hence, a despotic caliphate that keeps the Islamic peoples marooned in the eighth century is the Islamists' answer to all of these fears. Their solution is to eliminate Western liberal democracies that block the roadway for Islam's political and social change throughout the world. Already they have made headway, especially in Europe where Islamization and the creation of Eurabia are feeding the Islamist wolves a Europe's door. Saudi Arabia's religious fifth column is already grounded inside the United States [Chapter 13], while the Wahhabi theology is used to undermine of American liberties and democracy. The cultural war against the United States, supplemented by the sword of terrorism, is both a strategy and grand tactic to break down the American will to resist domination by the rule of Islam, including its religious law, civil code, and system of governance under a world caliphate.

The false idol of "multiculturalism," a concept contrived to support the radical Left's assault on American culture, self-destructs when it is exposed to the realism of militant Islam's perceptions of the West. The cultural chasm is massive between the American way of life, individual liberty, and democracy and Islam's civil code of a restricted social intercourse, autocratic laws in the *sharia*, and a worldwide governing system (the caliphate). As explained by Islamic scholar Bernard Lewis, ". . . the most powerful accusation of all against [the United States] is the degeneracy and debauchery of the American way of life, and the threat that it offers to Islam." These perceived threats to Islam, Professor Lewis explains, are "articles of faith in Muslim fundamentalist circles."[35] Osama bin Laden, for instance, after watching people come and go in early 1980s Beirut, commented that " 'this is a small America, with its *kufr* [infidels], filth, and whores, but soon things will change.' "[36] In February 1998, after witnessing American society and lack of what he perceived as moral values, bin Laden said, " 'all these crimes and sins committed by the Americans are a clear declaration of war on Allah, his messenger, and Muslims.' "[37]

When multiculturalism is confronted by Muslim theocracy and its fear of pluralistic liberty and the West's openness, respect for women, and culture founded on the principles of individual liberty flourishing in a robust democracies, the idea that "all cultures are equal" collapses on the basis of its own pseudo-logic. A cultural war is raging alongside the military conflict between Islamists and the West. The so-called "war on terror" is one of culture and of the sword. This demands that Americans engage Islamic fascists shouting "death to infidels" with a clear cultural message, as well as military engagement.

The abolishment of the caliphate in 1924, or the sultanate as its was known at the time, broke the continuous rule of Sunni Islam, though accommodating many changes along the way, that reached all the way back to Muhammad's death in 632 A.D. These fourteen centuries stand in silent testimony to Islam's role as a crucial "symbol of Muslim unity," which became important to Muslim identity across the centuries. As a consequence, Professor Lewis says, contemporary "Muslims . . . tend to see not a nation subdivided into religious groups but a religion subdivided into nations."[38]

This Islamic perspective of the religion flourishing in different lands has brought it into conflict with the West, whose nation-states exist on the basis of Western values and evolution of these territories under Western principles of international law. It should not be surprising that, when the West looks toward Islamic countries and their doctrine of autocratic rule under a world caliphate, it sees something akin to "fascism." President George W. Bush used the phrase "Islamic fascists" to describe those terrorists who plotted to blow up some ten airliners over the Atlantic in August 2006. His remarks set off a mini-flap. The Council on American-Islamic Relations (CAIR), a well-heeled, Saudi-funded Sunni lobbyist, was apoplectic over the President linking "Islam" and "fascism."

Although the harshness of "Islamic fascism" may rankle American senses a bit, it is a very descriptive phrase that accurately characterizes the religiously-based Wahhabi political assault on Western societies. The iron-hand of the restored caliphate envisioned by Osama bin Laden would certainly be used to clean up Osama's perceptions of "filth and whores" in American society and the West at-large. Extreme social regimentation would relegate

Jews and Christians to a sub-culture of second class residence in the newly conquered Muslim lands and those persons belonging to the Hindu and other religions would receive even harsher treatment, perhaps genocide. Make no mistake, the United States is at war and from the Islamic fascists' point of view it is a war to the death. Americans need to look behind the bombs and hijackings to the religious roots of Islamist behavior in order to better understand their motivation and how best to combine the West's counter-culture war and the sword to neutralize al-Qaeda's strengths.

Jihad

The Koran is the central authority of Islam. Muslims believe the Koran was dictated by Allah and delivered to the Prophet Muhammad by the Angel Gabriel. The roots of what it means to be a Muslim by the 1.2 billion believers around the world are secured deeply in the "Sacred Text." Islamic law, beliefs, and spiritual and ethical teachings are drawn from it. It is not surprising, therefore, that the Koran's authority is very strong, politically and socially in the Muslim world. Muslims today, as in the beginning, believe that the Koran is literally the word of God. Everything in the Koran's approximately 80,000 words, between 6,200 and 6,240 verses, and 114 suras is expressed in perfect Arabic and is considered eternal and created by the Great God. An important aspect of the Koran is that it dictates civil law (the *sharia*), assuring a fusion of state power and religious practices that continue to exist today. The caliph in the past was believed to be chosen by Allah to lead his people.

Muslim societies are not all alike, which has created political and religious differences and inconsistencies. Transnational extremist movements are dedicated to restoring world Islam in a caliphate that would reclaim past "Islamic lands," as well as extend the caliph's hegemony over lands held by non-believers. The caliphate, the extremists believe, would assure the political and social regimentation necessary for the *sharia* civil code to assure Muslim

unity in spite of cultural differences. Strict interpretation of the
Koran provides the code of conduct for carrying out such action.
Israel's Dore Gold presents a discomforting picture of Saudi
Arabia's contemporary religious teachings.

> Saudi mosques were serving [in the 1990s] as centers of vicious
> incitement, according to which Christianity was a 'distorted
> and tolerated religion.' Interfaith dialogue was called 'sinful,'
> and it was 'forbidden for man to bring together Islam and
> blasphemy, monotheism and polytheism . . . [and] Allah's
> straight path of righteousness and the satanic path of heresy.'
> Since Christians and Jews were infidels, it was permissible,
> according to Saudi religious textbooks, 'to demolish, burn, and
> destroy [their] bastions.'[39]

The idea of "Jihad" is central to all that is Islam. The first
recorded political use of jihad took place in the seventh century
during the military consolidation under the Prophet Muhammad.
From the beginning, Muslims established the rule of Islam to
conquered peoples under the guidance of jihad. Theology and
politics were one. So important was jihad regarded as an
"instrument of Islam" that the early Muslim leaders considered it
a sixth (unofficial) pillar of Islam (the five pillars of faith are
witness, prayer, pilgrimage, alms giving, and fasting). Jihad has
always held the connotation that all Muslims accepted duty to
spread the word of Islam.

The theology and practical use of jihad in spreading Islam is
well-rooted in the Koran:

> 9:73: O Prophet! Strive against the disbelievers and the
> hypocrites! Be harsh with them. Their ultimate abode is hell, a
> hapless journey's end.

9:123: O ye who believe! Fight those of the disbelievers who are near to you, and let them find harshness in you, and know that Allah is with those who keep their duty (unto Him).

2.191: And slay them whenever ye catch them, and turn them out from where they have turned you out . . . such is the reward of those who suppress faith.

8:12: . . . I will instill terror into the hearts of the unbelievers: smite ye above their necks smite all their finger-tips off them.

8:15, 16: O ye who believe! When ye meet the Unbelievers in hostile array never turn your back to them. If any to turn his back to them on such a day—unless it be in a stratagem of war, or retreat to do a troop (of his own)—draws on himself the wrath of Allah, and his abode is Hell,—an evil refuge (indeed)!

8:39: And fight them on until there is no more tumult or oppression, and there prevail justice and faith in Allah altogether and everywhere; but if they cease, verily Allah doth see all that they do.[40]

The jihad ideology defines enemies as those infidels who oppose the establishment or spread of Islam over the lands under their control or sovereignty. Spreading the faith by the power of the sword is an important duty to growing numbers in the contemporary Muslim world. The jihadists are religious devotees and their actions are rooted in the measures that led to the creation of the first Islamic state for than thirteen centuries ago. History serves as a guiding light for today's jihadists as they move toward restoration of the caliphate and engineering a reality that will allow Islam to embrace the entire world.[41] "In the universal Islamic polity as conceived by Muslims, there is no Caesar but only God, who is the sole sovereign and the sole source of law," Islamic scholar Bernard Lewis tells us. "Muhammad was His Prophet, who during his lifetime both taught and ruled on God's behalf."[42]

Osama bin Laden declared war on the Western world on
February 23, 1998, in his "Declaration of the World Islamic Front
for Jihad Against the Jews and the Crusaders." First, bin Laden
presented three "facts" that "are known to everyone." These
"facts" are used by bin Laden to create a phony script to
underwrite the rationale for his declaration and ensure that it met
the Koran's seventh century criteria for making war:

> First, for over seven years the United States has been occupying
> the lands of Islam in the holiest of places, the Arabian Peninsula,
> plundering its riches, dictating to its rulers, humiliating its people,
> terrorizing its neighbors, and turning its bases in the Peninsula
> into a spearhead through which to fight the neighboring Muslim
> peoples. . . . Second, despite the great devastation inflicted on the
> Iraqi people [1990–1991] by the crusader-Zionist alliance, and
> despite the huge number of those killed, which has exceeded 1
> million . . . despite all this, the Americans are once against trying
> to repeat the horrific massacres, as though they are not content
> with the protracted blockade imposed after the ferocious war on
> the fragmentation and devastation. . . . Third, if the Americans'
> aims behind these wars are religious and economic, the aim is
> also to serve the Jews' petty state and divert attention from its
> occupation of Jerusalem and murder of Muslims there. The best
> proof of this is their endeavor to fragment all the states in the
> region such as Iraq, Saudi Arabia, Egypt, and Sudan into paper
> statelets and through their disunion and weakness to guarantee
> Israel's survival and the continuation of the brutal crusade
> occupation of the Peninsula.

"All these crimes and sins committed by the Americans are a
clear declaration of war on Allah, his messenger, and Muslims," bin
Laden says in a sweeping conclusion. Osama bin Laden dropped
the first shoe: "On that basis, and in compliance with Allah's order,

we issue the following *fatwa* [ruling] to all Muslims: The ruling to kill all Americans and their allies—civilian and military—is an individual duty for every Muslim who can do it in any country in which it is possible to do it, in order to liberate the al-Aqsa Mosque and the holy mosque [Mecca] from their grip, and in order for their armies to move out of all the lands of Islam, defeated and unable to threaten any Muslim."[43]

Osama bin Laden's theological interpretation was a stroke of genius. Not only did he put the West and Israel on notice and open the door for development of a broader global-girdling terror network, but he checkmated any meaningful opposition by moderate Muslims. Robert Spencer explains: bin Laden's ". . . *theory of jihad* allows for the unchecked growth of militant groups in Islam—growth which outmanned and outgunned Islamic moderates are powerless to stop because to do so would be to turn Islam against itself."[44]

Al-Qaeda

Al-Qaeda was developed and flourished during the 1980s to bring Arab fighters into Afghanistan for the jihad against the Soviet Union for having seized Muslim land. Two years following the 1989 exit of the Soviets, the Persian Gulf War erupted, with infidels once again on Muslim lands—those foreign military forces based in Saudi Arabia were especially repugnant to Wahhabis, since Saudi territory was the home of two of Islam's most revered holy sites, Medina and Mecca.

Thanks to the quiet acceptance of terrorism by the Clinton Administration and its ineffective responses, and in some cases no response at all to the terrorist attacks during the 1990s, Osama bin Laden was emboldened to take more drastic steps. President Clinton's choice to view al-Qaeda'a terrorist acts as being nettlesome matters suitable for law enforcement (FBI) and prosecution strengthened Osama bin Laden's view of the U.S. being a "weak horse." With America's security door left open by the Clinton Administration, the September 11 attacks were inevitable. Many American counter-terrorism specialists in the 1990s advocated more direct responses, but their strong recommendations were brushed-off by the Administration. The only question open was where and when the big attack would occur.

There were many lonely voices trying to persuade the Clinton Administration to address terrorism as attacks on the sovereignty of the United States. Chasing down militant terrorists internationally is a soldier's job, not a policeman's, was the message offered by numerous counter-terrorism specialists in the 1990s. The rationale was simple: assigning the counter-terrorism job to law enforcement, though a couple of notable arrests and convictions were made, was insufficient to place the al-Qaeda organization nor Osama bin Laden personally at risk. In bin Laden's eyes, firing a few missiles at a base camp in Afghanistan in a roll-of-the-dice chance of killing him was another "weak horse" move. The situation was worsened by Clinton officials blabbing as to why they thought Osama was at the targeted Afghanistan camp in the first place. Result: loss of a valuable intelligence source.

Al-Qaeda is organized horizontally into a network rather than a vertical organizational chart showing top-down guidance and bottom-up feedback. Hence, chopping off the head of the "snake," Osama bin Laden, as some summarize the problem, while important, would not destroy al-Qaeda. Rather, al-Qaeda resembles more of an octopus whose tentacles or arms spread out. If one destroys a tentacle, the al-Qaeda octopus is poised to reconstitute itself. It can survive elimination of operational cells, going on to rebuild replacements. Chameleon-like, al-Qaeda is forever adapting to changing environments, organizing new fronts to mask its activities, and decentralizing the planning and execution terrorist attacks against the West. By assisting the radicalization of "homegrown" terrorists that support the jihad independently, al-

Qaeda has created a "wild card," though not under its direct control.

Al-Qaeda is a transnational organization or a borderless network of like-minded, though independently organized and led Islamists groups worldwide. It provides important direction in countering what Muslims see as the Western world's anti-Islam actions. While the West as a culture is the target of terrorism, the United States is singled out for particular attention. Al-Qaeda's pan-Islamic agenda also includes mobilizing the Muslim nation or *umma*. Reacting to an increase in the number of enemies after 9/11 and a well-founded respect for the destructive power of the weapons arrayed against them, al-Qaeda leaders encouraged Islamist groups to strike against foreign targets on their own soil, especially Americans and their resources. Sleeper cells may be present inside the United States and Western Europe. The secret groups are believed to have received training from al-Qaeda in Pakistan. Saudi-funded madrassas or religious schools, in Pakistan have brainwashed millions of young men to hate America, Israel, and India since the early 1990s. In order to mask its activities in garnering new recruits and supporters, al-Qaeda operates through mosques, madrassas, and cultural and community centers in the United States and Europe.[45]

Al-Qaeda's Strategy Against the Capitalist West

Al-Qaeda's holy war or jihad against the West is well-rooted in Islamic doctrine which precludes any chance of accommodation. The West's response, however, is not a holy war against Islam per se. But Islam is divided in two parts, one religious and the other political, the latter being the *sharia* or civil law and specific infringement of recognized civil liberties, especially those involving treatment of women and totalitarian governance. Wahhabism, the Islamic doctrine guiding al-Qaeda and its supporting groups, envisions restoration of the caliphate ruling the Islamic world. This is the political aspect of Islam, not the religious dimension. The West must be careful to respect the great world religion of Islam, while countering and defeating the political aspect inherent in Wahhabism. Easy words to scribble, but practically a very difficult task, since the sinews that bind religious and political Islam are not always evident.

To some extent, the dual aspect of religious-political Islam is a weak construct, since the two components are fused as one in the Koran and religious clarifications and statements over 1,400 years. But it was al-Qaeda that emerged from the fires of Salafism to inflict its anti-Western, pan-Islam vision of a world caliphate on non-Muslims. Islam in al-Qaeda's hands became a religious veil over what is clearly a political agenda of violence and totalitarian rule.

Al-Qaeda's strategy is based on waging a war against the West and Islam with the ultimate aim of restoring the traditional caliphate. The strategy demands first driving the Americans out of Iraq. Secondly, gathering numerous allied groups worldwide to assist the conflict in the name of pan-Islamic solidarity, and maneuvering to ensure Wahhabist leaders, especially Osama bin Laden, preserve positions of leadership. Thirdly, by extending a jihad to secular countries near Israeli borders. The next step would be creating a successful clash with Israel. Finally, Osama bin Laden would achieve totalitarian control in a restored of the caliphate that would extend to Islamic domination of the world.[46] Al-Qaeda's decentralized structure helps to attract and nurture new Islamic groups to integrate into the octopus-like network. These groups, scattered across the globe in a multitude of countries, are the building blocks of the full-scale Islamic war to come. Al-Qaeda's training of supporters in urban guerrilla and terrorist tactics, as well as assistance in picking targets, and sometimes resource support all help to build a solid network with loyalty to Osama bin Laden, Ayman Zawahiri, and other Islamist leaders.

Al-Qaeda's grand strategy is linked closely to its octopus-like network of dispersed sympathizers. These smaller, national-based groups hold a variety of beliefs consistent with Islam, and they are often swayed by al-Qaeda pronouncements for direct action against the United States. This centralized ideology of Islamic fundamentalism, Wahhabism and Salafism, provides an essential rationale for the decentralized execution of indigenous terrorist attacks against the West. The advent of "leaderless terrorism," according to Dennis Puchinsky, a former State Department official, was "premeditated" and has become a "permanent component of the global jihad movement." While this indigenous or "homegrown" terrorism has been growing, al-Qaeda has retained the capability to execute attacks of its own.[47]

Pakistan

Having been pushed out of Afghanistan in 2002, al-Qaeda and its Taliban allies set up operations in Waziristan, in rugged western Pakistan along the Afghan border. Although world maps show Waziristan being a part of Pakistan, the area is under quasi-control of the Islamabad government. Tribal leaders remain the supreme authorities in Waziristan. Movement from the region into Pakistan per se is quite easy, while entrance to the region from mainstream Pakistan can be made quite difficult by the ruling tribal leaders.

This is a perfect area for al-Qaeda, with ready access to a population filled with angry young men whose anti-Western beliefs make them ready for recruitment. Al-Qaeda is able to maintain clandestine training areas and at the same time have ready access to markets and stores, medical care, state-of-the art electronic technology. As a bonus, al-Qaeda faces relaxed security services, and they have ready access to regular air service to the West for foreign trainees and dispatch of terrorist cells. The Islamist jihad fighters live and operate openly—no one bothers them. Abdul Majadal, a Taliban commander wounded in a gun battle with British troops was evacuated from Afghanistan to Karachi for emergency care: " 'Until I return to fight, I'll feel safe and relaxed here," he told *Newsweek* writer Ron Moreau.[48]

Pakistan provides a perfect environment for combat jihadists. The country has been under military rule for forty of its sixty years, more than half of the 160 million people cannot read or write, annual per capita GDP is about $2,600 or about 75 percent below the world average, and, without public schools, poor parents send their children, some two million of them, to some 13,000 madrassas or Islamic religious schools. The madrassas emphasize memorization of the Koran and serve as recruitment centers for jihad.[49]

General Pervez Musharaff and the Pakistani Army made a half-hearted effort to eliminate the al-Qaeda and Taliban infrastructure present along Afghanistan's eastern border. After losing more than 1,000 troops, plus 3,000 wounded and 300 captured, the Pakistani government in 2006 decided to accommodate the jihadist presence. The war on terror took a major step backward when the northwest corner of Pakistan became an untested safe haven for al-Qaeda, the Afghan Taliban, and outlawed Pakistani jihadists.

Pakistan paid its own price for the al-Qaeda presence. Telecommunications intercepts confirmed that al-Qaeda members were responsible for the 2007 assassination of presidential candidate Benazir Bhutto, a declared enemy of the jihadists.[50] By early 2008, Western intelligence had concluded that al-Qaeda had reconstituted its massive network of operatives, logistics, communications, and couriers along the Afghan-Pakistan border. Al-Qaeda's adjustment to the U.S. success in Iraq included instructions for major operatives to leave the country. A renewed focused was being placed on mass-casualty attacks in Europe, with special attention placed on Germany and Spain. Illegal immigration in these two countries from Algeria and Morocco will provide the backbone for the planned attacks. The Pakistani government finally recognized that the United States was not the threat and that the cooperation between al-Qaeda and Pashtu separatism and extremism was a major internal threat.[51]

Europe

Among the indigenous terror events carried out independently in Europe within al-Qaeda guidelines were the urban transit attacks in Madrid in March 2003 by a Moroccan Islamist group and the radicalized "British boys" in London in July 2005. In the meantime, al-Qaeda money helped to persuade Algeria's Salafist Group for Combat and Call to make its jihadists available for bin Laden's operations. According to a statement by Ayman al-Zawahiri, the Algerian Salafist group would be available globally with cells and operations far from North Africa. In addition, al-Qaeda sleeper cells were developed in Canada, and Saudi money financed al-Qaeda's takeover of Somalia (2006). In the Balkans, al-Qaeda network was linked to indigenous groups, though it was a hard sell of Wahhabism meeting the needs of Balkan Muslims. Al-Qaeda fighters, however, for years have quietly infiltrated guerrilla forces in Kosovo, Bosnia, Croatia, and Macedonia. In Pakistan, al-Qaeda has schools and training facilities for use by foreign terrorists and relies on close relations with the Pakistani Islamist network. Al-Qaeda's operational ties also extend to allied groups in the Philippines, Malaysia, Indonesia, and elsewhere in South and Southeast Asia. Cross-connections with groups in Chechnya, Libya, Egypt, and elsewhere in the Caucasus and North Africa multiply the type and number of terrorist options available to al-Qaeda planners. In Latin America, al-Qaeda has a presence in the wide open and lawless "three-border region," which is made up of the cities of Puerto Igauzu, Argentina; Foz do Iguazu, Brazil; and Ciudad del Este, Paraguay.[52]

Europe is the favorite foreign lair for the Islamic terrorists. It has been regarded as a safe haven for terrorists who initially infected the host societies like a nasty cancer, and by 2007 they had metastasized into a sword wielded to Islamicize the whole of Europe. Al-Qaeda and its satellite groups find in Europe pliable societies that enable their funding, logistics, planning, and, in limited ways, training. Mosques are sites for radicalization and recruitment for creation of new terror cells; among the recruits are British, Spanish, and French citizens. In Britain, the use of the phrase "Londonistan" reflected the fact that, for whatever reason, the children and grandchildren of those brave Britons that stood up to Hitler and endured the Nazi Blitz have seemingly lost their will to stand up to the wicked. One might legitimately suspect that years of pounding by the radical progressives-socialists-marxists directed at tearing down the United Kingdom government has exacted a heavy price from British society. The London School of Economics, once a renowned institution of great pedagogical value, for example, was transformed a century ago into an anti-capitalist, anti-Western "mis-education" center. In recent years it has had a connection with some of the most brutal terrorists. Multiculturalism and political correctness, as is the case for many U.S. universities, advocated by Left-wing professors, journalists, and politicians further weakened love of country and the will to defend its values and traditional institutions.[53]

American journalist Tony Blankley, a clear thinking, graceful writer with roots in Britain, has gone to great lengths to warn of the impact on the United States, if Europe becomes an Islamicized "Eurabia."

> The threat of the radical Islamists taking over Europe is every bit as great to the United States as was the threat of the Nazis taking over Europe in the 1940s. We cannot afford to lose Europe. We cannot afford to see Europe transformed into a launching pad for Islamist jihad.[54]

London has long been a haven for al-Qaeda and others in the worldwide network of Islamic terrorism. Between 300 and 600 British citizens passed through Afghan training camps in the 1980s and 1990s. Many al-Qaeda members and supporters in Saudi

Arabia fled to London in the early 1990s when the House of Saud took action to break up dissidents in the kingdom. Meanwhile, the seeds of radical Islam began to take root in Britain and intensified over the years. Integration into the stratified British society was difficult for many Muslims. The apartheid reality in Britain trumped normative Left-wing mouthings of multilateralism and political correctness. In 2004, the unemployment rate of Muslims in Britain was about 28 percent or a bit more than twice as great as all Britons at nearly 13 percent.[55]

It is not surprising that al-Qaeda and its followers first penetrated those countries with lax asylum and immigration laws, including Spain, the Netherlands, Belgium, Germany, Denmark, Sweden, and Italy. Several hundred terrorists took up residence in the Netherlands by 2003.[56] The terrorist attacks on the mass transit systems in Madrid on March 11, 2004, and London on July 7, 2005, indicate a shift in al-Qaeda's strategy. Since being driven out of Afghanistan, it seems Osama bin Laden and his terrorist gang are finding direct attacks on Western targets more difficult. By enabling vicious attacks without al-Qaeda's hands-on involvement by satellite terrorist groups, including homegrown terrorists, al-Qaeda remains the head of the octopus while giving independence of action by its tentacles. In Madrid, for example, it is most likely that a Moroccan groups with ties to Islamic Combat Group and al-Qaeda bombed the commuter trains. In London, the terrorists were "British boys," as described in Melanie Phillips in her distressing book of reality, *Londonistan*—Muslim young adults who had been born and were a part of British society and knowledgeable of its values and traditions.[57]

Decentralization makes it more difficult for al-Qaeda to coordinate operations but multiplies the number of independent strikes possible. With al-Qaeda serving as the head of the global terrorist octopus, each of the tentacles reaching out worldwide become autonomous units. The proposition that all transnational terrorism events are interconnected, though not executed in a coordinated manner, has begun to take on an air of reality. The terrorist octopus is made more dangerous through such decentralization.[58]

Al-Qaeda also carries with it the burden to train their operatives in the techniques of intelligence collection, communications, and survival during covert presence and actions in Western countries. These are more than a list of "do's and don'ts." Complete manuals on terrorism subject areas and other relevant to terrorist operations are available to jihadists in the West. Among the undercover skills taught is how to go about creating and using forged documents and different names, and handling multiple passports and identity cards. The basics of developing alternative escape routes in the event they are needed, as well as techniques for detecting surveillance.[59]

The need for training is on-going since al-Qaeda continually attracts new recruits to its global network. Some terrorists over time will enter Paradise and others will be compelled to operate deeply underground for years before their covert actions are called upon for execution against Western targets. In addition, fresh faces are always in demand. New recruits are often found in prison where they convert to Islam, and, after they are released, to prove their faith by becoming a Holy Warrior (jihadist). Such recruitment is common in the United States and in Western Europe.[60] Although media speculation is that al-Qaeda may be attempting to create a "blond haired-blue eyed" army of jihadists, the reality is that such converts are few in number and useful mostly for propaganda purposes.[61]

Islamization in Europe is different than in the United States. Paul Belien, an adjunct fellow at the Hudson Institute, writes that the European Union is the primary promoter of massive Muslim immigration in the hope that a "'Euro-Arab symbiosis'" can be created. Egyptian-born Bat Ye'or, scholar and author of *Eurabia*, explains that European Union experts believe that such a symbiosis can be created "'through economic development, soft diplomacy and multiculturalism,'" which "'would guarantee Europe peace, markets and oil.'" Although Europeans are "extremely worried" by the Islamization process, Belien explains, it is being dictated to them by their political elite against their wishes.

Freedom of speech no longer exists in many countries. Laws said to be designed to curb "hate speech" forbid people to express their concerns about the massive immigration underway and the Islamization of their nations. Meanwhile, violent crimes are increasing, including knifings and rape, many by aliens, and ordinary people are prevented from carrying the means to protect themselves, including pepper spray.[62] When a popular restaurant in a small town outside of Amsterdam closed at 11 P.M., several members of the staff (young women) were discussing whose turn it was to be the designated driver for social activities in Amsterdam. This customer asked why they did not simply take the train. Answer: "Oh, we used to take the train but there have been so many rapes and robberies by immigrants recently that the trains are no longer safe."

Europeans are also facing official pressures under the Islamization process. In Antwerp, Belgium, a long-time civil servant who had worked in immigrant neighborhood for many years was pushed out of her job by newly arrived Salafist militants. The Salafists first set up youth groups, which were used to takeover the mosques. Since they were funded by the Saudis, the Salafists had money and used it in dealing with the Muslim community and city authorities. The Salafists demanded separate hours for Muslim women to use the municipal swimming pools and got their way. Worried immigrants went to the civil servant who had previously helped them before the Salafists arrived and expressed their misgivings. When the civil servant reported their concerns to her superior, she was told to "change her attitude." Soon after, she was replaced by one of the radical Salafists. She was also threatened by one of the Salafists of possible consequences, if she continued to speak out. Similar tactics have been used elsewhere in Europe where boasting that "Western Europe is becoming a hotbed of Salafism" can be heard.[63]

Islam is Europe's second-largest religion after Christianity and it is the fastest growing, a result of numerous mosque building programs. From Marseille to Creteil, France, to Rotterdam and Amsterdam, The Netherlands, to Cologne, Germany, and elsewhere throughout the continent, Europeans are waging campaigns against new mosques with their towering minarets against the skyline that dwarf Christian cathedrals built centuries ago. In Cologne, the city's Muslims began building a mosque "almost within the shadow" of the storied Cologne cathedral, a landmark survivor of intensive bombing during World War Two. The 2,000-person mosque will have twin minarets towering 170 feet. German hostility toward the mosque is met by 120,000 Muslims living in Cologne demanding their right to a place of worship visible to everyone.[64]

In the United Kingdom, the European-Muslim culture clash took a different direction in February 2008 when the archbishop of Canterbury called for applying *sharia* law in Britain in certain instances. Archbishop Rowan Williams, leader of the seventy-seven million Anglican Communion said that there was a place for "a constructive accommodation with some aspects of Muslim law in the United Kingdom. It is not clear that one can apply *sharia* law as if it were sliced up into various units. The *sharia* is a very complex legal system that follows the prescriptions of the Koran. The archbishop's comments created a firestorm of criticism, especially in light of British resentment over the fifty-two persons killed on July 7, 2005, by four bombs set off in the country's transportation system by Islamic terrorists. Prime Minister Gordon Brown issued a statement that said he believed that "British law should apply in this country, based on British values." The next day, many bishops joined the politicians in criticizing the archbishop's remarks and called for his resignation. Some of the bishops claimed that the archbishop was "undermining Christian faith."[65]

In June 2007, a report by the Virginia-based Jamestown Foundation revealed that jihadi networks and activities in and around Barcelona underscored Catalunya's new status as a European country for al-Qaeda terrorism operations.[66] The consolidation of the global Salafi-jihad in Catalunya, Spain's autonomously governed northern region, underwrites al-Qaeda's operations in Spain, Europe, North Africa, and the Middle East.

According to Spanish counter-terrorism officials and other terrorism experts, Catalunya has become the principal focus of jihadi terrorism in Spain and the largest recruitment center (some 300,000 Muslims, about one-third of them are from Morocco). Catalunya is the epicenter for jihadi meetings. Three cities— Badalona, Santa Coloma de Gramenet, and Sant Adria de Besos— serve as focal the points of the jihadi triangle for all of Europe. Every month three to five Muslim residents travel to Iraq, Chechnya, and Afghanistan. In March 2007, police found tapes by Osama bin Laden and for training in the city of Reus.

> The Salafi Islamist groups and their network in Catalunya have established regional operational cells and networks for recruiting jihadis and supporting terrorist activity, including criminal actions to gather funding.[67]

The bad news for Europe in the wake of al-Qaeda's losses in the Iraq War is that at least 200 foreign fighters (jihadists) have been ordered home to Europe. Britain, France, and Spain sent agents to Iraq to determine the identities and scope of the al-Qaeda blowback. Germany had already detected an increase in the number of Iraqis entering the country.[68]

In the meantime, al-Qaeda operated from North Africa (Algeria, Morocco, and Tunisia) in France, Germany, Italy, and The Netherlands. At the same time, operatives from South Asia have established jihadist cells in Britain and Switzerland. The new

European Police Organization, Europol, issued its first report in April 2007 stating that Islamic insurgency cells pose a greater threat than ever to European security.[69]

Religious converts in Europe are playing a growing role in jihadist networks. Two German converts to Islam, for instance, were arrested while planning to bomb American targets. A convert is among four defendants in Copenhagen being tried for plotting to blow up political targets in Sweden. Three converts await trial in Britain on charges of participating in a 2006 transatlantic airline plot. In some, cases converts feel pressured to prove their worthiness to serve their new faith and make bad decisions. Most European converts are good people who often promote interfaith understanding. But it is the jihadists, a tiny subset of converts that destroy property and injure people.[70]

European converts are of special interest to the al-Qaeda jihadists, since they can, as a rule, enter the United States more easily. It is not surprising that al-Qaeda continues to recruit European converts for explosives training in Pakistan. These trained Europeans have an extra edge in inserting operatives into the United States ". . . to carry out an attack that might be reminiscent of 9/11."[71]

Wahhabi presence in the Balkans is often open and disruptive, since they tend to challenge imams when they do not follow a strict interpretation of Islam. The clash with moderate Islam has resulted in gunfire and fatal confrontations with police. Those people being intimidated by the Wahhabi presence say that they need help against the violence.[72]

For the first time in the Balkan countries, people see Muslim women moving around in the hijab (Islamic headdress). This social change is a result of Saudi influence exerted through the Wahhabi presence, including those who marry local women. Saudis pressure Bosnian widows of those killed in the 1990s civil war to convert to Islam. Anyone who converts will be paid $50 per month.

Multiculturalism

When the Soviet Union collapsed in 1991, the European Left adopted multiculturalism as a new weapon to be used on re-shaping its own society. A secret partner in the "Marxist renewal and re-emergence" efforts, Gramsci's cultural transformation strategy was adopted by the Left to transform society and, over the long term, destroy capitalism. "They went directly from Communism to Multiculturalism as the continuation of Communism by other means," Fjordman, a Norwegian Internet Blogger, commented. "Leftists and Muslims have a mutual short-term interest in keeping Leftist parties in power, and a mutual long-term interest in weakening the traditional culture of Europe," Fjordman continued. ". . . Leftists from all over Europe seem to be opening the gates of Europe from within. 'You want to conquer Europe? That's ok. Just vote for us and help us get rid of capitalism and eradicate the Christian heritage in Europe, and we will let you in,'" Fjordman characterizes the European scene.[73]

Bat Ye'or outlined the "Eurabian ideology" that envisages a united Mediterranean culture based on "a symbiosis of the Northern and Southern shores through multiculturalism and a unifying process." The idea was to create a common Euro-Arab empire with a free circulation of goods and people and integration structures such as a common Euro-Arab parliament and universities. "Multiculturalism," Bat Ye'or says, "is in fact a crucial dimension of the Euro-Arab strategic alliance."[74]

Fjordman, agreeing with Bat Ye'or that the rise of Eurabia is tied to the policies of the European Union, offered a realistic perspective:

The tectonic plates of global power are now sifting in ways they haven't done for centuries. This is the retreat of the Western world order. Multiculturalism and the inability or unwillingness of Western nations to uphold their borders are viewed by

Muslims as a signal that their ancient Western rival is weak and
ripe for conquest. . . . Al-Qaeda strategists have earlier outlined
a schedule for awakening the Islamic world and overthrowing
the West with a timeline stretching over fifteen to twenty years.
A world war of sorts with the Islamic world is already
inevitable. . . . The only question is whether this will be a cold
or hot world war.[75]

Islamic multiculturalism or what ex-Muslim and writer Abdul
Kasem calls "Kafir mulitculturalism" (Kafir is the Islamic term for
non-Muslim) has opened a door for Islamists to turn the West's
policies to its advantage. Since the Western concept of
multiculturalism includes promotion of religious tolerance, freedom
of expression, and democracy, it opens the door for Islamists to
advance their agenda to create a pan-Islamic world. "All the
cardinal principles of Kafir Multiculturalism," Abdul Kasem
explains, "are working in favor of the Islamists."[76] The Islamists
support Kafir Multiculturalism as a ploy to mask their use of the
Western concept as a weapon against itself. The Islamists are
delighted to use the West's concepts of democracy, freedom of
expression, secularism, and respect for diversity of cultures,
religions, languages, and traditions to their advantage.

The jihadists have a "totally different idea of multiculturalism,"
Abdul Kasem explains. "The foundation of Islamic
Multiculturalism is solidly based on the supremacy of Islam,
primacy of the Arabs, and the global Islamic Ummah [community
of Muslim believers]." When Australia organized an "interfaith
dialogue," for instance, the Islamists were delighted to share the
"beauty" of Islam; the session and those following were funded by
the infidel taxpayers. For the jihadists, such "dialogues" have
served as the best platform to advance Islam in the West. Thanks
to those Westerners who are ignorant about Islam and are gullible
useful idiots," Abdul Kasem explains, "the Islamists are laughing

all the way to the mosque, knowing full well that Islam is totally safe in the hands of Western politicians."[77] The Islamists simply allow the kafirs to promote the agenda of imposing Islam on the infidel lands. The Koran is clear about Allah being the owner of infidel lands. A few verses from the Koran reinforce the point:

- *Islam is the perfect religion; it will dominate all other religions . . . 9:33*
- *Allah gradually reduces the land controlled by the unbelievers . . . 21.44*
- *Allah grabs the land of the unbelievers . . . 28:58*
- *The believers must make war on unbelievers and hypocrites and show firmness . . . 9:73*[78]

These verses from the Koran are a sample of those making the case that "Muslims are the legitimate owners and rulers of all infidel lands." When Islamists immigrate to infidel lands, therefore, they are not entering a foreign territory. Rather, they are simply occupying land that Allah had reserved for them.

Europe Is Dying

The twenty-seven member European Union and the United States are the principal champions in the capitalist West's geopolitical competition with Russia and the Islamic Middle East. The main problem is that the Europeans are faltering and unwilling to step out of their downward spiral. European military forces are paper thin and have shown themselves to be lacking in the self-confidence necessary to engage al-Qaeda and Taliban forces effectively in Afghanistan. Secondly, the Europeans have given up their Christian heritage, hamstringing themselves from being willing to sacrifice to preserve their way of life. And, thirdly, Europeans live for today and now as shown by their inability to sustain a birthrate sufficient to sustain the population.[79]

In early 2008, the U.S. had to send 3,200 more Marines to Afghanistan to backfill some 20,000 NATO allies—Germany, France, Spain, and Italy—unwilling to risk taking casualties. NATO political leaders insisted that the European forces were up to the task and performing well. Only the Britains and Canadians joined the United States in the heavy lifting against the Taliban. In addition, U.S. officials were adamant that NATO Europe countries had done little to train their military forces for counterinsurgency operations. The realities showed that only the U.S. was willing to risk its forces, more than half of the 42,000 allied troops, while NATO allies did very little. Yet, in early 2008, only six of Germany's 614 parliamentarians favor putting its 2,900 troops in Afghanistan in harms way. Spain, France, and Italy have also placed restrictions on how NATO may use their armed forces.[80] The reality of the situation is that if the NATO countries are unwilling to step up and do the job needed against the jihad, "that alliance no longer serves a useful purpose."[81]

The origin of the European disease that is leading it to its dying days is a result of a succession of rulers who were totalitarian in nature. Not only did they want to rule people's day-to-day activities but it wanted to control their minds and their souls. To do that, following Antonio Gramsci's prescription there had to be a systematic loss of faith the the Judeo-Christian God, Paul Belien explains. In real terms, the loss of faith and Judeo-Christian legacy opened the people's minds to the legitimacy of the state as the single source of order. As a result of "an ungodly state of affairs," Paul Belien writes:

Contemporary Europe is in crisis. Its welfare systems are running out of money. Its moral and legal order is breaking down, while the influence of radical Islam is growing. Its nation-states are being undermined by the European Union. Most Europeans look on passively. After three generations of welfare dependency, they have lost the ability to take their fate into their own hands.[82]

In what George Weigel has called "demographic suicide," the birthrates in Sweden, Spain, France, Italy, and Germany, for example, have fallen as low as 1.4 babies per woman. A 2.1 babies replacement rate is required simply to sustain the current population. At present birthrates, Europe's population will fall by 13 percent by 2050. During the same period. people of European stock in Europe will be down to 7.5 percent—overall, Caucasians that represented 31 percent of humankind in 1900 will be down to 11 percent by 2050. Time could run out for Europe. For many young Europeans already aware of living during Europe's final days have made elaborate immigration plans for implementation when the time is right. Many of them have visited friends and relatives in the United States for support of their evacuation from a Europe with a democratic deficit and an increasingly remote and ineffective European Union.[83]

Europeans do not enjoy freedom of speech in the same way that Americans do. Many restrictions apply to discussion about Islamization process underway and the large number of immigrants in their countries, but they dare not speak out. If people wish to express their worries about Islamization, they are inhibited by restrictive laws that call such discourse "hate speech."[84] The European Union, for instance, banned "jihad," "Islamic," and "fundamentalist" when referring to terrorism. Instead of using "jihadi fundamentalists," which has been declared a "sinful expression," the Eurocrats recommend using "violent extremism." Arnaud de Borchgrave concludes the obvious when he writes that "the European Union has gradually fallen into the paralyzing embrace of appeasement."[85]

America Is At War
The simple truth is that the United States is at war. It is a conflict we did not seek, one that we would rather not fight, and one

where the path to "victory" is uncertain. Yet it is a war we must win. The enemy is savage and celebrates his readiness to kill American men, women, and children in the name of God. There is little chance of a peaceful resolution. The war should be expected to go on for multiple generations, since the enemy's religious passions are unrelenting in the belief that Allah compels them to rule in His name over all the world's people. This is the third of the three global geopolitical competitors, militant Islam, whose violent jihad is aimed at Russia and its strategic partners, and the capitalist West dominated by the United States. The winner of this three-way world war will become evident sometime during the second half of this century.

The Islamic jihadists will not stop. Killing them, by their own religious beliefs, places them on a fast track to reaching "Paradise." The capitalist West needs a strength of purpose to protect itself against attack. But Americans are whining and tired of war after just six-and-a-half years into a decades-long struggle to protect themselves from militant Islam. The 2008 presidential elections shows one candidate promising to withdraw U.S. armed forces from the Middle East as quickly as possible in 2009, while the other possible national leader foresees a strategy that keep American military pressure against those jihadis dedicated with deep religious passion to do America harm. Meanwhile Europe is faltering and may soon leave the United States standing alone. Mark Steyn presents a distressing picture of a Europe that ". . . has all but succumbed to the dull opiate of multiculturalism. In its drowsy numbness, it stirs but has no idea what to do and so does nothing."[86] Is this America's future pathway?

The multi-generational war underway has already affected travel on the planet, re-directed huge sums of public resources to homeland security, and left numerous people fearful, uncertain, and insecure about their future. The jihadists are wielding a two-sided sword against the capitalist West. One edge is the "war" side, the sharper edge that promises endless assaults, bombings, decapitations, and similar great evils. The other is the "culture" side that uses immigration as a weapon to insert Muslim religious practices into Western countries for the specific purpose of transforming the non-Muslim ways of life into those acceptable to Islam (Chapter 13).

The "war" side of the sword is destructive in the sense the jihadists have met a technological barrier of conventional explosives. Yet, the jihadis are at work on developing or obtaining through theft or purchase an array of chemical, biological, radiological, and nuclear weapons. Iraq's murderous leader Saddam Hussein had developed a cookbook for the development of weapons of mass destruction. While Saddam's capabilities to produce and stockpile such weapons have been destroyed, the knowledge of "how to" build such weapons is common knowledge among the scientific and technological communities in the Middle East. Russia and the capitalist West have a similar fate: it is only a matter of time until these weapons are found in the hands of the jihadists. The difficulty for the West is that such weapons always confer an advantage to the jihadists, since they will always hold the initiative of where and when to execute first use.

Tolerating the jihadists is a poor option, for it plays into the hands of their long-term strategy where a combination of the "war" side and the "culture" side of the sword of Islam will meld into a winning position vis-a-vis Russia and the capitalist West. America is at war on two fronts and needs to coordinate its counter-strategies. Placing a continuous military pressure of the "war" side of the Islamic sword needs to be matched by strengthening U.S. resistance to the multicultural offensive against the American way of life inside the United States. In this regard, Americans have much to learn from the "salami-tactics" that have been used by Muslim immigrants so effectively in breaking the Christian back of Europe.

Finally, U.S. policies should take a clear account of the red-green alliance of the progressives-socialists-marxists (red) and Wahhabis/

Salafism (green, color of Arabia) in their mutual support for the transformation of American culture and society. Americans need to give the childish tactic of closing their eyes to unsavory realities and face the fact, as so wisely counseled by George Weigel: "The war against jihadism is a contest for the human future that will endure for generations."[87]

13

SAUDI ARABIA'S RELIGIOUS FIFTH COLUMN

You don't understand, you don't want to understand, that a Reverse Crusade is underway. A war of religion they call Holy War, Jihad. You don't understand, you don't want to understand, that for those Reverse Crusaders the West is a world to conquer and subjugate to Islam. Politically Correct, you don't realize or don't want to realize that a war of religion is being carried out. A war they call Jihad. A war that does not aim at the conquest of our territory maybe, (maybe?), but certainly aims at the conquest of our souls and the disappearance of our freedom. A war which is conducted to destroy our civilization, our way of living and dying, of praying or not praying, of eating and drinking and dressing and studying and enjoying Life.[1]

Oriana Fallaci, was one of the most trenchant observers of the world scene and accomplished political journalists. Originally from Italy, she lived many years in New York, and in 2002 wrote her first book in more than ten years, *The Rage and the Pride*.[2] Fallaci's tough-minded design for counter-terrorism—"Islamic hatred for the West [is] in a fire spread by the wind"—lays out the facts clearly for all to see. Some European countries, burdened by huge Muslim populations that are eroding the original cultures of their new European homelands, tried to ban her book, an effort she denounced as "intellectual terrorism."[3] Ms. Fallaci gave us all something to think about and to act upon.

Michael Barone concluded from his analysis of the facts of the Salafists/Wahhabis that "it may not be prudent yet to speak the truth out loud, that the Saudis are our enemies. But they should know that it is increasingly apparent to the American people that they are effectively waging war against us."[4] Writer and keen observer of the world scene Victor David Hanson observed that: "It is time for Washington to recognize its despotic, oil-rich 'ally' for what it is and act accordingly."[5]

War Against Infidels and Unbelievers

There should be no doubt that militant Islamists are conducting a crusade against all of those they consider "infidels" and "unbelievers." Al-Qaeda and other guerrilla groups are simultaneously waging conflict, with terrorism as a major weapon or tactic, against Christians and Jews in the United States and Europe, Hindus in Kashmir and elsewhere in India, Orthodox Russians in Chechnya, moderate Muslims in the Caucasus, and Buddhist Chinese in Xiniang. Militant Muslims connected with al-Qaeda are conducting war in Indonesia and the Philippines, hundreds were killed by Muslim-Christian violence in Nigeria over a beauty pageant and Danish cartoons. The "worldwide transnational Islamic revival" also extends to many countries where a presence is maintained for recruitment and to build a support structure. Examples might be Kenya, Bali, or the tri-border area between Paraguay, Argentina, and Brazil. The United States, however, remains the primary target with

Europe following close behind. During a September 11, 2002, celebration of the attacks a year earlier, for instance, Islamists in London praised Osama bin Laden as a hero and urged young men to join the effort for victory against "American efforts to dominate the world and snatch the Gulf oil fields."[6]

Millions of Muslims are people of bright and wonderful smiles. Many wish to be integrated into the modern world—tolerant of other religions and oriented toward democracy. Most Muslims are confident in practicing their faith, while learning from the non-Islamic communities. Islamists, on the other hand, are shrouded in darkness and fear and their supporters, a tiny minority, wish to hold the modern world at an arms length while they strive to re-create a seventh century milieu for the practice of a puritanical form of Islam, Wahhabi. "Though anchored in a religious creed," Daniel Pipes observes, "militant Islam is a radical utopian movement closer in spirit to other such movements such as communism and fascism than traditional religion." "By nature antidemocratic and aggressive, anti-Semitic and anti-Western," Pipes adds, "[militant Islam] . . . has great plans."[7] In a word, Wahhabism is driven by a political ideology shrouded inside a religious smokescreen.

Hatred of the United States is not so much for things Americans have done but for who we are. Educated Islamist radicals unleashed a laundry list of real and imagined U.S. policies as reflecting a form of racial and cultural arrogance against Muslims, such as support for Zionism, selfish support of corrupt regimes in the Arab world, and economic dominance and exploitation through globalization leading to poverty and tyranny. Yet, these ostensibly rational elements of American bad deeds are rooted more in the militant Arab world's own failings to devise a workable system of political Islam in which secular government can exist side-by-side with the Prophet Muhammad's teaching.

Muslims possess an intense historical awareness, Bernard Lewis, Princeton University's professor emeritus of Near Eastern studies counsels, that leads them to a much deeper and broader perspective of current events than Americans enjoy. In the eyes of Muslims, they are living participants of a profound historical tragedy. The richest and most powerful civilization on earth for centuries was founded on Islam. For 300 years a Muslim empire was accompanied by a great new civilization. A caliph, recognized as successor to The Prophet, was the supreme ruler of the Muslims. The caliph served as governor, as well as a leader in prayer and in battle. Islam's armies that took the Muslims across northern Africa and into the heart of Europe, including France and Austria. They colonized the Iberian Peninsula, except for some northern areas. Elsewhere, Muslims advanced into Asia Minor and through Iran into Central Asia. Teachers and traders, in their eyes, helped to bring "civilization and religion to the infidel barbarians who lived beyond the Muslim frontier."[8]

A small Turkish tribe, the Osmandis, conquered a large part of the Balkans in 1413 and captured Constantinople. In 1517, the Sultan Selim conquered Syria and Egypt and the Ottoman empire emerged as the universal governor of Islamic territories. The Ottoman campaign against Christian Europe was decisively defeated at the Battle of Vienna in 1683, which brought many Muslims, who were convinced of the superiority of their culture, to seek the reasons for their inferiority of power. The relative position of the Muslim world continued to deteriorate vis-a-vis Western civilization during the succeeding centuries. The resulting frustration of relentless pressures has found expression in contemporary times. Many Westerners are convinced of the superiority of their culture and believe that their advanced technology societies imposes an obligation on them to share their strengths throughout the world.[9]

A small group of Wahhabis and a descendant of ibn Saud formed a brotherhood (*Ikhwan*) in 1902 dedicated to re-establishing a purified faith by means of jihad. A decade later, Abdul Aziz ibn Saud, ruler of the Arabian District of Najd, sponsored a "spectacular revival" of the Wahhabi sect, which gave birth to a fierce warrior brotherhood: *Ikhwan* ("the Brethren"). An incredible breakdown in British intelligence occurred in 1915 when, at a Cabinet War Committee meeting Sir Mark Sykes expressed the view that Wahhabism "is a dying fire." Two years later, or five years after the warrior brotherhood began to form, Gilbert Clayton reported from Arabia to Sykes that there were indications that Wahhabi may have experienced some degree of revival. Clayton noted that he did not yet appreciate the strength of the movement but "it may modify the whole situation considerably."[10] The report recognized that Ibn Saud had an army of true Bedouins, the greatest warriors in Arabia. By the end of 1921, Ibn Saud's 150,000 strong fighting men were completing the conquest of Arabia. The following year brought the House of Saud into direct conflict with the British-backed Hashemite Kingdom of Jordan. The British, using aircraft and armored cars, turned back a force of 3,000 to 4,000 *Ikhwan* raiders just an hour's camel ride from Amman, today's capital of Jordan. In 1922, the British established boundaries upon Saudi Arabia, Iraq, and Kuwait.[11]

By 1924, a Saudi-Wahhabi conquest of Mecca turned out the Hashemite Kingdom, ensuring the Wahhabis the right to collect taxes and fees from pilgrims in *Hajj*. In 1925, the Saudi-Wahhabi reasserted power over the port of Jeddah and the Holy City of Medina. The latter was restored to Wahhabi control, and in 1926 a global Islamic conference was called by Ibn Saud to ratify his control over the two Holy Places.

With the discovery of oil by two Americans in 1931, Saudi Arabia passed from the British to the American sphere of influence. A year later the state of Saudi Arabia was formally established. The House of Saud and its religious co-conspirators, the Wahhabi, were soon transformed "into the world's richest and most powerful ruling elite."[12]

When the United States assumed Britain's previous oversight of the Middle East activities in 1945, American leaders wanted to show that they sympathized with the Arabs, Persians, and Muslims. The message was supposed to be "America was no imperialist power with self-seeking designs on the lands and wealth of other peoples." Following sixty-plus years, the United States has no real friends in the region. Why? According to a story told by Max Boot, the U.S. message about not being an "imperialist power" was actually seen by the Saudis as one of weakness. Perhaps Osama bin Laden best makes the case: "When people see a strong horse and a weak horse, by nature they will take the strong horse."[13]

In some ways, a host of past U.S. foreign actions and soft words had demonstrated a profound weakness and lack of resolve that led bin Laden's faulty perception that the U.S. was a "weak horse." He cited numerous events that showed Americans living a depraved and self-indulgent way of life had made them soft and unwilling to accept military casualties—a proverbial "weak horse." The litany of American weaknesses was repeated by al-Qaeda members over and over: the U.S. was driven from Vietnam under fire, U.S. Marines left Beirut quickly after a single bombing in 1983 had killed 241 men, and Americans bugged-out of Somalia after a ferocious gun battle that killed eighteen U.S. soldiers. "Hit them and they will run," bin Laden and others concluded. Their perception was reinforced by angry words but little U.S. action following the 1993 World Trade Center bombing, which killed six and injured more than a thousand people; seven American soldiers killed in a 1995 attack on the liaison mission to Riyadh, Saudi Arabia, but the Bill Clinton, gum-chewing strategists found the attacks an inconvenience. They did little more than give a huff-and-puff sound bite for the media. Nineteen American airmen were killed and more than 500 injured in a 1996 bombing of the Khobar military living quarters in Riyadh. The U.S. and Saudi Arabia moved the base for Americans to a remote area of desert, while Washington's terrorism investigators were stonewalled by the Saudis who were less than cooperative in identifying the perpetrators.

Two years later, 224 people were killed and 4,500 wounded in the bombings of the U.S. Embassies in Kenya and Tanzania (twenty U.S. cruise missiles were launched—mostly turning large rocks into pebbles at six al-Qaeda camps in northeastern Afghanistan and destroying a pharmaceutical plant in Somalia).[14] (Sandy Berger, President Clinton's national security advisor, could not keep his mouth shut and in the process babbled mindlessly, undermining the credibility of the strike against the pharmaceutical plant.). Seventeen sailors were killed in a 2000 attack on the *USS Cole*, a U.S. Navy vessel, while refueling in Yemen. Given this record of years of weak and ineffective responses, it should come as no surprise that the al-Qaeda attacks on September 11, 2001, were supposed to be the opening salvo of a large-scale campaign aimed at driving the U.S. and its allies out of Arabia and the rest of the Muslim world, overthrowing the corrupt tyrants supported by the United States, and preparing the ground for a final world struggle that would restore the predominance of Islam and its values.[15]

"These terrorists [militant Islamists] hate us for who we are, not what we have done," author Victor Davis Hanson explains. Al-Qaeda is about assuaging "the psychological wounds of hundreds of millions of Muslims who are without consensual government, freedom, and material security," Hanson continues. "Bin Laden is the ultimate representation of Islam's failure to come to grips with the dizzying . . . pace of globalization and the spread of popular Western culture."[16] For Osama bin Laden and his hate-mongering associates, the United States is a "demonic culture that dominates the world."[17]

"Traditional Islam seeks to teach human beings how to live in accord with God's will," Richard Pipes explains, "militant Islam aspires to create a new order."[18] Saudi Arabia's Wahhabi cultists have no moral constraints on the death and destruction left in the wake of their drive toward building one world of puritanical Islamic rule. Theirs is a "Reverse Crusade" against the West. The *Ikhwan* has not forgotten its original intention of engaging jihad against the infidel, nor have they forgotten that the sacred places had not been given to God but had been taken over by an earthly sovereign who named this holy territory after himself: Saudi Arabia.[19]

Civilizational Jihad

An analysis of the geopolitics of the Middle East yields insights often not readily apparent to the cursory eye. The Saudis are confronted with a revival of the Shia nation (culturally, not in the sense of a political state) that includes portions of Iraq, Syria, and Lebanon, and a potentially nuclear armed Iran. This emerging reality is the stuff worst-case scenarios are made of and keep kings and presidents alike awake at night. It is not surprising, therefore, that Riyadh plans to purchase more than $50 billion on weapons by 2013, $40 billion of the new armament will be in the form of aircraft and related equipment from the United States and Britain, with the remaining $10 billion in military expenditures going to France, Russia, and Pakistan. In exchange for its windfall oil revenues, Saudi Arabia exports "hate" to the capitalist West in the form of a civilizational jihad, which includes propaganda and disinformation against Christians, Jews, Shias, and moderate Muslims. The tacit boundaries of the Saudi-capitalist West geopolitical competition also includes the intolerant Wahhabi religious sect that legitimizes the rule of the Saudi royal family and exports global terrorism.[20]

The Muslim Brotherhood (*Ikhwan*) serves as the board of directors for the destruction of non-Islamic civilization in North America. This is hardly a new phenomenon. Israel's Dore Gold quotes Wilfred Cantwell Smith of McGill University who wrote in 1957, "most westerners have simply no inkling of how deep and fierce is the hate of the West that has gripped the modernizing Arab."[21]

The strategic goal of the Muslim Brotherhood in North America is civilizational jihad, which includes "the destruction of Western

civilization through long-term civilization-killing *Jihad* from within
. . . [by American and Canadian hands] and through sabotage ("the
hands of the believers") and, secondly, to support the global Islamic
movement to establish an Islamic super-state, the *caliphate*." This
civilization-killing process is described in a Muslim Brotherhood
memorandum dated May 22, 1991, which was accepted into
evidence in the *U.S. v Holy Land Foundation* trial held in Federal
Court: ***"The Ikhwan must understand that their work in America
is a kind of grand Jihad in eliminating and destroying the Western
civilization from within and "sabotaging" its miserable house by
their hands and the hands of believers so that it is eliminated and
Allah's religion is made victorious over all other religions."***[22]
[emphasis in original]

The Muslim Brotherhood has three main civilizational jihad
tools available to satisfy these strategic goals: infiltration of
supporters into America, multiculturalism as a tool for societal
transformation, and denial and deception through the Wahhabi
Lobby. These civilizational jihad measures are all made possible by
Saudi oil money and are backed up by the threat and possible
terrorist action with conventional, chemical, biological, and
radiological weapons and nuclear attacks.

Infiltrating America

The terrorist network in the United States since 1991 expanded to
more than fifty U.S. cities. Among the leading terrorist groups with
presence in multiple areas include the Muslim Brotherhood, al-
Qaeda, Hezbollah, Hamas, Armed Islamic Group (Algeria), and
several American homegrown cells. The New York and
Washington, D.C., metropolitan areas accommodate nine and six
terrorist groups, respectively. The Muslim Brotherhood was
represented in seven major urban areas in 2008. Al-Qaeda was well
represented at these locations and in Florida, Hamas was popular
in Texas, Louisiana, Mississippi, Missouri, Oklahoma, and Kansas.

On the West Coast, al-Qaeda maintained presence in Washington, Oregon, and California.[23] FBI Director Robert Mueller said in May 2008 that the Bureau had identified small groups of al-Qaeda terrorists in the United States.[24]

Muslims in the United States number about 2.35 million people or about 0.6 percent of the total population. According to a 2007 Pew Research Center survey of more than one thousand American Muslims, about one-quarter of those under thirty years of age condoned suicide bombings, at least under certain circumstances. Over-all, U.S. Muslims lean to the Democratic Party, six to one; income distribution for this group is close to the national norm. Twenty-eight percent of the survey respondents do not believe Arabs were responsible for the September 11, 2001, terror attacks. Two-thirds expressed an unfavorable view of al-Qaeda while five percent had a favorable opinion (115,000 people). Twenty-seven percent (621,000 people) said they had no opinion on al-Qaeda.[25]

Despite misgivings by many in the West, Islam is not the post-9/11 enemy of the capitalist West. "Rather," Dore Gold points out in *Hatred's Kingdom*, "the problem is the extremists in the Middle East who have manipulated Friday sermons in the mosques, textbooks in the schools, and state-controlled television to one end: to systematically prepare young people to condone the cold-blooded murder of innocent civilians."[26] The problem is that Wahhabism that has been allowed to spawn in Saudi Arabia and is now a thoroughly hate-filled ideology dedicated to mass murder in the United States. To underline the point, Dore Gold quoted an al-Qaeda spokesman, Sulaiman Abu Ghaith, as saying that " 'We have a right to kill 4 million Americans—2 million of them children—and to exile twice as many and wound and cripple hundreds of thousands.' "[27] Wahhabism has long legitimized extraordinary violence against noncombatants, including women and children, since its earliest days in the eighteenth and nineteenth centuries. The "unmitigated barbarism" that envelops Wahhabism to this day has been demonstrated many times. When a Wahhabi assault on the fortress of Taif in 1802 resulted in surrender, for instance, the Wahhabis took their swords to 367 men, women, and children, "cutting even the babies in cradles."[28]

The barbarity of Wahhabism in the current-day is expressed clearly in the willingness to conduct suicide bombings against combatants and non-combatants alike. A first step in fulfilling its commitment to destroy the United States "from the inside," al-Qaeda needs to infiltrate the numbers of its killers and with the right skills. Another major concern is "homegrown extremists" or those "inspired by militant Islamic ideology but without operational direction from al-Qa'ida."[29] With the much reported inadequacies of U.S. immigration and border controls, trace al-Qaeda's efforts also take advantage of the entry enforcement deficiencies. In Pakistan, al-Qaeda continues to provide explosives training to Europeans, since they can enter the United States more easily without a visa than those from other countries. David Horowitz laments the persistence of American weakness to shield the nation against al-Qaeda attacks.

> In future generations, students of history will marvel that Western civilization failed to believe that it had a right to vigorously defend itself from the sworn enemies who had proudly, unambiguously declared their genocidal intentions. They will marvel at the moral paralysis that prevented America from taking the easily identifiable steps necessary to prevent a recurrence of 9/11 or calamities far greater.[30]

Al-Qaeda uses as many guises to infiltrate operators into the United States. The student visa program is a favorite, especially if an agent was denied a U.S. entry visa. American authorities require colleges and universities to monitor such visitors more closely. However, one should take a large grain of salt with the idea that foreign students would ever be placed under effective monitoring by American institutions of higher learning.[31]

Al-Qaeda, many believe, are also using medical facilities across the country as a means of gaining entry to the United States. The State Department can issue visitors visas for the purpose of receiving medical treatment in the U.S. on the basis of letters from a valid clinic. In some cases, letters or e-mails to clinics have requested letters for themselves as groups as large as a dozen people. As of mid-2007, no post-9/11 restrictions on medical facilities issuing invitation letters for foreign national had been issued. Moreover, the State Department had not issued any cautions to the health care industry. Another problem is al-Qaeda operatives posing as medical aides to disabled persons, as well as those presenting themselves as disabled travelers.[32]

The Nation of Islam, a vibrant American Black Muslim group, was approached by Saudi Arabia-based Wahhabis who wished to buy their way in to a presence inside the United States. Working through the Saudi Arabian Embassy, the direct Wahhabi offer to the Nation of Islam included the Americans making five visits to Saudi Arabia, including a visit with the Saudi king, crown prince, and other members of the royal family. The Saudi's were persistent: "What do you need?," they asked.

The Saudis began by placing about $1 million in the Nation of Islam's coffers. The objective was to foster the conversion of Americans to Islam. The Nation of Islam was asked to find a land parcel of about twenty acres for construction of a mosque, two schools, and an information center on the outskirts of Chicago. The Saudi's also promised to fund four more of the centers for Wahhabism. In the meantime, the Saudi's funded several mosques across America, Canada, and Europe. The relationship with the Nation of Islam soured and the Saudis pulled out.[33]

Muslim-American activism preceded the terrorist events on September 11, 2001. A "New Millennium Conference" on America and Islam was held at Georgetown University in April 2000. More than fifty of the world's most prominent scholars, activists, and academicians joined their American counterparts and policymakers in Washington, D.C. Topics addressed included an "Islamic Vision for the 21st century," with a particular focus placed on "political Islam." Former speaker of the Jordanian parliament Dr. Abdul Latif Arabiyat believes that the Islamic world has a "right and obligation" to provide visions for the upcoming century. His commentary provided a comprehensive statement of the primary georeligious competition with Russia and the capitalist West in the twenty-first century: "This world suffers from tyranny, injustice, oppressive imperialism, and purposeful defamation of its thought, creed and human message," he said. "The Islamic world feels it has a massive treasure of global values and principles that humanity needs if it hopes to fix the foundations of modern civilization."[34]

The relationship between Islam and the West had become strained following 9/11, al-Qaeda's persistent terrorist threat, and the willingness of the Saudi government and royal family to fund the overseas activities of the Muslim Brotherhood and Wahhabi. Yet, for some, "money talks." Georgetown University, the Jesuit-run Roman Catholic institution, was quick to announce the receipt of a $20 million "gift" to endow the University's Center for Muslim-Christian understanding by Saudi Prince Alwaleed bin Talal, the new Center's namesake. The page one headline in *The Washington Times* was appropriate: "Saudis Buy a Campus Presence."[35] Another $20 million "gift" was ponied-up for a similar program at Harvard University.

Many believe that the size of the donations amount to little more than ". . . buying influence and creating bastions of non-critical pro-Islamic scholarship within academia." Clifford May, President of the Foundation for Defense of Democracies, pointed out that professors on Middle Eastern studies tend to reflect the concerns of Arab and Muslim rulers. In a word, those who do not play the game as defined by the "gifter" are unlikely to last long or gain a tenured position on college campuses. Clifford May adds that ". . . sometimes money is a bribe. Sometimes it is a tip."[36]

The Georgetown University's HRH Prince Alwaleed Bin Talal Center for Muslim-Christian Understanding drew considerable attention. Patrick Poole, writing for *FrontPageMagazine.com*, examined the Center's internal workings, noting that director John L. Esposito had a long history of ". . . vocal support and praise of his self-described 'good-friend,' convicted Palistinian Islamic Jihad leader Sami al-Arian."[37] Martin Kramer, a fellow at the Olin Institute at Harvard writes that John Esposito ". . . [has] proved that he is . . . a money magnet for Arab and Muslim money."[38] And, Winfield Myers writes that Esposito "blames the West for troubled relations with the Islam world [rather than] the way his benefactor's billions support the spread of the Wahhabi Islam around the globe—including the Georgetown section of Washington, D.C."[39]

Susan Douglass is the Center's educational consultant. She was an instructor at the Islamic Saudi Academy in Alexandria, Virginia, for many years, which is funded by the Saudi government and known among some media outlets as "Terror High." The U.S. Commission on International Religious Freedom notified the U.S. Senate in October 2007 that the academy of some 933 students was in violation of U.S. law. The Commission reported that the textbooks used at the Saudi academy contained "highly intolerant and discriminatory language, particularly against Jews, Christians and Shi`a Muslims." The textbooks teach students to "hate" Jews, Christians, "polytheists" and other "unbelievers." They also state, in line with the civilizational jihad, that violent jihad is a religious duty.[40]

Hadia Mubarak is the Georgetown Center's senior researcher. Like Susan Douglass, Mubarak has held top leadership positions in front organizations for the international Muslim Brotherhood. Mubarak is a former president of the Muslim Student Association and national broad member of the Council on American-Islamic

Relations (CAIR). Both organizations were identified in 2007 by the U.S. Department of Justice as unindicted co-conspirators and fronts for the Brotherhood.[41]

U.S. Representative Frank R. Wolf, a Georgetown graduate, wrote Dr. John J. DeGioia, the University president, and asked if the size of the gift could place the Center's academic independence in jeopardy. Congressman Wolf also expressed his concern that Georgetown University's role in training foreign service personnel and diplomats would be at odds with Saudi links to extremism and terrorism. Wolf also asked Dr. DeGioia to assess ". . . whether any of the Saudi-source funds have been used in the training, briefing or education of those going into or currently employed by the U.S. government."[42]

The HRH Prince Alwaleed Bin Talal Center for Muslim-Christian Understanding at Georgetown University is a case example for fostering civilizational jihad. It is all about destroying American culture from within and preparing for a time when Islam will emerge dominant over other religions inside the United States.

Multiculturalism

A second tool for civilizational jihad is the reversal of Western ideas about multiculturalism. Popular with those on the radical Left applying Antonio Gramsci's formula for transforming American culture, multiculturalism is also a two-sided coin in the hands of the Muslim Brotherhood.

Multiculturalism in the 1980s took a meaning in North America and Europe to support the "culture war" that would lead to of a progressive-socialist-marxist society. In the early 2000s, the idea of multiculturalism shed its anti-capitalist bias and assumed a revised meaning assimilation and ethnicity. Hege Storhaug, a Norwegian specialist on Islamic integration issues, explains that multiculturalism has been transformed from the idea of economic equality to cultural equality.[43] But, since 9/11, Europeans and Americans have come to increasingly regard immigrants, especially Muslims one, as being cultural threats, a source of hostility to the European and American ways of life, and a potential source or inspiration of additional terrorist attacks.[44]

The United States confronts two-faces of terrorist threats, one is external and reflected by al-Qaeda and the other are homegrown jihadists. Many of the latter group are drawn from Muslim communities in the West. Law enforcement officials have focused increasingly on the factors that are drawn into the radicalization process of the indigenous terrorists. Several commonalities in the pre-radicalization process have been identified from careful review of case studies.

The second phase of radicalization is "self-identification" in which individuals begin to examine the fundamentalism of Wahhabism. This "religious seeking" opens the individual to new world views and begins shifting their identity to associate with like-minded individuals and adopt jihad ideology and values as their own. Two indicators of progression along the radicalization continuum include a gravitation toward Wahhabi Islam and regular attendance to a Salafi mosque. Typical signatures of the self-identified include alienation from their former lives; affiliating with like-minded individuals or group to strengthen one's dedication to Wahhabi Islam; giving up cigarettes, drinking, gambling, and urban hip-hop gangster clothes; wearing traditional Islamic clothing; growing a beard; and involving themselves in social activism and community issues.

Stage three of the radicalization process involves "indoctrination." This is a big step by the individual toward intensifying his beliefs to the point that the jihadi-Wahhabi ideology is wholly adopted. It is at this point that the journeyman jihadist concludes, without question, that militant jihad action is required to further the Wahhabi cause. A "spiritual sanctioner" is critical during this phase: this person typically appears in the self-identification stage and remains a major influence through the indoctrination phase. Often a self-taught Islamic scholar, who transmits an "us" versus "them" world view.

Jihadization, phase four, occurs when the members of a cell see themselves as "holy warriors" or mujahedeen. The cell or cluster will begin planning for jihad or terrorists attacks. Target selection and operational planning will commence. Sometimes this will involve travels to a militant training camp overseas. The cell leaders typically pursue this travel, which serves as a catalyst for group action. Attack planning involves researching the Internet, reconnaissance and surveillance, acquiring explosive materials, creating an explosive device, and developing ingress and egress plans and procedures.[45]

The subtle methods applied to the radicalization process often do not involve law-breaking, placing law enforcement authorities at a disadvantage. In many ways, the radicalization continuum for a homegrown Wahhabi jihadist is very similar to the techniques used by communists in recruiting new members. Brian Michael Jenkins, a senior advisor to the president of the Rand Corporation, notes appropriately that

> . . . radicalization makes little noise. It borders on areas protected by the First and Fourth Amendments. It takes place over a long period of time. It therefore does not lend itself to a traditional criminal investigations approach.[46]

Another important aspect of the civilizational jihad is through use of multiculturalism in subverting America's public schools. Stanley Kurtz, a National Review Online contributing editor, offers a simple proposition: "Unless we counteract the influence of Saudi money on the education of the young, we're going to find it difficult to win the war on terror."[47] The "young" Mr. Kurtz is referring to are those in K-12 education in the United States.

The Saudis have coopted and seized control over Middle Eastern and Islamic studies in the United States with surprising ease. According to Stanley Kurtz's analysis, the Saudi's subverted Title VI of the U.S. Higher Education Act by using it as a "trojan horse." The federal government subsidizes centers for Middle Eastern studies to design lesson plans and seminars for K-12 teachers in American schools. In the absence of effective federal oversight, the university-distributed teaching aids for K-12 find their way into the curricula without public vetting. But the Saudis beforehand "bought and paid for" those curricula. "Meanwhile," Mr. Kurtz explains,

. . . the American government is asleep at the wheel—paying scant attention to how its federally mandated public outreach programs actually work. So without ever realizing it, America's taxpayers end up subsidizing—and providing official federal approval for—K-12 educational materials on the Middle East that have been created under Saudi auspices.[48]

The common denominator of this slight of hand is Saudi money. The "educational materials" bypassing school boards, fooling the Federal government, and taking advantage of America's goodwill sometimes praise and promote Islam, while they criticize Judaism and Christianity. Stanley Kurtz quotes a 2005 investigative report by the Jewish Telegraphic Agency: "Believing they're importing the wisdom of places like Harvard or Georgetown . . . [Americans] are actually inviting into their schools whole curricula and syllabuses developed with the support of Riyadh."[49]

Saudi efforts to propagandize American K-12 students about Middle Eastern studies and Islam, while pouring a sewer line of disinformation and hatred about Jews, Christians, Shias, and others is not limited to lesson plans and teacher training. Saudi money influence is also exerted through textbooks for public school children K-12. Susan L. Douglass is one of those at the center of the textbook storm. For at least ten years a teacher at the notorious Islamic Saudi Academy in Alexandria, Virginia, which teaches Wahhabism through textbooks, is now a senior staff member of Georgetown University's Prince Alwaleed Bin Talal Center. According to Paul Sperry, Douglass ". . . has convinced American textbook publishers and educators to gloss over the violent aspects of Islam to make the faith more appealing to non-Muslim children."[50]

William J. Bennetta, a fellow of the California Academy of Sciences and president of the Textbook League wrote in the summer 2000 that Prentice-Hall's high school text, *World Culture: A Global Mosaic*, "serves as a vehicle for Muslim propaganda" and that Houghton Mifflin's seventh grade text, ". . . *Across the Centuries,* is loaded with Muslim religious propaganda."[51] In addition, a textbook published by the Teacher's Curriculum Institute, *History Alive! The Medieval World and Beyond*, was removed from the Scottsdale, Arizona, school district in 2005 for misrepresenting and glorifying Islamic beliefs and history. In February 2008, the textbook caused a controversy in California. At the center was a gentleman named al-Qazzaz, a specialist in Middle East studies, who was a contributor to *History Alive!* And one of those who approved its use in public middle schools.[52]

Beyond curriculum and textbook issues, America's schools are being increasingly besieged by "special requests" to accommodate Muslim "religious needs." Americans schools are sensitive to religious requirements and usually can be found to be seeking responsible ways to satisfy students needs. Some things, such excusing Muslim children from gym class during Ramadan fasting are easy to accommodate, including separate lunch areas for reduced-diet students or alternative locations where children can pray.

On the other hand, some religious groups complain that special arrangements are made available to Muslim students that would not be open to Christians at an equivalent level. The allegation of a double standard was raised when Muslim students were given a break to pray in the classroom, a class time praying session by Christians would never have been allowed.

The University of Michigan at Dearborn was criticized in 2007 for planning to install foot baths in two restrooms to make it easier for Muslim students to cleanse before daily prayers. It was reported in September 2007 that schools in Oak Lawn, Illinois, might cancel Halloween and Christmas activities after complaints were received that they were offensive, especially to Muslim students.[53]

Attacks against existing American culture are an unending tactic of civilizational jihad. The Saudi offensive to coopt and control of the curricula, textbooks, and special privileges in American schools is all about replacing Kafir (non-Muslim) multiculturalism with Islamic multiculturalism. Each step is one more toward the uncompromising goal of establishing "the supremacy of Islam, primacy of Arabs, and the global Islamic Ummah [Muslim community]." As Abdul Kasem observed, "the Islamists have nothing to worry about in terms of their agenda to eventually impose Islam on the infidel lands. The politicians of the infidel territories are doing their job for them (i.e., promoting Islam)."[54]

Denial and Deception ("Wahhabi Lobby")

The Muslim Brotherhood—the *al-Ikhwan al-Muslimin*—consists of about seventy U.S. national organizations, each with their own agendas within broad guidelines of an international directorate. The Brotherhood's shared creed is: "God is our objective; the Koran is our constitution; the Prophet is our leader; *jihad* is our way; and death for the sake of God is the highest of our operations."[55]

The Muslim Brotherhood in North America operates behind a series of front groups typified by what is called the "Wahabbi Lobby" by American and Canadian analysts. The goal of the Brotherhood's denial and deception efforts has little to do with civil rights, anti-discrimination, student associations, and similar "soft" activities. Rather, this cover is used to hide its true goal in the world's shadows: ". . . destroy the United States from the inside and work for the establishment of a global Islamist society."[56]

The Brotherhood's strategic concept is sound and well-thought out. It is oriented to a patient, long-term organizational approach toward creating and "developing organizations and networks that implement 'civilizational jihad.'" The Brotherhood in America has been implementing this strategy since 1962, beginning with establishing its first Muslim Student Union through a program of conferences and camps." By the 1970s, the *Ikhwan* began establishing affiliated vocational and professional organization, such as Muslim Doctors, Social Workers, and Science and Engineer syndicates. In 1981 the Brotherhood in North America founded the Islamic Association of Palestine whose work is linked with the Palestinian Intifada and the Hamas terror organization.[57] Rod Dreher, *Dallas Morning News*, says that the Brotherhood "'operates as a self-conscious revolutionary vanguard in the United States.'"[58]

The "axis" of the Brotherhood are Islamic religious and educational centers. The Centers serve as the hub "for a small Islamic society," which mirrors the *Ikhwan*'s key organizations. These Centers serve social and family needs of the Muslim community, but also are placed in service of the political goals of destroying existing American culture establishing a caliphate in North America. The Centers also are propaganda and disinformation houses to keep any wayward thinking in line. They are instrumental in maintaining the Brotherhood's internal structure, discipline, recruitment, and "special work" or military work aimed at securing the group's security against outside dangers, including U.S. and state law enforcement and intelligence, "Zionism," and other American fronts.[59]

A network of Wahhabi-sponsored propaganda and disinformation organizations underwrite the Muslim Brotherhood's goal of transforming America into an Islamic-loving caliphate in the new geopolitical order later in the twenty-first century. Through use of numerous and inventive salami-tactics, the Wahhabi Lobby operating under the guidance of the Muslim Brotherhood is dedicated to developing a fifth column of support for militant Islam in America and establishing an Islamic caliphate. Eight lobby organizations, six in particular, provide the basis for the Brotherhood's operations.

1. Council for American-Islamic Relations (CAIR)

This element of the Saudi-Wahhabi "religious militia" was modeled after an American Jewish organization, the Anti-Defamation League.[60] CAIR's 1994 charter is a model of moderation: "promote interest and understanding among the general public with regards to Islam and understanding among the general public with regards to Islam and Muslims in North America." A spin-off of the Islamic Association of Palestine, CAIR generally lays claim to representing the Muslim viewpoint in America.

CAIR provides support for militant Islamists and their spewing of anti-Semitism and anti-Israel disinformation. For instance, CAIR co-sponsored a rally at Brooklyn College in May 1998, providing a platform for Wagdy Ghuneim, a radical cleric from Egypt. Among his racist remarks, he led the audience in a song with the lyrics: "no to the Jews, descendants of the apes." When billboards around Los Angeles depicting Osama bin Laden with the headline "The Sworn Enemy" was posted in October 1998 by a local television station, CAIR stated that they were "an insult to the hundreds of thousands of Muslims who live in Southern California."

CAIR is a major front in the network of political Islam organization dedicated to civilizational jihad inside the United States. "[Jihad] means the legal, compulsory, communal effort to expand the territories ruled by non-Muslims," Daniel Pipes explains. "The purpose of Jihad . . . is not directly to spread the Islamic faith but to extend sovereign Muslim power. . . ."[61]

CAIR enjoys a key position in the Wahhabi Lobby: "Despite its mainstream and wholesome appearance," Daniel Pipes and Sharon Chadha summarized, "the Council on American-Islamic Relations is the leading Islamist apologist in the United States and, as such is a major influence on the enemy's side in the war on terror."[62]

2. Islamic Society of North America (ISNA)

The Union of Orthodox Jewish Congregations, analysts Stephen Schwartz says, provided the model for the creation of ISNA, the second element of the Saudi-Wahhabi "religious militia" inside the United States.[63] Located in Plainfield, Indiana, ISNA is the largest Muslim Organization in the United States. It was founded in 1981. The Society operates as an "umbrella organization" or "clearinghouse" for networking all Saudi-Wahhabi activities in the United States. This hub of the Saudi fifth column provides a large percentage of the Wahhabi theological indoctrination materials to a significant percentage of the more than 2,500 mosques in North America. Many of these mosques were built with Saudi money. Among the strings attached to the Saudi money is that those who take the cash are bound to strictly follow the instruction of Wahhabi imams. These strings include the toeing-the-line on the tone and content of sermons delivered in the Saudi-paid-for mosques, assuring that the books and periodicals made available in mosque libraries or sold in its bookstores are drawn from Saudi-approved sources, and following the Saudi policies governing the suppression of dissenters within the congregations.[64]

Steven Emerson, a courageous investigative journalist focused on Wahhabi extremism in North America is very careful to avoid accusing ISNA of having a direct involvement in terrorism. He does say, however, that ". . . ISNA has sponsored extremists, racists, people who call for *Jihad* against the United States."[65]

3. Muslim Students Association

Islamic extremism has been reported as growing at universities and colleges for several years. The increased activities of the Muslim Students Association result from a presence on at least 600 campuses, about 150 of which are affiliated with the national organization. The national and local chapters of the MSA are loosely associated. It is not rare to find the positions of specific chapters differing in some ways from the national association. A 1991 Muslim Brotherhood memorandum, however, made it quite clear the MSA was one of its like-minded "organizations of our friends"—members and associates of the Saudi "religious militia" or Wahhabi Lobby.[66]

4. Islamic Circle of North America (ICNA)

Boiling in a caldron of fierce hatred for Jews, the ICNA consists of a radical Islamic organization—the Pakistani Jamaat e-Islami—that helped to establish the Taliban. ICNA also enjoys direct ties with al-Qaeda terrorists. It offers high praise for terrorist attacks, highly critical commentary of Western values and policies, and advocates the imposition of Islamic law (the *Sharia*). Anti-American, radical Islamists are often invited to ICNA's annual conferences. It also has ties with Muslim organizations that that find suicide bombings as being "justifiable."[67]

5. Muslim American Society (MAS)

Founded in 1993, the Muslim American Society is a major front for the Muslim Brotherhood in North America, and, as such, is dedicated to placing the United States under the governance of the *Sharia*, or Islamic law. Adopting a version of Antonio Gramsci's formula, the gradual approach to achieving Islamic rule is advocated: "first you change the person, then the family, then the community, than the nation." That is to say, first you "convert Americans to Islam" and then you "elect like-minded Muslims to political office."[68] The modus operandi was very simple: MAS and the Brotherhood would deny any affiliation, while their strategy, though being prosecuted under different names, was the same: the transformation of American society "through the spread of Islam, with the ultimate goal of establishing Islamic rule in America."[69]

The following snapshot of the Islamic cultural assault against the United States exposes the Wahhabi Lobby efforts to satisfy Saudi Arabia's geopolitical drive to dominate America and the world through the imposition of Islam and global rule of the *Sharia*:

> Working for Islam equally means to form a society that is committed to the Islamic way of thinking and Islamic way of life, which means to form a government that implements principles of justice embodied in the shariah to guard the rights of every person and community, and establish truth and justice, and at the same time call others toward Islam—truth, peace, and justice. These three responsibilities are obligatory not merely for the entire Muslim community but for every individual Muslim until we have established a system of governance adequate to the task. Until the nations of the world have functionally Islamic governments, every individual who is careless or lazy in working for Islam is sinful. These sins of omission will not be forgiven until they take a quick action to carry out all their responsibilities and Islamic duties.[70]

6. Muslim Public Affairs Council (MPAC)

This organization is a rather weak Saudi-Wahhabi imitation of the American Israel Public Affairs Committee (AIPAC).[71] MPAC was founded in 1988 in Los Angeles as a non-profit social welfare organization claiming to be "a public service agency working for the civil rights of American Muslims, for the integration of Islam into American pluralism, and for a positive, constructive relationship between American Muslims and their representatives."[72]

During an October 2000 rally in Washington, D.C., MPAC's political advisor, Dr. Mahdi Bray was seen excitedly professing his support for Hamas and Hezbollah, two of the most deadly terrorist organizations. In December 2000, Mahdi Bray organized a rally outside the White House. The crowd chanted in Arabic to the emcee leading them: "*Khaybar, Khatbar* oh Jews, the Army of Muhammad is coming for you!," posters equated the Star of David with the Nazi Swastika, and anti-Semitic literature was distributed. When fifteen people, including six children were killed in a suicide bombing of a pizza parlor in Jerusalem in August 2001, MPAC issued a press release calling the bombing ". . . the expected result of the reckless policy of Israeli assassination that did not spare children and political figures. . . ." MPAC also said Hezbollah's truck bombing of the U.S. Marine Barracks in Beirut as a "military operation" rather than a terrorist attack.[73] MPAC joined the anti-war organization CodePink for Peace. The organization also worked closely with International ANSWER and the Marxist-Leninist Workers World Party.

7. Arab-American Institute (AAI)

This self-described "nonpartisan group" is not a part of the Saudi-Muslim Brotherhood conspiracy to transform the United States and others in the capitalist West to a dhimmitude status under Islamic governance. In fact it is dominated by Christians; Muslims account for only about a quarter of its membership. Yet, many share concerns about the conflicts in the Middle East and the wartime accommodations to the realities of post 9/11 America that have triggered fear and uncertainty among some Arab Americans.[74]

8. American-Arab Anti-Discrimination Committee (ADC)

James Zogby and Senator James Abourezk, the first Arab-American to serve in the U.S. Senate, 1973 to 1979, founded this non-religious civil rights group in 1980. It opposes the U.S. war on terror and Patriot Act, ethnic profiling of Arab-Americans, and "supports Palestinian 'martyrdom' campaigns in Israel. In 2003, it was a signatory to a letter for members of Congress exhorting them to oppose the Patriot Act II. Other signatories from the radical Left included the American Civil Liberties Union, American Library Association, Center for Constitutional Rights, National Lawyers Guild, and People for the American Way. The Committee is heavily funded by Wahhabist Saudi Prince Alwaleed Bin Talal.[75]

Senator Abourezk, a senior advisor for presidential candidate Barack Obama, stirred up some animosities in 1979 when he signed on to serve as the American lawyer for Ayatollah Ruhollah Khomeini revolutionary Islamic Government during the Iran hostage crisis.[76] Abourezk in 2002 asked Saul Landau, a fellow at the Institute for Policy Studies, to join him and others on a "humanitarian mission" to Iraq being organized by U.S. Representative Nick Rahall, a Democrat from West Virginia. During the "show and tell" propaganda tour in Baghdad, Abouresk and Rahall stepped aside for private talks with Iraq Deputy Prime Minister Tariq Aziz.[77] In 2007, he explained that the 9/11 attacks were all about a handful of hapless Arabs who were exploited by Zionists who were really responsible. The attacks were based on the Arabs unknowing cooperation with the Zionists; it was all about racism to Senator Abourezk. Meanwhile, the senator has always been quick to dismiss the acts of violence by Muslims and the bloody deeds of Hamas and Hezbollah. These ravings, Robert Spencer suggests, ". . . is evidence of a man who has lost his moral compass."[78]

Weapons of Mass Destruction

Unfortunately for humankind, the proliferation horse is out of the barn. The undersecretary of defense for intelligence, retired Lt. Gen. James Clapper told a joint hearing of House armed services and intelligence committees that, "al Qaeda has and will continue to attempt visually dramatic mass casualty attacks here at home, and they will continue to attempt to acquire chemical, biological, radiological, and nuclear materials," adding that if they are successful "we believe they would use them."[79]

The possibility of terrorist groups, such as al-Qaeda, being in possession of weapons of mass destruction and with the will to use them against soft, mass casualty targets presents nightmare scenarios that Western leaders must deal with. Since the United States is "target number one" for the Islamic fascists, no stone can be left unturned in rooting out and destroying their mass-killing capabilities. The consequences of failure could mean the death of tens of thousands of Americans and Europeans, perhaps even hundreds of thousands of lives. The sarin nerve gas attacks against the Tokyo commuter train system in 1995 showed how effective chemical weapons can be, even when delivered in a less than optimal manner. The anthrax attacks through the mails in the United States by persons unknown following the September 11, 2001, demonstrated the ease of covert delivery of biological weapons.

Osama bin Laden has been less than bashful since the 1990s about his desire to obtain weapons of mass destruction. According to press reports, bin Laden was known to have been seeking nuclear capabilities. Although Pentagon analysts believe he was unsuccessful, the Arab press was full of speculation in 1999 as to whether al-Qaeda had gained access to twenty nuclear "suitcase bombs" allegedly developed by the Soviet Union during the Cold War. Rumors of the disappearance of these bombs (more the size of a steamer trunk than a suitcase) further inflamed the Arab media's speculation. One senior Pentagon official said in late 2001 that al-Qaeda had already developed a " 'crude chemical and possibly biological capability.' "[80] The CIA reported in 2004 that al-Qaeda had an interest in radiological dispersal devices for "dirty bombs."[81]

In November 2002, British authorities arrested an al-Qaeda operative named Rahbah Kadri for plotting a chemical attack on the London subway system. Questioning Rabah, as Kenneth Timmerman recounts the events, led authorities to a French-Algerian dual national, Marwan Ben-Ahmed, who had collected all of the ingredients necessary for building a bomb to have been delivered during the Christmas holidays, perhaps against the U.S. or Russian embassies in Paris. Ben-Ahmed was operating in coordination with al-Qaeda cells in Britain and elsewhere. French police raided a housing project just outside Lyon on Christmas Eve, and they seized "more than four" al-Qaeda operatives. They also found lists of chemicals needed to make cyanide, the same agent that was to have been used against the London subway system. The cyanide was to be released from propane tanks in the hopes of killing hundreds or thousands of people.[82]

More than forty al-Qaeda sites were identified in Afghanistan in late 2001 by General Tommy Franks, commander of U.S. forces, that ". . . represent potential for WMD (weapons of mass destruction) research or things of that sort." Nothing specific about chemical, biological, or nuclear weapons, however, could be found.[83] Subsequent exploitation of the al-Qaeda data captured led the CIA to report that the group was focused on anthrax for mass killing.[84]

A year later, Pakistani authorities reported three small al-Qaeda laboratories for the development of weapons of mass destruction had been discovered in a village near Karachi. According to the report, al-Qaeda had moved much of its lab equipment to other countries in the region with the help of gold smugglers. The local terrorists near Karachi had been trained in Afghanistan before September 11 and had been working with al-Qaeda since the fall of the Taliban.[85]

The Polish press reported in May 2004 that al-Qaeda terrorists obtained nuclear and biological materials from the Solntsevo organized crime gang. Semen Mogilevich heads this notorious Russian crime group that traffics in nuclear materials, drugs, prostitutes, precious gems, and stolen art. Three members of the Solntsevo gang were arrested on their way to Munich with seventeen ounces of smuggled plutonium.[86]

Osama bin Laden's quest to develop chemical, biological, and nuclear weapons did not start from zero. At hand was an extensive knowledge base in Iraq and Pakistan of how to develop WMD clandestinely and deliver them with devastating consequences.

During the Cold War in the 1980s, East Germany maintained a 12,000-acre terrorist training camp, at Massow, located not far from Berlin. Massow did not officially exist, yet several Iraqi agents were trained there in the use of chemical and biological weapons; these WMD first mass casualty seeds planted in Islamic countries. East Germany's secret police—the Stasi—are reported to have trained Iraq hit squads and other terrorist groups in the art of placing explosives, poisoning water reservoirs, and planning chemical and biological weapons attacks, including Baghdad resident and international terrorist Abu Nidal. Much of the concrete facility was underground and a maze of tunnels led to the hidden training building with a ventilation system, steel double doors, and the poison gas was controlled with the help of tight seals. The Massow terrorist school operated through 1988.[87] This training of Saddam Hussein's secret terrorist army has been linked by British journalist Gwynne Roberts with the nerve gas poisoning of Kurds in the 1980s. The Stasi training of the Iraqis was later shifted to Iraq by Stasi officers who chose not to return to the newly unified Germany. Iraqis were taught with an emphasis on nerve gases and their terrorist uses. Discussion also focused on the possibilities of bacterial weapons, such as anthrax, pneumonic diseases, and hepatitis. Chemical attacks against airports, train stations, and public events were also a part of the curricula in East Germany and later in Iraq during the 1990s.[88]

The Stasi, an extension of the KGB, was supporting Soviet policies during the 1970s by training and sometimes equipping foreign terrorists and then returning them to their countries with the freedom to carry out their own terrorist attacks to destroy Western democracies. This model appears to be the framework of the "new al-Qaeda" that emerged after being chased out of Afghanistan. The late investigative journalist Claire Sterling put it this way: "In effect, the Soviet Union had simply laid a loaded gun on the table, leaving others to get on with it."[89] Since the collapse of the Soviet Union, one might paraphrase and say: "In effect, Iraq had simply laid the expertise about WMD on the table, leaving others to get on with it."

The UN inspections following the 1991 Gulf War found twenty-three chemical facilities in Iraq that were producing nerve agents tabun, sarin, and VX, as well as mustard gas. VX is the most deadly agent—a single pinhead-sized droplet can result in death. The UN supervised the destruction of 480,000 liters of chemical agents of which 28,000 liters were filled in munitions (bombs, artillery rounds). Another 1.8 million liters of chemical precursors were also destroyed.

Unlike Iraq's chemical weapons, the country's biological weapons program was easy to hide. Iraq had seven core biological weapons sites, twenty-two storage bunkers, and numerous dual-use, civilian and military, sites (perhaps as many as seventy-nine). These dual-use sites included vaccine and pharmaceutical facilities, research and university facilities, breweries, distilleries, dairies, and diagnostic laboratories. Following discovery of the clandestine biological weapons program in 1995, the UN Special Commission on Iraq destroyed what the Iraqis declared: 19,000 liters of botulinum toxin with nearly 10,000 liters in munitions; 8,500 liters of concentrated anthrax with some 6,000 liters filled in munitions; and 2,200 liters of aflatoxin (a cancer-causing agent) with 1,580 filled munitions. Theoretically, the killing power of the botulinum toxin alone was enough to kill fifteen billion people.

Saddam Hussein also was well down the path toward building his own nuclear weapons. After the Gulf War and extent of the nuclear program fully exposed, Western scientists estimated that Iraq was twelve to eighteen months away from having nuclear weapons. Saddam had pumped $10–12 billion in building three uranium enrichment programs and the large foreign procurement program operating through deceptive practices. All told, fifty-six nuclear production sites were identified by the UN Special Commission of Iraq. These sites included uranium mining, production, and processing sites. Saddam Hussein's program is believed to have produced nuclear triggers, two of which are unaccounted for. Hans Blix, director on the UN International Atomic Energy Administration said that he was "shocked" by the enormity of Iraq's nuclear weapons program.[90]

Richard Danzig, a former Secretary of the Navy, probably best characterized the West's current situation: "only a thin wall of terrorist ignorance and inexperience now protects us."[91] Al-Qaeda may have already penetrated the "thin wall" protecting Western societies from biological attacks. One must simply assemble the brainpower of scientists and engineers necessary to make deadly biological agents suitable for dissemination against Western targets. Delivery vehicles could be used by of suicide terrorists seeking a one-way pass to Paradise. According to the courtroom testimony of Egyptian Islamic Jihad member, Ahmad Ibrahim al-Najjar, Osama bin Laden paid $10,000 for anthrax and other germs, such as e-coli and salmonella, from private laboratories in East European and Southeast Asia. One was a Czech factory that turns out germs to fill mail orders and sells to anyone who pays in advance; the germ source in Southeast Asia is cheaper.[92] A jihadist website in March 2008 posted instructions on making anthrax suitable for biological weapons: " 'The wait has been long, but the time has arrived, God willing. It is glad tidings of being able to use biological weapons against the enemies of God. So, allow me to present to you a simple recipe for making anthrax, God willing.' "[93]

Britain's intelligence service, MI5, reported in June 2003 that it was only a matter of time until al-Qaeda developed radiological weapons, while the CIA issued a report in May 2003 that suggested al-Qaeda and other terrorist groups were already capable of making an improvised nuclear device capable of producing a nuclear explosion.[94]

As reported by Steve Coll, a managing editor at the *Washington Post*, Osama bin Laden since at least the late 1990s has been quietly working on chemical and biological weapons while far more open on his nuclear weapons goals in public. His inspiration is drawn from the American atomic bombing at Nagasaki and Hiroshima, which shocked the Japanese government into surrendering . . . a course they may not have otherwise taken. Hence, Coll explains, bin Laden ". . . wants to do to American foreign policy what the United States did to Japanese surrender policy."[95]

The open question is how would al-Qaeda go about getting the bomb or perhaps *he has already obtained nuclear bombs*. Basically, two realistic pathways are open to al-Qaeda: buy or steal existing weapons or buy enough plutonium or highly enriched uranium to build its own improvised nuclear devices. The most plausible route might be to build a crude, yield-producing device using uranium stolen from the former Soviet Union. U.S. counter-terrorism experts believe that Osama bin Laden would prefer buying weapons from criminal sources in Russia and Pakistan with inside assistance on how to detonate them.

Al-Qaeda and other terrorist groups might best apply a gun-type fission device to trigger an explosion, similar to the bomb dropped on Hiroshima. The bomb dropped on Nagasaki was an implosion device, which is more difficult to make. The gun-type device contains two sub-critical masses, gunpowder, and an explosive device that sets off the gunpowder, causing one piece of the sub-critical uranium to hit the other, creating a critical mass and an explosion.[96]

Numerous news reports and unclassified intelligence reports make it quite clear that al-Qaeda is attempting to obtain nuclear capability (or it already has such a capacity). Some allege connections with the secretive Pakistani nuclear bomb-maker Abdul Qadeer Khan and other nuclear scientists, as well as obtaining materials illegally from Pakistan, others claim that bin Laden got his hands on former Soviet "suitcase nukes," and some report the Balashikha Russian criminal gang and other crime groups as supplying al-Qaeda with small amounts of uranium over time.

Nuclear 9/11

Nuclear proliferation is a fact of life in the twenty-first century. Not only have Israel, North Korea, India, and Pakistan joined the nuclear club since late in the last century, but Saddam Hussein was only eighteen months away from a nuclear capability when the Gulf War broke out in 1991. Iran stands on the threshold of developing nuclear weapons. Rumors persist that Japan has a standby capability for rapid break out, and Brazil is believed to be giving thought to resurrecting its earlier flirtation with the possible development of nuclear materials and perhaps weapons.

These are all serious possibilities and concerns on this crowded planet. Especially bothersome is a dream scenario shared by Osama bin Laden and Ayman al-Zawahir, al-Qaeda's primary leaders, to strike the United States with nuclear weapons on its soil. According to former CIA director George Tenet, bin Laden and al-Zawahiri went so far as early as 1996 to hire an Egyptian physicist to work on nuclear and chemical projects in Sudan.[97] Tenet writes:

> But of all al-Qa'ida's efforts to obtain other forms of WMD, the main threat is the nuclear one. I am convinced that this is where UBL [Usama bin Laden] and his operatives desperately want to

go. They understand that bombings by cars, trucks, trains, and planes will get them some headlines, to be sure. But if they manage to set off a mushroom cloud, they will make history. Such an event would place al-Qa'ida on a par with the superpowers and make good Bin Laden's threat to destroy our economy and bring death into every American household. Even in the darkest days of the cold war, we could count on the fact that the Soviets, just like us, wanted to live. Not so with terrorists. Al-Qai'da boasts that while we fear death, they embrace it.[98]

Despite rigorous efforts by the United States and other major powers, the nuclear proliferation horse had burst out of the barn and was at a full gallop in mid-2008. The pressures are especially intense in the Middle East where the prospect of a nuclear armed Iran (Shia) is distressing to several Sunni states in the region, including Saudi Arabia. Syria, increasingly drawn into Tehran's political orbit, contracted with North Korea to build it a copy of its Yongbyon Reactor at al-Kibar, which was destroyed by Israel before completion in September 2007.[99]

At the same time, A. Q. Khan, the head of Pakistan's nuclear program and a man with a burning hatred toward the United States, operated a covert smuggling ring in the Middle East. He sold blueprints for development of advanced nuclear weapons suitable for delivery by ballistic missiles, as well as associated technology and components to Iran, Libya, and North Korea. Khan's digitized bomb designed turned up in the computer files of Swiss smugglers in 2004, and at least one official at the UN International Atomic Energy Agency expressed a belief that the Swiss were not the only ones in possession of Khan's nuclear designs.[100] Perhaps Joseph Cirincione at the Carnegie Endowment for International Peace summarized the nuclear proliferation situation in 2008 best: "In the last year, we've uncovered probably the most significant hemorrhaging of nuclear weapons technology since the Soviets penetrated the Manhattan Project [1947]."[101]

These selected examples of ongoing nuclear proliferation activities raise the obvious question as to whether Al-Qaeda has participated in A. Q. Khan's nuclear smuggling network. The answer is affirmative, if one believes at least the broad outline of the attack scenario presented by a said-to-be Al-Qaeda operative, Al-Asuquf, presented in the appendix. It quotes in chilling detail the anatomy of a nuclear 9/11 attack plan against the United States. The scenario has been rolling around in the Internet since 2002 but some have been reluctant to publish it for lack of corroboration. It could be a hoax, if one could not prove its authenticity. But no one has been able to prove or disprove the accuracy of the scenario, though its analytical assessment of the U.S. economy is sound. Hence, it is suspended in uncertainty, and we dare not take it off the table. If Al-Qaeda was the source, it would have been prepared somewhere in western Pakistan, placed on a computer memory stick, passed through several hands to disguise the source, and finally an operative would have sent the message into the Internet world from an Internet café somewhere in the Middle East to a password protected Web site. From there it could have been sent to numerous destinations.[102]

14

FACELESS INTERNATIONAL

WHAT WILL THE WORLD look like at the end of the twenty-first century? Which geopolitical competitor will wield dominant political authority over all of the world's six billion people? The choices are stark: autocracy, democracy, or theocracy.

Russia and its strategic partners are already moving down a pathway toward Lenin's vision of a Party-State autocracy at the core of a geopolitically successful Marxism. In Gramsci's formula, Lenin's geopolitical structure does not provide a framework for conquering the world as was the case with Soviet Marxism-Leninism. Rather, Gramsci accommodated Lenin's geopolitical vision in a far more subtle way. Gramsci's focus is on conquering "the mind of civil society," or acquiring "a Marxist hegemony over the minds of the population that must be won." The key for Russia, and America's homegrown progressive-socialist-marxist collaborators, is "to change the cultural outlook . . . the outward face of the . . ." of the people in the capitalist West toward socialist-marxist governance.[1]

The power to control the minds of the people is a prerequisite for transforming the culture and changing their world view is key to their embracing global socialist governance.

In order to win the geopolitical competition with the capitalist West and militant Islam, Russia would have to mute its ideological rhetoric. "For starters," Malachi Martin counsels in *The Keys of This Blood*, "Marxists would have to drop all Leninist shibboleths. It wouldn't do to rant about 'revolution' and 'dictatorship of the proletariat' and 'Workers Paradise.' Instead, according to Gramsci, Marxists would have to exalt such ideas as 'national consensus' and 'national unity' and 'national pacification.' "[2]

When the Soviet Union dissolved itself in 1991 and evolved politically into the Russian Federation, it also abandoned Marxism-Leninism as its official governing ideology and adopted the cultural Marxism of Antonio Gramsci as a guide for its relations with the United States and others in the capitalist West. Suffering through the transition years in the 1990s, Russia regained its feet under Vladimir Putin, who painstakingly rebuilt Russia in the image of the Soviet Union without the nuisance value of Marxism-Leninism. For the Kremlin, the exercise of mind control over the Russian people was possible through state-controlled capitalism in a new Party-State governing system. Since an extension of global dictatorship by military means had become impossible in a nuclear-armed world, Gramsci's formula for cultural revolution provided the right political medicine to win control of the minds of all the world's people. Christopher Story, editor of the British-based *Soviet Analyst*, explains how the phony coup against Mikhail Gorbachev in August 1991 resulted in a "cosmetic ban" of the Soviet Communist Party, a move that could be "unbanned." "Today," Story says, "the existence of the CPSU [Communist Party of the Soviet Union] is openly acknowledged by Soviet/Russian and Western Communist sources."[3]

Soviet-Russia has not given up on creating a communist world order. Rather, Gorbachev, in implementing the "Andropov Plan," flipped from the military confrontational tactics of Marxism-Leninism to Antonio Gramsci's far more subtle cultural revolution to win control of the minds of peoples in targeted countries. In order to make this grand stage-play realistic, Gorbachev choreographed a top-to-bottom restructuring of the Soviet-Russian Communist Party. Christopher Story explains that the Party was splintered ". . . into factions across the entire political spectrum [creating controlled opposition] to establish the conditions for 'democratism'—fake democracy."[4] The play acting was extended to the Soviet republics, whose new independent status would be later fashioned into "a new internationalist unity," one that in 2008 is quite evident in Central Asia and some of the East European countries. Georgia, Poland, and the Baltic states appear most troublesome for Moscow but its flood of energy cash offers the Kremlin new political options. Meanwhile, the Russians are moving confidently toward an eventual "convergence" with Europe. Warning the Russian people in May 2007 of a dangerous global environment, Vladimir Putin said: ". . . in our time, these threats are not diminishing. . . . [and] in these new threats, as during the time of the Third Reich, are the same contempt for human life and the same claims of exceptionality and diktat in the new world."[5] There is little doubt Putin's reference to a modern-day Third Reich is a codeword for the United States.

By 2008, one could marvel at the changes in the new Russia, while at the same time acknowledging that the key pillars of the Soviet system remained in place. The privileged elite, the *nomenklatura*, remained intact and, thanks to the economic boom fueled by higher energy prices, they have more money than they ever could have dreamed of possessing. The KGB changed its name to the FSB, and former members Soviet intelligence and security services became key decision-makers at all levels of the Russian government—the *Siloviki*. And the Communist Party, which had disappeared with the demise of the Soviet Union, reappeared in Gramscian mufti during the December 2007 elections for the State Duma (parliament).

The United Party, winning nearly two-thirds of the popular vote, assured a continuation of Vladimir Putin's rule, this time as prime minister. With the United Party's dominance the familiar Soviet-Russia Party-State is back in power. Prime Minister Putin has a clear pathway for rebuilding Russia's ground and air forces, restoring a naval presence in the Mediterranean, exercising initiatives to bring about a Russian-European convergence using transformation tools straight out of Antonio Gramsci's cultural Marxism, and waging a long-term geopolitical competition vis-a-vis the capitalist West and militant Islam.

The secret Soviet-Russian International Department, which is now Gramsci-oriented, or "today's Comintern" as Christopher Story calls it, is located in Moscow and at the Presidio, a former military base in San Francisco. It is from the latter location that Gorbachev's foundation is linked with the Institute for Policy Studies and its "solar system of organizations."

Curiously, the Gorbachev Foundation was created under a cover name, "Tamalpais Institute," at the Presidio in San Francisco on April 10, 1991, *four months before* the ostensible August KGB coup against Mikhail Gorbachev. Following the dissolution of the Soviet Union and disappearance of the Communist Party on December 31, 1991, the Tamalpais Institute's name was changed to the Gorbachev Foundation.[6] Many of the Foundation's large staff were former members of the International Department of the Central Committee of the Communist Party, which was responsible for many "active measures" carried out against the West.

Golitsyn explained how Gorbachev adopted Lenin's instructions in 1921 for Party members to be prepared to "resort to all sorts of stratagems, manoeuvers, illegal methods, evasions, and subterfuge" in carrying out the recycled New Economic Policy. "Gorbachev," Golitsyn emphasized, "is a committed Leninist who is carrying out a Communist renewal as a means towards the ultimate conquest of Western democracies."[7]

Boilerplate aside, the Gorbachev Foundation was created to cast grand global images on the wall of Plato's cave depicting humanity coming together in a geopolitical design of world socialist governance. Elevating Antonio Gramsci's secular solution from a national to an international level, Mikhail Gorbachev spun a picture of worldwide happiness in which all humankind would join hands and skip through a green meadow in the freshness of a spring sun. The reality outside of the cave, however, revealed Gorbachev's world socialism and governance to be one in which liberty would become an all but a remote memory and humanity impoverished to levels below today's worst imagination. The supposedly crazy-man Anatoliy Golitsyn warned the CIA in 1989 that, as Russia entered *perestroika,* Moscow would ". . . intensify the efforts of Gorbachev . . . to engage the American elite in cooperation over the environment, space, disarmament and the joint 'solution' of social, political, economic, environmental, military and international problems."[8] Golitsyn also said that "Soviet [Russian] agents of influence in the United States will redouble their attempts to act as catalysts in promoting 'restructuring' and convergence."[9] These actions by the Kremlin would be equivalent to Gramsci's Marxist formula of moving quietly into open societal spaces to position oneself for an eventual ascent to power.

Mikhail Gorbachev, riding the crest of a wave of popularity as the man who dared to slay the communist dragon and end the Cold War, immediately went about the process of undermining political loyalty to American democratic principles and national sovereignty by spinning an image of global governance (with socialism tucked away in the shadows). He began his propaganda campaign in an address to the United Nations—appropriately on December 7, 1988, the forty-seventh anniversary of Japan's sneak-attack on Pearl Harbor. General Secretary of the Soviet Communist Party Gorbachev outlined some of the major disinformation themes that would flow in different guises in the days to come.

Further world progress is now possible only through the search for consensus of all mankind, in movement toward a new world order. . . . The world community must learn to shape and direct the process in such a way as to preserve civilization, to make it safe for all and more pleasant for normal life. It is a question of cooperation that could be more accurately called 'co-creation' and 'co-development.' The formula of development 'at another's expense' is becoming outdated. In light of present realities, genuine progress by infringing upon the rights and liberties of man and peoples, or at the expense of nature, is impossible.[10]

In this quotation, Mr. Gorbachev calls for humankind to find the consensus necessary to move toward a new world order and a "coming together" (read: an end to sovereignty). What he called "co-creation" and "co-development" masked an intent to bring about a convergence of capitalism and socialism, first in Europe and then in North America. The "development 'at another's expense'" is a criticism of Europe's partnership agreements with African states and U.S. free trade policies in Latin America. It is a short tip-toe through the enchanted forest of socialism from these comments to reach the far Left's fiery anti-globalization movement. In retrospect, the contemporary geopolitical competition between Russia, the capitalist West, and the Salafists/Wahhabists began with Gorbachev's 1988 "new world order" speech at the United Nations.

Gorbachev's propaganda effort shifted to the Gorbachev Foundation after the dissolution of the Soviet Union. The Foundation was financed by millions of dollars from Americans with deep-pockets who were "honored" to be recognized as being one of America's elite by the former General Secretary of the Soviet Communist Party. The money was used to underwrite rather extravagant gatherings of these supposed opinion-makers in the

"State of the World Forum," whose meetings were designed to lead the attendees to the image of a new world order.

A third element of the propaganda strategy was satisfied by the Gorbachev Foundation nerve center in Moscow, which had a large supporting staff. In the words of Britisher Christopher Story, a former aide to Prime Minister Margaret Thatcher, ". . . the former International Department of the CPSU Central Committee has been relabelled the Gorbachev Foundation [which] indicates Gorbachev's continuing importance as an implementer of the [Andropov] strategy."[11]

Fourth, Christopher Story discovered a replacement Marxist doctrine to have been drawn from Antonio Gramsci's revisionism and at the core of "restructuring" right from the beginning. Gorbachev removed the shackles from the economic dependency of Eastern Europe as the Soviet Union faced bankruptcy and had no realistic way of dodging an on-coming economic train wreck. Sometimes a winning strategy is to lose at the beginning, in a controlled way, so as to pick up a new direction and win later.

And, fifth, Mr. Gorbachev's new book, *To Understand Perestroika,* was published in the Russian language in 2006. Reviews in English reported how Gorbachev discusses *perestroika* and accounts for some of the miscalculations made in implementing policy. He also revealed the evolution of his views on socialism, which led him to embrace a "social-democratic" scenario in Russia's development. Curiously, the book was right on time to try to smooth the ruffled feathers in the West about Russia's increasing tilt toward authoritarian governance. First, "miscalculations" as expressed by Gorbachev in the 2006 interviews were steeped in disinformation of what he wanted people to believe. After all, he's the guy that killed communism, or at least that is what many believe. Secondly, "social-democratic" is a euphemism for the weak-wristed socialist governments in Europe, all members of the Socialist International. Convergence with Europe is Moscow's initial step in trying to erase the European transatlantic alliance with the United States.[12]

One can also trace Mr. Gorbachev's propaganda line through the proceedings hosted by the "State of the World Forum" meetings from the San Francisco-based Gorbachev Foundation operation. Founded in 1995, the World Forum's boilerplate states that it works ". . . with partners worldwide to gather together the creative genius on the planet in a search for solutions to critical global challenges."[13] Co-chairs numbered twenty or so, including some moderates, but heavily tilted to the Left, including Ruud Lubbers, Rigoberta Menchu Tum, Ted Turner, Maurice Strong, and others. Strikingly successful in raising money for the World Forum proceedings, about 260 "partner" corporations, government agencies, foundations, and individuals donated. Included among the cash cows were the usual Left-wing suspects: Heinz Foundation, John D. and Catherine T. MacArthur Foundation, John Merck Fund, Ploughshares Fund, Union of Concerned Scientists, W. Alton Jones Foundation, and others with pronounced left-wing orientations. Many hard-nosed, profit-oriented, major businesses also took the bait.

Gorbachev used the State of the World Forum to promote a "paradigm shift," a model amenable to the cultural Marxism ideology of Antonio Gramsci." "Again and again," writer and analyst Berit Kjos explains, "the Communist leader and his hand-picked 'council of the wise' or 'global brain trust' told the assembly of more than 1000 guests and participants that new inclusive universal values must replace the Judeo-Christian world view." The unstated socialist view would replace familiar trappings of the sovereignty-based, Westphalia system with new values in the definition of a new global perspective. For Gorbachev, "the old beliefs and political systems," as writer Berit Kjos observed, "must be abandoned."[14]

By guiding State of the World Forum discussion to "correct" answers, albeit with a variety of perspectives allowed, Gorbachev strived to motivate a thousand or so "elites" toward endorsement of the new global paradigm. Gorbachev needed to screen out contradictory points during the sessions, especially the Judeo-Christian values at the root of American liberal government. Another filter might screen out the idea of national sovereignty as being immutable. He also tried to inculcate the idea that individual freedom guaranteed behind sovereign borders was an outmoded concept.

Berit Kjos summarized Mr. Gorbachev's "Plan for a United World" in a telling conclusion:

> This new paradigm turns all our American values upside down. Gorbachev may tout 'consensus' and 'synthesis' as the means to peace and security, but his ambiguous blends would drown Western capitalism in the sea of **global socialism**. Remember, his idea of 'democratizing' the world eliminates all the human rights guaranteed by the US Constitution. He demands the abolition of poverty everywhere, but at the cost of American resources. He wants equality for all—except the elite ruling class.[15]

In July 2006 an apparently frustrated Mikhail Gorbachev struck out against the United States. "Americans have a severe disease—worse than AIDS. It's called the winners's complex," he said, "you want an American-style [of government] here [in Russia]. That will not work."[16] A year later, Gorbachev was back on his high horse, plugging global socialist governance and railing about the United States trying to build an empire after the Cold War: "The Americans . . . gave birth to the idea of a new empire, world leadership by a single power, and what followed? What has followed are unilateral actions . . . wars . . . ignoring the UN Security Council . . . international law and . . . the will of the people, even the American people."[17]

In April 2008, President Vladimir Putin, just a few weeks before he became prime minister addressed the Russian people:

'Throughout history, Russia and her citizens have accomplished, and today are still accomplishing, a truly historic task. Maintaining the governance of a vast territory, preserving a unique commonwealth of peoples while occupying a major place in world affairs, calls not only for enormous toil. It calls also for enormous sacrifices and privations on the part of our people. Such has been Russia's thousand-year history. Such is the way in which it has retained its place as a mighty nation. We do not have the right to forget this.'[18]

The meaning of Putin's words for the Russian mind-set is explained by Andrei Piontkovsky of the Hudson Institute: the speech served as "the fateful sounding of the nationalist trumpet, a secret signal to his supporters that he would propel 'our Revolution, a conservative, nationalistic revolution' which would lead to 'a renaissance of the Fatherland's worldwide imperial greatness.' "[19]

Piontkovsky's analysis was right on target. When taking the oath of office on May 8, 2008, Putin told the assembled legislators assembled at the Duma that "our resources are sufficient to achieve even more complex, even more ambitious tasks and goals. I'm using our accumulated potential effectively and judiciously."[20] A World War Two Victory Parade was held at Red Square on May 9, 2008, the first such demonstration since 1990, revealing a broad range of technologically outdated tanks, missiles, bombers, and fighter planes (naval forces are also in disrepair and in need of updating). Putin promised to reverse the deterioration of Russian military forces. As a down payment, the Russian military budget has risen from $2 billion in 2002 to $42 billion in 2008. The West should take Prime Minister Putin's promise to upgrade Russia's military readiness in the immediate future with a grave seriousness.

Russia's grand theatrical production, "The Andropov Plan," drew its final curtain in the wake of the Army's heavy-handed, bloody crushing of tiny Georgia in August 2008. For more than two decades, the Kremlin's play acting had presented a Potemkin image of an internationally responsible democratic government. The stage play, based on deception and deceit, was the key ingredient for buying the time necessary for Soviet-Russia's Marxist renewal and restructuring the Kremlin's influence over its foreign agents of influence.

Act I brought an end to the Cold War marked by mutual nuclear deterrence and an armed standoff in Europe. The Berlin Wall tumbled down, captive nations inside the Soviet empire were freed, and nuclear weapons pared back. Communism in its Marxist-Leninist form disappeared. The Federation of Russia emerged from the controlled crumbling of the Soviet Union. These were heady times.

Act II was focused in the wild and wooly 1990s as momentous economic turmoil and crime dominated the stage. Behind the scenes, however, one could find previous Soviet power centers operating very actively. While the KGB moved the country's treasury out the back door to overseas banks and investments, nomenklatura (about 1.5 million elites of the former Soviet Communist Party, those holding senior positions in the government and the enterprises) moved through the front door to purchase Soviet state industries for pennies on the dollar. Millionaires were created overnight and a few took their ill-gotten gains to billions of dollars. As Act II came to its closing scene at the end of the 1990s, a seemingly pedestrian and controllable former KGB officer strolled onto the stage. After a stint as chief of the Federal Security Service (FSB), a happy face KGB, Vladimir Putin became President of Russia in March 2000.

Act III opened with a bang as President Putin moved quickly to tame the excesses of the 1990s and instill discipline in the politics and economy of the state. After he chased two billionaires out of the country and jailed another, the other fell into line—there was a new sheriff in town. Quasi-independent regional governors were cashiered and Putin's men put them in their place. The free press was silenced as a dozen or more journalists and writers met untimely deaths at the hands of persons unknown. President Putin danced with President Bush, looking into the American president's eyes Putin saw a man he could dupe. Meanwhile, world demand for oil and natural gas soared, raising prices with them and filling Russia's coffers and the pockets of the *nomemklatura*. Hundreds of former KGB men, the *siloviki*, found second careers at all levels of government, solidifying Putin's iron-fist.

Marxism-Leninism was dead, but secretly the Soviet-Russians flipped to adoption of Antonio Gramsci's cultural Marxism, which is hidden inside the Gorbachev Foundation in Moscow and San Francisco. Gramsci's stealthy formula for revolution, which allows the creation of mind control over the targeted people by destroying their cultural values and replacing them with socialist principles, will allow the Kremlin to "Marxize" their enemies without firing a shot. Moscow's strategy is to achieve global dominance over time through its agents of influence in countries throughout the capitalist West. The relationship between Russia and the Gramscists in Europe, the United States, and elsewhere is not a direct or mechanical one. Rather, it is an organic structure in which Russian and foreign elements of Gramsci's cultural Marxism are integrated naturally into a unified organic whole. They are mutually supportive in destroying the societal values in their respective countries and replacing them with Marxist principles through a new societal mind control ("hegemony").

Act IV opened in December 2007 with a huge victory by the United Russia Party in the Duma (parliament) that allowed Vladimir Putin to change governing chairs from president to prime minister, thereby preserving the fiction of a democratic Russia. During the same period, the "Campaign for America's Future," a front for the Washington, D.C.-based Institute for Policy Studies (IPS), began a political campaign toward "Building a New Majority for Real

Change." The radical left IPS , a close friend of the Soviet Union during the Cold War, since 1963 had created a vast 'solar system of organizations" following the Gramsci formula for cultural revolution at the federal, state, municipal, county, and community levels throughout the United States. The culture war to destroy American values is aimed at "Marxizing" America and making it possible to win political power through the ballot-box when the brainwashing toward socialist governance will begin in earnest.

Russia's long-planned, ruthless assault on Georgia turned off the theater lights. The two decades-old stage play was over. The new Russia based on a Party-State, Gramscian Marxism, government-owned industries, and an urge to bully its neighbors back into line are but the first steps of the Kremlin's long-range strategy. In conjunction with its foreign agents of influence, Russia is striving to create a one-world socialist governance by the end of the century without firing a shot.

The capitalist West, the second competitor for world dominance, will be able to rival Russia and its strategic partners by emphasizing its democratic strengths and defending its culture against the assaults from the far Left. Economic globalization, individual liberty, and democracy are the centerpiece activities and strengths of the capitalist West and, if relations with countries in the southern hemisphere are managed on a fair and balanced basis, it could provide a winning edge for the great democracies over the long-term. The capitalist West, however, is also vulnerable to inroads by cultural Marxism in Europe and the United States. The progressives-socialists-marxists strive to corrupt the Judeo-Christian cultures and substitute their own hard Left mind-control framework to guide the societies toward global socialist governance. Europe is already under the strong influence of the radical Left and may disintegrate under the demographic pressure of a plummeting birthrate and a rapidly growing Muslim population from the Middle East and Africa.

The far Left's war against America, the "culture war," has been underway since the 1960s using Antonio Gramsci's formula for cultural transformation leading to the staircase of power. The Left's ideological soldiers have successfully penetrated much of American society, including the public schools and universities across the nation. Progressives-socialists-marxists also have taken over the Democrat Party, a longstanding goal. From its current position, the radical Left envisions gaining political control through the ballot box and then putting into place a series of wealth redistribution measures, curbs on free economics, and an eventual end of U.S. national sovereignty as the country joins others in creating socialist world governance. Gramsci exhorted his followers to join the capitalists in the West—"Participate in their profit-seeking, in their social 'do-gooding,' in their international peace-making and peace-keeping structures, in health standards and living standards, and yes, even in their profession of ethical and religious goals," Malachi Martin explains. "Become members of the global home they are building, genuine members of their human family, collaborating in liberating all men from slavery and meaninglessness of daily life."[21] Progressive-socialist-marxists are encouraged to take this path, not for the sake of penetrating capitalist countries, but to corrupt their "Christian cultural basis," the strength and superstructure of their Judeo-Christian cultures—do this as a prerequisite to exercise control over peoples' minds. This makes socialist politics at the mass level possible and encourages an eventual extension toward socialist world governance.

During the Cold War, the Institute for Policy Studies and its broad solar system of "shining stars" were " . . . of enormous assistance to adversaries of the United States." Scott Steven Powell, from his experience of working inside IPS, stated in no uncertain terms: "In addition to generating programs that support active-measures campaigns, the IPS network produces enormous volumes of literature presenting ideas on a full range of issues which often reflect the Soviet line, but which are written in contemporary terms and style that appeal to popular American sentiments."[22] Powell took his analysis one step further by listing seven specific Soviet aims, each of which are unchanged and now reflect Russia's strategic goals:

'1. To influence world and American public opinion against U.S. military and political programs by suggesting they are the major cause of international conflict and crisis. 2. To demonstrate that the U.S. is an aggressive, 'colonialist' and 'imperialist' power, and demonstrate that its policies and goals are incompatible with the ambitions of the underdeveloped world. 3. To isolate the United States from its allies and friends and discredit those who cooperate with the U.S. 4. To discredit U.S. policies and representatives in the eyes of its citizens and the world by creating or exacerbating splits within the nation. 5. To discredit and weaken American intelligence services and expose their personnel. 6. To confuse world public opinion regarding the aggressive nature of . . . [Russian] policies. 7. To create a favorable environment for the execution of . . . [Russian] foreign policy.'[23]

Powell concluded in 1987 that: *"From its inception IPS, in its words and in its activities, has assisted the Soviet Union in attaining these seven objectives."*[24] [emphasis added] There is no evidence that this IPS-Kremlin relationship has changed significantly since the dissolution of the Soviet Union three years later (December 1990). On the contrary, a German journalist reported that in the mid-1980s Gorbachev was consulting with a member of the Transnational Institute and other American-European collaborators associated with IPS during his final preparations for implementing the Andropov Plan. This accounts for the madness unleashed among European radicals during the early 1990s in striving to understand and apply

Gramsci's cultural revolution formula to their open activities. Moreover, the anti-globalization campaign and the anti-war protests in the United States, Europe, and elsewhere all supported Russian goals as enumerated as "Soviet aims" by S. Steven Powell in 1987. IPS and its henchmen played instrumental roles in the planning and conduct of both the anti-globalization and anti-war protests since the terrorist attacks on September 11, 2001. Each of the major protests in the United States were planned by Marxist-Leninists (World Workers Party/ANSWER) and Marxists (United for Peace and Justice/IPS). The same was true in Europe where Anarcho-Communists also played a major role in the protests.

The Institute for Policy Studies also has worked hard since its inception to penetrate and influence the U.S. House of Representatives and the Senate. The objective from the beginning has been to influence the policy-making process of the United States. "The cord that binds the multitude of I.P.S. projects and activities," John Rees of the Maldon Institute wrote in 1983, "is its effort to influence U.S. policies along the lines ultimately favorable to the interests of the Soviet Union."[25] The IPS umbilical was refreshed in the 1990s and is still connected to the Kremlin through the Gorbachev Foundation, a Russian front for integrating international cooperation in support of the Gramscian project to develop a socialist world governance led by Moscow.

The U.S. Congress remains a target for facilitating progress toward progressive-socialist-marxist political dominance inside the United States for the purpose of triggering a cultural revolution that will lead the American people to accept a government headed by a cabal of socialists and Marxists. Not only are IPS collaborators flooded throughout congressional staffs, they are also working closely with members of the House and Senate. The key instrument for influencing U.S. policy is the seventy-plus Representatives and one Senator that make up the Congressional Progressive Caucus, which is largely owned and operated by the Institute for Policy Studies.

The IPS "solar system of organizations" has marshaled all of its resources for the 2008 presidential election. Based on the belief that the collapse of conservatism has finally opened the door for their accession to power, the progressive-socialist-marxist radical Left is driving many of the social and foreign policy debates. Convinced that conservatives have formed a "circular firing squad," Robert Borosage, co-director of the Campaign for America's Future, says that "its time for a change . . . a new era has begun. . . ."[26] "The . . . Campaign for America's Future is convinced that Democrats are going to win big this November [2008], but it's not taking any chances," Joseph D'Agostino writes. "The group has moved to the forefront of progressive activism and is pushing for a permanent political realignment that would usher in a new era of Big Government.[27]

The Institute for Policy Studies and its "solar system of organizations" have a major influence on policy-making in the Congress, many state legislatures, and municipalities. With its international reach to Europe and Russia through the Gorbachev Foundation, constellations of "shining stars" also influence U.S. foreign policy. With the exception of President Jimmy Carter and, to some degree, Bill Clinton the progressive-socialist-marxist movement has been shut out of the White House. The IPS directors and members of their network are drooling to once again have one of their acolytes as President of the United States. With the assistance of George Soros and his gang of fellow plutocrats, the far Left has taken over by developing fronts inside a "shadow party" secreted within the Democrat Party. It was from here that the radical Left placed all its chips on Barack Obama.

Presidential candidate Barack Obama, offers Americans "Change We Can Believe In." Obama's background reveals that he has been steeped in the organizational and battle tactics for social revolution by the renowned "community organizer" Saul Alinsky. The late Alinsky (he died in 1972) developed a whole set of tactics to touch-off a successful cultural revolution—"a wholesale revolution whose ultimate objective is the systematic acquisition of power by a purportedly oppressed segment of the population, and the radical transformation of America's social and economic structure." He adds that "the goal is to foment enough public discontent, moral confusion, and outright chaos to spark the social upheaval . . . a revolution whose foot soldiers view the status quo as fatally flawed and wholly unworthy of salvation."[28] The idea is to energize the poor and less fortunate, or what Marx might have called the "lumpen proletariat." Barack Obama taught workshops in the 1980s on the Alinsky method, took part in "community organizing," and conducted training activities for "future leaders" while he was with ACORN, an IPS far Left collaborator.

For the radical Left, thirsting more than two decades, Barack Obama is the perfect front man for advancing the progressive-socialist-marxist program for transforming American culture. Obama align himself with the radical Left from the beginning of his career. His "community organizing" for ACORN became his early school house to entering the IPS solar system and stunning the personalities inside with his exceptional rhetorical skills. While he was busy internalizing a radical policy perspective and preparing for a future in politics, the far Left groomed him for what may become his future in the White House. When one combines the perspective of Obama in the White House and with the Institute for Policy Studies helping to shape policies in the U.S. House and Senate, plus several state legislatures, one might believe that it is "game over" for America's traditional culture embracing liberty and liberal democratic government.

Militant Islam, the third geopolitical competitor for dominant global authority, is focused on restoration of a world Islamic caliphate. Wielding a double-edged sword, one side sharpened for terrorist attacks and the other dulled for waging a theocratic "civilizational jihad," or "a kind of grand jihad in eliminating and destroying the Western civilization from within . . . so that . . . Allah's religion is made victorious over all other religions."[29] A major success for militant Islam is in Europe, where, from all indications, the growing Muslim presence will be in a position to win political control through the ballot box in fifteen to twenty years.

The capitalist West is already at war against Islamic jihadism. George Weigel argues persuasively that ". . . the twenty-first century will be one in which rapidly advancing modernization coincides with an explosion in religious conviction and passion," which will pose ". . . a specific and mortal threat to the civilization of the West, and to the United States as the lead society of the West."[30]

The 9/11 attacks created a strategic moment for Americans. The echo of Paul Revere's warning rolled across the land, prompting Americans to take up arms and attempt to help Iraq achieve democratic governance that would serve as a demonstration effect to the Islamic world: how democracy could resolve their concerns about modernity and offer a preferable alternative to endless war against the West. But America's effort was undermined by the centuries old differences between Shiite and Sunni Muslims, intervention by Iran, and the far Left's anti-war, anti-democratic actions that prompted many Americans to take to the streets in protest against the conflict.

This "grand jihad" of destroying Western civilization from the inside is rightly characterized by Bruce Bawer as a "cultural jihad." Militant Islam touts *sharia* law as having dominion over all Muslims, even when their infractions of the law, including murder, occur in non-Muslim countries. At the same time militants have choreographed an attack on Western freedoms of speech and expression by the brutal 2004 murder of Theo Van Gogh in Amsterdam for his film about oppression of women and the publication of satirical cartoons in Danish newspapers in 2005 through riots, mayhem, and even killings worldwide. Western societies learned to censor themselves out of fear or sympathy for Islam's followers. No matter how repressive a foreign regime may be, the West, including Americans, have allowed their concern for what Islamists may think or do to influence their words and actions. Intimidation, even implied threats, are enough for self-censoring, resulting in a loss of liberties previously enjoyed. Already militant Islam has set the train of civilizational jihad into motion. The United States, like Europe, is accommodating the Muslim *sharia* demands. This has become a kind of "self-dhimmitudization" similar to what has been occurring in Europe. Accommodating the cultural practices of others is about good manners. But such accommodations under the threat of physical harm, real or implied, or verbal denunciation leads in infringement of basic liberties enjoyed by all Americans. By rendering deferential preference to Muslims under pressure is what Bruce Brawer correctly calls "cultural surrender."[31]

To make matters worse, the U.S. Departments of State and Homeland Security have designed their own politically correct words for use in describing Islamic terrorism—officials are being advised to use vague terms like "terrorist" or "violent extremist," while avoiding such descriptive terms as "jihadists" or "Islamofacist" to describe American enemies.[32]

There always seems to be someone in the room, when discussing the Muslim word "jihad," that hastens to make the point that it refers to the internal struggle to follow's God's guidance. True enough. But Andrew C. McCarthy, author of *Willful Blindness: A Memoir of the Jihad* says that ". . . if *jihad* truly were a sublime summons to become a better person, it is not entirely clear how plowing jumbo jets into skyscrapers and mass murdering civilians could achieve the sheen of the sacerdotal in the eyes of the faithful . . . simply stated, jihad is and has always been about forcible conquest." He adds that "the jihadist project . . . is to remove all barriers to the establishment of the sharia," which is a prerequisite for Islam's dominance.

Columnist Diana West calls the new government guide *Words that Work and Words that Don't* "crazy" and for good reason. The latest nonsense from government bureaucrats would label the war on "Islamic terror" as being "a Global Struggle for Security and Progress." References to "caliphate" are banned and substituted with "global totalitarian state." In addition, "jihad" is censored and so is "Islamofascist." Diana West has it right: "animating the directive, written with considerable input from unidentified American Muslim 'experts,' is the delusional belief that what we say (or don't say) has transformative power over Muslim attitudes and behaviors regarding Islamic terrorism, the Islamic caliphate, the advance of Islamic law (sharia) and the so-call war on (Islamic) terror. . . ."[33] Americans are not Europeans—one should expect the public to reject such bureaucratic derangement in the U.S. government.

The war against America by Islamic terrorists is both violent and psychological. Propaganda and disinformation in the soft civilizational jihad is dedicated to preparing Americans for rule under the Islamic sharia. Islam, as a religion, provides a smokescreen for both the violent and soft jihads. Playing word games and defining politically correct terms that soft-pedal the images of violent and civilizational jihad is a crucial first step toward acceptance of dhimmitude.

The Departments of State and Homeland Security seemingly do not understand that words count in a propaganda and disinformation war. It is vital for Americans to withstand the temptations of political correctness and refer to things as they are. Instead of playing shadow puppets on the walls of Plato's cave, government officials should stay focused on the realities of the violent and soft dimensions of jihad. Playing the game of hurt feelings by some Muslims brings the kind of results that has led Europe into the hell of dhimmitude.

"Things can and do, get worse," George Weigel counsels, "especially when cultural morale declines: much of Europe today exhibits a kind of cultural exhaustion that does not bode well for the future."[34] Will Americans follow the European decline or will they fight back to defend their way of life? Once the culture is torn, Americans may never find their way back to the societal values that have provided more than two centuries of greatness to the nation's democratic experiment of individual freedom and limited government. Moreover, the absence of a coherent culture would compromise the ability of the United States to lead the capitalist West successfully in its twenty-first century geopolitical competition with Russia and militant Islam. A politically socialized and "Marxized" United States would leave the world hanging between autocracy and theocracy. In either case, a victory by Russia or the Islamists would be America's death knell . . . an end of its rich culture based on democracy and individual liberty.

APPENDIX

SOMETIMES IN THE SHADOW world of deceit, deception, and disinformation, a truth is wrapped in an apparent hoax, a hidden truth of an attack to come could be a warning notice. Or, it could simply by a propaganda ploy to scare the American people. We are uncertain. We do know that A. Q. Khan's nuclear smuggling involved a far greater proliferation of nuclear technology and knowledge that had been previously expected. To this writer, the attack scenario looks like a long-term set of goals and strategy to guide Al-Qaeda's nuclear development efforts.

The consequences would be so great if the attack plan was executed that we have little choice but to keep the alleged Al-Qaeda scenario on the table, despite our misgivings. A ten-kiloton nuclear bomb detonated near the White House, for instance, could kill about 100,000 people and pulverize downtown buildings—thousands more could die from short-term and long-term radioactive fallout over a vast area. Assistance for surviving victims could be delayed for hours. "These people are going to be on their own," said the University of Georgia's Cham E. Dallas. "There's no white horse to ride to the rescue."[1]

Mohammad Al-Asuquf—Interview (2002)

Al-Jazeera: What is the objective of the Al Queda network?

Al-Asuquf: To destroy the Great Satan, that is, the United States and Israel.

Al-Jazeera: Why?

Al-Asuquf: The USA over the past 60 years has been impregnating [infecting] the world with its arrogance, greed and malfeasance. It is the incarnation of all that is evil. The people of this planet don't deserve this torture.

Al-Jazeera: Isn't this view somewhat one-sided?

Al-Asuquf: No; one only has to observe recent events. The disrespect of the Kyoto treaty; the case of the Permanent Court of International Justice, their inaction with regards to our Palestinian brothers; the financial greed and absurd speculations in Third World countries; the complete indifference to other oppressed people and countless other situations which all of the world's leaders well know. And on top of all that, the Bush doctrine of "shoot first and ask questions later." This is an unacceptable abuse and will therefore have very grave consequences.

Al-Jazeera: But isn't the development and influence of America the fruit of its own competence?

Al-Asuquf: Competence in extortion, competence in subjugation, competence in lying. After the Second World War, the USA was the only industrialized country with its manufacturing infrastructure intact. Loaning money like a good loan shark, it ended up becoming a very rich and powerful country; however, its greed remained undiminished. Today, Americans live like maharajas, wasting more than any other people, spending more than $80 billion per year just on gambling. They've lost any notion of spirituality and live in constant sin. With each passing day the USA demonstrates that it doesn't know how to live with other peoples; for this, it deserves destruction.

Al-Jazeera: Wouldn't it be easier to simply assassinate President George Bush?

Al-Asuquf: In the first place, it would do no good, other than turning him into a martyr. When you face a powerful enemy, the best strategy is not to kill him, but to make him lose his leadership due to his incompetence, and let him live to watch this unfold.

Al-Jazeera: Does the Al Queda network have the military capacity to make war on the United States?

Al-Asuquf: If we analyze history, we will see that all great wars, before they were started, were based on previously established concepts [of war]. But if we observe well, we will see that these concepts and strategies came to nothing, since a new type of war was ultimately waged. An example is the construction of the Maginot line by the French before the First [*sic* Second] World War, which, in reality proved to be completely useless against the invading forces. Aircraft carriers, nuclear submarines, and spy satellites will be useless in the next war.

Al-Jazeera: American authorities hold more than 1,000 people suspected of terrorism since September 11th. Won't this compromise Al Queda's plans?

Al-Asuquf: Of those imprisoned, perhaps 20 to 30 percent belong to Al Queda. Moreover, they are from the second echelon. We have more than 500 members in the first echelon and 800 from the second inside the United States.

Al-Jazeera: What do you mean by first and second echelons?

Al-Asuquf: In the first echelon are Al Queda members who have been in the United States for more than 10 years, many married with children. They have detailed knowledge of our plans and are just waiting for a phone call. They are also known as "sleepers." Those of the second echelon have arrived in the last five years and have no idea of our plans.

Al-Jazeera: Are even those who are married, with children, ready to die with their families?

Al-Asuquf: Yes. All of them are ready to die. Long live September 11th.

Al-Jazeera: What was September 11th to Al Queda's overall plans?

Al-Asuquf: As a general step, it was just the beginning. It was a way of calling the world's attention to what is still to come.

Al-Jazeera: How many members does Al Queda have?

Al-Asuquf: In the first echelon, about 5,000; in the second, about 20,000 all over the world.

Al-Jazeera: In the detention camp at Guantanamo, are there any members of the first echelon?

Al-Asuquf: No, in fact many of those there are not even Al Queda members.

Al-Jazeera: How does Al Queda intend to destroy the most powerful nation in history?

Al-Asuquf: It's a question of logistics. Using its own poison, that is, attacking the heart of what they consider the most important thing in the world: money.

Al-Jazeera: How so?

Al-Asuquf: The American economy is an economy of false appearances. There is no real economic ballast to the American economy. The American GDP is something around $10 trillion, of which just 1 percent represents agriculture, and just 24 percent represents industry. Therefore, 75 percent of the American GDP is service and most of this is financial speculation. For those who understand economics, and it appears that the American Secretary of the Treasury, Paul O'Neil, doesn't or doesn't see it, it's enough to say the USA acts like a huge "dot.com," and dollars, strictly speaking, are its shares.

Al-Jazeera: How can you be so sure of this?

Al-Asuquf: The value of a company's shares is directly proportional to the profitability of the enterprise. When a business is just a service provider and doesn't produce any durable goods, the values of its shares depends on its credibility. Which is to say that if the credibility of the USA were shaken, its shares (the dollar) would fall with incredible rapidity and the entire American economy would begin to collapse.

Al-Jazeera: How can you be sure of this?

Al-Asuquf: On a smaller scale, it's exactly what large financial groups do to the countries of the third world to reap profits in one month that Swiss banks couldn't get in four or five years.

Al-Jazeera: So how will Al Queda shock the American economy to this point?

Al-Asuquf: By provoking a deficit of between $50 and $70 trillion dollars, the equivalent of the United States GDP for five to seven years.

Al-Jazeera: How will this be done?

Al-Asuquf: With the destruction of the seven largest American cities, along with other measures.

Al-Jazeera: By what means will this be done?

Al-Asuquf: Using atomic bombs.

Al-Jazeera: With all of the security in the USA, how, hypothetically, will these bombs be smuggled onto American soil?

Al-Asuquf: They won't be smuggled in, they're already there.

Al-Jazeera: What are you saying?

Al-Asuquf: There are already seven nuclear devices on American soil which were put in place before September 11th and are ready to be detonated.

Al-Jazeera: How did they get in to the USA?

Al-Asuquf: Before September 11, American security was a fiasco, and even after, were it necessary, we could manage to smuggle bombs into the United States. They entered through seaports, as normal cargo.

Al-Jazeera: How is that possible?

Al-Asuquf: A nuclear device is no bigger than a refrigerator; therefore, it can be easily camouflaged as one. Millions of cargo containers arrive in seaports each day, and no matter how efficient security is, it's impossible to check, search through and examine each container.

Al-Jazeera: Where did these atomic bombs come from?

Al-Asuquf: They were purchased on the black market.

Al-Jazeera: From whom?

Al-Asuquf: We bought five from the defunct Soviet Union and two more from Pakistan.

Al-Jazeera: How is it possible to buy an atomic bomb? Isn't there security?

Al-Asuquf: Before 1989 it was practically impossible, however after fall of the Berlin Wall, the Russian army began a process of self destruction, and some high generals began to lose their privileges, and therefore, highly susceptible to corruption. Even General Lebed, now deceased, and Hans Blix, the head of the arms inspection commission of the United Nations, have stated this, notwithstanding denials by Russian Defense Minister Seguey Ivanov.

Al-Jazeera: How much does a nuclear bomb cost?

Al-Asuquf: Somewhere around $200 million.

Al-Jazeera: How did Al Queda get this money?

Al-Asuquf: We have numerous sponsors.

Al-Jazeera: Who are they?

Al-Asuquf: There are a number of countries which support us, and also numerous wealthy individuals.

Al-Jazeera: Are all of these countries Arab?

Al-Asuquf: No, there are some European countries as well which have an interest in the fall of the USA.

Al-Jazeera: Who are these wealthy individuals?

Al-Asuquf: People who are also tired of watching the USA suck the wealth out of the rest of the world.

Al-Jazeera: Is Saddam Hussein one of them?

Al-Asuquf: You could say that he's just one of the collaborators, through Abdel Tawab Mullah Hawaish, his vice-prime minister and the person responsible for Iraq's arms program.

Al-Jazeera: Are these atomic bombs powerful ones?

Al-Asuquf: The five Russian devices are from the old T-3 missiles, also are well known as RD-107s, and their potency is something around 100 kilotons each, that is, 5 times as powerful as the Hiroshima bomb. The Pakistan bombs are less powerful, somewhere around 10 kilotons.

Al-Jazeera: Can't the bombs be detected and disarmed by American authorities?

Al-Asuquf: No, in spite of their age they've undergone modernization and are well hidden. Even if they were found, they have autodetonation provisions should anything get close to them. Even electromagnetic pulses would be incapable of deactivating them.

Al-Jazeera: Don't they emit radiation? Can't they be detected?

Al-Asuquf: No. They are wrapped in thick leaden cases.

Al-Jazeera: A suspected Pakistani ship was recently searched and all that was found were lead bars. Does this have anything to do with the bombs?

Al-Asuquf: Yes, however that lead was just an extra layer, and was not essentially necessary.

Al-Jazeera: How will the bombs be detonated?

Al-Asuquf: There are numerous methods, a cell-phone, radio frequency, seismic shocks or by timer.

Al-Jazeera: Once detonated, how many deaths will be caused by these bombs?

Al-Asuquf: It depends, since our plans are very malleable.

Al-Jazeera: So what is the entire plan?

Al-Asuquf: The beginning will be the detonation of a nuclear device, which will cause the death of between 800 thousand and one million people and create chaos on a scale never seen before. During this chaos, two or three cropsprayers that are now dismantled and stored in graneries (silos?) close to little-used highways in the countryside will take off on suicide missions to spray two or three large American cities with smallpox. That means that once the smallpox has been identified, all airports and seaports will be closed by quarantine. Land borders will likewise be shut down. Not one airplane, ship or vehicle will enter or leave the United States. This will cause total chaos. . . .

Al-Jazeera: But the American government has guaranteed that within five days it could produce enough smallpox vaccine to inoculate the entire population.

Al-Asuquf: There will be simultaneous suicide attacks against the vaccine production plants.

Al-Jazeera: Which will be the first city?

Al-Asuquf: The first city will be that in which optimal conditions present themselves, for example, clear skies, and winds of eight miles-per-hour or less in the direction of the country's center so that radioactive dust can contaminate the maximum possible area.

Al-Jazeera: Will this annihilate the USA?

Al-Asuquf: No. But the process will have begun. Who will buy food products from the United States knowing they may have been contaminated by radiation? Who will travel to the United States knowing the possibility of contracting smallpox? Who will continue to invest in American institutions? Just as with the World Trade Center, it will be simply a question of time before the entire economic structure collapses and turns to dust. If our objectives are reached with one bomb and the smallpox, probably we'll save the lives of others, however that's risky [unlikely], and it's probable that six more bombs will be detonated, one per week, and other attacks with chemical weapons will be carried out.

Al-Jazeera: How many innocent people will die?

Al-Asuquf: According to estimates made by me and Ayman Al-Zawahiro, somewhere around 15 million due to the atomic bombs and their radiation. Of those exposed to smallpox, 25 percent will die, approximately five million, and many more due to the ensuing chaos and disorder.

Al-Jazeera: What about the American military response?

Al-Asuquf: There will practically be none. Even if five or ten cities were chosen at random to be destroyed, that would still be a small price to pay. The problem is the economic despair will be so great that even economizing by not using arms unnecessary will occur, since the liquidity of American goods will be almost zero and at that point the United States will make more selling its Nimitz-class aircraft carriers, which cost about five billion dollars, to Turkey or Italy for one billion dollars, since the country will so urgently need to recapitalize, though it will be too late. Moreover, how will the morale of American soldiers be knowing that their entire families have died and their country no longer exists. Fight for what?

Al-Jazeera: And won't the global economy also be ruined?

Al-Asuquf: In the beginning it will be very difficult; a serious economic crisis will ensue. However, without the United States, the world will soon arise in a more just and fraternal manner.

Al-Jazeera: And Israel?

Al-Asuquf: As they say . . . it will be dessert.

Al-Jazeera: Does bin Laden's spokesman, Sulaiman Abu Gheith, know you are giving this interview?

Al-Asuquf: It was he and bin Laden who suggested I give it.

Al-Jazeera: Osama bin Laden is still alive?

Al-Asuquf: He is quite healthy, alongside his commanders Mohammed Atef and Khalid Shaik Mohammed and Mullah Omar.

Al-Jazeera: Aren't you fearful that Al Queda's plans will be discovered?

Al-Asuquf: The plan is ready in its countdown, and nothing can stop it.

Al-Jazeera: Not even if the United States asks forgiveness and changes its attitudes?

Al-Asuquf: That won't happen, and even if it did, it's too late.

Al-Jazeera: When will the attack begin?

Al-Asuquf: I can't reveal that. Allah Akbar.[2]

NOTES

Introduction

1. ". . . evolution from a Judeo-Christian civilization, with important post-Enlightenment secular elements, into a post-Judeo-Christian civilization that is subservient to the ideology of Jihad and the Islamic powers that propagate it. The new . . . civilization in the making can be called a 'civilization of dhimmitude.' The term dhimmitude comes from the Arabic word 'dhimmi.' It refers to subjugated non-Muslim individuals or people that accept the restrictions and humiliating subordination to an ascendant Islamic power to avoid enslavement or death." Note: author Bat Ye'or wrote these words to describe the looming dilemma faced by Europeans in 2005, but she also said that "similar developments . . . have been discerned in America. . . ." Bat Ye'or, Eurabia: The Euro-Arab Axis (Cranbury, N.J.: American University Press, 2005), pp. 9, 13.
2. Malachi Martin, *The Keys of This Blood: The Struggle for World Dominion Between Pope John Paul II, Mikhail Gorbachev, and the Capitalist West* (New York: Simon and Schuster, 1990), pp. 15–16.
3. *Ibid.*, p. 16.

Chapter 1

1. Louise Ropes Loomis, trans., *Plato*, Book VII: "Figure of Mankind in the Dark Cave . . .," (Roslyn, N.Y.: Walter J. Black, 1943), pp. 398–400.
2. Alberto M. Piedra, "Weapons of the Left & the Right," *Touchstone*, 14-3 (April 2001).
3. David Horowitz and Richard Poe, *The Shadow Party: How George Soros, Hillary Clinton, and the Sixties Radicals Seized Control of the Democratic Party* (Nashville, Tenn.: Nelson Current, 2006).
4. Arnaud de Borchgrave, "Capitalism's 'Unacceptable' Aspects," *Washington Times* (August 23, 2001), p. A14.
5. Samuel P. Huntington, *The Clash of Civilizations and the Remaking of World Order* (New York: Simon & Schuster, 1996), pp. 209–18.
6. Dinesh D'Souza, *The Enemy at Home: The Cultural Left and Its Responsibility for 9/11* (New York: Doubleday, 2007), p. 14.
7. Huntington, *Clash of Civilizations*, p. 213.
8. Walid Phares, *Future Jihad: Terrorist Strategies Against America* (New York: Palgrave Macmillan, 2005), p. 14.
9. Bat Y'or, *Eurabia*, p. 265.
10. Arnaud de Borchgrave, "Osama's Saudi Moles," *Washington Times* (August 1, 2003), p. A19.
11. Phil Kent as quoted by Michael Carney, "Dark Side's Critic," *Washington Times* (July 3, 2003), p. A2.
12. As quoted by Matthew Riemer, "Shifting Sands and the House of Saud," *Asia Times Online* (May 29, 2003).
13. When General Emilio Mola Vidal was marching on Madrid during the fall of 1936 in the early days of the Spanish Civil War (1936–1939), journalists asked which of his four columns of troops would capture the city. He replied that the seizure of Loyalist Spain's capital city would fall to his "fifth column," which was already inside the city. General Mola's remark has since been used to describe the activities of agents of influence, terrorists, spies, saboteurs, and civilian sympathizers behind the lines or those positioned inside a target country. When Madrid finally fell to General Franciso Franco's fascist armies in 1939, thousands of Madridenos in black shirts and hundreds of black flags greeted the victorious troops. Hugh Thomas claimed in 1977 that the term was probably first used by Russian Marshal Alexsandr Suvorov in 1790, when his forces captured Izmail from the Ottoman Empire with the active assistance of Slavs inside the besieged city. See Trevor N. Dupuy, Colonel, editor-in-chief, *International Military and Defense Encyclopedia*, Vol. 2 (New York: Brassey's, 1993), pp. 934–35.
14. As quoted by John Mintz, "Saudi Strain of Islam Faulted," *Washington Post* (June 27, 2003), p. A11.

15. Senator Carl Levin, "Lawmakers: Report to Show al Qaeda-Saudi Ties," *CNN.com* (July 13, 2003), http://cnn.com, and Daniel Klaidman, Mark Hosenball, Michael Isikoff, and Evan Thomas, "Al Qaeda in America: The Enemy Within," *Newsweek* (July 23, 2003).

16. Dore Gold, *Hatred's Kingdom: How Saudi Arabia Supports the New Global Terrorism* (Washington, D.C.: Regnery, 2003), p. 15. See also Olivier Roy, *Failure of Political Islam*, trans. by Carol Volk (Cambridge, Mass.: Harvard University Press, 1994), pp. 1–2.

17. Oriana Fallaci coined the phrase "Reverse Crusade" in *The Rage and the Pride* (New York: Rizzoli, 2001).

18. William Kristol, "The Long War," *Weekly Standard* (March 6–13, 2006), p. 9.

19. Martin, *Keys of This Blood*, p. 31.

20. Tony Blankley, *The West's Last Chance: Will We Win the Clash of Civilizations?* (Washington, D.C.: Regnery Publishing, 2005), pp. 20–21.

Chapter 2

1. "Progressive" is a far Left code word for "socialist," and "socialism" is often used synonymously with "marxism" (lower case to differentiate it from the Cold War uses). The writer, therefore, has opted to use the awkward contraction "progressive-socialism-marxism" because it is impossible to differentiate between them. With apologies to the reader.

2. Association for Economic and Social Analysis, *The Party's Not Over: Marxism 2000* (Amherst, Mass.: University of Massachusetts, Department of Economics, September 2000).

3. **Radicals** advocate drastic or revolutionary changes to fundamental political, economic, and social dimensions of society and often use direct methods to achieve their goals; **socialism** conceptually has a large number of variants but all include some degree of restriction on individual liberty, a strong central government to confiscate individual wealth through taxation or other means to "share" it with other members of society, and redefines individual property rights—"socialism" is often used by communists to describe the transition period to a fantasy world of total egalitarianism; **anarchism** considers the state the root of all evil and the source of everything wrong in society; and **syndicalists** believe, like anarchists, that the state always represents the economic class in power, capitalists, against the interests of the working class, and the state is always the focus of their hatred of capitalism. See Bernard K. Johnpoll and Harvey Klehr, ed., *Biographical Dictionary of the American Left* (New York: Greenwood, 1986), pp. ix–xi.

4. Alice Widener, *Teachers of Destruction: Their Plans for a Socialist Revolution* (Washington, D.C.: Citizens Evaluation Institute, 1970), pp. 23, 13, 16.

5. *Ibid.*, pp. 223, 231.

6. The term "radical" to describe a secretive, largely undefined group of Leftists is appropriate since these socialists, Marxists, Marxist-Leninists, anarchists, Gramcists, and Trotskyites and others distinguish themselves from transnational social activists trying to do good in the world through honest efforts aimed at assisting the less fortunate.

7. John Earl Haynes and Harvey Klehr, *In Denial: Historians, Communism & Espionage* (San Francisco: Encounter Books, 2003), p. 46.

8. Widener, *Teachers of Destruction*, backcover quote.

9. Douglas Kellner, *Critical Theory, Marxism and Modernity* (Baltimore: Johns Hopkins University Press, 1989), pp. vii, 1.

10. *Ibid.*, p. 44.

11. *Ibid.*, p. 45.

12. *Ibid.*, p. 46.

13. Gerald Atkinson, "What is the Frankfurt School?" (August 1, 1999), http://newtotalitarianians.com/FrankfurtSchool.html.

14. Mary Jo Buhle, Paul Buhle, and Dana Georgakas, eds., *Encyclopedia of the American Left*, 2d ed. (New York: Oxford University Press, 1998), pp. 248–49, 477–79, 603, 617; Francis X. Gannon, *Biographical Dictionary of the Left*, consolidated Vol. I (Belmont, Mass.: Western Islands, 1969), pp. 336–37, 435–36; and Douglas Brown, "History of the Frankfurt School," Illuminations: the Critical Theory Website (December 1998), http://uta.edu/huma/illuminations.

15. Herbert Marcuse, *One-Dimensional Man: Studies in the Ideology of Advanced Industrial Society* (Boston: Beacon, 1964).

16. *Ibid.*, p. xv.

17. David Horowitz, *The Professors* (Washington, D.C.: Regnery, 2006), pp. xxxvii–xxxviii.

18. As quoted by Atkinson, "What Is the Frankfurt School?"

19. Monica Stillo, *Antonio Gramsci* (University of Leeds, United Kingdom: Institute of Communications Studies, 1999), http://theory.org.uk/ctr-gram.htm; Frank Rosengarten, *An Introduction to Gramsci's Life and Thought*, Sociology Department, Queens College of the City of New York (undated), http://soc.qc.edc/gramsci/intro/engbio.html; and *Why Read Gramsci?* (undated), http://charm.net/~vacirca/PNoverv.html.

20. John Vennari, "Russia Hearkens to Gramsci's Ghost," text of speech delivered to Catholic Bishops in Mexico City and published by *The Fatima Crusader*, 48 (Winter 1995). See http://fatima.org/library/cr48pg14.html.

21. *Ibid.*

22. *Ibid.*, p. 7.

23. Lynne Lawner, "Introduction," *Antonio Gramsci: Letters from Prison* (New York: Noonday Press, 1989), p. 51.

24. The key element of Gramsci's blueprint for the global victory rested on Hegel's distinction between what was "inner" or "immanent" to man and what man held to be outside and above him and his world—a superior force transcending the limitations of individuals and of groups both large and small. For Gramsci, the IMMANENT and the TRANSCENDENT were unavoidably paired and yoked. Marxism's "transcendent" was the utopian ideal. But the Marxist transcendent was too foreign to the Christian mind and Christian culture. So, Gramsci argued that since the immanent and the transcendent are paired, then unless you can systematically touch what is *immanent* and *immediate* to individuals and groups and societies in their daily lives, you cannot convince them to struggle for the transcendent. Vennari, "Russia Hearkens to Gramsci's Ghost."

25. Stephane Courtois and others, *The Black Book of Communism: Crimes, Terror, and Repression*, trans. by Jonathan Murphy and Mark Kramer (Cambridge, Mass.: Harvard University Press, 1999), p. 727. (First published in French as *Le Livre noir du Communisme: Crimes, terreur, repression*, 1997).

26. David Horowitz, *The Politics of Bad Faith: The Radical Assault on America's Future* (New York: Free Press, 1998), p. 62.

27. David Horowitz, *Radical Son* (New York: Simon & Schuster, 1997), p. 106.

28. Peter Collier and David Horowitz, *Destructive Generation: Second Thoughts About the Sixties* (New York: Summit Books, 1989), pp. 14, 146, 149.

29. Horowitz, *Politics of Bad Faith*, pp. 62, 83.

30. Harvey Klehr, *The Heyday of American Communism* (New York: Basic Books, 1984), p. xi.

31. Horowitz, *Radical Son*, p. 63.

32. David Horowitz, "Spies Like Us" (October 20, 1997), http://salon.com.

33. Horowitz, *Radical Son*, p. 109.

34. Courtois and others, *Black Book of Communism*, pp. 647–64.

35. Harvey Klehr, *Far Left of Center: The American Radical Left Today* (New Brunswick: Transaction Books, 1988), p. 23.

36. Horowitz, *Radical Son*, p. 105.

37. Martin Carnoy and Derek Shearer, *Economic Democracy: The Challenge of the 1980s* (Armonk, N.Y.: M. E. Sharpe, 1980), p. 385.

38. *Ibid.*, pp. 3–5.

39. Harry C. Boyte, *The Backyard Revolution: Understanding the New Citizen Movement* (Philadelphia: Temple University Press, 1981), pp. 204–05.

40. Rael Jean Isaac and Erich Isaac, *The Coercive Utopians: Social Deception by America's Power Players* (Chicago: Regnery Gateway, 1983), pp. 2, 294.

41. G. William Domhoff, "How to Commit Revolution in Corporate America" in Jeremy Rifkin and John Rossen, *How to Commit Revolution American Style*, an anthology (Secaucus, N.J.: Lyle Stuart, 1973), pp. 162–214. See also G. William Domhoff, "Blueprints for a New Society," *Ramparts* (February 1974).

42. G. William Domhoff, "Power at the National Level," *Who Rules America?* (April 2005) *(*First published in 1967 and in 2005 in its 5th edition), http://sociology.ucsc.edu/whorulesamerica/power/who_has_the_power.html.

43. Collier and Horowitz, *Destructive Generation*, pp. 15, 16.

44. Gramsci did not use "passive revolution" to describe his own formula but actions taken by the bourgeoisie. The phrase is flipped here to boomerang, since it so clearly defines Gramsci's own pragmatic blueprint.

45. Horowitz, *Professors*, p. xxxvi.

46. Martin, *Keys of This Blood*, p. 250.

47. *Ibid.*, p. 251.

48. Alberto M. Piedra, "Weapons of the Left & the Right," *Touchstone*, 14-3 (April 2001).

49. *Ibid.*

50. E. J. Dionne, Jr., "Cardinal Ratzinger's Challenge," *Washington Post* (August 19, 2005), p. A19.

51. Jennifer Harper, "Church a Way of Life in Dixies," *Washington Times* (April 28, 2006), pp. A1, A20.

52. Anonymous e-mail of a flyer showing Marines in prayer and ACLU commentary (November 2004).

53. Joseph Caquette, Chairman, National Americanism Commission, American Legion, and Joseph Infranco, Senior Vice President, Alliance Defense Fund, "Public Money and the ACLU;" and Letters to the Editor, *Washington Times* (June 3, 2007), p. B3.

54. Burt Prelutsky, "ACLU and the Holiday Spirit," *Washington Times* (November 23, 2004), p. A17.

55. John Gibson, *The War on Christmas: How the Liberal Plot to Ban the Sacred Christian Holiday Is Worse Than You Think* (New York: Sentinel, 2005), pp. ix–xi.

56. Michael Novak as quoted by David Limbaugh in *Persecution: How Liberals Are Waging War Against Christianity* (Washington, D.C.: Regnery, 2003), p. 331.

57. Joshua O. Haberman, Rabbi, "The Bible Belt Is America's Safety Belt," as quoted by Don Feder, "The Anti-Christian League," http://frontpage magazine.com (December 13, 2005).

58. Phil Stewart, "Pope Raps Policies 'Hostile' to Families," *Washington Times* (January 2, 2008), p. A1.

59. Piedra, "Weapons of the Left & the Right."

60. Bill O'Reilly, *Culture Warrior* (New York: Broadway Books, 2006), p. 123.

61. David Horowitz, *Hating Whitey: and Other Progressive Causes* (Dallas: Spence, 1999), pp. 225–31, and Tammy Bruce, *New Thought Police: Inside the Left's Assault on Free Speech and Free Minds* (Roseville, Calif.: Prima Publishing, 2003), pp. 15–16.

62. Bruce, *New Though Police*, p. 46.

63. *Ibid.*, pp. 116–17.

64. Kate O'Beirne, *Women Who Make the World Worse and How Their Radical Feminist Assault Is Ruining Our Families, Military, Schools, and Sports* (New York: Sentinel, 2006), p. 5.

65. Lisa MacDonald, "Women's Liberation and the Fight for Socialism," *Links*, No. 18 (May–August 2000), p. 69.

66. Daniel Williams and Alan Cooperman, "Vatican Letter Denounced 'Lethal Effects' of Feminism," *Washington Post* (August 1, 2004), p. A17; and "Feminism Denounced As a Threat to Families," *Washington Times* (August 1, 2004), p. A5.

67. Midge Decter, "Forward" in Kimberly Schuld, *Guide to Feminist Organizations* (Washington, D.C.: Capital Research Center, 2002), p. vii.

68. *Ibid.*, pp. 11–14.

69. Tammy Bruce, *The Death of Right and Wrong: Exposing the Left's Assault on Our Culture and Values* (Roseville, Calif.: Prima Publishing, 2003), p. 83.

70. *Ibid.*, p. 124, and Buhle, Buhle, and Georgakas, *Encyclopedia of the American Left*, p. 777.

71. *Ibid.*, pp. 1–7.

72. Henry Mark and Erika Holzer, *Aid and Comfort* (Jefferson, N.C.: McFarland & Company, 2002), p. 14.

73. *Ibid.*, p. 21.

74. O'Beirne, *Women Who Make the World Worse*, pp. 157–58.

75. "Two Front Battle," *Washington Times* (May 19, 2005), p. A2.

76. Daniel J. Flynn, *Why the Left Hates America* (Roseville, Calif.: Prima Publishing, 2002), pp. 70–71.

77. Bruce, *Death of Right and Wrong*, pp. 194–95.

78. Alan Sears and Craig Osten, *The Homosexual Agenda: Exposing the Principal Threat to Religious Freedom Today* (Nashville, Tenn.: Broadman & Holman, 2003), pp. 18–27.

79. "Vatican Officials Comment on Homosexuality Causes Stir," *Arlington Catholic Herald* (June 19, 2003), pp. 11, 28, and Julia Duin, "Criticism of Gays Riles Georgetown," *Washington Times* (May 30, 2003), pp. A1, A12.

80. Sears and Osten, *Homosexual Agenda*, p. 47.

81. *Ibid.*, p. 48.

82. *Ibid.*, p. 49.

83. *Ibid.*, p. 96.

84. Cheryl Wetzstein, "Scandinavian Marriage Scorned As a Model for U.S.," *Washington Times* (March 10, 2004), pp. A1, A12.

85. *Ibid.*

86. Deep Babingtom, "Italian Families Rally for Tradition," *Washington Times* (May 13, 2007), pp. A1, A14.

87. Cheryl Wetzstein, "Syphilis Rates Up on Gay Male Sex," *Washington Times* (March 13, 2008), p. A3.
88. O'Reilly, *Culture Warrior*, p. 121.
89. Judith Levine, *Harmful to Minors: The Perils of Protecting Children From Sex* (New York: Thunder's Mouth Press, 2002), pp. 25, 225. See also, as quoted by Bruce, in *Death of Right and Wrong*, p. 193.
90. *Ibid.*, p. 238.
91. As quoted in Sears and Osten, *Homosexual Agenda*, pp. 83–84.
92. O'Reilly, *Culture Warrior*, pp. 205–06.
93. Bruce, *Death of Right and Wrong*, pp. 205–06.
94. Levine, *Harmful to Minors*, pp. i–ii.
95. "Bolshevik Schools," *Washington Times* (February 22, 2001), p. A2 (reprinted from "The American Educational Soviet," *New American* , February 26, 2001).
96. Martin, *Keys of This Blood,* p. 254.
97. Piedra, "Weapons of the Left & the Right."
98. Michael Savage, *Savage Nation: Saving America from the Liberal Assault* (Nashville: WND books, 2002), pp. 156–58.
99. As quoted by Bruce, *Death of Right and Wrong*, p. 166. See also http://frontpagemag.com/Content/read.asp?ID=10.
100. Ronald Radosh, *Commies* (San Francisco: Encounter, 2001), p. 204.
101. "American Lefties Say U.S. Deserved 9–11," *NewsMax.com* (June 14. 2002).
102. Peter Drier and Dick Flacks, "Patriotism's Secret History," *Nation* (June 3, 2002), pp. 39–42.

Chapter 3

1. J. R. Nyquist, "Plotting Global Conquest," JRN Blog (January 15, 2005), http://jrnnyquist_2002_0115.htm. Mr. Nyquist is a contributor to WorldNet, a WorldNetDaily monthly magazine.
2. Anatoliy Golitsyn, *The Perestroika Deception* (New York: Edward Harle Limited, 1998), p. 10.
3. Christopher Andrew and Vasili Mitrokhin, *Sword and the Shield: The Mitrokhin Archive and the Secret History of the KGB* (New York: Basic Books, 1999), pp. 5–7, 132, 251, 254.
4. Andrew and Mitrokhin, *Sword and the Shield*, pp. 203, 204.
5. Herman and Dohrs, "In Stalin's Footsteps."
6. Hedrick Smith, *The New Russians* (New York: Random House, 1990), pp. 72–76.
7. *Ibid.*, p. 427.
8. Golitsyn, *Perestroika Deception*, pp. 13–15.

9. J. Michael Waller, *Secret Empire: The KGB in Russia Today* (Boulder: Westview, 1994), p. 3.

10. As quoted from Mitrokhin's notes in Christopher Andrew and Vasili Mitrokhin, *The World Was Going Our Way* (New York: Basic Books, 2005), p. 19.

11. Anatoliy Golitsyn, *New Lies for Old* (New York: Dodd, Mead, 1984), pp. 4, 12–13.

12. *Ibid.*, pp. 13–17.

13. *Ibid.*, pp. 15–16.

14. Mark Reibling, *Wedge: The Secret War Between the FBI and CIA* (New York: Knopf, 1994), p. 187.

15. *Ibid.*, pp. 407–08.

16. Andrew and Mitrokhin, *Sword and Shield*, pp. 184–85.

17. *Ibid.*, p. 367.

18. Golitsyn, *Perestroika Deception,* p. xvii.

19. Peter Reddaway and Dmitri Glinski, *Tragedy of Russia's Reforms: Market Bolshevism Against Democracy* (Washington, D.C.: United States Institute of Peace Press, 2001), p. 122.

20. *Ibid.*

21. Golitsyn, "Memorandum to the CIA: March 1990,"*Perestroika Deception,* p. 87

22. Golitsyn, "Memorandum to the CIA: 26 March & 12 October 1993,"*Perestroika Deception*, pp. 163, 224.

23. Christopher Story, "Foreword by the Editor," in Golitsyn, *Perestroika Deception*, p. xxii.

24. Christopher Story, Editor's Note No. 44, in Golitsyn, "Memorandum to the CIA—March 1990," *Perestroika Deception*, pp. 116–17.

25. *Ibid.*

26. *Russia: My Way!* (Washington, D.C.: Maldon Institute, January 11, 2005), p. 14.

27. *Ibid.*

28. Stephen Handelman, *Comrade Criminal: Russia's New Mafiya* (New Haven: Yale University Press, 1995), p. 96.

29. *Ibid.*, p. 102.

30. Paul Klebnikov, *Godfather of the Kremlin: Boris Berezovsky and the Looting of Russia* (New York: Harcourt, 2000), p. 56.

31. *Ibid.*, pp. 65–66.

32. Veselovsky memo, as quoted by Klebnikov, *Godfather of the Kremlin*, p. 59.

33. Reddaway and Glinski, *Tragedy of Russia's Reforms,* pp. 248, 266.

34. *Ibid.*, p. 259.

35. *Ibid.*, pp. 194, 204.

36. Golitsyn, "Memorandum to the CIA: 26 August 1991," p. 141.

37. *Ibid.*
38. Reddaway and Glinski, *Tragedy of Russia's Reforms,* pp. 142–43.
39. *Ibid.,* p. 204.
40. Handelman, *Comrade Criminal,* p. 105.
41. Klebnikov, *Godfather of the Kremlin,* pp. 56, 74–75.
42. As quoted by Smith, *New Russians,* p. 450.
43. Reddaway and Glinski, *Tragedy of Russia's Reforms,* pp. 16, 607, 614–16.
44. As quoted by Andre Piontkovsky, *Another Look Into Putin's Soul* (Washington, D.C.: Hudson Institute, 2006), p. 3.
45. William Safire, "Siloviki Versus Oligarchy," *New York Times* (November 5, 2003), http://nytimes.com/2003/1105/opinion/05SAFI.html, and David Warsh, ed., *economicprincipals.com* (September 12, 2004), http://economicprincipals .com/issues/04.09.12.html.
46. Warsh, "Meet the Siloviki."
47. Anna Politkovskaya, *Putin's Russia: Life in a Democracy,* trans. by Arch Tait (New York: Metropolitan Books, 2004), p. 68.
48. Ol'ga Kryshtanovskaya, *Nova gazeta* (August 30, 2004) as quoted by John B. Dunlop, "Putin as a State-Builder?," Center on Democracy, Development, and the Rule of Law, Stanford Institute on International Studies, No. 39 (February 24, 2005), http://cddrl.stanford.edu.
49. Fred Weir, "KGB Influence Still Felt in Russia," *Christian Science Monitor* (December 2003), and "Kremlin Riddles with Former KGB Agents," *Speigel Online* (December 14, 2006), http://speigel.de/international/0,1518,454486,00. html.
50. Michael McFaul, "Vladimir Putin's Grand Strategy," *Weekly Standard* (November 17, 2003), pp. 17–19.
51. Peter Finn, "Jailed Russian Oil Tycoon Faces More Charges," *Washington Post* (February 6, 2007), p. A10.
52. Kevin Sullivan and Peter Finn, "Russia Charges Exiled Tycoon," *Washington Post* (April 14, 2007), pp. A10, A11; and Peter Finn, "New Charges for Jailed Russian Tycoon and Kremlin Foe," *Washington Post* (July 1, 2008), p. A7.
53. Ben Bolton, "Why Are Putin's Enemies Dying?," *NewsMax* (May 2007), pp. 48–49.
54. Steve Forbes, "Paul Klebnikov, 1963–2004," *Forbes.com* (July 12, 2004), and "Paul Klebnikov," *Economist* (print edition) (July 15, 2004), http:// economist.com/people/displayStory.cfm?story_id=2921517.
55. Politkovskaya, *Putin's Russia,* pp. 234, 68.
56. As quoted by Peter Finn, "Difficulties Arise in Probe of Russian Reporter's Death," *Washington Post* (September 5, 2007), p. A16, and Anton Troianovski, "Russian Arrests 10 in Slaying of Outspoken Journalist," *Washington Post* (August 28, 2007), p. A7.

57. The amount of Polonium-210 that entered Litvenenko's body was of a microscopic size. He died after twenty-two agonizing says in the hospital, Peter Finn, "Poisoning of Ex-Agent Sets Off Alarm Bells, *Washington Post* (January 7, 2007), p. A16.

58. Wesley Prudon, "A Hit Job Worthy of the KGB," *Washington Times* (November 28, 2006), p. A4; Michael Hirsh and Owen Matthews, "Spy Poisoning: How Dangerous is Russia?," *Newsweek* (December 11, 2006); Caroline Davies, "Was He Sacrificed to Embarrass Putin?," *Telegraph* (UK) (November 11, 2006); Mary Jordan and Peter Finn, "Russian Billionaire's Bitter Feud with Putin a Plot Line in Poisoning," *Washington Post* (December 9, 2006), pp. A1, A16; Scott Shane, "When an Ex-K.G.B. Man Says They're Out to Get Him . . .," *New York Times* (December 10, 2006); Charles Krauthammer, "That Murder in London," *Washington Post* (December 8, 2006), p. A39; and David Stringer, "Ex-KGB Spy Laid to Rest in London," *Washington Times* (December 8, 2006), p. A17.

59. Mary Jordan and Peter Finn, "Britain Seeks Extradition of Ex-KGB Agent," *Washington Post* (May 23, 2007), pp. A1, A14, and Mike Franchettei, "Putin the Terrible, We Love You," *Sunday Times* (Britain) (May 27, 2007).

60. Peter Finn, "Murder Suspect to Run for Parliament in Russia," *Washington Post* (September 17, 2007), p. A14.

61. Handelman, *Comrade Criminal*, p. 105.

62. Michael Kozakavich, "Russia's SVR: The Leaner If Not Meaner Successor to the KGB's First Directorate," *Prism*, 3–8, Jamestown Foundation (May 30, 1997).

63. As quoted by Waller, *Secret Empire*, p. 48.

64. *Ibid.*, p. 57.

65. "Russia Steps Up Espionage," *Jane's Intelligence Digest* (November 29, 2002), pp. 1, 4.

66. Leon Aron, "The Man Who Knew Russia Too Much," *Washington Post* (December 24, 2006), p. B4.

67. Politkovskaya, *Putin's Russia*, p. 82.

68. *Ibid.*

69. *Ibid.*

70. Beichman, "Russia's Press Perils," p. A17.

71. Mikhail Gorbachev, "Interview" with Charlie Rose (October 18, 2006).

72. As quoted by Fred Weir, "Putin's Russia: Better or Worse," *Christian Science Monitor Online* (December 4, 2006), http://csmonitor.com/2006/1204/p01s04-woeu.html.

73. Steven Pearlstein, "Putin Is Free to Manage Capitalism," *Washington Post* (December 10, 2003), p. E1.

74. Michael Mainville, "Kasparov Makes Putin Play Defense," *Washington Times* (December 28, 2006), pp. A1, A15; and Peter Baker, "Russia! Which Way Did It Go?," *Washington Post* (December 24, 2006), pp. B1, B5.

75. Fred Hiatt, "Kasparov's Gambit," *Washington Post* (February 12, 2007), p. A17.

76. Peter Finn, "Russia Turns New Law Against Kremlin Critics," *Washington Post* (September 26, 2007), pp. A14, A16.

77. Peter Finn, "New Manuals Push a Putin's-Eye view in Russian Schools," *Washington Post* (July 20, 2007), pp. A1, A16.

78. Mansur Mirovalov, "Russia Youth Camp Grooms New Putins," *Washington Times* (July 23, 2007), pp. A1, A11.

79. Sarah E. Mendelson and Theodore P. Gerber, "Young Russia's Enemy No. 1," *Washington Post* (August 3, 2007), p. A15.

80. Anna Zakatnova, "On the Left . . ., " *Russian Beyond the Headlines*, U.S. Edition, an advertising supplement to the *Washington Post* (October 31, 2007), p. H8.

81. Andrew Richards, "Russian Economy Booming," *Washington Times* (October 29, 2007), p. A2.

82. Christian Lowe, *Washington Times* (December 20, 2006), p. A15.

83. Baker, *"Russia!,"* p. B5

84. Masha Lipman, "Putin Cements His Grip," *Washington Post* (October 6, 2007), p. A21. See also James Hackett, "Permanent President Putin," *Washington Times* (September 4, 2007), p. A13.

85. Steve Gutterman, "Putin Backer Sweeps Election," *Washington Times* (March 3, 2008), p. A11; Anne Applebaum, "Why Russia Holds 'Elections,'" *Washington Post* (March 3, 2008), p. A17; Arkady Ostrovsky, "Putin's Pyramid," *Economist: The World in 2008*, p. 92; and David Satter, "Russia Incorporated," *Weekly Standard* (December 17, 2007), pp. 26–29.

86. As quoted by Reuben F. Johnson, "Change You Cannot Believe In," *Weekly Standard* (March 17, 2008), pp. 16–17.

87. Dominic O'Connell, "Gazprom: How We Will be the First Trillion-Dollar Firm," *Sunday Times* (July 8, 2007), p. 1 (bus.), and Irwin M. Stelzer, "Putin's Oily Politics," *Weekly Standard* (June 11, 2007), pp. 16–17.

88. Stelzer, "Putin's Oily Politics," p. 17.

89. *Ibid.*

90. Vladimir Isachenkov, "Putin to Discuss Merger with Belarus," *Washington Times,* (December 9, 2007), p. A4; Jim Heintz, Russia and Serbia Tighten Their Ties with Multi-Billion Dollar Energy Deal," *Washington Post* (January 26, 2008), p. A18; and David R. Sands, "Serbian Deal to Give Gazprom Further Control," *Washington Times* (January 25, 2008), p. A13.

91. Keith C. Smith, "Putin Checkmate's Europe's Energy Hopes" (June 2007) and "Europe's Response to Russia's Energy Policies" (April 2007) (Washington, D.C.: Center for Strategic and International Studies).

92. The Marquis de Custine, *Custine's Eternal Russia*, ed. and trans. by Phyllis Penn Kohler (Coral Gables, Fla.: University of Miami, 1976), pp. 114, 120.

Chapter 4

1. Martin, *Keys of this Blood*, p. 31.
2. Olesya Dmitracova, "Russia, India Partnership Solidifies Nuclear Ties," *Washington Times* (January 26, 2007), p. A17.
3. Sultan Shahin, "Three of a Kind: India, China, and Russia," *Asia Times Online* (September 27, 2003).
4. An interview of Yevgeny Primakov by Vladimir Bogdanov, "Superpowers' Roles Evolve With the End of the Cold War," *Trendline Russia* (November 15, 2006), a Russian Federation official advertising supplement to the *Washington Post* (November 15, 2006), p. H1.
5. Judith Ingram, "Kremlin on Offensive Over Sales of Weapons," *Washington Times* (March 26, 2003), p. A17, and Bill Gertz, "Bush Presses Putin to Stop Arms Sales," *Washington Times* (March 25, 2003), pp. A1, A11.
6. Stephen Blank, "Russian Weapons and Foreign Rogues," *Asia Times Online* (March 25, 2003).
7. "Russia Issues Blunt Warnings to Arab Allies on U.S. Plans," *WorldTribune .com* (June 28, 2002).
8. "Intelligence Service Says 'No Comment' on Reports of Cooperation with Baghdad," *RFE/RL Newsline*, 7–71, Part 1 (April 14, 2003).
9. David Harrison, "Revealed: Russia Spied on Blair for Saddam," *Sunday Telegraph* (April 13, 2003).
10. Robert W. Chandler, *Tomorrow's War, Today's Decisions* (McLean, Va.: AMCODA Press, 1996), p. 61.
11. Bill Gertz, "Pentagon Ousts Official Who Tied Russia, Iraq Arms," *Washington Times* (December 30, 2004), p. A3.
12. As quoted by Stephen Hayes, "Saddam's Dangerous Friends," *Weekly Standard* (March 24, 2008), p. 18.
13. *Ibid.*, pp. 18–25.
14. Elisabeth Sieca-Kozlowski, "The Russian Army: Strategies for Survival and Individuals and Joint Modalities of Action in a Situation of 'Chaos,'" *Culture & Conflict*, 24 (1997), as reported by Lieutenant Colonel Alain Porchet, *Do Recent Changes in Russia's Military Machine Spell the Country's Return as a Major Power?*, European Strategic Intelligence and Security Center (January 9, 2008).
15. *Ibid.*, pp. 3–4 (as quoted by Porchet).
16. *Ibid.*, p. 4 (as quoted by Porchet).
17. Peter Finn, "Putin Withdraws Russia From Major Arms Area," *Washington Post* (December 1, 2007), p. A8.
18. Sergei Blagov, "Russian Rhetoric Serves Short-term Goals" (February 2, 2008), *International Relations and Security Network (ISN)*, http://isn.ethz.

19. *Ibid.*

20. David R. Sands, "Putin Accuses U.S., NATO of Renewing an 'Arms Race,'" *Washington Times* (February 9, 2008), pp. A1, A7.

21. Mansur Mirovalev, "Medvedev Not Easier to Deal With, Putin Says," *Washington Times* (March 9, 2008), p. A6.

22. Uday, "Putin's Global Game: Containing the US," *South China Morning Post* (December 12, 2002).

23. "Russia's Defense Industry Announces Revised Defense Exports Record," *Geostrategy-Direct.com* (March 21, 2007).

24. "Belarus Extends Russia's Reach to Countries Where Moscow 'is unwilling to go,'" *Geostrategy-Direct.com* (July 11, 2007), and "Russia Aggressively Pursuing Mideast Reconnaissance Market," *Geostrategy-Direct.com* (September 12, 2007).

25. "Extreme Censorship Silences Another Dissenting Voice in Russia," *Geostrategy-Direct.com* (March 21, 2007); "Russian Journalist Was Investigating Belarus Arms Deal," *Geostrategy-Direct.com* (April 11, 2007); and "Suited and Booted," *Economist* (March 15, 2005), p. 73.

26. "Iran Brokers Syria's Weapons Deals with China, Russia, N. Korea," *Geostrategy-Direct.com* (February 13, 2008).

27. "Report: Secret High Tech Torpedo from Russia Transferred to Iran," *Geostrategy-Direct.com* (November 21, 2007).

28. Alex Vatanka and Richard Weitz, "Russian Roulette—Moscow Seeks Influence Through Arms Exports," *Jane's Intelligence Review* (January 2007), pp. 36–41.

29. "U.S. Intelligence Cites Covert Russian, N. Korean Aid for Burma Nuclear Facilities," *Geostrategy-Direct.com* (November 28, 2007).

30. Bill Gertz, "China, Russia Hit Sanctions as 'Wrong,'" *Washington Times* (January 11, 2007), p. A3.

31. As quoted by Jim Hoagland, "Don't Give Up on Russia," *Washington Post* (November 17, 2006), p. A35.

32. As quoted by Thom Shanker and Mark Landler, "Putin Says U.S. Is Undermining Global Stability," *New York Times* (February 11, 2007). See also Thomas Rice and Craig Whitlock, "Putin Hits U.S. Over Unilateral Practices," *Washington Post* (February 11, 2007), pp. A1, A23.

33. Duncan Lennox, "On the Defensive," *Jane's Intelligence Review* (August 2007), pp. 40–45.

34. As quoted by Peter Finn, "Antimissile Plan by U.S. Strains Ties with Russia," *Washington Post* (February 21, 2007), p. A10.

35. Mike Eckel, "Putin Likens Missile Plan to Cold War," *Washington Times* (October 27, 2007), pp. A1, A6.

36. "Russia Expands Spy Network in Mideast," *Geostrategy-Direct.com* (August 8, 2007); and "Russia to Increase Military Might and Spy Efforts," *New York*

Times (July 26, 2007).

37. As quoted by David R. Sands, "Russia Expanding Navy into Mediterranean Sea," *Washington Times* (August 7, 2007), pp. A1, A16; and "Russian Navy Eyes Syria Bases to Expand Mideast Presence," *Geostrategy-Direct.com* (August 15, 2007).

38. Bill Gertz, "Russia Exercise Included Strategic Cruise Missile Attack on U.S.," *Geostrategy-Direct.com* (September 19, 2007).

39. Andrew Borowiec, "Russia Boasts Buzzing U.S. Base in Cold War-Style Assertiveness," *Washington Times* (August 10, 2007), pp. A1, A12; Anton Troianovski, "Russia Resumes Its Long-Range Air Patrols," *Washington Post* (August 18, 2007), p. A7; and "SCO Exercise Highlight Growing Co-operation," *Jane's Intelligence Review* (September 2007), p. 7.

40. David R. Sands, "Kyrgyzstan Says Alliance Not Aimed at U.S.," *Washington Times* (August 18, 2007), p. A6.

41. Ariel Cohen, "Russia's Race for the Arctic," *Washington Times* (August 7, 2007), p. A12; and John Carey, "Cold War Redux?, *Washington Times* (August 22, 2007), p. A15.

42. Nadezhda Sorokina, "Ice War," *Russia Beyond the Headlines*, U.S. Edition, an advertisement supplement to the *Washington Post* (September 30, 2007), p. G5.

43. As quoted from "Greetings from China," *Isvestiya* (Russia) (February 12, 2007), translated in an essay, "Russia, 2007" by Andrei Piontkovsky, Hudson Institute (Washington, D.C.: unpublished).

44. Patrick E. Tyler, "Russia and China Sign Friendship and Cooperation Treaty: A Strategic Shift in Eurasia?," *Backgrounder*, No. 1459, Heritage Foundation (July 18, 2001).

45. Colonel Stanislav Lunev, "Sino-Russian Alliance Challenges U.S. Interests," *Newsmax.com* (January 13, 2002), http://newsmax.com/archives/articles/2002/1/13/132400.shtml.

46. Richard Weitz, "Shanghai Summit Fails to Yield NATO-Style Defence Agreement," *Jane's Intelligence Review* (August 2006), p. 41.

47. Stephen Blank, "China's Emerging Nexus with Central Asia," 6–13, *China Brief*, Jamestown Foundation (June 21, 2006); "China's Emerging Energy Nexus with Central Asia," 6–15, *China Brief*, Jamestown Foundation (July 19, 2006); and Pan Guang, "China and Central Asia: Charting a New Course for Regional Cooperation," conference paper, Jamestown Foundation (February 2007).

48. Paul Hare, "China in Angola: An Emerging Energy Partnership," *News*, Jamestown Foundation (November 13, 2006).

49. "A Ravenous Dragon," *Economist*, Special Report on China's Quest for Resources (March 15, 2008), p. 16.

50. James Kirchick, "Africa's New Hegemon," *Weekly Standard* (March 5, 2007), pp. 14–16.

51. Charles R. Smith, "Red China's Growing Influence," *NewsMax* (May 2006), p. 68.

52. Gabe Collins, "China Seeks Oil Security With New Tanker Fleet," *Oil & Gas Journal* (October 9, 2006), pp. 20–26, and Gabriel B. Collins and Andrew S. Erickson, "Tanking Up the Commercial and Strategic Significance of China's Growing Tanker Fleet," *Geopolitics of Energy*, 29-8 (August 2007). See also China's new energy policy directions in Wenran Jiang, "Beijing's 'New Thinking' on Energy Security," 6–8, *China Brief*, Jamestown Foundation (April 12, 2006).

53. Ed Lanfranco, "China Boosts Defense Fund As Talks End,: *Washington Times* (March 5, 2007), pp. A1, A10; and Edward Cody, "China Boosts Military Spending," *Washington Post* (March 5, 2007), p. A12.

54. Patrice Hall, "Chinese Powering World Economy," *Washington Times* (July 26, 2007), pp. A1, A11.

55. Joachim Bamrud, "China's Big Spending Spree in Latin America," *Newsmax* (February 2008), p. 46.

56. "China's Military Build-Up," *Jane's Intelligence Digest* (August 8, 2003), p. 2.

57. John Pomfret, "China to Buy 8 More Russian Submarines," *Washington Post* (June 28, 2002), p. A15; "U.S. Intelligence Takes Softer Line on China . . . But the DIA Sees China Buildup as Threat," Northeast Asia Report, *Geostrategy-Direct.com* (January 24, 2007); and Wayne Allard, "Another Great Wall," *Washington Times* (June 28, 2007), p. A17.

58. Edward Lanfranco, "China Warns U.S., Japan Against Missile Defense," *Washington Times* (June 6, 2007), p. A12.

59. Edward Cody, "China Offers Glimpse of Rationale Behind Its Military Policies," *Washington Post* (December 30, 2006), p. A17.

60. "Beijing Decries Sanctions Placed on Its Companies," *Washington Times* (January 26, 2006), p. A5; Bill Gertz, "Exporting Weapons Draws U.S. Sanctions," *Washington Times* (May 20, 2002), pp. A1, A14; and Bill Gertz, "Firms in Arms Sales to Iran Identified," *Washington Times* (July 26, 2002), p. A10.

61. "U.S. Believes Russia Is Using Chinese Fronts," *Geostrategy-Direct.com* (June 18, 2002).

62. Thomas Woodrow, "China Opens Pandora's Nuclear Box," 2–4, *China Brief*, Jamestown Foundation (December 10, 2002).

63. David R. Sands, "Chinese-Iranian Trade Fueled by Distrust of U.S.," *Washington Times* (July 27, 2005), p. A13.

64. Elaine Kurtenbach, "China Close to Oil Deal with Iran," *Washington Times* (February 18, 2006), p. 7, and Xuecheng Liu, "China's Energy Security and the Grand Strategy," *Policy Analysis Brief*, Stanley Foundation (September 2006).

65. John Calabrese, "China and Iran: Mismatched Partners," *Occasional Paper*, Jamestown Foundation (August 2006), p. 15.

66. George Jahn, "Iran Defies Nuclear Ultimatum," *Washington Times* (February 23, 2007), pp. A1, A20.

66. John J. Tkacik, Jr., "The Arsenal of the Iraq Insurgency," *Weekly Standard* (August 13, 2007), pp. 16–17.

67. Bill Gertz, "Inside the Ring—China Arming Terrorists," *Washington Times* (June 15, 2007), p. 9.

68. Henry Kissinger, "The Next Steps with Iran," *Washington Post* (July 31, 2006), p. A15.

69. Abbas Amanat, "The Persian Complex," *New York Times* (May 25, 2006), p. A27.

70. Peter Baker, "Putin's Concessions to U.S. Are Limited By the Bottom Line," *Washington Post* (April 16, 2002), p. A15, and David R. Sands, "Aid to Iran Seen Diluting U.S. Effort," *Washington Time* (October 10, 2002), p. A14.

71. Pavel K. Baev, "Moscow Insists on Seeing No Evil in Iran," *Eurasian Daily Monitor*, Jamestown Foundation (December 3, 2005).

72. Peter Baker, "Putin Won't Support U.N. Action Against Iran," *Washington Post* (September 17, 2005), p. A6.

73. "Russia Trains 1,000 Iranians as Nuclear Technicians to Operate Bushehr Plant," *Geostrategy-Direct.com* (March 22, 2005), and Dana Priest, "Iran's Emerging Nuclear Plant Poses Test for U.S.," *Washington Post* (July 29, 2002), pp. A1, A6.

74. "Germans, Swiss, Russians Linked to Iran Nukes," *Geostrategy-Direct.com* (March 8, 2005).

75. "MI6 Identified Dual-Use British Fronts Supplying Iran's Nuke Programs," *Geostrategy-Direct.com* (June 27, 2007).

76. Bill Gertz, "Iran Imported 'P-2 Centrifuges from Asian Suppliers,'" *Geostrategy-Direct.com* (June 22, 2004).

77. George Jahn, "Iran to Install Centrifuges with Potential for Nuke Arms," *Washington Times* (January 27, 2007), p. A17.

78. "Iran Leading Mideast Nuke Race; IAEA Plans Inspections," *Geostrategy-Direct.com* (December 17, 2002); "Report: North Korea, Iran Collaborating on Warheads, Long-Range Missile," *Geostrategy-Direct.com* (August 19, 2003), and "Iran, North Korea Seen Closely Coordinating on Strategy, Nuclear Development," *Geostrategy-Direct.com* (October 18, 2006).

79. "Iran Readies Missile Test that Could Strike Europe, Gets Help from China, N. Korea and Russia," *Geostrategy-Direct.com* (April 11, 2007), and Nasser Karimi, "Iran Says It Is Now Running 3,000 Uranium Centrifuges," *Washington Post* (September 3, 2007), p. A12.

80. "Show But Don't Tell: Iran Puts Six Missiles on Display at Parade," *Geostrategy-Direct.com* (September 30, 2003); "Iran 'Ecstatic' with Chinese Missile Navigation System Based on GPS," *Geostrategy-Direct.com* (August 24, 2004);

Bill Gertz, "N. Korea, Iran Cooperate on Missiles," *Washington Times* (January 30, 2007), pp. A1, A11; and "Bush Announces New Intelligence Assessment on Iran's ICBM Capability," *Geostrategy-Direct.com* (November 7, 2007).

81. "Iran Briefed on Russian SU-30 Fighters as Counters to U.S. F-15," *Geostrategy-Direct.com* (August 8, 2007).

82. Patrick E. Tyler, "Russians Question Wisdom of Their Coziness with Iran," *New York Times* (March 16, 2001), and "Russia Accelerates Deliveries of SAM Systems to Iran, Syria," *Geostrategy-Direct.com* (January 17, 2007).

83. Michael Wines, "Putin to Sell Arms and Nuclear Help to Iran," *New York Times* (March 13, 2001), p. A7.

84. Bill Gertz, "Reports of Sale to Iran of Su-30s Rattle Israelis," *Geostrategy-Direct.com* (August 15, 2007).

85. Jephraim P. Gundzik, "Resurgent Russia Challenges US," *Asia Times* (March 17, 2005).

86. Arnaud de Borchgrave, "Putin's Tehran Junket," *Washington Times* (October 19, 2007), p. A18; David R. Sands, "Putin Urges U.S. Not to Strike Iran," *Washington Times* (October 17, 2007), pp. A1, A12; and "U.S. Intelligence Studying List of Targets in Iran" and "Iran Constructing New Nuclear Site Inside Mountain," *Geostrategy-Direct.com* (October 17, 2007).

87. Ayelet Savyon, "Inquiry and Analysis—Iran," *Middle East Media Research Institute (MEMRI)*, No. 128 (March 28, 2003), http://memri.org/ein/opener_latest.cgi?ID=1A12803.

88. "U.S. Signals Gulf States that Attack on Iran is Possible this Year," *Geostrategy-Direct.com* (January 24, 2007).

89. "Iran's Links to 9/11, al Qaeda Come to Light," *Geostrategy-Direct.com* (June 28, 2004).

90. "Captured Documents Confirm Iran Backing for All Sides Against U.S. in Iraq," *Geostrategy-Direct.com* (January 17, 2007).

91. "U.S. Military Says It Captured 5 Iranians Linked to Group That Arms Insurgents in Iraq," *Washington Post* (January 14, 2007), p. A16.

92. Dafna Linzer, "Troops Authorized to Kill Iranian Operatives in Iraq," *Washington Post* (January 26, 2007), pp. A1, A16; Gethin Chamberlain, "Iran Arming Insurgents," *Washington Times* (February 12, 2007), pp. A1, A20; and Joshua Partlow, "Military Ties Iran to Arms in Iraq," *Washington Post* (February 12, 2007), pp. A1, A13.

93. "Lacking Support, Syria's Assad Imports 100,000 Shi'ites from Iran," *Geostrategy-Direct.com* (March 28, 2007).

94. Anahi Rama, "Ortega Gives Iranian Leader Tour of Slums," *Washington Times* (January 15, 2007), p. A13.

95. Andy Webb-Vidal, "Oiling the Axis," *Jane's Intelligence Review* (August 2007), pp. 32–35.

96. Andrew and Mitrokhin, *World Was Going Our Way*, pp. 1, 10.

97. "Iran Accelerates Efforts in America's Backyard," *Geostrategy-Direct.com* (July 7, 2007).

Chapter 5

1. Georgie Anne Geyer, "Resurgence of Leftists in Latin America," *Washington Times* (September 21, 2001), p. A25; Traci Cari, "Latin America's Leftists Redefine Political Labels," *Washington Times* (March 21, 2006), p. A14; and Georgie Anne Geyer, "Split Opens Hemisphere to World," *Washington Times* (November 7, 2006), p. A12.

2. Stephen Marks, "Montevideo Sao Paulo Forum," *Links*, 6 (January-April 1996), p. 7.

3. *Ibid.*, p. 8.

4. Communist Party of Cuba, "Contemporary Capitalism and the Debate Over the Alternatives," Ninth Meeting of the Sao Paulo Forum, trans. by Dick Nichols (Managua, Nicaragua: February 19–21, 2000) in *Links*, 16 (December 2000), p. 16.

5. Final Declaration of the Tenth Meeting of the Forum of Sao Paulo, "Forum of Sao Paulo: 'A Battle of Ideas for a Better World'" (Havana, Cuba: December 4–7, 2001) in *Links*, 21 (May-August 2002), pp. 108–11.

6. Phil Brennan, "Communism Thrives South of the Border," *NewsMax.com* (August 2003), pp. 62–63.

7. Constantine Menges, "Castro's Axis Dominates 223 Million," *NewsMax* (May 2004), p. 68.

8. Dana Rohrabacker, Benjamin Gilman, Dan Burton, Christopher Smith, Darrell Issa, Walter Jones, Wally Herger, and Jim Gibbons, plus five added signatures, Members of Congress, Letter to the Honorable George W. Bush (October 2, 2002).

9. Commentary by Francis Fukuyama, Johns Hopkins University; Anibal Romero, Simon Bolivar University in Caracas, Venezuela; and Julio Cirino, Director of International Relations with the Fundacio Pensa in Buenos Aires, Argentina, at a panel discussion on "Radical Populism in Latin America," Hudson Institute (November 6, 2007).

10. Seventy-seven developing countries established the Group of 77 (G-77) on June 15, 1964, at the end of the first session of the United Nations Conference on Trade and Development (UNCTAD) in Geneva. The G-77 provides a means for the developing world to articulate and promote its collective economic interests. See http://g77.org.

11. Fidel Castro, "Message to the September 1999 G77 Ministerial Meeting" as quoted by Peter Boyle, "The Politics of the New Movement for Global

Solidarity," *Links*, 17 (January–April 2001), pp. 6–7.

12. *Ibid.*, p. 7.

13. Fidel Castro, "Complete Text of President Castro's Speech at the Opening Session of the South Summit, April 12, 2000," http://zmag.org/CrisisCurEvts/Globalism/castrosouth.htm.

14. Fabiola Sanchez, "Castro Honored on 75th Birthday," *Washington Times* (August 12, 2001), p. A7.

15. "Venezuela Now Almost a Cuban Satellite," *NewsMax* (June 14, 2001).

16. Anthony Boadle, "Castro Warns of Attack on Chavez," *Washington Times* (February 13, 2005), p. A6.

17. Bill Gertz, "Hundreds of Cuban Agents taking Key Posts in Venezuela," *Geostrategy-Direct.com* (August 9, 2005).

18. "Raul Castro Reiterates Cuba's Support for China's Unity Quest with Taiwan," *Prens Latina* (July 13, 2001).

19. "Cuba Military Delegation Visits North Korea," *Geostragey-Direct.com* (July 17, 2001), and "China Steps Up Military Cooperation with Cuba," *Geostragey-Direct.com* (May 3, 2005).

20. "Castro Visits Iran, Seeks to Strengthen Ties," *USA Today* (May 8, 2001).

21. As quoted by John J. Miller, "In Castro's Service," *National Review* (November 5, 2001), p. 47.

22. J. Michael Waller, "Iran and Cuba Zap U.S. Satellites," *Insight* (September 1, 2003), pp. 34–37.

23. Scott Wilson, "Brazil Elects Lula in a Landslide," *Washington Post* (October 28, 2003), p. A13, and J. Michael Waller, "Beware Risks to a Democratic Future," *Insight* (January 21–February 3, 2003), pp. 27–28.

24. Constantine Menges, "Lula da Silva, Castro and China," *Washington Times* (December 10, 2002), p. A15, and Waller, "Beware risks to a Democratic Future," p. 29.

25. Alan Clendenning, "Lula da Silva Welcomes Leftists Chavez, Castro," *Washington Times* (January 3, 2003), p. A13.

26. "Brazil's Left Leader," *International Reports: Early Warning*, 20-9 (Washington, D.C.: Maldon Institute, May 31, 2002), p. 2.

27. "Crisis in Brazil," *International Reports: Early Warning*, 20-11 (Washington, D.C.: Maldon Institute, June 28, 2002), p. 10.

28. Faith Whittlesey, "Brazil's Gathering Clouds," *Washington Times* (October 1, 2002), p. A17.

29. Eduardo Gudynas, "The Paths of the South American Community of Nations, America's Program" (Silver City, N.M.: International Relations Center, April 21, 2005), http://americaspolicy.org/columns/gudynas/2005/0504sac.html, and Mary Turck, "South America Community of Nations," Americas.org (March 9, 2007), http://americas.org/item_17137.

30. "Brazil's Crime Wave" and "Land Invasion," *International Reports: Early*

Warning (Washington, D.C.: September 3, 2004, and February 4, 2005, respectively).

31. Monte Reel, "Cash Aid Program Bolsters Lula's Reelection Prospects," *Washington Post* (October 29, 2006), p. A14.

32. Patrick Hall, "U.S. Not Sure About Lula's Leanings," *Washington Times* (October 30, 2002), p. C9; Anthony Faiola, "Brazil's Leader Seeks to Ease U.S. Concerns About Policies," *Washington Post* (December 10, 2002), p. A18; and David R. Sands, "U.S. Concerns Lessen on New Brazil Leader," *Washington Times* (October 30, 2002), p. A13.

33. Vivian Sequere, "Lula Has Big Plan in 2nd Term," *Washington Times* (January 2, 2007), p. A13.

34. "Lula Uses Davos Podium in Plea for World's Poor," *Washington Times* (January 16, 2003), p. A16.

35. "The New Inter-Hemispheric Alliance," *Memorandum to File*, No. 2004-85 (Washington, D.C.: Maldon Institute, December 3, 2004).

36. Deroy Murdock, "Brazil Could Join the Axis of Evil," Hudson Institute (October 4, 2002), http://hudson.org/index.cfm?fuseaction=publication_details&id=1992.

37. Martin Parry, "Lula Courts Beijing During Official Visit," *Washington Times* (May 25, 2004), p. A12.

38. "China, Inc. and Latin America," *International Reports: Early Warning*, 22-3 (Washington, D.C.: Maldon Institute, March 4, 2005), p. 6.

39. Todd Benson, "Brazil Muslim Support in Tri-Border Area of S. America?," *Sun* (August 3, 2003); Stan Lehman, "Arab Roots Grow Deep in Brazil's Rich Melting Pot," *Washington Times* (July 12, 2005), p. A14; "U.S. Presses Brazil to Move Against Terrorists in 'Triple Frontier' Area," *Geostrategy-Direct.com* (November 20, 2001); "Suspected Terrorist From Egypt Arrested in Southern Brazil," *Geostrategy-Direct.com* (April 30, 2002); and "Brazil Investigates Report Hizbollah Met in Outlaw Region," *Geostrategy-Direct.com* (November 26, 2002).

40. "Leftist Brazil Plans Military Buildup," *Geostrategy-Direct.com* (September 19, 2007).

41. Arnaud de Borchgrave, "A New Castro with Big Money," *Washington Times* (August 25, 2005), p. A19.

42. Ian James, "Crowds Lining Up for Food Basics," *Washington Times* (November 22, 2007), p. A12.

43. Juan Forero, "Chavez, Assailed on Many Fronts, Is Riveted by 19th Century Idol," *Washington Times* (February 23, 2008), p. A10.

44. "Global-Venezuela," *International Reports: Early Warning*, 21-6 (Washington, D.C.: Maldon Institute, April 18, 2003), p. A12.

45. Alfonso Daniels, "Chavez Recruits Populist Army to Defeat Civic Woes," *Washington Times* (April 22, 2007), pp. A1, A5; and Juan Forero,

"Venezuela Lets Councils Bloom," *Washington Times* (May 17, 2007), pp. A10, A14.

46. Andy Wedd-Vidal, "Cuba's Political Future Lies in Venezuela's Hands," *Jane's Intelligence Review* (September 2006), pp. 30–31.

47. Scott Wilson, "General Strike Leader Arrested in Venezuela," *Washington Post* (February 21, 2003), p. A16.

48. Martin Arostegui, "Chavez Consolidates Control Over Military," *Washington Times* (August 6, 2007), p. A13.

49. "Venezuelan Strongman Chavez Seizes Control of Media," *NewsMax* (February 2005), p. 65.

50. Jim Meyers, " 'Second Fidel' Starts Latin Al-Jazeera," *NewsMax* (July 2005), p. 60.

51. As quoted Blanquita Cullem, "Chavez vs. Free Speech," *Washington Times* (June 12, 2007), p. A17.

52. Christian Oliver, "Thousands Say No to Chavez's Bid to Silence RCTV, " *Washington Times* (May 22, 2007), p. A12; Christopher Toothaker, "Protesters Call TV Closure Political," *Washington Times* (May 27, 2007), p. A5; "Chavez Channel Prompts Protests," *Washington Times* (May 29, 2007), pp. A1, A10; and Christian Oliver, "Chavez Targets News Channel," *Washington Times* (May 30, 2007), p. A13.

53. As quoted by Cullem, "Chavez vs. Free Speech," p. A17.

54. Christopher Toothaker, "Chavez Offers Plan to Revise Constitution," *Washington Times* (August 16, 2007), p. A11.

55. Juan Forero, "New Chapter Would Widen Chavez's Reach," *Washington Post* (October 31, 2007), pp. A12, A15; and "Crackdown in Venezuela Called a Ploy," *Washington Post* (November, 9, 2007), p. A17.

56. Juan Forero, "Chavez Chastened in Venezuelan Vote," *Washington Post* (December 4, 2007), pp. A1, A7; Martin Arostegui, "Chavez Vows to Turn a Defeat Into a Victory," *Washington Times* (December 4, 2007), pp. A1, A12; and "The Wind Goes Out of the Revolution," *Economist* (December 8, 2007), p. 30.

57. As quoted by "Chavez Slows to a Trot," *Economist* (January 12, 2008), p. 32.

58. *Ibid.*

59. Juan Forero, "Pulling the Plug on Anti-Chavez TV," *Washington Post* (January 18, 2007), p. A16, and Blanquita Cullum, "Hasta La Vista, Free Speech," *Weekly Standard* (March 5, 2007), pp. 18–19.

60. Georgia Anne Geyer, *Washington Times* (January 23, 2003), p. A17.

61. Barbara J. Fraser, "In Latin America, Church Still Influences State," *Arlington Catholic News* (February 8, 2007), p. 8.

62. Robert A. Sirico, "Liberation Theology," *Dow Jones Reprints* (December 31, 2007), http://online.wsj.com.

63. Samuel Gregg, "Chavez's Holy War," *Washington Times* (January 17, 2007), p. A14.

64. David Forgacs, ed., *The Antonio Gramsci Reader* (New York: New York University Press, 2000), p. 426.

65. Juan Forero, "Venezuela Preparing to Give Land to the Peasants," *New York Times* (October 15, 2001), p. A3.

66. Sharon Behn, "Seizure, Redistribution of Land in Venezuela Slammed," *Washington Times* (September 13, 2005), pp. A1, A19

67. Juan Forero, "Chavez Sets Plans for Nationalization," *Washington Post* (January 9, 2007), p. A7.

68. Ian James, "Chavez to Nationalize 'Strategic Sectors,' " *Washington Times* (January 9, 2007), pp. A1, A11, and Steve Mufson, "Victim of His Power Grab," *Washington Post* (January 18, 2007), pp. D1, D8.

69. Nicholas Kralev, "Chavez Hit for Meddling in Neighbor's Elections," *Washington Times* (June 6, 2006), p. A12, and Kelly Hearn, "S. America Nations Eye Alternative to IMF," *Washington Times* (July 14, 2006), p. A15.

70. Jackson Diehl, "Chavez's War of Words," *Washington Post* (August 7, 2006), p. A1; Paul Crespo, "Hugo Chavez's Diabolical Ways," *NewsMax* (December 2006), p. 4; Mansur Mirovalev, "Chavez Seeks Investment, Submarines from Russia," *Washington Times* (June 30, 2007), p. A9; Dave Eberhart, "Hugo Chavez Spends $4 Billion on Weapons," *NewsMax* (May 2007), pp. 50–51; and Martin Arostegui, "Chavez Consolidates Control Over Military," *Washington Times* (August 6, 2007), p. A13.

71. Irwin M. Selzer, "The Axis of Oil," *Weekly Standard* (February 7, 2005), pp. 25–28.

72. "Chavez Touts $3B China Trade Deal," *NewsMax* (February 2005), p. 68.

73. Bill Gertz, "U.S. Eyes Chavez Ties to China," *Washington Times* (August 25, 2006), pp. A1, A20.

74. Bill Gertz, "Venezuelan Defector Says Chavez Backed Taliban," *Geostrategy-Direct.com* (January 21, 2003).

75. Martin Arostegui, "Chavez Deploys Forces," *Washington Times* (March 3, 2008), pp. A1, A18; David R. Sands, "Ecuador Cuts Colombia Ties," *Washington Times* (March 4, 2008); and "The War Behind the Insults," *Economist* (March 8, 2008), p. 12.

76. Martin Arostegui, "Chavez Plans for Terrorist Regime," *Insight* (January 20, 2003), pp. 22–24.

77. Bill Gertz, *Geostrategy-Direct.com* (February 18, 2003).

78. "Bolivia's Putsch by Degrees," *International Reports: Early Warning*," 19-7 (Washington, D.C.: Maldon Institute, May 4, 2001), p. 9.

79. Adam Saytanides, *In These Times* (November 16, 2003).

80. Chris Smith, "Bolivia Teeters Under Populism," *Jane's Intelligence Review* (November 2004), pp. 32–35.

81. Adriana Barrera, "Presidential Victor Pans U.S. Policy," *Washington Times*

(December 30, 2005), p. A12.

82. Martin Arostegui, "Morales Invites Teacher Chavez," *Washington Times* (May 11, 2006), p. A15.

83. Helen Popper, "Bolivia to Get New Constitution," *Washington Times* (March 6, 2006), p. A13.

84. Fraser, "Church Still Influences State," p. 29.

85. Martin Arostegui, "Evo Morales: A New Security Command in Bolivia," *Washington Times* (January 31, 2006), p. A13.

86. Ban Keane, "Bolivia's Land Reform Off to Shaky Start," *Washington Times* (January 16, 2007), p. A12.

87. Martin Arostegui, "Stringent Restrictions on Press Proposed," *Washington Times* (February 6, 2006), p. A11.

88. Martin Arostegui, "ETA Activity in Bolivia Eyed," *Washington Times* (March 9, 2007), p. A15.

89. Martin Arostegui, "Leftist Leaders Unite After Bolivia's Energy Takeover," *Washington Times* (May 5, 2006), pp. A1, A12, and Juan Forero, "Step 1 in Bolivian Takeover: Audit of Foreign Companies," *New York Times* (May 4, 2006), p. A13.

90. Monte Reel, "Bolivian President Seizes Gas Industry," *Washington Post* (May 2, 2006), pp. A1, A6; and Dan Keane, "Bolivia, Firms Reach Deal Nationalizing Industry," *Washington Post* (October 30, 2006), p. A14.

91. Bill Gertz, "China Proposes Missile Replacement for Bolivia," *Washington Times* (February 27, 2006), p. A3.

92. Monte Reel, "Bolivia's Political Fissures Force Morales to Shift Course," *Washington Post* (January 22, 2007), p. A13.

93. Martin Arostegui, "Morales Demands 4 Supreme Court Justices Resign," *Washington Times* (May 25, 2007), p. A15.

94. Martin Arostegui, "Rivalries Split Indian Coalition," *Washington Times* (August 30, 2007), p. A11.

95. Martin Arostegui, "Bolivians Foil Morales," *Washington Times* (October 23, 2007), p. A17.

96. "The Judges Revolt," *International Reports: Early Warning* (Washington, D.C.: Maldon Institute, January 7, 2005), pp. 12–14; Monte Hayes, "Officials Remove President Gutierrez," *Washington Times* (April 21, 2005), p. A15; and Monte Reel, "Ecuadoran Congress Ousts President," *Washington Times* (April 21, 2005), pp. A14, A20.

97. Juan Forero, "Presidential Race in Ecuador Heads to Second Round," *Washington Post* (October 16, 2006), p. A15.

98. Juan Forero, "Ecuador's Leftist Front-Runner," *Washington Post* (October 15, 2006), p. A15; Monte Hayes, "Ecuador Election Adds Weight to Leftists Tilt," *Washington Times* (November 28, 2006), p. A12; and Fernando Bustamante, "Hostile House," *Jane's Intelligence Review* (January 2007), pp. 48–49.

99. "Ecuador's Hugo Chavez?," *Washington Post* (October 1, 2007), p. A19.

100. "Correa Promised Iranian Protection," *Washington Times* (January 16, 2007), p. A11.

101. Martin Arostegui, "Uruguay Caught Buying Iran Arms," *Washington Times* (October 12, 2007), p. A1, A11.

102. Radosh, *Commies*, pp. 172–96.

103. "State Dept. Kept Quiet About Sandinista Links to '93 World Trade Center Bombing," *Geostrategy-Direct.com* (December 4, 2001).

104. Gerald Brant, "Communists Return to Nicaragua," *NewsMax* (November 2003), pp. 56–59.

105. Tom Carter, "U.N.-Brokered Accord Avoids 'Coup' in Nicaragua," *Washington Times* (January 22, 2005), p. A7.

106. Hector Tobar and Alex Renderos, "After Long Hiatus, Ortega Returns to Office in Nicaragua," *Washington Post* (January 11, 2007), p. A21; Traci Cari, "Ortega Returns Pushing Peace, Good U.S. Links," *Washington Times* (November 14, 2006), p. A15; and Philip Sherwell, "Nicaragua's Ortega Favored to Win," *Washington Times* (October 17, 2005), p. A17.

107. Lindsay, "Left-Leaning Argentina Challenges U.S. Role," *Washington Times* (January 13, 2004), p. A12.

108. *Ibid.*, and Keyy Hearn, "Argentina Cuts Debt," *Washington Times* (March 15, 2005), p. A13.

109. Monte Reel and Michael A. Fletcher, "Anti-U.S. Protests Flare at Summit," *Washington Post* (November 5, 2005), pp. A1, A15.

110. "Marital Bliss," *Economist* (December 15, 2007), p. 43.

111. Bill Cormier, "Argentine First Lady Leads Exit Polls," *Washington Times* (October 29, 2007), pp. A1, A9.

112. Silene Ramirez, "Leftists Gather for First Female Leader's Swearing-In," *Washington Times* (March 12, 2006), p. A6.

113. Saul Landau, *The Pre-Emptive Empire: A Guide to Bush's Kingdom* (Sterling, Va.: Pluto Press, 2003), pp. 94–95.

Chapter 6

1. According to an Official Report to the U.S. House Committee on Un-American Activities, Rubin registered in New York City as a communist for the 1936 general election. S. Steven Powell, *Covert Cadre: Inside the Institute of Policy Studies* (Ottawa, Ill.: Green Hill Publishers, 1987), pp. 15, 16, 24, 391.

2. *Ibid.*, p. 16.

3. David Horowitz, as edited by Jamie Galzov, *Left Illusions: An Intellectual Odyssey* (Dallas: Spence, 2003), p. 339.

4. John Rees, "The Institute for Policy Studies: Transnational Intrigue and Revolutionary Terrorism," unpublished manuscript with permission to use as a source document (Washington, D.C.: Maldon Institute, circa 2000), p. 19.

5. *Ibid.*, p. 4.

6. "Samuel Rubin (1901–1978)," *TNI History*, Transnational Institute (http://tni.org/persons/rubin.htm). See also Carey McWilliams, "Second Thoughts," *Nation* (January 6–13, 1979), p. 7.

7. Powell, *Covert Cadre*, pp. 15, 391.

8. "Samuel Rubin on the Founding of the Transnational Institute," Closerie des Lilas, Paris (1972), TNI History, http://tni-org/archives/rubin/rubin72htm.

9. Ronald Radosh, Mary R. Habeck, and Grigory Sevostianov, *Spain Betrayed: The Soviet Union in the Spanish Civil War* (New Haven: Yale University Press, 2001), pp. xvii, 422–25.

10. Andrew and Mitrokhin, *Sword and the Shield*, pp. 74–75.

11. Stephane and others, *Black Book of Communism*, pp. 334–35.

12. *Ibid.*, pp. 340–49.

13. *Ibid.*, pp. 350–51.

14. John Train, "Invective From the Left," *Forbes* (August 3, 1981), p. 110.

15. Ambergris, a morbid secretion of the sperm whale intestine, can be found floating on the ocean or along the shoreline. When this opaque, ash-colored substance is heated, it becomes very fragrant and is used in perfumery.

16. James L. Tyson, *Target America: The Influence of Communist Propaganda on U.S. Media* (Chicago: Regnery Gateway, 1981), p. 40.

17. Harvey Klehr, John Earl Haynes, and Frederick Igorevich Firsov, *The Secret World of American Communism* (New Haven: Yale University Press, 1995), p. 27.

18. Soviet KGB officer Victor Taltz (1983 and 1984); Soviet Third secretary and KGB officer Valeriy Likarev who served as chief liaison between IPS and the Soviet Institute for Study of USA and Canada; Georgi Arbatov, head of the Soviet Institute and assistant to Mikhail Gorbachev (1985); Vladimir I. Strokin, a third secretary at the Soviet Embassy; Soviet U.N. diplomat Igor Mishchenko; a journalist for the Soviet Literary Gazette; and two unidentified members of the Eastern bloc at IPS (1984). See Powell, *Covert Cadre*, center section (photographs).

19. U.S., Federal Bureau of Investigation, Memo to Washington Field Office from Director, FBI; Subject: Institute for Policy Studies, Bureau File No. 100-447935 (August 6, 1968).

20. U.S., Federal Bureau of Investigation, Memo, Washington Field Office; Subject: Institute for Policy Studies, Bureau File No. 100-46784 (March 14, 1969).

21. U.S., Federal Bureau of Investigation, Washington Field Office; letter sent to the U.S. Attorney General and Director, FBI, Subject: Institute for Policy

Studies (July 22, 1969).

22. Powell, *Covert Cadre*, pp. 15–16. The House of Faberge, under the direction of Peter Carl Faberge, had served its imperial patrons Czars Alexander III (1882–94) and Nicholas II (1894–1917 with objects of great imaginative design and craftsmanship through the subtle use of contrasting materials, such as golds, enamels, silver, gemstones, ivory, and semi-precious stones. The most famous, of course, are the Faberge imperial eggs.

23. "Samuel Rubin Foundation," European Platform for Conflict Prevention and Transformation, http://euforic.org/euconflict/guides/orgs/fund/110.htm.

24. Tyson, *Target America*, pp. 40–41.

25. Carla Hall, "Perfume Philanthropist Samuel Rubin's Lifetime Work for the Poor," *Washington Post* (September 22, 1978). See TNI in the Media, http://tni-org/interviews/lm-int.htm.

26. Judy Kaplan and Linn Shapiro, eds., *Red Diapers: Growing Up in the Communist Left* (Chicago: University of Illinois Press, 1998), p. 3.

27. *Ibid.*, p. 10.

28. John Barron, *KGB Today: The Hidden Hand* (New York: Reader's Digest Press, 1983), p. 283; and Tyson, *Target America*, p. 58.

29. Lionel Chetwynd, "Semper Fi: Twenty-Five Years Later the Sacrifice and Faith of Our Vietnam POWs Is Mostly Forgotten. Shame On Us," *National Review* (February 23, 1998).

30. Michael Tremoglie, "Red Queen of 'Peace,'" *FrontPageMagazine.com* (December 11, 2002).

31. Joshua Muravchik, "The Think Tank of the Left," *New York Times* (April 26, 1981).

32. Robert Morris, *Self Destruct: Dismantling America's Internal Security* (New York: Arlington House, 1979), pp. 82–83; and Tyson, *Target America*, p. 116.

33. Barron, *KGB Today*, p. 283.

34. Powell, *Covert Cadre*, p. 295.

35. *Ibid.*, p. 296.

36. *Ibid.*, pp. 290–301.

37. *Ibid.*, p. 312.

38. *Ibid.*, p. 317.

39. *Ibid.*, pp. 320–22.

40. *Ibid.*, pp. 322–23.

41. Cora Weiss, "Lay Down Your Arms-a Peaceful World is Possible: The Challenge for Educators," 4th European Congress for Peace Education, speech June 30, 2003, http://ipb.org. Emphasis added.

42. Peter Weiss, Biography, TNI website, 1999, http://tni.org.

43. Both the National Lawyers Guild and the National Emergency Civil Liberties Committee were cited as Communist fronts by the Congress in the 1960s. See

Powell, *Covert Cadre*, p. 11.

44. Susan Braudy, *Family Circle: The Boudins and the Aristocracy of the Left* (New York: Knoph, 2003), pp. 71, 76.

45. Powell, *Covert Cadre*, p. 181.

46. At the time of the founding of IALANA, among those on the LCNP consultative council were Richard Barnet, Institute for Policy Studies; Goler T. Butcher, Howard University, who headed the Carter administration's Agency for International Development Africa program; Ramsey Clark, a CCR cooperating attorney and former U.S. Attorney General, as well as a member of IADL; Robert F. Drinan, S.J., Georgetown University, Jesuit priest and later a U.S. Congressman from Massachusetts and head of Americans for Democratic Action; Richard A. Falk, Princeton University, long active with the IADL and partner of Richard Barnet in a number of IADL-related projects such as the Lawyers Committee on Vietnam; Ann Fagan Ginger, Meikeljohn Civil Liberties Institute, veteran NLG activist and a leader of the IADL's Havana-based affiliate, the American Association of Jurists (AAJ); Sean MacBride, International Peace Bureau (Geneva) and winner of the Lenin Peace Prize and the Nobel Peace Prize; Saul Mendlovitz, Rutgers, World Policy Institute [formerly Institute for World Order]; Elliott L. Meyrowitz, NLG, New York; John B. Quigley, Jr., Ohio State, former NLG national vice president; IADL activist Marcus G. Raskin, IPS; and Edith Tiger, National Emergency Civil Liberties Committee (NECLC), a CPUSA front.

47. Braudy, *Family Circle*, pp. 73, 78–79; and Powell, *Covert Cadre,* p. 51.

48. John Earl Haynes and Harvey Klehr, *VENONA: Decoding Soviet Espionage in America* (New Haven: Yale University Press, 1999), p. 9.

49. Marcus Raskin came to Washington in 1959 as legislative assistant to radical Democrat U.S. House Representative Robert Kastenmeier. Richard Barnet served in the State Department as a Soviet specialist in the Arms Control and Disarmament Agency during the Kennedy Administration.

50. Richard J. Barnet, *The Economy of Death* (New York: Atheneum, 1970), pp. 57–128.

51. *Ibid.*, p. 131.

52. Institute for Policy Studies, "Winter 2001 Schedule of Classes" (Washington, D.C.: 2001).

53. Marcus G. Raskin, *Liberalism: The Genius of American Ideals* (New York: Rowman & Littlefield, 2004), pp. 1–3.

54. Gannon, *Biographical Dictionary of the Left,* p. 386.

55. John Train, "The Source," *Forbes* (November 24, 1980), p. 51.

56. Rees, "Institute for Policy Studies," p. 8.

57. *Ibid.*, p. 17.

58. Rael Jean Isaac, "The Institute for Policy Studies: Empire on the Left," *Midstream* (June/July 1980), p. 2.

59. Powell, *Covert Cadre*, p. 24.
60. Rees, "Institute for Policy Studies," p. 85.
61. Peter Watson, "Lost in a Swamp of Modernity (Ideas, Fundamentalism, and Cultural Contexts)," *New Statesman* (October 29, 2001).
62. Eqbal Ahmad, *Confronting Empire*, interviews with David Barsamian (Cambridge, Mass.: South End Press, 2000), pp. xi–xii, 24–25; Rael Jean Isaac, *America the Enemy: Profile of a Revolutionary Think Tank* (Washington, D.C.: Ethics and Public Policy Center, circa 1981); and *Middle East Report*, MERIP, Spring 2004, No. 230. See also Fred Halliday, "New World, But the Same Old Disorder," *The Observer* (March 10, 2002), http://tni.org/archives/halliday/disorder.htm.
63. Powell, *Covert Cadre*, pp. 11, 150.
64. Eqbal Ahmad, "An Interview with Lissette Lewin on the Foundation of the Transnational Institute," *NRC Handelsblad* (November 24, 1973), http://tni.org/history/ahmad/nrc73uk.htm.
65. *21st Century Levellers* (Maldon Institute), p. 40.
66. Susan George, "Acceptance Speech for the Doctorado Honoris Causa in Political Science and Sociology" at the Universidad Nacional de Educacion a Distancia, Madrid (April 25, 2007), http://tni.org/detail_page.phtml?&-&act_id=1675.
67. Transnationals Information Exchange, *Meeting the Corporate Challenge*, TIE Report 18/19 (Amsterdam, The Netherlands: circa 1984), p. 6.
68. Transnationals Information Exchange, "Press Release—European Workshop on Transnational Corporations" (May 19–21, 1978) and "International Trade Secretariats" (February–April 1981).
69. Julio de Santa Ana, World Council of Churches, letter to J. H. Scheavesande (March 11, 1982) (Loosdrecht, The Netherlands: Zozzaro Archive).
70. Julio de Santa Ana, World Council of Churches, letter to selected non-governmental organizations (August 15, 1982) (Loosdrecht, The Netherlands: Zozzaro Archive).
71. Dan Smith, Director, *The Transnational Institute: Report on Activities in 1991/1992* (Amsterdam, The Netherlands: November 1992).
72. Joel Rocamora, Fellow, Transnational Institute, letter to "Dear Friends" (October 8, 1992).
73. Susan George, "Stop! Another World Is Possible," *Nation* (February 18, 2002), pp. 11–13.
74. Powell, *Covert Cadre*, pp. 68–69, 150.
75. Jarol B. Manheim, *The Death of a Thousand Cuts: Corporate Campaigns and the Attack on the Corporation* (Mahwah, N.J.: Lawrence Erbaum Associates, 2001), pp. 173–74; and Erik Leaver and John Cavanagh, "Controlling Transnational Corporations," *Foreign Policy in Focus*, Interhemispheric Resource Center and the Institute for Policy Studies, 1–6 (November 1996).

76. Manheim, *Death of a Thousand Cuts,* pp. 176–77.
77. Joshua Karlinen, Corporate Executive Director, "Issue Library: Globalization 191," *CorpWatch* (December 10, 2001), extract from *The Corporate Planet: Ecology and Politics in the Age of Globalization* (Sierra Club Books, 1997), and "Corporate Globalization Fact Sheet," *CorpWatch* (March 22, 2001).
78. George McGovern, "Foreword," in Landau, *Pre-Emptive Empire,* p. viii.
79. Radosh, *Commies,* p. 78.
80. Horowitz, *Radical Son,* p. 201.
81. "Saul Landau," http://geocities.com/CapitolHill/Senate/1777/landau.htm.
82. Landau's relationship with Fidel Castro began in the summer of 1959 when he spent three months in Cuba where he met with communist officials and Castro himself. See Horowitz, *Radical Son,* p. 114.
83. Saul Landau's letter to Cuba's intelligence chief, Pablo Fernandez (September 13, 1976).
84. Tyson, *Target America,* p. 48. See also John Rees, "A K.G.B. Agent in Washington," *Review of the News* (April 27, 1977), pp. 31–42.
85. Powell, *Covert Cadre,* p. 244.
86. *Ibid.,* pp. 63–70.
87. Isaac and Isaac, *Coercive Utopians,* p. 266.
88. Powell, *Covert Cadre,* p. 258.

Chapter 7

1. Powell, *Covert Cadre,* pp. 359–60.
2. Boggs, *Gramsci's Marxism,* p. 119.
3. *Ibid.,* p. 122.
4. *Ibid.,* p. 60.
5. *Ibid.,* pp. 17, 30, 33, 39–40, 71.
6. As quoted in the "Introduction" to Antonio Gramsci, *The Modern Prince and Other Writings* (New York: International Publishers, 1957), p. 13.
7. Carl Marzani, trans., *The Open Marxism of Antonio Gramsci* (New York: Cameron Associates, 1957), pp. 19–20.
8. Boggs, *Gramsci's Marxism,* p. 126.
9. *Ibid.,* p. 17.
10. Culture and Media Institute, *National Cultural Values Survey—America: A Nation in Moral and Spiritual Confusion,* values survey conducted December 4–8, 2006 (Alexandria, Va.: Media Research Center, 2007), p. 2.
11. *Ibid.,* pp. 13–15, 19.
12. Boggs, *Gramsci's Marxism,* pp. 33, 74–76.
13. *Ibid.,* pp. 77–78.
14. Horowitz, *Radical Son,* p. 405.

15. Phil Brennan, "Dangerous Minds: How Activists Mislead Students," *NewsMax* (April 2006), p. 70.

16. Wes Vernon, "Hard Left Dominates Campuses: Time to Fight Back?," *NewsMax.com* (September 5, 2002).

17. *Ibid.*

18. As quoted in "Campus 'Corruption,'" *Washington Times* (March 17, 2006), p. A2.

19. Thomas Sowell, "Sheep in Training," *Washington Times* (March 12, 2000), p. B3.

20. Bruce, *New Thought Police,* pp. xv–xvi.

21. Courtois and others, *Black Book of Communism.*

22. Haynes and Klehr, *In Denial*, pp. 1–2. See also David Evanier, "Invincible Ignorance," *Weekly Standard* (November 17, 2003), p. 38.

23. *Ibid.*, p. 8. See also Haynes and Klehr, *VENONA: Decoding Soviet Espionage.*

24. *Ibid.*, pp. 13, 17–18, 27–28, 59, 68.

25. American Communists and their Leftist supporters used the congressional committee investigating their actions as propaganda. They re-ordered the words of the "House Committee on Un-American Activities" to the "House Un-American Activities Committee" (HUAC), which over time, with constant reinforcing propaganda, became the common phrase of the day.

26. Haynes and Klehr, *In Denial*, pp. 89, 193, 205.

27. *Ibid.*, pp. 8–9.

28. As quoted by Jennifer Harper, "Diminished Values Tied to Media Diet," *Washington Times* (June 7, 2007), p. A4.

29. Boggs, *Gramsci's Marxism*, p. 33.

30. Harper, *"Diminished Values,"* p. A4.

31. *Ibid.*

32. Brian Fitzpatrick, *The Media Assault on American Values: The Conflict Between the Media, Personal Responsibility and Respect for Religion* (Alexandria, Va.: Culture and Media Institute, 2007), p. 6.

33. Kevin Sullivan, "Blair Likens News Media to 'Feral Beast,'" *Washington Post* (June 13, 2007), p. A17.

34. Steve Brill as quoted by Bernard Goldberg, *Bias: A CBS Insider Exposes How the Media Distort the News* (Washington, D.C.: Regnery, 2002), p. v.

35 Goldberg, *Bias*, p.1.

36. Lowell Ponte, "The ABC's of Media Bias," *FrontPageMagazine.com* (October 14, 2004).

37. L. Brent Bozell III, *Weapons of Mass Distortion* (New York: Three Rivers Press, 2004), pp. 4, 9–10, 17.

38. *Ibid.*, p. 103.

39. *Ibid.*, p. 107.

40. *Ibid.*, pp. 191, 200.

41. William McGowan, *Coloring the News: How Political Correctness Has Corrupted American Journalism* (San Francisco, Calif.: Encounter Books, 2002), pp. 31, 34.

42. *Ibid.*, p. 243.

43. Bob Kohn, *Journalistic Fraud: How 'The New York Times' Distorts the News and Why It Can No Longer Be Trusted* (Nashville: WND Books, 2003), p. 4.

44. Kohn, *New York Times*, pp. 45–94.

45. Mallard Fillmore, as drawn and quoted by Bruce Tinsley, *Washington Times* (October 18, 2007), p. A2.

46. Tyson, *Target America*, p. 35.

47. Powell, *Covert Cadre*, p. 105.

48. *Ibid.*, pp. 105–06.

49. Michael P. Tremoglie, *Philadelphia Inquirer* (February 8, 2007), http://thebulletin .us/site/news.cfm?newsid=17827093&BRD-2737&461&dept_id=580169 &rfi=6.

50. Christopher Andrew and Oleg Gordievsky, *KGB: The Inside Story of its Foreign Operations from Lenin to Gorbachev* (New York: HarperCollins, 1990), p. 581.

51. *Ibid.*, pp. 599–600.

52. Powell, *Covert Cadre*, p. 305.

53. William Arkin, http://DiscoverTheNetwork.org; Powell, *Covert Cadre*, pp. 24, 90, 98, 269, 305, 343, and 362; and Rees, "Institute for Policy Studies," pp. 52, 78.

54. Craig Whitlock, "From CIA Jails, Inmates Fade Into Obscurity," *Washington Post* (October 27, 2007), p. A1.

55. David Horowitz and Jacob Laskin, "The Worst School in America," *FrontPageMagazine.com* (September 9, 2007).

56. For profile of Angela Davis see http://DiscoverTheNetwork.org.

57. Jennifer Verner, "Post Reporter Dana Priest's Troubling Connections," *Accuracy in Media*, Special Report (May 9, 2006), http://aim.org/special_report_print/4557_0_8_0.

58. Powell, *Covert Cadre*, p. 66.

59. Isaac and Isaac, *Coercive Utopians*, p. 267, and an editorial in the *Covert Action Information Bulletin* as cited by Powell, *Covert Cadre*, p. 69.

60. Lieutenant General Ricardo Sanchez, as quoted by Jack Kelly, "What Gen. Sanchez Also Said," *Washington Times* (October 18, 2007), p. A16.

61. Powell, *Covert Cadre*, pp. 144–45.

62. Horowitz, *Radical Son*, p. 321.

63. Victor Navasky is publisher, editorial director, and co-owner of *The Nation.*, He is the principal after-the-fact defender of Alger Hiss and the Rosenberg spies, and he wrote *Naming Names,* a left-wing review of the anti-Communist blacklist era. Navasky's views on journalism, which are reflected in *The*

Nation, are colored by his Left-wing politics and his antipathy against corporate ownership of media outlets. "Navasky and other long-time apologists for Communism, have never apologized for enabling an ideology of class hatred that in the last century killed 100 million innocent people." On the other hand, how could one really apologize for the deaths of so many people when their only sin was living during a time when those like Navasky held but an "idea" as supreme? According to Navasky, copies of *The Nation* are distributed on 160 college campuses. Urging students to subscribe, and the magazine sponsors speakers and debates on campuses, plus "Radio Nation" broadcasts on forty college radio stations. Source: http://DiscoverTheNetwork.org (September 28, 2007).

64. These themes were expressed in subscription offers from *The Nation* in 2003 and 2004 received by the writer.
65. *The Nation* (May 7, May 14, and June 11, 2007) issues.
66. Al Franken, "CNN Rushes Rush," *Nation* (September 3, 2001), p. 51.
67. See the *Nation* (August 6, 2001), p. 46; (December 24, 2001), p. 42; and (January 28, 2002), p. 32.
68. Matthew Rothschild, "12 Reasons to Subscribe to the *Progressive,*" subscription flyer, n.d., circa 2003.
69. Quoted in "Dear Subscriber" letters from Matthew Rothschild, editor, *The Progressive,* n.d., circa 2003.
70. Kirk Nielsen, "The Army Goes on Spring Break," *Progressive* (June 2007), p. 25.
71. Powell, *Covert Cadre,* p. 148.
72. *Ibid.,* p. 149.
73. Norman Soloman, "Cracking the Media Walls," *In These Times* (October 22, 2003).
74. Powell, *Covert Cadre,* pp. 147–48.
75. See MotherJones.com (July 27, 2001; March 4, 2002; January/February 2002; July 14, 2003; and July/August 2007).
76. *People's Weekly World,* 18–50 (May 29–June 4, 2004).
77. Powell, *Covert Cadre,* pp. 126–27.
78. John Cavanagh, "Dear Friend of the Institute," Institute for Policy Studies (November 2004).
79. Richard Rahn, "Weapons of Mass Disinformation," *Washington Times* (March 21, 2005), p. A15.
80. As quoted in Katrina vanden Heuvel and Robert L. Borosage, *Taking Back America and Taking Down the Radical Right* (New York: Nation Books, 2004), pp. xi–xii.
81. Boggs, *Gramsci's Marxism,* pp. 32–35.
82. *Ibid.,* p. 26.
83 Newt Gingrich, "FoxNews *Sunday,*" *FoxNews* (July 29, 2007).

84. Gar Alperovitz, "Taking the Offensive on Wealth," *Nation* (February 21, 2005).

85. Lance Selfa, "U.S. Politics Shifts Leftward," *International Socialist Review*, 53 (May–June 2007).

86. Powell, *Covert Cadre*, pp. 353, 359.

87. Jennifer Yachin, "Progressives Boast of New Clout," *Roll Call* (May 21, 2007).

88. "Rocking House," *Nation* (February 6, 2006), http://thenation.com.

89. Martin, *Keys of This Blood*, pp. 249–50.

90. Ethelbert Miller and John Cavanagh, "Dear IPS Friends," *Ideas Into Action for Justice and the Environment*, Institute for Policy Studies, 2004 Annual Report.

91. Powell, *Covert Cadre*, pp. 56, 136.

92. *Ibid.*, p. 353.

Chapter 8

1. As quoted by Herbert Romerstein, *Heroic Victims: Stalin's Foreign Legion in the Spanish Civil War* (Washington, D.C.: Council for the Defense of Freedom, 1994), p. 91.

2. Institute for Policy Studies, *"Ideas Into Action,"* p. 3.

3. John Feffer, principal author, *Just Security: An Alternative Foreign Policy Framework* (Washington, D.C.: Foreign Policy in Focus, 2007), p. 5.

4. Powell, *Covert Cadre*, p. 18.

5. Institute for Policy Studies, *Ideas Into Action*, p. 7.

6. Rees, "Institute for Policy Studies," pp. 17–18.

7. The environment or "environmental justice" is a Left-wing code word for political activism against transnational corporations and is used to encourage radical approaches to programs for economic redistribution. Environmental justice movements also combat asymmetrical power relations in such areas as race, class, culture, and gender inequalities. See "Environmental Justice," a summary of course CMMU 110 at the University of California (Santa Cruz) in David Horowitz and Jacob Laskin, "The Worst School in America" (September 7, 2007), http://FrontPageMagazine.com.

8. Institute for Policy Studies, *Ideas Into Action*, p. 4.

9. Powell, *Covert Cadre*, p. 10.

10. Institute for Policy Studies, "Overview" (2007), http://ips-dc.org/overview.htm.

11. Boggs, *Gramsci's Marxism*, pp. 76, 77.

12. Powell, *Covert Cadre*, p. 10.

13. Boggs, *Gramsci's Marxism*, p. 108.

14. John Barron, *Operation Solo: The FBI Man in the Kremlin* (Washington, D.C.: Regnery, 1996).

15. John Bactell, "The Movements Against War and Capitalist Globalization," Communist Party USA (July 17, 2003), http://cpusa.org/article/articlesview/568/1/3.
16. Sam Webb, National Chair, CPUSA, *The Nature, Role, and Work of the Communist Party* (New York: circa 2007), pp. 7, 11.
17. Angela Davis, http://discoverthenetworks.org/printindividuaProfile.asp?indid=1303.
18. Harry Targ, http://discoverthenetworks.org/printindividuaProfile.asp?indid=2243.
19. Leslie Cagan, http://discoverthenetworks.org/printindividuaProfile.asp?indid=629.
20. Workers World Party, "Party Overview" and "Official Platform Statement," http://workersworld.org.
21. Workers World Party, "About Workers World," http://workers.org/wwp.php.
22. World Workers Party, http://discoverthenetworks.org/printindividuaProfile.asp?grpid=6603.
23. As quoted by Derrick Johnson, interviewer, "Neighborhood Bully: Ramsey Clark on American Militarism," *Sun Magazine* (November 2000), http://thesunmagazine.org/bully.html.
24. Manny Goldstein, "The Mysterious Ramsey Clark: Stalinist Dupe or Ruling-Class Spook?," *The Shadow* (underground newspaper) (undated, circa 2000), http://shadow.autono.net/sin001/clark.htm.
25. Ramsey Clark, "Why I'm Willing to Defend Hussein," *Los Angeles Times* (January 24, 2005).
26. Advertisement, "Dangerous Times Demand Courageous Voices. Bob Avakian is Such a Voice," *Nation* (June 25, 2007).
27. H. Bruce Franklin, http://discoverthenetworks.org/printindividuaProfile.asp?indid=2207.
28. Revolutionary Communist Party, http://discoverthenetworks.org/printindividuaProfile.asp?grpid=6197.
29. Andrew Hammer, "Towards a Truly Global Anti-Capitalism" (undated), http://dsausa.org/news/al6report.html. See also "The Organization" (http://dsa.org/text/about/org.html) and "Where We Stand: The Political Perspective of DSA" (http://dsausaorg/text/about/dsapp.2.html).
30. "Socialists in Congress" (August 31, 2001), http://restoringAmerica.org/documents/socialists_in_congress.html, and Chuck Morse, "How Red is the Progressive Caucus?," (2002), http://chuckmorse.com/how_red_are_progressives.html.
31. Barbara Ehrenreich, http://discoverthenetworks.org/printindividuaProfile.asp?indid=1058.
32. As quoted by Powell, *Covert Cadre*, pp. 85–86.
33. John Barron, *Operation Solo: The FBI Man in the Kremlin* (Washington,

D.C.: Regnery, 1996). pp. xiv–xv.

34. *Ibid.*, p. 55.
35. *Ibid.*, p. xxi.
36. Feffer, *Just Security*, p. 5.
37. *Ibid.*, p. 67.
38. Powell, *Covert Cadre*, p. 53.
39. *Ibid.*, p. 57.
40. Powell, *Covert Cadre*, p. 57, and Robert L. Borosage and John Marks, eds., *The CIA File* (New York: Grossman, 1976), p. 216
41. *Ibid.*
42. *Ibid.*, pp. 59–62.
43. Tyson, *Target America,* p. 51.
44. Center for National Security Studies, "Mission and History," http://cnss.org.
45. Rees, "The Institute for Policy Studies," p. 76.
46. Tyson, *Target America,* pp. 50–53, 206.
47. Powell, *Covert Cadre*, p. 216.
48. New FN: Dateline D.C., "Barack's Advisors," *Pittsburgh Tribune-Review* (March 2, 2008).
49. Rees, "Institute for Policy Studies," pp. 43, 78, 137.
50. Tyson, *Target America*, p. 238.
51. Powell, *Covert Cadre*, p. 73.
52. David Horowitz and Richard Poe, *The Shadow Party: How George Soros, Hillary Clinton, and the Sixties Radicals Seized Control of the Democratic Party* (Nashville, Tenn.: Nelson Current, 2006), pp. 22–23.
53. Powell, *Covert Cadre*, pp. 269–70.
54. J. R. Dunn, "The Generals and CDI," *American Thinker* (April 26, 2006).
55. "Generals for Peace and Disarmament," brochure (Lttervoort, the Netherlands: n.d.).
56. Isaac and Isaac, *Coercive Utopians*, p. 223.
57. Powell, *Covert Cadre*, p. 236.
58. *Ibid.*, p. 48n.
59. "The National Security Archive," http://gwu-edu/~narchiv/nsa/archive/support .htm.
60. Susan Huck, *Legal Terrorism* (New World Publishing, 1989), p. 62.
61. Shirley Christian, *Nicaragua: Revolution in the Family* (New York: Random House, 1985), pp. 189–91.
62. Tim Robbins, HBO's "Real Time" with Bill Maher, quoted from the *Weekly Standard* (November 10, 2007).
63. Bruce Bawer, "The Peace Racket," *Los Angeles Times* (September 2, 2007), as reported in the *Washington Times* (September 11, 2007), p. A2.
64. Marcus G. Raskin, *The Politics of National Security* (New Brunswick, N.J.:

Transaction Books, 1979), p. 32.

65. Miller and Cavanagh, "Dear IPS Friends.

66. As quoted in "War Resisters League," http://discoverthenetworks.org. See also Maldon Institute, *Take Back America*, p. 26.

67. American Friends Service Committee, http://discoverthenetworks.org.

68. As quoted in Women's International League for Peace and Freedom, http://discoverthenetworks.org.

69. Maldon Institute, *Take Back America Conference*, p. 21.

70. Fellowship for Reconciliation, *Vision and Mission Statements* (2004), http://forusa.org/vismis.html, and *History and Supporters* (2007), http://forusa.org/about/history.html.

71. Maldon Institute, *Vietnam Veterans Against the War* (Washington, D.C.: April 28, 2004), p. 4.

72. John F. Kerry, *Vietnam Veterans Against the War Statement*, Senate Committee of Foreign Relations (April 23, 1971), http://lists.village.virginia.edu/sixties/HTM_docs/Resources/Primary/Manifestos/VVAW.

73. "Kerry Photo Shocker: Candidate Teamed Up With 'Hanoi' Jane Fonda," *NewsMax.com* (February 9, 2004), http://newsmax.com/archives/ic/2004/2/9/134218.s.html.

74. "Iraq Veterans Against the War," http://discoverthenetworks.org.

75. Feffer. *Just Security*, pp. 41, 43.

76. Klehr, *Far Left of Center*, p. 163.

77. As quoted by Herbert Romerstein, "The Ultra Left's Secret Agenda," *Washington Times* (November 11, 2001).

78. Rachel Zabarkes Friedman, "Lawyers of Jihad," *National Review* (August 13, 2004), pp. 29–31.

79. Powell, *Covert Cadre*, pp. 11, 17.

80. Manheim, *Death of a Thousand Cuts*, p. 105.

81. Buhle, Buhle, and Georgkas, eds., *Encyclopedia of the American Left*, pp. 532–33.

82. Powell, *Covert Cadre*, p. 331.

83. "About CCR" (2004), http://ccr.ny.org, and "Center for Constitutional Rights (CCR)," http://discoverthenetworks.org.

84. Center for Constitutional Rights, "Legal Programs," http://ccr.ny.org (2004). See also Tyson, *Target America*, p. 38.

85. *Ibid.*

86. "Assata Shakur," *AfroCubaWeb* (2004), http://afrocubaweb.com/assata.htm.

87. Michael Powell and Michelle Garcia, "Sheik's U.S. Lawyer Convicted of Aiding Terrorist Activity," *Washington Post* (February 11, 2005), pp. A1, A10; Gail Appleson, "Lawyer Accused of Plotting with Sheik," *Washington Post* (December 30, 2004), p. A2; and "Center for Constitutional Rights (CCR)," http://discoverthenetworks.org.

88. As quoted by Matthew Vadum, "The Terrorists' Legal Team; Case by Case, the Center for Constitutional Rights," *Capital Research Center* (September 2006), p. A6.

89. John Perazzo, "CCR: Fifth Column Law Factory," *FrontPageMagazine.com* (July 31, 2002).

90. *Ibid.*

91. Ralph de Toledano, "What the ACLU Doesn't Want You to Know," *Insight* (July 1–8, 2002), and Pat Boone, "ACLU Mullahs," *Washington Times* (September 4, 2006), p. A2.

92. "The ACLU: Who We Are" and "What We Do" (September 2004), http:// aclu.org.

93. Nadine Stroessen, President, ACLU, "Invitation to the Writer to Join the ACLU" (2003), and Lonnae O'Neal Parker, "Code Orange for Liberty," *Washington Post* (June 12, 2003), pp. C1, C8.

94. Bill O'Reilly, "Terror Tactics of the ACLU," *NewsMax* (April 2005), p. 38, and "Real ID," a flyer compiled by the ACLU Washington Legislative Office (2007).

95. Amos Oz, "Rights on the Line," *Nation"* (April 22, 2002), pp. 4–5.

96. Wayne Parry, "ACLU to Provide Free Legal Help for Muslims Facing Questioning," *Newsday.com* (December 14, 2001).

97. Robert Carlson and Peter Ferrara, "ACLU Joins the Security Fray," *Washington Times* (January 2, 2002), p. 11, and Guy Taylor, "ACLU Sues Patriot Act, Says FBI Has Too Much Power," *Washington Post* (July 31, 2003), p. A6.

98. Frank J. Murray, "High Court Rejects Challenge to Spy Laws," *Washington Times* (March 25, 2003), p. A4; Victoria Toensing, "Constitutional Surveillance," *Weekly Standard* (March 6/13, 2006), pp. 19–20; and Andrew C. McCarthy, "The ACLU Loses in Court," *Weekly Standard* (July 23, 2007), pp. 15–18.

99. Nat Hentoff, " 'Hype, Hysteria and the Patriot Act,' " *Washington Times* (September 15, 2003), p. A21.

100. Michelle Malkin, "Leftist War on the FBI," *Washington Times* (August 24, 2004), p. A14.

101. Bill O'Reilly, "Is the ACLU Bin Laden's Best Ally?," *FoxNews Channel* (August 5, 2005), http://foxnews.com.

102. As quoted by William H. McIlhany, "Betrayal at the Top: The Record of the American Civil Liberties Union," (August 2004, date downloaded), http:// members.tripod.com/~BioLeft/aclu.htm.

103. Isaac and Isaac, *Coercive Utopians*, p. 239.

104. The National Conference of Black Lawyers is an association of lawyers, judges, legal workers, law students, and legal activists. A bar association, its program is of concern to the broader Black community, http://ncbl.org.

105. Isaac and Isaac, *Coercive Utopians*, pp. 25, 239.

Chapter 9

1. As quoted by Michael Otten and Dan Walters, " How 1960s Radicals Joined the System in Their Efforts to Give It a Facelift," *Sacramento Union* (May 2, 1982).
2. Powell, *Covert Cadre*, pp. 359–60.
3. Boggs, *Gramsci's Marxism*, p. 125. Professor Boggs, Antioch University at Los Angeles and National University, was listed in the IPS Speakers Bureau for 2003 under the rubric of "Military, National Security, & Intelligence." Among his specialized expertise indicated were militarism and culture and Hollywood and American culture.
3. "A small but highly active band of college students calling themselves Students for a Democratic Society are doing everything they can to dispense with both democracy and society," Eugene H. Methvin wrote in an October 1968 *Reader's Digest* article. The SDS may not have started out as a gang of far Left radicals but in the end, Mr. Methvin explains, they were hard core revolutionaries dedicated to tearing down American liberal democracy and society. Indeed, ". . . the SDSers marched to the red flag of communist revolution and black flag of anarchy. . . ." Mr. Methvin wrote about the reality of SDS in 1968: "Their [the SDSers] ultimate goal is nothing less than destruction of society itself." The communist "flavor" inside SDS became quite apparent when Barack Obama's friend Bernardine Dohrn, at age 26, told the 1968 SDS convention in East Lansing, Michigan, that "I consider myself a revolutionary communist." At that the audience of 500 rose in cheers." See Eugene H. Methvin, "SDS: Engineers of Campus Chaos," *Reader's Digest* (October 1968), pp. 103–08. After years of violence and mayhem, the SDS members "Marxized" themselves before they faded into mainstream America. Many of today's SDSers have continued their mission of destroying American democracy by serving as professional revolutionaries embracing Antonio Gramsci's formula for cultural revolution. One notable SDSer is Wade Rathke, founder of ACORN, Barack Obama's school house for community organizing. Another is Andy Stern, president of the Service Employees International Union; other SDSers are in key positions supporting the Institute for Policy Studies "solar system of organizations."
4. *Ibid.*, p. 53.
5. *Ibid.*, p. 39. See also Alberto Luzarraga, "Gramsci and the U.S. Body Politic—Who is Antonio Gramsci? You'd Better Learn!!!," *FreeRepublic.com* (December 29, 2000).
6. *Ibid.*, p. 17.
7. *Ibid*, p. 16.
8. Martin, *Keys of This Blood*, pp. 377–78.
9. Bogg's, *Gramsci's Marxism*, p. 134n.

10. Powell, *Covert Cadre*, pp. 277–78.
11. "About World Peacemakers," *World Peacemakers: Gospel for a New Millennium*, http://worldpeacemakers.org.
12. World Council of Churches, *What is the World Council of Churches?* and *Towards a Common Understanding and Vision of the World Council of Churches* (2004), http://wcc-coe.org/wcc/who/index-e.html. See also letter to Etienne de Jonghe, General Secretary of Pax Christi International, from Konrad Raiser, General Secretary of the World Council of Churches, dated February 9, 1994, entitled "Conversations About Ways to Resolve the Conflict in Former Yugoslavia."
13. Iain Colquhoun, "Who Is Behind the Fatima 'Multi-Faith Plan?," *Fatima Crusader* 76 (Spring 2004).
14. Cora Weiss as quoted by S. Steven Powell, *Covert Cadre*, pp. 303–04.
15. Powell, *Covert Cadre*, p. 178.
16. *Ibid.*, p. 290.
17. National Council of Churches, *NCC At a Glance: Who Belongs. How It Works and What It Does* (August 2004), http://ncccusa.org, and Powell, *Covert Cadre*, p. 290.
18. Isaac and Isaac, *Coercive Utopians*, p. 25.
19. *Ibid.*
20. Horowitz, *Radical Son*, p. 194; Manheim, *Death of a Thousand Cuts*, p. 6; and Powell, *Covert Cadre*, pp. 152, 173, 176, 229–30.
21. J. Bryan Hehir, "Papal Foreign Policy," *Foreign Policy* (Spring 1990) as quoted by Scott Appleby, "Pope John Paul II," *Foreign Policy* (Summer 2000), p. 14.
22. "Gorbachev Signed JPII Death Warrant," *Wprost* (April 27, 2008), announcing the book release of John O. Kohler, *Chodzi o Papieza. Szpiedzy w watykanie* (*About the Pope: Spies in the Vatican*), http://polskieradio.pl/the news/news.?ID=81176.
23. Pax Christi International, "About Us" and "Pax Christi's Member Organizations Worldwide" (2005), http://paxchristi.net.
24. End the Arms Race (Canada), "The World Trade Organization and War: Making the Connection," *Catholic Peace Voice*, Pax Christi USA (newspaper), 25-1 (Winter 2000), p. 9.
25. "Michael Lerner," http://discoverthenetworks.org.
26. Horowitz, *Radical Son*, p. 176.
27. "Michael Lerner," http://discoverthenetworks.org.
28. "Sojourners," http://discoverthenetworks.org.
29. As quoted by Powell, *Covert Cadre*, pp. 281–85.
30. "Sojourners," http://discoverthenetworks.org
31. Boggs, *Gramsci's Marxism*, pp. 20–21.
32. *Ibid.*, p. 123.

33. David Walls, *The Activist's Almanac* (New York: Fireside, 1993), p. 15.

34. Peter B. Levy, *The New Left and Labor in the 1960s* (Champagne, Ill.: University of Illinois Press, 1994), p. 154.

35. "The Port Huron Statement of the Students for a Democratic Society," courtesy of the office of Tom Hayden, http://coursea.matrix.msu.edu/ ~hst306/documents/huron.html.

36. William Greider, "Rolling Back the Twentieth Century," *Taking Back America*, Katrina vanden Heuvel and Robert L. Borosage, eds. (New York: Nation Books, 2004), p. 10.

37. As quoted in "John Sweeney," http://discoverthenetworks.org.

38. Linda Chavez and Daniel Gray, *Betrayal: How Union Bosses Shake Down Their Members and Corrupt American Politics* (New York: Crown Forum, 2004), p. 21.

39. "Linda Chavez-Thompson," http://discoverthenetworks.org.

40. "Midwest Academy (MA)," http://discoverthenetworks.org.

41. "Service Employees International Union (SEIU)," http://discoverthenetworks.org.

42. Bob Herbert, "Anxious About Tomorrow," *New York Times* (September 1, 2007).

43. William R. Hawkins, "SEIU's Hostile Leftist Takeover," *FrontPageMagazine .com* (December 24, 2004).

44. William R. Hawkins, "The Radical Power Behind the Democrats," *FrontPageMagazine.com* (August 5, 2004).

45. Chavez and Gray, *Betrayal*, p. 92.

46. Powell, *Covert Cadre*, pp. 14, 149, 358.

47. Chavez and Gray, *Betrayal*, p. 6.

48. As quoted, *Ibid.*

49. Powell, *Covert Cadre*, p. 358.

50. Mark W. Henrickson, "The Union Tomorrow," *FrontPageMagazine.com* (June 28, 2007).

51. Manheim, *Death of a Thousand Cuts*, p. 129.

52. George Archibald, "Teacher's Union Call for Defeat of Bush," *Washington Times* (July 4, 2004), pp. A1, A7.

53. "Who We Are" and "A Vision that Endures, http://aft.org. See also Jay Matthews, "Teachers Union President to Retire," *Washington Post* (July 14, 2004), p. A17.

54. Chavez and Gray, *Betrayal*, p. 110.

55. As quoted, *Ibid.*, pp. 117–23.

56. Chavez and Gray, *Betrayal*, p. 119.

57. Boggs, *Gramsci's Marxism*, p. 35.

58. Bernie Horn, ed., *Progressive Agenda for the States 2008: Leadership for America* (Washington, D.C.: Center for Policy Alternatives, December 2007), p. iv.

59. Rees, "Institute for Policy Studies," p. 55.

60. Boggs, *Gramsci's Marxism*, pp. 108, 110.

61. Buhle, Buhle, and Georgakas, eds., *Encyclopedia of the American Left*, pp. 18–19.

62. Hillary D. Rodham, "'There Is Only the Fight . . .' An Analysis of the Alinsky Model," a thesis submitted to partial fulfillment of the requirements for the Bachelor of Arts degree under the Special Honors Program, Wellesley College (Wellesley, Mass.: 1968), p. 55. Available at Gopublius.com.

63. Saul Alinsky, a conversation with Marion K. Sanders, "The Professional Radical, 1970," *Harper's Magazine* (January 1970). See also Wm. F. Buckley Jr., "Is There an Alinsky in Your Future?," *National Review* 18–44 (November 1, 1966), and Saul D. Alinsky, *Reveille for Radicals*, with a 1969 introduction and afterword (New York: Vintage Books, 1969).

64. William T. Poole, *The New Left in Government: From Protest to Policy-Making*, Heritage Institutional Analysis No. 9 (Washington, D.C.: Heritage Foundation, November 1978), p. 13.

65. Carnoy and Shearer, *Economic Democracy*, pp. 362–63.

66. John C. Boland, "Nader Crusade—The Anti-Business Lobby Is Alive and Kicking," *Barron's* (October 12, 1981), p. 20; as quoted and cited by Rees, "Institute for Policy Studies, p. 133. See also Isaac and Isaac, *Coercive Utopians*, p. 131.

67. Gar Alperovitz and Jeff Faux, *Rebuilding America* (New York: Pantheon, 1984), p. ix.

68. *Ibid.*, back cover and p. 271.

69. Powell, *Covert Cadre*, p. 26.

70. In 1978, Gar Alperowitz, one of the initial IPS fellows, and Christopher Jencks created and IPS spinoff, the Cambridge Institute in Massacusetts. With IPS help, this organization, in turn, created the Center for the Study of Public Policy, the Center for Community Development, and the Huron Institute. These IPS "shining stars" collected millions of dollars of federal money for examination of a host of socialist schemes. Next Alperovitz, with local church support, spun an "IPS grandchild" organization, the Exploratory Project for Economic Alternatives, which obtained a $300,000 grant from the U.S. Department of Housing and Urban Development. In 1978, Ralph Nader and Gar Alperowitz created a coalition called the Consumers Opposed to Inflation in the Necessities (COIN), which argued that inflation was due to prices rises by giant energy companies and utilities, not OPEC's impact on oil prices and the ripple effect through the economy. From their COIN soapbox, Nader and Alperovitz argued for public ownership of large corporations and for "confronting 'the need for public control over major economic decisions now in the hands of the private sector.'" See Isaac and Isaac, *Coercive Utopians*, pp. 87–88, 110, 130, 131, 182, and Powell, *Covert Cadre*, pp. 18, 26, 192, 199, 205, 206, 207. See also Gar Alperovitz, *America Beyond Capitalism:*

Reclaiming Our Wealth, Our Liberty, and Our Democracy (Hoboken, N.J.: John Wiley & Sons, 2005).

71. Horowitz, *Radical Son*, p. 391.

72. Michelle Malkin, "Mighty Hoax from Little ACORN?," *Washington Times* (June 27, 2008), p. A23.

73. "Association of Community Organizations for Reform Now (ACORN)," "ACORN's Continuing Pattern of Voter Fraud," "New Report Reveals Truth About ACORN," http://discoverthenetworks.org; and John H. Fund, "Grapes of Rathke: Acorn, a Liberal Activist Group, Comes Under Scrutiny. About Time," *Jewish World Review* (November 8, 2006).

74. Malkin, "Mighty Hoax," p. A23.

75. Dateline D.C., "Barack Obama's Men," *Pittsburgh Tribune-Review* (February 10, 2008) and "Barack's Advisors," *Pittsburgh Tribune-Review* (March 8, 2008).

76. Http://citiesforprogress.org.

77. "Center for Community Change," http://discoverthenetworks.org.

78. As quoted by Powell, *Covert Cadre*, p. 191.

79. "New World Foundation," http://discoverthenetworks.org.

80. Tim McFeely, "Dear Friends," *Progressive Agenda for the States 2008: Leadership for America* (Washington, D.C.: Center for Policy Alternatives, December 2007), p. ii.

81. Boggs, *Gramsci's Marxism*, pp. 121–22.

82. *Ibid.*

83. Richard Poe, "Soros Vows to 'Puncture American Supremacy,'" *NewsMax* (May 2004), p. 18.

84. George Soros, "The Age of Open Society," *Foreign Policy* (Summer 2000), p. 52.

85. David N. Bossie, "George Soros Exposed," *Washington Times* (November 24, 2004).

86. The term "Shadow Party" seems to have escaped its anonymous originator and fell into general use by American journalists and commentators.

87. Laura Blumenfeld, "Soros Deep Pockets vs. Bush," *Washington Post* (November 11, 2003), p. A3, and David Horowitz and Richard Poe, "The Shadow Party I," *FrontPageMagazine.com* (October 6, 2004), p. 7.

88. "George Soros' Secret Meeting: 5-Year Plan Hatched for Combat," *NewsMax* (June 2005), p. 54.

89. James Dellinger and Matthew Vadum, "George Soro's Democracy Alliance: In Search of a Permanent Democratic Majority," *Foundation Watch* (Washington, D.C.: Capital Research Center, December 2006), p. 2; Matthew Vadum and James Dellinger, "Billionaires for Big Government: What's Next for George Soros's Democracy Alliance?," *Foundation Watch* (Washington, D.C.: Capital Research Center, January 2008), pp. 1–9; and About the Democracy Alliance, http://democracyalliance.org.

90. Ben Johnson, "'Charitable Foundations: ATMs for the Left," *FrontPageMagazine.com* (March 2, 2004): "Tides Foundation and Tides Center," http://discoverthenetworks.org; Kent, *Foundations of Betrayal*, pp. 87–88; and "About Tides," http://tides.org.

91. "About MoveOn.org Political Action," http://moveon.org, and "Billionaires Join Soros to Defeat Bush," *NewsMax* (April 2004), p. 49.

92. As quoted by Gabriel Schoenfeld, "Jews, Muslims, and the Democrats," *Commentary* (January 2007) and in "'Alarming Clue,'" *Washington Times* (December 27, 2006), p. A2.

93. Horowitz and Poe, *Shadow Party*, pp. 183–87

94. "Who We Are," http://mediamatters.org.

95. Horowitz and Poe, *Shadow Party*, p. 190.

96. Rondi Adamson, "Soros-Funded Media Matters Attacks Conservatives," *Human Events.com* (October 29, 2007), http://humanevents.com/article .php?print=yes&id=23079.

97. As quoted by Cliff Kincaid, *Communism in Hawaii and the Obama Connection* (Owings, Md.: America's Survival, Inc., May 2008), p. 5. See also Elias Crim and Matthew Vadum, *Barack Obama: A Radical Leftist's Journey from Community Organizing to Politics* (Washington, D.C.: Capital Research Center, June 2008), pp. 4–6.

98. California Legislature, Fourth Report of the Senate Fact-Finding Committee On Un-American Activities, *Communist Front Organizations* (Sacramento, Calif.: California Senate, 1949), p. 353.

99. Barack Obama, *Dreams from My Father* (New York: Crown Publishers, 2004), pp. 100–01. See also Kincaid, *Communism in Hawaii and the Obama Connection*, pp. 4, 20; and Crim and Vadum, *Barack Obama: A Radical Leftist's Journey*, pp. 6–7.

100. Dateline D.C., "Barack's Advisers," *Pittsburgh Tribune-Review* (March 2, 2008).

101. As quoted in Isaac and Isaac, *Coercive Utopians*, pp. 168–69.

102. Hank De Zutter, "What Makes Obama Run?, *Chicago Reader* (December 8, 1995), http://chicagoreader.com/features/stories/archive/barackobama.

103. "Cloward-Piven Strategy," http://discoverthenetworks.org/groupProfile.asp? grpid=6967.

104. "The Acorn Indictments," *Wall Street Journal* (November 3, 2006).

105. Braudy, *Family Circle*, pp. 216, 353.

106. Anne E. Kornblut and Dan Balz, "Obama Pressed in Pa. Debate," *Washington Post* (April 17, 2008), pp. A1, A6.

107. Braudy, *Family Circle*, p. 377.

108. U.S., Senate, Committee on the Judiciary, Subcommittee to Investigate the Administration of Internal Security Act and Other Internal Security Laws, *Terroristic Activity: Inside the Weatherman Movement*, 93rd cong., 2nd

sess., Part 2—October 2, 1974 (Washington, D.C.: Government Printing Office, 1975), p. 106.

109. William Kristol, "The Mask Slips," *New York Times* (April 14, 2008). See also Ann Coulter, "Obama Woos Gun-Toting God Nuts," *FrontPageMagazine.com* (April 17, 2008).

110. The Soviet Union created a multitude of Fronts during the Cold War to carry its propaganda and disinformation into the West. Twelve or thirteen were most important; all of them were granted official status as "independent" non-government organizations or civil society groups by the United Nations. Since the disintegration of the Soviet Union and the dissolution of the International Department of the Central Committee of the Soviet Communist Party, which controlled the most important Fronts, one would think they would have lost their mission and left in the dust pile of history. But such is not the case. The World Peace Council and International Association of Democratic Lawyers are two of the most important of at least eight of the original thirteen-plus Soviet front organizations that are still operating and were validated by the United Nations in 2007. "Where do the old Soviet structures hide?," Hans Graf Huyen, a German expert on Soviet deception asks in a private paper circulated in November 1994. His answer: "'The Gorbachev Foundation . . . has somehow taken over the tasks—and the personnel—of the International Department of the Central Committee of the CPSU.'"

111. "Life Under Socialism: An Afro-American Journalist in the U.S.S.R.," *People's Daily World* (June 19, 1986), p. 18-A. See also the president of the U.S. Peace Council, Al Marder, in *People's Weekly World* (June 2, 2007), and U.S. Peace Council, "Mission," http://uspeacecouncil.org.

112. Frank Chapman, letter to *People's Weekly World,* as quoted by David Gilbert and David Loud, *Communism in Chicago and the Obama Connection* (Owings, Md.: America's Survival, Inc., May 2008).

113. As quoted by Powell, *Covert Cadre*, p. 29.

114. Dateline, D.C., "Barack Obama's Men," *Pittsburgh Tribune-Review* (February 10, 2008).

115. Christina Bellantoni and S. A. Miller, "Clinton Revisits Wright's Role," *Washington Times* (April 17, 2008), pp. A1, A12.

116. Stanley Kurtz, "'Context' You Say?," *National Review* (May 19, 2008), p. 28.

117. Kathy Shaidle, "Obama's Church: Gospel of Hate," *FrontPageMagazine* (April 7, 2008).

118. As quoted by Kurtz, "'Context' You Say?," pp. 30, 32.

119. *Ibid.*, p. 34.

120. Jacob Laskin, "Obama's World, Part III," *FrontPageMagazine* (May 9, 2008).

121. *Ibid.*

122. "The Black Manifesto" in Gayraud S. Wilmore and James H. Cone, eds., *Black Theology: A Documentary History, 1966–1979* (Marynoll, N.Y.: Orbis Books, 1979), p. 82.

123. As quoted in Jamie Glazov, "Symposium: The Unknown Obama," *FrontPageMagazine* (April 4, 2008).

124. Barack Obama, Senator, "One Nation . . . Under God?," *Soujourners Magazine*, 35–10 (November 2006), pp. 43–47.

Chapter 10

1. Susan George in *Anti-Capitalism: A Guide to the Movement*, Emma Bircham and John Charlton, eds. (London: Bookmarks, August 2001), p. vi.

2. Institute for Policy Studies, *Just Security*, pp. 43, 51, 55.

3. Boggs, *Gramsci's Marxism*, p. 16.

4. *Peoples Global Action*, Bulletin No. 5, UK edition (February 2000).

5. "Appendix 1: Brief History of Peoples' Global Action" in the invitation to the upcoming Third International PGA Conference in Cochabamba, Bolivia (September 16–24, 2001), http://nadir.org/iniativ/agp/new/cocha.htm.

6. Albert Meltzer, *Anarchism: Arguments for and Against* (San Francisco: AK Press, 1996), pp. 80–81.

7. Maldon Institute, "PGA's Cochabamba Conference," *The International Reports: Early Warning*, 19–18 (October 12, 2001), p. 10.

8. Maldon Institute, "PGA's Cochabamba Conference."

9. "Fourth Conference of People's Global Action (PGA): Food Sovereignty and Gender," notice of planned conference at Kathmandu, Nepal, September 17–21, 2005, "PGA Hallmarks."

10. Rob Portman, as quoted by Jeffrey Sparshott, "House Defeats Bill to Cut WTO Ties," *Washington Times* (June 10, 2005), p. C10.

11. Tony Clarke, *By What Authority! Unmasking and Challenging the Global Corporations' Assault on Democracy through the World Trade Organization*, with contributions by John Cavanagh, Institute for Policy Studies, Richard Grossman, David Korten, and others of the International Forum on Globalization (IFG) committee on corporations (joint publication by the IFG and Polaris Institute, n.d., circa 2000), pp. 1–3.

12. The World Trade Organization was created by sovereign governments in 1995 at the Uruguay Round of GATT (General Agreement on Tariffs and Trade) negotiations. From the beginning, the 135-member WTO (149 in 2006) was established to set the rules for international commerce and settle trade disputes through a basic set of principles: trade should be made as free as possible, all of a countries trading partners should be treated equally, and discrimination between domestic and foreign products, services or people should be avoided. The U.S. government view that the WTO provides "an

important framework for a fair, rules-based, international system of trade that we benefit from everyday."

13. Debi Barker and Jerry Mander, *Invisible Government—The World Trade Organization: Global Government for the New Millennium?* (Sausalito, Calif.: International Forum on Globalization (IFG), October 1999), p. 2.

14. *Ibid.*

15. John S. Sweeney, president of the American Federation of Labor-Congress of Industrial Unions (AFL-CIO), provided leadership for the union members present in Seattle. Among the most heavily represented unions were the International Brotherhood of Teamsters (IBT), United Steelworkers of America (USWA), Union of the Needle Trades (UNITE), International Association of Machinists (IAM), International Brotherhood of Electrical Workers (IBEW), Service Employees International Union (SEIU), Hotel and Restaurant Employees Union (HERE), and American Federation of State, County, and Municipal Employees Union (AFSCME). Well-known radical Left unions present in Seattle also included two prominent AFL-CIO members—United Electrical (UE) and the International Longshore and Warehouse Union (ILWU). A third radical Left group that sent members to help shut down the WTO was the National Educational Association (NEA). *Battle in Seattle: Strategy and Tactics Behind the WTO Protests* (Washington, D.C.: Maldon Institute, December 10, 1999), pp. 1–2.

16. *Ibid.*, pp. 4–5.

17. Lou Niles as quoted by Craig Pittman, "Ruckus Society Campers Train for Disobedience," *Washington Post* (March 19, 2000), p. C6.

18. *Ibid.*, and David Hogberg, "Nonprofit Ruckus," *American Spectator* (April, 8, 2005).

19. *Legal Issues Relating to Protest Activities*, Seattle Chapter of the National Lawyers Guild, http://nlg.org/wto/nlgmanual.html (no date; circa November 1999), 18 pages.

20. Michael M. Weinstein and Steve Charnovitz, "The Greening of the WTO," *Foreign Affairs* (November/December 2001), p. 147.

21. James Sheehan, *Global Greens: Inside the International Environmental Establishment*, Foundation Watch (Washington, D.C.: Capital Research Center, July 2003), p. 5.

22. David Hogberg, "The Rainforest Action Network" (*Foundation Watch*, Washington, D.C.: Capital Research Center, May 2005), pp. 1–3.

23. Peter Siebelt, *Econostra: Het Netwerk Achter Volkert van der Graaf* (Soesterberg, The Netherlands: Uitgeverji Aspekt, 2003).

24. ConsumerFreedom.com, advertisement ("Greenpeace") in *National Review* January 28, 2002), p. 5.

25. John Passacantando, Executive Director, Greenpeace (Washington, D.C.: n.d., circa 2003).

26. "Derail the 5th Ministerial of the WTO," *Mexico Solidarity Network* (Internet

Access August 1, 2003), http://mexiconsolidarity.org/cancun_call.html.

27. Kevin Sullivan, "Rich-Poor Rift Triggers Collapse of Trade Talks," *Washington Post* (September 15, 2003), pp. A1, A17.

28. John Cavanagh and Robin Broad, "A Turning Point for World Trade" (September 18, 2003) in Transnational Institute, *WTO Ministerial*, 11–14 September 2003, Cancun, Mexico, http://tni-org/globecon/wto/docs/news.htm.

29. "The Global Rulemakers," *Global Exchange*, http://globalexchange.org/economy/rulemakers.

30. *Multinational Monitor,* 21-4 (April 2000).

31. *Spring Rites Return: Protests Against the IMF/World Bank* (Washington, D.C.: Maldon Institute, April 7, 2000), p. 7.

32. *Ibid.,* p. 4.

33. "Zapatista Coffee (Denver, Colo.: http://thehumanbean.com, 2005), Catholic Relief Services, *CRS Fair Trade Program*, handout (Baltimore, Md., 2005).

34. Friends of the Earth, *The IMF: Selling the Environmental Short* (Washington, D.C.: Friends of the Earth, March 2000).

35. Global Exchange, *World Bank/IMF Fact Sheet* (April 2000), http://globalexchange.com/wbimf.html.

36. Darryl Fears, "For the Men in Black, Anarchy Makes Sense," *Washington Post* (April 17, 2000), p. A6.

37. Michael W. Lynch, "The Battle After Seattle," *Reason Online* (April 17, 2000, http://reason.com/bi/lynch4-16.html.

38. Steven Pearlstein and Manny Fernandez, "World Bank Defends Policies," *Washington Post* (April 28, 2001), pp. E1, E8.

39. Manny Fernandez and David A. Fahrenthold, "Police Arrest Hundreds in Protests," *Washington Post* (September 28, 2002), pp. A1, A14; and Matthew Cella, Guy Taylor, and Jim Keary, "Cops Handle Protesters: City Stays Open," *Washington Times* (September 28, 2002), pp. A1, A4.

40. "Preemptive Arrests Mark Unprecedented Attack on Civil Liberties by DC Police," Press Release, Anti-Capitalist Convergence (September 28, 2002), http://abolishthebank.org.

41. "Editorials—Protesters Put Down," *Washington Times* (September 28, 2002), p. A11.

42. Protestors and legal experts began an immediate debate whether the mass arrests, especially at Pershing Park, were lawful. Many believed that the anarcho-communists gave probable cause to the police by announcing their goal to "shut-down the city" through violent action. Lawsuits were filed, the Metropolitan police denied violating protestor rights. Finally, the matter was settled in January 2005 when the District of Columbia government agreed to pay $425,000 to seven people caught up in the mass arrest at Pershing Park. It seems that the police made no order for the protestors to disperse

and therefore did not have justification for making arrests. The seven plaintiffs, five protestors and two bystanders each was paid about $50,000 with the remainder going to the ultra-Left oriented National Lawyers Guild, American Civil Liberties Union, and the law firm of Covington & Burling, which had teamed up to represent the seven. See Carol D. Leonnig and Del Quentin Wilber, "D.C. Settles with Mass Arrest Victims," *Washington Post* (January 25, 2005), pp. A1, A5.

43. Mobilization for Global Justice, "Global Justice Activists Successfully Quarantine Infectious Policies of World Bank/IMF and Corporate Led Globalization," Press release (September 28, 2002).

44. Erik Kirschbaum, "Protesters Claim Victory in Disrupting G-8 Summit," *Washington Times* (June 9, 2007), p. A6, and Joseph Curl and David R. Sands, "G-8 Debuts Friendlier Cast," *Washington Post* (June 3, 2007), pp. A1, A5.

45. Ira Straus, "Tolerance of anti-G-8 Violence: A Failure of the West" (June 2007), a paper presented at a Panel on Heiligendamm G-8 Summit, Hudson Institute (Washington, D.C.: June 5, 2007).

46. *World Social Forum: Revitalizing Anti-Global Action* (Washington, D.C.: Maldon Institute, February 9, 2001), pp. 1–2.

47. Joao Pedro Stedile, "Brazil's Landless Battalions" in Tom Mertes, ed., *A Movement of Movements* (New York: Verso, 2004), p. 26.

48. *Porto Alegre's World Social Forum* (Washington, D.C.: Maldon Institute, March 7, 2002), pp. 8–9, and "WSF Trumps WEF," *The International Reports: Early Warning*, 20-2 (Washington, D.C.: Maldon Institute, February 15, 2002), pp. 1–3.

49. *Porto Alegre's World Social Forum*, p. 10.

50. Marc Cooper, "From Protest to Politics: A Report from Porto Alegre," *Nation* (March 11, 2002), p. 13.

51. *21st Century Levellers—2003 World Social Forum: Porto Alegre* (Washington, D.C.: Maldon Institute, February 7, 2003), pp. 14–15.

52. Among the key speakers in Mumbai were Samir Amin (Egypt, neo-Marxist), Luis Ayala (Socialist International), Mustafa Barghouti (Palestinian leader), Maude Barlow (Canada, activist), Ahmed Ben-Bella (first president of Algeria), Alejandro Bedana (Nicaragua, Sandinista), Walden Bello, (IPS and Focus on the Global South), Fausto Bertinotti (Italy, Refounded Communist Party), Nguyen Thi Binh (Vietnam, communist vice president), Anuradha Mittal (IPS and Institute for Food and Development Policy), Mary Robinson (Ireland, former president and UN high commissioner), Joseph Stiglitz (U.S., former World Bank economist turned criticizer), and Alexander Zharikov (Russia, World Federation of Trade Unions). Source: World Social Forum 2004, "Key Speakers," http://wsfindia.org/announce_pressdetails.php?id=2.

53. *The World Social Forum 2004: Bombay, India* (Washington, D.C.: Maldon Institute, January 31, 2004), p. 17.

54. "The World Social Forum, Brazil, 2005," *Memorandum to File*, No. 2005-21 (Washington, D.C.: Maldon Institute, February 3, 2005), p. 4.

55. Socialist International, *Socialist International Meetings at the World Social Forum, 26–31 January 2005)*, http://socialistinternational.org/main.html.

56. Michelle Garcia, "A 'Movement on Fire' Plays Well in Caracas," *Washington Post* (January 29, 2006), p. A20, and Humberto Marquez, "World Social Forum: A Loud, Multicolored 'No' to Imperialism and War," Inter Press Service News Agency (January 25, 2006), http://ipsnews.net/news.asp?idnews=31911.

57. Carlos Torres, "Threats and Challenges: The VI World Social Forum Caracas 2006," *Alternatives* (December 14, 2005), http://alternatives.ca/article 2279.html.

58. Jose Correa Leite, *The World Social Forum: Strategies of Resistance*, trans. by Carolina Gil (Chicago, Ill.: Haymarket Books, 2005), pp. 9–13, 18, 102.

59. Institute for Policy Studies, *Ideas Into Action*, p. 4.

60. Radosh, *Commies*, p. 89.

61. *The Iraq Antiwar Movement* (Washington, D.C.: Maldon Institute, October 9, 2002).

62. Ramsey Clark's International Action Center, which is staffed by the Workers World Party (Marxist-Leninist) runs International ANSWER (an acronym for "Act Now to Stop War and End Racism"); "International ANSWER," http://discoverthenetworks.org.

63. Libby Copeland, "Protesting for Peace With a Vivid Hue and Cry," *Washington Post* (June 10, 2007), pp. D1, D7.

64. Jean Pearce, "Code Pinko" (March 26, 2003), http://frontpagemag.com from excerpts quoted in "Culture, *et cetera,*" *Washington Times* (March 28, 2003), p. A2.

65. *International Iraq Antiwar Protests: A Briefing Paper* (Washington, D.C.: Maldon Institute, January 17, 2003).

66. Peter Siebelt of Loosdrecht, The Netherlands, was the first to use this phrase.

67. *International Iraq Antiwar Protests* (Maldon Institute), p. 9.

68. Robert Stacy McCain, "Communists, Go Home," *Washington Times* (September 27, 2001), p. A5.

69. "Anti-Capitalist Convergence Issues New Call to Action," http://abolishthe bank.org/en/new_call.html (accessed 09/25/01).

70. "National March Against War and Racism," http://iacenter.org/main.htm (accessed 09/19/01).

71. John J. Tierney, *The Politics of Peace: What's Behind the Anti-War Movement?* (Washington, D.C.: Capital Research Center, 2005), p. 21.

72. *The Iraq Anti-war Movement: Analysis of the January 18–19 Protests* (Washington, D.C.: Maldon Institute, January 24, 2003), p. 9.

73. Susan Webb, Progressive Caucus Introduces Comprehensive Bill to Exit Iraq,"

People's Weekly World, 21–30, newspaper of the Communist Party, USA (January 20–26, 2007), pp. 1, 14.

74. Tarek Fatah, "Defining Progressive," *Comments*, http://members.tripod.com/progressivemuslims/Communts.html.

75. Muslim American Society, Freedom Foundation, http://masnet.org/freedom.htm, accessed January 17, 2003.

76. *The Iraq Anti-war Movement: Analysis of the January 18–19 Protests* (Washington, D.C.: Maldon Institute, January 24, 2003), pp. 10–13.

77. *Iraq War: Protest and Civil Disobedience: A Briefing Paper* (Washington, D.C.: Maldon Institute, March 21, 2003), pp. 2–3.

78. Thomas E. Ricks and Bradley Graham, "Around the Globe, Protest Marches," *Washington Post* (March 23, 2003), p. A10.

79. Glenn Frankel, "Thousands Protest Across Europe, Asia," *Washington Post* (March 23, 2003), p. A28; "Australia: Protestors Denounce U.S.-Led War in Iraq," *Washington Times* (March 24, 2003), p. A17; and Geir Moulson, "Worldwide Protests Continue," *Washington Post* (March 30, 2003), p. A30.

80. Petula Dvorak, "Storm's Devastation Fans Antiwar Flame," *Washington Post* (September 8, 2005), p. A17; and Petula Dvorak, "Antiwar Rally Will Be a First for Many," *Washington Post* (September 23, 2005), pp. B1, B4; and James G. Lakely, "War Protesters Linked to Radical Left-Wing Groups," *Washington Times* (September 22, 2005), p. A13.

81. Dana Milbank and Alan Cooperman, "Politics: Conservative Author Is Seeing Red in America," *Washington Post* (August 31, 2005, p. A5 [please note that the *Post* tried to denigrate the facts of John J. Tierney, Jr.'s remarks by tagging him as a "conservative author" rather than simply an "author."]. See also Bill Sammon, "Liberals Drop Public Sheehan Role," *Washington Times* (August 31, 2005), p. A4.

82. Editorial, *Voice of Revolution*, newspaper of the U.S. Marxist-Leninist Organization (August 24, 2007), p. 3.

83. David Horowitz, "The Fifth Column Left Declares War" (March 17, 2003), http://FrontPageMagazine.com.

Chapter 11

1. United Nations, Department of Public Information, "The United Nations and Civil Society" (2005), http://un.org/issues/civilsociety, and http://un.org/unfip/2004/Website/index.htm.

2. H. G. Wells, *The Outline of History: Being a Plain History of Life and Mankind*, Vol. II (London: George Newnes Limited, n.d., circa 1922), pp. 752–53.

3. Dore Gold, *Tower of Babble: How the United Nations Has Fueled Global Chaos* (New York: Crown Forum, 2004), pp. 3–10, 19–20, 158.

4. Nat Hentoff, "United Nations Uselessness: Failing Innocent People in Darfur," *Washington Post* (October 17, 2005), p. A19.

5. Gold, *Tower of Babble,* pp. 173–74.

6. *Ibid.,* pp. 238, 239.

7. Joseph A. Klein, *Global Deception: The UN's Stealth Assault on America's Freedom* (Los Angeles: World Ahead, 2005), pp. 1–3.

8. Joseph Klein, "Re-Arranging the Deck Chairs at the UN," *FrontPage Magazine.com* (January 23, 2008).

9. Chris Eisendrath, "Rising Force in Advancing World Peace," *Philadelphia Inquirer* (May 27, 2000).

10. United Nations, "Secretary-General's Address to the 51st Annual DPI-NGO Conference," (New York: September 14, 1998).

11. United Nations, *On 50th Anniversary of Conference of Non-Governmental Organizations, Deputy Secretary-General Says NGOs Serve As Global Conscience,* Press Release DSG/SM/38 (December 3, 1998).

12. Thomas Carothers, "Civil Society: Think Again," *Foreign Policy* (Winter 1999–2000), p. 19.

13. United Nations, "NGOs in Consultative Status with ECOSOC" (July 25, 2005), accessed on January 30, 2008.

14. Robert Huberty and David Riggs, "NGO Accountability: What the U.S. Can Teach the U.N.," *Foundation Watch* (Washington, D.C.: Capital Research Center, July 2003), pp. 1–4.

15. Kofi A. Annan, Secretary-General of the United Nations, *We the Peoples* (New York: UN Department of Public Information, 2000), p. 67.

16. United Nations, General Assembly, "Arrangements and Practices for the Interaction of Non-Governmental Organizations in All Activities of the United Nations System," 53d sess., A/53/150 (July 10, 1998).

17. World Federalist Movement, "Statement of Purpose" (http://worldfederalist.org/VISION/SoP.html).

18. Ronald Baily. "International Man of Mystery: Who Is Maurice Strong," *National Review* (September 1, 1997), http://iresist.com/cbg/strong.html.

19. National Center for Public Policy Research, "Dossier: Maurice Strong" (September 1997), http://nationalcenter.org/DossierStrong.html.

20. *Ibid.*

21. Claudia Rosett, "The Buck Still Hasn't Stopped: The Volcker Report on Oil-for-Food is Sadly Incomplete," *Weekly Standard* (October 3, 2005), pp. 10–12.

22. "About the UN Millennium Project," http://unmillenniumproject.org.

23. Millennium Project, Commissioned by the UN Secretary General and Supported by the UN Development Group, "About the UN Millennium Project;" "About the Goals: What they Are;" and "Task Force Reports" (June 2006), http://unmillenniumproject.org. See also Richard Jerome and Mary Green, "A Family's Fight for Life," *People* (March 13, 2006).

24. Klein, *Global Deception,* pp. 51–58.

25. David R. Sands, "G-8 Faces Setbacks to U.N. Development Goals," *Washington Times* (July 7, 2008), pp. A1, A16.
26. *Ibid.*, p. 64.
27. U.S., Federal Bureau of Investigation, "American POWs/MIAs in Southeast Asia," released under the Freedom of Information-Privacy Act, http://goia.fbi .gov/foiaindex/powmias.htm, accessed March 6, 2006.
28. Horowitz, *Radical Son*, pp. 302–03.
29. *Ibid.*, p. 394.
30. *Ibid.*, p. 400.
31. *Ibid.*, pp. 400, 403.
32. Peter Weiss, "A Background Paper for The Hague Appeal for Peace" (http://haguepeace.org).
33. Hague Appeal for Peace, "The Hague Agenda for Peace and Justice for the 21st Century," conference edition, http://haguepeace.org. Also distributed as a UN document, UN Ref A/54/98.
34. http://wfm.org.
35. William R. Pace, Secretary General, Hague Appeal for Peace, "Conference of '99—Closing Plenary" (May 1999), http://haguepeace.org/showPage.php?url= closing.inc.
36. http://ipb.org.
37. Stacy Lu, "Peace Conference; Peace Power to the People," *ABC News World Service* (June 1, 1999). Available at http://haguepeace.org/show/Page.php? url=articles/art6.inc.
38. http://ippnw.org.
39. http://ialana.net.
40. Yoko Furuyama, comments at the Closing Plenary of the Hague Appeal for Peace (May 1999).
41. Peace Boat, "Voyages," http://peaceboat.org/english/voyg/index.html (accessed January 19, 2008).
42. Conference of Mayors for Peace, 7th Executive Conference (2007), http:// mayorsforpeace.org.
43. Peace Boat US, "Who We Are," http://peaceboat-US.org.
44. United Nations, *The Hague Appeal for Peace and Justice for the 21st Century,"* UN Ref A/54/98. (New York: http://haguepeace.org, n.d.), pp. 9, 13.
45. Cora Weiss, President, Hague Appeal for Peace, "Centennial of the Russian Initiative: From the First Peace Conference 1899–to the Third 1999," address at St. Petersburg, Russia (June 22, 1999), http://haguepeace.org/html/weiss russia.html.
46. Cora Weiss, "Hamburg Speech: Challenge for Peace Educators," 4th European Congress for Peace Education, Hamburg, Germany (June 30, 2003), http://ipb.org/web/noticia.php?id=605.
47. Hague Appeal for Peace, *Sample Learning Units: Book 2*, "Learning to

Abolish War: Teaching Toward a Culture of Peace (New York: 2002), p. 12.

48. *Ibid.*, pp. 22, 34.
49. Jacques Ellul, *Propaganda: The Formation of Men's Attitudes* ["Introduction" by Konrad Kellen], trans. from French by Konrad Kellen and Jean Lerner (New York: Alfred A Knopf, 1971), p. vi.
50. Terence H. Qualter, *Propaganda and Psychological Warfare* (New York: Random House, 1962), pp. 9, 14, 15.

Chapter 12

1. As quoted by Anton La Guardia, "Fanatics Around the World Dream of the Caliph's Return" (January 8, 2005), http://telegraph.co.uk.
2. As quoted by Daniel Pipes, "What Do the Terrorists Want? [a Caliphate]," *New York Sun* (July 26, 2005).
3. *Ibid.*
4. George Weigel, *Faith, Reason, and the War Against Jihadism: A Call to Action* (New York: Doubleday, 2007), pp. 35–36.
5. *Ibid.*, p. 7.
6. *Ibid.*, p. 22, and Huntington, *Clash of Civilizations,* pp. 210–13. See also Robert Spencer, *The Truth About Muhammad: Founder of the World's Most Intolerant Religion* (Washington, D.C.: Regnery, 2006).
7. *Ibid.*, pp. 14, 16.
8. *Ibid.*, p. 60.
9. *Ibid.*, pp. 56–57, 59.
10. Akbar Ahmed, *Journey Into Islam: The Crisis of Globalization* (Washington, D.C.: Brookings Institution, 2007), p. 1.
11. Spencer, *The Truth About Muhammad*, p. 182.
12. *Ibid.*, p. 85.
13. Walid Phares, *Future Jihad* (New York: Palgrave Macmillan, 2005), p. 2.
14. Weigel, *Faith, Reason, and the War Against Jihadism*, p. 8.
15. Gold, *Hatred's Kingdom*, p. 76.
16. Trevor Stanley, "Understanding the Origins of Wahhabism and Salafism," *Terrorism*, 3014 (July 15, 2005), http://jamestown.org.
17. Phares, *Future Jihad*, p. 59.
18. *Ibid.*, p. 179.
19. Robert Spencer, *Islam Unveiled* (San Francisco: Encounter Books, 2002), p. 12.
20. Phares, *Future Jihad*, p. 61. See also Fromkin, *A Peace to End All Peace*, pp. 425–26, 513–14, 560.
21. *The Wahhabi Connection* (Washington, D.C.: Maldon Institute, October 2003), p. 3.
22. Gold, *Hatred's Kingdom*, p. 55.

23. Peter L. Bergen, *Holy War, Inc.* (New York: Touchstone, 2002), p. 203.
24. Gold, *Hatred's Kingdom*, pp. 100–01.
25. Bernard Lewis, *The Crisis of Islam* (New York: Modern Library, 2003), pp. 78–79.
26. Robert Spencer, *The Politically Incorrect Guide to Islam (and the Crusades)* (Washington, D.C.: Regnery, 2005), pp. 41–42.
27. Lydia Khalil, "Al-Qaeda & the Muslim Brotherhood: United by Strategy, Divided by Tactics," *Terrorism Monitor,* 4–6 (March 23, 2006), p. 1, http://jamestown.org.
28. Although Wahhabism and Salafism have different historical roots, they are often used interchangeably. Salafism is an early twentieth century reform-oriented movement. It is not a separate "sect" nor a unified movement. Wahhabis sometimes use "Salafi" as a cover for their activities. Christopher M. Blanchard, *The Islamic Traditions of Wahhabism and Salafiyya*, CRS Report for Congress RS21695 (January 25, 2006), and Stephen Schwartz, "Wahhabis or 'Salafis? What's in a Name . . ." (December 20, 2006), http://islamicpluralism.org.
29. Olivier Roy, Research Director, Centre National de la Recherche Scientifique, Paris, "Neo-Fundamentalism," Social Science Research Council, http://ssrg .org/sept11/essays/roy_text_only.htm.
30. Weigel, *Faith Reason, and the War Against Jihadism*, p. 50.
31. As quoted by Spencer, *Politically Incorrect Guide to Islam*, p. 111.
32. *Ibid.*, p. 80.
33. *Ibid.*, pp. 36, 183–90.
34. Victor Davis Hanson, "Excuse After Excuse," *Washington Times* (August 19, 2006), p. A9.
35. Lewis, *Crisis of Islam*, pp. 80–81.
36. As quoted by Phares, *Future Jihad*, p. 117.
37. As quoted in Spencer, *Islam Unveiled*, p. 167.
38. Bernard Lewis, "The Revolt of Islam," *New Yorker* (November 19, 2001), p. 51.
39. Gold, *Hatred's Kingdom*, pp. 13–14. See also Ibn Warraq, *Why I Am Not a Muslim* (Amherst, N.Y.: Prometheus Books, 1995), pp. 11, 105, and Spencer, *Islam Unveiled,* p. 95.
40. As quoted in "Jihad in the Qur'an" in Andrew G. Bostom, ed., *The Legacy of Jihad: Islamic Holy War and the Fate of Non-Muslims* (Amherst, N.Y.: Prometheus Books, 2005), pp. 125–26 (extracts also from the Koran: 9.5, 9.29, 9.111, 4.74, 4.76, 4.95, 2.216, 2.217, 2.218, 8. 41, 8.65, and 48.20. Taken from "The Noble Qur'an," Muslim Students Association, University of Southern California, http://usc.edu/dept/MSA/quran.).
41. Phares, *Future Jihad*, pp. 48–51; and Ye'or, *Eurabia*, pp. 31–34.
42. Lewis, *Crisis of Islam*, p. 7.
43. Osama bin Laden, "Declaration of the World Islamic Front for Jihad Against

the Jews and the Crusaders" (February 23, 1998), http://fas.org/irp/world/para/docs/980223-fatwa.htm.

44. Spencer, *Islam Unveiled*, pp. 168, 59–75.

45. Rohan Gunaratna, "Confronting the West: Al-Qaeda's Strategy After September 11," *Jane's Intelligence Review* (July 2002), pp. 27–29.

46. Claude Salhani, "Bin Laden's Blueprint," *Washington Times* (September 9, 2006), p. A11.

47. " 'Homegrown' Terrorism, Leaderless Islamic Jihadism Replacing Al Qaida" (July 2006), http://geostrategy-direct.com/geostrategy-direct/secure/2006/07_12ba.asp.

48. Ron Moreau, "Where the Jihad Lives Now," *Newsweek* (October 29, 2007).

49. Fred Gedrich, "Invest in Pakistan, *Washington Times* (February 5, 2008), p. A19, and Arnaud de Borchgrave, "Perils of Pakistan," *Washington Times* (November 6, 2007), p. A16.

50. Sami Yousafzai and Ron Moreau, "Al Qaeda's Newest Triggerman," *Newsweek* (January 14, 2008).

51. "Al Qaida Rebuilds Its Network Along Afghan-Pakistani Border" and "Pakistan New Sees Porous Border Area with Afghanistan as Direct Threat," *Geostrategy-Direct.com* (February 20, 2008).

52. David Ing, "Moroccan Islamist Group Linked to Madrid Bombs," *Jane's Intelligence Review* (April 2004), pp. 4–5; "Bankrolled by Bin Laden, Algeria's Salafists Eye U.S. Targets" (October 15, 2002), http://geostrategy-direct.com/geostrategy-direct/secure/2002/10_15/dos.asp; Dana Priest and DeNeen L. Brown, " 'Sleeper Cell Contacts Revealed By Canada," *Washington Post* (December 25, 2002), pp. A1, A24; "Saudi Money Financed Al Qaida Takeover in Somalia" (July 2006), http://geostrategy-direct.com/geostrategy-direct/secure/2006/07_12/3.asp; Jamie Dettmer, "Al-Qaeda's Links in the Balkans," *Insight* (July 22, 2002), pp. 22–23; Yoshie Furuhashi, "Bin Laden's Balkan Connections," http://csf.colorado.edu/soc/m-fem/2001/msg00440.html; "The New Al Qaida: More Urbane But Dependent on Pakistan's 'Hardcore Militant' Underground" (August 30, 2006), http://geostrategy-direct.com/geostrategy-direct/secure/2006/08_30/do.asp; Rohan Gunaratna, "Al-Qaeda's Operational Ties With Allied Groups," *Jane's Intelligence Review* (February 2003), pp. 20–22; Rajiv Chandraskaran, "Al Qaeda's Southeast Asian Reach," *Washington Post* (February 3, 2002), pp. A1, A16; and Jeffrey Fields, "Islamist Terrorist Threat in the Tri-Border Region," Center for Nonproliferation Studies (October 2002).

53. Michael Radu, "The Problem of 'Londonistan': Europe, Human Rights, and Terrorists," *E-Notes*, Foreign Policy Research Institute (April 12, 2002), http://fpri.org/enotes/americawar.20020412.radu.londonistan.html.

54. Tony Blankley, "An Islamist Threat Like the Nazis," *Washington Times* (September 12, 2005), pp. A1, A22.

55. Kevin Sullivan and Joshua Partlow, "Young Muslim Rage Takes Root in Britain," *Washington Post* (August 13, 2006), pp. A1, A14.
56. "Al-Qaeda: The Link and Threat to Europe," *Terrorism & Security Monitor* (January 2003), p. 11 (jtsm.janes.com).
57. Christopher Jasparro, "Madrid Attacks Point to Sustained Al-Qaeda Direction," *Jane's Intelligence Review* (August 2004), pp. 30–33, and Phillips, *Londonistan.*
58. Bill Gertz, "Terror Cells at Liberty to Strike," *Washington Times* (September 18, 2002), pp. A1, A18; and Hsin-Hsien Sheena Wong, "Hoekstra Warns of European Tourists," *Washington Times* (September 23, 2006), p. A6.
59. Neil Livingstone, "Words and Bullets: Al Qaeda's Testbook for Terror," *DomesticPreparedness.com* (September 7, 2005), http://domprep.com/index .lasso?PGID=3.WID=996.
60. Daveed Gartenstein-Ross, "Wahhabi Prison Fellowship," *Weekly Standard* (September 25, 2005), pp. 17–19.
61. Alison Pargeter, "Western Converts to Radical Islam: The Global Jihad's New Soldiers?," *Jane's Intelligence Review* (August 2006), p. 20.
62. Paul Belien, "Bowing to the Islamists," *Washington Times* (October 24, 2007), p. A21.
63. Paul Belien, "Islamization of Antwerp," *Washington Times* (March 14, 2007), p. A21.
64. Molly Moore, "In a Europe Torn Over Mosques, A City Offers Accommodation," *Washington Post* (December 9, 2007), pp. A1, A29, and Harry de Quetteville, "Construction of Mosque Ignites German Hostility," *Washington Times* (June 25, 2007), pp. A1, A13.
65. Julia Duin, "Anglican Head Backs Some Islamic Rules," *Washington Times* (February 8, 2008), pp. A1, A11, and Jonathan Petre, "Islamic Support Jeopardizes Archbishop," *Washington Times* (February 9, 2008), pp. A1, A7.
66. The name of the autonomous northern region of Spain is no longer called "Catalonia" in the English language. Rather, the name of the region is now spelled and pronounced "Catalunya," which is based on a decision by the Catalan Omni Cultural organization.
67. Kathryn Haahr, "Catalonia: Europe's New Center of Global Jihad," *Terrorism Monitor*, V-11 (June 7, 2007), http://jamestown.org.
68. "Al Qaida Iraq War Veterans Filtering Back to Europe Organize New Cells," *Geostrategy-Direct.com* (February 13, 2008).
69. "EU: Al Qaida Cells from North Africa Putting Down Roots Throughout Europe," *Geostrategy-Direct.com* (June 13, 2007).
70. Craig Whitlock, "Converts to Islam Move Up in Cells," *Washington Post* (September 15, 2007), pp. A10, A12.
71. "Al Qaeda Recruits Europeans to Train," *Washington Times* (September 26, 2007), p. A9.

72. Stephen Schwartz, "The Balkan Front," *Weekly Standard* (May 14, 2007), pp. 14–17.
73. Fjordman in Jamie Glazov, "Symposium: The Death of Multiculturalism?, *FrontPageMagazine.com* (September 8, 2006).
74. Bat Ye'or in Jamie Glazov, "Symposium: The Death of Multiculturalism?, *FrontPageMagazine.com* (September 8, 2006).
75. Fjordman in Jamie Glazov, "Symposium: The Death of Multiculturalism?, *FrontPageMagazine.com* (September 8, 2006).
76. Abdul Kasem, commentary in Jamie Glazov, "Islamic Multiculturalism," *FrontPageMagazine.com* (February 11, 2008).
77. *Ibid.*
78. *Ibid.*, as quoted.
79. Walter A. McDougall, "Will 'Europe' Survive the 21ˢᵗ Century? A Meditation on the 50th Anniversary of the European Community," Foreign Policy Research Institute (August 3, 2007), http://fpri.org.
80. Arnaud de Borchgrave, "Europe: The Weak That Was," *Washington Times* (February 16, 2008), p. A9.
81. "The Week . . .," *National Review* (February 25, 2008), p. 6, and Sara A. Carter, "NATO Seen Cool to Hot Spots in Afghanistan," *Washington Times* (January 17, 2008), pp. A1, A10.
82. Paul Belien, "Europe's Dreaded Affliction," *Washington Times* (August 1, 2007), p. A17.
83. McDougall, "Will 'Europe' Survive the 21st Century?"
84. Paul Belien, "Bowing to the Islamists," *Washington Times* (October 24, 2007), p. A21.
85. De Borchgrave, "Europe: The Weak That Was," p. A9.
86. Mark Steyn, *America Alone* (Washington, D.C.: Regnery, 2006), p. xxix.
87. Weigel, *Faith, Reason, and the War Against Jihadism*, p. 71.

Chapter 13

1. Oriana Fallaci, *The Rage and the Pride* (New York: Rizzoli, 2001), pp. 27, 84.
2. Oriana Fallaci, passed away in Florence, Italy, on September 15, 2006.
3. Tom Carter, "Italian Author Slams Islam's 'hate' for West," *Washington Times* (October 23, 2002), pp. A1, A2, and Suzanne Fields, "Jihad and the Anti-West Culture War," *Washington Times* (October 28, 2002), p. A21.
4. Michael Barone, "Our Enemies the Saudis," *U.S. News & World Report* (June 3, 2002), and http://defenddemocracy.org.
5. Victor Davis Hanson, "Our Enemies, the Saudis," *Commentary* (July/August 2002).

6. Dennis Mullin, "Call It by Any Other Name, It Still Adds Up to a Crusade," *Washington Post* (January 3, 2003), p. B2, and Paul Martin, "Radical Muslims Urge Campaign Against U.S.," *Washington Times* (September 12, 2002), pp. A1, A7.

7. Daniel Pipes, *Militant Islam Reaches America* (New York: W. W. Norton, 2002), pp. 39, 47.

8. Bernard Lewis, "The Revolt of Islam," *New Yorker* (November 19, 2001), http://newyorker.com; Hugh Seton-Watson, *Nations and States: An Enquiry into the Origins of Nations and the Politics of Nationalism* (Boulder, Colo.: Westview, 1977), pp. 240–41; and David Fromkin, *A Peace to End All Peace* p. 104.

9. Huntington, *Clash of Civilizations*, pp. 217–18.

10. Roger Scruton, "The Political Problem of Islam," *Intercollegiate Review*, 38-1 (Fall 2002), p. 4, and Fromkin, *A Peace to End All Peace*, p. 326n.

11. Gold, *Hatred's Kingdom*, pp. 44–47.

12. Stephen Schwartz, *The Two Faces of Islam* (New York: Doubleday, 2002), pp. 92–93, 110–11.

13. As quoted by Max Boot, "The End of Appeasement," *Weekly Standard* (February 10, 2002), p. 21.

14. Rashid, *Taliban*, p. 75.

15. Lewis, "Revolt of Islam," and "Targeted by a History of Hatred," *Wall Street Journal* (September 10, 2002) and available at http://defenddemocracy.org.

16. Victor Davis Hanson, *An Autumn of War: What America Learned from September 11 and the War on Terrorism* (New York: Anchor, 2002), pp. 15, xiv.

17. Robert Satloff, "Terror Against America: Assessment and Implications (Part I)" in *Peacewatch Policywatch: Anthology 2001—A Year of Terror* (Washington, D.C.: Washington Institute for Near East Policy, 2002), pp. 336–37.

18. *Militant Islam Reaches America*, pp. 10, 20; Roy, *Failure of Political Islam*, p. 202; and Abdullah II, King of Jordan, "The True Voice of Islam," *Washington Post* (December 7, 2002), p. A25.

19. Scruton, "Political Problem of Islam," p. 12.

20. "How the Saudis Spend Their Petrodollars" (November 14, 2007), http://geostrategy-direct.com, and Gold, *Hatred's Kingdom*, pp. 12, 62.

21. As quoted in Gold, *Hatred's Kingdom*, pp. 93–94.

22. As quoted by Stephen Coughlin, "Analysis of Muslim Brotherhood's General Strategic Goals for North America Memorandum" (September 7, 2007), available at http://investigationproject.org.

23. "The Terrorist Network in America, 1991–2007 [cumulative]," http://investigativeproject.org.

24. "Mueller Cofirms Stateside Al Qaida Cells," *Geostrategy-Drect.com* (May 7, 2008).

25. Alan Cooperman, "Survey: U.S. Muslims Assimilated, opposed to Extremism," *Washington Post* (May 23, 2007), p. A3; Fred Lucas, "Survey

of U.S. Muslims' Views Pleases, Worries Islamic Groups," CNS.com (May 24, 2007); and Robert Spencer, "300,000 supporters of Suicide Attacks in America," *FrontPageMagazine.com* (May 30, 2007).

26. Gold, *"Hatred's Kingdom*, p. 7.
27. *Ibid.*, p. 13.
28. *Ibid.*
29. Michael McConnell, Director of National Intelligence, *Annual Threat Assessment of the Director of National Intelligence for the Senate Select Committee on Intelligence* (February 5, 2008), p. 9, available at http://investigativeproject.org. See also Lolita C. Baldor, "General: al-Qaida Making New Cells in US," *ABCNews.go.com* (July 25, 2007), http://abcnews.go.com/Politics/wirestory?id=3411341.
30. David Horowitz, "Al-Qaida Exploits Lax Immigration Controls," "FrontPageMag.com (September 26, 2007).
31. Jim Meyers, "Plan to Use Student Visas Failed by FBI," *NewsMax* (April 2007), p. 20.
32. "Al-Qaeda Infiltrating America as Patients," *WorldNetDaily* (July 15, 2007), http://worldnetdaily.com/news/article.asp?ARTICLE_ID=56693.
33. E. D. Hill, commentator, "Islam vs. Islamists: Voices from the Muslim Center," *FoxNews* (October 20, 2007).
34. "America, Islam, and the New Millennium Conference," *Washington Report on Middle East Affairs"* (July 2000), pp. 87–90; http://WRMEA.com.
35. Julia Duin, "Saudis Buy a Campus Presence," *Washington Times* (December 10, 2007), pp. A1, A10.
36. As quoted by Duin, "Saudis Buy a Campus Presence," pp. A1, A10.
37. Patrick Poole, "Georgetown's Wahhabi Front," *FrontPageMag.com* (February 19, 2008).
38. *Ibid.*
39. Winfield Myers, "John Esposito Blames Christians," *FrontPageMag.com* (November 29, 2007).
40. *Ibid.*, See also Julian Duin, "Religion Monitor: Shut Saudi School," *Washington Times* (October 18, 2007), p. A8; and Jacqueline L Salmon and Valerie Strauss, "State Dept. Urged to Shut Saudi School in Fairfax," *Washington Post* (October 19, 2007), pp. A1, A12.
41. Poole, "Georgetown U's Wahhabi Front."
42. Frank R. Wolf, Member of Congress, memorandum for Dr. John J. DeGioia, President, Georgetown University (February 14, 2008).
43. Hege Storhaug, commentary in Jamie Glazov, "Symposium: The Death of Multiculturalism?," *FrontPageMagazine.com* (September 8, 2006).
44. McDougal, "Will Europe Survive the 21st Century?"
45. Mitchell D. Silber and Arvin Bhatt, *Radicalization in the West: The Homegrown Threat* (New York: Police Department, City of New York, NYPD Intelligence Division, 2007), pp. 23, 30–38, 43–53.

46. Brian Michael Jenkins, "Outside Expert's View" in Silber and Bhatt, *Radicalization in the West: The Homegrown Threat*, p. 11.
47. Stanley Kurtz, "Saudi in the Classroom," *National Review Online* (July 25, 2007), http://nationalreview.com.
48. *Ibid.*
49. Jewish Telegraphic Agency, as quoted in Kurtz, "Saudi in the Classroom."
50. Paul Sperry, "Look Who's Teaching Johnny About Islam," *WorldNetDaily* (February 19, 2008), http://worldnetdaily.com.
51. William J. Bennetta, "Houghton Mifflin's Islamic Connection," *The Textbook League*, letter (July-August 2000).
52. Cinammon Stillwell, "Promotion of Islam in Our Schools," *FrontPage Magazine.com* (February 13, 2008).
53. Amy Fagan, "Muslims' Needs Roiling Schools," *Washington Times* (October 2, 2007), p. A8.
54. Kasem, "Islam Multiculturalism."
55. As quoted by Douglas Farah and Ron Sandee, "The Ikhwan in North America: A Short History," *NEA Foundation* (n.d.), p. 2, http://nefafoundation.
56. *Ibid.*, p. 1.
57. Joseph Myers, "Homeland Security Implications of the Holy Land Foundation Trial, *American Thinker* (September 18, 2007, http://americanthinker.com).
58. As quoted by Myers, *American Thinker*.
59. Myers, "Homeland Security Implications," and Farah and Sandee, *Ikhwan in North America*.
60. Schwartz, *Two Faces of Islam*, pp. 233, 240.
61. Daniel Pipes as quoted in "Muslim Charities: Moderate non-Profits or Elaborate Deceptions?," *A Judicial Watch Special Report* (2007), p. 2.
62. Daniel Pipes and Sharon Chadha, *The Council on American-Islamic Relations* (Washington, D.C.: Capital Research Center, August 2005), p. 1.
63. Schwartz, *Two Faces of Islam*, pp. 233, 240.
64. "Muslim Charities, *Judicial Watch Special Report*, pp. 4–5, and "Islamic Society of North America (ISNA)," http://DiscoverTheNetwork.org.
65. "Islamic Society of North America (ISNA)," http://DiscoverTheNetwork.org.
66. "Muslim Students Association of the U.S. and Canada (MSA)," http://discoverthenetworks.org, and "Muslim Students Association: The Investigative Project on Terrorism," dossier (n.d., circa August 2007), http://investgativeproject.org.
67. "Muslim Charities," *Judicial Watch Special Report*, pp. 5–6.
68. *Ibid.*, p. 8.
69. "Muslim American Society: The Investigative Project on Terrorism," (n.d., circa 2007).
70. *Ibid.*, pp. 36–37.
71. Schwartz, *Two Faces of Islam*, p. 233.

72. "Muslim Public Affairs Council (MPAC)," http://discoverthenetworks.org.
73. *Ibid.*, pp. 210–13.
74. "Arab-American Institute (AAI)," http://discoverthenetworks.org.
75. "American-Arab Anti-Discrimination Committee (ADC)," (May 26, 2003), http://discoverthenetworks.org, and "CAIR and ADC Praise Pelosi Trip ME as Ellison Meets Terror Inciting Mufti of Al Aqsa," *MilitantIslamMonitor.org*.
76. *New York Times* (August 3, 1987). See also Dateline D.C., "Barack Obama's Men," *Pittsburgh-Review* (February 10, 2008).
77. Saul Landau, "Doom in Baghdad," *Progressive* (November 2002), pp. 18–20.
78. Robert Spencer, "Abourezk and the ADC: Apologists for Terror," *FrontPageMagazine.com* (November 16, 2007).
79. Bill Gertz, "Al Qaeda Seen in Search of Nukes," *Washington Times* (July 26, 2007), p. A4.
80. William J. Broad, Stephen Engelberg, and James Glanz, "Assessing Risks, Chemical, Biological, Even Nuclear," *New York Times* (November 7, 2001), pp. B1, B7.
81. "CIA: 33 Groups Preparing for WMD Terrorism," *Geostrategy-Direct.com* (December 7, 2004).
82. Kenneth R. Timmerman, "France Uncovers Al-Qaeda Bombers," *Insight* (January 21–February 3, 2003), pp. 22–23.
83. "US Identifies 40 Afghan Sites Tied to Weapons of Mass Destruction," *Hindustan Times* (November 28, 2001), http://hindustantimes.com.
84. "CIA: 33 Groups Preparing for WMD Terrorism," *Geostrategy-Direct.com* (December 7, 2004), http://geostrategy-direct.com/geostrategy-direct/2004/12_07/ba.asp.
85. Ralph Joseph, "Chemical Labs Show al Qaeda Still Active," *Washington Times* (October 6, 2002), p. A6.
86. "Al Qaida Sought Nuclear, Biological Goods From Russian Mob Organization," *Geostrategy-Direct.com* (May 25, 2004), http://geostrategy-direct.com/geostrategy-direct/secure/2004/5_25/ba.asp, and Robert I. Friedman, *Red Mafiya: How the Russian Mob Has Invaded America* (New York: Little, Brown, 2000), p. 238.
87. Elaine Landau, *Terrorism: America's Growing Threat* (New York: Lodestar Books, 1992), pp. 78–80.
88. " 'Auschwitz in the Sand' Feed Fears—Iraqis Reportedly Trained At Ex-East German Camp," *Seattle Times* (February 28, 1991), pp. 12–13, and "Now, What About Saddam?: By Sea, Air & Land; a Present Danger?," *PrimeTime Thursday*, ABC News (February 28, 1991).
89. Claire Sterling, *The Terror Network: The Secret War of International Terrorism* (New York: Holt, Rinehart and Winston, 1981), p. 293.
90. Robert W. Chandler, *Tomorrow's War, Today's Decisions: Iraqi Weapons of Mass Destruction and the Implications of WMD-Armed Adversaries*

for Future U.S. Military Strategy (McLean, Va.: AMCODA Press, 1996), pp. 21–61.

91. John Mintz, "Technical Hurdles Separate Terrorists From Biowarfare," *Washington Post* (December 30, 2004), pp. A1, A6.

92. Katty Kay, "Bin Laden Link to 'Mail Order Germs,'" *Times* (London) (October 25, 2001).

93. "Jihadist Posts Anthrax-Making Instructions," *Geostrategy-Direct.com* (April 2, 2008).

94. "Al-Qaeda and the Bomb," *Jane's Intelligence Digest* (July 4, 2003), p. 1.

95. Steve Coll, "What Bin Laden Sees in Hiroshima," *Washington Post* (February 6, 2005), pp. B1, B5.

96. Dafna Linzer, "Nuclear Capabilities May Elude Terrorists, Experts Say," *Washington Post* (December 24, 2004), pp. A1, A6.

97. George Tenet, *At the Center of the Storm: My Years at the CIA* (New York: HarperCollins, 2007), p. 102.

98. *Ibid.*, p. 279.

99. "Syria Has 'A Lot of Explaining to Do' About Its Nuclear Program," *Geostrategy-Direct.com* (June 25, 2008).

100. Peter Grier, "Did Rogue Network Leak Nuclear Bomb Design?," *Christian Science Monitor* (June 18, 2008).

101. "Blueprints on Swiss Computers Link Khan to Iran's Nukes," *Geostrategy-Direct.com* (June 25, 2008).

102. Craig Whitlock, "Al-Qaeda's Growing Online Offensive," *Washington Post* (June 24, 2008), pp. A1, A12.

Chapter 14

1. Martin, *Keys of This Blood*, p. 249.

2. *Ibid.*

3. Christopher Story, interview with William F. Jasper, "Red March to Global Tyranny," *The New American* (1995), http://jbs.org/tna.htm; also available at http://reformed-theology.org/html/issue09/perestroika_03.htm. Mr. Story is also editor of Anatoliy Golitsyn's book *The Perestroika Deception*.

4. *Ibid.*

5. As quoted by Anne Applebaum, "The Hitler Analogy," *Washington Post* (May 20, 2008), p. A13.

6. Golitsyn, "Memorandum to the CIA: March 1989," *Perestroika Deception*, p. 31.

7. *Ibid.*, p. 19.

8. Golitsyn, *Perestroika Deception*, p. 30.

9. *Ibid.*

10. Mikhail Gorbachev, "United Nations Address—M. Gorbachev," *United Nations* (December 7, 1988), http://writespirit.net/inspirational_talks/Mikhail_Gorbachev/united_nations_ad. . . .

11. Christopher Story, ed., in Golitsyn, *Perestroika Deception*, p. 139n. See also Judi McLeod, "Nancy Pelosi: One of Mikhail Gorbachev's Most Useful Idiots," AmericanNewssource.com/2006/cover-new111506.htm.

12. Gorbachev Foundation of North America, http://gfna.net/newsdetail.php?newsid=19&.

13. Http//worldforum.org/about/main.htm.

14. Berit Kjos, "Gorbachev's Plan for a United World" (October 1995), http://crossroad.to/text/articles/gorb10-95.html.

15. *Ibid.*

16. Claire Shipman, "Gorbachev: 'Americans have a Severe Disease,'" *ABCNews* (July 12, 2006), http://abcnews.go.com/GMA/story?id=2182020&page=1.

17. "Gorbachev Says U.S. Sowing World Disorder," *Washington Times* (July 28, 2007), p. A6.

18. As quoted by Andrei Piontkovsky in "The Hubris of Russia's Governing Elite," *Insight* (April 23, 2008); also available at http://hudson.org.

19. *Ibid.*

20. As quoted by Peter Finn, "Putin Sets Plans for Tenure as Premier," *Washington Post* (May 9, 2008), p. A14.

21. Martin, *Keys of This Blood.*, p. 377.

22. Powell, *Covert Cadre*, p. 359.

23. *Ibid.*, p. 360.

24. *Ibid.*

25. John Rees, "Marxist Plans to Co-Opt Congress," *Review of the NEWS* (March 2, 1983).

26. Robert L. Borosage, "Straight Talk 2007," Take Back America 2007 Conference, Campaign for America's Future (June 18, 2007).

27. Joseph A. D'Agostino, "The Campaign for America's Future: A Left-Wing Network Flush with Money," *Organization Trends* (Washington, D.C.: Capital Research Center, July 2008), p. 1.

28. John Perazzo, "Democrats' Platform for Revolution," *FrontPageMagazine.com* (May 5, 2008).

29. As quoted by Coughlin, "Analysis of Muslim Brotherhood's General Strategic Goals."

30. Weigel, *Faith, Reason, and the War Against Jihadism*, p. 3.

31. Bruce Brawer, "An Anatomy of Surrender," *City Journal* (Spring 2008), as summarized and quoted in "Culture *et cetera*," *Washington Times* (May 5, 2008), p. A2.

32. Victor Davis Hanson, *Washington Times* (May 5, 2008).

33. Diana West, "A New Language Code," *Washington Times* (May 9, 2008),

p. 21.

34. Weigel, *Faith, Reason, and the War Against Jihadism*, p. 15.

Appendix

1. Gary Emerling, "Nuclear Attack on D.C. a Hypothetical Disaster," *Washington Times* (April 16, 2008), pp. A1, A8.
2. Source: http://fencing.net/forums/thread4945.html.

INDEX